THE INFORMATION SOCIETY

THE INFORMATION SOCIETY

Critical Concepts in Sociology

Edited by
Robin Mansell

Volume IV
Everyday Life

LONDON AND NEW YORK

First published 2009
by Routledge
2 Park Square, Milton Park, Abingdon, Oxon, OX14 4RN, UK

Simultaneously published in the USA and Canada
by Routledge
270 Madison Avenue, New York, NY 10016

Routledge is an imprint of the Taylor & Francis Group, an informa business

Editorial material and selection © 2009, Robin Mansell; individual owners retain copyright in their own material

Typeset in 10/12pt Times NR MT by Graphicraft Limited, Hong Kong
Printed and bound in Great Britain by
the MPG Books Group

All rights reserved. No part of this book may be reprinted or reproduced or utilised in any form or by any electronic, mechanical, or other means, now known or hereafter invented, including photocopying and recording, or in any information storage or retrieval system, without permission in writing from the publishers.

British Library Cataloguing in Publication Data
A catalogue record for this book is available from the British Library

Library of Congress Cataloging in Publication Data
The information society : critical concepts in sociology / edited by Robin Mansell.
p. cm. — (Critical concepts in sociology)
Includes bibliographical references and index.
ISBN 978-0-415-44308-1 (set, hardback) — ISBN 978-0-415-44309-8 (volume 1, hardback) — ISBN 978-0-415-44310-4 (volume 2, hardback) — ISBN 978-0-415-44311-1 (volume 3, hardback) — ISBN 978-0-415-44312-8 (volume 4, hardback)   1. Information society.   I. Mansell, Robin.
HM851.I5324 2009
303.48′33—dc22
2008042128

ISBN 10: 0-415-44308-3 (Set)
ISBN 10: 0-415-44312-1 (Volume IV)

ISBN 13: 978-0-415-44308-1 (Set)
ISBN 13: 978-0-415-44312-8 (Volume IV)

Publisher's Note

References within each chapter are as they appear in the original complete work.

CONTENTS

VOLUME IV EVERYDAY LIFE

Acknowledgements	ix
Introduction to Volume IV ROBIN MANSELL	1

PART 9
Everyday life online and offline 15

66	Transnational virtual community? Exploring implications for culture, power and language GUSTAVO LINS RIBEIRO	17
67	Multiple subjectivity and virtual community at the end of the Freudian century SHERRY TURKLE	28
68	Social implications of the Internet PAUL DIMAGGIO, ESZTER HARGITTAI, W. RUSSELL NEUMAN, AND JOHN P. ROBINSON	42
69	Theorizing globalization DOUGLAS KELLNER	76
70	Media literacy and the challenge of new information and communication technologies SONIA LIVINGSTONE	105
71	Complicity and collusion in the mediation of everyday life ROGER SILVERSTONE	118
72	Identities: traditions and new communities JESÚS MARTÍN-BARBERO	137

CONTENTS

73 The three ages of Internet studies: ten, five and zero years ago 158
    BARRY WELLMAN

74 Where information society and community voice intersect 165
    RAMESH SRINIVASAN

75 Nation and diaspora: rethinking multiculturalism in a
    transnational context 186
    KARIM H. KARIM

PART 10
Gender and the cyborg 205

76 Gender and the information society: a socially structured silence 207
    SUE CURRY JANSEN

77 A cyborg manifesto: science, technology, and socialist-feminism
    in the late twentieth century 228
    DONNA J. HARAWAY

78 What do we know about gender and information technology
    at work? A discussion of selected feminist research 272
    JULIET WEBSTER

79 Reflections on gender and technology studies: in what state
    is the art? 291
    JUDY WAJCMAN

80 An interrupted postcolonial/feminist cyberethnography:
    complicity and resistance in the "cyberfield" 310
    RADHIKA GAJJALA

81 Gendering the Internet: claims, controversies and cultures 330
    LIESBET VAN ZOONEN

PART 11
Privacy and surveillance 347

82 The surveillance society: information technology and
    bureaucratic social control 349
    OSCAR H. GANDY, JR.

CONTENTS

83 An electronic panopticon? A sociological critique of surveillance theory 366
DAVID LYON

84 The distribution of privacy risks: who needs protection? 388
CHARLES D. RAAB AND COLIN J. BENNETT

85 Tactical memory: the politics of openness in the construction of memory 412
SANDRA BRAMAN

86 The secret self: the case of identity theft 433
MARK POSTER

Index 456

ACKNOWLEDGEMENTS

The publishers would like to thank the following for permission to reprint their material:

Sage Publications for permission to reprint Gustavo L. Ribeiro (1997). Transnational Virtual Community? Exploring Implications for Culture, Power and Language. *Organization*, 4(4): 496–505.

Blackwell Publishing for permission to reprint Sherry Turkle (1997). Multiple Subjectivity and Virtual Community at the End of the Freudian Century. *Sociological Inquiry*, 67(1): 72–84.

Annual Reviews, Paul DiMaggio, W. Russell Neuman and John P. Robinson for permission to reprint Paul DiMaggio, Eszter Hargittai, W. Russell Neuman and John P. Robinson (2001). Social Implications of the Internet. *Annual Review of Sociology*, 27: 307–336. © 2001 by Annual Reviews www.annualreviews.org.

Blackwell Publishing for permission to reprint Douglas Kellner (2002). Theorizing Globalization. *Sociological Theory*, 20(3): 285–305.

Taylor & Francis for permission to reprint Sonia Livingstone (2004). Media Literacy and the Challenge of New Information and Communication Technologies. *The Communication Review*, 7(1): 3–14.

The Johns Hopkins University Press for permission to reprint Roger Silverstone (2002). Complicity and Collusion in the Mediation of Everyday Life. *New Literary History*, 33(4): 761–780. © New Literary History, The University of Virginia.

Sage Publications for permission to reprint Jesús Martín-Barbero (2002). Identities: Traditions and New Communities. *Media, Culture & Society*, 24(5): 621–641.

Sage Publications and Barry Wellman for permission to reprint Barry Wellman (2004). The Three Ages of Internet Studies: Ten, Five and Zero Years Ago. *New Media & Society*, 6(1): 123–129.

ACKNOWLEDGEMENTS

Taylor & Francis for permission to reprint Ramesh Srinivasan (2006). Where Information Society and Community Voice Intersect. *The Information Society*, 22(5): 355–365.

Blackwell Publishing for permission to reprint Sue C. Jansen (1989). Gender and the Information Society: A Socially Structured Silence. *Journal of Communication*, 39(3): 196–215.

Sage Publications for permission to reprint Juliet Webster (1995). What Do We Know about Gender and Information Technology at Work? A Discussion of Selected Feminist Research. *European Journal of Women's Studies*, 2(3): 315–334.

Sage Publications for permission to reprint Judy Wajcman (2000). Reflections on Gender and Technology Studies: In What State Is the Art?, *Social Studies of Science*, 30(3): 447–464.

Sage Publications for permission to reprint Liesbet van Zoonen (2002). Gendering the Internet: Claims, Controversies and Cultures. *European Journal of Communication*, 17(1): 5–23.

Blackwell Publishing for permission to reprint Oscar H. Gandy Jr. (1989). The Surveillance Society: Information Technology and Bureaucratic Social Control. *Journal of Communication*, 39(3): 61–76.

Blackwell Publishing for permission to reprint David Lyon (1993). An Electronic Panopticon? A Sociological Critique of Surveillance Theory. *Sociological Review*, 41(4): 653–678.

Taylor & Francis for permission to reprint Charles D. Raab and Colin J. Bennett (1998). The Distribution of Privacy Risks: Who Needs Protection? *The Information Society*, 14(4): 263–274.

Sandra Braman for permission to reprint Sandra Braman (2006). Tactical Memory: The Politics of Openness in the Construction of Memory. *First Monday*, 11(7).

Disclaimer

The publishers have made every effort to contact authors/copyright holders of works reprinted in *The Information Society (Critical Concepts in Sociology)*. This has not been possible in every case, however, and we would welcome correspondence from those individuals/companies whom we have been unable to trace.

INTRODUCTION TO VOLUME IV

Robin Mansell

These 'ways of operating' constitute the innumerable practices by means of which users reappropriate the space organized by techniques of sociocultural production ... to bring to light the clandestine forms taken by the dispersed, tactical, and make-shift creativity of groups or individuals already caught in the nets of 'discipline'. Pushed to their ideal limits, these procedures and ruses of consumers compose the network of an antidiscipline.

(Certeau 1984: xiv–xv)

Everyday life online and offline

The Information Society is discussed in the academic literature from many disciplinary perspectives. Empirical research, drawing upon sociological and political theories of power, reveals insights about why some developments in today's multifaceted information societies are variously welcomed or resisted. Research carried out in the 1980s and early 1990s exhibited a fascination with the virtual, often neglecting the offline environments in which participants in online communities live their lives.[1]

One of the first online communities was The WELL or Whole Earth 'Lectronic Link in the United States, which was created by Stewart Brand and Larry Brilliant in 1985. Originally established as an electronic bulletin board, by the early 1990s it had become a fully interactive Internet-based online discussion site. The WELL was bought by the Salon Media Group in 1999, a small Internet company based in California, offering online news and entertainment. The group has since experienced considerable losses, finding it difficult to attract sufficient subscription advertising to some of its other services, and in the late 2000s is hoping to take advantage of the opportunities offered by Web 2.0 developments. Participation in the WELL has declined, but the profile of its users remains predominantly American (more than 80 per cent), well-educated (more than 79 per cent with university degrees) citizens.

This illustration could be used to exemplify the rise and fall of innumerable Internet start-up companies and high-profile large corporations that are hosting online community sites today. There is a vast body of research on online business models and the factors contributing to their success and failure. The 'everyday life' research tradition is concerned with the use of these sites, rather than with their production. Although some research focuses on the affordances (e.g. qualities such as shape, colour, etc.) or design of these sites, the principal focus is on the everyday lives of those who interact within online communities and how, in turn, this influences meaning construction, the representation of self and others and, in some cases, action in the 'real' world.

Countless virtual community websites cater to an enormous variety of human interests. Blogging has created opportunities for online publishing and discussion and online gaming, and the use of avatars in virtual spaces, such as Second Life, and numerous online art sites means that there is an almost limitless opportunity for online experience, assuming a user has the access and resources required to enter websites and participate. How do these virtual opportunities influence people's lives? In what ways do the new spaces of socio-technical production combine with older modes of information production and communicative practice to alter people's everyday lives, and with what consequences?

Virtuality and identity

The implications of information societies vary depending on the situation in which they are encountered. In the United States, writer and critic Harold Rheingold's interactions within the WELL informed his insights published in *The Virtual Community: Homesteading on the Electronic Frontier* (1993), where he maintained that with the development of online interaction every user becomes a potential publisher. This book became a classic and a touchstone for further investigation of the way virtual communities may be implicated in people's lives.

One major line of research has focused on the way interactions in 'cyberspace' or electronic spaces, such as those supported by the Internet and Web 2.0 developments, influence identity construction. Sherry Turkle's (1995) pathbreaking work *Life on the Screen* focused on the implications of the multiple identities that avatars may assume on behalf of their creators. Her early studies of users of Multi-User Dungeons (MUDs) (Turkle 1997) were informed by psychoanalytic theory and she found that users of online games were likely to cycle through different characters and genders as they adopted flexible identities. More recent work, by Constance Steinkuehler and Dimitri Williams (2006), for example, has examined 'third spaces' where identity creation occurs online, while Sal Humphreys (2005) demonstrated some of the ways in which online gaming communities are challenging the sustainability of conventional media.

There are disputes about the implications of virtual engagement for social engagement offline and for intra-psychic experience. In 2008 an American psychiatrist, Jerald Block argued that 'Internet addiction appears to be a common disorder that merits inclusion in DSM-V [the American Psychiatric Association's manual listing mental illnesses and diagnoses]' (2008: 306). He acknowledged that there were no reliable data in the United States, drawing instead on evidence of a link between intense Internet use and rates of suicide and depression in South Korea and China. Al Cooper *et al.*'s (2000) reviews of studies of online sexual compulsivity, however, suggest that such behaviour should not be perceived as a major problem and, similarly, Robert Kraut *et al.* (2002) found for the United States that intensive use of the Internet is generally consistent with perceptions of well-being. Nevertheless, these findings have been called into question[2] and the jury is out on the balance between positive and negative intra-subjective experiences of virtual spaces and their consequences for people's everyday lives.

Online engagement patterns

Another line of research employs surveys to explain the determinants of Internet use. An early contribution using this method was William Dutton *et al.*'s (1987) examination of personal computer use in American households, which highlighted the characteristics of different types of adopters. Survey-based research includes the Pew Internet and American Life project surveys in the United States,[3] and the World Internet Project surveys, which encompass a growing number of countries.[4] There are also occasional surveys, illustrated by Jonathan Gershuny's (2003) work on time use. Surveys have also been developed by Barry Wellman and Caroline Haythornthwaite's (2002) work on *The Internet in Everyday Life*, and to support Wellman's (2004) extensive research on online intimacy and perceptions of social capital and online collaborative working.

Online activism

Although some of this research compares different patterns of use of the Internet on a national relative basis, it is limited to countries with the resources to conduct such research and by the questions that can be asked in survey instruments. There are many case studies of the use of information and communication technologies (ICT) and the media in support of development goals, as illustrated by Ramesh Srinivasan's (2006) review.[5] Some of this work is linked to critical theories of learning and theories about the role of culture, power and language within dispersed networked communities, as in the case of Gustavo Ribeiro's emphasis on the role of these technologies in enabling 'witnessing' as a form of political action:

> Witnessing from a distance is not new; but, in the age of information dominated by immediacy of image, it operates more profoundly

than ever before. Witnessing – besides being an existential force – activates different forms of commitment embedded in moral and sometimes religious values.

(Ribeiro 1997: 503; see also Ribeiro 1998)

Ribeiro makes it clear that the outcomes of cyberactivism are governed by offline power relationships enacted in the real rather than the cyber world. Similarly, Karim Karim's (2007) work focuses on the potential for virtual communities to engage diasporas to create new connections that may lead to the possibility of 'globalization from below'. Lilie Chouliaraki's (2006) research addresses whether life as represented on the screen may be alienating spectators in a way that inhibits their inclination towards public action.

Mediation in information societies

The connections between public action and mediated life online are central to research building on the tradition of 'everyday life' studies in sociology. Case studies are employed in research that focuses on the strategies and tactics of what Michel de Certeau, the French social theorist, called 'ways of operating'. This is an approach with a long history in the sociological literature.[6] Henri Lefebvre, a French sociologist and a major contributor to studies in this research tradition, observed that 'there can be no knowledge of the everyday without knowledge of society in its entirety' (1962/2002: 4). In the field of media research, Roger Silverstone, a British sociologist, worked within this tradition to analyse the mediation of people's lives by older and newer media, with the aim of understanding both the detailed nature of their experiences as well as the wider politics and societal consequences. Silverstone (1994, 1999), David Morley (Morley and Silverstone 1990) and Leslie Haddon (2006; Silverstone) and Haddon (1996) developed these ideas to focus on people's strategies and tactics for accommodating and resisting the new digital technologies, including standalone computers, social networking sites and mobile phones, resulting in a distinctive approach to the 'domestication' of ICT and into the way diasporic communities embrace the technologies of information societies, an approach also developed by Maria Bakardjieva (2003).

Like Jesus Martin-Barbero, who understands that 'the network society is not, then, purely a phenomenon composed of technological connections, but rather the systemic disjunction of the global and the local' (2002: 622), Silverstone (2002, 2005a, 2005b) was interested in how we can relate the local to the global in societies where individualization seems to take increasing precedence over communal interests, arguing that it is through everyday experience of mediated relationships that a common humanity is created. The concept of mediation refers broadly to the way meaning and value are constructed through interaction with technology and media content.[7] In

Media and Morality: On the Rise of the Mediapolis, he argued that 'mediated connection and interconnection define the dominant infrastructure for the conduct of social, political and economic life across the globe' (Silverstone 2007: 26) and that this dominance has profound ethical and moral implications which call for public action to ensure that disadvantaged people are not excluded or harmed.

One of the difficulties of understanding the implications of information societies, which embrace intensive use of newer media, including the Internet, mobile phones and other applications, is that there is a gap between situated, qualitative micro-level studies and those with a macro-level perspective. Paul DiMaggio *et al.* (2001), in their review of the literature on the social implications of the Internet, show that the main issues that have been studied are concerned with inequality, community and social capital, political participation and organizational change or the economy, with few connections with the everyday lives of Internet users. They argue, as have I (Mansell 1999, 2004b), that this aspect needs to be addressed. So far, there are few instances of convergence between the different approaches in the literature. An exception is the work of Nick Couldry *et al.* (2007), whose book *Media Consumption and Public Engagement: Beyond the Presumption of Attention*, brings qualitative and quantitative research methods to bear on questions of civic engagement.

Literacy

In the era of conventional broadcasting, concerns were raised about product marketing to children and their capacities to discern advertising from the entertainment content of the media (Melody and Ehrlich 1974). Policy initiatives were taken in the United States to protect children and to increase their literacy or ability to distinguish been different types of media content. These measures are less effective in relation to the new media platforms that are hosting advertising that is almost indistinguishable from entertainment or education content. Current concerns over literacy extend far beyond children's exposure to advertising and beyond traditional capabilities for reading and writing in a given language. The spread of the Internet has brought literacy issues to the forefront of policy concerns at national and international levels, many of which have been addressed by Sonia Livingstone (2003, 2004) and others, such as David Buckingham (2003) and Gunther Kress (2003). Literacy in information societies is associated with confidence in using digital platforms of all kinds in creative ways that are perceived as meaningful by users.

The findings of research in this area are contested by many as they raise questions about which literacies are aligned with different cultural and discursive practices, as indicated by Phil Graham (1999; Graham and Goodrum 2007). Hopeton Dunn and Sheena Johnson-Brown's (2007) review of the literature on literacy highlights the importance of research on the multiplicity of information society literacies that are essential for an understanding, from the perspective of the 'global South', of the hegemonic impositions of social, cultural, political and market-oriented norms that are being imposed in line with the Information Society vision.

Gender and the cyborg

Some but by no means all of the foregoing domains of research are undertaken with sensitivity to gender issues. Studies of information societies generally lack such sensitivity despite their importance and clear evidence that it is an issue notwithstanding the possibilities to participate anonymously in virtual spaces or to play with gender identity online. Donna Haraway's 'Cyborg Manifesto' (1991), first published in 1985, discusses the politics of feminism when social reality conceives of human beings as hybrids of machine and organism. She argues that 'we are living through a movement from an organic, industrial society to a polymorphous, information system' leading to a more strongly bimodal social structure. She suggests, however, that, despite the repressive aspects, 'if we learn how to read these webs of power and social life, we might learn new couplings, new coalitions'. Women and other disadvantaged groups need to take responsibility for the relations between science and technology and embrace 'the skilful task of reconstructing the boundaries of daily life, in partial connection with others, in communication with all our parts' (Haraway 1991: 162, 171, 181).[8]

Judy Wajcman (2000, 2004) insists that all aspects of the technologies underpinning information societies should be regarded as open and contingent and shaped by both the symbolic and the material aspects of technoscientific practice and politics. She argues that Haraway's approach tends to permit semiotic analysis to take precedence over the material, with the risk that the social action required to promote the changes in gendered power relations to enable women to take greater advantage of the possibilities of the Internet is not sufficiently emphasized. Juliet Webster's (1995: 319) survey showed that changes involving technologies are often introduced by management in order to achieve a desired work organization. In this sense, ICTs are not 'gender neutral'. Sue Jansen's (1989) discussion of the invisibility of gender in research on communication and technology highlights processes enabling the reproduction of power in the social distribution of knowledge; similar observations can be found in Liesbet van Zoonen's (2002) work.

Radhika Gajjala offers an evocative commentary on the challenge of undertaking ethnographies of women's use of networks. She highlights the dangers of researcher complicity and the need to differentiate between '"speaking for," "speaking to," "speaking with," and "speaking about" human subjects of research' (2002: 183):

In cyberspace there is a less clear line between 'legitimate' and 'illegitimate,' authorized and unauthorized public spaces. Yet the fact that cyberspace is still characterized by Anglo-American (masculine) academic and corporate hegemony sees to it that the few inconsistencies are either erased or ignored in various re-writings and re-wirings of cyberspace.

(Gajjala 2002: 184)

Aida Opoku-Mensah (2000) also points out that there is no simplistic way in which these technologies can work in the service of democratization or in the interests of women.

Privacy and surveillance

In 2008 the wealthy countries of the OECD were calling for renewed focus on policy measures for the 'Internet Economy' (OECD 2008), some related to privacy protection and surveillance. Ideas vary across regions of the world about the extent to which individual privacy – the right to be left alone – should be a priority for policy, over the collective interest in information about individuals for commercial or safety purposes. In 1980 (revised in 2007) the OECD countries introduced guidelines for the protection of privacy and transborder flows of personal data. However, social networking and Web 2.0 applications are leading to renewed concerns among the OECD countries and other countries as well. While it is acknowledged that behavioural advertising can offer benefits to users, this advertising method relies on the accumulation of personal data, creating risks for individual privacy, and numerous data gathering activities undertaken for military purposes are increasingly being sanctioned by national and international law.

Charles Raab and Colin Bennett (1998, 2003; Rabb 1999) have undertaken comparative research on the changing conceptions and treatments of citizen privacy, documenting legislative measures and privacy protection practices. They note that risks to privacy are unevenly distributed throughout populations, which can give rise to new forms of inequality. Anthony Fitzpatrick (2000) provides an overview of the debates over information rights in cyberspace.

Monitoring consumer purchasing behaviour is not a new activity. However, companies and governments are monitoring consumer and citizen behaviour for targeted marketing and surveillance purposes. Oscar Gandy and Jonathan Baron's (Gandy 1993; Gandy and Baron 1998) work and the study by Anthony Danna and Gandy (2002) highlight the potential for intrusions into the everyday lives of citizens in the United States and consider the potential for resistance to surveillance. Mark Poster's (2007) work on identity theft is indicative of the need for caution in making assumptions about links between privacy and identity. He points to the dual aspects of identity – consciousness and informational – suggesting that identity theft discourses need to be understood as a new means of 'governmentality' in the interests of those who collect information about individuals.

Oscar Gandy and David Lyon consider surveillance in terms of Jeremy Bentham's Panopticon, as discussed by Michel Foucault (1977) in his analysis of the prison and discipline. Lyon observes that 'how far electronic panopticism will develop . . . before the dialectic of control starts to swing more decisively in favour of its subjects, and what difference *can* be made by those subjects' is the crucial issue (1993: 674). In a later work Lyon (2006) has turned to the problems of surveillance that are occurring on a global basis.

Sandra Braman's work calls attention to the way political strategies and tactics involving surveillance and privacy intrusions are implicated by the scale of the Internet and a shift towards a 'panspectron'.[9] She observes that 'in the panopticon environment the subject knows that the watcher is there, in the panspectron environment one may be completely unaware that information is being collected' (2006: n.p.). When no one knows who is storing and processing personal information for corporate or security purposes, and stories released by authorities are misleading, she argues that there is a need to use open Internet spaces to construct alternative narratives, a point also made by Michael Dillon (2002). My work with Brian Collins (Mansell and Collins, 2005) reviews a substantial body of literature in the social sciences and in science and engineering which examines the trustworthiness and risks associated with these developments in information societies.

Conclusion

Everyday life is ever more intensely mediated in information societies – and within a period of intense globalization. Douglas Kellner observes that globalization is best understood as 'a highly complex, contradictory, and thus ambiguous set of institutions and social relations, as well as one involving flows of goods, services, ideas, technologies, cultural forms, and people' (2002: 286). In this volume the focus is on how people connect with and experience those flows in their everyday lives, and especially on the varied strategies and tactics of accommodation and resistance to online and offline social relationships. These occur locally, but they are interpenetrated by manifestations of the global in complex ways involving power relations which, at least potentially, enable new opportunities for learning and diversity while also reaching shared understandings and conclusions. Whether these opportunities make a profound difference in people's lives and whether they are understood as helpful are questions that the scholarly community must continue to assess.

Notes

1 Orgad (2007) provides an overview of the way the interrelationships between the online and the offline have come to be understood.
2 See papers in *CyberPsychology & Behavior*, e.g. Boles *et al.* (2004), Palandri and Green (2000).
3 See http://www.pewinternet.org/, (accessed 23 August 2008).
4 See http://www.digitalcenter.org/pages/site_content.asp?intGlobalId=26, (accessed 23 August 2008).
5 This field of research is not included in this volume, but see Mansell (2004a) and http://www.gg.rhul.ac.uk/ict4d/collective.html (accessed 23 August 2003).
6 The origin of studies of 'everyday life' in sociology research can be traced to Georg Lukács (1920/71), influenced by Georg Simmel; to Henri Lefebvre (1962/2002, 1971/84) and Michel de Certeau (1984); and to Irving Goffman (1959) and Harold Garfinkel (1967) (see Bennett and Watson 2002). For a review of application to the study of media and ICT, see Haddon (2004).
7 Different ways in which mediation is used in the literature can be found in Mansell and Silverstone (2002).
8 For cyborg literature see, http://www.unizar.es/departamentos/filologia_inglesa/garciala/bibliography/Subjects/8.Cybernetics/Cyborgs.doc (accessed 22 August 2008), and for the science fiction genre, see Hacking (1998), Gray (1996, 2002) and Haraway (2008).
9 See Hookway *et al.* (2000) for a discussion of panspectron.

References

Bakardjieva, M. (2003). 'Virtual Togetherness: An Everyday-life Perspective'. *Media Culture & Society*, 25(3): 291–313.
Bennett, T. and Watson, D. (2002). *Understanding Everyday Life*. Oxford: Blackwell.
Block, J. J. (2008). 'Issues for DSM-V: Internet Addition'. *American Journal of Psychiatry*, 165(3): 306–7.
Boles, S. C., Cooper, A. and Osborne, C. S. (2004). 'Variations in Internet-related Problems and Psychosocial Functioning in Online Sexual Activities: Implications for Social and Sexual Development in Young Adults'. *CyberPsychology & Behavior*, 7(2): 207–30.
Braman, S. (2006). 'Tactical Memory: The Politics of Openness in the Construction of Memory'. *First Monday*, 11(7): n.p.
Buckingham, D. (2003). *Media Education: Literacy, Learning and Contemporary Culture*. Cambridge: Polity.
Certeau, M. de (1984). *The Practice of Everyday Life* (S. Rendall, trans.). Berkeley CA: University of California Press.
Chouliaraki, L. (2006). 'Towards an Analytics of Mediation'. *Critical Discourse Studies*, 3(2): 153–78.
Cooper, A., Delmonico, D. L. and Burg, R. (2000). 'Cybersex Users, Abusers, and Compulsives: New Findings and Implications'. *Sexual Addiction & Compulsivity*, 7(1–2): 5–29.
Couldry, N., Livingstone, S. and Markham, T. (2007). *Media Consumption and Public Engagement: Beyond the Presumption of Attention*. Basingstoke: Palgrave Macmillan.
Danna, A. and Gandy Jr, O. H. (2002). 'All That Glitters Is Not Gold: Digging Beneath the Surface of Data Mining'. *Journal of Business Ethics*, 40(4): 373–86.

Dillon, M. (2002). 'Network Society, Network-centric Warfare and the State of Emergency'. *Theory Culture & Society*, 19(4): 71–9.
DiMaggio, P., Hargittai, E., Neuman, W. R. and Robinson, J. P. (2001). 'Social Implications of the Internet'. *Annual Review of Sociology*, 27: 307–36.
Dunn, H. and Johnson-Brown, S. (2007). 'Information Literacies and Digital Empowerment in the Global South'. In R. Mansell (ed.), *Media, Communication and Information: Celebrating 50 Years of Theories and Practice* (pp. 78–102). Paris: Reports prepared for UNESCO on the occasion of the International Association of Media and Communication Research (IAMCR) 50th Anniversary Conference, 2007.
Dutton, W. H., Rogers, E. M. and Jun, S. H. (1987). 'Diffusion and Social Impacts of Personal Computers'. *Communication Research*, 14(2): 219–50.
Fitzpatrick, A. (2000). 'Critical Cyberpolicy: Network Technologies, Massless Citizens, Virtual Rights'. *Critical Social Policy*, 20(3): 375–407.
Foucault, M. (1977). *Discipline and Punish: The Birth of the Prison*. New York: Random House.
Gajjala, R. (2002). 'An Interrupted Postcolonial/Feminist Cyberethnography: Complicity and Resistance in the "Cyberfield". *Feminist Media Studies*, 2(2): 177–93.
Gandy Jr, O. H. (1993). 'Toward a Political-Economy of Personal Information'. *Critical Studies in Mass Communication*, 10(1): 70–97.
—— and Baron, J. (1998). 'Inequality – It's All in the Way You Look at It'. *Communication Research*, 25(5): 505–27.
Garfinkel, H. (1967). *Studies in Ethnomethodology*. Englewood Cliffs, NJ: Prentice-Hall.
Gershuny, J. (2003). 'Web Use and Net Nerds: A Neofunctionalist Analysis of the Impact of Information Technology in the Home'. *Social Forces*, 82(1): 141–68.
Goffman, I. (1959). *The Presentation of Self in Everyday Life*. London: Penguin Books.
Graham, P. (1999). 'Critical Systems Theory – A Political Economy of Language, Thought and Technology'. *Communication Research*, 26(4): 482–507.
—— and Goodrum, A. A. (2007). 'New Media Literacies: At the Intersection of Technical, Cultural, and Discursive Practices'. In R. Mansell, C. Avgerou, D. Quah and R. Silverstone (eds), *The Oxford Handbook of Information and Communication Technologies* (pp. 473–93). Oxford: Oxford University Press.
Gray, C. H. (1996). *The Cyborg Handbook*. New York: Routledge.
—— (2002). *Cyborg Citizen: Politics in the Posthuman Age*. New York: Routledge.
Hacking, I. (1998). 'Canguilhem amid the Cyborgs'. *Economy and Society*, 27(2–3): 202–16.
Haddon, L. (2004). *Information and Communication Technologies in Everyday Life*. Cambridge: Berg.
—— (2006). 'The Contribution of Domestication Research to In-home Computing and Media Consumption'. *The Information Society*, 22(4): 195–203.
Haraway, D. (1991). 'A Cyborg Manifesto: Science, Technology and Socialist-Feminism in the Late Twentieth Century'. In *Simians, Cyborgs and Women* (pp. 149–81). New York: Routledge (published initially in 1985 in *Socialist Review*, 15: 65–107, titled '. . . in the 1980s').
—— (2008). *When Species Meet*. Minneapolis, MI: University of Minnesota Press.

Hookway, B., Kwinter, S. and Mau, B. (2000). *Pandemonium: The Rise of Predatory Locales in the Postwar World*. Princeton, NJ: Princeton Architectural Press.

Humphreys, S. (2005). 'Productive Players: Online Computer Games' Challenge to Conventional Media Forms'. *Communication and Critical/Cultural Studies*, 2(1): 37–51.

Jansen, S. C. (1989). 'Gender and the Information Society – A Socially Structured Silence'. *Journal of Communication*, 39(3): 196–215.

Karim, K. H. (2007). 'Nation and Diaspora: Rethinking Multiculturalism in a Transnational Context'. *International Journal of Media and Cultural Politics*, 2(3): 267–82.

Kellner, D. (2002). 'Theorizing Globalization'. *Sociological Theory – Cambridge*, 20(3): 285–305.

Kraut, R., Kiesler, S., Boneva, B., Commings, J., Helgeson, V. and Crawford, A. (2002). 'Internet Paradox Revisited'. *Journal of Social Issues*, 58(1): 49–74.

Kress, G. (2003). *Literacy in the New Media Age*. London: Routledge.

Lefebvre, H. (1962/2002). *Critique of Everyday Life*. New York: Verso.

—— (1971/84). *Everyday Life in the Modern World* (S. Rabinovitch, trans.). New Brunswick, CT: Transaction Publishers.

Livingstone, S. (2003). 'Children's Use of the Internet: Reflections on the Emerging Research Agenda'. *New Media & Society*, 5(2): 147–66.

—— (2004). 'Media Literacy and the Challenge of New Information and Communication Technologies'. *Communication Review*, 7(1): 3–14.

Lukács, G. (1920/71). *History and Class Consciousness*. London: Merlin Press.

Lyon, D. (1993). 'An Electronic Panopticon – A Sociological Critique of Surveillance Theory'. *Sociological Review*, 41(4): 653–78.

—— (2006). *Theorizing Surveillance: The Panopticon and Beyond*. Uffcolm, Devon: Willan Publishing.

Mansell, R. (1999). 'New Media Competition and Access: The Scarcity–Abundance Dialectic'. *New Media & Society*, 1(2): 155–82.

—— (2004a). 'ICTs for Development: What Prospects and Problems?' *Southern African Journal of Information and Communication*, 5: 1–22.

—— (2004b). 'Political Economy, Power and New Media'. *New Media & Society*, 6(1): 74–83.

—— and Collins, B. S. (eds) (2005). *Trust and Crime in Information Societies*. Cheltenham: Edward Elgar Publishers.

—— and Silverstone, R. (eds) (2002). *Inside the Communication Revolution: New Patterns of Social and Technical Interaction*. Oxford: Oxford University Press.

Martin-Barbero, J. (2002). 'Identities: Traditions and New Communities'. *Media Culture & Society*, 24(5): 621–41.

Melody, W. H. and Ehrlich, W. (1974). 'Children's TV Commercials – Vanishing Policy Options'. *Journal of Communication*, 24(4): 113–25.

Morley, D. and Silverstone, R. (1990). 'Domestic Communication – Technologies and Meanings'. *Media Culture & Society*, 12(1): 31–55.

Organization for Economic Cooperation and Development (OECD) (2008). *Shaping Policies for the Future of the Internet Economy*. Report prepared for the OECD Ministerial Meeting on the Future of the Internet Economy, Seoul, Korea, 17–18 June. Paris: OECD.

Opoku-Mensah, A. (2000). 'ICTs as Tools of Democratization: African Women Speak Out'. In E. M. Rathgeber and E. O. Adera (eds), *Gender and the Information Revolution in Africa* (n.p.). Ottawa: International Development Research Centre (IDRC).

Orgad, S. (2007). 'The Interrelations between Online and Offline: Questions, Issues and Implications'. In R. Mansell, C. Avgerou, D. Quah and R. Silverstone (eds), *The Oxford Handbook of Information and Communication Technologies* (pp. 514–36). Oxford: Oxford University Press.

Palandri, M. and Green, L. (2000). 'Image Management in a Bondage, Discipline, Sadomasochist Subculture: A Cyber-Ethnographic Study'. *CyberPsychology & Behavior*, 3(4): 631–41.

Poster, M. (2007). 'The Secret Self – The Case of Identity Theft'. *Cultural Studies*, 21(1): 118–40.

Raab, C. D. (1999). 'From Balancing to Steering: New Directions for Data Protection'. In C. Bennett and R. Grant (eds), *Visions of Privacy: Policy Approaches for the Digital Age* (pp. 68–93). Toronto: University of Toronto Press.

—— and Bennett, C. J. (1998). 'The Distribution of Privacy Risks: Who Needs Protection?' *The Information Society*, 14(4): 263–74.

—— and Bennett, C. (2003). *The Governance of Privacy: Policy Instruments in Global Perspective*. Sudbury, MA: Dartmouth Publishing Co.

Rheingold, H. (1993). *The Virtual Community: Homesteading on the Electronic Frontier*. Reading, MA: Addison-Wesley.

Ribeiro, G. L. (1997). 'Transnational Virtual Community? Exploring Implications for Culture, Power and Language'. *Organization*, 4(4): 496–505.

—— (1998). 'Cybercultural Politics, Political Activism at Distance in a Transnational World'. In S. Alvarez, E. Dagnino and A. Escobar (eds), *Cultures of Politics, Politics of Cultures: Re-visioning Latin American Social Movements* (pp. 325–52). Boulder, CO: Westview Press.

Silverstone, R. (1994). *Television and Everyday Life*. London: Routledge.

—— (1999). *Why Study the Media?* London: Sage.

—— (2002). 'Complicity and Collusion in the Mediation of Everyday Life'. *New Literary History*, 33(4): 761–80.

—— (2005a). 'Mediation and Communication'. In C. Calhoun, C. Rojek and B. Turner (eds), *The Sage Handbook of Sociology* (pp. 188–207). London: Sage.

—— (ed.) (2005b). *Media, Technology and Everyday Life in Europe: From Information to Communication*. Aldershot: Ashgate.

—— (2007). *Media and Morality: On the Rise of the Mediapolis*. Cambridge: Polity Press.

—— and Haddon, L. (1996). 'Design and the Domestication of Information and Communication Technologies: Technical Change and Everyday Life'. In R. Mansell and R. Silverstone (eds), *Communication by Design: The Politics of Information and Communication Technologies* (pp. 44–74). Oxford: Oxford University Press.

Srinivasan, R. (2006). 'Where Information Society and Community Voice Intersect'. *The Information Society*, 22(5): 355–65.

Steinkuehler, C. and Williams, D. (2006). 'Where Everybody Knows Your (Screen) Name: Online Games as "Third Places"'. *Journal of Computer-Mediated Communication*, 11(4): n.p.

Turkle, S. (1995). *Life on the Screen: Identity in the Age of the Internet*. New York: Simon and Schuster.
—— (1997). 'Multiple Subjectivity and Virtual Community at the End of the Freudian Century'. *Sociological Inquiry*, 67(1): 72–84.
van Zoonan, L. (2002). 'Gendering the Internet: Claims, Controversies and Cultures'. *European Journal of Communication*, 17(1): 5–23.
Wajcman, J. (2000). 'Reflections on Gender and Technology Studies: In What State Is the Art?' *Social Studies of Science*, 30(3): 447–64.
—— (2004). *TechnoFeminism*. Cambridge: Polity Press.
Webster, J. (1995). 'What Do We Know about Gender and Information Technology at Work – A Discussion of Selected Feminist Research'. *European Journal of Womens Studies*, 2(3): 315–34.
Wellman, B. (2004). 'The Three Ages of Internet Studies: Ten, Five and Zero Years Ago'. *New Media & Society*, 6(1): 123–30.
—— and Haythornthwaite, C. A. (2002). *The Internet in Everyday Life*. Oxford: Blackwell.

Part 9

EVERYDAY LIFE ONLINE AND OFFLINE

66

TRANSNATIONAL VIRTUAL COMMUNITY?

Exploring implications for culture, power and language

Gustavo Lins Ribeiro

Source: *Organization* 4(4) (1997): 496–505.

Introduction: transnationalism as an issue

My interest in transnationalism derives from several sources. Earlier I studied the political economy of transnational corporations and its effects upon politics, development, migration, levels of integration and social actors' identities (Ribeiro, 1994). Later, following the implications of my work for a critique of development, I started to discuss environmentalism and sustainability as new ideologies and utopias in the late 20th century (Ribeiro, 1992). Particularly relevant for me were the claims of universality, of planetary integration and of the creation of a global citizenship often present in these discourses.

My trajectory has made it gradually clearer that what is at stake, besides many other classical anthropological subjects such as local and supra-local relationships, is an issue that has long been central for anthropology: the modes of representing membership in socio-cultural and political economic units. Why revisit this question now? Precisely because these modes of representation are suffering tremendous impacts caused by the presence of new transnational forces, and are experiencing a transition period where previous models and institutions are not sufficient to make sense of the world. In a context of deterritorialization, fragmentation, globalization of industrial and financial capitals, transnational migration and massive flows of planetary information, space and territory have become entities that need to be rethought.[1]

Space and territory are central terms of the equation 'the modes of representing membership to socio-cultural and political economic units'. 'Where are you from?' is a question we cannot stop asking. Political loyalties are often bounded by territories and technologies of identifying 'authorized users' and 'citizens' that have become common in the modern world (ID card, social security number, passport, driver's license, credit cards, passwords, etc.). The representation of membership in some spatial unit is often organized in terms of an inclusive logic that can be simplified as follows: local, regional, national and international levels. As cultural, political and historical constructs these classificatory categories are subject to change. Apparently, the reorganization of the forms of conceiving the relationships between territory, politics, economy and culture involves a tremendous amount of social energy and imagination, since such a reorganization is simultaneously playing with the construction of subjectivities and collectivities of 'imagined communities' (Anderson, 1991). The appearance of novel forms in this domain is, thus, always potentially threatening to the status quo, for historically it has meant a process of domination of larger areas and of more people.

This is where the discussion on transnationalism becomes particularly important. The appearance of novel forms of relating space to politics (the nation-state, for instance) generally puts into jeopardy the previously existing ones. But transnationalism does not obey the same logic of inclusivity as do the older forms. It crosscuts, as a transversal axis, the different levels of integration in such a manner that it is highly difficult to relate transnationalism to a circumscribed territory. Its space can only be conceived as diffused, disseminated in a web or a network. Thus we can say that a transnational level of integration does not correspond to spatial realities as do the other levels. In fact, transnationalism corresponds to a different articulation of 'real space' and to the creation of a new domain of political contestation and cultural ambiance that are not equivalent to space as we experience it.

A significant number of anthropologists and sociologists are explicitly working with transnationalism or with globalization, its close relative.[2] Some of the issues involved are central for the understanding of the contemporary world and for the social sciences as a whole. Discussions of fragmentation, the emergence of the global fragmented space, of many polymorphic arrangements of interactions and determinations between global and local phenomena are having different repercussions on studies of identity, integration, diffusion, the understanding of the international division of labor, world system theories, etc. The dialectics of homogenization and heterogenization may be approached from economic or cultural perspectives, varying from the crude power games between powerful political and economic agencies to the circulation of international pop culture and commodities with the politics of signs that create the sense of 'we are the world'.

Here I want to call attention to the intertwining of technological and symbolic factors that will allow me to discuss the existence of a virtual-imagined transnational community. I also want to explore some of the implications of transnationalism on culture, language and power. I do not pretend, however, given the vast array of intervening issues, to be covering all possible facets and problems directly or indirectly involved.

Internet: virtuality and the symbolic-cultural basis of the transnational community

There are many social and symbolic processes concurrent to the formation of the transnational condition, many of them already mentioned by authors such as Sklair (1991), Appadurai (1991) and Basch *et al.* (1994). They include the presence of transnational actors and practices, of different 'scapes', and of processes of deterritorialization. But the main basis for the emergence of what I call the transnational virtual community is the global computer network. Benedict Anderson (1991) could, in retrospect, show how important print capitalism was to creating an imagined community that would develop into a nation-state. I can now suggest that electronic and computer capitalism is the necessary environment for the development of a transnation.

Perhaps the most impressive turning-point in the recent history of computers was their transformation into a powerful communication machine. Internet (and the World Wide Web), the network of networks, is presently interconnecting millions of people all over the globe and has become a powerful symbolic transnational means of interactive communication. Since the electronic frontier is always expanding, once more in human history the possibilities seem endless. Virtual reality now exists in an 'on-line', 'parallel' world, a sort of hyper postmodern universe, where time, space and geography are nonexistent or not important (Escobar, 1994; Laquey & Ryer, 1994; Feenberg, 1990).

I want to explore global computer networks as the techno-symbolic basis for the transnational community, especially in relation to the emergence of its own culture and space, that are frequently, but not exclusively, designated as cyberculture and cyberspace (Escobar, 1994). Later, I will consider the problem of a transnational language, or a means of linguistic exchange, that is central to the creation and reproduction of this community within its own environment.

Virtuality is a key concept in understanding the type of culture of the transnational community. Sensitivity to virtuality seems to be a general characteristic of human beings, since we are capable of being symbolically transported to other places, imagining what is not here and, more, to create realities from structures that are purely abstractions before they become empirical facts.[3] Virtual communities and apparatuses have existed before the one created by computer networks. Movie spectators, radio listeners,

TV watchers, radio amateurs, can be listed amongst those. One result of the development of technology is the quantitative and qualitative enhancement of the virtual universe. The importance of virtuality in our daily lives is growing. Virtual university, virtual politics, virtual weddings and virtual sex, spark the attention of journalists eager for novelties in contemporary social behavior.

I want to further discuss my designation of the transnational community as imagined and virtual. Actually, the difference between imagination and virtuality is very thin. I will try to be faithful to its subtlety. This difference is often measured against a common background: the status of reality, in its hard sense. Imagination maintains an empirical basis upon which it elevates itself and from which it may even take off: the image of objects. Virtuality refers more to the potentiality and possibility of being, of becoming a force in the real world. If we can use the two words in the same reasoning, I would say that virtuality is imagination in the process of reaching completeness. The relationship between imagination, virtuality and reality is a complex one, and needs to be seen as a relation of transit and not of opposition. Reality stimulates imagination, things imagined can become reality, virtuality influences the real world, and vice versa.

But, then, what is the difference between an imagined community and a virtual one? The difference lies in the fact that an imagined community is an abstraction, symbolically and politically constructed, while the virtual community, besides being that, is a reality of a different kind, a sort of intermediate, parallel state between reality and abstraction, where simulation and simulacra have lives of their own. The virtual reality is 'there', it can be experienced, manipulated and lived as if it were real. Your presence in the virtual universe over, you can re-enter the real 'physical' world. There is a 'hybridization' between the 'real and the virtual, between the synthetic and the natural' (Queau, 1993: 96).

Yet Philippe Queau, in his discussion of the era of the virtual, issues also a warning:

> A tendency to de-realization invades all persons that adhere too much to the clean perfection of mathematics or to the playful rigor of computers. The technology of virtual simulation cannot but reinforce this risk of de-realization, by giving a pseudo-concrete and pseudo-palpable character to imaginary entities. . . . On one hand, thus, they constitute tools to command complexity, propitiating a better intelligibility, on the other they have a certain propensity to encourage latent forms of illusion and even of schizophrenia. The more we recur to simulation as a scriptural means and as a way of inventing the world, the greater the risk to confound the world with the representations we make of it.
>
> (Queau, 1993: 98–9)

Fetishes, illusion and power in cyberspace

As many members of other political imagined communities, the members of the transnational one, especially its ideologues, tend to have hyperbolic opinions about their role in the real world (see, for instance, Laquey and Ryer, 1994). Homeless minds and faceless people now communicate in a decentralized web that covers the planet, dissolving space and time. They think of themselves as capable of freely manipulating the system, once they are signed up as 'users' of this new order, just as, I imagine, people felt in the pre-history of bourgeois democracy, nation-states and the 'free market'. Indeed, this virtual community shares, so far, 'primordial sentiments', ties that are more characteristic of emerging new states (Geertz, 1963) than of civil ones. Children both of globalism and of the Computer Age, they see themselves as creating a new world; a situation mediated by hi-tech, where access to the network is, at the same time, a sort of postmodern liberation and the experiencing of new democratic means. Means that empower people to flood the world system with information, thereby checking the abuses of the powerful. Nongovernmental organizations everywhere, for instance, praise this potential of liberation.

What NGOs and other members of this community often do not see is that every technological innovation is ambiguous, containing within itself the potential for both Utopia and dystopia (Feenberg, 1990). Perhaps it is a common characteristic of all imagined communities to give the impression that everyone is equal once endowed with the necessary competence. However, underneath the prototype of a first transnation may lie the prototype of the first transstate.

The Internet does not fit the image of a liberal free market, uncontrolled, or responsive only to individual manipulation. Although we should explore the idea of decentralized control, it may be argued that the network is controlled by a 'hierarchy of connections' whose highest points are located within the American state, in scientific and in security agencies, as well as in corporations linked to the development of electronic/computer capitalism, that in case of necessity may always exercise their electronic power. More than ever we should be wary of cyberpanopticism.

The implementation of virtual democracy is also limited by the cost of computers, related equipment and services; access to network codes; education; proficiency in English; and the control of the functioning of the system by many different computer centers. The consolidation of a transnational community needs to advance towards a political discussion on the exercise of democracy on a global scale that does not misrepresent the disparities existing within the world system power game, nor the new technologies and sociabilities they engender with new fetishes and illusions.

Arthur Kroker and Michael Weinstein (1994) point to the advent of new fetishes and power systems, of the 'wired body', of what they call the Virtual class'. Notwithstanding their quasi-delirious rhetoric and hypercriticism, that sometimes reify technopower, these authors are incisive demolishers of cyber-authoritarianism and of the hysteria created by technotopia, which favors the controllers of Internet — the privileged space for the exercise of power by the virtual class, the dominant class in the electronic and computer era. Mainly composed of 'pure capitalists' and 'visionary capitalists specialized in computers', such a class is grounded in the communication industry. Once the electronic frontier is installed and expanding, the virtual class seeks to subdivide cyberspace for the purposes of capitalist accumulation and political control. What is at stake is the competition for rights to intellectual property.

Language and the transnational community

The influence of computing in the construction of subjectivity, in communication processes, and in the emergence of new forms of capitalism and power, is an area hotly debated. Besides the appearance of new fetishes and power systems, there are also subtle forms of exercising micropower based upon individual competence. Some studies (Weber, 1994; Edwards, 1994; Stone, 1992, for instance) indicate that people have to be 'socialized' into news groups, or conference groups. 'Lurkers', i.e. people who observe news groups without interacting, 'first write in an apologetic and respectful fashion. Their writers may ask for welcome or claim membership. They explicitly acknowledge the rules and conventions ... [of the newsgroup], and the need for "safety" on the group' (Weber, 1994: 2). In fact, the culture of the network, with its codes, protocols and emerging writing styles, presupposes the existence of a language and access to it, i.e. a linguistic competence, something that, as Bourdieu noted (1983: 161 and following) cannot be separated from power analysis. Who speaks, to whom, through what media and in what constructed circumstances, are vital elements of any communication process.

Indeed, the interest in understanding computer impacts on writing styles and in the capacity and modes of communication, attracted the attention of linguists and literary critics. George P. Landow (1992: 2), for instance, initially inspired by the paradigm shifts promoted by Jacques Derrida, Theodor Nelson, Roland Barthes and Van Dan, agrees that 'we must abandon conceptual systems founded upon ideas of center, margin, hierarchy, and linearity and replace them with ones of multilinearity, nodes, links, and networks'. According to Landow, 'almost all parties to this paradigm shift, which marks a revolution in human thought, see electronic writing as a direct response to the strengths and weakness of the printed book. This response has profound implications for literature, education, and politics' (pp. 2–3).

This new medium promotes radical alterations in the roles of author and reader. It equally promotes changes in the student/teacher relationship permitting access to malleable and countless sources of information that may be manipulated by the student without the teacher's authoritative mediation. Academic power and its internal relationships, pedagogical norms of linear and sequential use of information, the definition of producers and consumers of knowledge and information, the editorial industry, various types of hierarchies of status and power, find themselves facing a challenge often compared to that represented by Gutenberg's revolution. We are confronted, once again, with the power/technology equation.

It is true that the diffusion of information is positively correlated to the democratization of access to power. Yet, despite the fact that the dissemination of the Internet is occurring at a much faster rate than that of the printed book, we cannot assume that it will one day become available for everyone. If we take into consideration that books, public education and the emergence of the mass media destroyed neither the profound existing social inequalities nor power abuses, why should we assume that networks of hypertexts, grounded in the illusion of interaction and infinite availability of information, will represent a panacea for liberation? In spite of virtual reality's growing importance in the contemporary world, power is, in the last instance, defined by social, economic and political relationships that are enacted in the real world.

As a transnational communication means, Internet raises the interesting question about the emergence of an 'international auxiliary language', to phrase it as Edward Sapir did in 1931. Sapir was interested in the creation of a constructed natural language, something closer to Esperanto, since he recognized that the transformation of a certain national language into an international means of linguistic exchange clashed with different national susceptibilities. However, today, much more than in 1931, English can be thought of as the creole of the world system, and within Internet it provides a most important basis from which grammatical and lexical structures arise. The existence of today's computer-English, a transnational creole that will not supersede the many other national languages, does not satisfy all of Sapir's expectations but is very close to another of his statements: 'It is a good thing that the idea of an international language is no longer presented in merely idealistic terms, but is more and more taking on the aspect of a practical and technological problem and of an exercise in the cleaning up of the thought process' (1956: 63–4).

Computer-English is also evidence of an ongoing process of 'debabelization' occurring within the virtual imagined transnational community. Yet we do not know what will happen with language within cyberspace. There are at least three possible scenarios. In the first, English gains autonomy as the Internet language, backed up by the consolidation of its commercial, military and diplomatic functions, and other phenomena of globalization such as the expansion of cable TV and of international pop culture, hegemonized by American productions. A second, and less likely scenario is that 'computerese' gains autonomy, through user-friendly softwares, mainly based upon the utilization of icons. Finally, a third possibility is the development of a Tower of Babel' software, capable of translating all languages used on the Net. In cyberspace the socio-linguistic issue is rapidly becoming a political matter. Debabelization may be a technological possibility, but Babel was not exclusively constructed over linguistic differences.

Conclusions

As an emerging mode of representing membership to socio-cultural units, transnationalism catapults to paroxysm the already complicated coexistence of heterogeneous and homogeneous configurations. It calls for individual and collective actors that can endure the constant and ambiguous paradox of living with proto-uniform global forces (such as electronic/computer capitalism, consumer culture, and English as the world system creole) and being, at the same time, flexible, and sensitive to the value of difference. This paradox may be simplified as being equivalent to the tension between centralizing and decentralizing forces. The outcomes of such a tension are regulated by the differentiated amounts of power actors have in a given scenario.

Transnationalism also scrambles the structuring capabilities of different levels of integration, in particular that of the nation-state. Its distinct operation is to render impossible or irrelevant the tracing of national origins of people, capital, information, culture and commodities. In so doing, it reconstructs social and individual identities, creating different allegiances and making us face new political subjects, that express themselves through new political discourses, networks and power systems. Given that many of these ongoing transformations are being carried out by powerful actors, such as transnational corporations and multilateral agencies that are, in different and contradictory ways, related to the interests of the expansion of global capitalism, global civil society stands out as a possible countervailing response to these prevailing trends.

I argued in this article that we can already anticipate the existence of a virtual-imagined transnational community. Whether this community will give shape to an effective global political body, that will invigorate the cause of social justice, is an open question that might be defined by political conflicts and alliances over time. But there are some positive signs. For instance, many political ideologies and organizations, fostering the existence of the virtual-imagined transnational community, are linked to movements that defend human rights and the environment worldwide.

Furthermore, I contend that the virtual power of the transnational community is increasingly noticeable. I coined the expressions 'witnessing' and 'political activism from a distance' to designate two capabilities that members of the virtual-imagined transnational community exercise within the

Internet (Ribeiro, 1997). Witnessing from a distance is not new; but, in the age of information dominated by immediacy of image, it operates more profoundly than ever before. Witnessing — besides being an existential force — activates different forms of commitment embedded in moral and sometimes religious values. But witnessing from a distance cannot only be conceived as a segment of a moral economy that appeals to the indignation of enlightened individuals. The way the Zapatistas, for example, used the Internet showed how this form of communication facilitates instantaneous, collective, decentered 'activism from a distance' capable of intervening in the course of real events.

At the same time, every world region, given its diverse existing characteristics, is a part of the processes of globalization and transnationalism in a different manner and with different consequences for itself and for the world system. While the need to go beyond the grid of regional studies is implicit in the idea of global and transnational studies, this does not mean, however, that transnationalism cannot be studied in a given circumscribed world region nor that regional studies are outmoded. In reality the latter refer to supranational levels of integration of a different sort, something between the international and transnational levels.

Despite the fact that the idea of Latin America, for instance, is itself a geopolitical construct, marked by specific power conflicts and history, it is also obviously true that the different parts of the region share a series of common characteristics. In an era where the relationships between difference and democracy have become a crucial issue fostered by the actual experiencing of social and ethnic diversity promoted by globalization, Latin American intellectuals need to look at the region's diverse political and cultural histories to devise our possible contributions to global political culture. I agree with Néstor García Canclini (1996) that the clue is perhaps to be found under the term 'hybridity'.

Finally, I am convinced that the current ascendance of transnationalism makes its understanding mandatory for the creation of means through which new forms of citizenship can be conceived and constructed in a globalized world, as novel forms of hegemony unfold. It is true that there is much speculation in the present debate, but this does not invalidate the ongoing discussions. Quite the contrary. Exercising discursive control over the future is, for powerful elites, as important as controlling the past. We know that the future is, in many ways, a battleground for the present.

Notes

This text is based upon a paper that I originally read at the session 'Rethinking the Cultural: Beyond Cultural Imperialisms and Parochialisms of the Past', organized by Dr Rob Borofski, at the 93rd Meeting of the American Anthropological Association, Atlanta, 1 December 1994. It was significantly enhanced to be presented as a

'Distinguished Alumni Lecture' at the Graduate Center of the City University of New York, on 6 April 1995. I thank Dr Jane Schneider for honoring me with the invitation to expose my ideas within the stimulating environment of my alma mater, and Paul E. Little for his many suggestions.

1 This is certainly one of the reasons why geographers are amongst the leading discussants of globalization. They are joined by economists, sociologists, political scientists, anthropologists and regional planners.
2 For the purposes of making an analytical distinction, I consider globalization mostly as a historical economic process directly related to the expansion of capitalism, to the 'shrinking of the world' (Harvey, 1989). Although it obviously has political implications, globalization differs from transnationalism in the sense that politics and ideology are the privileged realms of the latter. The organization of people within imagined communities, their relationships to power institutions, the reformulation of identities and subjectivities, as well as of the relationships between the private and public spheres, are the main thrust of the discussion on transnationalism. Citizenship, thus, is an issue more pertinent to transnationalism than to globalization.
3 Allucquère Roseanne Stone (1992: 609) defines cyberspace as 'a physically inhabitable, electronically generated alternate reality, entered by means of direct links to the brain — that is, it is inhabited by refigured human "persons" separated from their physical bodies, which are parked in "normal" space. The physical laws of "normal" space need not apply in cyberspace, although some experiential rules carry over from normal space —for example, the geometry of cyberspace is, in most depictions, Cartesian. The "original" body is the authenticating source for the refigured person in cyberspace: no "person" exists whose presence is not warranted by a physical body back in "normal" space.'

References

Anderson, Benedict (1991) *Imagined Communities: Reflections on the Origins and Spread of Nationalism*, revised edn. London: Verso.

Appadurai, Arjun (1991) 'Global Ethnoscapes: Notes and Queries for a Transnational Anthropology', in Richard Fox (ed.) *Recapturing Anthropology: Working in the Present*, pp. 191–210. Santa Fe: School of American Research Press.

Basch, Linda, Glick Schiller, Nina and Szanton Blanc, Cristina (1994) *Nations Unbound: Transnational Projects, Postcolonial Predicaments and Deterritorialized Nation-States*. Langhorne: Gordon & Breach.

Bourdieu, Pierre (1983) 'A economia das trocas linguisticas', in Renato Ortiz (ed.) *Pierre Bourdieu*. São Paulo: Editora Atica.

Edwards, David B. (1994) 'Afghanistan, Ethnography, and the New World Order', *Cultural Anthropology* 9(3): 345–60.

Escobar, Arturo (1994) 'Welcome to Cyberia: Notes on the Anthropology of Cyberculture', *Current Anthropology* 35: 211–31.

Feenberg, Andrew (1990) 'Post-Industrial Discourses', *Theory and Society* 19(6): 709–37.

García Canclini, Néstor (1996) 'Anthropology and Cultural Studies: An Agenda for the End of the Century', paper presented at the 95th Meeting of the American Anthropological Association, San Francisco, November.

Geertz, Clifford (1963) 'The Integrative Revolution. Primordial Sentiments and Civil Politics in the New States', in Clifford Geertz (ed.) *Old Societies and New States*.

The Quest for Modernity in Asia and Africa, pp. 105–57. New York: The Free Press.

Harvey, David (1989) *The Condition of Post-Modernity.* Oxford: Basil Blackwell.

Kroker, A. and Weinstein, M. (1994) *Data Trash: The Theory of the Virtual Class.* New York: St Martin's Press.

Landow, George P. (1992) *Hypertext. The Convergence of Contemporary Critical Theory and Technology.* Baltimore, MD and London: The Johns Hopkins University Press.

Laquey, Tracy and Ryer, Jeanne C. (1994) *O manual da Internet. Um guia introdutorio para acesso as redes globais.* Rio de Janeiro: Editora Campus.

Queau, Philippe (1993) 'O tempo do virtual', in Andre Parente (ed.) *Imagem-Maquina*, pp. 91–9. Rio de Janeiro: Editora 34.

Ribeiro, Gustavo Lins (1992) 'Ambientalismo e desenvolvimento sustentado. Nova ideologia/utopia do desenvolvimento', *Revista de Antropologia* 34: 59–101.

Ribeiro, Gustavo Lins (1994) *Transnational Capitalism. Hydropolitics in Argentina.* Gainesville: University Press of Florida.

Ribeiro, Gustavo Lins (1997) 'Cybercultural Politics: Political Activism at a Distance in a Transnational World', in Sonia Alvarez, Evelina Dagnino and Arturo Escobar (eds) *Culture of Politics/Politics of Culture: Revisioning Latin American Social Movements.* Boulder, CO: Westview Press.

Sapir, Edward (1956) 'The Function of an International Auxiliary Language', in E. Sapir, *Culture. Language and Personality*, ed. D. G. Mandelbaum, pp. 45–64. Berkeley: University of California Press.

Sklair, Leslie (1991) *Sociology of the Global System.* Baltimore, MD: The Johns Hopkins University Press.

Stone, Allucquère Roseanne (1992) 'Virtual Systems', in Jonathan Crary and Sanford Kwinter (eds) *Incorporations*, pp. 609–21. New York: Zone.

Weber, H. L. (1994) 'The Social Organization of an Electronic Community: a Case Study', paper presented at the 93rd Meeting of the American Anthropological Association, Atlanta, November.

67

MULTIPLE SUBJECTIVITY AND VIRTUAL COMMUNITY AT THE END OF THE FREUDIAN CENTURY

Sherry Turkle

Source: *Sociological Inquiry* 67(1) (1997): 72–84.

Online experiences challenge what many have traditionally called "identity"; on the Internet many people recast identity in terms of multiple windows and parallel lives. In this way, today's life on the screen dramatizes and concretizes larger cultural trends that encourage thinking about identity in terms of multiplicity and flexibility.

Long before there were computers, the Internet, or virtual communities, Walt Whitman wrote: "There was a child went forth every day. And the first object he looked upon, that object he became." These few lines speak directly to the theoretical commitment behind my research as I explore the role of technology in shaping individuals and communities: We construct our objects and our objects construct us.[1] In this spirit, it is appropriate to ask what we are becoming when some of the first objects we look upon exist only on computer screens. The objects may exist in the virtual spaces of simulation games or they may be online representations of ourselves in virtual communities on the Internet. In either case, Whitman was prescient about their effects when he further wrote: "Do I contradict myself? Very well then I contradict myself. I am large. I contain multitudes." Online experiences challenge what many people have traditionally called "identity"; a sense of self is recast in terms of multiple windows and parallel lives. Online life is, of course, not the only factor pushing in this direction. Today's life on the screen dramatizes and concretizes larger cultural trends that encourage people to think about identity in terms of multiplicity and flexibility.

Online personae

Through networked software known as MUDs (short for Multi-User Dungeons or Multi-User Domains), people all over the world, each at his or her individual machine, join online virtual communities that exist only through the space created by the computer. The key element of "MUDding," from the perspective of "identity-effects" is the creation and projection of a "persona" into a virtual space. This element characterizes far more "banal" online communities as well, such as bulletin boards, newsgroups, and chat rooms on commercial services.

You join a MUD through a command that links your networked computer to one on which the MUD software and database reside. When you start, you create a character or several characters; you specify their genders and other physical and psychological attributes. Other players in the MUD can see this description. It becomes your character's self-presentation. The created characters need not be human (you can write and deploy a program in MUD that presents itself as a person or, if you wish, as a robot), and there may be more than two genders.

Players create characters who have casual and romantic sex, hold jobs, attend rituals and celebrations, fall in love and get married. To say the least, such goings-on are gripping: "This is more real than my real life," says a character who turns out to be a man playing a woman who is pretending to be a man. As players participate in MUDs, they become authors not only of text but of themselves, constructing selves through social interaction.

In traditional role-playing games in which one's physical body is present, one steps in and out of a character. MUDs, in contrast, offer a parallel life. The boundaries of the game are fuzzy; the routine of playing them becomes part of their players' everyday lives. MUDs blur the boundaries between self and game, self and role, self and simulation. One player says: "You are what you pretend to be ... you are what you play." Players sometimes talk about their real selves as a composite of their characters and sometimes talk about their MUD characters as means for working on their "real" lives. An avid participant in the online "talk channels" known as Internet Relay Chat describes a similar feeling: "I go from channel to channel depending.... I actually feel a part of several of the channels, several conversations.... I'm different in the different chats. They bring out different things in me."

Often the most avid participants in online communities are people who work with computers all day at their "regular" jobs. As they play on MUDs, for example, they will periodically put their characters "to sleep," remaining logged on to the game but pursuing other activities. From time to time they return to the online space. In this way they break up their work days and experience their lives as a "cycling-through" between the real world and a series of simulated ones. This same sort of cycling-through characterizes how people use newsgroups, Internet Relay Chat, bulletin boards, and chat rooms.

This kind of interaction with virtual environments is made possible by the existence on the computer of what have come to be called "windows." Windows are a way of working with a computer that makes it possible for the machine to place you in several contexts at the same time. As a user, you are attentive to only one of the windows on your screen at any given moment, but in a certain sense, you are a presence in all of them at all times. You might be writing a paper for a bacteriology journal and using your computer in several ways to help you: You are "present" to a word-processing program in which you are taking notes and collecting thoughts, you are present to communications software that is in touch with a distant computer for collecting reference materials, and you are present to a program that is charting the growth of simulated bacterial colonies when a new organism enters their ecology. Each of these activities takes place in a window and your identity on the computer is the sum of your distributed presence.

This certainly is the case for Doug, a Dartmouth College junior who plays four characters distributed across three different MUDs. One is a seductive woman. One is a macho, cowboy type whose self-description stresses that he is a "Marlboros rolled in the tee shirt sleeve kind of guy." Then there is "Carrot," a rabbit of unspecified gender who wanders its MUD introducing people to each other. Doug says, "Carrot is so low-key that people let it be around while they are having private conversations. So I think of Carrot as my passive, voyeuristic character."

Doug's fourth character is one that he plays on a FurryMUD (MUDs on which all the characters are furry animals). "I'd rather not even talk about that character because its anonymity there is very important to me," Doug says. "Let's just say that on FurryMUDs I feel like a sexual tourist." Doug talks about playing his characters in windows that have enhanced his ability to "turn pieces of my mind on and off."

> I split my mind. I'm getting better at it. I can see myself as being two or three or more. And I just turn on one part of my mind and then another when I go from window to window. I'm in some kind of argument in one window and trying to come on to a girl in a MUD in another, and another window might be running a spreadsheet program or some other technical thing for school.... And then I'll get a real-time message (that flashes on the screen as soon as it is sent from another system user), and I guess that's RL. It's just one more window.

The development of windows for computer interfaces was a technical innovation motivated by the desire to help people work more efficiently. Windows encourage users to cycle through different applications much as time-sharing computers cycle through the computing needs of different people. In practice, windows are a potent metaphor for thinking about the self as a multiple, distributed, "time-sharing" system. The self is no longer simply playing different roles in different settings, something that people experience when, for example, one wakes up as a lover, makes breakfast as a mother, and drives to work as a lawyer. The life practice of windows is of a distributed self that exists in many worlds and plays many roles at the same time. MUDs extend the metaphor. Now, in Doug's words, "RL" [real life] can be just "one more window."

This particular notion of a distributed self undermines many traditional notions of identity. Identity, after all, from the Latin *idem,* refers to the sameness between two qualities. In MUDs, however, one can be and usually is many.

Online experiences of playing multiple aspects of self are resonant with theories that imagine the self as multiple and fragmented, or as a society of selves. In the late 1960s and early 1970s, I was first exposed to such ideas. I came into contact with the notion that the self is constituted by and through language, that sex is the exchange of signifiers, and that there is no such thing as "the ego." I was taught that each of us is a multiplicity of parts, fragments, and desiring connections. These lessons took place in the hot-house of Parisian intellectual culture whose gurus included Jacques Lacan, Michel Foucault, Gilles Deleuze, and Félix Guattari. But despite such ideal conditions for learning, my "French lessons" remained abstract exercises. These theorists of poststructuralism addressed the history of the body but quite frankly, from my point of view, had little to do with my own.

Today, twenty years later, I use the personal computer and modem on my desk to access MUDs. Anonymously, I travel their rooms and public spaces (a bar, a lounge, a hot tub). I create several characters (some not of my biological gender), who are able to have social and sexual encounters with other characters (some of my virtual gender, others not of my virtual gender). My textual actions are my actions—my words make things happen. In different MUDs I have different routines, different friends, different names.

In this context, the Gallic abstractions of poststructuralist theory seem uncannily concrete. In my computer-mediated worlds, the self is multiple, fluid, constituted by machinelike connectivity; the self is made and transformed by language; sexual congress is an exchange of signification; understanding follows from navigation and tinkering rather than analysis. Maps of MUD cyberspaces are rare and if they exist they are usually out of date. MUDs require active, trial-and-error exploration.

One day on a MUD, I come across a reference to a character named "Dr. Sherry," a cyber-psychotherapist who has an office in the rambling house that constitutes this MUD's virtual geography. There, I am informed, Dr. Sherry administers questionnaires and conducts interviews about the psychology of MUD-ding. I have every reason to believe that the name

Dr. Sherry refers to my fifteen-year career as a student of the psychological impact of technology. But I didn't create this character. Dr. Sherry is a character name someone else created in order to quickly communicate an interest in a certain set of questions about technology and the self. I experience Dr. Sherry as a little piece of my history spinning out of control. I try to quiet my mind; I tell myself that surely one's books, one's public intellectual persona, are pieces of oneself in the world for others to use as they please. Surely this virtual appropriation is flattering. But my disquiet continues. Dr. Sherry, after all, is not an inanimate book, an object placed in the world. Dr. Sherry is a person, or at least a person behind a character who is meeting with others in the world. Well, in the MUD world at least.

I talk over my disquiet with a friend who poses the conversation-stopping question: "Well, would you prefer if Dr. Sherry were a bot (short for online, virtual robot) trained to interview people about life on the MUD?" This had not occurred to me, but in a flash I realize that this, too, is possible. It is even likely to be the case. Many bots roam this MUD. Characters played by people are mistaken for these little artificial intelligences. I myself have made this mistake several times when a character's responses seemed too automatic. Sometimes bots are mistaken for people. I have made this mistake, too, and been fooled by a bot that offered me directions or flattered me by remembering our last interaction. Dr. Sherry could indeed be one of these. I am confronted with a double that could be a person or a program.

Life on the screen thus offers concrete experiences of the abstract theories that had intrigued yet confused me during my intellectual coming of age. Experiences on the Internet, and more generally with contemporary computing, can serve as objects-to-think-with that encourage the appropriation of poststructuralist ideas.

Objects-to-think-with

Appropriable theories, ideas that capture the imagination of the culture at large, tend to be those with which people can become actively involved. They tend to be theories that can be "played" with. So one way to examine the social appropriability of a given theory is to ask whether it is accompanied by its own objects-to-think-with, objects that can help the theory move beyond intellectual circles.[2]

For instance, the popular appropriation of Freudian ideas had little to do with scientific demonstrations of their validity. Freudian ideas passed into the popular culture because they offered robust objects-to-think-with. The objects were almost-tangible ideas such as dreams and slips of the tongue. People were able to play with such Freudian "objects." They became used to looking for them and manipulating them, both seriously and not so seriously. As they did so, the idea that slips and dreams betray the unconscious started to feel natural.

In *Purity and Danger,* the British anthropologist Mary Douglas (1966) examined how the manipulation of food, a concrete material, could organize cultural understandings of the sacred and profane. Other scholars had tried to explain the Jewish dietary laws, the kosher rules, instrumentally in terms of hygiene (i.e., pork carries disease), or in terms of wanting to keep the Jewish people separate from other groups. Douglas argued that the separation of foods taught a fundamental tenet of Judaism: Holiness is order and each thing must have its place. For Douglas, every kosher meal embodies the ordered cosmology, a separation of heaven, earth, and seas. In the story of the Creation, each of these realms is allotted its proper kind of animal life. Two-legged fowls fly with wings, four-legged animals hop or walk, and scaly fish swim with fins. It is acceptable to eat these "pure" creatures, but those that cross categories (such as the lobster that lives in the sea but crawls upon its floor) are unacceptable. The foods themselves carry a theory of unbreachable order.[3]

For Freud's work, dreams and slips of the tongue carried ideas. For Douglas, food carries ideas. Today, computational experiences carry ideas. Take the case of the Internet:[4] People decide that they want to interact with others online. They get an account on a commercial network service. They think that this will provide them with new access to people and information and of course it does. But it does more. They may find themselves in virtual communities taking on multiple roles; they may find themselves playing characters of different ages, attitudes, personalities, and genders. They may be swept up by experiences that enable them to explore previously unexamined aspects of their sexuality or that challenge their ideas about a unitary self.

When people adopt an online persona, they cross a boundary into highly charged territory. Some feel an uncomfortable sense of fragmentation, some a sense of relief. Some sense the possibilities for self-discovery, even self-transformation. A twenty-six-year-old graduate student in history says: "When I log on to a new MUD and I create a character and know I have to start typing my description, I always feel a sense of panic. Like I could find out something I don't want to know." A woman in her late thirties who just got an account with America Online used the fact that she could create five account "names" as a chance to "lay out all the moods I'm in—all the ways I want to be in different places on the system." Another individual named one of her accounts after her yet-to-be-born child. "I got the account right after the amnio, right after I knew it would be a girl. And all of a sudden, I wanted that little girl to have a presence on the net; I wrote her a letter and I realized I was writing a letter to a part of me." A twenty-year-old undergraduate says: "I am always very self-conscious when I create a new character. Usually, I end up creating someone I wouldn't want my parents to know about. It takes me, like, three hours." Online personae are objects-to-think-with when thinking about identity as multiple and decentered rather than unitary.

With this last comment, I am not implying that MUDs or computer bulletin boards or chat rooms are causally implicated in the dramatic increase of people who exhibit symptoms of multiple personality disorder (MPD), or that people on MUDs have MPD, or that participating in a MUD is like having MPD. What I am saying is that the many manifestations of multiplicity in our culture, including the adoption of online personae, are contributing to a general reconsideration of traditional, unitary notions of identity. Online experiences with "parallel lives" are part of the cultural context that supports new theorizations about multiple selves.

Trojan horses: from flexibility to multiplicity

The history of a psychiatric symptom is inextricably tied up with the history of the culture that surrounds it. When I was a graduate student in psychology in the 1970s, clinical psychology texts regarded the symptom of multiple personality as so rare as to be barely worthy of mention. I remember being told that perhaps one in a million people might manifest this symptom. In these rare cases, there was typically one alter personality in addition to the host personality. Today, cases of multiple personality are much more frequent and typically involve up to sixteen alters of different ages, races, genders, and sexual orientation (Hacking, 1995). Many current theories of the genesis of MPD suggest that traumatic events cause various aspects of the self to congeal into virtual personalities. These personalities represent "ones" often hiding from the "others" and hiding too from that privileged alter, the host personality. Sometimes, the alters are known to each other and to the host; some alters may see their roles as actively helping others. Such differences in the transparency of the self system led the philosopher Ian Hacking to write about a "continuum of dissociation." The differences also suggest a continuum of association among the many parts of the self.

If the disorder in MPD stems from a need for rigid walls to block secrets, then the notion of a continuum of association or accessibility helps us conceptualize healthy selves that are not unitary but that have flexible access to their many aspects. "Multiplicity" is a term that carries with it several centuries of negative associations; contemporary American theorists such as Kenneth Gergen (1991), Emily Martin (1994), and Robert Jay Litton (1993) are having an easier time with descriptions of contemporary identity that stress the virtue of flexibility. In my view, the notion of a flexible self serves as a kind of Trojan Horse for ideas about identity as multiplicity.

Flexibility is a more acceptable concept; but it definitely introduces the notion of a healthy self as one that cycles-through its multiple states of being. From there, I would argue, the distance to multiplicity as a normal state of self is short—a matter of semantics. For the essence of the "acceptable," flexible self is not unitary; even its aspects are ever-changing. The philosopher Daniel Dennett (1991) speaks of the flexible self in his "multiple drafts" theory of consciousness. Dennett's notion of multiple drafts is analogous to the experience of several versions of a document open on a computer screen where the user is able to move among them at will. Knowledge of these drafts encourages a respect for the many different versions, while it imposes a certain distance from them. The historian and social theorist Donna Haraway (1991) equates a "split and contradictory self" with a "knowing self" and is optimistic about its possibilities: "The knowing self is partial in all its guises, never finished, whole, simply there and original; it is always constructed and stitched together imperfectly and is therefore able to join with another, to see together without claiming to be another." What most characterizes the Dennett and Haraway models of the self is that the lines of communication between its various aspects are always open. This open communication is presented as encouraging an attitude of respect for the many within us and the many within others.

Increasingly, psychoanalytic theorists are also using a notion of flexibility and transparency as a way of introducing nonpathological multiplicity. They are thinking about healthy selves whose resilience and capacity for joy come from having access to their many aspects. For example, the psychoanalyst Philip Bromberg insists that our ways of describing "good parenting" must now shift away from an emphasis on confirming a child in a "core self" and onto helping a child develop the capacity to negotiate fluid transitions between self states. Bromberg believes that dissociation is not fundamentally trauma driven. It is a part of normal psychological development, necessary to the "necessary illusion of being one self." The healthy individual knows how to be many, but smoothes out the moments of transition between states of self. Bromberg (1995) says: "Health is when you are multiple but feel a unity. Health is when different aspects of self can get to know each other and reflect upon each other. Health is being one while being many." Here, within the American psychoanalytic tradition, is a model of multiplicity without dissociation—that is, multiplicity as a conscious, highly articulated cycling-through.

Self states and avatars

Case, a thirty-four-year-old industrial designer, reports that he likes participating in online virtual communities (MUDding) as a female because (some would think paradoxically) it makes it easier for him to be aggressive and confrontational. Case's several online female personae—strong, dynamic, "out there" women—remind him of his mother, whom he describes as a strong, "Katherine Hepburn type." His father was a mild-mannered man, a "Jimmy Stuart type." Case says that in "real life" he has always been more like his father, but he came to feel that he paid a price for his low-key ways. When he discovered MUDs, he saw the possibility to experiment:

> For virtual reality to be interesting it has to emulate the real. But you have to be able to do something in the virtual that you couldn't in the real. For me, my female characters are interesting because I can say and do the sorts of things that I mentally want to do, but if I did them as a man, they would be obnoxious. I see a strong woman as admirable. I see a strong man as a problem. Potentially a bully.

For Case, if you are assertive as a man, it is coded as "being a bastard." If you are assertive as a woman, it is coded as "modern and together."

> My wife and I both design logos for small businesses. But do this thought experiment. If I say "I will design this logo for $3,000, take it or leave it," I'm just a typical pushy businessman. If she says it, I think it sounds like she's a "together" woman. There is too much male power-wielding in society, and so if you use power as a man, that turns you into a stereotypical man. Women can do it more easily.

Case's gender swapping has given him permission to be more assertive within the MUD and more assertive outside of it as well:

> There are aspects of my personality—the more assertive, administrative, bureaucratic ones—that I am able to work on in the MUDs. I've never been good at bureaucratic things, but I'm much better from practicing on MUDs and playing a woman in charge. I am able to do things—in the real, that is—that I couldn't have before because I have played Katherine Hepburn characters.

Case says his Katherine Hepburn personae are "externalizations of a part of myself." In one interview with him, I use the expression "aspects of the self," and he picks it up eagerly, for MUDding reminds him of how Hindu gods could have different aspects or subpersonalities, all the while having a whole self.

> You may, for example, have an aspect who is a ruthless business person who can negotiate contracts very, very well, and you may call upon that part of yourself while you are in tense negotiation, to do the negotiation, to actually go through and negotiate a really good contract. But you would have to trust this aspect to say something like, "Of course, I will need my lawyers to look over this," when in fact among your "lawyers" is the integrated self who is going to do an ethics vet over the contract, because you don't want to violate your own ethical standards and this (ruthless) aspect of

yourself might do something that you wouldn't feel comfortable with later.

Case's gender swapping has enabled the different aspects of his inner world to achieve self-expression without compromising the values he associates with his "whole person." Role playing has given the negotiators practice; Case says he has come to trust them more. In response to my question "Do you feel that you call upon your personae in real life?" Case responds:

> Yes, an aspect sort of clears its throat and says, "I can do this. You are being so amazingly conflicted over this and I know exactly what to do. Why don't you just let me do it?" MUDs give me balance. In real life, I tend to be extremely diplomatic, nonconfrontational. I don't like to ram my ideas down anyone's throat. On the MUD, I can be, "Take it or leave it." All of my Hepburn characters are that way. That's probably why I play them. Because they are smart-mouthed, they will not sugarcoat their words.

In some ways, Case's description of his inner world of actors who address him and are capable of taking over negotiations is reminiscent of the language of people with MPD. But the contrast is significant: Case's inner actors are not split off from each other or his sense of "himself." He experiences himself very much as a collective self, not feeling that he must goad or repress this or that aspect of himself into conformity. He is at ease, cycling through from Katherine Hepburn to Jimmy Stuart. To use Bromberg's language, online life has helped Case learn how to "stand in the spaces between selves and still feel one, to see the multiplicity and still feel a unity." To use the computer scientist Marvin Minsky's (1987) phrase, Case feels at ease in his "society of mind."

We are dwellers on the threshold between the real and the virtual; we are unsure of how to cycle-through between our online and offline lives. Our experience recalls what the anthropologist Victor Turner (1966) termed a "liminal moment," a moment of cultural passage when new formulations and new meanings are most likely to emerge. Liminal moments are times of tension, extreme reactions, and great opportunity. When Turner talked about liminality, he understood it as a transitional state, but living with flux may no longer be temporary. It is fitting that the story of a technology that is bringing postmodernism down to earth refuses any simple resolutions and requires an openness to multiple viewpoints.

Cycling-through

Whether or not the term is used, the idea of cycling-through is increasingly important for thinking about identity in our culture of simulation. As recently as the 1980s, when first confronted with computers and computational objects, children's thoughts about whether these objects were alive did not center on their physical movement, as they had for the objects of Jean Piaget's (1960) day, but on their psychology. Children of that time took a new world of objects and imposed a new world order, constructing a coherent story about what is alive. More recently, computational objects that evoke evolution have strained that order to the breaking point. Faced, for example, with widely available computer programs such as The Blind Watchmaker, Tierra, and SimLife—objects that explicitly evoke the notion of artificial life—children still try to impose strategies and categories, but they do so in the manner of theoretical bricoleurs, making do with whatever materials are at hand, with whatever theory can fit the rapidly changing circumstances. When children confront these new objects and try to construct a theory of what is alive, we see a form of cycling-through, this time cycling-through theories of "aliveness."

My current collection of children's comments about the aliveness of simulation games includes the following: "The 'Tierrans' are not alive because they are just in the computer, could be alive if they got out of the computer, are alive until you turn off the computer and then they're dead, are not alive because nothing in the computer is real." I have also heard, "The 'Sim' creatures are not alive but almost-alive, would be alive if they spoke, would be alive if they traveled, are alive but not real, are not alive because they don't have bodies, are alive because they can have babies, and finally, they're not alive because the babies in the game don't have parents."

These theories about what is alive are strikingly heterogeneous. Different children comfortably hold different theories, and individual children are able to hold different theories at the same time. In the short history of how the computer has changed the way we think, children have often led the way. Today, children are pointing the way toward multiple theories in the presence of the artifacts of artificial life.

One fifth-grade girl jumped back and forth from a psychological to a mechanistic language when she talked about a small robotic creature she had built out of Lego blocks and programmed with the Logo computer language. Sometimes she called it a machine, sometimes a creature. She talked about it in ways that referenced it as a psychological being, as an intentional self, and as an instrument of its programmer's intentions. These perspectives are equally present for her; for different purposes, she finds one or another of them more useful. Adults find themselves in a similar situation. One forty-year-old woman, an interior designer, confronted with a computer program that simulates the evolution of simple creatures, cycled-through views of it as alive, as "alive in a way" but not alive like humans or animals, as information but not body, as body but not the right kind of body for life, as alive but not spiritually alive, or as our creature but not God's creature, thus not alive. A thirty-seven-year-old lawyer found the same software not alive because life "isn't just replicating bits of information"; alive "like a virus"; not alive, because "life in a parallel universe shouldn't count as life"; alive "but not real life."

In his history of artificial life, the author Steven Levy (1992) suggested that when we think about computer programs that can evolve we might envisage a continuum in which an evolving program would be more alive than a car, but less alive than a bacterium. My observations of how people are dealing with the lifelike properties of computational objects suggest that they are not constructing hierarchies but multiple definitions of life, which they "alternate" through rapid cycling. Multiple and alternating definitions, like thinking comfortably about one's identity in terms of multiple and alternating aspects of self, become a habit of mind.

In *Listening to Prozac,* the psychiatrist Peter Kramer (1993) wrote about an incident in which he prescribed an antidepressant medication for a college student. At the next therapy session, the patient appeared with symptoms of anxiety. Since it is not unusual for patients to respond with jitters to the early stages of treatment with antidepressants, Kramer was not concerned. Sometimes the jitters disappear by themselves; sometimes the prescribing physician changes the antidepressant, or adds a second, sedating medication at bedtime. Kramer says:

> I considered these alternatives and began to discuss them with the young man when he interrupted to correct my misapprehension: He had not taken the antidepressant. He was anxious because he feared my response when I learned he had "disobeyed" me.
>
> As my patient spoke, I was struck by the sudden change in my experience of his anxiety. One moment, the anxiety was a collection of meaningless physical symptoms, of interest only because they had to be suppressed, by other biological means, in order for the treatment to continue. At the next, the anxiety was rich in overtones ... emotion a psychoanalyst might call Oedipal, anxiety over retribution by the exigent father. The two anxieties were utterly different: the one a simple outpouring of brain chemicals, calling for a scientific response, however diplomatically communicated; the other worthy of empathic exploration of the most delicate sort.
>
> (p. xii)

Kramer experienced this alternation of perspective because his patient did not take his medication. Other people experience such alternations when they do take medication. They commonly have moments when they equate their personality with their chemistry. But even as they do so, they do not abandon a sense of themselves as made up of *more than* chemistry. Rather, they cycle through "I am my chemicals" to "I am my history" to "I am my genes."

It may in fact be in the area of genetics that we have become most accustomed to cycling-through. In *Listening to Prozac,* Kramer tells a story about how genetics is causing us to cycle through different views of identity. About to express praise for his friends' two children with a comment such as "Don't the genes breed true?", Kramer stopped himself when he remembered that both children were adopted. "Since when had I—I, who make my living through the presumption that people are shaped by love and loss, and above all by their early family life—begun to assume that personality traits are genetically determined?" [p. xiii]. In fact, Kramer hadn't begun to assume this, he just sometimes did. Cycling-through different and often opposing theories has become how we think about our minds and about what it means to be alive, just as cycling-through different aspects of self have become a way of life as people move through different characters and genders when they move from window to window on their computer screens.

Notes

1 This essay is drawn from Turkle (1995).
2 And, of course, the traffic does not flow in only one direction. In our current situation, science fiction informs social criticism; theme parks such as Disneyland become not simply objects of analysis, but exemplars of theory. The notion of ideas moving out may be heuristically useful, but it is too simple. Postmodern theory has underscored the traffic between diverse and seemingly separate realms. With it, high culture comes to contemplate advertising, science fiction fandom, and the romance novel.
3 Douglas's analysis begins with Genesis and the story of the creation, in which a threefold classification unfolds. There is earth, water, and sky. Leviticus, where the kosher rules are set out, takes up this scheme, says Douglas, and "allots to each element its proper kind of animal life." She states: "Holiness is exemplified by completeness. . . . Holiness means keeping distinct the categories of creation" (p. 53). It follows that "any class of creatures which is not equipped for the right kind of locomotion in its element is contrary to holiness" (p. 55).

If the proposed interpretation of the forbidden animals is correct, the dietary laws would have been like signs which at every turn inspired meditation on the oneness, purity, and completeness of God. By rules of avoidance holiness was given a physical expression in every encounter with the animal kingdom and at every meal (p. 57).
4 I could also have taken the case of people's relationships with the interfaces of contemporary personal computers. In that case, people decide that they want to buy an easy-to-use computer. They are attracted by a consumer product—say, a computer with a Macintosh-style interface. They think they are getting an instrumentally useful product, and there is little question that they are. But now it is in their home and they interact with it every day. And it turns out they are also getting an object that teaches them a new way of thinking and encourages them to develop new expectations about the kinds of relationship they and their children will have with machines. I see the Macintosh as a concrete emissary for significant elements of postmodern thought, most dramatically for the willingness to accept opacity and dialogue with machines. And it would not be an exaggeration to say

that, to date, the Macintosh style of simulated desktop has been our most widely disseminated cultural introduction to virtual reality. The sociologist of science Bruno Latour (1988) stresses the importance of such concrete emissaries or "foot soldiers."

References

Bromberg, P. 1994. "Speak That I May See You: Some Reflections on Dissociation, Reality, and Psychoanalytic Listening." *Psychoanalytic Dialogues* 4(4): 517–547.

Dennett, D. 1991. *Consciousness Explained.* Boston: Little Brown.

Douglas, M. 1966. *Purity and Danger: An Analysis of the Concepts of Pollution and Taboo.* London: Routledge, ARK.

Gergen, Kenneth. 1991. *The Saturated Self: Dilemmas of Identity in Contemporary Life.* New York: Basic Books.

Hacking, I. 1995. *Rewriting the Soul: Multiple Personality and the Sciences of Memory.* Princeton, NJ: Princeton University Press.

Haraway, D. 1991. "The Actors Are Cyborg, Nature Is Coyote, and the Geography Is Elsewhere: Postscript to 'Cyborgs at Large.'" In *Technoculture*, edited by C. Penley and A. Ross. Minneapolis: University of Minnesota Press.

Kramer, P. 1993. *Listening to Prozac: A Psychiatrist Explores Antidepressant Drugs and the Remaking of the Self.* New York: Viking.

Latour, B. 1988. *The Pasteurization of France*, translated by A. Sheridan and J. Law. Cambridge, MA: Harvard University Press.

Levy, S. 1992. *Artificial Life: The Quest for the New Frontier.* New York: Pantheon.

Lifton, Robert Jay. 1993. *The Protean Self: Human Resilience in an Age of Fragmentation.* New York: Basic Books.

Martin, Emily. 1994. *Flexible Bodies.* Boston: Beacon.

Minsky, M. 1987. *The Society of Mind.* New York: Simon and Schuster.

Piaget, J. 1960. *The Child's Conception of the World*, translated by J. Tomlinson and A. Tomlinson. Totowa, NJ: Littlefield, Adams.

Turkle, S. 1995. *Life on the Screen: Identity in the Age of the Internet.* New York: Simon and Schuster.

———. 1984. *The Second Self: Computers and the Human Spirit.* New York: Simon and Schuster.

Turner, V. 1966. *The Ritual Process: Structure and Antistructure.* Chicago: Aldine.

68
SOCIAL IMPLICATIONS OF THE INTERNET

Paul DiMaggio, Eszter Hargittai, W. Russell Neuman, and John P. Robinson

Source: *Annual Review of Sociology* 27 (2001): 307–36.

Abstract

The Internet is a critically important research site for sociologists testing theories of technology diffusion and media effects, particularly because it is a medium uniquely capable of integrating modes of communication and forms of content. Current research tends to focus on the Internet's implications in five domains: 1) inequality (the "digital divide"); 2) community and social capital; 3) political participation; 4) organizations and other economic institutions; and 5) cultural participation and cultural diversity. A recurrent theme across domains is that the Internet tends to complement rather than displace existing media and patterns of behavior. Thus in each domain, utopian claims and dystopic warnings based on extrapolations from technical possibilities have given way to more nuanced and circumscribed understandings of how Internet use adapts to existing patterns, permits certain innovations, and reinforces particular kinds of change. Moreover, in each domain the ultimate social implications of this new technology depend on economic, legal, and policy decisions that are shaping the Internet as it becomes institutionalized. Sociologists need to study the Internet more actively and, particularly, to synthesize research findings on individual user behavior with macroscopic analyses of institutional and political-economic factors that constrain that behavior.

Introduction

By "Internet" we refer to the electronic network of networks that links people and information through computers and other digital devices allowing person-to-person communication and information retrieval. Although the late 1960s saw the inception of an ancestral network dedicated to scientific (and, after 1975, military) communication, the Internet did not emerge until 1982; it began its rapid ascent only in the early 1990s, when graphical interfaces became widely available and commercial interests were allowed to participate (Abbate 1999, Castells 2001). Access to and use of the medium diffused widely and swiftly. The number of Americans online grew from 25 million in 1995 (when only 3% of Americans had ever used the Internet) (Pew Research Center for People and the Press 1995) to 83 million in 1999 (Intelli-Quest 1999), with 55 million Americans going online on a typical day in mid-2000 (Howard *et al*, forthcoming). The amount of information available on the World Wide Web has also risen exponentially, from fewer than 20,000 Web sites in 1995 (Prettejohn 1996) to over 10 million in 2000 (Netcraft 2000), representing over two billion Web pages, with as many as two million pages added daily (Lake 2000).

Our focus in this chapter is on the Internet's implications for social change. The Internet presents researchers with a moving target: Agre (1998a) describes it as "a meta-medium: a set of layered services that make it easy to construct new media with almost any properties one likes." We use Internet to refer both to technical infrastructure (public TCP/IP networks, other large-scale networks like AOL, and foundational protocols), and to uses to which this infrastructure is put (World Wide Web, electronic mail, online multiperson interactive spaces). We focus primarily on general, public uses. Among the topics we do not address systematically are the use of digital technologies for communication *within* formal organizations, the technology's potential contribution to the conduct of social-science research and scholarly communication, or the much broader topic of social antecedents and consequences of computerization.

Many observers allege that the Internet is changing society. Perhaps not surprisingly, given the novelty of the new digital media, there is little agreement about what those changes are. Our purpose here is to summarize research by social scientists about the Internet and to encourage more sociologists to contribute actively to such research. We believe that it is important for sociologists to address these issues for three reasons. First, the medium's rapid growth offers a once-in-a-lifetime opportunity for scholars to test theories of technology diffusion and media effects *during the early stages of a new medium's diffusion and institutionalization.* Second, the Internet is unique because it integrates both different modalities of communication (reciprocal interaction, broadcasting, individual reference-searching, group discussion, person/machine interaction) and different kinds of content (text, video, visual images, audio) in a single medium. This versatility renders plausible claims that the technology will be implicated in many kinds of social change, perhaps more deeply than television or radio. Finally, choices are being made—systems developed, money invested, laws passed, regulations promulgated—that will shape the system's technical and normative structure for decades to come. Many of these choices are based on behavioral assumptions about how people and the Internet interact. We believe such assumptions should represent more than guesswork.

Theoretical context

Sociology's major theoretical traditions emphasize different aspects of electronic media. For Durkheimians, point-to-point communications media like telephones reinforce organic solidarity, while broadcast media like radio or television yield powerful collective representations (Alexander 1988). Marxists focus upon exploitation of communications media to enhance elite control of both politics and production through cultural hegemony and enhanced surveillance (Schiller 1996, Davis *et al* 1997). Weberians attend to the ways in which point-to-point media advance rationalization by reducing limits of time and space, and broadcast media provide the elements of distinctive status cultures (Collins 1979).

Other traditions also offer perspectives on the digital media. Technological determinists suggest that structural features of new media induce social change by enabling new forms of communication and cultivating distinctive skills and sensibilities (McLuhan 1967, Eisenstein 1979). In the 1960s, students of social change suggested that in the face of new developments in communications technology, industrial society would yield to the "information society," with consequences in every institutional realm (Machlup 1962, Bell 1973). Critical theorists problematize the effects of technological change on political deliberation and the integrity of civil society (Habermas 1989, Calhoun 1998).

Daniel Bell (1977) appears to have been the first sociologist to write about the social impact of digital communications media themselves. Bell predicted that major social consequences would derive from two related developments: the invention of miniature electronic and optical circuits capable of speeding the flow of information through networks; and the impending integration of computer processing and telecommunications into what Harvard's Anthony Oettinger dubbed "compunications" technology. Anticipating the democratization of electronic mail and telefaxing, as well as digital transmission of newspapers and magazines, Bell explored the policy dilemmas these changes would raise, calling "the social organization of the new 'compunications' technology" the most central issue "for the post-industrial society" (1977:38).

More recently, Manuel Castells has argued that the world is entering an "information age" in which digital information technology "provides the material basis" for the "pervasive expansion" of what he calls "the networking form of organization" in every realm of social structure (1996:468). According to Castells, the Internet's integration of print, oral, and audio-visual modalities into a single system promises an impact on society comparable to that of the alphabet (p. 328), creating new forms of identity and inequality, submerging power in decentered flows, and establishing new forms of social organization.

The comprehensive visions of Bell and Castells, like the other theoretical traditions we have described, suggest a range of empirical questions one must answer to understand the Internet's influence upon society. From the Marxian and Weberian traditions come concerns about power and inequality in the access to the new technology. The Durkheimian perspective sensitizes us to the new media's impact on community and social capital. The work of Habermas and Calhoun leads us to ask how the Internet may alter the practice of politics. The Weberian tradition raises the question of the effect of Internet technology on bureaucracy and economic institutions. Critical theory raises important questions of how the Internet may affect the arts and entertainment media.

We address each of these five topics in turn, summarizing the results of research undertaken by social scientists and other investigators. In most of these areas, the research literature is limited, and many questions remain. But there is a pattern: Early writings projected utopian hopes onto the new technology, eliciting a dystopian response. Research on each topic yields two conclusions. First, the Internet's impact is more limited than either the utopian or dystopian visions suggest. Second, the nature of that impact will vary depending upon how economic actors, government regulation, and users collectively organize the evolving Internet technology.

Major research questions

The Internet and inequality: opportunity or reproduction?

Enthusiasts predicted that the Internet would reduce inequality by lowering the cost of information and thus enhancing the ability of low-income men and women to gain human capital, find and compete for good jobs, and otherwise enhance their life chances (Anderson *et al* 1995). By contrast, cyber-skeptics suggest that the greatest benefits will accrue to high-SES persons, who may use their resources to employ the Internet sooner and more productively than their less privileged peers, and that this tendency would be reinforced by better Internet connections and easier access to social support (DiMaggio & Hargittai 2001).

As in other areas, early research results suggest that the outcome is more complex than either of these predictions, and that the Internet's effects on inequality will depend on the social organization of its use. In this section, we examine research on individual-level inequality among users, as well as cross-national differences in Internet penetration and inequality in effective Internet access for content producers.

The "digital divide" in the United States

Anderson *et al* (1995) were among the first to highlight the potential of inequality in Internet access to limit people's opportunities to find jobs, obtain education, access government information, participate in political dialog, and build networks of social support. By "digital divide," we refer to inequalities in access to the Internet, extent of use, knowledge of search strategies, quality of technical connections and social support, ability to evaluate the quality of information, and diversity of uses. Although some speculate that current intergroup differences will evaporate as the Internet diffuses (Compaine 2000), Schement (1999) points out that inequalities in access to information services (e.g. telephone, cable) tend to persist in contrast to the rapid diffusion of information goods (e.g. radio, television, VCRs) that reach near saturation relatively quickly. This is because the former require ongoing expenditures, whereas the latter are based on one-time purchases. For example, although 94% of all American households have telephones, this figure drops below 80% for the low-income elderly and female-headed households below the poverty level (Schement 1996).

Because sociologists have conducted so little research on the digital divide, to chart the dimensions of inequality we must rely primarily on studies reporting bivariate statistics. Reports of the National Telecommunications and Information Administration (NTIA 1995, 1998, 1999, 2000) documented differences in Internet access favoring the college educated, the wealthy, whites, people under the age of 55 and, especially in earlier years, men and urban dwellers. (Moreover, less affluent and less well-educated users are more likely to become nonusers after trying it out [Katz & Aspden 1997].) Interestingly, despite the focus of early reports on income differences, the impact of educational attainment on Internet use is twice that of income after multivariate controls (Robinson *et al* 2000b). Research has also found that Internet non-users report as reasons for not going online that they are not computer users, they do not want their children to have Internet access, they lack time or interest, or they cannot afford it (Strover & Straubhaar 2000). There is some evidence that measures of access reflect resource control, whereas measures of intensity of use are driven more by demand. Thus teenagers are less likely to report Internet access than adults between the ages of 25 and 54 (NTIA 1998); but when homes have Internet access, teenagers are online much more than adults (Kraut *et al* 1996).

Patterns of inequality are likely to reflect such changing factors as public connection availability, private subscription price, services available, and the technology necessary to access them effectively, as well as the diffusion of knowledge and the evolution of informal technical-support networks. Therefore, it is crucial to examine change in inequality over time. Three surveys conducted between 1996 and 1998 found that the gap in access between whites and African Americans had increased over time (Hoffman *et al* 2000), but NTIA surveys (1998, 2000) found that divide diminishing between 1998 and 2000. Wilhelm (2000) reports that significant differences persist in Internet use among racial and ethnic groups, with socioeconomic status held constant, and he argues that access to telecommunications tools and lack of easy access to Spanish-language content explain lower usage rates among Hispanics. By contrast, broad evidence suggests that two gaps, the advantage of men over women and of the young over the old, have declined as the technology has diffused and become more user-friendly (Roper Starch 1998, Clemente 1998, Bimber 2000, NTIA 2000, Howard *et al* forthcoming). Other evidence suggests that late adopters have less formal education and lower incomes than earlier cohorts (Howard *et al*, forthcoming, Katz *et al*, forthcoming).

Several exemplary studies go beyond description to analysis. In a study notable for its use of multivariate analysis and multiple outcome measures, Bimber (2000) found that the gap between men and women in *access* to the Internet reflected male/female differences in income and other resources; but that women with access used the Internet less frequently than did otherwise similar men, a result he attributed to the fact that full-time employment had a significant effect on frequency of use for men, but not for women. In a study exemplary for tying individual-level inequality to institutional arrangements, Strover (1999) compared dial-up Internet connectivity in four rural US counties, concluding that low levels of commercial investment in telecommunications infrastructure in sparsely populated areas limits use by generating less choice among service providers and higher connection fees.

Other research has focused on public settings that provide Internet access for pesons unable to reach the Internet at home or work. A national survey of public libraries reported that urban libraries are almost three times as likely as rural libraries to offer high-speed Internet connections; and that because many urban libraries serve high-poverty areas, access to high-speed connections is relatively available to the urban poor (Bertot & McClure 1998). An evaluation of Internet access programs at two public libraries and two community centers indicated that effectiveness was a function of the extent to which staff were trained to assist Internet users and potential users found the atmosphere welcoming and nonthreat-ening (Lentz *et al* 2000). Research on schools, another key site for public access, indicates that the proportion of US public schools offering Internet access rose from 3% in 1994 to 63% in 1999 (US Department of Education 2000), but that training and support staffing necessary for teachers to incorporate the technology effectively in instructional plans has lagged behind (Bolt & Crawford 2000).

Much research and policy assumes that people can convert Internet access into other valued goods, services, and life outcomes. Researchers have not yet tested this premise for Internet access, but research on general computer use sustains its plausibility, while leaving much to be done. Krueger (1993) reported a substantial wage premium accruing to workers who use computers. Attewell & Battle (1999) found that home computer use was significantly related to students' test scores in mathematics and reading, with higher returns for boys, whites, and the well-to-do.

The global digital divide

The number of Internet users globally skyrocketed from 16 million in 1995 to almost 360 million by mid-2000 (NUA 2000a). Despite this rapid diffusion, this number represents just 5% of the world's population. As is the case with other communications devices, access across countries is very uneven, with 97% of Internet host computers located in developed countries (ITU 1998). With respect to content, US producers dominate the Web, creating and hosting a large percentage of the most visited Web sites (OECD 1997) and so establishing English as the Internet's dominant language.

Studies of cross-national variation in levels of Internet connectivity and use are few. Most reports on global Internet diffusion present little more than descriptive statistics, emphasizing correlations with national wealth and education (ITU 1997, 1999, Partridge & Ypsilanti 1997). Cross-national differences reflect differences in the availability of local-language programming, but not that alone. Hargittai (1996) called attention to institutional factors, reporting that in 1995 three quarters of highly developed countries, but only 10% of LDCs, had commercial access providers (an indicator of private-sector involvement and thus additional impetus for diffusion). Although data quality constrains generalization, the divide between developed and less developed nations appears not to have lessened as the Internet has diffused.

Better data make it possible to analyze Internet diffusion in OECD countries in more detail. Using multivariate analyses of OECD nations, Hargittai (1999) demonstrated that national wealth and competition in the telecommunications sector (and regulatory environments fostering competition) were the strongest predictors of connectivity (see also Guillén & Suarez 2001).

Wilson (2000) distinguishes between "formal access" (physical availability) and "effective access" (affordable connectivity and diffusion of skills people need to benefit from the technology). In-depth case studies help develop this distinction. Rao et al (1999) suggest that lack of local content in native languages in South Asia discourages use. Based on a detailed review of statistics and case reports, Norris (2001) concludes that the Internet is reproducing cross-national inequalities in use of newspapers, telephones, radio, and television because diffusion largely depends on economic development and research and development investments that are unequally distributed across societies.

Yet a case study of Trinidad reports that by 1999 penetration was deep (approximately 30% of households had at least one regular user) and, while stratified by income, relatively broad. The authors attribute this both to

Trinidad's comparatively strong communications infrastructure and healthy economy, and equally important, to the premium placed on email by residents of an island nation that exports its most successful young people abroad (Miller & Slater 2000). Technologies shape themselves to the contours of local priorities and ways of life: Just as some less developed countries were vanguard adopters of sound cassettes and cell phones, some may embrace the Internet relatively quickly, especially as wireless transmission creates convergence between Internet and cell phone technologies.

Inequality in content providers' access to attention

Sociologists should be concerned not only with inequality in access to the Internet, but with inequality in access to the attention of those who use the Internet. By dramatically reducing the cost of the replication and distribution of information, the Internet has the potential to create arenas for more voices than any other previous communication medium by putting product dissemination within the reach of the individual.

Information abundance creates a new problem, however: attention scarcity (Goldhaber 1997). Content creators can only reach large audiences if online gatekeepers—Web services that categorize online information and provide links and search facilities to other sites—channel users to them (Hargittai 2000b). Yet Internet traffic is highly concentrated: 80% of site visits are to just .5% of Web sites (Waxman 2000a). As was the case with broadcast media, the growth and commercialization of the Internet has been accompanied by a commodification of attention. A rapidly evolving mosaic of search engines and point-of-entry sites compete for dominance (NUA 2000a), playing a pivotal role in channeling users' attention toward some contents and away from others (Hargittai 2000b).

During the late 1990s, entrepreneurs developed comprehensive and strongly branded "portals"—Web sites containing search engines, category guides, and various shopping and information services—to match users and content. Such sites now account for one in four of the most visited destinations of the Web (Waxman 2000b). The search engines they feature are often biased in their identification and, especially, ranking of sites in response to user queries (Introna & Nissenbaum 2000). The effects of bias are compounded by the tendency of engine users to employ simple search terms and to satisfice by terminating searches at the first acceptable site. [A 1998 analysis of almost one billion queries on the Altavista search engine revealed that 77% of sessions included but one query and 85% of users viewed only the first screen of search results (Silverstein *et al* 1998)] . Thus, Web destinations that are displayed prominently on portal sites or ranked high by search engines are likely to monopolize the attention of all but the most sophisticated and committed Internet users. Understanding the processes by which such display opportunities and ranks are awarded is an important research tack.

Research on inequality in access to and use of the Internet—among individual users, groups, organizations, countries, and content creators—should be an important priority for sociologists. At the individual level, the priority should be on using multivariate methods to explore the determinants of different measures of inequality: not just whether or not one has "access," but inequality in location of access (home, work, public facilities); the quality of hardware, software, and connections; skill in using the technology; and access to social support networks. Because inequality reflects the technology's organization, not inherent qualities, special priority should be placed on studies of how inequality is affected by such factors as government programs, industry structure and pricing policies, and approaches to the provision and organization of content.

Impact on time use and community: social isolation or social capital formation

Initial enthusiasts anticipated that the Internet would boost efficiency, making people more productive and enabling them to avoid unnecessary transportation by accomplishing online tasks like banking, shopping, library research, even socializing online. The results (less stress, more time, new online contacts) would make individuals more fulfilled and build social capital for society at large. More recently, two studies have suggested that the Internet may induce anomie and erode social capital by enabling users to retreat into an artificial world (Kraut *et al* 1998, Nie & Erbring 2000). In this section, we explore research on what Internet users do with their time, how the Internet affects their well-being, and how the Internet influences communities, both real and virtual.

Time displacement

Much of the debate over social capital is about whether the Internet attenuates users' human relationships, or whether it serves to reinforce them. Experience with earlier communications technologies suggests that Internet users may substitute time online for attention to functionally equivalent social and media activities (Weiss 1970). Thus, when television appeared in the United States, it had rapid impact on use of other media: Audiences abandoned their radio sets, movie theaters closed, and general-interest magazines stopped publishing fiction and eventually folded. Early studies documented reductions in time spent going to the movies, listening to radio, and reading fiction as television viewing time increased (Coffin 1954, Bogart 1956). Subsequent research replicated these results cross-nationally and also documented significant declines in out-of-home socializing, in-home conversation, housework, personal care activities, and even sleep (Robinson & Godby 1999).

If television, a unidirectional mass medium, displaced so many activities, then it stands to reason that the Internet, which permits interactive as well as oneway communication, might substitute for even more. Observers have expressed particular concern that Internet users may reduce the time devoted to off-line social interaction and spend less time with print media, as well as with television and other media (Nie & Erbring 2000).

The functional-equivalence model that described the effects of television thus far appears *not* to fit the experience of Internet users. Analyses of 1995 and 1998 national surveys by the Pew Center for the People and the Press, which asked respondents about activities "yesterday," have found Internet use to be unrelated or positively associated with social interaction (Robinson *et al* 1997, 2000a). Moreover, analysis of 1997 data from the federal Survey of Public Participation in the Arts indicates that Internet users (with appropriate controls) read more literature, attended more arts events, went to more movies, and watched *and* played more sports than comparable nonusers (Robinson & Kestnbaum 1999). A more recent study based on 1998 Pew Center data indicates intriguing changes associated with the Internet's diffusion: Among users who had been early adopters, Internet use was associated with *greater* use of print media. Among new Internet users, however, this relationship had disappeared (Robinson *et al* 2000b). No significant decline in TV viewing was found after demographic controls. Overall, then, these analyses provide scant support for time displacement due to functional equivalence with respect to other media. (See also Cole 2000, who found lower TV use among Internet users but slightly higher use of other media).

The situation with respect to social interaction is more complicated. Two well-publicized studies reported indications that Internet use substituted for other interactions. Kraut *et al* (1998), who used a rare longitudinal design to study 169 Pittsburgh-area families who were given computers and Internet connections over a two-year period, reported that higher levels of Internet use were "associated with declines in communication with family members, declines in social circles, and increased loneliness and depression." The authors inferred that heavy users substituted interactions with weak ties on the Internet for time spent with close friends and relatives. Yet as the researchers followed their sample they discovered that, except for increased stress, negative psychological effects decayed to statistical insignificance and some positive outcomes emerged. They attribute these changes to increases in experience and competence and, more speculatively, to the Internet's greater utility in the later period and to a change in sign of network externalities from negative to positive as more of these users' friends and family went online (Kraut *et al* forthcoming).

An innovative study that used special use-logging software to compare the online behavior of experienced and novice Web users reinforces the notion that the effect of Internet use may vary with user competence. Compared to experienced Internet users, the novices engaged in more aimless surfing, were less successful in finding information, and were more likely to report feeling a souring of affect over the course of their sessions. Their negative reactions reflected not the Internet experience per se but the frustration and sense of impotence of the inexperienced user without immediate access to social support (Neuman *et al* 1996).

Nie & Erbring (2000) surveyed four thousand Internet users online and asked how the Internet had changed their lives. Most reported no change, but heavier users reported declines in socializing, media use, shopping, and other activities. By contrast, analyses of national (off-line) sample surveys (from both 1995 and 1998) using more fine-grained activity measures indicate that Internet users are no less likely (with controls) to engage in social visiting or to call friends on the telephone. More recent surveys (online *and* off) have revealed that Internet users have *higher* levels of generalized trust and larger social networks than nonusers (Uslaner 1999, Robinson *et al* 2000b, Hampton & Wellman 2000, Cole 2000). Results from survey analyses also suggest that Internet use serves to complement rather than substitute for print media and offline socialization. Indeed, a detailed time diary study also found Internet users to be no less active media users or offline socializers than nonusers, though they did do less housework, devote less time to family care, and sleep less (Robinson *et al* 2000b).

Community

Wellman (2001) argues that the Internet has contributed to a shift from a group-based to a network-based society that is decoupling community and geographic propinquity, and thus requiring new understandings and operationalizations of the former. Consistent with this insight, Katz *et al* (forthcoming) report that Internet users visit friends more and talk with them by telephone more frequently, but that they also travel more and have fewer friends in their immediate neighborhoods.

To some extent, whether one views the Internet as corrosive to or supportive of community depends in part on how one evaluates the things people do with it. For example, Nie & Erbring (2000, p. 4) view moderate to heavy-users' self-reported substitution of email for telephone contact as part of their loss of "contact with their social environment." By contrast, Lin (2001) regards online communication, including email, as markedly expanding the stock of social capital.

Indeed, an increasing body of literature suggests that the Internet enhances social ties defined in many ways, often by reinforcing existing behavior patterns. A report on a national survey of users (Howard *et al* forthcoming) revealed that the Internet puts users in more frequent contact with families and friends, with email being an important avenue of communication. This study also suggests that research on Internet use and social capital should distinguish among different types of Internet use: The Internet seems particularly unlikely to corrode the social capital of women, more of whom than men employ the medium as a complement to other channels of social interaction. Similarly, a longitudinal study by Kraut *et al* (forthcoming) found that Internet use increased interaction with family members and reported closeness to friends, especially for users whose perceived social-support networks were strong *before* they began using the Internet.

The Internet is unique among media in making it easy for people to assemble (at a distance) and communicate with many others at the same time in such settings as chat rooms or online discussion forums. "Online communities" come in very different shapes and sizes, ranging from virtual communities that connect geographically distant people with no prior acquaintance who share similar interests, to settings that facilitate interactions among friendship networks or family members, to community networks that focus on issues relevant to a geographically defined neighborhood (Smith & Kollock 1999, Wellman & Gulia 1999, Preece 2000). Research on "online community" should distinguish among these forms, lest results appear contradictory and confusing.

Early studies tended to focus on online role-playing games [e.g. multi-user dungeons or MUDs (Turkle 1995)] and newsgroups (Hauben & Hauben 1997). These were among the first online communities and are still popular research sites, in part because researchers can obtain full transcripts of discussions and events. Such "online ethnography" has provided useful insights into issues of identity formation (Paccagnella 1997) and the status and concerns of particular groups (e.g., Kolko *et al* 2000 on race in cyberspace). But as the technology matures, ever smaller percentages of Internet users participate in online games and newsgroups. Increasingly, researchers must follow users into newer kinds of online communities based on shared interests or (physical) community networks.

The number of case studies of online communities is large and growing. Participants value such online settings for making it easy (and inexpensive) to communicate across large distances, providing opportunities for participation by the homebound aged or infirm, and enabling people with minority interests or lifestyles to find companionship and counsel unavailable in their communities of residence (Etzioni & Etzioni 1997). Rheingold's (1993) classic study of an online community emphasized the capacity of online networks to provide their members with social support. And other researchers have noted that, compared to real-life social networks, online communities are more often based on participants' shared interests rather than shared demographic characteristics or mere propinquity (Wellman & Gulia 1999). Nonetheless, issues related to racial, gender, and sexual dynamics do permeate and complicate online interactions [e.g. requiring communities to establish norms for dealing with intimidating or offensive language (Lessig 1999, Silver 2000)] .

Whereas some studies focus on "virtual" communities, others explore the impact of the Internet on geographic communities. An exemplary study of a highly wired residential community underscores the importance of examining online interactions in the context of offline everyday life (Hampton & Wellman 2000). It revealed that Internet users maintain community ties through both computer-mediated communication and face-to-face interaction. Although they maintain more long-distance relationships than do non-Internet users, they communicate even more with their neighbors—and are acquainted with three times as many of their neighbors as are their unwired peers. A study of a similar community revealed that residents make much use of the Internet for "social-capital building activities," but that individual-level community involvement and attachment increased only for residents who were already very active at the experiment's inception (Kavanaugh & Patterson forthcoming). Similarly, a study of scholarly networks found that although the Internet helps maintain contact over long distances, most email contacts are between people who also interact face-to-face (Koku *et al* 2001). In other words, research suggests that the Internet sustains the bonds of community by complementing, not replacing, other channels of interaction.

Social capital

Many scholars believe that the Internet facilitates the creation of social capital and other public goods by making information flow more efficiently through residential or professional communities (Lin 2001, Wellman 2001). Yet Putnam (2000) reports that, after demographic controls, Internet users are no different than non-users on measures of civic engagement. He notes, however, that it is premature to project this result onto future user cohorts, and he is agnostic about the Internet's contribution to social capital at the community level. Putnam calls attention to the need to understand qualitative differences between mediated and face-to-face interaction and to explore a tension between the technology's potential and the dangers of unequal access and "cyberbalkanization" (Putnam 2000:177; for an operationalization, see Van Alstyne & Brynjolfsson 1997).

Other studies indicate that, under some circumstances at least, Internet use may enhance social capital. In a longitudinal study of Pittsburgh residents, Kraut *et al* (forthcoming) found Internet use associated with greater participation in community activities and more trust (though less commitment to remaining in their community), with the positive effects greater for more extroverted participants. An analysis of online survey respondents from the United States, United Kingdom, Canada, and Australia found that increased Internet use tended to have a direct positive effect on social capital (operationalized as participation in community networks and activities) and a positive indirect effect (through social capital) on political participation (Gibson *et al* 2000).

There is much anecdotal evidence that the Internet provides significant benefits to people with unusual identities or concerns (e.g., rare medical conditions). But there is some evidence that "social capital" produced by less focused networks is rather thin. For example, a survey of users of Amsterdam's "Digital City," a multi-use space created to encourage Internet access and public-spirited interaction, found that, despite soaring membership figures, most users participated relatively infrequently and for recreational purposes (Van den Besselaar & Beckers 1998).

It has also been argued that the Internet builds social capital by enhancing the effectiveness of community-level voluntary associations, but little research evaluates this claim. The Internet has also been described as an inexpensive and effective means of organizing oppositional social movement. Lin (2001) describes the fascinating case of China's Falun Gong organization, which used the Internet to establish a powerful, hierarchical religious movement under the noses of an authoritarian regime. Whether similar movements will follow suit will depend on the success of states in monitoring and controlling such activities.

We draw five morals from the research to date. First, the Internet has no intrinsic effect on social interaction and civic participation. This nonfinding should challenge scholars to understand the circumstances under which different effects are produced, which will doubtless lead them to distinguish different profiles of Web use and different orientations of users. Second, Internet use tends to intensify already existing inclinations toward sociability or community involvement, rather than creating them ab initio. Third, we need to know more than we do about the qualitative character of online relationships. Fourth, we know that virtual communities exist in large number, but we know relatively little about their performance. Research on how virtual communities address problems of commitment and trust (like Kollock's [1999] innovative study of institutionalized reputation on E-Bay and Usenet barter sites) is necessary to understand the limits and possibilities of community online. Fifth, we need more systematic studies of how civic associations and social movements use the Internet, so that we can move beyond single cases to understanding the institutional conditions that encourage or discourage successful exploitation of this technology for collective ends.

Impact on politics: renewed public sphere or electronic battleground?

In the political domain we again find utopians and doomsayers at odds. Enthusiasts find early evidence of a re-engaged, more deliberative, more equitable political community (Browning 1996, Hill & Hughes 1998, Negroponte 1995). Skeptics foresee the re-emergence of an unresponsive commercial sphere dominated by the usual corporate players—but with an increased capacity to invade the privacy of individual citizens (Beniger 1996, Lessig 1999). Most research suggests that effects thus far have been mixed and modest.

Drawing conclusions at such early stages of technology diffusion before the emergence of stable norms is risky because it is difficult to disentangle: 1) the unique characteristics of early adopters from the characteristics of the medium in question; 2) the primitive limitations of the early Web from the technology's mature characteristics; and 3) the Web's explosive growth from other political trends (Rogers 1995, Bimber 1999). As with other topics, the literature about politics on the Internet has progressed through three stages: unjustifiable euphoria, abrupt and equally unjustifiable skepticism, and gradual realization that Web-based human interaction really does have unique and politically significant properties.

An informed public

Empirical research on mass political knowledge in industrial democracies, and particularly in the United States, has drawn heavily on the 'information cost' perspective of Downs (1957) and Schumpeter (1947) to explain why the public is so poorly informed. Because it takes time and energy to seek out, interpret, and remember political information, it may be rational to free-ride on the civic attentiveness of others. The political promise of the Internet is that it significantly lowers the behavioral costs of finding, storing, and communicating specific and personally relevant political information at convenient, timely intervals.

The literature reveals, however, that after controlling for education and political interest, there is little evidence of an effect of Internet use on political knowledge. Those who seek political information online are generally well informed to begin with, politically oriented, and heavy users of other media (Bimber 2000, Johnson & Kaye 1998). At present, the Internet supplements and complements rather than replaces traditional sources of political information (Pew 1998, 1999, Robinson *et al* 2000b). A June 2000 survey revealed that 33% of US adults (and 46% of those under thirty) go online for news at least once a week, compared to 20% in 1998, and 15% they say do so every day. About half say they seek out political news, fewer than report that they look for weather, technology, business, and sports news (Howard *et al* forthcoming). In some cases they access news not readily available through print or broadcast media, but often the Web is a supplementary medium through which conventional news organizations distribute information available through other means.

An engaged public

The economic and psychological dynamics of Web-based human communication, however, are potentially distinct enough from those of traditional print and broadcast news media that in time we may see evidence of an Internet effect. For example, news sites often provide interactive links that encourage users to "send a copy of this article to a friend or colleague." The capacity for horizontal interpersonal communication, to rebroadcast a news article with personal commentary, enhances the capacity for discussion, engagement, and the two-step flow that serves as the critical antidote to anomic mass communication (Kornhauser 1968). Evolving third-voice technologies would permit users to unilaterally convert every mass-medium Web site into an open public discussion (Dibbell 1999). Discussion groups on the Web at present lack the selective, highly edited character of letters to the editor and citizen op-eds. But though they may not achieve the ideal of deliberative discourse envisioned by Habermas (1981, Elster 1998), they would appear to be a step in that direction.

There is great concern about the political malaise and disengagement presumably reflected in low voter turnouts in US national elections. Will reduced costs of gathering political information produce higher voting rates? Probably not, due to the complex and tangled influences of multiple historical, cultural and economic trends, which render bivariate analyses of relationships between media use and electoral participation ill advised. Schudson (1998) points out that US electoral participation rates were highest in the second half of the nineteenth century, when citizens were generally uninformed and uneducated, the media were limited and sensationalistic, and quality of public debate was largely undistinguished. Bimber (2000) argues that political impact derives less from the character of the medium than from the character of information and the day-to-day culture of its use. The successful Jesse Ventura candidacy in Minnesota is widely cited as an example of grass-roots Internet populism; but in that case the Net was primarily used to organize the already engaged, not to mobilize disaffected or uninterested voters (Stromer-Galley 2000). Online financial contributions and voting online by the already politically active may prove more significant in the long run (Mintz 2000).

Political polarization

Perhaps the most central question for sociological analysis of changing technical structures of interpersonal and mass communication is the tension between forces of social integration and polarization (Neuman 2000). Many fear that the Internet will weaken the cultural center and "political commons" that network television and metropolitan newspapers provided

(Neuman 1991, Hirsch 1978). Negroponte, for example, predicts that an artificially intelligent Web-based Daily Me will select news and information based on the predilections and prejudices of the individual cybercitizen and further displace the cultural commons (Negroponte 1995).

Research on earlier media, however, indicates that individuals tend to be aware of the most popular cultural artifacts and to monitor the latest hot programs and motion pictures (Neuman 1991). Ideologically inclined individuals do choose to attend to media that reinforce their prejudices (e.g., conservatives listen to conservatively oriented radio talk shows), but expose themselves as well to opposing views (Freedman & Sears 1965, Frey 1986). The Net's capacity for anonymous communication may heighten the level of extremist and hate speech in the early stages of diffusion. But institutions of self-regulation may emerge to constrain such expression in cyberspace, as they have in nonelectronic public forums (Lessig 1999).

Deliberative democracy

Web proponents may concede that historically apolitical social strata are unlikely to be mobilized overnight by Internet political content, and agree that there are few signs thus far that the Internet has increased political fragmentation and polarization. But they insist that the Internet will enhance the quality of political discussion and the viability, meaningfulness, and diversity of the public sphere by lowering the access barrier to meaningful public speech. No longer is it necessary to own a newspaper or television station to participate: The Web is a two-way medium, and every Internet receiver can be a publisher as well (Compaine & Gomery 2000, Todreas 1999). Such claims provide critics of commercial (and especially American) dominance of the mass media and the international flow of news and culture with a new focal point for inquiry (Bennett 1995, Bourdieu 1999, Garnham 1990, McChesney 1996, Schiller 1989).

Can the Web make a real difference? It is clear that the Internet significantly lowers entry barriers and other Downsian cost factors for participation in the electronic public sphere. Bimber finds that many of the distortions of group discussion resulting from dominant personalities and group dynamics are reproduced in cyberspace, but he concludes that virtual political space (notably Usenet-style threaded discussion groups) has its place as a significant supplement to, if not replacement for, the face-to-face discussions of Habermas' idealized nineteenth-century salon (Bimber 2000, Hill & Hughes 1998, Schneider 1996). Lowering the economic costs to initiate and sustain an accessible political voice—compare a teenager's bedroom-based Web site to the cost of sustaining a printed magazine or broadcasting facility—can lower access barriers for minority voices, as well.

Skeptics argue that the commercial incentives of advertising-based media may lead ultimately to an Internet culturally indistinguishable from modern commercial television (Davis 1998, Margolis & Resnick 1999, Rheingold 1993). This debate is particularly interesting in the case of Web-based political campaigning in the United States, where by 2000, most candidates had their own Web sites, many with detailed issue and policy information unavailable through traditional media (Schneider 2000b). Will such diverse sites attract sufficient traffic to sustain themselves? Or will dominant commercial portals like AOL or specialized startups like *voter.com* dominate attention, paying for access to the public sphere through political advertising? As of this writing the jury is out, but researchers are actively studying elite and mass behavior (Schneider 2000a).

The politics of the Internet

A final note: It may be that the battle for control of the Net and for dominance in the electronic marketplace of ideas will prove to be the most fruitful arena for sociological inquiry. The tension between political ideals of openness and the strong economic incentives to sustain and protect scarcity and its corresponding economic return should sustain significant scholarship in this domain for years to come (Lessig 1999, Neuman *et al* 1998, Shapiro 1999).

Impact on organizations: flexible networks or panopticons?

Some management writers depict information technology as transforming organizations: replacing hierarchical bureaucracy with flat, networked structures in which local initiative supplants authoritative command; and replacing formal organizations themselves with "network organizations" in which agency is interstitial and strategy constantly renegotiated (Tapscott 1999). Others suggest that digital telecommunications may increase management control by permitting unprecedented degrees of surveillance (Zuboff 1989). In this section, we focus primarily on organizations' use of the public Internet, rather than on communications networks internal to the firm (the use of which is reviewed in Sproull & Kiesler 1991, Wellman *et al* 1996, and O'Mahoney & Barley 1999).

Limits on Internet impact

Little research bears directly on these claims, and what there is finds limited effects for three reasons. First, authors who make the strongest claims often conflate different types of digital technology, including workplace applications, local area networks, and the Internet. The Internet is less central to some notable organizational trends (e.g., the shrinkage of middle management) than computerization of internal functions (Board on Science, Technology & Economic Policy 1999).

Second, many structural changes associated with the "networked firm" predate the rise of information technologies alleged to have caused them (Powell 2001, Castells 1996). Although some argue that the Internet causes large firms to devolve into loosely integrated production networks by reducing information and transaction costs (Brynjolfsson et al 1994), the move toward network organizations was under way before the Internet became popular. (The Internet, though not determinant, is important. Although network forms emerged in response to competitive environments, new information technologies contributed to their rapid development [Castells 1996].)

Third, technology's effects reflect *not* its inherent potential, as futurists assume, but active choices that are shaped by technology owners' perceived interests, existing organizational structures and routines, and by cultural norms (O'Mahoney & Barley 1999, Orlikowski & Iacono 2000). Many traditional firms heavily constrain use of email and the Internet, especially by clerical and service employees, and such firms often implement systems that facilitate surveillance rather than enabling flexible, decentralized interaction (Zuboff 1989, Wellman et al 1996, Frenkel et al 1999).

Telecommuting, once predicted to rise exponentially, is a good example. Of a national sample of 1050 workers interviewed in late 1999, 41% believed they could work effectively from home, but only 10% reported their employers provided that option (and 9% reported doing so at least once a week) (Heldritch Center 2000). Other evidence suggests that most employees use home Internet connections to supplement hours at the workplace, not to substitute for them (O'Mahony & Barley: 131).

Work group effects

Research on work groups (much of it in laboratory settings) suggests that electronic communications influence interaction style and work flow. Use of electronic mail compared to telephones, for example, enables workers to control the pace of their response and thus facilitates multitasking. Digital conferencing may make employees less risk-averse and render group decision-making less predictable, more time-consuming, and more egalitarian (Sproull & Kiesler 1991, Wellman et al 1996). Whether such effects enhance organizational performance or will persist as the technologies evolve is uncertain, in part because they depend on details of system design and implementation (Sproull & Kiesler 1991, O'Mahony & Barley 1999). In vivo research suggests that formally egalitarian "network" structures may coexist with substantial hierarchy and centralization in patterns of communication (Ahuja & Carley 1998).

Firm structure effects

There is little evidence that the Internet is reshaping organizational structures. O'Mahoney & Barley report that "whether information technologies further centralization or decentralization" varies depending on how managements uses them. The few empirical studies of the relationships between digital technology and organizational size, buy-or-sell decisions, and organizational boundaries are anecdotal or inconclusive (O'Mahoney & Barley 1999: 143–45). The Internet may induce change, but we will not know until researchers undertake large-sample studies that specify changes precisely, treat separately different kinds of information technology, and distinguish effects on different kinds of workers and different business functions.

Take, for example, technology's impact on interfirm networks. Most electronic networks complement, rather than substitute for, more intimate media. For many "network organizations" propinquity is crucial in breeding trust and rapport among participants, for example enabling companies in small-firm networks to share information and exchange specialized assets (Harrison 1994). Spatial agglomeration is also central to the success of biotechnology firms (and to venture capitalists who sustain them) (Powell 2001). The most thorough review of technology-transfer research emphasizes the role of "the mobility and activity of technically trained people" over that of impersonal networks (Board on Science, Technology & Economic Policy 1999). Digital telecommunications seem most important for routine transactions (e.g., inventory systems in which multiple firms share a data base) and for communication among knowledge workers accustomed to scientific norms of exchange (e.g., R&D), and least sufficient when interactions entail risk and require interpersonal judgment.

Industry specific effects

Studies of specific industries indicate that digital telecommunications can facilitate transformative change when market pressures require it and organizational resources and structures render it possible. For example, when fierce competition and deregulation provoked change and rising demand made it profitable, trucking firms used the Internet (with such other technologies as global positioning) to develop logistics capacity and reposition themselves as transportation-services companies (Nagarajan Bander & White 2000). Hospitals and medical practices have used the Internet to pool information across entities, enabling the emergence of the "integrated healthcare systems" that are transforming many regional healthcare markets (Scott et al 2000, Starr 1997). Other industries that have used Internet technology to effect significant change are banking and financial services (Rochlin 1997) and, with distance learning, higher education (Brown & Duguid 2000:25).

In each case, firms adapted the technology to specific strategies, rather than yielding to general technological imperatives.

Thus, the Internet is implicated in profound changes in organizational structures, practices, and strategies. But the extent and nature of these changes—which business functions they restructure, which employees they affect—vary markedly by industry. And rather than causing change, digital technologies are ordinarily pressed into the service of developments to which managers are already committed. The area is ripe for both organizational case studies that focus on the Internet's use in particular industries and organizational surveys that permit confident generalization.

The Internet is also implicated in organizational change in the public sector, where enthusiasts have hailed its potential for saving tax dollars, reducing red tape, and making government more responsive. In an empirically detailed and theoretically sophisticated study, Fountain (2001a,b) has demonstrated both the potential and impediments to its realization. Implementing digital technology saves governments money, but how much depends on network externalities. It reduces some aspects of bureaucratic rigidity but strengthens others by embedding them in code. It enhances the flow of information to citizens and enables government workers to cut through red tape, but in expanding the latter's discretion, it risks imposing new forms of inequality among citizens in their relations with the state (Fountain 2001a,b).

Impact on culture: bountiful diversity, hypersegmentation, or massification?

Many sociologists feared that the original mass media (general-interest magazines, radio, and television) would inexorably "massify" taste, as profit-seeking firms produced only those homogeneous and banal programs or texts with the greatest audience appeal (Shils 1963). Since 1980, changes in consumer demand have combined with new media technologies to segment markets and differentiate cultural goods, enabling individuals and groups to individualize their media habits. As an "interconnected network of audio, video, and electronic text communication that will blur the distinction between interpersonal and mass communications and between public and private communications" (Neuman 1991, p. 12), the Internet seems designed to take these trends to their logical conclusion.

Not surprisingly, early observers viewed the new technology as profoundly liberating, opening up outlets for the creative energies of people of every taste and persuasion (Barlow 1996). Because posting information on the Web is so inexpensive, the technology's enthusiasts believed it would virtually eliminate barriers to entry in fields like music recording, book publishing, and even filmmaking. In this view, the Internet would democratize the flow of information, supplanting top-down dependence on traditional news and media organizations with bottom-up sharing among consumers themselves.

Such optimistic scenarios assume that the Internet's only impact is a direct one on costs (of cultural goods to consumers and of publication to producers). But a second, perhaps more important, effect of the Internet may be to induce the restructuring of the culture industries themselves. When goods are distributed on the Internet, they can be repackaged in many ways: newspapers, for example, can be disassembled, their parts distributed separately; recorded music can come with more textual documentation than will fit in a CD jewel box. New distribution systems may also alter the size distribution of firms within industries, the relative power of gatekeepers and artists, and the nature of competitive strategies. The Web's earliest cultural impact has been in the music industry, where it has reinforced existing trends toward deconcentration, product differentiation, and the multiplication of market channels (Dowd 2000, Caves 2000).

Some observers suggest that economic imperatives will keep the Internet from realizing its technical potential as a font of cultural abundance (Neuman 1991, Castells 1996). True, barriers to entry are formally lower; but savage competition for users' limited attention may erect new barriers based on investments in marketing and production. The major media producers are developing the Internet commercially after the model of earlier media (albeit with more interactivity), with the expectation that Internet content, broadcast entertainment, and news will soon enter homes through a single system (Castells 1996, but see Owen 1999).

A third position holds that corporate power will overwhelm the Web's liberating potential by radically accelerating long-term trends toward narrower market segmentation and more fine-grained product customization. In this view, Web sites' ability to use "cookies" to track users' browsing habits provides an unprecedented opportunity for targeting appeals. Marketers will divide the public into countless market segments and bombard them with messages that reinforce dispositions and tastes their previous browsing-and-buying patterns have revealed, engendering isolation and myopia (Turow 1997).

We have little purchase on which perspective is right for two reasons. First, aside from industry reports that many users have robust appetites for free music and sexual images, we know little about cultural practice on the Web. To be sure, the Web offers a remarkable smorgasbord of free cultural products and services. But we know little about who uses them, due to the lack of scholarly research on the extent to which, and ways in which, Internet users listen to music, visit museum sites, or read literature online. Nor do social scientists know to what extent culture consumers use the Web to cultivate existing tastes or, instead, to explore unfamiliar genres.

Second, we cannot yet tell to what extent (and how) media firms will be able to wring profits from Web-based entertainment. They will develop the Web as mass medium only if consumer demand for entertainment suffices to justify large investments (Castells 1996:365). Tendencies toward cultural fragmentation may be repelled by cultural omnivores: well-educated consumers with eclectic tastes for many (finely differentiated) genres (Peterson & Kern 1996). Government will influence the outcome through legislation and court rulings (e.g., the Napster injuncion) that define intellectual property rights.

The Internet's cultural effects may vary among user groups. Because marketers are most interested in reaching people who consume the most, their "fragmenting" efforts may focus on the well-to-do; but such users, especially when they are highly schooled, are the ones most likely to use sophisticated search strategies, so their online behavior may be less easily affected. Castells (1996:371) predicts a Web "populated by two essentially distinct populations, the *interacting and the interacted*," the first using the medium's full capacity, the latter limited to a "restricted number of pre-packaged choices."

The evolving Internet

Research on technological change teaches us that the relationship between technology and society is never unidirectional. Rather technologies are often developed in response to the agendas of powerful social actors. Initially, they shape themselves to the contours of custom; ultimately, they follow paths selected through struggles among groups seeking to turn technologies to their own interests (McGuire & Granovetter 1998).

We see this malleability in the history of the telephone, which was created as a business tool (and even a broadcasting device), but which became an instrument of sociable interaction (Fischer 1992). We see it especially in the history of radio, which emerged as an interactive medium tailored to the needs of military communication, grew into a point-to-point communications device linking amateur enthusiasts, developed into a commercial broadcast system beaming a standardized mass culture across national societies, and finally, under the impact of television's competition, transformed itself into a finely differentiated medium specializing in broadcasting musical genres to narrowly defined subcultural market segments (Douglas 1988, Hargittai 2000a, Owen 1999).

If anything, the Internet is even more pliant because it combines point-to-point and broadcast capability within a single network (Robinson *et al* 2000b, Wellman 2001). It can be a telephone: literally, or through email, chat rooms, and other forms of real-time communication between individuals. It can serve as a library: specialized Web sites "narrowcast" information to users interested enough to use search engines to find them. It can act as a soapbox for individuals expressing themselves to e-lists and discussion forums. Or it can operate as a conventional mass medium: Internet Service Providers like AOL and services like RealMedia let providers broadcast information to huge user publics simultaneously. Precisely because *it can be all of these things at once*—because it affords users choices among multiple *modes of appropriation* that coexist at any given time—the Internet is unprecedentedly malleable. This malleability raises the stakes for actors who wish to shape its evolution (Hargittai 2000b).

The findings of individual-level research on Internet use reflect the technology as it has emerged, not patterns intrinsic to the medium itself. Economic competition and public policies will shape the extent to which the Internet develops as point-to-point communicator, library, or mass medium; and this, in turn, will alter the incentives and opportunities for different kinds of individuals to use it. Thus, the social impact of the Internet depends on the impact of society on what the Internet becomes. It follows that sociologists should be studying carefully the organization of the Internet field, as well as the manner in which different ways of organizing content shape patterns of use, because such research holds the key to anticipating and understanding the Internet's effects.

Sociologists have been largely remiss in meeting this challenge. A useful exception is Aldrich's (1999:312) analysis of the Web from the standpoint of community, in which he distinguishes among governance structures (regulators and informal consortia), commercial users, service providers to those users, browser developers, and other "infrastructural populations" (hardware and software firms, ISPs, search engines, and portal sites) that occupy niches in the Web's ecology. Owen (1999: ch. 11) presents a useful overview of the Internet industry from an economics perspective, with a particularly thorough treatment of the underlying technology and of the firms that maintain the network and offer connection services. A small but interesting literature explores the Internet's emergent structure through analysis of the network created by the hyperlinks that Web sites send to one another (Zook forthcoming). Early studies using huge data sets were able to map sites onto coherent topical clusters (Larson 1996) and also reported high levels of integration, with most sites reachable from most others at a path distance of four or less (Jackson 1997).

The Internet's future, and thus its social impact, will be influenced by the resolution of three crucial policy issues. The first, establishing equality in Internet access, is necessary to ensure that less well-to-do or technically sophisticated citizens are not excluded from the political, economic, and social opportunities that the Internet increasingly provides. As our discussion of empirical work on this issue demonstrates, a sociological perspective calls attention to the need to go beyond the conventional focus on access per se to explore inequality in the combination of technical and social resources required for effective participation (DiMaggio & Hargittai 2001).

The second, establishing meaningful and enforceable norms of privacy for Internet users, involves the quest for balance between the functionality that people and businesses seek from the Internet and the sacrifice of access to personal information that the technology currently requires people to offer in exchange (Lessig 1999). Sociological research on the beliefs and practices of Internet users, online vendors, and service providers is necessary to inform policy deliberations in this area.

The third, defining rules governing intellectual property for a world in which copying and transmitting cultural works is essentially costless, entails the search for a balance between incentives necessary to motivate creative workers and the interest of society in maximizing access to works of the mind (Computer Science and Telecommunications Board 2000). Currently the pendulum has swung far in the direction of the companies that control rights to intellectual property, with implications not just for music-loving teenagers but for social scientists eager to access formerly public data bases as well (Lessig 1999). Sociologists can contribute to this debate by testing behavioral assumptions about motivations of creative workers and the requirements of markets sufficient to sustain production of intellectual goods.

Lessig (1999) makes a valuable distinction among three ways that states and private interests can regulate communications media: law, norms, and code. The Internet, he argues, is distinctive in that code—the details of the programs that facilitate the exchange of messages and information—is a particularly powerful source of social control, with direct regulation relatively less effective. His work calls attention to the importance of studying aspects of the technology that remain invisible to most observers (and of the need for sociologists studying the Web to acquire sufficient technical expertise to address these questions.).

Conclusion

Sociology has been slow to take advantage of the unique opportunity to study the emergence of a potentially transformative technology in situ. Too much of the basic research has been undertaken by nonacademic survey organizations, yielding theoretically unmotivated description at best, and technically flawed and/or proprietarily-held data at worst. (Fortunately, this is changing with such new data-collection efforts as the 2000 General Social Survey's topical module on Internet use, and with increased accessibility of data, much of which is now available on the statistically interactive web site *www.webuse.umd.edu*.) The relatively few sociologists who study the Internet have focused disproportionately on virtual communities, a worthy topic, but not the only one. And in that area, as well as in research on the Internet's impact on inequality, politics, organizations, and culture, we need to develop explanatory models that distinguish between different modes of Internet use and that tie behavior directly to social and institutional context.

Research has suffered, as well, from a disproportionate emphasis on individuals, implicitly treating the nature of the Internet itself as fixed. This is regrettable because this protean technology's character and effects will reflect the outcome of ongoing struggles among powerful economic and political actors. Yet few sociologists have examined the Internet's institutional structure, industrial organization, or political economy. Some sociologists *are* doing important work; but unless their numbers grow, a magnificent opportunity to build and test theories of social and technical change may go unexploited.

If sociology needs the Internet as a laboratory, policy makers need sociology to illuminate the collective choices that will shape the Internet's future. As Philip Agre (1998b:19) has written, discussions of the Internet are often informed less by positive knowledge than by "the cultural system of myths and ideas that our society projects onto the technology." Social science remains the best hope for substituting knowledge for myth and informing public discourse about current conditions and policy alternatives.

Acknowledgments

We are grateful to Phil Agre, Philip Howard, and Barry Wellman for wise and helpful comments on earlier drafts, and we take full responsibility for persistent defects and limitations. Research support to the authors from the National Science Foundation (grants SBR9710662, SES9819907, and IIS0086143), the Russell Sage Foundation, the Markle Foundation, and the Pew Charitable Trusts is gratefully acknowledged.

Literature cited

Abbate J. 1999. *Inventing the Internet.* Cambridge, MA: MIT Press

Agre P. 1998a. *The Internet and public discourse. First Monday 3.* http://www.firstmondaydk/issues/issue3_3/agre/index.html.

Agre P. 1998b. Presentation in *Proceeding of a Congressional Breakfast Seminar on Information Technology and Social Change*, pp. 14–19. Washington, DC: Consortium of Soc. Sci. Assoc.

Ahuja M. K., Carley K. M. 1998. Network structure in virtual organizations. *J. Computer-Mediated Commun.* http://www.ascusc.org/jcmc/vol3/issue4/ahuja.html

Aldrich H. 1999. *Organizations Evolving.* Beverly Hills, CA: Sage

Alexander J. C., ed. 1988. *Durkheimian Sociology: Cultural Studies.* New York: Columbia Univ. Press

Anderson R. H., Bikson T. K., Law S. A., Mitchell B. M. 1995. *Universal Access to E-Mail—Feasability and Societal Implications.* Santa Monica, CA: RAND

Attewell P., Battle J. 1999. Home computers and school performance. *Info. Soc.* 15:1–10

Barlow J. P. 1996. *A Declaration of the Independence of Cyberspace.* http://www.eff.org/~barlow/Declaration-Final.html

Bell D. 1973. *The Coming of Post-Industrial Society: A Venture in Social Forecasting.* New York: Basic

Bell D. 1977 [1980]. Teletext and technology: new networks of knowledge and information in postindustrial society. In *The Winding Passage: Essays and Sociological Journeys, 1960–1980*, ed. D. Bell, pp. 34–65. New York: Basic

Beniger J. R. 1996. Who shall control cyberspace? In *Communication and Cyberspace: Social Interaction in an Electronic Environment*, ed. L. Srate, R. Jacobson, S. B. Gibson, pp. 49–58. Cresskill, NJ: Hampton

Bennett W. L. 1995. *News: The Politics of Illusion.* New York: Longman. 3rd ed.

Bertot J. C., McClure C. R. 1998. *The 1998 National Survey of U.S. Public Library Outlet Internet Connectivity: Final Report.* Washington, DC: Am. Library Assoc. Natl. Com. on Libraries & Info. Sci.

Bimber B. 1998. The Internet and political transformation: populism, community and accelerated pluralism. *Polity* 31:133–60

Bimber B. 1999. The internet and citizen communication with government: Does the medium matter. *Polit. Commun.* 16:409–28

Bimber B. 2000a. The gender gap on the Internet. *Soc. Sci. Q.* 81:868–76

Bimber B. 2000b. The study of information technology and civic engagement. *Polit. Commun.* 17: In press

Bimber B. 2001. Information and civic engagement in America: The search for political effects of the Internet. *Polit. Res. Q.*

Board on Science, Technology and Economic Policy. National Research Council. 1999. *Securing America's Industrial Strength.* Washington, DC: Natl. Acad. Press

Bogart L. 1956. *The Age of Television: A Study of Viewing Habits and the Impact of Television on American Life.* New York: Ungar

Bolt D., Crawford R. 2000. *Digital Divide: Computers and Our Children's Future.* New York: TV Books

Bourdieu P. 1999. *On Television.* New York: New Press

Brown J. S., Duguid P. 2000. *The Social Life of Information.* Boston: Harvard Bus. School Press

Browning G. 1996. *Electronic Democracy: Using the Internet to Influence American Politics.* Wilton CT: Pemberton

Brynjolfsson E., Malone T., Gurbaxani V., Kambil A. 1994. Does information technology lead to smaller firms? *Mgmt. Sci.* 40:1628–44

Calhoun C. 1998. Community without propinquity revisited: communication technology and the transformation of the urban public sphere. *Soc. Inquiry* 68: 373–97

Castells M. 1996. *The Rise of the Network Society.* Vol. 1 of *The Information Age: Economy, Society and Culture.* Oxford, UK: Black-well's

Castells M. 2001. *Internet Galaxy: Reflections on the Internet, Business and Society.* New York: Oxford Univ. Press. Forthcoming

Caves R. 2000. *Creative Industries: Contracts Between Art and Commerce.* Cambridge: Harvard Univ. Press

Clemente P. C. 1998. *State of the Net: The New Frontier.* New York: McGraw Hill

Coffin T. 1955. Television's impact on society. *Am. Psychol.* 10:630–41

Cole J. 2000. *Surveying the Digital Future.* Los Angeles: UCLA Ctr. Telecommun. Policy (www.ccp.ucla.edu)

Collins R. 1979. *The Credential Society.* New York: Academic

Compaine B. 2000. *Re-examining the digital divide.* Pap. pres. 28th Annual Telecommun. Policy Res. Conf., Arlington, VA

Compaine B., Gomery D., eds. 2000. *Who Owns the Media? Competition and Concentration in the Mass Media Industry.* Mahwah, NJ: Erlbaum

Computer Science and Telecommunications Board, National Research Council. 2000. *The Digital Dilemma: Intellectual Property in the Information Age.* Washington, DC: Natl. Acad. Press

Davis J., Hirschl T., Stack M., eds. 1997. *Cutting Edge: Technology, Information Capitalism, and Social Revolution.* New York: Verso

Davis R. 1998. *The Web of Politics: The Internet's Impact on the American Political System.* New York: Oxford Univ. Press

Dibbell J. 1999. Let third voice be heard. *Intellectual Capital* (August 19). http://www.intellectualcapital.com/issues/issue282/item-6125.asp

DiMaggio P., Hargittai E. 2001. From the 'Digital Divide' to digital inequality: studying Internet use as penetration increases. Work. Pap, Ctr. for Arts Cult. Policy Stud., Princeton Univ.

Douglas S. 1987. *Inventing American Broadcasting, 1899–1922.* Baltimore: Johns Hopkins Univ. Press

Dowd T. 2001. Musical diversity and the mainstream recording market, 1955–1990. *Rassegna Italiana di Sociol.* Forthcoming

Downs A. 1957. *An Economic Theory of Democracy.* New York: Harper & Row

Eisenstein E. L. 1979. *The Printing Press as an Agent of Change.* Cambridge Univ. Press

Elster J. ed. 1998. *Deliberative Democracy.* New York: Cambridge Univ. Press

Etzioni A., Etzioni O. 1997. Communities: virtual vs. real. *Science* 277:295

Fischer C. 1992. *America Calling: A Social History of the Telephone to 1940.* Berkeley: Univ. Calif. Press

Fountain J. E. 2001a. The economic impact of the Internet on the government sector. In *The Economic Payoff from the Internet Revolution*, Rep. Brookings Task Force on the Internet. Washington, DC: Brookings Inst.

Fountain J. E. 2001b. *Building the Virtual State: Information Technology and Institutional Change.* Washington, DC: Brookings Inst.

Freedman J. L., Sears D. 1965. Selective exposure. In *Advances in Experimental Social Psychology*, ed. L. Berkowitz, 2:58–98. Orlando: Academic Press

Frenkel S. J., Korczynski M., Shire K. A., Tam M. 1999. *On the Front Line: Organization of Work in the Information Economy.* Ithaca, NY: Cornell Univ. Press

Frey D. 1986. Recent research on selective exposure to information. *Adv. Exp. Soc. Psychol.* 19:41–80

Garnham N. 1990. *Capitalism and Communication: Global Culture and the Economics of Information.* Newbury Park, CA: Sage

Gibson R. K., Howard P. E. N., Ward S. 2000. Social capital, Internet connectedness and political participation: A four-country study. Pap. pres. 2000 Int. Polit. Sci. Assoc. Meet., Quebecé, Canada

Guillén M., Suarez S. 2001. Developing the Internet: entrepreneurship and public policy in Ireland, Singapore, Argentina and Spain. *Telecommun. Policy* 25

Goldhaber M. H. 1997. The attention economy and the Net. *First Monday*

Habermas J. 1981. *The Theory of Communicative Action*, Vol. 1. *Reason and the Rationalization of Society.* Boston: Beacon

Habermas J. 1989. *The Structural Transformation of the Public Sphere.* Cambridge MA: MIT Press

Hampton K., Wellman B. 2000. Examining community in the digital neighborhood: early results from Canada's wired suburb. In *Digital Cities: Experiences,*

Technologies and Future Perspectives, ed. T. Ishida, K. Isbister, pp. 475–92. Heidelberg, Germany: Springer-Verlag

Hargittai E. 1996. *Holes in the Net: The Internet and International Stratification.* Senior Honors Thesis. Smith College. (http://cs. smith.edu/~hargitta/Thesis)

Hargittai E. 1999. Weaving the Western Web: Explaining difference in Internet connectivity among OECD countries. *Telecommun. Policy* 23:701–18

Hargittai E. 2000a. Radio's lessons for the Internet. *Commun. ACM* 43:50–57

Hargittai E. 2000b. Open portals or closed gates? Channeling content on the World Wide Web. *Poetics.* 27:233–53

Harrison B. 1994. *Lean and Mean: The Changing Landscape of Corporate Power in the Age of Flexibility.* New York: Basic

Hauben M., Hauben R. 1997. *Netizens: On the History and Impact of Usenet and the Internet.* Los Alamitos, CA: IEEE Computer Soc. Press

Heldritch Center for Workforce Development (Rutgers Univ.) and Center for Survey Research and Analysis (Univ. Conn.). 2000. *Nothing but Net: American Workers and the Information Economy.* New Brunswick NJ: Heldritch Ctr.

Hill K. A., Hughes J. E. 1998. *Cyberpolitics: Citizen Activism in the Age of the Internet.* Lanham, MD: Rowman & Littlefield

Hirsch P. M. 1978. Television as a national medium: Its cultural and political role in American society. In *Handbook of Urban Life*, ed. David Street, pp. 389–427. San Francisco: Jossey-Bass

Hoffman D. L., Novak T. P., Schlosser A. 2000. The evolution of the Digital Divide: How gaps in Internet access may impact electronic commerce. *J. Computer-Mediated Commun.* 5 March.

Howard P. E. N., Rainie L., Jones S. 2001. Days and nights on the Internet: the impact of a diffusing technology. Special issue of *Am. Behav. Sci.* ed. B. Wellman, C. Haythornthwaite. Forthcoming

Intelli-Quest. 1999. Intelliquest study shows 83 million U.S. Internet users and 56 million online shoppers. Press release, April 19. http://www.intelliquest.com/press/release78.asp

ITU (International Telecommunications Union) 1997. *Challenges to the Network: Telecoms and the Internet.* Geneva: ITU Press

ITU. 1998. *World Telecommunication Development Report.* Geneva: ITU Press

ITU. 1999. *Challenges to the Network: Internet for Development 1999.* Geneva: ITU Press

Introna L., Nissenbaum H. 2000. Shaping the Web: Why the politics of search engines matters. *Info. Soc.* 16

Jackson M. 1997. Assessing the communication structure of the World Wide Web. *J. Computer-Mediated Commun.* 3. http://www.ascusc.org/jcmc/vol3/issue1 jackson.html

Johnson T. J., Kaye B. K. 1998. A vehicle for engagement or a haven for the disaffected? Internet use, political alienation and voter participation, In *Engaging the Public: How Government and the Media Can Reinvigorate American Democracy*, ed. T. J. Johnson, C. E. Hays, S. P. Hays. New York: Rowman & Littlefleld

Katz J. E., Aspden P. 1997. Motives, hurdles and dropouts. *Commun. ACM* 40:97–102

Katz J. E., Rice R., Aspden P. 2001. The Internet, 1995–2000: Access, civic involvement and social interaction. Special issue of *Am. Behav. Sci.* ed. B. Wellman, C. Haythorn-Waite.

Kavanaugh A. L., Patterson S. J. 2001. The impact of community computer networks on social capital and community, involvement. Special issue *of Am. Behav. Sci.*, ed. B. Wellman, C. Haythornthwaite. Forthcoming

Koku E., Nazer N., Wellman B. 2001. International scholarly networks. *Am. Behav. Sci.* Forthcoming.

Kolko B. E., Nakamura L., Rodman G. B. 2000. *Race in Cyberspace.* New York: Routledge

Kollock P. 1999. The production of trust in online markets. *Adv. Group Processes* 16:99–123

Kornhauser W. 1968. Mass society. In *The Encyclopedia of the Social Sciences*, ed. D. Sills. New York: Free Press/Macmillan

Kraut R., Scherlis W., Mukhopadhyay T., Manning J., Kiesler S. 1996. The HomeNet field trial of residential Internet services. *Commun. ACM* 39:55–63

Kraut R., Patterson M., Lundmark V., Kiesler S., Mukophadhyay T., Scherlis W. 1998. Internet paradox: A social technology that reduces social involvement and psychological well-being? *Am. Psychol.* 53:1011–31

Kraut R., Kiesler S., Boneva B., Cummings J., Helgeson V. 2001. Internet paradox revisited. *J. Soc. Issues.* Forthcoming

Krueger A. B. 1993. How computers have changed the wage structure: evidence from micro data. *Q. J. Econ.* 108:33–60

Lake D. 2000. The Web: growing by 2 million pages a day. *Indust. Standard* Feb 28

Larson R. 1996. Bibliometrics of the World Wide Web: an exploratory analysis of the intellectual structure of Cyberspace. Ray R. Larson. In *ASIS '96 Proceedings of the 59th ASIS Annu. Mtg.*, ed. S. Hardin. Baltimore, MD, Oct 21–24, 1996. Medford, NJ: Info. Today, http://sherlock.berkeley.edu/asis96/asis96.html

Lentz B., Straubhaar J., LaPastina A., Main S., Taylor J. 2000. *Structuring access: the role of public access centers in the "Digital Divide."* Pap. pres. Annu. Meet. Int. Commun. Assoc, Acapulco, June.

Lessig L. 1999. *Code and Other Laws of Cyberspace.* New York: Basic

Lin N. 2001. *Social Capital: A Theory of Social Structure and Action.* New York: Cambridge Univ. Press

Machlup F. 1962. *The Production and Distribution of Knowledge in the United States.* Princeton, NJ: Princeton Univ. Press

Margolis M., Resnick D. 1999. *Taming the Cyber-Revolution: How Money and Politics Domsticate the Web.* Thousand Oaks, Calif: Sage

McChesney R. W. 1996. The Internet and U.S. communication policy-making in historical and critical perspective. /. *Commun.* 46:98–124

McGuire P., Granovetter M. 1998. *Business and bias in public policy formation: the National Civic Federation and the social construction of electric utility regulation, 1905–1907.* Pap. pres. meet. Am. Sociol. Assoc, San Francisco

McLuhan M. 1967. *Understanding Media: The Extensions of Man.* New York: McGraw Hill

Miller D., Slater D. 2000. *The Internet: An Ethnographic Approach.* New York: Berg

Mintz J. 2000. McCain camp enjoys a big Net advantage. *Washington Post.* Feb 9

Nagarajan A., Bander J. L., White C. C. 2000. Trucking. In *U.S. Industry in 2000: Studies in Competitive Performance*, ed. Board on Sci., Technol. Econ. Policy, Natl. Res. Coun., pp. 123–53. Washington, DC: Natl. Acad. Press

NTIA (National Telecommunications and Information Administration). 1995. *Falling Through the Net: A Survey of the 'Have Nots' in Rural and Urban America.* Washington, DC: US Dep. Commerce

NTIA. 1998. *Falling Through the Net II: New Data on the Digital Divide.* Washington, DC: US Dep. Commerce

NTIA. 1999. *Falling Through the Net III: Defining the Digital Divide.* Washington, DC: US Dep. Commerce

NTIA. 2000. *Falling through the Net: Toward Digital Inclusion.* Washington, DC: US Dep. Commerce

Negroponte N. 1995. *Being Digital.* New York: Knopf

Netcraft. 2000. *The Netcraft Web Server Survey.* Online document available at http://www.netcraft.com/survey/ (last accessed Aug. 25, 2000)

Neuman W. R. 1991. *The Future of the Mass Audience.* New York: Cambridge Univ. Press

Neuman W. R. 2000. The impact of the new media: fragmentation, stratification and political evolution. In *Mediated Politics: Communication in the Future of Democracy*, ed. W. L. Bennett, R. M. Entman. New York: Cambridge Univ. Press

Neuman W. R., McKnight L. W., Solomon R. J. 1998. *The Gordian Knot: Political Gridlock on the Information Highway.* Cambridge: MIT Press

Neuman W. R., O'Donnell S. R., Schneider S. M. 1996. The Web's next wave: a field study of Internet diffusion and use patterns. Ms., MIT Media Lab.

Nie N. H., Ebring L. 2000. *Internet and Society: A Preliminary Report.* Stanford, CA; Inst, for Quant. Stud. Soc.

Norris P. 2001. *Digital Divide? Civic Engagement, Information Poverty and the Internet in Democratic Societies.* New York: Cambridge Univ. Press

NUA. 2000a. How many online? *NUA Internet Surveys.* Online document available at http://www.nua.ie/surveys/how_many_online/world.html

NUA. 2000b. February 14. Portals draw lion's share of audiences. *NUA Internet Surveys.* http://www.nua.ie/surveys/?f=VS&art_id=905355592&rel=true

O'Mahony S., Barley S. R. 1999. Do digital telecommunications affect work and organization? The state of our knowledge. *Res. Org. Behav.* 21:125–61

OECD. 1997. *Webcasting and Convergence: Policy Implications.* Paris: OECD. (http://www.oecd.org/dsti/sti/it/cm/prod/e_97-221.htm)

Orlikowski W. J., Iacono C. S. 2000. The truth is not out there: an enacted view of the 'digital economy.' In *Understanding the Digital Economy: Data, Tools, and Research*, ed. E. Brynjolfsson, B. Kahin, pp. 352–80. Cambridge, MA: MIT Press

Owen B. M. 1999. *The Internet Challenge to Television.* Cambridge: Harvard Univ. Press

Paccagnella L. 1997. Getting the seats of your pants dirty: strategies for ethnographic research on virtual communities. *J. Computer-Mediated Commun.* http://www.ascusc.org/jcmc/vol3/issue1/paccagnella.html

Paltridge S., Ypsilanti D. 1997. A bright outlook for communications. *OECD Observer.* 205:19–22

Peterson R. A., Kern R. M. 1996. Changing highbrow taste: from snob to omnivore. *Am. Sociol. Rev.* 61:900–7

Pew Center for the People and the Press. 1995. *Technology in the American household.* Washington, DC http://www.people-press.org/tech.htm

Pew Center for the People and the Press. 1998. *Internet news takes off.* http://www.people-press.org/med98rpt.htm.

Pew Center for the People and the Press. 1999. *The Internet news audience goes ordinary.* January. Washington DC, Pew Res. Ctr. for People & Press

Powell W. W. 2001. The capitalist firm in the 21st century: emerging patterns. In *The 21st Century Firm: Changing Economic Organization in International Perspective,* ed. P. DiMaggio. Princeton, NJ: Princeton Univ. Press

Preece J. 2000. *On-line Communities Designing Usability and Supporting Sociability.* New York: Wiley

Prettejohn M. 1996. *The first year: August 1995–August 1996.* Netcraft. http://www.net-craft.com/survey/year1.html

Putnam R. D. 2000. *Bowling Alone: The Collapse and Revival of American Community.* New York: Simon & Schuster

Rao M., Rashid I., Rizvi H., Subba R. 2000. *Online content in South Asia.* South Asia Networks Organisation. Online document http://www.sasianet.org/onlinecont.html last accessed August 26

Rheingold H. 1993. *The Virtual Community: Homesteading on the Electronic Frontier.* Reading, MA: Addison-Wesley

Robinson J. P., Barth K., Kohut A. 1997. Personal computers, mass media, and use of time. *Soc. Sci. Computer Rev.* 15:65–82

Robinson J. P., Kestnbaum M. 1999. The personal computer, culture and other uses of free time. *Soc. Sci. Computer Rev.* Summer: 209–216

Robinson J. P., Godbey G. 1999. *Time for Life.* State College, PA: Perm State Univ. Press. 2nd ed.

Robinson J. P., Kestnbaum M., Neustadtl A., Alvarez A. 2000. *IT, the Internet, and time displacement.* Pap. pres. Annu. Meet. Am. Assoc. Pub. Opin. Res, Portland, OR, May 2000

Rochlin G. I. 1997. *Trapped in the Net: The Unanticipated Consequences of Computerization.* Princeton: Princeton Univ. Press

Rogers E. M. 1995. *Diffusion of Innovations,* New York: Free Press. 4th ed.

Roper Starch Worldwide Inc. 1998. *America Online Roper Starch Cyber study 1998.* New York

Sandvig C. 2000. *The information apologue: play and Internet access in the children's library.* Pap. pres. Int. Commun. Assoc. Annu. Meet., Acapulco, Mexico. June 1–5

Schement J. 1996. *Beyond Universal Service: Characteristics of Americans without Telephones, 1980–1993.* Commun. Policy Work. Pap. No. 1. Washington, DC: Benton Found.

Schement J. 1999. Of gaps by which democracy we measure. *Info. Impacts.* Dec.

Schiller H. I. 1989. *Culture, Inc.: The Corporate Takeover of Public Expression.* New York: Oxford Univ. Press Schiller H. 1996. *Information Inequality: The Deepening Social Crisis in America.* New York: Routledge

Schneider S. M. 1996. Creating a democratic public sphere through political discussion: a case study of abortion conversation on the Internet. *Soc. Sci. Computer Rev.* 14:373–93

Schneider S. M. 2000a. *Political portals and democracy: threats and promises.* May.nete-lection.org/commentary/2000015.php3

Schneider S. M. 2000b. *The dot-not candidates.* July, netelection.org/commentary/2000023.php3

Schudson M. 1998. *The Good Citizen: A History of American Civic Life.* New York: Free Press

Schumpeter J. A. 1947. *Capitalism, Socialism and Democracy.* New York: Harper & Row

Scott W. R., Ruef M., Mendel P., Caronna C. A. 2000. *Institutional Change and Organizations: Transformation of a Healthcare Field.* Chicago: Univ. Chicago Press.

Shapiro A. L. 1999. *The Control Revolution: How the Internet is Putting Individuals in Charge and Changing the World We Know.* New York: Century Found.

Shils E. 1963. The theory of mass society. In *American as a Mass Society*, ed. P. Olson, pp. 30–50. Glencoe, IL: Free Press

Silver D. 2000. Margins in the wires: looking for race, gender and sexuality in the Blacksburg Electronic Village. In *Race in Cyberspace*, ed. B. E. Kolko, L. Nakamura, G. B. Rodman. New York: Routledge

Silverstein C., Henzinger M., Marais H., Moricz M. 1998. Analysis of a very! large AltaVista query log. *SRC Tech. Note* 1098-014. Oct 26

Smith M., Kollock P., eds. 1999. *Communities in Cyberspace.* London: Routledge

Sproull L. S., Kiesler S. B. 1991. *Connections: New Ways of Working in the Networked Organization.* Boston: MIT Press

Starr P. 1997. Smart technology, stunted policy: developing health information networks. *Health Affairs* 15:91–105

Stoll C. 1995. *Silicon Snake Oil: Second Thoughts on the Information Highway.* New York: Doubleday

Stromer-Galley J. 2000. Online interaction and why candidates avoid it. *J. Commun.* 50. In press

Strover S. 1999. *Rural Internet Connectivity.* Rural Policy Res. Inst. Rep. P99-13. http://www.rupri.org/pubs/archive/reports/P99-13/

Strover S., Straubhaar J. 2000. *E-Government Services and Computer and Internet Use in Texas. A Report from the Telecommunications and Information Policy Institute.* Austin, TX. http://www.utexas.edu/research/tipi/reports/dk_final2.htm

Tapscott D. 1999. Introduction. *Creating Value in the Network Economy*, ed. D. Tapscott, pp. vii–xxvi. Boston: Harvard Bus. School Press

Todreas T. M. 1999. *Value Creation and Branding in Television's Digital Age.* Westport CT: Quorum

Turkle S. 1995. *Life on the Screen: Identity in the Age of the Internet.* New York: Simon & Schuster

Turow J. 1997. *Breaking Up America: Advertisers and the New Media World.* Chicago: Univ. Chicago Press

US Dep. Education. 2000. Internet access in U.S. public schools and classrooms: 1994–1999. Stats in Brief. Nat. Ctr. Educ. Stat. Feb

Uslaner E. 2001. The Internet and social capital. *Proc. ACM.* Forthcoming

Van Alstyne M., Brynjolfsson E. 1997. *Global village or cyberbalkans.* http://web.mit.edu/marshall/www/papers/CyberBalkans.pdf.

Van den Besselaar P., Beckers D. 1998. Demographics and sociographics of the "Digital City." In *Community Computing and Support Systems Social Interaction in Networked Communities*, ed. T. Ishida. Heidelberg: Springer, http://www.swi.psy.uva.nl/usr/beckers/publications/kyoto.html

Waxman J. 2000a. *The Old 80/20 Rule Take One on the Jaw. Internet Trends Report 1999 Review.* San Francisco: Alexa Res.

Waxman J. 2000b. *Leading the Pack... Internet Trends Report 1999 Review.* San Francisco: Alexa Res.

Weber M. 1968 [1924]. *Economy and Society*, ed. G. Roth, C. Wittich. New York: Bedminster

Weiss R. 1970. Effects of mass media of communication. In *Handbook of Social Psychology*, ed. G. Lindzey, E. Aronson, 5:77–195. Reading, MA: Addison-Wesley.

Wellman B. 2001. Physical place and cyber-place: Changing portals and the rise of networked individualism. *Int. J. Urban Regional Res.* Forthcoming

Wellman B., Salaff J., Dimitrova D., Garton L., Gulia M., Haythornwaite C. 1996. Computer networks as social networks: collaborative work, telework, and virtual community. *Annu. Rev. Sociol.* 22:213–38

Wellman B., Gulia M. 1999. Net surfers don't ride alone: virtual community as community. In *Networks in the Global Village*, ed. Barry Wellman, pp. 331–67. Boulder, CO: Westview

Wilhelm A. 2000. *Democracy in the Digital Age.* New York: Routledge

Wilson E. J. 2000. *Closing the Digital Divide: An Initial Review. Briefing the President.* Washington, DC: Internet Policy Inst. May. http://www.internet policy, org/briefing/ErnestWilson0700.html

Zook M. 2001. Old hierarchies or new networks of centrality? The global geography of the Internet content market. *Am. Behav. Sci.* 44: Forthcoming

Zuboff S. 1988. *In the Age of the Smart Machine: The Future of Work and Power.* New York: Basic

69

THEORIZING GLOBALIZATION

Douglas Kellner

Source: *Sociological Theory* 20(3) (2002): 285–305.

> I sketch aspects of a critical theory of globalization that will discuss the fundamental transformations in the world economy, politics, and culture in a dialectical framework that distinguishes between progressive and emancipatory features and oppressive and negative attributes. This requires articulations of the contradictions and ambiguities of globalization and the ways that globalization both is imposed from above and yet can be contested and reconfigured from below. I argue that the key to understanding globalization is theorizing it as at once a product of technological revolution and the global restructuring of capitalism in which economic, technological, political, and cultural features are intertwined. From this perspective, one should avoid both technological and economic determinism and all one-sided optics of globalization in favor of a view that theorizes globalization as a highly complex, contradictory, and thus ambiguous set of institutions and social relations, as well as one involving flows of goods, services, ideas, technologies, cultural forms, and people.

Globalization appears to be the buzzword of the 1990s, the primary attractor of books, articles, and heated debate, just as postmodernism was the most fashionable and debated topic of the 1980s. A wide and diverse range of social theorists are arguing that today's world is organized by accelerating globalization, which is strengthening the dominance of a world capitalist economic system, supplanting the primacy of the nation-state with transnational corporations and organizations, and eroding local cultures and traditions through a global culture.[1] Marxists, world-systems theorists, functionalists, Weberians, and other contemporary theorists are converging on the position that globalization is a distinguishing trend of the present moment.

Moreover, advocates of a postmodern break in history argue that developments in transnational capitalism are producing a new global historical configuration of post-Fordism, or postmodernism, as an emergent cultural logic of capitalism (Harvey 1989; Soja 1989; Jameson 1991; Gottdiener 1995). Others define the emergent global economy and culture as a "network society" grounded in new communications and information technology (Castells 1996, 1997, 1998). For others, globalization marks the triumph of capitalism and its market economy.[2] Some theorists see the emergence of a new transnational ruling elite and the universalization of consumerism (Sklair 2001), while others stress global fragmentation of "the clash of civilizations" (Huntington 1996). Driving "post" discourses into novel realms of theory and politics, Michael Hardt and Antonio Negri (2000) present the emergence of "Empire" as producing fresh forms of sovereignty, economy, culture, and political struggle that open the new millennium to an unforeseeable and unpredictable flow of novelties, surprises, and upheavals.

Indeed, globalization is one of the most hotly debated issues of the present era. For some, it is a cover concept for global capitalism and imperialism and is accordingly condemned as another form of the imposition of the logic of capital and the market on ever more regions of the world and spheres of life. For others, it is the continuation of modernization and a force of progress, increased wealth, freedom, democracy, and happiness. Its defenders present globalization as beneficial, generating fresh economic opportunities, political democratization, cultural diversity, and the opening to an exciting new world. Its critics see globalization as harmful, bringing about increased domination and control by the wealthier overdeveloped nations over the poor underdeveloped countries, thus increasing the hegemony of the "haves" over the "have-nots." In addition, supplementing the negative view, globalization critics assert that globalization produces an undermining of democracy, a cultural homogenization, and increased destruction of natural species and the environment.[3] Some imagine the globalization project—whether viewed positively or negatively—as inevitable and beyond human control and intervention, whereas others view it generating new conflicts and new spaces for struggle, distinguishing between globalization from above and globalization from below (Brecher, Costello, and Smith 2000).

In this study, I sketch aspects of a critical theory of globalization that will discuss the fundamental transformations in the world economy, politics, and culture in a dialectical framework that distinguishes between progressive and emancipatory features and oppressive and negative attributes. This requires articulations of the contradictions and ambiguities of globalization and the ways that globalization both is imposed from above and yet can be contested and reconfigured from below. I argue that the key to understanding globalization is theorizing it as at once a product of technological revolution and the global restructuring of capitalism in which economic, technological, political, and cultural features are intertwined. From this perspective, one should avoid both technological and economic determinism and all one-sided optics of globalization in favor of a view that theorizes globalization as a highly complex, contradictory, and thus ambiguous set of institutions and social relations, as well as one involving flows of goods, services, ideas, technologies, cultural forms, and people (see Appadurai 1996).

Finally, I will raise the question of whether debates centered around the "post" (e.g., postmodernism, postindustrialism, post-Fordism, and so on) do or do not help elucidate the phenomenon of globalization. I argue in the affirmative, claiming that discourses of the "post" dramatize what is new, original, and different in our current situation, but that such discourses can be and are easily misused. For the discourse of postmodernity, for example, to have any force, it must be grounded in analysis of scientific and technological revolution and the global restructuring of capital, or it is just an empty buzzword (see Best and Kellner 1997, 2001). Thus, to properly theorize postmodernity one must articulate globalization and the roles of technoscience and new technologies in its construction. In turn, understanding how scientific and technological revolution and the global restructuring of capitalism are creating unique historical configurations of globalization helps one perceive the urgency and force of the discourse of the "post."

Globalization, technological revolution, and the restructuring of capitalism

For critical social theory, globalization involves both capitalist markets and sets of social relations *and* flows of commodities, capital, technology, ideas, forms of culture, and people across national boundaries via a global networked society (see Castells 1996, 1997, 1998; Held *et al.* 1999). The transmutations of technology and capital work together to create a new globalized and interconnected world. A technological revolution involving the creation of a computerized network of communication, transportation, and exchange is the presupposition of a globalized economy, along with the extension of a world capitalist market system that is absorbing ever more areas of the world and spheres of production, exchange, and consumption into its orbit. The technological revolution presupposes global computerized networks and the free movement of goods, information, and peoples across national boundaries. Hence, the Internet and global computer networks make possible globalization by producing a technological infrastructure for the global economy. Computerized networks, satellite-communication systems, and the software and hardware that link together and facilitate the global economy depend on breakthroughs in microphysics. Technoscience has generated transistors, increasingly powerful and sophisticated computer chips, integrated circuits, high-tech communication systems, and a technological revolution that provides an infrastructure for the global economy and society (see Gilder 1989, 2000; Kaku 1997; Best and Kellner 2001).

From this perspective, globalization cannot be understood without comprehending the scientific and technological revolutions and global restructuring of capital that are the motor and matrix of globalization. Many theorists of globalization, however, either fail to observe the fundamental importance of scientific and technological revolution and the new technologies that help spawn globalization or interpret the process in a technological determinist framework that occludes the economic dimensions of the imperatives and institutions of capitalism. Such one-sided optics fail to grasp the co-evolution of science, technology, and capitalism and the complex and highly ambiguous system of globalization that combines capitalism and democracy, technological mutations, and a turbulent mixture of costs and benefits, gains and losses.

In order to theorize the global network economy, one therefore needs to avoid the extremes of technological and economic determinism. Technological determinists frequently use the discourse of postindustrial or postmodern society to describe current developments. This discourse often produces an ideal-type distinction between a previous mode of industrial production, characterized by heavy industry, mass production and consumption, bureaucratic organization, and social conformity, and a new postindustrial society, characterized by "flexible production" or post-Fordism, in which new technologies serve as the demiurge to a new postmodernity (Harvey 1981).

For postmodern theorists such as Jean Baudrillard (1993), technologies of information and social reproduction (e.g., simulation) have permeated every aspect of society and created a new social environment. In the movement toward postmodernity, Baudrillard claims that humanity has left behind reality and modern conceptions, as well as the world of modernity. This postmodern adventure is marked by an implosion of technology and the human, which is generating a new posthuman species and postmodern world.[4] For other less extravagant theorists of the technological revolution, the human species is evolving into a novel, postindustrial technosociety, culture, and condition in which technology, knowledge, and information are the axial or organizing principles (Bell 1976).

There are positive and negative models of technological determinism. A positive discourse envisages new technologies as producing a new economy interpreted affirmatively as fabricating a fresh wealth of nations. On this affirmative view, globalization provides opportunities for small business and individual entrepreneurs, empowering excluded persons and social groups. Technophiles claim that new technologies also make possible increased democratization, communication, education, culture, entertainment, and other social benefits, thus generating a utopia of social progress.

Few legitimating theories of the information and technological revolution, however, contextualize the structuring, implementation, marketing, and use of new technologies in the context of the vicissitudes of contemporary capitalism. The ideologues of the information society act as if technology were an autonomous force and either neglect to theorize the co-evolution of capital and technology or use the advancements of technology to legitimate market capitalism (i.e., Gilder 1989, 2000; Gates 1995, 1999; Friedman 1999). Theorists such as Kevin Kelly, the executive editor of *Wired*, think that humanity has entered a postcapitalist society that constitutes an original and innovative stage of history and economy at which previous categories do not apply.[5] Or, like Bill Gates (1995, 1999), defenders of the "new economy" imagine computer and information technologies producing a "friction-free capitalism," perceived as a highly creative form of capitalism that goes beyond its previous contradictions, forms, and limitations.

By contrast, a negative version of technological determinism portrays the new world system as constituted by a monolithic or homogenizing technological system of domination. German philosopher and Nazi supporter Martin Heidegger talked of the "complete Europeanisation of the earth and man" (Heidegger 1971:15), claiming that Western science and technology were creating a new organization or framework, which he called *Gestell* (or "enframing"), that was encompassing ever more realms of experience. French theorist Jacques Ellul (1964) depicted a totalitarian expansion of technology—what he called *la technique*—imposing its logic on ever more domains of life and human practices. More recently, a large number of technophobic critics have argued that new technologies and global cyberspace constitute a realm of alienation and reification in which humans are alienated from our bodies, other people, nature, tradition, and lived communities (Borgmann 1994, 1999; Slouka 1995; Stoll 1995; Shenk 1997; Virilio 1998).

In addition to technologically determinist and reductive postindustrial accounts of globalization, there are economic determinist discourses that view it primarily as the continuation of capitalism, rather than its restructuring through technological revolution. A large number of theorists conceive globalization simply as a process of the imposition of the logic of capital and neoliberalism on various parts of the world, rather than seeing the restructuring process and the enormous changes and transformations that scientific and technological revolution are producing in the networked economy and society. Capital-logic theorists, for instance, portray globalization primarily as the imposition of the logic of capital on the world economy, polity, and culture, often engaging in economic determinism, rather than seeing the complex new configurations of economy, technology, polity, and culture and the attendant forces of domination and resistance. In the same vein, some critical theorists depict globalization as the triumph of a globalized hegemony of market capitalism, where capital creates a homogeneous world culture of commercialization, commodification, administration, surveillance, and domination (Robins and Webster 1999).

From these economistic perspectives, globalization is merely a continuation of previous social tendencies—that is, the logic of capital and domination by corporate and commercial interests of the world economy and culture. Defenders of capitalism, by contrast, present globalization as the triumph of free markets, democracy, and individual freedom (Fukuyama 1992; Friedman 1999). Hence, both positive and negative versions of economic and technological determinism exist. Most theories of globalization, therefore, are reductive, undialectical, and one-sided, either failing to see the interaction between technological features of globalization and the global restructuring of capitalism or failing to articulate the complex relations between capitalism and democracy. Dominant discourses of globalization are thus one-sidedly for or against globalization, failing to grasp the contradictions and the conflicting costs and benefits, upsides and downsides, of the process. Hence, many current theories of globalization do not capture the novelty and ambiguity of the present moment, which involves both innovative forms of technology and economy and emergent conflicts and problems generated by the contradictions of globalization.

In particular, an economic determinism and reductionism that merely depicts globalization as the continuation of market capitalism fails to comprehend the emergent forms and modes of capitalism itself, which are based on novel developments in science, technology, culture, and everyday life. Likewise, technological determinism fails to note how the new technologies and new economy are part of a global restructuring of capitalism and are not autonomous forces that themselves are engendering a new society and economy that breaks with the previous mode of social organization. The postindustrial society is sometimes referred to as the "knowledge society" or "information society," in which knowledge and information are given more predominant roles than in earlier days (see the survey and critique in Webster 1995). It is now obvious that the knowledge and information sectors are increasingly important domains of our contemporary moment, and that the theories of Daniel Bell and other postindustrial theorists are thus not as ideological and far off the mark as many of his critics on the left once argued. In order to avoid the technological determinism and idealism of many forms of this theory, however, one should theorize the information or knowledge "revolution" as part and parcel of a new form of *technocapitalism* marked by a synthesis of capital and technology.

Some poststructuralist theories that stress the complexity of globalization exaggerate the disjunctions and autonomous flows of capital, technology, culture, people, and goods. Thus, a critical theory of globalization grounds globalization in a theory of capitalist restructuring and technological revolution. To paraphrase Max Horkheimer, whoever wants to talk about capitalism must talk about globalization, and it is impossible to theorize globalization without talking about the restructuring of capitalism. The term "technocapitalism" is useful to describe the synthesis of capital and technology in the present organization of society (Kellner 1989a). Unlike theories of postmodernity (e.g., Baudrillard's) or the knowledge and information society, which often argue that technology is *the* new organizing principle of society, the concept of technocapitalism points to both the increasingly important role of technology *and* the enduring primacy of capitalist relations of production. In an era of unrestrained capitalism, it would be difficult to deny that contemporary societies are still organized around production and capital accumulation and that capitalist imperatives continue to dominate production, distribution, and consumption, as well as other cultural, social, and political domains.[6] Workers remain exploited by capitalists, and capital persists as the hegemonic force—more so than ever after the collapse of communism.

Moreover, with the turn toward neoliberalism as a hegemonic ideology and practice, the market and its logic come to triumph over public goods, and the state is subservient to economic imperatives and logic. Yet the term "technocapitalism" points to a new configuration of capitalist society in which technical and scientific knowledge, computerization and automation of labor, and information technology and multimedia play a role in the process of production analogous to the function of human labor-power, mechanization of the labor process, and machines in an earlier era of capitalism. This process is generating novel modes of societal organization, forms of culture and everyday life, conflicts, and modes of struggle.

The emergence of innovative forms of technology, politics, culture, and economy marks a situation parallel to that confronted by the Frankfurt school in the 1930s. These German theorists, who left Nazi Germany, were forced to theorize the new configurations brought about by the transition from market to state-monopoly capitalism (Bronner and Kellner 1989; Kellner 1989a). In their now classic texts, the Frankfurt school analyzed: the emergent forms of social and economic organization, technology, and culture; the rise of giant corporations and cartels and the capitalist state in "organized capitalism," in both its fascist and "democratic" state capitalist forms; and the culture industries and mass culture that served as new modes of social control, powerful forms of ideology and domination, and novel configurations of culture and everyday life.

Today, critical theorists confront the challenge of theorizing the emergent forms of technocapitalism and novelties of the present era constructed by syntheses of technology and capital in the formation of a new stage of global capitalism. The notion of technocapitalism attempts to avoid technological or economic determinism by guiding theorists to perceive the interaction of capital and technology in the present moment. Capital is generating innovative forms of technology, just as its restructuring is producing novel configurations of a networked global economy, culture, and polity. In terms of political economy, the emergent postindustrial form of technocapitalism is characterized by a decline of the state and the increased power of the market, accompanied by the growing power of globalized transnational corporations and governmental bodies and the declining power of the nation-state and its institutions—which remain, however, extremely important players in the global economy, as the responses to the terror attacks of September 11 document.

Globalization is also constituted by a complex interconnection between capitalism and democracy that involves positive and negative features and both empowers and disempowers individuals and groups, undermining and yet creating potential for fresh types of democracy. Yet many theories of globalization present it as either primarily negative, a disaster for the human species, or positive, as bringing a wealth of products, ideas, and economic opportunities to a global arena. Hence, I would advocate development of a critical theory of globalization that would dialectically appraise its positive and negative features. A critical theory is sharply critical of globalization's oppressive effects and skeptical of legitimating ideological discourse, but it also recognizes the centrality of the phenomenon in the present age. And it affirms and promotes globalization's progressive features (such as the Internet, which, as I document below, makes possible a reconstruction of education and more democratic polity, as well as increasing the power of capital), while noting contradictions and ambiguities.

The contradictions of globalization

The terrorist acts on the United States on September 11 and the subsequent Terror War dramatically disclose the downsides of globalization—the ways that global flows of technology, goods, information, ideologies, and people can have destructive as well as productive effects. The disclosure of powerful anti-Western terrorist networks shows that globalization divides the world as it unifies, that it produces enemies as it incorporates participants. The events disclose explosive contradictions and conflicts at the heart of globalization and the fact that the technologies of information, communication, and transportation that facilitate globalization can also be used to undermine and attack it, to generate instruments of destruction as well as production.[7]

The experience of September 11 points to the objective ambiguity of globalization: that positive and negative sides are interconnected, that the institutions of the open society unlock the possibilities of destruction and violence as well as those of democracy, free trade, and cultural and social exchange. Once again, the interconnection and interdependency of the networked world was dramatically demonstrated, as terrorists from the Middle East brought local grievances from their region to attack key symbols of American power and the very infrastructure of New York. Some saw terrorism as an expression of the dark side of globalization, while I would conceive it as part of the objective ambiguity of globalization that simultaneously creates friends and enemies, wealth and poverty, and growing divisions between the "haves" and "have-nots." Yet the downturning of the global economy, intensification of local and global political conflicts, repression of human rights and civil liberties, and general increase in fear and anxiety have certainly undermined the naïve optimism of globaphiles who perceived globalization as a purely positive instrument of progress and well-being.

The use of powerful technologies as weapons of destruction also discloses current asymmetries of power and emergent forms of terrorism and war, as the new millennium has exploded into dangerous conflicts and interventions. As technologies of mass destruction become more available and dispersed, perilous instabilities have emerged that have elicited policing measures to stem the flow of movements of people and goods both across borders and internally. In particular, the U.S. Patriot Act has led to repressive measures that are replacing the spaces of the open and free information society with new forms of surveillance, policing, and repression.

Ultimately, however, the abhorrent terror acts by Osama bin Laden's network and the violent military response to the al-Qaeda terrorist acts by the Bush Administration may be an anomalous paroxysm, whereby a highly regressive premodern Islamic fundamentalism has clashed with an old-fashioned patriarchal and unilateralist Wild West militarism. It could be that such forms of terrorism, militarism, and state repression will be superseded by more rational forms of politics that globalize and criminalize terrorism and that do not sacrifice the benefits of the open society and economy in the name of security. Yet the events of September 11 may open a new era of Terror War that will lead to the kind of apocalyptic futurist world depicted by cyberpunk fiction (see Kellner forthcoming).

In any case, the events of September 11 have promoted a fury of reflection, theoretical debates, and political conflicts and upheaval that put the complex dynamics of globalization at the center of contemporary theory and politics. To those skeptical of the centrality of globalization to contemporary experience, it is now clear that we are living in a global world that is highly interconnected and vulnerable to passions and crises that can cross borders and can affect anyone or any region at any time. The events of September 11 also provide a test case to evaluate various theories of globalization and the contemporary era. In addition, they highlight some of the contradictions of globalization and the need to develop a highly complex and dialectical model to capture its conflicts, ambiguities, and contradictory effects.

Consequently, I want to argue that in order to properly theorize globalization, one needs to conceptualize several sets of contradictions generated by globalization's combination of technological revolution and restructuring of capital, which in turn generates tensions between capitalism and democracy and "haves" and "have-nots." Within the world economy, globalization involves the proliferation of the logic of capital, but also the spread of democracy in information, finance, investing, and the diffusion of technology (see Friedman 1999; Hardt and Negri 2000). Globalization is thus a contradictory amalgam of capitalism and democracy in which the logic of capital and the market system enter ever more arenas of global life, even as democracy spreads and more political regions and spaces of everyday life are being contested by democratic demands and forces. But the overall process is contradictory. Sometimes globalizing forces promote democracy and sometimes they inhibit it. Thus, both equating capitalism and democracy and simply opposing them are problematic. These tensions are especially evident, as I will argue, in the domain of the Internet and the expansion of new realms of technologically mediated communication, information, and politics.

The processes of globalization are highly turbulent and have generated new conflicts throughout the world. Benjamin Barber (1996) describes the strife between McWorld and Jihad, contrasting the homogenizing, commercialized, Americanized tendencies of the global economy and culture with traditional cultures, which are often resistant to globalization. Thomas Friedman (1999) makes a more benign distinction between what he calls the Lexus and the Olive Tree. The former symbolizes modernization, affluence and luxury, and Westernized consumption; the latter symbolizes roots, tradition, place, and stable community.

Barber's model oversimplifies present world divisions and conflicts and does not adequately present the contradictions within the West or the "Jihad" world, although he postulates a dialectical interpenetrating of both forces and sees both as opposed to democracy. His book does, however, point to problems and limitations of globalization, noting serious conflicts and opponents, unlike Thomas Friedman's harmonizing duality of *The Lexus and the Olive* (1999), which suggests that both poles of capitalist luxury and premodern roots are parts of the globalization process. In an ode to globalization, Friedman assumes the dual victory of capitalism and democracy, a la Fukuyama, while Barber demonstrates contradictions and tensions between capitalism and democracy within the New World (Dis)Order, as well as the antidemocratic animus of Jihad.

Hence, Friedman (1999) is too uncritical of globalization, caught up in his own Lexus high-consumption lifestyle, failing to perceive the depth of the oppressive features of globalization and the breadth and extent of resistance and opposition to it. In particular, he fails to articulate contradictions between capitalism and democracy and the ways that globalization and its economic logic undermine democracy as well as circulating it. Likewise, he does not grasp the virulence of the premodern and Jihadist tendencies that he blithely identifies with the Olive Tree, or the reasons why many parts of the world so strongly resist globalization and the West.

Consequently, it is important to present globalization as a strange amalgam of both homogenizing forces of sameness and uniformity *and* heterogeneity, difference, and hybridity, as well as a contradictory mixture of democratizing and antidemocratizing tendencies. On the one hand, globalization unfolds a process of standardization in which a globalized mass culture circulates the globe, creating sameness and homogeneity everywhere. On the other hand, globalized culture makes possible unique appropriations and developments everywhere, thus encouraging hybridity, difference, and heterogeneity to proliferate.[8] Every local context involves its own appropriation and reworking of global products and signifiers, thus encouraging difference, otherness, diversity, and variety (Luke and Luke 2000). Grasping that globalization embodies these contradictory tendencies at once—that it can be a force of both homogenization and heterogeneity—is crucial to articulating the contradictions of globalization and avoiding one-sided and reductive conceptions.

My intention is to present globalization as conflictual, contradictory, and open to resistance and democratic intervention and transformation, not just as a monolithic juggernaut of progress or domination, as in many discourses. This goal is advanced by distinguishing between "globalization from below" and the "globalization from above" of corporate capitalism and the capitalist state, a distinction that should help us to get a better sense of how globalization does or does not promote democratization.

"Globalization from below" refers to the ways in which marginalized individuals and social movements resist globalization and/or use its institutions and instruments to further democratization and social justice. While on one level globalization significantly increases the supremacy of big corporations and big government, it can also give power to groups and individuals who were previously left out of the democratic dialogue and terrain of political struggle. Such potentially positive effects of globalization include increased access to education for individuals excluded from entry to culture and knowledge and the possible opportunity for oppositional individuals and groups to participate in global culture and politics through access to global communication and media networks and to circulate local struggles and oppositional ideas through these media. The role of new technologies in social movements, political struggle, and everyday life forces social movements to reconsider their political strategies and goals and democratic theory to appraise how new technologies do and do not promote democratization (Kellner 1997, 1999b), social justice, and other positive attributes. Indeed, the movements against capitalist globalization that I would endorse are those that oppose oppressive institutions of capitalist globalization such as the WTO, IMF, and certain transnational corporations and that are for positive values such as social justice, labor and human rights, and ecology.

In their magisterial book *Empire*, Hardt and Negri (2000) present contradictions within globalization in terms of an imperializing logic of "Empire" and an assortment of struggles by the "multitude," creating a contradictory and tension-filled situation. As in my conception, Hardt and Negri present globalization as a complex process that involves a multidimensional mixture of production and effects of the global economy and capitalist market system, new technologies and media, expanded judicial and legal modes of governance, and emergent modes of power, sovereignty, and resistance.[9] Combining poststructuralism with "autonomous Marxism," Hardt and Negri stress political openings and possibilities of struggle within *Empire* in an optimistic and buoyant text that envisages progressive democratization and self-valorization in the turbulent process of the restructuring of capital.

Many theorists, by contrast, have argued that one of the trends of globalization is depoliticization of publics, the decline of the nation-state, and the end of traditional politics (Boggs 2000). While I would agree that globalization is promoted by tremendously powerful economic forces and that it often undermines democratic movements and decisionmaking, I would also argue that there are openings and possibilities for a globalization from below that inflects globalization for positive and progressive ends, and that globalization can thus help promote as well as undermine democracy.[10] Globalization involves both a disorganization and reorganization of capitalism, a tremendous restructuring process, which creates openings for progressive social change and intervention. In a more fluid and open economic and political system, oppositional forces can gain concessions, win victories, and effect progressive changes. During the 1970s, new social movements, new nongovernmental organizations (NGOs), and new forms of struggle and solidarity emerged that have been expanding to the present day (Hardt and Negri 2000; Burbach 2001; Foran forthcoming).

The present conjuncture, I would suggest, is marked by a conflict between growing centralization and organization of power and wealth in the hands of the few and opposing processes exhibiting a fragmentation of power that is more plural, multiple, and open to contestation than was previously the case. As the following analysis will suggest, both tendencies are observable; it is up to individuals and groups to find openings for political intervention and social transformation. Thus, rather than just denouncing globalization or engaging in celebration and legitimation, a critical theory of globalization reproaches those aspects that are oppressive while seizing upon opportunities to fight domination and exploitation and to promote democratization, justice, and a progressive reconstruction of the polity, society, and culture.

Against capitalist globalization from above, there have been a significant eruption of forces and subcultures of resistance that have attempted to preserve specific forms of culture and society against globalization and homogenization and to create alternative forces of society and culture, thus exhibiting resistance and globalization from below. Most dramatically, peasant and guerrilla movements in Latin America, labor unions, students, and environmentalists throughout the world, and a variety of other groups and movements have resisted capitalist globalization and attacks on previous rights and benefits.[11] Several dozen people's organizations from around the world have protested World Trade Organization (WTO) policies, and a backlash against globalization is visible everywhere. Politicians who once championed trade agreements like the General Agreement on Tariffs and Trade (GATT) and the North American Free Trade Agreement (NAFTA) are now often quiet about these arrangements. At the 1996 annual Davos World Economic Forum, its founder and managing director presented a warning entitled "Start Taking the Backlash Against Globalization Seriously." Reports surfaced that major representatives of the capitalist system expressed fear that capitalism was getting too mean and predatory, that it needs a kinder and gentler state to ensure order and harmony, and that the welfare state might make a come-back (see *New York Times* 1996:A15).[12] One should take such reports with the proverbial grain of salt, but they do express fissures and openings in the system for critical discourse and intervention.

Indeed, by 1999, the theme of the annual Davos conference centered around making globalization work for poor countries and minimizing the differences between the "haves" and the "have-nots." The growing divisions between rich and poor were worrying some globalizers, as was the wave of crises in Asian, Latin American, and other developing countries. In James Flanigan's report in the *Los Angeles Times* (Flanigan 1999), the "main theme" is to "spread the wealth. In a world frightened by glaring imbalances and the weakness of economies from Indonesia to Russia, the talk is no longer of a new world economy getting stronger but of ways to 'keep the engine going'" (p. A13). In particular, the globalizers were attempting to keep economies growing in the more developed countries and capital flowing to developing nations. U.S. Vice President Al Gore called on all countries to spur economic growth, and he proposed a new U.S.–led initiative to eliminate the debt burdens of developing countries. South African President Nelson Mandela asked: "Is globalization only for the powerful? Does it offer nothing to the men, women and children who are ravaged by the violence of poverty?" (ibid.).

The global movement against capitalist globalization

No clear answer emerged to Mandela's question as the new millennium opened, and with the global economic recession and the Terror War erupting in 2001, the situation of many developing countries has worsened. Yet as part of the backlash against globalization over the past years, a number of theorists have argued that the proliferation of difference and the move to more local discourses and practices define the contemporary scene. In this view, theory and politics should shift from the level of globalization and its accompanying, often totalizing, macrodimensions in order to focus on the local, the specific, the particular, the heterogeneous, and the microlevel of everyday experience. An array of theories associated with poststructuralism, postmodernism, feminism, and multiculturalism focuses on difference, otherness, marginality, the personal, the particular, and the concrete over more general theory and politics that aim at more global or universal conditions.[13] Likewise, a broad spectrum of subcultures of resistance have focused their attention on the local level, organizing struggles around identity issues such as gender, race, sexual preference, and youth subculture.

It can be argued that such dichotomies as those between the global and the local express contradictions and tensions between crucial constitutive forces of the present moment, and that it is therefore a mistake to reject focus on one side in favor of exclusive concern with the other (Cvetkovich and Kellner 1997). Hence, an important challenge for a critical theory of globalization is to think through the relationships between the global and the local by observing how global forces influence and even structure an increasing number of local situations. This requires analysis of how local forces mediate the global, inflecting global forces to diverse ends and conditions and producing unique configurations of the local and the global as the matrix for thought and action in the contemporary world (see Luke and Luke 2000).

Globalization is thus necessarily complex and challenging to both critical theories and radical democratic politics. However, many people operate with binary concepts of the global and the local and promote one or the other side of the equation as the solution to the world's problems. For globalists, globalization is the solution and underdevelopment, backwardness, and provincialism are the problems. For localists, globalization is the problem and localization is the solution. Less simplistically, however, it is the mix that matters, and whether global or local solutions are most fitting depends on the conditions in the distinctive context that one is addressing and the specific solutions and policies being proposed.

For instance, the Internet can be used to promote capitalist globalization or struggles against it. One of the more instructive examples of the use of the Internet to foster movements against the excesses of corporate capitalism occurred in the protests in Seattle and throughout the world against the World Trade Organization (WTO) meeting in December 1999. Behind these actions lay a global protest movement, using the Internet to organize resistance to the WTO and capitalist globalization while championing democratization. Many Web sites contained anti-WTO material, and numerous mailing lists used the Internet to distribute critical material and to organize the protest. This resulted in the mobilization of caravans from all over the United States to take protestors, many of whom had never met and had been recruited through the Internet, to Seattle. There were also significant numbers of international participants in Seattle, which exhibited labor, environmentalist, feminist, anticapitalist, animal rights, anarchist, and other groups organized to protest aspects of globalization and form new alliances and solidarities for future struggles. In addition, protests occurred throughout the world, and a proliferation of material against the extremely secret WTO spread throughout the Internet.[14]

Furthermore, the Internet provided critical coverage of the event, documentation of the various groups' protests, and debate over the WTO and globalization. Whereas the mainstream media presented the protests as "antitrade," featuring the incidents of anarchist violence against property while minimizing police violence against demonstrators, the Internet provided pictures, eyewitness accounts, and reports of police brutality and the generally peaceful and nonviolent nature of the protests. While the mainstream media framed the protests negatively and privileged suspect spokespeople such as Patrick Buchanan as critics of globalization, the Internet provided multiple representations of the demonstrations, advanced reflective discussion of the WTO and globalization, and presented a diversity of critical perspectives.

The Seattle protests had some immediate consequences. The day after the demonstrators made good on their promise to shut down the WTO negotiations, Bill Clinton gave a speech endorsing the concept of labor rights enforceable by trade sanctions, thus effectively making impossible any agreement and consensus during the Seattle meetings. In addition, at the World Economic Forum in Davos a month later, there was much discussion of how concessions on labor and the environment were necessary if consensus over globalization and free trade were to be possible. Importantly, the issue of overcoming divisions between the information-rich and poor and improving the lot of the disenfranchised and oppressed—bringing the benefits of globalization to these groups—were also seriously discussed at the meeting and in the media.

More significantly, many activists were energized by the new alliances, solidarities, and militancy and continued to cultivate an antiglobalization movement. The Seattle demonstrations were followed by struggles in April 2000 in Washington, DC, to protest the World Bank and the International Monetary Fund (IMF), and later in the year against capitalist globalization in Prague and Melbourne. In April 2001, an extremely large and militant protest erupted against the Free Trade Area of the Americas summit in Quebec City, and in summer 2001 a large demonstration took place in Genoa.

In May 2002, a surprisingly large demonstration took place in Washington, DC against capitalist globalization and for peace and justice, and it was apparent that a new worldwide movement was in the making, uniting diverse opponents of capitalist globalization throughout the world. The anticorporate globalization movement favored globalization from below, which would protect the environment, labor rights, national cultures, democratization, and other goods from the ravages of uncontrolled capitalist globalization (Brecher, Costello, and Smith 2000; Steger 2002).

Initially, the incipient antiglobalization movement was precisely that—antiglobalization. The movement itself, however, was increasingly global, was linking together diverse movements into global solidarity networks, and was using the Internet and instruments of globalization to advance its struggles. Moreover, many opponents of capitalist globalization recognized the need for a global movement to have a positive vision and to stand for such things as social justice, equality, labor, civil liberties and human rights, and a sustainable environmentalism. Accordingly, the anticapitalist globalization movement began advocating common values and visions, and began referring to itself in positive terms, like the social justice movement.

In particular, the movement against capitalist globalization used the Internet to organize mass demonstrations and to disseminate information to the world concerning the policies of the institutions of capitalist globalization. The events made clear that protestors were not against globalization per se, but opposed neoliberal and capitalist globalization, rejecting specific policies and institutions that produce intensified exploitation of labor, environmental devastation, growing divisions among the social classes, and the undermining of democracy. The emerging antiglobalization-from-above movements are contextualizing these problems in the framework of a restructuring of capitalism on a worldwide basis for maximum profit with zero accountability and have made clear the need for democratization, regulation, rules, and globalization in the interests of people, not profit.

The new movements against capitalist globalization have placed the issues of global justice and environmental destruction squarely in the center of important political concerns of our time. Hence, whereas the mainstream media failed to vigorously debate or even report on globalization until the eruption of a vigorous antiglobalization movement and rarely, if ever, critically discussed the activities of the WTO, the World Bank, and the IMF, there is now a widely circulating critical discourse and controversy over these institutions. Stung by criticisms, representatives of the World Bank in particular are pledging reform, and pressures are mounting concerning proper and improper roles for the major global institutions, highlighting their limitations and deficiencies and the need for reforms such as debt relief for overburdened developing countries to solve some of their fiscal and social problems.

Opposing capital's globalization from above, cyberactivists have thus been promoting globalization from below, developing networks of solidarity and propagating oppositional ideas and movements throughout the planet. Opposing the capitalist international of transnational corporate-led globalization, a Fifth International—to use Waterman's (1992) phrase—of computer-mediated activism is emerging that is qualitatively different from the party-based socialist and communist internationals. Such networking links labor, feminist, ecological, peace, and other anticapitalist groups, providing the basis for a new politics of alliance and solidarity to overcome the limitations of postmodern identity politics (see Dyer-Witheford 1999; Burbach 2001; Best and Kellner 2001).

Of course, right-wing and reactionary forces have used the Internet to promote their political agendas as well. In a short time, one can easily access an exotic witch's brew of Web sites maintained by the Ku Klux Klan and myriad neo-Nazi assemblages, including the Aryan Nation and various militia groups. Internet discussion lists also disperse these views, and right-wing extremists are aggressively active on many computer forums as well as radio programs and stations, public-access television programs, fax campaigns, video, and even rock-music productions. These organizations are hardly harmless, having carried out terrorism of various sorts from church burnings to the bombings of public buildings. Adopting quasi-Leninist discourse and tactics for ultraright causes, these groups have successfully recruited working-class members devastated by the developments of global capitalism, which has resulted in widespread unemployment in traditional forms of industrial, agricultural, and unskilled labor. Moreover, extremist Web sites have influenced alienated middle-class youth as well (a 1999 HBO documentary on *Hate on the Internet* provides a disturbing number of examples of how extremist Web sites influenced disaffected youth to commit hate crimes).

Indeed, a recent twist in the saga of technopolitics seems to be that allegedly "terrorist" groups are now increasingly using the Internet and Web sites to promote their causes. An article in the *Los Angeles Times* (2001:A1, A14) reports that groups like Hamas use their Web site to post reports of acts of terror against Israel, rather than calling newspapers or broadcasting outlets. A wide range of groups labeled as "terrorist" reportedly use e-mail, listserves, and Web sites to further their struggles—causes including Hezbollah and Hamas, the Maoist group Shining Path in Peru, and a variety of other groups throughout Asia and elsewhere. For instance, the Tamil Tigers, a liberation movement in Sri Lanka, offers position papers, daily news, and free e-mail service. According to the *Times*, experts are still unclear about "whether the ability to communicate online worldwide is prompting an increase or a decrease in terrorist acts." There have been widespread discussions of how bin Laden's al-Qaeda network used the Internet to plan the September 11 terrorist attacks on the United States, how the group communicated with each other, got funds and purchased airline tickets via the Internet, and used flight simulations to practice their hijacking. In the contemporary era, the Internet can thus be used for a diversity of political projects and goals ranging from education, to business, to political organization and debate, to terrorism.

Moreover, different political groups are engaging in cyberwar as an adjunct to their political battles. Israeli hackers have repeatedly attacked the Web sites of Hezbollah, while pro-Palestine hackers have reportedly placed militant demands and slogans on the Web sites of Israel's army, foreign ministry, and parliament. Pakistani and Indian computer hackers have waged similar cyberbattles against the Web sites of opposing forces in the bloody struggle over Kashmir, while rebel forces in the Philippines have taunted government troops with cell phone calls and messages and have attacked government Web sites.

The examples in this section suggest how technopolitics makes possible a refiguring of politics, a refocusing of politics on everyday life, and the use of the tools and techniques of new computer and communication technology to expand the field and domain of politics. In this conjuncture, the ideas of Guy Debord and the Situationist International are especially relevant, with their stress on the construction of situations, the use of technology, media of communication, and cultural forms to promote a revolution of everyday life and to increase the realm of freedom, community, and empowerment.[15] To some extent, the new technologies *are* revolutionary and *do* constitute a revolution of everyday life, but it is often a revolution that promotes and disseminates the capitalist consumer society and involves new modes of fetishism, enslavement, and domination yet to be clearly perceived and theorized.

Concluding comments

The Internet is thus a contested terrain, used by left, right, and center to promote their own agendas and interests. The political battles of the future may well be fought in the streets, factories, parliaments, and other sites of past struggle, but politics is already mediated by broadcast, computer, and information technologies and will increasingly be so in the future. Those interested in the politics and culture of the future should therefore be clear on the important role of the new public spheres and intervene accordingly, while critical pedagogues have the responsibility of teaching students the skills that will enable them to participate in the politics and struggles of the present and future.

And so, to paraphrase Foucault, wherever there is globalization from above—globalization as the imposition of capitalist logic—there can be resistance and struggle. The possibilities of globalization from below result from transnational alliances between groups fighting for better wages and working conditions, social and political justice, environmental protection, and more democracy and freedom worldwide. In addition, a renewed emphasis on local and grassroots movements has put dominant economic forces on the defensive in their own backyards, and the broadcasting media and the Internet have often called attention to oppressive and destructive corporate policies on the local level, putting national and even transnational pressure for reform upon major corporations. Moreover, proliferating media and the Internet make possible a greater circulation of struggles and new alliances and solidarities that can connect resistant forces that oppose capitalist and corporate-state elite forms of globalization from above (Dyer-Witheford 1999).

In a certain sense, the phenomena of globalization replicates the history of the United States and most so-called capitalist democracies in which tension between capitalism and democracy has been the defining feature of the conflicts of the past 200 years. In analyzing the development of education in the United States, Samuel Bowles and Herbert Gintis (1986) and Aronowitz and Giroux (1986) have analyzed the conflicts between corporate logic and democracy in schooling, Robert McChesney (1995 and 1997), myself (Kellner 1990, 1992, 2001, forthcoming), and others have articulated the contradictions between capitalism and democracy in the media and public sphere, and Joshua Cohen and Joel Rogers (1983) and many others argue that contradictions between capitalism and democracy are defining features of U.S. polity and history.

On a global terrain, Hardt and Negri (2000) have stressed the openings and possibilities for democratic transformative struggle within globalization, or what they call "Empire." I argue that similar arguments can be made in which globalization is not conceived merely as the triumph of capitalism and democracy working together, as it was in the classical theories of Milton Friedman or more recently in Francis Fukuyama. Nor should globalization be depicted solely as the triumph of capital, as in many despairing antiglobalization theories. Rather, one should see that globalization unleashes conflicts between capitalism and democracy and, in its restructuring processes, creates new openings for struggle, resistance, and democratic transformation.

I would also suggest that the model of Marx and Engels, as deployed in the "Communist Manifesto," could be usefully employed to analyze the contradictions of globalization (Marx and Engels 1978:469ff). From the historical materialist optic, capitalism was interpreted as the greatest, most progressive force in history for Marx and Engels, destroying a retrograde feudalism, authoritarian patriarchy, backwardness and provincialism in favor of a market society, global cosmopolitanism, and constant revolutionizing of the forces of production. Yet capitalism was also presented in the Marxian theory as a major disaster for the human race, condemning a large part of the race to alienated labor and regions of the world to colonialist exploitation and generating conflicts between classes and nations, the consequences of which the contemporary era continues to suffer.

Marx deployed a similar dialectical and historical model in his later analyses of imperialism, arguing, for instance, in his writings on British imperialism in India that British colonialism was a great productive and progressive force in India at the same time as it was highly destructive (Marx and Engels 1978:653ff). A similar dialectical and critical model can be used today that articulates the progressive elements of globalization in conjunction with its more oppressive features, deploying the categories of negation and critique, while sublating (*Aufhebung*) the positive features. Moreover, a dialectical and transdisciplinary model is necessary to capture the complexity and multi-dimensionality of globalization today, one that brings together in theorizing globalization, the economy, technology, polity, society, and culture, articulating the interplay of these elements and avoiding any form of determinism or reductivism.

Theorizing globalization dialectically and critically requires that we analyze both continuities and discontinuities with the past, specifying what is a continuation of past histories and what is new and original in the present moment. To elucidate the latter, I believe that the discourse of the postmodern is useful in dramatizing the changes and novelties of the mode of globalization. The concept of the postmodern can signal that which is fresh and original, calling attention to topics and phenomena that require novel theorization and intense critical thought and inquiry. Hence, although Manuel Castells (1996, 1997, 1998) does the most detailed analysis of new technologies and the rise of what he calls a networked society, by refusing to link his analyses with the problematic of the postmodern, he cuts himself off from theoretical resources that enable theorists to articulate the novelties of the present that are unique and different from the previous mode of social organization.[16]

Consequently, although there is admittedly a lot of mystification in the discourse of the postmodern, it signals emphatically the shifts and ruptures in our era—the novelties and originalities—and dramatizes the mutations in culture, subjectivities, and theory that Castells and other theorists of globalization or the information society gloss over. The discourse of the postmodern in relation to analysis of contemporary culture and society is just jargon, however, unless it is rooted in analysis of the global restructuring of capitalism and analysis of the scientific-technological revolution that is part and parcel of it (see Best and Kellner 1997, 2001).

As I have argued in this study, the term "globalization" is often used as a code word that stands for a tremendous diversity of issues and problems and serves as a front for a variety of theoretical and political positions. While it can function as a legitimating ideology to cover and sanitize ugly realities, a critical globalization theory can inflect the discourse to point precisely to these deplorable phenomena and can elucidate a series of contemporary problems and conflicts. In view of the different concepts and functions of globalization discourse, it is important to note that the concept of globalization is a theoretical construct that varies according to the assumptions and commitments of the theory in question. Seeing the term as a construct helps rob it of its force of nature as a sign of an inexorable triumph of market forces and the hegemony of capital, or, as the extreme right fears, of a rapidly encroaching world government. While the term can both describe and legitimate capitalist transnationalism and supranational government institutions, a critical theory of globalization does not buy into ideological valorizations and affirms difference, hybridity, resistance, and democratic self-determination against forms of global domination and subordination.

Globalization should thus be seen as a contested terrain, with opposing forces attempting to use its institutions, technologies, media, and forms for their own purposes. There are certainly negative aspects to globalization that strengthen elite economic and political forces over and against the underlying population. However, as I suggest above, there are also positive possibilities. Other beneficial openings include the opportunity for greater democratization, increased education and health care, and new possibilities within the global economy that provide entry to members of races, regions, and classes previously excluded from mainstream economics, politics, and culture within the modern corporate order.

Furthermore, there is utopian potential in the new technologies, as well as the possibility for increased domination and the hegemony of capital. While the first generation of computers were large mainframe systems controlled by big government and big business, later generations of personal computers and networks have created a more decentralized situation in which ever more individuals own their own computers and use them for their own projects and goals. A new generation of wireless communication could enable areas of the world that do not even have electricity to participate in the communication and information revolution of the emergent global era. This would require, of course, something like a Marshall Plan for the developing world, which would necessitate help with disseminating technologies that would also address problems of world hunger, disease, illiteracy, and poverty.

In relation to education, the spread and distribution of information and communication technology signifies the possibility of openings of opportunities for research and interaction not previously accessible to students who did not have the privilege of access to major research libraries or institutions. Although it has its problems and limitations, the Internet makes available more information and knowledge to more people than any previous institution in history. Moreover, the Internet enables individuals to participate in discussions and to circulate their ideas and work in ways that were previously closed off to many excluded groups and individuals.

A progressive reconstruction of education that is done in the interests of democratization would demand access to new technologies for all, helping to overcome the so-called digital divide and divisions of the "haves" and "have-nots" as well as teaching information literacy to provide the skills necessary to participate in the emerging cybersociety (see Kellner 2000). Expanding democratic and multicultural reconstruction of education forces thus educators and citizens to confront the challenge of the digital divide, in which there are divisions between information and technology "haves" and "have-nots," just as there are class, gender, and race divisions in every sphere of the existing constellations of society and culture. Although the latest surveys of the digital divide indicate that the key indicators are class and education and not race and gender, making computers a significant force of democratization of education and society will nonetheless require significant investment and programs to assure that everyone receives the training, literacies, and tools necessary to properly function in a high-tech global economy and culture.[17]

Hence, a critical theory of globalization presents globalization as a product of capitalism and democracy, as a set of forces imposed from above in conjunction with resistance from below. In this optic, globalization generates new conflicts, new struggles, and new crises, which can be seen in part as resistance to capitalist logic. In the light of the neo-liberal projects to dismantle the welfare state, colonize the public sphere, and control globalization, it is up to citizens and activists to create new public spheres, politics, and pedagogies, to use the new technologies to discuss what kinds of society people today want, and to oppose the society against which people resist and struggle. This involves, minimally, demands for more education, health care, welfare, and benefits from the state and a struggle to create a more democratic and egalitarian society. But one cannot expect that generous corporations and a beneficent state are going to make available to citizens the bounties and benefits of the globalized new information economy. Rather, it is up to individuals and groups to promote democratization and progressive social change.

Thus, in opposition to the globalization from above of corporate capitalism, I would advocate a globalization from below, one which supports individuals and groups using the new technologies to create a more multicultural, egalitarian, democratic, and ecological world. Of course, the new technologies might exacerbate existing inequalities in the current class, gender, race, and regional configurations of power and give the major corporate forces powerful new tools to advance their interests. In this situation, it is up to people of good will to devise strategies to use the new technologies to promote democratization and social justice. For as the new technologies become ever more central to every domain of everyday life, developing an oppositional technopolitics in the new public spheres will become more and more important (see Kellner 1995a, 1995b, 1997, 2000). Changes in the economy, politics, and social life demand a constant reconceptualization of politics and social change in the light of globalization and the technological revolution, requiring new thinking as a response to ever-changing historical conditions.

Notes

1 Attempts to chart the globalization of capital, decline of the nation-state, and rise of a new global culture include the essays in Featherstone (1990), Giddens (1990), Robertson (1991), King (1991), Bird *et al.* (1993), Gilroy (1993), Arrighi (1994), Lash and Urry (1994), Grewal and Kaplan (1994), Wark (1994), Featherstone, Lash, and Robertson (1995), Axford (1995), Held (1995), Waters (1995), Hirst and Thompson (1996), Axtmann (1998), Albrow (1996), Cvetkovich and Kellner (1997), Kellner (1998), Friedman (1999), Held *et al.* (1999), Hardt and Negri (2000), Lechner and Bali (2000), Steger (2002), and Stiglitz (2002).
2 See apologists such as Fukuyama (1992) and Friedman (1999), who perceive this process as positive, while others, such as Mander and Goldsmith (1996), Eisenstein (1998), and Robins and Webster (1999) portray it as negative.
3 What appeared at the first stage of academic and popular discourses of globalization in the 1990s tended to be dichotomized into celebratory globophilia and dismissive globophobia. See Best and Kellner (2001). There was also a tendency on the part of some theorists to exaggerate the novelties of globalization, and on the part of others to dismiss these claims by arguing that globalization has been going on for centuries and not that much is new and different. For an excellent delineation and critique of academic discourses on globalization, see Steger (2002).
4 See Baudrillard (1993) and the analyses in Kellner (1989b, 1994).
5 See Kelly (1994, 1998) and the critique in Best and Kellner (1999).
6 In his extreme postmodern stage, Baudrillard (1993) argued that "simulation" had replaced production as the organizing principle of contemporary societies, marking "the end of political economy" (p. 955). See the critique in Kellner (1989b). In general, I am trying to mediate the economic determinism in some neo-Marxian and other theories of globalization and the technological determinism found in Baudrillard and others.
7 I am not able, in the framework of this paper, to theorize the alarming expansion of war and militarism in the post–September 11 environment. For my theorizing of war and militarism, see Kellner (2002, forthcoming).
8 For example, as Ritzer (1996) argues, McDonald's imposes not only a similar cuisine all over the world, but circulates processes of what he calls "McDonaldization" that involve a production/consumption model of efficiency, technological rationality, calculability, predictability, and control. Yet, as Watson *et al.* (1997) argue, McDonald's has various cultural meanings in diverse local contexts, as well as different products, organization, and effects. However, the latter source goes too far toward stressing heterogeneity, downplaying the cultural power of McDonald's as a force of a homogenizing globalization and Western corporate logic and system; see Kellner (1999a, 2003).
9 While I find *Empire* an extremely impressive and massively productive text, I am not sure what is gained by using the word "Empire" rather than the concepts of global capital and political economy. While Hardt and Negri (2000) combine categories of Marxism and critical social theory with poststructuralist discourse derived from Foucault and Deleuze and Guattari, they frequently favor the latter, often mystifying and obscuring the object of analysis. I am also not as confident as are they that the "multitude" replaces traditional concepts of the working class and other modern political subjects, movements, and actors, and I find their emphasis on nomads, "New Barbarians," and the poor as replacement categories problematical. Nor am I clear on exactly what forms their poststructuralist politics would take. The same problem is evident, I believe, in an earlier decade's provocative and post-Marxist text by Laclau and Mouffe (1985),

who valorized new social movements, radical democracy, and a postsocialist politics without providing many concrete examples or proposals for struggle in the present conjuncture.

10 I am thus trying to mediate in this paper between those who claim that globalization simply undermines democracy and those, such as Friedman (1999), who claim that globalization promotes democratization. I should also note that in distinguishing between globalization from above and globalization from below, I do not want to say that one is good and the other is bad in relation to democracy. As Friedman shows, capitalist corporations and global forces might very well promote democratization in many arenas of the world, and globalization from below might promote special interests or reactionary goals, so I criticize theorizing globalization in binary terms as primarily "good" or "bad." While critics of globalization simply see it as the reproduction of capitalism, its champions, like Friedman, do not perceive how globalization undercuts democracy. Likewise, Friedman does not engage the role of new social movements, dissident groups, or the "have-nots" in promoting democratization. Nor do concerns for social justice, equality, and participatory democracy play a role in his book.

11 On resistance by labor to globalization, see Moody (1997); on resistance by environmentalists and other social movements, see the studies in Mander and Goldsmith (1996). I provide examples below from several domains.

12 Friedman (1999:267ff) notes that George Soros was the star of Davos in 1995, when the triumph of global capital was being celebrated, but that the next year Russian Communist Party leader Gennadi A. Zyuganov was a major media focus when unrestrained globalization was being questioned. Friedman does not point out that this was a result of a growing recognition that divisions between "haves" and "have-nots" were becoming too scandalous and that predatory capitalism was becoming too brutal and ferocious.

13 Such positions are associated with the postmodern theories of Foucault, Lyotard, and Rorty and have been taken up by a wide range of feminists, multiculturalists, and others. On these theorists and postmodern politics, see Best and Kellner (1991, 1997, 2001) and the valorization and critique of postmodern politics in Hardt and Negri (2000) and Burbach (2001).

14 As a December 1 *ABC* News story titled "Networked Protests" put it, "Disparate groups from the Direct Action Network to the AFL-CIO to various environmental and human rights groups have organized rallies and protests online, allowing for a global reach that would have been unthinkable just five years ago." As early as March, activists were hitting the news groups and list-serves—strings of e-mail messages people use as a kind of long-term chat—to organize protests and rallies.

In addition, while the organizers demanded that the protesters agree not to engage in violent action, one Web site urged WTO protesters to help tie up the WTO's Web servers, and another group produced an anti-WTO Web site that replicated the look of the official site (see RTMark's Web site, http://gatt.org/; the same group produced a replica of George W. Bush's site with satirical and critical material, winning the wrath of the Bush campaign). For compelling accounts of the anti-WTO demonstrations in Seattle and an acute analysis of the issues involved, see Hawkens (2000) and Klein (2000).

15 On the importance of the ideas of Debord and the Situationist International to make sense of the present conjuncture, see Best and Kellner (1997: chap. 3); on the new forms of the interactive consumer society, see Best and Kellner (2001).

16 Castells claims that Harvey (1989) and Lash (1990) say about as much about the postmodern as needs to be said (Castells 1996:26ff). With due respect to their

excellent work, I believe that no two theorists or books exhaust the problematic of the postmodern, which involves mutations in theory, culture, society, politics, science, philosophy, and almost every other domain of experience and is thus inexhaustible (Best and Kellner 1997, 2001). Yet one should be careful in using postmodern discourse to avoid the mystifying elements, a point made in the books just noted as well as in Hardt and Negri (2000).

17 "Digital divide" has emerged as the buzz word for perceived divisions between information technology "haves" and "have-nots" in the current economy and society. A U.S. Department of Commerce report released in July 1999 claimed that the digital divide is dramatically escalating in relation to race, and the Clinton Administration and media picked up on this theme (U.S. Department of Commerce, NTIA 1999). A critique of the data involved in the report emerged, claiming that it was outdated; more recent studies by Stanford University, Cheskin Research, ACNielson, and the Forester Institute claim that education and class are more significant factors than race in constructing the divide (see Cyberatlas for a collection of reports and statistics on the divide).

In any case, it is clear that there is a gaping division between information-technology "haves" and "have-nots," that this is a major challenge to developing an egalitarian and democratic society, and that something needs to be done about the problem. My contribution involves the argument that empowering the "have-nots" requires the dissemination of new literacies, thus empowering groups and individuals previously excluded from economic opportunities and socio-political participation (see Kellner 2000).

References

Albrow, Martin. 1996. *The Global Age.* Cambridge, England: Polity Press.
Appadurai, Arjun. 1996. *Modernity at Large.* Minneapolis, MN: University of Minnesota Press.
Aronowitz, Stanley, and Henry Giroux. 1985. *Education Under Siege.* New York: Bergin and Garvey.
Aronson, Ronald. 1983. *The Dialectics of Disaster.* London, England: Verso.
Arrighi, Giovanni. 1994. *The Long Twentieth Century.* London, England, and New York: Verso.
Axford, Barrie. 1995. *The Global System.* Cambridge, England: Polity Press.
Axtmann, Roland, ed. 1998. *Globalization in European Context.* London, England: Cassells.
Baudrillard, Jean. 1993. *Symbolic Exchange and Death.* London, England: Sage.
Bell, Daniel. 1976. *The Coming of Post-Industrial Society.* New York: Basic Books.
Best, Steven, and Douglas Kellner. 1991. *Postmodern Theory: Critical Interrogations.* London, England, and New York: Macmillan and Guilford.
———. 1997. *The Postmodern Turn.* London, England, and New York: Routledge and Guilford Press.
———. 1999. "Kevin Kelly's Complexity Theory: The Politics and Ideology of Self-Organizing Systems." *Organization and Environment* 12:141–62.
———. 2001. *The Postmodern Adventure.* London, England, and New York: Routledge and Guilford Press.
Bird, Jon, Barry Curtis, Tim Putnam, and Lisa Tickner, eds. 1993. *Mapping the Futures: Local Cultures, Global Change.* London, England, and New York: Routledge.

Boggs, Carl. 2000. *The End of Politics.* New York: Guilford Press.
Borgmann, Albert. 1994. *Across the Postmodern Divide.* Chicago, IL: University of Chicago Press.
———. 1999. *Holding onto Reality.* Chicago, IL: University of Chicago Press.
Bowles, Samuel, and Herbert Gintis. 1986. *On Democracy.* New York: Basic Books.
Brecher, Jeremy, and Tim Costello. 1994. *Global Village or Global Pillage: Economic Reconstruction from the Bottom Up.* Boston, MA: South End Press.
Brecher, Jeremy, Tim Costello, and Brendan Smith. 2000. *Globalization from Below.* Boston, MA: South End Press.
Bronner, Stephen Eric, and Douglas Kellner, eds. 1989. *Critical Theory and Society: A Reader.* New York: Routledge.
Burbach, Roger. 2001. *Globalization and Postmodern Politics: From Zapatistas to High-Tech Robber Barons.* London, England: Pluto Press.
Castells, Manuel. 1996. *The Information Age: Economy, Society, and Culture.* Vol. 1, *The Rise of the Network Society.* Oxford, England: Blackwell.
———. 1997. *The Information Age: Economy, Society, and Culture.* Vol. 2, *The Power of Identity.* Oxford, England: Blackwell.
———. 1998. *The Information Age: Economy, Society, and Culture.* Vol. 3, *End of Millennium.* Oxford, England: Blackwell.
Cohen, Joshua, and Joel Rogers. 1983. *On Democracy.* New York: Penguin.
Cvetkovich, Ann, and Douglas Kellner. 1997. *Articulating the Global and the Local: Globalization and Cultural Studies.* Boulder, CO: Westview Press.
Cyberatlas, http://cyberatlas.internet.com/big-picture/demographics.
Drew, Jesse. 1998. "Global Communications in the Post-Industrial Age: A Study of the Communications Strategies of U.S. Labor Organizations." Ph.D. dissertation, University of Texas.
Dyer-Witheford, Nick. 1999. *Cyber-Marx: Cycles and Circuits of Struggle in High-Technology Capitalism.* Urbana and Chicago, IL: University of Illinois Press.
Eisenstein, Zillah. 1998. *Global Obscenities: Patriarchy, Capitalism, and the Lure of Cyberfantasy.* New York: New York University Press.
Ellul, Jacques. 1964. *The Technological Society.* New York: Knopf.
Featherstone, Mike, ed. 1990. *Global Culture: Nationalism, Globalization, and Modernity.* London, England: Sage.
Featherstone, Mike, Scott Lash, and Roland Robertson, eds. 1995. *Global Modernities.* London, England: Sage.
Flanigan, James. 1999. *Los Angeles Times*, February 19.
Foran, John, ed. Forthcoming. *The Future of Revolutions: Rethinking Radical Change in the Age of Globalization.* London, England: Zed Books.
Fredericks, Howard. 1994. "North American NGO Networking Against NAFTA: The Use of Computer Communications in Cross-Border Coalition Building." XVII International Congress of the Latin American Studies Association, pp. 1–24.
Friedman, Thomas. 1999. *The Lexus and the Olive Tree.* New York: Farrar Straus Giroux.
Fukuyama, Francis. 1992. *The End of History and the Last Man.* New York: Free Press.
Gates, Bill. 1995. *The Road Ahead.* New York: Viking.
———. 1999. *Business@the Speed of Thought.* New York: Viking.

Giddens, Anthony. 1990. *Consequences of Modernity.* Cambridge, England: Polity Press; Palo Alto, CA: Stanford University Press.

Gilder, George. 1989. *Microcosm.* New York: Simon and Schuster.

———. 2000. *Telecosm.* New York: Simon and Schuster.

Gilroy, Paul. 1993. *The Black Atlantic: Modernity and Double Consciousness.* Cambridge, MA: Harvard University Press.

Grewal, Inderpal, and Caren Kaplan, eds. 1994. *Scattered Hegemonies: Postmodernity and Transnational Feminist Practices.* Minneapolis, MN: University of Minnesota Press.

Gottdiener, Mark. 1995. *Postmodern Semiotics.* Oxford, England: Blackwell.

Hardt, Michael, and Antonio Negri. *Empire.* 2000. Cambridge, MA: Harvard University Press.

Harvey, David. 1989. *The Condition of Postmodernity.* Cambridge, MA: Blackwell.

Hawkens, Paul. "What Really Happened at the Battle of Seattle." http://www.purefood.org/Corp/PaulHawken.cfm.

Heidegger, Martin. 1971. *The Question Concerning Technology.* New York: Harper and Row.

Held, David. 1995. *Democracy and the Global Order.* Cambridge, England: Polity Press; Palo Alto, CA: Stanford University Press.

Held, David, Anthony McGrew, David Goldblatt, and Jonathan Perraton. 1999. *Global Transformations.* Cambridge, England: Polity Press; Palo Alto, CA: Stanford University Press.

Hirst, Paul, and Grahame Thompson. 1996. *Globalization in Question.* Cambridge, England: Polity Press.

Huntington, Samuel. 1996. *The Clash of Civilizations and the Remaking of World Order.* New York: Simon and Schuster.

Jameson, Fredric. 1991. *Postmodernism, or the Cultural Logic of Late Capitalism.* Durham, NC: Duke University Press.

Kaku, Michio. 1997. *Visions: How Science Will Revolutionize the 21st Century.* New York: Anchor Books.

Kellner, Douglas. 1989a. *Critical Theory, Marxism, and Modernity.* Cambridge, England: Polity Press; Baltimore, MD: Johns Hopkins University Press.

———. 1989b. *Jean Baudrillard: From Marxism to Postmodernism and Beyond.* Cambridge, England: Polity Press; Palo Alto, CA: Stanford University Press.

———. 1990. *Television and the Crisis of Democracy.* Boulder, CO: Westview Press.

———. 1992. *The Persian Gulf TV War.* Boulder, CO: Westview Press.

———, ed. 1994. *Jean Baudrillard: A Critical Reader.* Oxford, England: Basil Blackwell.

———. 1995a. *Media Culture.* London, England, and New York: Routledge.

———. 1995b. "Intellectuals and New Technologies." *Media, Culture, and Society* 17:201–17.

———. 1997. "Intellectuals, the New Public Spheres, and Technopolitics." *New Political Science* 41–42:169–88.

———. 1998. "Multiple Literacies and Critical Pedagogy in a Multicultural Society." *Educational Theory* 48:103–22.

———. 1999a. "Theorizing McDonaldization: A Multiperspectivist Approach," Pp. 186–206 in *Resisting McDonaldization*, edited by Barry Smart. London: Sage Publications.

———. 1999b. "Globalization from Below? Toward a Radical Democratic Technopolitics." *Angelaki* 4:101–13.
———. 2000. "New Technologies/New Literacies: Reconstructing Education for the New Millennium." *Teaching Education* 11:245–65.
———. 2001. *Grand Theft 2000*. Lanham, MD: Rowman and Littlefield.
———. 2002. "Postmodern War in the Age of Bush II." *New Political Science* 24(1): 57–72.
———. 2003. *Media Spectacle*. London, England, and New York: Routledge.
———. Forthcoming. "September 11, Terror War, and the New Barbarism." Available online at http://www.gseis.ucla.edu/faculty/kellner/papers/sept11kell.htm.
Kelly, Kevin. 1994. *Out of Control: The New Biology of Machines, Social Systems, and the Economic World*. New York: Addison Wesley.
———. 1998. *New Rules for the New Economy*. New York: Viking.
King, Anthony D., ed. 1991. *Culture, Globalization, and the World-System: Contemporary Conditions for the Representation of Identity*. Binghamton, NY: SUNY Art Department.
Klein, Naomi. 2000. "Were the DC and Seattle Protests Unfocused, or Are Critics Missing the Point?" *The Nation* online, July 10. http://past.thenation.com/cgi-bin/framizer.cgi?url=http://past.thenation.com/issue/000710/0710klein.shtml.
Laclau, Ernesto, and Chantel Mouffe. 1985. *Hegemony and Socialist Strategy: Toward a Radical Democratic Politics*. London, England: Verso.
Lash, Scott. 1990. *Sociology of Postmodernism*. London and New York: Routledge.
Lash, Scott, and John Urry. 1994. *Economies of Signs and Space*. London, England: Sage.
Latouche, Serge. 1996. *The Westernization of the World*. Cambridge, England: Polity Press.
Lechner, Frank J., and John Boli. 2000. *The Globalization Reader*. Malden, MA and Oxford, UK: Blackwell.
Luke, Allan, and Carmen Luke. 2000. "A Situated Perspective on Cultural Globalization." Pp. 275–98 in *Globalization and Education*, edited by Nicholas Burbules and Carlos Torres. London, England, and New York: Routledge.
Mander, Jerry, and Edward Goldsmith. 1996. *The Case Against the Global Economy*. San Francisco, CA: Sierra Club Books.
Marx, Karl, and Frederick Engels. 1978. *The Marx-Engels Reader*. 2d ed. Edited by Robert C. Tucker. New York: W. W. Norton.
McChesney, Robert. 1995. *Telecommunications, Mass Media, and Democracy: The Battle for the Control of U.S. Broadcasting, 1928–1935*. New York and Oxford: Oxford University Press.
———. 1997. *Corporate Media and the Threat to Democracy*. New York: Seven Stories Press.
Moody, Kim. 1988. *An Injury to One*. London, England: Verso.
———. 1997. "Towards an International Social-Movement Unionism." *New Left Review* 225:52–72.
Polyani, Karl. [1944] 1957. *The Great Transformation*. Boston, MA: Beacon Press.
Ritzer, George. 1996. *The McDonaldization of Society*. Thousand Oaks, CA: Pine Forge Press.
Robertson, Roland. 1991. *Globalization*. London, England: Sage.

Robins, Kevin, and Frank Webster. 1999. *Times of the Technoculture.* London, England, and New York: Routledge.

Shenk, David. 1997. *Data Smog: Surviving the Information Glut.* New York: HarperCollins.

Sklair, Leslie. 2001. *The Transnational Capitalist Class.* Cambridge: Blackwell.

Slouka, Mark. 1995. *War of the Worlds.* New York: Harper and Row.

Soja, Edward. 1989. *Postmodern Geographies.* London, England: Verso.

Steger, Manfred. 2002. *Globalism: The New Market Ideology.* Lanham, MD: Rowman and Littlefield.

Stiglitz, Joseph E. 2002. *Globalization and Its Discontents.* New York: Norton.

Stoll, Clifford. 1995. *Silicon Snake Oil: Second Thoughts on the Information Highway.* New York: Doubleday.

U.S. Department of Commerce, National Telecommunications and Information Administration (NTIA). 1999. "Falling Through the Net: Defining the Digital Divide." http://www.ntia.doc.gov/ntiahome/fttn99/contents.html (last accessed 29 June 2002).

Virilio, Paul. 1998. *The Virilio Reader.* Edited by James Der Derian. Maiden, MA, and Oxford, England: Blackwell Publishers.

Waters, Malcolm. 1995. *Globalization.* London, England: Routledge.

Wark, McKenzie. 1994. *Virtual Geography: Living with Global Media Events.* Bloomington and Indianapolis, IN: Indiana University Press.

Waterman, Peter. 1992. "International Labour Communication by Computer: The Fifth International?" Working Paper Series 129, Institute of Social Studies, The Hague.

Watson, James L., ed. 1997. *Golden Arches East: McDonald's in East Asia.* Palo Alto, CA: Stanford University Press.

Webster, Frank. 1995. *Theories of the Information Society.* London, England, and New York: Routledge.

MEDIA LITERACY AND THE CHALLENGE OF NEW INFORMATION AND COMMUNICATION TECHNOLOGIES

Sonia Livingstone

Source: *The Communication Review* 7(1) (2004): 3–14.

Within both academic and policy discourses, the concept of media literacy is being extended from its traditional focus on print and audiovisual media to encompass the internet and other new media. The present article addresses three central questions currently facing the public, policy-makers and academy: What is media literacy? How is it changing? And what are the uses of literacy? The article begins with a definition: media literacy is the ability to access, analyse, evaluate and create messages across a variety of contexts. This four-component model is then examined for its applicability to the internet. Having advocated this skills-based approach to media literacy in relation to the internet, the article identifies some outstanding issues for new media literacy crucial to any policy of promoting media literacy among the population. The outcome is to extend our understanding of media literacy so as to encompass the historically and culturally conditioned relationship among three processes: (i) the symbolic and material representation of knowledge, culture and values; (ii) the diffusion of interpretative skills and abilities across a (stratified) population; and (iii) the institutional, especially, the state management of the power that access to and skilled use of knowledge brings to those who are 'literate'.

Renewed debates over media literacy

The concept of media literacy, like that of literacy itself, has long proved contentious (Luke, 1989). The hugely significant skills of reading and writing have been augmented by the also-significant skill of "reading" audiovisual material from the mid-twentieth century onward. Today, as we witness a further major shift in information and communication technology (ICT), a new form of literacy is emerging, uneasily termed computer literacy or Internet literacy. This new form of literacy, if it is indeed "new," and if it is appropriately labeled "literacy," lies at the heart of a series of lively debates intersecting the academy, the policy community, and the public.

A casual search of bookshops makes plain the explosion of academic interest in questions of literacy, with titles exploring literacy in the electronic era (Snyder, 1998), the information age (Kubey, 1997), the digital era (Warnick, 2002), the digital world (Tyner, 1998) or even cyberliteracy (Gurak, 2001). These volumes draw together a multidisciplinary mix of specialists in literacy, culture, media education, human-computer-interaction, and social studies of technology (Kellner, 2002; Kubey, 1997; Poster, 2001; Tyner, 1998). Meanwhile, policymakers are determining regulatory frameworks required to produce an ICT-literate population, at times turning to the academy for guidance.

This mix of disciplines and stakeholder interests is perhaps generating more heat than light at present. This is exacerbated by the fact that so far, research has been mainly analytic, for few have explored new literacies empirically. Indeed, only recently has the majority of the public even had the chance to come to terms with the new skills required of them not just in their leisure, as with television, but crucially also at work, in education and in their community (Livingstone, 2002). This brief article takes the opportunity to draw out a series of key intellectual challenges posed by the introduction of new information and communication technologies for our thinking about media literacy.

Is "literacy" a useful term?

History tells us that even the narrow and common sense meaning of the term "literacy"—being able to read and write—masks a complex history of contestation over the power and authority to access, interpret, and produce printed texts (Luke, 1989). Such scope for contestation is magnified as the materiality of symbolic texts increasingly relies on audiovisual and computer-based technologies. In theorizing people's interpretations of media, old and new, are we now dealing with one or many literacies? Are the literacies required for today's communication and information environment an extension of, or a radical break with, past traditions of knowledge and learning? Should the academy be guiding, or critiquing, the implementation of media literacy policy (Sterne, 2002)?

Some might argue that we should leave the somewhat opaque, contested term "literacy" to its origins in high culture (Williams, 1976), rejecting its association with the world of authoritative printed books and its tendency to stigmatize those who lack it. Doubtless the spawning of new literacies—computer literacy, cyber-literacy, Internet literacy, network literacy, digital literacy, information literacy—is infelicitous. And how do these relate to the existing literacy terms—print literacy, audiovisual literacy, critical literacy, visual literacy, oral literacy, cultural literacy, or social literacy (Freire & Macedo, 1987; Hirsch, 1987; Street, 1995)? When the dominant media shifted from print-based to audiovisual media, communication scholars shifted their conceptual vocabulary away from reading and literacy to audience reception and interpretation. So why now, faced with new computer-based media, revert to literacy? I suggest that the terms "audience" and "reception" do not work so well for media which are socially diversified (rather than mass), technologically converged (rather than distinct) and interactive (rather than one-to-many, with producer and receiver separate).

The crucial point is not that computers are replacing television, just as television did not replace print; rather, people now engage with a media environment which integrates print, audiovisual, telephony, and computer media. Hence, we need a conceptual framework that spans these media. Literacy seems to do the work required here: It is pan-media in that it covers the interpretation of all complex, mediated symbolic texts broadcast or published on electronic communications networks; at the same time, because historically it has been tied to particular media forms and technologies, literacy foregrounds the technological, cultural, and historical specificity of particular media as used in particular times and places.

What is media literacy?

When a single term is used across diverse domains, confusions arise. How media literacy is defined has consequences for the framing of the debate, the research agenda and policy initiatives. At present, definitions range from the tautological (computer literacy is the ability to use computers) to the hugely idealistic: "The term literacy is shorthand for cultural ideals as eclectic as economic development, personal fulfillment, and individual moral fortitude" (Tyner, 1998, p. 17). Nonetheless, in a key conference a decade ago, a clear, concise and widely adopted definition emerged: Media literacy—indeed literacy more generally—is the ability to access, analyze, evaluate, and create messages in a variety of forms (Aufderheide, 1993; Christ & Potter, 1998). These four components—access, analysis, evaluation, and content creation—together constitute a skills-based approach to media literacy. Each component supports the others as part of a nonlinear, dynamic learning process: Learning to create content helps one to analyze that produced professionally by others; skills in analysis and evaluation open the doors to new uses of the Internet, expanding access, and so forth.

For the moment, let us agree that this is a useful definition—although I argue later that these are necessary but not sufficient components for literacy—and ask, how far is it possible or desirable to adapt what we know of print and audiovisual media literacy in order to map a research agenda for new forms of literacy in today's changing media environment?

Access

Understanding barriers to access has been long debated in relation to print media (raising concerns about education and social mobility) and telephony (centering on universal service provision to ensure social participation). It has posed fewer problems for audiovisual media, although today the diversification and commercialization of television channels puts universal participation in a shared culture and the provision of free-to-all public service content back on the agenda. In relation to new media, the digital divide debate examines the challenges of ensuring that ICT provision facilitates rather than undermines equality in education, participation and culture (Kellner, 2002; Norris, 2001; Rice, 2002). As research on the domestic appropriation of ICT has revealed, access is a dynamic and social process, not a one-off act of hardware provision, to be evaluated in terms of the ongoing quality of provision in media contents and services (Facer, Sutherland, Furlong, & Furlong, 2001; Livingstone, 2002; Ribak, 2001). Moreover, while it is becoming clear that media access underdetermines use, a more sophisticated account is required of how the two are linked. Much could be learned here from television literacy, where research shows that the social context in front of the screen frames and directs the nature of the engagement with and learning from what is shown on the screen (Buckingham, 2000; Silverstone, 1994; Singer & Singer, 2001).

Analysis

Questions of equality in knowledge, culture, and participation through media are not simply to be resolved by addressing the question of access. A sustained and satisfactory engagement with symbolic texts rests on a range of analytic competencies (Eco, 1979): Readers and viewers must be literate in the sense of being competent in and motivated toward relevant cultural traditions and values. While the reader-response theorists (Iser, 1980) identified competencies for the reader of literary works, media scholars identified parallel interpretative skills to decode audiovisual media (Hall, 1980; Hodge & Tripp, 1986; Liebes & Katz, 1995; Livingstone, 1998); it is these skills that media education programs teach to children. Buckingham (1998), building on Bazalgette's (1999) work, outlines a six-fold scheme that teaches students to address questions of media agency, media categories, media technologies, media languages, media audiences, and media representations. If we treat this as an initial specification of the analytic competence for effective use of new media, this could offer a valuable framework for new media literacies. On the other hand, it could be argued that our analytic repertoire—genre, narrative, authorial voice, modality, literary merit—is heavily dependent on its historical origins in print, being therefore only poorly applicable to new media.

Evaluation

Evaluation is crucial to literacy: Imagine the World Wide Web user who cannot distinguish dated, biased, or exploitative sources, unable to select intelligently when overwhelmed by an abundance of information and services. Being able to evaluate content is no simple skill; rather, critical evaluation rests on a substantial body of knowledge regarding the broader social, cultural, economic, political, and historical contexts in which media content is produced (Bazalgette, 1999). The challenge is exacerbated for the World Wide Web, produced in an age of information abundance, even overload. Compare this with print and audiovisual texts, produced in a context of scarcity, with few people having access to the systems of production and distribution. As this maintained the distinction between producers and consumers, with key filters operating to select material to be distributed in accordance with criteria of cultural quality, ideology, market pressure or professional production values, it was the operation and consequences of these filters that formed the centerpiece of critical media literacy teaching. Now that almost anyone can produce and disseminate Internet contents, with fewer—and different kinds of—filters, the basis of critical literacy must alter.

In this fast-changing production context, teaching users to question the authority, objectivity or quality of mediated knowledge becomes ever more crucial. How much contextual and critical knowledge is required? What are the appropriate and legitimate grounds for criticism—aesthetic, political, ideological, and/or economic? How do or should these relate to the values of those providing ICT resources and teaching media literacy? To answer this, media literacy programs must address the broader relation between literacy and critique, particularly given shifting criteria of quality, authority, and standards. Buckingham (1998) argues that throughout the history of media literacy education, differing versions of the tension between a positive approach to education-as-democratization and a defensive or paternalist approach to education-as-discrimination (or cultural demarcation) have been played out, often undermining the media educator. Exactly this tension continues to shape contemporary discussions over the appropriate uses of newly gained ICT literacy, with the vague term, "empowerment," ambiguously open to both democratic and defensive constructions.

Content creation

Not all definitions of media literacy include the production of symbolic texts. Generally, ordinary people are positioned as receivers but not senders of messages. Indeed, the history of print literacy shows that, while teaching the population to read was itself highly contentious, teaching people to write required yet a further struggle between the elitist interests of the establishment and the democratizing trends of the enlightenment (Kintgen, Kroll, & Rose, 1988). In audiovisual media education, a parallel struggle has been apparent, often argued in terms of pedagogic effectiveness; supposedly children understand the conventions and merits of professionally produced material if they have experience making it themselves (Hobbs, 1998; Sefton-Green, 1999). For others, the argument for content creation is rather that of giving the tools for communication to the "voiceless," furthering the rights of self-expression and cultural participation. In advancing policy, it would clarify matters to disentangle three arguments: the pedagogic argument that people learn best about media through making it; the employment argument that those with new media skills are increasingly needed as the information sector expands; and the cultural politics argument that citizens have the right to self-representation and cultural participation.

In key respects, content creation is easier than ever: One and the same technology can be used for sending and receiving, with desktop publishing software, easy-to-use web creation software, digital cameras and webcams putting professional expertise into the hands of everyone. Many are already content producers, developing complex literacy skills through the use of e-mail, chat, and games. The social consequences of these activities—participation, social capital, civic culture—serve to network (or exclude) today's younger generation. At present, cementing content creation within media literacy programs requires further research to establish the relation between reception and production in the new media environment, together with further clarification of the benefits to learning, cultural expression, and civic participation.

Beyond a skills-based approach

Thus far I have developed a skills-based approach to new media literacies that applies across all media, relying on media-neutral terms. This has the advantages of generality and historical continuity, focusing on interpretative skills long valued in Western culture. In a media environment characterized by rapid change, a pan-media definition of literacy is surely practical. But problematically, this also implies that the ability to access, analyze, evaluate, and create communication content is common across the book, television, the Internet. If, instead, it seems that new media, especially online media, represent a radically new information and communication environment, then an account of a literate engagement with this environment must encompass the technological interface as well as the user's skills. In other words, to focus solely on questions of skill or ability neglects the textuality and technology that mediates communication. In consequence, it unwittingly supports a universalist, cognitive framework, thereby neglecting in turn the historical and cultural contingency of both media and the social knowledge processes that interpret them. Visualize someone reading a book, watching television, playing a computer game, searching the World Wide Web—evidently there is not only skill involved but also an interpretative relationship with a complex, symbolically-encoded, technologically-mediated text. I suggest that, as people engage with a diversity of ICTs, we must consider the possibility of literacies in the plural, defined through their relations with different media rather than defined independently of them. In the language of audience research, the conceptual shift is from an exclusive focus on the viewer to a focus on the interaction between text and reader or between inscribed and actual viewer/user.

From print to screen

So, once we claim that technology makes a difference, then a purely individual, skills-based model will not suffice. Instead we must ask how literacy changes—and becomes plural—as the technology changes. For the centuries during which literacy meant print literacy, we became accustomed to taking for granted the specificity of this medium and, therefore, the specificity of literacy *qua* print literacy. Nonetheless, being able to read and write has implied familiarity with a set of historically and culturally specific conventions. For example, the author (together with a biography or institutional affiliation), the publisher, and the date of publication are all set out clearly at the beginning of a book, inviting decoding in terms of cultural value, authority, datedness, etc; the layout, including the balance between words and images, sequencing of segments or chapters, use of contents page, subheadings, bibliography and index, similarly invites a conventional interpretation.

What then of literacy today? If one sees the computer as merely requiring a minimal technical proficiency from its users, and if one thinks that the Internet merely makes already-familiar contents accessible online, then literacy would neither be dependent on, or changed by, the technological shift from page to screen. But if, through its mediating role, ICT is seen to transform knowledge and culture, then this minimal conception of literacy is only the beginning of the story. The challenges ahead will extend beyond the promotion of technical proficiency to reconsidering some deeply-entrenched notions of thinking, learning and authority (Poster, 2001; Rice, 2002; Snyder, 1998; Turkle, 1995; Tyner, 1998).

What's new?

Attempts to specify just what is technologically new about the Internet include analyses of multimedia texts, hypertextuality, anarchic organization, synchronous communication, interactivity, cultural diversity and inclusivity, visual aesthetics, use of bricolage, and so forth, all contrasted with the traditional, linear, hierarchical, logical, rule-governed conventions of print and, by and large, audiovisual media (Castells, 2002; Fornas, Klein, Landendorf, Suden, & Sveningsson, 2002; Lievrouw & Livingstone, 2002; McMillan, 2002; Newhagen & Rafaeli, 1996; Poster, 2001). Although advocates of the "changing literacies" view appear to endorse technological determinism, careful reading repudiates simple causal claims regarding the impact of technology on society (MacKenzie & Wajcman, 1999). Rather, they refer to the supposed underlying shift from modernity to postmodernity, with both technology and literacy being shaped by this grander transformation. For example, Johnson-Eilola (1998) posits a generation gap in understanding "a game" thus: "where modernists are compelled to understand the rules before playing a game—or at best, must be able to discern simple, clear rules by trial and error—postmodernists are capable of working such chaotic environments from within, movement by movement" (p. 195). So, are transformations in literacy indeed so dramatic as to contribute to the shift from modern to postmodern culture (Poster, 2001)?

The counterargument holds that claims made for the transformative nature of the Internet are exaggerated, even false. Perhaps, instead, further research will reveal continuities with the literacies of past decades and centuries. Arguably, much that is now claimed to be intrinsically new to the Internet—heterogeneity of sources, competing authorities, nonlinear or visual forms of representation and so forth—has long applied to libraries, encyclopedias, textbooks, and the like. And the dismay of parents and teachers in contemplating the activities of the younger generation is hardly the sign of a radical break with the past. While the "no change" view ascribes few if any social consequences to the new forms of textuality and technology, it must be acknowledged that the arguments are as yet inconclusive on both sides.

Changing literacies

These accounts of "what's new" include, implicitly if not explicitly, a series of speculations regarding the nature of the user's engagement with the Internet. Stimulating though these are, they are reminiscent of semiotic analyses of film and television before the advent of audience reception studies, full of assumptions about the interpretative role of the reader (Eco, 1979), which are rarely subjected to empirical investigation. Also problematic, at present we lack a sophisticated analysis of the new media environment in terms of text, technology and cultural form, unlike the early days of audience reception studies when a subtle reading of audiovisual texts—whether based on literary criticism, ideology critique, semiotics, and so on—was already in place. So, research must now identify, in textual terms, how the internet mediates the representation of knowledge, the framing of entertainment, and the conduct of communication. And, in tandem with this analysis, it must investigate the emerging skills and practices of new media users as they meaningfully appropriate ICT into their daily lives. How do people variously "read" the World Wide Web? What practices surround the use of the Web, e-mail, chat, and so forth? What literacies are people thereby developing? A top-down definition of media literacy, developed from print and audiovisual media, while a useful initial guide, should not pre-empt learning from users themselves, as was fruitfully the case for audience research (Livingstone, 1998). When considering how the medium matters —is the message, perhaps—the medium must not be understood solely in terms of technology, it must also be "read" in cultural and political terms. Audiovisual media literacy programs have long been concerned to disabuse their students of the myth of technology's neutrality, the favorite exam question being, "Television is a window on the world: Discuss." Yet in today's popular discourse, we are told that the World Wide Web offers a world of information, that the Internet provides an open channel for societal participation. Analogous work to identify the technological characteristics, textual preferences, normative assumptions, biased framing and skewed modes of address of the world wide web is just beginning (e.g., Burbules, 1998). Notwithstanding the optimism, enthusiasm, and even the radical potential of the medium itself, there is also evidence that—online, through attempts of content-providers to re-impose hierarchical, print-based models of authoritative information (Castells, 2002) and offline, through attempts to perpetuate traditional methods of teaching, learning, and assessment (Loveless & Ellis, 2001)—there is a considerable counterforce holding back socially and technologically-inspired moves towards a radical break in the history of literacy. As critical analysis progresses, we will gain a better idea of whether "the Internet is a window on the world" and, assuming the answer is negative, a better sense of the task of promoting critical media literacy.

Individual and institutional uses of literacy

Not only does a skills-based definition of literacy focus on users to the neglect of text and technology, it also prioritizes the abilities of the individual over the knowledge arrangements of society. Yet, as Hartley (2002) argues, "literacy is not and never has been a personal attribute or ideologically inert 'skill' simply to be acquired by individual persons...It is ideologically and politically charged—it can be used as a means of social control or regulation, but also as a progressive weapon in the struggle for emancipation" (p. 136). If literacy is not an end in itself, so what are its social and institutional uses? How are these managed by media, governmental, educational, and commercial bodies? And what kind of critical stance should the academy take as policy is developed (Sterne, 2002)? These questions are currently pressing for those of us in the U.K., for the new

Communications Bill (2003) sets a government regulator the unprecedented brief of "promoting media literacy." What does, could, and should this mean?

As we move into an information society, is media literacy increasingly part of citizenship, a key means, a right even, by which citizens participate in society? Or is literacy primarily a means of realizing ideals of self-actualization, cultural expression, and aesthetic creativity? Will these goals be subordinated to the use of media literacy to support the competitive cultural and economic advantages vital in a globalized, information society? This seems plausible insofar as media literacy, in the U.K. at least, is part of a package of measures to lighten top-down media regulation by devolving responsibility for media use from the state to individuals, a move that can be interpreted either as "empowering" or, more critically, as part of a Foucauldian shift from centralized government to individual governance (Foucault, 1991). Perhaps even these economic goals will be undermined by the reproduction of the divisive standards and values of the established cultural elite. Of the research task explored in this article, namely to extend our understanding of access, analysis, critical evaluation, and content creation from familiar to new media, interestingly it is the latter two which have proved more contentious; yet these are the most crucial to the democratic agenda. Only if these are firmly foregrounded in a definition of media literacy will people be positioned not merely as selective, receptive, and accepting but also as participating, critical; in short, not merely as consumers but also as citizens.

Conclusion

This article has argued that literacy concerns the historically and culturally conditioned relationship among three processes, no one of which is sufficient alone: 1) the symbolic and material representation of knowledge, culture and values; 2) the diffusion of interpretative skills and abilities across a (stratified) population; and 3) the institutional, especially, the state management of the power that access to and skilled use of knowledge brings to those who are "literate." As we extend conceptions of literacy to embrace new media, the first process—that of representation—is barely addressed in the research literature: Until we have a robust account of the media in which people might be judged literate, we can say little about the nature or uses of their literacy. The second process—that of skilled interpretation—has much to learn from the well-established traditions of readership and audience reception in two respects. First, media literacy has developed a sophisticated account of the individual skills involved in decoding media texts, although these have yet to be applied to the new media. Second, audience research has developed an interactive view of the relationship between reader and text which, in the context of new ICTs, must also encompass questions of technology. Literacy, by extension, cannot be conceived solely as a feature of the user but must also be seen as medium-dependent, a co-production of the interactive engagement between technology and user. Further, this paper has argued that, to claim that literacy is changing with the widespread introduction of ICT, research must establish that the literacy associated with the new media, especially the Internet, differs significantly from that of print and audiovisual media.

The third process—that of the institutional uses of literacy—invites a more critical take on literacy, particularly insofar as academic research is used to inform policy. Crucially, however, it is the *relationship* among textuality, competence, and power that sets those who see literacy as democratizing, empowering of ordinary people against those who see it as elitist, divisive, a source of inequality. Today's anxieties over the digital divide merely represent the latest steps in a long-standing struggle between critical and enlightenment positions whose outcome will influence who will have the power to benefit from information and communication in a technologically-mediated twenty-first century.

References

Aufderheide, P. (Ed.). (1993). *Media literacy: A report of the national leadership conference on media literacy*. Aspen, CO: Aspen Institute.

Bazalgette, C. (1999). *Making movies matter*. London: British Film Institute. Available at: www.bfi.org.uk

Buckingham, D. (1998). Media education in the UK: Moving beyond protectionism. *Journal of Communication, 48*, 33–42.

Buckingham, D. (2000). *After the death of childhood: Growing up in the age of electronic media*. Cambridge: Polity Press.

Burbules, N. C. (1998). Rhetorics of the Web: Hyperreading and critical literacy. In I. Snyder (Ed.), *Page to screen: Taking literacy into the electronic era* (pp. 102–122). New York: Routledge.

Castells, M. (2002). *The Internet galaxy: Reflections on the Internet, business, and society*. Oxford: Oxford University Press.

Christ, W. G., & Potter, W. J. (1998). Media literacy, media education, and the academy. *Journal of Communication, 48*, 5–15.

Eco, U. (1979). *The role of the reader: Explorations in the semiotics of texts*. Bloomington, IN: Indiana University Press.

Facer, K., Sutherland, R., Furlong, R., & Furlong, J. (2001). What's the point of using computers? The development of young people's computer expertise in the home. *New Media and Society, 3*, 199–219.

Fornas, J., Klein, K., Ladendorf, M., Sunden, J., & Sveningsson, M. (2002). *Digital borderlands: Cultural studies of identity and interactivity on the Internet*. New York: Peter Lang.

Foucault, M. (1991). Governmentality. In G. Burchill, C. Gordon, & P. Miller (Eds.), *The Foucault effect: Studies in governmentality* (pp. 87–104). Chicago: University of Chicago Press.

Freire, P., and Macedo, D. (1987). *Literacy: Reading the word and the world*. South Hadley, MA.: Bergin and Garvey.
Gurak, L. J. (2001). *Cyberliteracy: Navigating the Internet with awareness*. New Haven, CT: Yale University Press.
Hall, S. (1980). Encoding/decoding. In S. Hall, D. Hobson, A. Lowe, & P. Willis (Eds.), *Culture, media, language*. London: Hutchinson.
Hartley, J. (2002). *Communication, cultural and media studies: The key concepts*. London: Routledge.
Hirsch, E. D. (1987). *Cultural literacy: What every American needs to know*. Boston: Houghton Mifflin.
Hobbs, R. (1998). The seven great debates in the media literacy movement. *Journal of Communication, 48*, 6–32.
Hodge, R., & Tripp, D. (1986). *Children and television: A semiotic approach*. Cambridge: Polity.
Iser, W. (1980). Interaction between text and reader. In S. R. Suleiman & I. Crosman (Eds.), *The reader in the text: Essays on audience and interpretation*. Princeton, NJ: Princeton University Press.
Johnson-Eilola, J. (1998). Living on the surface: Learning in the age of global communication networks. In I. Snyder (Ed.), *Page to screen: Taking literacy into the electronic era* (pp. 185–210). New York: Routledge.
Kellner, D. (2002). New media and new literacies: Reconstructing education for the new millenium. In L. Lievrouw & S. Livingstone (Eds.), *The handbook of new media* (pp. 90–104). London: Sage.
Kintgen, E. R., Kroll, B. M., and Rose, M. (Eds.). (1988). *Perspectives on literacy*. Carbondale, IL: Southern Illinois University Press.
Kubey, R. (Ed.). (1997). *Media literacy in the information age*. New Brunswick, NJ: Transaction Publishers.
Liebes, T., & Katz, E. (1995). *The export of meaning: Cross-cultural readings of DALLAS*. Cambridge: Polity Press.
Lievrouw, L., & Livingstone, S. (2002). The social shaping and consequences of ICTs. In L. L. Lievrouw (Ed.), *Handbook of new media: Social shaping and consequences of ICTs* (pp. 1–15). London: Sage.
Livingstone, S. (1998). *Making sense of television: The psychology of audience interpretation* (2nd ed.). London: Routledge.
Livingstone, S. (2002). *Young people and new media*. London: Sage.
Loveless, A., & Ellis, V. (Eds.). (2001). *ICT, pedagogy and the curriculum: Subject to change*. London: Routledge.
Luke, C. (1989). *Pedagogy, printing, and protestantism: The discourse on childhood*. New York: State University of New York Press.
MacKenzie, D., & Wajcman, J. (Eds.). (1999). *The social shaping of technology* (2nd ed.). Buckingham: Open University Press.
McMillan, S. (2002). Exploring models of interactivity from multiple research traditions: Users, documents, and systems. In L. Lievrouw & S. Livingstone (Eds.), *The handbook of new media* (pp. 164–175). London: Sage.
Newhagen, J. E., and Rafaeli, S. (1996). Why communication researchers should study the Internet: A dialogue. *Journal of Communication, 46*, 4–13.
Norris, P. (2001). *Digital divide: Civic engagement, information poverty, and the Internet worldwide*. Cambridge: Cambridge University Press.

Poster, M. (2001). *What's the matter with the Internet?* Minneapolis, MN: University of Minnesota.

Ribak, R. (2001). "Like immigrants": Negotiating power in the face of the home computer. *New Media and Society, 3*, 220–238.

Rice, R. (2002). Primary issues in Internet use: Access, civic and community involvement, and social interaction and expression. In L. L. Lievrouw (Ed.), *Handbook of new media: Social shaping and consequences of ICTs* (pp. 105–129). London: Sage.

Sefton-Green, J. (Ed.). (1999). *Young people, creativity and new technologies: The challenge of digital arts.* London: Routledge.

Silverstone, R. (1994). *Television and everyday life.* London: Routledge.

Singer, D. G., and Singer, J. L. (Eds.). (2001). *Handbook of children and the media.* Thousand Oaks, CA: Sage.

Snyder, I. (1998). Beyond the hype: Reassessing hypertext. In I. Snyder (Ed.), *Page to screen: Taking literacy into the electronic era* (pp. 125–143). London: Routledge.

Sterne, J. (2002). Cultural policy studies and the problem of political representation. *The Communication Review, 5*, 59–89.

Street, B. (1995). *Social literacies: Critical approaches to literacy in development, ethnography and education.* London: Longman.

Turkle, S. (1995). *Life on the screen: Identity in the age of the Internet.* New York: Simon & Schuster.

Tyner, K. (1998). *Literacy in a digital world.* Mahwah, NJ: Lawrence Erlbaum.

Warnick, B. (2002). *Critical literacy in a digital era: Technology, rhetoric, and the public interest.* Mahway, NJ: Lawrence Erlbaum.

Williams, R. (1976). *Keywords: A vocabulary of culture and society.* London: Fontana.

71

COMPLICITY AND COLLUSION IN THE MEDIATION OF EVERYDAY LIFE*

Roger Silverstone

Source: *New Literary History* 33(4) (2002): 761–80.

> On the 2nd we were at the Wenglers in the afternoon. It once again made an enormous impression on me when they put on the wireless and leapt from London to Rome, from Rome to Moscow etc. The concepts of time and space are annihilated. One must become a mystic. For me radio destroys every form of religion and at the same time gives rise to religion. Gives rise to it twice over: a) because such a miracle exists, b) because the human intellect invests, explains, makes use of it. But this same human intellect puts up with the Hitler government.[1]

This essay investigates everyday life as a moral and a social space. It presumes that it is in the everyday, and above all in the detail of the relationships that are made with others and which constitute everyday life's possibility, that our common humanity is created and sustained. It also presumes that it is through the actions and the interactions that make up the continuities of daily experience that an ethics of care and responsibility is, or is not, enabled. I argue that no ethics of, and from, the everyday is conceivable without communication, and that all communication involves mediation, mediation as a transformative process in which the meaningfulness and value of things are constructed.

The modern world has witnessed, and in significant degrees has been defined by, a progressive technological intrusion into the conduct of everyday life, of which the most recent and arguably the most significant manifestations have been our media technologies. These technologies, principally broadcast technologies in the twentieth century, have become increasingly central to the ways in which individuals manage their everyday lives: central in their capacity, in broadcast schedules and the consistencies of genre, to create a framework for the ordering of the everyday, and central too in their capacity to provide the symbolic resources and tools for making sense of the complexities of the everyday.

These technologically enabled processes of communication and meaning construction are processes of mediation.[2] Mediation, in the sense in which I am using the term, describes the fundamentally, but unevenly, dialectical process in which institutionalized media of communication (the press, broadcast radio and television, and increasingly the World Wide Web) are involved in the general circulation of symbols in social life. That circulation no longer requires face-to-face communication, though it does not exclude it.

Mediation is dialectical because while it is perfectly possible to privilege those mass media as defining and perhaps even determining social meanings, such privileging would miss the continuous and often creative engagement that listeners and viewers have with the products of mass communication. And it is uneven, precisely because the power to work with, or against, the dominant or deeply entrenched meanings that the media provide is unevenly distributed across and within societies.

Mediation, in this sense of the term, is both technological and social. It is also increasingly pervasive, as social actors become progressively dependent on the supply of public meanings and accounts of the world in attempting to make sense of their own. As such, mediation has significant consequences for the way in which the world appears in and to everyday life, and as such this mediated appearance in turn provides a framework for the definition and conduct of our relationships to the other, and especially the distant other—the other who only appears to us within the media.

I intend to argue that there are profound moral and ethical issues to be addressed in confronting the mediation of everyday life. I also intend to argue that insofar as the persisting representational characteristics of contemporary media, above all in our media's representation of the other, remain unchallenged—as for the most part they are—then those who receive and accept them are neither mere prisoners of a dominant ideology nor innocents in a world of false consciousness; rather they are willing participants, that is, complicit, or even actively engaged, that is, collusive, in a mediated culture that fails to deliver its promises of communication and connection, with enduring, powerful and largely negative consequences for our status as human beings.

This critique juxtaposes the media and everyday life while at the same time arguing that the media and everyday life are in significant ways inseparable. One can no longer conceive of the everyday without acknowledging the central role that increasingly the electronic media (but also books and the press) have in defining its ways of seeing, being, and acting. My argument presupposes that the media take as their paramount reality, in terms of their orientation, the everyday life world of its audiences, readers, and users. Of course neither the media nor everyday life are unitary phenomena, nor do they have a singular relationship to each other. Notwithstanding these differences of individual and institutional practice, as well as differential possibilities for both resistance and transcendence, the media are becoming a second order paramount reality, fully equivalent to, though not reducible to, the "world in which the acts of our activity are objectified and the world in which these acts actually proceed and are actually accomplished once and only once."[3]

This second order paramount reality, that of the media, does not replace the world of lived experience, as Jean Baudrillard, with his notion of the simulacrum, imagined it did, but it runs through that experiential world, dialectically engaged with it, eternally intertwined.[4] The lived and the represented consequently become the warp and the weft of the everyday, and what is at stake in any investigation of their interrelationship is the historical and sociological specificity of the ensuing fabric, its strengths and its weaknesses, its coincidences and its contradictions: the touch and the feel of culture—the ethics and aesthetics of experience.

From this perspective mediation is already a crucial constituent of everyday life. One cannot inquire into one without simultaneously inquiring into the other.

Mediating the everyday

I want to approach this inquiry through a discussion of four dimensions of the mediated everyday: its ambiguity and paradoxicality, its physicality, its sociability, and its ethics.

Critical accounts of everyday life have come to acknowledge and defend, among other things, the essential paradoxicality of everyday life.[5] Everyday life is seen as a site for the toleration, indeed celebration, of ambiguity: a site for creativity and the transcendence—playful, political, or otherwise—of the constraints imposed by an increasingly dominant and strategic system of technological rationality, administrative order, and capitalist commodification. Everyday life is a site for the heterological, the unpredictable, and the tactical.

These accounts are palpable misreadings. Paradox, like history, is a luxury of the elite. Ambiguities are threats not comforts in the material struggles of the everyday. Indeed it is arguably the case that everyday life within modernity, but also earlier, consists in a continuous battle against uncertainty and for clarity and confidence in the conduct of daily existence. Everyday life is tough for most people most of the time. Even Bakhtin's carnival, with its famous refusal of the singular orderings of dominant culture and its playful celebration of the disorder of the popular, nevertheless gains its meaning from its own precise and predictable order. In this sense it cannot escape the ritual frames that are a central dimension of popular culture, even more perhaps than of high culture. So insofar as paradox and ambiguity persist within the lived cultures of everyday life, as opposed to the representations or aestheticizations of everyday life, then it might be suggested that they express a degree of failure, failure to control the contradictory demands of daily life in modernity.

The media are crucially implicated in this refusal of paradox, for in their own forms of ordering, in narrative and schedule above all, they provide a framework for the resolution of ambiguity, the reduction of insecurity, and the creation of a degree of comfort. Thus the predominant genres and modes of representation (news, chat show, soap opera) meet the needs and the desires for order of, and in, the everyday, and even in those areas of media production and consumption where it may be suggested that there is scope for both resistance and ambiguity (and there is evidence, for example, in popular music culture and in some online networks and bulletin boards that this is the case), it could still be argued that what is at stake is not the embrace of ambiguity and paradox but the search, perhaps the impossible search, for different kinds of order.[6]

It is an order grounded in the body. Everyday life is bodily life: life that is gendered and aged; life both enabled and limited by material resources, by circumstance and fate. Bakhtin's recovery of the everyday was through the celebration of the popular, and the popular was Rabelaisian, turning its back on the ascetic and the refined. The everyday has its own smells, its own desires, and in its refusals of the antiseptic orderings of high culture, the everyday also refuses the Cartesian dualism in which bodies and minds are separated and where bodies come a distinct second in the creation of social value. Theories of everyday life, no less than empirical investigations into its conduct, require getting involved in the nitty-gritty of the physical world. The body is seen, consequently, as the site for resistance, notwithstanding the increasingly insistent pressures of a "bureaucratic society of controlled consumption," for without that resistance the social as well as the physical body itself would atrophy.[7] The viability as well as the value of everyday life consists in our physical capacity to engage fully with what the system throws at us. Indeed the utopianism in the writing on everyday life privileges the capacity of the individual to construct his or her own reality, albeit from a position of structural weakness, as she transforms the abstract structures of language into the vivid discourses of daily speech or the alienating spaces and times of the city into something like home.[8]

The world of the everyday is above all a vivid world, and that vividness is grounded in bodily experience and sensibility. And it is through the vivid face-to-face that socially meaningful and robust relations are sustained: in places and across generations, reproduced through time.

Bodies, however, require comfort and security, both material and symbolic. It is in the repetitiveness of the everyday, its very familiarity and predictability, that such securities are sought and sometimes found. Amongst the disturbances caused during the modern period are disturbances that have affected the body mightily. The body has been subject to increased and terrifying risk. It has been incorporated into the technological, undergoing a cyborg fusion that many have seen as being transformative of our capacity to act in the world. The body, finally, has been seen to be the site of the exercise of power, inscribed, as Nikolas Rose has argued in his work on governmentality, with the ink of states and nations.[9]

The experience of everyday life, however, is no longer containable within physical space, even if it ever was. The media have provided an increasingly available and increasingly insistent alternative: the possibility of bodily transcendence through identifications with characters, the seductions of narrative, obsessional gaming, and Internet chat. Though the media do this, of course, at a price. In the palpable dematerialization of the body, our own but crucially that of the other, the media have created a space in which the lack of physical contact destroys a sense of meaningful difference between bodies. Of course this lack is a constant in all forms of imaginative and aesthetic experience. But in the electronic media it is disguised, if not denied, in the constant presence of the other in the images and voices of mediated representation and interaction. Many have complained about the homogenizing power of the media and the cultural industries behind them, but here is a particular manifestation of that homogeneity, one in which representational distancing draws the sting from the face-to-face, the pain of recognition, and, as I shall argue shortly, the demands on the person of a grounded ethics.

On the one hand, then, the threat of uniformity but on the other the threat of fragmentation and individualisation: what is also at stake in the mediation of everyday life is the relationship between the individual and the social. Manuel Castells, in extensive discussions of the revolutionary consequences of the Internet on social life and behavior, points to a fit between the increasing individualism of late modernity and the emergence of such a networking technology. He suggests that while this emergence keeps nodes and participants separate it also simultaneously links them together in intense forms of sociability. On the one hand he points to the triumph of the individual, on the other to the possibility that this triumph will in turn lead, with technologically enabled mediation, to the creation of a new kind of network society.[10]

The quality of everyday life is often seen to be threatened by modernity and above all by the relentless rise of individualism as both an ideology and reality. Capitalism and industrialism, both, have undermined secondary social groupings—family, church, community—and the possibility for solidarity and the sharing of common experience that they offered. These institutions and groupings were once seen to have enabled a shared body of commonsense beliefs and assumptions, unquestioned though they may have been, which in turn enabled and sustained traditional forms of collective life.

On the other hand modernity is seen to have generated the conditions for a multiplicity of perspectives and positions which in turn enabled a new kind of publicness, or at least the opportunity for it. As Hannah Arendt notes, comparing the value of public and private spaces through an observation of the centrality of difference:

> For though the common world is the common meeting ground of all, those who are present have different locations in it, and the location of one can no more coincide with the location of another than the location of two objects. Being seen and being heard by others derive their significance from the fact that everybody sees and hears from a different position. This is the meaning of public life, compared to which even the richest and most satisfying family life can offer only the prolongation or multiplication of one's own position with its attending aspects and perspectives.[11]

The possibility of public life depends on the mutuality of seeing and hearing, and seeing and hearing in turn depends on the recognition of both difference and identity amongst those involved in the interaction. Such is Arendt's gold standard for an ethics of public participation and responsibility.

However modernity has yet another tale to tell. Individualism has promoted difference without commonness. And technological rationality, an equivalent condition on the same march of modernity, has promoted commonness without difference.[12] Manuel Castells implies, and to a degree he follows Raymond Williams in the logic of his argument, that new media technologies arise, and are accepted, in modernising societies precisely as a way of mediating this contradiction.[13] For Williams radio and then television emerged not only to fulfill capitalism's pressing need for efficient and speedy communication but in order to provide an inclusive framework for national culture and public participation amongst geographically and socially mobile populations. Similarly, now, the Internet provides the framework, only this time on a global scale. The imagined community of print and broadcasting is to be replaced by the fragmented network of the Internet, but with what consequences for everyday life?[14]

Again, much has been written on the capacity of networking technologies to create, or enable, new forms of sociability. There is an increasing amount of empirical work purporting to show how forms of on-line connectivity, chat and the sharing of enthusiasms or anxieties, can and do provide meaningful contact, sufficient for those involved to feel engaged and supported, to make friends, and even to transfer their virtual mutuality into the real world.[15] Some times these new connectivities are seen as providing compensating alternatives to the weakening infrastructures of everyday life, patching the thinning ozone layer of sociability in the daily round.[16] On the other hand, such on-line sociability is decried for its limited singularity; a monochrome of lifestyles and interests, it is unsustainable beyond the narrow confines of mutual identification.[17] On-line relationships consequently are always provisional and essentially voluntaristic; they can break down under the slightest pressure.

At best, therefore, one can see these networks as involving the privatization of sociability: an until-further-notice, rather than a taken-for-granted, kind of thing. The me-centered network survives for only as long as I do.[18] It has little capacity for reproduction, nor does it have the patience for the struggle with contradiction. And while bulletin boards and chat-rooms provide a space for debate, they do so on the narrow terrain of a prior identification of singular agendas and particular interests. They do not, in these manifestations, create even a pale imitation of the face-to-faceness of everyday life, however romantic such a notion is seen to be. What is offered by such networks, and for the most part gladly accepted, is what can only be described as an illusion of connection.

And illusions, of course, though they have their costs, can be massively sustaining. The illusion of connection is grounded in the refusal of otherness. It is based on the private masquerading as the public, the separate masquerading as the shared, the different masquerading as the same, the distant masquerading as the close-at-hand, the unequal masquerading as the equal. In all these dimensions the masquerade is profound in its ethical consequences.

Indeed the quality and authenticity of everyday life stands or falls in its capacity to define and sustain a viable ethics. Numerous social theorists ground their critical position on the degree to which rationality, the creation of value, the capacity to make meaningful choices and distinctions, and the acceptance of responsibility for the other are, or are not, preserved or at least redeemable in the ongoing activities of modern everyday life.[19]

At the heart of such an enquiry into the ethics of everyday life must be a concern with our relationships to each other.[20] And these relationships need to be premised on a recognition of difference, on the legitimate and indelible differences between us. This is, I believe, what Arendt is arguing in the quotation already cited above, and it is, of course, the core of the ethical position taken by Emmanuel Levinas. Levinas writes:

> The absolutely other is the Other. He and I do not form a number. The collectivity in which I say "you" or "we" is not a plural of the "I." I, you—these are not individuals of a common concept. Neither possession nor the unity of number nor the unity of concepts link me to the Stranger, the Stranger who disturbs the being at home with oneself. But stranger also means free one. Over him I have no *power*. He escapes my grasp by an essential dimension,

even if I have him at my disposal. He is not wholly in my site.... We are the same and theother.

(*TI* 39)

There is something quite terrifying in this modest observation. Levinas is arguing that impotence and vulnerability lie at the core of any defensible notion and practice of humanity. As Kenneth Cmiel points out, for Levinas it is communication's failure, its impossibility, its breakdown, that is its saving grace.[21] Communication can never incorporate the other fully, nor should it aim to. The resistance of the other to inclusion, and indeed also to exclusion, is seminal. We are neither all alike nor all implacably different. In the recognition of this intransigence lies an ethical position that, in its application to, and within, the domain of everyday life requires that we take responsibility for the stranger in an inevitably discomforting world. It is a world we can never claim fully to know nor fully to understand; it is a world which requires of us, as a consequence, a certain humility. The other, as Other, will always be trouble, but such trouble is a necessary precondition of what it means to be human. The Other cannot be erased.

The media are crucially implicated in the representation of the other, in his or her presence or absence in contemporary society. While our screens and speakers are daily suffused with the images and voices of worlds and peoples of which we would otherwise have no knowledge, the nature of that representation and the quality of the relationship that is offered to us as listeners and viewers is fundamentally constrained. It is constrained by the character of the media as doubly connecting and disconnecting, as simultaneously both engaging and disengaging. Two related dimensions of this process of mediation appear to be particularly salient: distance and trust.

Distance and trust

Communication and mediation are both means to transcend distance. The distance that separates one being from another in the face-to-face encounter is arguably as significant and profound, and as ultimately unbridgeable, as that which separates two cultures across differences of global space and of fundamental belief. Electronically mediated communication, however, has the problem of time-space distanciation to deal with (a problem which, one hardly needs to be reminded, the media themselves have largely created).[22] The dislocation of communication has, of course, been a gradual process; and it might be suggested that the instantaneity and vividness of both broadcast and Net-based media have at long last solved the problems that were posed initially by the compass, the steam engine, and the telegraph. That is, connection, true connection, across intangible space, is at last possible. The space between the "as if" of representation and narrative and the "real" appears to have finally been bridged by the immediate, the live and interactive. It hardly needs to be said, of course, that such transcendence is illusory. Such mediations not only preserve separation in the same breath as they appear to deny it, but such illusory connection has significant consequences for how we understand the world, and above all how we relate to the mediated other in a world where more and more of our significant others are indeed mediated.

Distance remains a huge problem in this mediated world and for our management of everyday life, especially because the persistence of distance is of such moral import. As Kevin Robins has noted in his discussion of the psychodynamics of the representation of the Gulf War, "the screen exposes the ordinary viewer to harsh realities, but it screens out the harshness of those realities. It has a certain moral weightlessness: it grants sensation without demanding responsibility, and it involves us in a spectacle without engaging us in the complexity of its reality."[23] This observation is both familiar and unfamiliar. It is familiar insofar as spectacle has, at least since Guy Debord, been seen as a major component of the media's totalitarian occupation of the spaces of the everyday;[24] but it is less familiar insofar as it provides the basis for taking an ethical position, one that engages the problem of mediated distance as being a crucial component of the morality of the everyday.

The problem of distance is also a problem of proximity. Contemporary mediation veers towards two contrasting, compatible, but equally indefensible modes of representation in the mediation of the other. The first involves pushing the other beyond the pale: defining alterity as beyond reach and comprehension. The images of celebrating Palestinians that were persistently screened after the bombing of the World Trade Center could only reinforce the perception of them and what they represented as totally alien. Subsequent representations of Islam, both geographically distant as well as close to home, likewise reinforce that sense of unreachable otherness which creates anxiety and in turn legitimates repression. The dominance of such images, and the absence of alternatives or contextualizations, as is well known, powerfully sustain a culture of suspicion and hostility, in which moral judgements, that is, judgements which involve sensibility and responsibility for the other, become impossible.[25]

The second representational strategy involves exactly the opposite. It denies difference altogether. Images of the other are incorporated into entirely familiar and taken-for-granted narratives and frames, those of advertising or of the talk show, or even the documentary. Laughing Africans and Caribbeans sell cars and alcohol. The poor are not poor unless they have swollen bellies and flies in their eyes. Jerry Springer and Ricki Lake offer fifteen minutes of fame to the otherwise marginal and invisible: they are tamed but not respected through their display. The domestication of otherness is necessarily a refusal of otherness.

Mediated distance therefore continually swings between incorporation (that is denial of both difference and distance) or annihilation (that is denial of both a common humanity and closeness). In both cases the other appears on our screens, and therefore, on the face of it, is seen and seen to be present. Yet in both cases the possibility of approaching that otherness with any degree of comprehension and sensibility is, with obvious individual exceptions, fundamentally compromised.

In a related paper to this one I have discussed these issues within a framework defined by what I have called the notion of *proper distance*.[26] This refers to the importance of understanding the more or less precise degree of proximity required in our mediated interrelationships if we are to create and sustain a sense of the other sufficient not just for reciprocity but for a duty of care, obligation, and responsibility. Proper distance would preserve the other through difference as well as through shared identity.

Luc Boltanski, in a similarly focused discussion of the mediated representation of suffering, argues that one of the central components of the distancing in mediated communication is the inability of the receiver to know about, or interrogate, the context or the intention of those who initiate the communication: "The media situation, by not only distancing the spectator from the unfortunate but also from the person who presents the unfortunate's suffering to him (without necessarily having witnessed them), makes more exacting the necessary conditions of trust which, as many experimental studies have shown, are broadly dependent upon an effect of presence."[27]

A major characteristic of modernity lies in our increasing trust in abstract systems. This, together with what Anthony Giddens calls the sequestration of experience—that is, the committing of madness, criminality, sickness and death, and sexuality and nature, to the institutionalized margins of everyday life—define, from another perspective, an essentially practical disengagement from the disturbances and traumas of otherwise naked reality.[28] Trust in abstract systems, indeed trust in the technologies that enable and make manifest those abstract systems, is yet another challenge to the morality of everyday life.

Trust, and trustworthiness, is as crucial a component in the mediation of everyday life as it is in other dimensions of social life. But here, if recent commentators are to be believed, it is in increasingly short supply. While it is obviously the case that the everyday is unsustainable unless we do trust in abstract systems, those institutions, the media, that are not just to be trusted in themselves but to be trusted to enable trust in others, are doubly significant. The decline in support for, and trust in, the democratic process in the developed societies can be seen to be, at least in part, as Onora O'Neill argues, a consequence of our increasing lack of trust in the media's representation of that process.[29]

However the media, like all those involved in relations of trust, operate in a skewed economy; for while it is rarely difficult to find evidence of untrustworthiness, it is virtually impossible to prove its opposite: I can not prove that you are trustworthy, only, should the case arise, that you have broken that trust. And once broken it is difficult, often impossible, to rebuild.

Trust then is a slippery thing; it is always conditional, requiring continuous maintenance and evidence of fulfilment. There is a paradox, however in the mediation of trust and in the creation and sustaining of our trust in the media, for such trust is beset with ambiguity. Much of our media has palpably an unstable, not to say from time to time an exploitative, relationship to reality and to truth. The boundaries are daily crossed between the so-called purity of information and entertainment. The distinction between descriptive and analytic reporting is blurred, and the op-ed has become a feature of the world's press. Reality TV and docu-soaps visibly and playfully massage the boundary between reality and fiction. Spontaneous chat shows are rehearsed. Live transmissions from the world's hot-spots are pre-recorded. How can we trust in a fake, especially one we know to be a fake? Or to put it another way, the question is not so much about the absence of trust within the processes of mediation but our acceptance of those absences, our willing refusal to challenge manifest breaches of trust. How come we don't seem to mind?

One answer to this question is provided by Max Horkheimer and Theodor Adorno who end their critique of the culture industries with an observation on the power of advertising. Consumers, they say, "feel compelled to buy and use its products even though they see through them."[30] This suggests that there is no alternative, and indeed their pessimism relies on a sense of the omnipotence of such forms of communication. My own argument differs from theirs in one key respect. While it acknowledges the representational power that the media wield, it nevertheless suggests that if we are to maintain not only an intellectual but also a political position that insists on our capacity for agency, then we have to recognize that media power can and must be challenged. If we are to be acknowledged as willing participants in mediated culture then there has to be some meaning in the notion of *willing*.

So the question of our acceptance of such dominant forms of mediation is a real one and much more complex than contemporary claims of irresponsibility and dumbing down tend to assume. One way of addressing this question might be to indicate how both the everyday and its manifestation in popular culture have consistently refused to take the mediated representation of the world entirely at face value. The serious minded do not recognize the profound centrality of play at the heart of media culture, a playfulness recognized and indulged in by both parties to the communication. Play offers a different and distinct basis for the exercise (or breach) of trust. Instead of a betrayal of the facts, what counts in play is essentially a betrayal of the rules. Instead of the liar is the cheat. The conventions and rules of playfulness define a set of limits and practices which are only challenged, and distrusted, in their breach. Media representation, of the so-called popular kind, plays, by and large, according to rules, though the rules are not always clear-cut; they are not fixed, nor are they unregulated by states. The playfulness of popular culture to which mediated culture is heir has always been misunderstood, distrusted, and also quite often feared by those in authority. The history of Victorian Britain was certainly in part a history of the struggle to regulate and contain the playfulness of the popular, seeking to constrain its anarchic streak and bringing it safely into the confines of, increasingly, commodified culture.[31] Yet, in many of the strands of popular television, as well as in the tabloid and yellow press, these forms of play live on. The playfulness of mediated culture is not simply, then, a postmodern invention. It has a history, and a logic.

There is a difference between trust in a narrative or a report, that is trust in factual accuracy, and trust in the media's enabling structures, where accuracy might take second place, even in factual reporting, to aesthetics and to the authority of genre. In the former there is a concern with content, and with the singularity of a representational claim. In the latter there is a concern with the quality and reliability of the enabling structures, and the rules that govern them. Here reports can be misleading, but only if they are misread. Contemporary mediation involves both, often contradictory, kinds of textuality and both kinds of claims on audiences and viewers. The literal and the playful overlay and complicate the relationship between the factual and the fictional. The knowingness that audiences can bring to their media consumption is a crucial part of the trust that is generated in their relationship to what they see and hear, though it would of course be wrong to suggest that such knowingness is uniform or invulnerable. Audiences can make mistakes, and media can, wittingly or otherwise, lead them astray.

The play theory of mediation still has, however, significant implications for media ethics.[32] For in play there is a profound displacement of responsibility. While there is no game without our participation, the game itself, as play, can be seen to inoculate its players from accepting responsibility for anything other than what takes place within its own clearly bounded framework. "It's only a game." We trust in the other within the game to play fairly, but we do not take responsibility for the game itself. We leave that to others. However notions of trust based on play have to involve a shared responsibility, for there is no game without all participants. Mediation, too, is a shared activity, involving reciprocity and mutuality, albeit in a highly skewed political infrastructure. We, the audience, cannot walk away if the game is to continue; the game cannot continue without us.

Complicity and collusion

Recent media research has been at pains to demonstrate the degree to which audiences for a wide range of broadcast material must be considered active. Choices are made between programs, and meanings are not predefined by either producers or texts.[33] An understanding of the reader-text relationship requires the recognition that both at the point of impact and in subsequent social and cultural discourses audiences are at work, actively engaged with the significant continuities (and the continuous significance) of otherwise one-way communication. Such activity, of course, becomes interactivity in the world of the computer and the network with, consequently, a sense of even stronger kinds of participation.

I want to argue, in this final section of the essay, that such presuppositions necessarily have a moral consequence, one that has hitherto been almost completely ignored. If audiences are active and if the notion of activity has any meaning at all, then they must be presumed to have to take responsibility for their actions. If audiences refuse to take that responsibility, then they are morally culpable. And we are all audiences now.[34]

It follows that the weaknesses of our media, which are both structural and circumstantial, do not just impinge on everyday life, impose on our daily values and practices like men or women from Mars. They emerge and are accepted as components of a shared culture. Without challenge, without interrogation, and above all without our willingness to take responsibility for them, they both fail us and, crucially, we them.

The notion of the active audience is limited insofar as it does not move beyond the immediate experience of the individual, and insofar as it does not move beyond the reception of content.[35] Tamar Liebes and Elihu Katz, in their cross-cultural research on the reception of the television series *Dallas*, are unusual in identifying some audiences who actually engage with both the presumed intentions of producers and the structures of production.[36] These audiences do not just relate what they see to their everyday lives, but they relate critically to the rules of media engagement, the rules of the game in which they are participating by watching the program. This kind of critical relationship to the media is a precondition for any ethical or moral interrogation of the media. It is a precondition, too, for our ability to take responsibility for mediation. Without such informed interrogation, audiences become complicit with the media's representational strategies.

In a sophisticated and challenging essay on the relationship between the anthropologist and his or her subject in a postcolonial global world, George Marcus finds in complicity the figure with which to address both the ethical dilemmas within the practice of ethnographic fieldwork and the means to move beyond the limits of the singularly local as its container. Complicity, "being an accomplice," "partnership in an evil action," but also, more generally, "the state of being complex or involved" (*OED*), emerges when both partners in the ethnographic project are in some senses aware of, but do not fully acknowledge or question, those aspects of the world which are material to that relationship and to the two cultures which sustain it. Both parties privately know that an explanation for the reality in front of them depends on moving outside it, to other sites and settings in time and space. They are complicit in a project of knowledge generation which both know is inadequate but which both are willing to accept.

From one perspective this kind of complicity is a terminally disabling dimension of the anthropological project, ethically and morally.[37] However rather than seeing complicity as the death-knell of ethnography Marcus argues that once recognized and understood, complicity provides a route into a new kind of multi-sited ethnography, an ethnography which requires the anthropologist, at least, to follow the trails and explore the contexts necessary to engage properly with the other.

Students of media and everyday life can learn from this dilemma in anthropological practice and the kinds of reflexivity it generates. In the context of this essay the notion of complicity turns on questions of distance and of representation. Complicity figures as an irony of position, in which neither the participants in the interaction (the represented and the representing) quite know enough about the other, quite understand enough about each other's power, to create a secure collaborative relationship, but they nevertheless proceed on the basis that they actually do know enough. Together they share knowledge of a material absence, but in the half-light of their inevitably time-limited interaction, they leave well enough alone.

However, the anthropological critique, perhaps for understandable reasons, stops one step short, for it does not consider the third party to this interaction, the party who reads the anthropologist's text. To include her, and to include her in her plurality and in the context of the everyday, infinitely complicates the complicity of mediation, which involves, always, not two but three parties: the represented, the representing, and the witnesses to the representation. Documentary filmmaking and news reporting, indeed any attempt within the media to claim a reality and thereby to claim a truth, involves a complicity in which all involved participate; a refusal to recognize that the process in which they are all engaged, as subjects/objects, as producers/writers, as receivers/audiences—albeit from different positions of power—is inadequate and compromised by its own contradictions. Audiences, producers, and, increasingly, participants and subjects of representation are complicit in this representational practice when they fail to challenge it, and when they fail to reflect on those of its aspects that, by default, risk betraying the world.

Subjects are complicit when they play according to the rules, when they accept the limitations of genre, when they fail to recognize the impossibility, and partiality, of representation.[38] Producers are complicit likewise when they fail to reflect on the limitations of their practice and fail to communicate these both to their subjects and their audiences. Audiences are complicit insofar as they uncritically accept the media's representational claims and insofar as their knowing acknowledgement of its limitations remains tacit.

There is, then, a close link between this dimension of complicity in everyday life and the will to power in mediation, that is, the need to believe in our ability to know the other fully and our need to believe in the reality and authority of the facts about her or him. Participants in media culture are complicit insofar as they accept the media as necessary for both our understanding of the world and our capacity to value the other, as the media indeed are; but also as sufficient, which they cannot be.

Our complicity relies on this mutual misrecognition and of course it sustains it, too. It provides us with comfort, at least until such time as events in the world break through the tissue of representation.[39] That comfort, in turn, inoculates us against the challenges of the real and against our need ever, fully, to take responsibility for the other.

The boundary between complicity and collusion is a permeable one. But whereas I have argued that complicity is a kind of substrate in the relationship we have both to the other and to our media, as well as to the other through our media, collusion, "secret agreement or understanding for purposes of trickery or fraud" (literally, and instructively, "playing together") (*OED*) can be seen to be more direct in its moral consequences. This is particularly the case where we are confronted by images and narratives of suffering and pain. Stanley Cohen, in reflecting on the process of mediation in his recent, trenchant account of denial in the face of human suffering, notes an important paradox. It is worth quoting him at length:

> Television is the primary channel through which the agonies of distant others reach the consciences of the more privileged, safe and comfortable.... These images belong to a hyper-reality, a continuous set of paradoxes about the observer's view of what is "really" happening.... But there is also a fathomless distance, not just the geographical distance from the event, but the unimaginability of this happening to you or your loved ones.... On the one hand, immediacy breaks down the older barriers to knowledge and compassion, the TV news becoming "a hopeful example of the internationalisation of conscience." But, on the other, its selectivity, promiscuity and short attention time span, make viewers into "voyeurs of the suffering of others, tourists amidst their landscapes of anguish."[40]

Whereas one can read the ambivalence of this as a sign of hope, and indeed increasing international responsiveness to distant suffering is certainly hopeful, it would be a mistake to ignore its inverse. For it is the intransigence of the distant and the ephemeral that provides the raw material for collusive denial. If the "as if" of representation brings tragedy and trauma in to the front room it nevertheless also makes it easy to deposit them both outside the back door.

Collusion, therefore, involves such shared denial. Indeed, as Cohen notes, denials draw on shared cultural vocabularies to be credible. Collusions, "mutually reinforcing denials that allow no meta-comment, work best when we are unaware of them" (64). Just as families can deny the presence of an alcoholic member because it would be too painful to acknowledge, so too can societies deny the presence of problems and traumas that they would otherwise have to confront. Media images enable a collusive illusion that the appearance of the other in crisis on the screen is sufficient for us to believe that we are fully engaged with him or her in that crisis.

Indeed, in this crucial matter of our relationship to the other, and our capacity to care, we are confronted by the sharing of, and our complicity and collusion with, two kinds of cultural vocabularies. The first is shared between us and our media: the vocabulary and discourse of representation, narrative, and report. The second is amongst ourselves: the related vocabularies and discourses of everyday life—its talk, its memories, and its forgettings. Complicity depends on our willing acceptance of the media's capacity to translate the properly challenging other both into the comforting frames of the familiar and into excommunicated banishment. Collusive denial depends on our capacity, and our desire, both to ignore and to forget the reality of the other's otherness. Complicity is implicated in our relationship to the forms and processes of mediation, collusion to its content.

Our domestic and entirely understandable desire for simplicity, comfort, and order in our everyday lives, has, then, a lot to answer for. The media, in their collusion with that desire, do too. But our complicity and collusion lie even deeper than this, for they lie at the heart of the media's mediation of the realities of the world and in the "as if" of its representational practices. The mediated symbolic is not imposed upon us as a space of no escape. It is one, historically, we have chosen, one that we choose on a daily basis, and one whose choice we have chosen to deny. Choice involves agency. Agency involves the possibility of challenge and refusal. This is not say that we can walk away from our media-saturated culture. Manifestly we cannot. But we can begin to understand it and in that understanding take responsibility for it. We can then challenge and change it.

Our media allow us to frame, represent, and see the other and his or her world. They do not, by and large, in their distancing, invite us to engage with the other, nor to accept the challenge of the other. In effect they provide a sanctuary for everyday life, a bounded space of safety and identity within and around it. But sanctuaries insulate and isolate as well as protect.

Notes

* I am extremely grateful to Rita Felski for her trenchant and helpful comments on an earlier draft of this essay.

1 Victor Klemperer, 9 November 1935, *The Klemperer Diaries 1933–45* (London, 2000), p. 133. Victor Klemperer, expelled from his tenure as Professor of Romance Languages at the Technical University of Dresden in 1935, miraculously

survived both Nazi persecution and the British bombing of his city. His diary chronicles both his own daily existence in its increasing deprivation and persecution, and also the rise and fall of Hitler's Germany from the point of view of his own everyday life experience.

2 Mediation (Thompson uses the term mediazation) indicates the specific character and dynamics of, especially, the electronic media in enabling arguably distinct forms of communication in public and private cultures, see John B. Thompson, *Media and Modernity* (Cambridge, 1995), and Roger Silverstone "Mediation and Communication" in *The International Handbook of Sociology*, ed. Craig Calhoun, Chris Rojek, and Bryan S. Turner (London, in press).

3 M. M. Bakhtin, *Toward a Philosophy of the Act*, ed. Michael Holquist and Vadim Liapunov (Austin, 1993), p. 2.

4 Jean Baudrillard, *Simulations* (New York, 1983).

5 Two recent reviews provide overlapping but often quite distinct accounts of the major theoretical contributions to twentieth-century writing on everyday life; both, as it happens, studiously ignore the role of the media: Michael Gardiner, *Critiques of Everyday Life* (London, 2000); Ben Highmore, *Everyday Life and Cultural Theory* (London, 2002).

6 Order but also power: compare Couldry who examines the micro-sociology of media power and Downing who looks at a broader politics of alternative media: Nick Couldry, *The Place of Media Power: Pilgrims and Witnesses of the Media Age* (London, 2000); John H. Downing, *Radical Media: Rebellious Communication and Social Movements* (London, 2001); on the significance of ritual as a framework for approaching the relationship between order and power in media, see Eric Rothenbuehler, *Ritual Communication: From Everyday Conversation to Mediated Ceremony* (Thousand Oaks, 1998).

7 Henri Lefebvre, *Everyday Life in the Modern World* (New Brunswick, 1984), pp. 68–109.

8 Michel de Certeau, *The Practice of Everyday Life* (Berkeley, 1984); Michel de Certeau, Luce Girard, and Pierre Mayol, *The Practice of Everyday Life Vol. 2: Living and Cooking* (Minneapolis, 1998).

9 On risk, see Ulrich Beck, *Risk Society* (London, 1992); on the cyborg, see Donna J. Haraway, *Simians, Cyborgs and Women* (London, 1991); and for the key texts in an increasing literature on governmentality, see Nikolas Rose, *Governing the Soul: The Shaping of the Private Self* (London, 1990) and *Powers of Freedom: Reframing Political Thought* (Cambridge, 1999).

10 Manuel Castells, *The Internet Galaxy* (Oxford, 2001), p. 133.

11 Hannah Arendt, *The Human Condition* (Chicago, 1958), p. 57.

12 This is clearly a trope in the writing of the Frankfurt School and those influenced by them: see Agnes Heller, *Everyday Life* (London: 1984) and Herbert Marcuse, *One-Dimensional Man* (London, 1964).

13 Castells, *Internet Galaxy*, p. 133. See also Raymond Williams, *Television: Technology and Cultural Form* (London, 1974).

14 The "imagined community" is that of the nation state, created by the collective reading of the morning press: see Benedict Anderson, *Imagined Communities: Reflections on the Origins and Spread of Nationalism* (London, 1984).

15 There is a burgeoning literature on the Internet as a site for the construction of community as well as individual and shared identities. On the increasingly complex relationship between the on-line and off-line as spaces for sociality and sociability, see, for example: Nancy Baym, *Tune In, Log On: Soaps, Fandom and Online Community* (Thousand Oaks, 2000); *Cybersociety: Computer Mediated Communication and Community*, ed. Steven G. Jones (Thousand Oaks, 1995);

Virtual Culture: Identity and Communication in Cybersociety, ed. Steven G. Jones (Thousand Oaks, 1997); *Cybersociety 2.0: Revisiting Computer Mediated Communication and Community*, ed. Steven G. Jones (Thousand Oaks, 1998).
16 Barry Wellman, *Networks in the Global Village: Life in Contemporary Communities* (Boulder, 1999).
17 Craig Calhoun, "Community without Propinquity Revisited: Communications Technology and the Transformation of the Urban Public Sphere," *Sociological Inquiry*, 68 (1998), 373–97; Stephen Doheny-Farina, *The Wired Neighborhood* (New Haven, 1998).
18 Barry Wellman and Milena Gulia, "Virtual Communities as Communities: Net Surfers Don't Ride Alone," in *Communities in Cyberspace*, ed. Marc A. Smith and Peter Kollock (London, 1999), pp. 167–94.
19 Perhaps the most significant contemporary articulation of these arguments is provided, but by no means exclusively, by the work of Emmanuel Levinas and Zygmunt Bauman; see especially, Emmanuel Levinas, *Totality and Infinity: An Essay on Exteriority* (Pittsburgh, 1969); hereafter cited in text as *TI*; Zygmunt Bauman, *Postmodern Ethics* (Cambridge, 1993); but see also Agnes Heller, *Everyday Life* (London, 1984), and Jürgen Habermas, *The Theory of Communicative Action: Lifeworld and System* (Boston, 1984).
20 "Ethical thought consists of the systematic examination of the relations of human beings to each other, the conceptions, interests and ideals which human ways of treating one another spring, and the systems of value on which such ends of life are based." Isaiah Berlin, *The Crooked Timber of Humanity* (London, 1990), p. 1.
21 Cmiel's perceptive critique and appreciation compares both Levinas's and Arendt's responses to postwar social science's approaches to communication, indicating the value of their alternative and so far marginalized ways of thinking about both communication's politics and its ethics; see Kenneth Cmiel, "On Cynicism, Evil and the Discovery of Communication in the 1940s," *Journal of Communication*, 46.3 (1996), 88–107.
22 Anthony Giddens, *The Consequences of Modernity* (Cambridge, 1990); hereafter cited in text as *CM*.
23 Kevin Robins, "The Haunted Screen," in *Culture on the Brink: Ideologies of Technology*, ed. Gretchen Bender and Timothy Druckrey (Seattle, 1994), p. 313.
24 Guy Debord, *The Society of the Spectacle* (London, 1977).
25 The work of George Gerbner and his colleagues on what has come to be known as cultivation theory, has shown, perhaps unsurprisingly, that high exposure to mainstream television both limits worldviews and, given the particularity of its culture, also generates higher degrees of anxiety that in turn can be translated into political conservatism. For a recent but broadly sympathetic review, see James Shanahan and Michael Morgan, *Television and its Viewers: Cultivation Theory and Research* (Cambridge, 1999).
26 Roger Silverstone, "Proper Distance: Towards an Ethics for Cyberspace," in *Innovations*, ed. Gunnar Liestol, Andrew Morrison, and Terje Rasmussen (Cambridge, in press).
27 Luc Boltanski, *Distant Suffering: Morality, Media and Politics* (Cambridge, 1999), p. 151.
28 Anthony Giddens, *Modernity and Self-Identity* (Cambridge, 1991), pp. 144–80.
29 Onora O'Neill, *A Question of Trust* (Cambridge, 2002), pp. 88–100. This is the text based on her BBC Reith Lectures given in the early part of 2002.
30 Max Horkheimer and Theodor Adorno, *Dialectic of Enlightenment* (New York, 1972), p. 167.

31 Peter Burke, *Popular Culture in Early Modern Europe* (London, 1978) provides an historical background to the relationship between high and popular culture; Cornel Sandvoss, *Football Fandom and Television in the Triangle of Universalisation, Globalisation and Rationalisation* (Ph.D. diss., University of London, 2001) traces the nineteenth- and twentieth-century domestication of soccer.
32 William Stephenson, *The Play Theory of Mass Communication* (New Brunswick, 1988).
33 The literature is vast, especially, but not exclusively, from within the British tradition of media and cultural studies; see Nicholas Abercrombie and Brian Longhurst, *Audiences* (London, 1998); Sonia Livingstone, *Making Sense of Television: The Psychology of Audience Interpretation*, 2nd edition (London, 1998); David Morley, *Television Audiences and Cultural Studies* (London, 1992); Ellen Seiter, *Television and New Media Audiences* (Oxford, 1999).
34 See Abercrombie and Longhurst, *Audiences*.
35 Roger Silverstone, *Television and Everyday Life* (London, 1994), pp. 132–58.
36 Tamar Liebes and Elihu Katz, *The Export of Meaning* (Oxford, 1993).
37 Renato Rosaldo, *Culture and Truth: The Remaking of Social Analysis* (Boston, 1989); Rosaldo's arguments are discussed in George E. Marcus, *Ethnography Through Thick and Thin* (Princeton, 1998), pp. 114–16.
38 Complicity turns to collusion, when, as increasingly is the case, media subjects seek, in their understanding of the process, to manipulate the setting in order to guarantee participation and visibility.
39 Roger Silverstone, "La médiatisation de la catastrophe," *Dossiers de l'Audiovisuel*, 104 (2002), 60–64.
40 Stanley Cohen, *States of Denial: Knowing about Atrocities and Suffering* (Cambridge, 2001); hereafter cited in text. Cohen cites and discusses Michael Ignatieff, *The Warrior's Honour: Ethnic War and the Modern Conscience* (London, 1998), pp. 10 and 11.

72

IDENTITIES

Traditions and new communities*

Jesús Martín-Barbero

Source: *Media, Culture & Society* 24(5) (2002): 621–41.

> The re-emergence of the subject as a result of its 'death' brings with it a proliferation of concrete finitudes whose limitations are the very source of their power. [...] And this is not abstract speculation; on the contrary, it is an intellectual path opened up by the terrain onto which history has thrown us: the multiplication of new and not-so-new identities, the explosion of national and ethnic identities, multicultural protest, and the whole variety of forms of struggle associated with the new social movements.
>
> (Laclau, 1996: 65)

The thick texture of the identity debate

The upsurge in the wave of identity politics that we are presently witnessing is no single movement, nor is it conceivable as arising from a single cause. The reasons and motives are enmeshed in a web consisting of neglected historical grievances, land claims, ingrained biological prejudices, religious fervour, sudden memory-lapses, long-standing battles for recognition and, criss-crossing all these elements and bringing them to the boil, new and old struggles for power. Given the welter of presuppositions it contains, as well as the range of positions it covers, this highly diverse configuration has resulted in confused thinking about these various phenomena. Consequently, we need to work on a sketch that clarifies and articulates the principal axes of the debate. This is the focus of the first part. We then proceed to an analysis of three strategic areas of the Latin American situation: those of the traditional communities, of national identity, and of urban communities.

On fundamentalisms as modes of resistance and belonging

Perhaps the most central line of debate is that which – opposing one extreme to another – considers the emergence of identity fundamentalisms as the form in which collective subjects react to the threat which befalls them due to a globalization interested more in 'basic instincts' – impulses of power and strategic calculations – than in identities. This is a globalization that aspires to dissolve society as a community of meaning, replacing it with a world comprising markets, networks and flows of information. The form in which individuals and groups situated in peripheral nations feel this pressure is to be sought in the disconnection which more and more openly translates into social and cultural exclusion, into the majority's ever-decreasing standards of living, into the breaking of the social contract between work, capital and the state, and into the destruction of the solidarity that once made social security possible.

> What men, women, and children share is a deeply felt fear of the unknown, which becomes all the more menacing when rooted in the day-to-day basis of their personal lives: they are terrorized by solitude and uncertainty in an individualistic, ferociously competitive society
>
> (Castells, 1998: 49)

Manuel Castells analyses thus the coordinates of a fundamentalism that consists simultaneously of furious resistances and feverish quests for meaning. These consist of resistances to the processes of individualization and social atomization, and to the intangibility of flows whose interconnections blur the limits of belonging and destabilize the spatial and temporal fabric of work and life. These are also quests for a social and personal identity which, 'based on images of the past and projected onto a utopian future, allow them to overcome an intolerable present' (Castells, 1998: 48). The network society is not, then, purely a phenomenon composed of technological connections, but rather the systemic disjunction of the global and the local brought about by the fracturing of their respective temporal frameworks of experience and power: faced with an elite which inhabits an atemporal space of global networks and flows, the majority in our countries still inhabit the local space-time of their cultures, and, faced by the logic of global power, they themselves take refuge in the logic of communal power.

Before it became a topic on academic agendas, multiculturalism designated the awakening and explosion within cultural communities that responded to the threat of the global (Kymlicka, 1996; Monguin, 1995a, 1996). This has occurred as much as a result of the singularity of each culture as from the need which people today feel to exercise some control over their sociocultural environment. Thus, multiculturalism simultaneously encompasses two separate yet deeply interwoven movements: that of resistance to implosion and that of the need to be constructive.

We may see an entrenchment of everything that contains or expresses some collective form of identity: from the ethnic and territorial to the religious and national, as well as their multiple overlapping. Globalization aggravates and distorts basic identities whose roots reach deep into history. What we have seen in Sarajevo and Kosovo is the self-delusion of identities that are struggling to be recognized but whose recognition is complete only when all others have been expelled from their land, allowing them to become self-enclosed. From a Sarajevo where once the Christian orthodox and Muslim worlds coexisted alongside other faiths and cultures, we have arrived at a confrontation between neighbours in the same street who overnight discovered that their ethnic purity was endangered, and that to save it they were allowed to denounce, expel or destroy the others, despite their having been lifelong neighbours. This is of course closely linked to the enmity – deriving from an identity crisis – shown by citizens of the rich nations towards the immigrants arriving from 'the South'. It is as if – due to migratory pressure and a techno-economic logic – frontiers which, for centuries, demarcated diverse worlds, distinct political ideologies and different cultural universes had totally collapsed. The contradictions of the universalist discourse of which the West has felt so proud were there to be discovered. And then each country or community of countries, each social group, almost every single individual, all need to ward off the threat created by the proximity of the other, of others of all shapes and countenances, reshaping an exclusion so it no longer depends on frontiers (which would be an obstacle to the flows of commodities and information). Instead, it now takes the form of imposing of distances that keep 'everyone in their place'.

Today the implosive force of the ghettos is proportionate to the explosive potential of the mix of old resentments and new powers, whence its capacity to disarticulate the social and the regression to the most racist and xenophobic particularisms that bring about the negation of the other, of all others.

Nevertheless, in the revival of identity politics it is not only revenge and intolerance that speak. Its profound ambiguity opens the path for other voices raised against today's thousand-and-one forms of cultural, social and political exclusion. If many identity movements start with self-recognition *qua* reaction and isolation, they may also function as spaces of memory and solidarity, as places of refuge in which individuals encounter a moral tradition (Bellah, 1985: 286). Whether communitarian or libertarian, this is where the search for alternatives begins, a search capable of overturning the mainly exclusionary meaning which the technological networks have for most, transforming them instead into potential sources of social and personal enrichment.

Disenchantment with the world and collective demoralization

A second axis of the debate locates globalization at the heart of the dual reflection upon the legitimation crisis of the social system and the confrontation of today's societies with the limits of modernity. What the legitimation crisis lays bare is that the administrative production of meaning does not exist. According to Habermas, the crisis is constituted by three tendencies marking the structural transformation of images of the world: the dominant elements of the cultural tradition cease to be of value as interpretations of history in its entirety; practical questions no longer refer to the sphere of truth, and values lose their very rationality; secular ethics have become uncoupled from the rational notion of natural right, thus undermining the utopian content of that tradition. The fracturing of the world-images throws the disintegration of the social into relief: both individual and group identities lose their foundations, so that social conflict takes psychic forms. 'Are we witnessing the birth-pangs of a completely new form of socialization?', asks Habermas (1975: 155), responding with his own investigation into the pathologies of subjectivity in a society in which 'the state autonomously sets itself up against the life-world, constituting a fragment of sociality devoid of normative content, and opposes the imperatives of reason guiding the life-world with its own imperatives based on the preservation of the system' (Habermas, 1989: 412). The schism between system and life-worlds is brought about by the junction between the subsystems of money and power, market and state, a differentiation which, while facilitating novel forms of integration into the system, also creates within the life-worlds and social movements new forms of resistance based less in terms of governance than on the fortification of collective identities.

In recent years, the analysis of the ways in which the pathologies of modernity have obstructed the construction of identities has been enriched by reflections upon the risk society, and its critical correlate, reflexivity. Thus, what we are now witnessing is the problematization of society itself, the increasing awareness of its 'structural ambiguity' when our own knowledge of modernity puts at risk the whole of each and every society on the planet. What enters into crisis are the institutions and 'wellsprings of meaning' upon, and with which, industrial modernity was built: work, politics, the family, that is to say 'the nervous-system of our day-to-day social order', the very basis of common life (Beck, 1998: 95). It is the interior world, the intimacy between people (Giddens, 1995, 1997), the sphere of subjectivity and identity, which are most deeply affected by this discontent. Where the malaise – the unease of the 'I' – appears in its most disconcerting form is among the young. This is apparent, on the one hand, by their rejection of society and their taking refuge in ecstatic oblivion, and, on the other hand, in neotribal fusion (Follari and Lanz, 1998: 19–37): millions of youngsters throughout the world come together not to speak, but to be side-by-side, in silence, to listen to heavy metal, merging with the rage and fury fermented and projected by much contemporary music, indicating to us the contradictory mixture of passivity and aggression that constitutes the 'we'-experience among today's youth.

Without being integrated into tradition and social experience, instrumental, specialized knowledge self-validates itself by reference to the techno-scientific system, free of all relations to social existence (Lipovetsky, 1992; Maldonado, 1997; Postman, 1994; Serres, 1990). Thus, by another route, society is exposed to the self-same paradox: the growth of technology, which strives to abolish insecurity, actually serves to intensify control without supplying security. Post-rational, the risk society sees the return of uncertainty, corroding not only the intellectual sphere but also the emotional, and, in so doing, destabilizing the foundations of every moral code. Such a society delegates to the individual the search for the cohesive values and contexts of trust that can be used to face the 'ethical aridity' (Bauman, 1993; 1998) which today devastates values and spheres of action that have been opened up by technology but are irreducible to technical decisions. How, in such inclement conditions, in such an ethical and interpersonal wasteland, do we prevent the formation of self-destructive identities?

New identities: other sites of subject-formation

The crisis of identity that we are at present witnessing is not solely coloured by the motifs of disenchantment and demoralization. It also defines the space of emergence for the upsurge in identities being renewed by the current predicaments of the human condition. Habermas (1989: 424) highlights the decentralization suffered by complex societies through the absence of a central instance of regulation and self-expression, in which 'collective identities are subject to oscillations in the flux of interpretations, taking on more the image of a fragile network than that of a stable centre of self-reflection'. For his part, Stuart Hall (1999) assumes the shattering of all that we took to be fixed and the destabilization of all that we believed to be unitary: 'A new type of structural change is fragmenting the cultural landscapes of class, gender, ethnicity, race, and nationality, which had in the past provided us with solid locales as social individuals. Such transformations are also changing our personal identities.' This change points especially to the multiplication of referents through which subjects come to identify themselves, since this decentralization not only affects society, but also individuals who now live with a partial and precarious integration of the multiple dimensions that shape them. The individual is now no longer indivisible, and whatever unity is postulated has more than a whiff of an 'imaginary unity' about it.

The above should not be confused with the celebration of difference-cum-fragmentation proclaimed by most postmodernist discourse and exploited by the market. The celebration of weak identities is closely related to the celebration of market de-regulation demanded by the neoliberal ideology which presently steers the course of globalization. David Harvey (1989: 296) has relevantly noted the paradox that 'as spatial barriers become less decisive, the sensitivity of capital towards differences in place grows all the more, increasing the incentive for places to make themselves distinct in order to attract capital.' Local identity is thus compelled to transform itself into a marketable representation of difference: it becomes subject to makeovers, which reinforce its exoticism, and to hybridizations, which neutralize its most conflictual features. This is the other face of a globalization that accelerates the de-racination through which it endeavours to inscribe identities with the logic of flows, a device for translating all cultural differences into the *lingua franca* of the techno-financial world and rendering identities volatile so that they may then float freely in a moral vacuum, a space of cultural indifference. The complementarity of the movements upon which this treacherous translation is based could not be more clear: while the movement of images and goods goes from centre to periphery, the millions of emigrants subject to exclusion make the opposite journey from periphery to centre. This occasions the – often fundamentalist – reworking of the original cultures inside 'ethnic enclaves' dotted across the large cities of the northern countries.

It is to the feminist movement that we owe the production of a radically new perspective on identity which, countering all forms of essentialism, affirms the divided, decentred nature of the subject while at the same time refusing to accept an infinitely fluid and malleable conception of identity (Mouffe, 1996; Pimentel, 1996). This permits us not only to inscribe the 'politics of identity' within the political project of human emancipation, but also to rethink the very meaning of politics, postulating 'the creation of a new type of political subject'. The subject becomes newly illuminated by the way in which feminism, with the maxim 'the personal is political', subverts the metaphysical *machismo* of the Left and, in recent years, has incorporated into the same movement a sense of damage and victimization alongside that of recognition and empowerment. This last sentiment recovers for the process of identity construction not only those power struggles produced in the materiality of social relations, but also those located within the realm of the imaginary. As with the multiplicity of rival identities, the affirmation of a decentred, split subject appears in feminism not as a theoretical postulate but as the result of an exploration of the concrete experience of oppression.

Close to, and enriching, the feminist perspective is the proposal for a politics of recognition developed from a highly disconcerting standpoint by Charles Taylor (1998), who contends that, while in classical Greco-Roman antiquity it was the law which endowed a people with its personality, in the very foundations of political modernity is lodged the idea that the people already have an identity prior to any political structuration. The idea of recognition, according to its Hegelian formulation, is thereby crystallized in the distinction between traditional 'honour' as a concept and hierarchical principle, and modern 'dignity' as an egalitarian principle. Identity, then, is not what is attributed to someone by mere virtue of group membership – as with the caste-system – but, rather, it is the expression of what gives meaning and value to the life of the individual. It is upon the expressive turn taken by an individual or collective subject that identity depends, drawing life from the recognition of others, being constructed through processes of dialogue and exchange, for it is here that individuals and groups feel despised or acknowledged by others. Modern identities – as opposed to those that were ascribed by virtue of a pre-existing structure, such as the nobility or the plebs – are constructed through negotiations for recognition by the other.

The relationship between expressivity and the recognition of identity concerning cultural rights (whether of minorities or of entire peoples) is rendered splendidly visible in the polysemy of the Spanish verb '*contar*': there is at the same time a right to recount [*contarnos*] our own histories, and to count in [*contar en*] economic and political decisions. In order that the plurality of cultures be taken politically into account, it is imperative that the diversity of identities can be recounted, narrated. Thus, there is a constitutive relationship between identity and narration, there being no cultural identity which is not recounted (Bhabha, 1990). This in turn marks the new understanding of identity as a relational construction. And this occurs in every language, not least in the multimediatic idiom within which today's translations are played out – whether oral, written, audio-visual or informatic – and also in that even more complex and ambiguous idiom of appropriations, and miscegenations [*mestizajes*]. In its densest and most challenging sense, the idea of multiculturalism points towards the configuration of societies in which the dynamics of the economy and world-culture mobilize not only the heterogeneity of groups and their retooling to meet global pressures, but also bring about the coexistence of very diverse narratives and codes within those self-same societies, causing an immense upheaval in our experience to date of identity.

The secret universality of which particularisms are made

The third axis of the debate centres on the highly problematical relationship which today exists between particularism and universalism. The present diversification of cultural identities – with no little prompting from postmodernist discourse – drives towards the radical exaltation of difference. Because this has burst open the floodgates, it has destroyed any societal articulation with the national, and even less with the universal. But, wonders Ernesto Laclau (1996: 46), 'Is particularism conceivable solely as such, leaving aside the differences that it affirms? Are the relations between universalism and particularism mutually exclusive?'

He responds with an historical analysis of three moments in which the West has lived out this relationship. First is ancient-classical philosophy. Here, either the particular in itself realizes the universal – forming part of it – or else the particular negates the universal, affirming itself as particularism, thus rendering universality a particularity defined by a limitless exclusion. The second moment is Christianity, in which universality refers to the events that bind eschatology together. Between the universal and the particular – which is the body in which the universal is incarnate – there is no possibility of mediation outside of God. But it is just that possibility of the *incarnation* of the universal in the particular which serves to introduce to history a logic which, once having being secularized, will indelibly brand the West: the logic of the 'privileged agent of History, whose particular body was the vehicle of a universality that transcended it' (Laclau, 1996: 48). Here, fully formed, is the 'universal class' of Marxism – incarnate in the proletariat, represented by the party, and made word inthe voice of the autocrat of the day. And also it is Eurocentrism, with its imperialist expansion converted into the universal function of civilization and modernization that condemns those 'peoples without history' whose resistance to modernization betrays their inability to accede to the universal.

The third moment is that of contemporary thought, which is capable of assuming that pure particularisms offer no exit from the political and cultural conflicts that we are living through. The particular – say, an ethnic minority – is regarded as only fully able to constitute itself within a context of rights, which historically has been provided by the nation-state since

> ... its claims cannot be formulated in terms of difference, but only in those of certain universal principles which the minority shares with the rest of society: the right to good schools, to a decent life, to participate in the public space of citizenship, etc.
> (Laclau, 1996: 56)

Laclau's contribution to the understanding of a democratic multiculturalism proves decisive here since, faced with the weighty old baggage of a renascent messianism and the particularisms trapped in the logic of apartheid, he affirms a universal which emerges from the particular, not as something already present, but rather as an always-distant horizon, the symbol of an absent plenitude which mobilizes societies more and more to extend equal rights. There is no difference that can become apparent as such outside of the community with which it shares those rights upon which its claims are based. And without universal values there is no possibility of coexistence between the identities of particular groups.

What multiculturalism demonstrates is that liberal-democratic institutions have remained too narrow to welcome a cultural diversity that is tearing apart our societies for the very reason that it cannot be contained within that institutional structure. This tearing apart can only be stitched together by a politics that extends universal rights and values to all those sectors of the population which have previously lived outside the application of those rights, be they women or ethnic minorities, evangelists or homosexuals. Michel Wiewiorka (1997) thus refuses to have to choose between the universalism inherited from the Enlightenment, which excludes whole sectors of the population, and the tribal differentiation affirmed in racist, xenophobic segregation – a choice that is fatal for democracy.

It is at this point that the identity debate achieves its maximum tension. In an article bordering on a manifesto, Eric Hobsbawm (1996) wonders what identity politics has to do with the emancipatory project of the Left. Identities today appear more a matter of fashion than the colour of your skin. They are interchangeable, chameleon-like, and mix-and-match. By contrast, the classic Left was mobilized by 'grand and universal' causes. Identity politics are, for Hobsbawm, a problem for minorities, and the alliances forged among minorities who cluster around negatively defined identities will always be in danger of disintegrating in the face of the slightest internal conflict. From a left-feminist perspective, Chantal Mouffe (1996) identifies today's project of emancipation with a deepening of democracy, the key to which is to be found in multiculturalism. It is not only cultural but also political questions that are at play in the diversity and conflict of identities: these are today the site and object of political struggles, and, moreover, they shape the primordial terrain in which hegemony is exercised.

However, in order to arrive at this point in the debate it is necessary to clear some cluttered terrain. On one hand, there is a liberal rationalism for which the world of passions and the violence of antagonisms are considered archaic and irrational; and on the other hand, there is the blindness of those liberal illusions of a 'consensus without exclusions' that might somehow be arrived at by way of engaging in discourse (see the Habermasian 'communicative rationality of reciprocal understanding'). Chantal Mouffe (1996: 27) formulates an illuminating question: 'What type of relationship can be established between identity and otherness that might defuse the danger of exclusion?' As a demarcation between an 'us' and a 'them', every identity implies the temptation to turn the other into an enemy who threatens my own (personal and group) identity. Therefore, in order to respond to the question formulated, it is necessary to distinguish *the political* – the dimension of hostility and antagonism between human beings – from *politics*: the construction of an order that organizes and facilitates an always-conflictual human coexistence. The impossibility of conceiving of a totally conflict-free human order makes the most crucial challenge facing democracy today one of how to transform itself into a 'pluralist democracy': it must be capable of taking on the us/them distinction so that 'they' are also recognized as legitimate. This, in turn, implies that the passions are not relegated to the private sphere but rather kept in play through argument: that is, by struggles which do not seek to annihilate the other, since the other also has a right to recognition and, therefore, to life. When democracy requires us to maintain the tension between our identity as individuals and as citizens it becomes the site of emancipation, since only out of this tension will it be possible to sustain collectively the other tension between difference and equivalence (equality). And then we will abandon the illusory search for the reabsorption of otherness in a unified totality. Just as otherness is irreducible, so must 'pluralist democracy' regard itself as an 'impossible good' – a regulative idea that exists only insofar as it cannot be perfectly realized.

Old and new cultural communities: a rough guide

There was a time when we used to believe we knew with certainty what we were speaking of when we designated, dichotomously, the traditional and the modern, since anthropology was the discipline in charge of 'primitive' cultures whereas sociology looked after 'modern' ones. This implied two opposed views of culture. For the anthropologist culture is *everything*, since in the primordial magma inhabited by the primitives 'the cultural' is as much the axe as it is myth, the effects of invasion as much as kinship or the repertories of medicinal plants or ritual dance. But for the sociologist, culture is *only* special types of objects and activities, products and practices, almost always pertaining to the canon of arts and letters. But in our late modernity, the separation which once underscored that double idea of culture is becoming blurred. There is the growing movement in the communicative specialization of 'the cultural', now 'organized in a system of machines which produce and transmit symbolic goods to their consuming public' (Brunner, 1996:134). It is what the school does with its pupils, the press with its readers, television with its viewers, even the church with its congregation. At the same time, culture is living out another, radically opposed movement: this concerns a trend toward *anthropologization*, through which social life itself becomes, or is converted into, culture. Nowadays, the subject/object of culture is as much health care as it is the arts, work as much as violence; there is also political culture and the culture of drug trafficking; there are organizational, urban, youth, professional, audio-visual, scientific and technological cultures, etc. It is as though, while the relentless machine of modernizing rationalization was rolling along – trying to keep things separate and specialized – culture escaped all compartmentalization, completely flooding the social field.

Something similar is happening to the dichotomy between the rural and the urban, since the urban used to be the opposite of the rural. Today, this dichotomy is being dissolved, not only in analytical discourse but also in social experience due to its reshaping by processes of deterritorialization and hybridization. The urban is now no longer solely identified with the city (Monguin, 1995b), but also with what to a greater or lesser extent permeates the world of the peasant. The 'urban' is the movement that inserts the local into the global, whether because of the economy or the mass media. Even the most robustly local cultures undergo changes that affect the various ways of living out one's identity or sense of belonging to a particular territory. We are dealing here with the same movements that displace the old frontiers between the traditional and the modern, the popular and the mass, the local and the global. Today, these changes and movements are crucial for an understanding of how identities survive and are recreated in traditional, national and urban communities.

Ruling conventions and reconfigurations in traditional communities

When dissecting the indigenous image the face of the *mestizo* appears, since the Indians in the photographs not only blindly look at us, they are also mute. Although we live surrounded by pre-Hispanic imagery our culture lends no ear to aboriginal tongues. [...] We have grown accustomed to strolling through a gallery of curios, and we enjoy ourselves increasingly by using our platonic camera obscura to observe the shadows that Western thought casts on the museum walls.

(Bartra, 1999: 108)

When we speak of traditional communities in Latin America we normally refer to the pre-Hispanic cultures of indigenous peoples. We may also use this denomination to cover black and peasant cultures; however, in this text we refer only to the indigenous peoples. For centuries, these peoples were regarded – particularly in the view of the *indigenistas* – as 'the natural fact of this continent, the kingdom of the historyless peoples, the fixed starting-point from which modernity is measured' (Lauer, 1982). During the 1970s, that view seemed to have been superseded by a non-linear conception of time and development, but today we discover that the process of globalization is re-establishing and sharpening a developmentalist mentality for which modernity and tradition seem irreconcilable once more, to such an extent that, in order to contemplate the future, it is necessary to stop looking at the past. Conversely, postmodernist discourse idealizes indigenous difference as an untouchable world, endowed with an intrinsic truth and authenticity that separates it from everything else and is self-enclosed. Meanwhile, another postmodern discourse makes hybridity the category that allows us to announce the painless disappearance of the conflicts underlying cultural resistance.

Yet it is only within an historical dynamic that the indigenous can be understood in all its cultural complexity, in all its temporal diversity, living on in certain nomadic ethnic groups of the Amazonian forests, in their conquered, colonized indigeneity, the diverse modes and entry-points of their modernization, and also in the forms and movements of miscegenation and hybridization. We must work from a re-created pre-Hispanicity – the social value of work, the virtual absence of the notion of the individual, the profound unity between man and nature, widespread reciprocity – to those figures which today comprise the plot of modernity and its cultural discontinuities, those memories and imaginaries which wrap together the indigenous, the rural and the folkloric with the urban-popular, with mass culture.

Every day, indigenous peoples renew their cultural and political modes of affirmation and it is only the prejudice of a covert ethnocentrism, which often even permeates anthropological discourse, that prevents us from perceiving the diverse meanings of development in these ethnic communities. The transformation of identities emerges especially in the processes of appropriation that are expressed in the changes occurring to festivals and handicrafts. It is through these that communities appropriate an aggressive economy and a standardizing jurisprudence and continue to connect with their memories and utopias. This is demonstrated by the diversification and development of artesanal production in open interaction with modern design, even taking on certain logics of the cultural industries (García Canclini, 1982); the development of an indigenous common law increasingly recognized by national and international norms (Sánchez Botero, 1998); the growing presence of TV and radio stations scheduled and directed by the communities themselves (Alfaro, 1998); and even, following Comandante Marcos's exhortation, the promotion via the Internet of the rights of the indigenous Zapatista movement to a utopia which not only seeks to provide a local alternative, but also aspires to reorientate the current democratic movements in Mexico (Rojo Arias, 1996).

The current reconfiguration of these cultures – indigenous, peasant, black – responds not only to the evolution of certain modes of domination at the heart of globalization, but also to one of its effects: the intensification of those communities' communication and interaction with other cultures from all over the world (Bayardo and Lacarrieu, 1997). From within these communities, such communication processes are simultaneously perceived as another form of threat to their cultural survival – a long and deeply embedded experience of the traps of domination makes any exposure to the other heavy with suspicion. However, at the same time, communication is lived as a possible way of breaking down exclusion and as an experience of interaction which, while risky, also opens up new models of the future. All of this makes it possible for the dynamics of traditional communities to bypass the framework of interpretation developed by the *folcloristas*. There is less nostalgic complaisance about tradition than is supposed and actually a greater awareness of the indispensable symbolic re-elaboration required to construct the future.

Today, traditional communities have a strategic role as reminders for the modern societies in which they live: they help us to confront the purely mechanical transplantation of cultures at the same time as they represent, in their diversity, a fundamental challenge to the supposedly dehistoricized universality of modernization and its homogenizing pressures. Yet, for this to be of value, we need a cultural politics which, instead of preserving these cultures (that is, keeping them preserved), stimulates in them a capacity for self-development and renewal. We need to comprehend fully all that challenges us in these communities, all that dislocates and subverts our hegemonic sense of time, a time absorbed in an autistic present which claims to be self-sufficient. What emerges from the weakening of the past and of historical consciousness is a version of time fabricated by the media, and ultimately reinforced by the velocities of cyberspace. Without the past, or with a past divorced from memory and turned into mere citation – a sepia-tinted adornment of the present in nostalgic mode (Jameson, 1992: 45) – our societies sink into a bottomless and horizonless present. In order to confront the inertia that hurls us into a future converted into mere repetition, the lucid yet disconcerting conception of time proposed by Walter Benjamin (1970: 255–66) – in which the past remains open since not everything in it has been realized – may prove decisive. The past, for Benjamin, is not formed solely by facts, that is by the 'already-done', but is also shaped by what remains to be done, by potentialities that await their realization, by seeds scattered on barren terrain. There is a forgotten future in the past that it is necessary to redeem, liberate, and mobilize anew. This implies that Benjamin understood the present as 'now-time', the spark that connects the past with the future, completely the opposite of our own fleeting and anaesthetized present. The present, then, is that 'now' from which it is possible to unhitch a past tethered by the pseudo-continuity of history and to construct a future. Faced with a historicism which believed it possible to resuscitate tradition, Benjamin (1989) rethought tradition as an inheritance – neither cumulative nor as heritage, but rather as something of radically ambiguous value whose appropriation is under permanent dispute, re-interpreted and re-interpretable, shot through with, and shaken by change, and in perpetual conflict with the inertia of each age. The memory that takes charge of tradition is not one that transports us back to some static epoch; rather it brings to mind a past that destabilizes us.

Avatars of national communities

> The history of Latin America could be told as a continuous and reciprocal land occupation. There are no stable borders recognized by all. No physical frontier or social boundary guarantees security. Thus in each generation is born and internalized an ancestral fear of the invader, of the other, of the different, from wheresoever they might come.
>
> (Lechner, 1990: 120)

Despite the abundance of discussions, national identity is not in danger. It is a changing identity, continuously being enriched by marginal voices, the contributions of the mass media, academic rethinking, ideological debate,

Americanization, and resistance to the growth of misery, but it is also being weakened by a reduction in the capacities of systems of education and the institutionalization of resignation due to the absence of cultural stimuli.
(Monsiváis, 1992: 192)

Where the social order is precarious, and at the same time idealized as ontologically pre-constituted, rather than as politically constructed on a daily basis, pluralism is perceived as disintegration and as undermining order, difference is associated with rebellion, and heterogeneity is considered to be the source of contamination and deformation of cultural purity. Hence, the tendency is to conceive of the nation-state as hierarchical and centralist in order to counter societal weaknesses and centripetal tendencies. Defined by the various populisms in terms of the elemental and racial, the authentic and ancestral, 'the national' has come to mean the permanent substitution of the people by the state, much to the detriment of civil society (Flifisch, 1984; Lechner, 1981). The preservation of national identity becomes confused with the preservation of the state, as happened during the 1970s in pursuit of the 'doctrine of national security'. The defence of 'national interests' pursued in spite of social demands will end up justifying the suppression/ suspension of democracy. Latin American countries have a long experience of that distortion of meaning whereby national identity is pressed into the service of a chauvinism which both rationalizes and masks the crisis of the nation-state as a subject incapable of realizing a unity that might articulate popular demands and truly represent diverse interests. The crisis is disguised by the various populisms and developmentalisms yet remains active in the way in which nations have been conceived: they have not taken on board difference but have subordinated it to a state whose tendencies have been to centralize rather than to integrate.

The history of the dispossessions and exclusions that have marked the formation and development of Latin American nation-states have been one of the aspects of culture least studied by the social sciences. It was only in the mid-1980s when cultural studies began to investigate the relationship between nation and narration, that is, the founding stories of the national (Bhabha, 1990; González Stephan *et al.*, 1995). That is how, beginning with the successive constitutions as well as through the various 'endowments and established museums, the educated class have endeavoured to give a literary embodiment to a collective feeling, to construct a national imaginary.' What is in play is 'the discourse of memory produced by power', a power constituted in 'the same violence of representation that depicts a white, masculine, and at best a *mestizo* nation' (Achugar, 1997). Excluded from this 'national' representation were the indigenous and black peoples, women, and all those whose difference has hindered and impeded the construction of a homogeneous national subject. Consequently, everything about the founding representation has the air of a simulacrum: a representation without the very reality that it represents, deformed images and distorting mirrors in which the majority cannot recognize themselves. The exclusionary forgetfulness and the mutilating representation are at the very origins of the narratives that founded these nations.

However, because they were constituted as nations through the rhythms of their transformation into 'modern countries', it is hardly surprising that one of the most contradictory dimensions of Latin American modernity is to be found in the projects of, and the dislocations by, the national. Since the 1920s, the national has been proposed as a synthesis of cultural particularity and the body politic which 'transforms the diverse cultures' multiplicity of desires into a single desire to participate in (form part of) the national sentiment' (Novaes, 1983: 10). In the 1950s, nationalism transmuted itself into populisms and developmentalisms which consecrated the state's dominance to the detriment of civil society, a dominance rationalized as modernizing by both the Left's ideologies and the Right's practice. During the 1980s, the affirmation of modernity, now identified with the substitution of the state by the market as chief agent in the construction of hegemony, resulted in a profound devaluation of the national (Schwarz, 1987).

From the outset of the modern project, what has been undermining the state/nation relationship in Latin America, emptying it of significance, has been the impossibility of conceiving of the national as existing outside a state-imposed centralized unity. As Norbert Lechner states in the introductory quotation, due to the lack of a physical frontier capable of conferring security, we Latin Americans have internalized an ancestral fear of the other and of difference, no matter from whence this might come. That fear even expresses itself in the widespread tendency among politicians of perceiving difference as disintegration and as the breakdown of order, and among intellectuals concerned with cultural purity of regarding heterogeneity as a source of contamination and deformity. Thus, in our countries, authoritarianism is not a perverse tendency among the military and political classes, but rather a response to the precariousness of the social order, to the weakness of civil society and its complex sociocultural mix. Until very recently, for both Left and Right, the idea of the national was incompatible with the idea of difference: the people was a single indivisible entity, society a subject without textures or internal articulations, and politico-cultural debate shuttled between national essences and class identity (Sábato, 1989; Schmúcler, 1988).

Carlos Monsiváis obliges us constantly to shift our view as to how the national is configured to inspect the character of the popular as both subject and actor in the construction of a nation which the politicians and intellectuals think that they alone have built. From the point of view of the populace, the nation:

> ... has implied the willingness to assimilate and reshape 'concessions' before turning them into daily life, the willingness to adapt

the secularizing efforts of liberals to the requirements of superstition and hoarding, the relish with which the recently 'converted' use new technological breakthroughs. One thing brought about the other: the arrogant nation did not accept pariahs while the latter surreptitiously made it their own.

(Monsiváis, 1981: 38)

Nevertheless, the people to whom Monsiváis refers is one that stretches from paid-up revolutionaries to the urban masses of today. What we are trying to grasp above all is the popular capacity to incorporate into identity that which comes as much from their memory as from pillaging modern cultures: the national is not being opposed to the international, but continually recomposed through its mixing of reality and mythology, computers and oral culture, television and romances. This identity is more a question of *method* than content, a way of internalizing what comes from 'outside' without doing grave damage to the psychical, cultural or moral realms.

The contradictory movement of globalization and the fragmentation of culture simultaneously involves the revitalization and worldwide extension of the local. The devaluation of the national does not stem solely from the deterritorialization that globally interconnected circuits of the economy and world-culture bring about, but is also an effect of the internal erosion that produces the freeing up of differences, particularly those that are regional and generational. From the perspective of a global culture, the national appears provincial and encumbered with statist baggage; viewed from within the diversity of local cultures, the national is identified with centralizing homogenization and bureaucratic officialdom. The idea of the national in culture overflows in both directions, thus re-establishing the meaning of *frontiers*. What sense can geographical boundaries have in a world where satellites can 'photograph' the riches under the earth's surface and in which information critical to economic decisions can circulate through informal networks? Of course, frontiers will remain. But are not the 'old' borders of class and race, as well as the new technological and generational borders, even less salvageable today than are national frontiers? This does not suggest that the national has lost its validity as the historical site of mediation for popular memory – which is precisely what makes intergenerational communication possible. But this is only on condition that the continued existence of the national does not become confused with the intolerance today manifested by certain nationalisms and particularisms that are perhaps inflamed by the dissolution of frontiers, as is especially evident in the Western world.

New (urban) communities in the virtual city

Our thought still ties us to the past, to the world as it existed in our infancy and youth. Born and raised before the electronic revolution, many of us do not understand what this signifies. On the other hand, the young people of the new generation are just like members of the first generation born in a new country. Thus, we have to *resituate the future*. In order to build a culture in which the past is useful and not coercive, between us we must establish the future as something that is already here, ready for us to help and protect it before it is born, because it is too late to oppose it.

(Mead, 1971: 65)

When speaking of new urban cultures we refer in particular to the changes which are today affecting our ways of being together, changes which respond to brutally accelerated urbanization processes that are intimately linked to the imaginaries of a modernity identified with the speed of the traffic and the fragmentary nature of the languages of information. At the same time, we inhabit cities inundated not only with informational flows, but also with the flows that the pauperization of peasants continues to produce. The contradictions of urbanization could not be clearer: while this process permeates life in the countryside, our cities undergo a de-urbanization that has two characteristics. First, each day more and more people – bereft of cultural referents, insecure and lacking in confidence – are using less and less of the city, restricting themselves to ever-diminishing spaces, staying in the places they know, while tending to disregard what lies beyond. Second, with brutally rising levels of unemployment, more people are surviving informally in the city, which is to say using knowledge and skill brought from the countryside.

The virtual city in formation is constituted in the space of a new sensorium, the emergence of which is closely linked to the movement that connects the expansion/explosion of the city with the growth/concentration of electronic networks and media. 'It is through the logic of the audiovisual networks that a new diagram of urban space and interchange is brought about' (García Canclini, 1982: 49). This dispersal/fragmentation of the 'dense' city intensifies mediation and technological experience to the point where they become a substitute for, and render vicarious, social and personal experience: as Baudrillard (1981, 1984, 1994) tirelessly insists, in today's city all experience would be a mere *simulacrum*, the simulation of an impossible real. It is in this new communicative space – no longer woven from encounters and crowds but from connections, flows and networks – that I see the emergence of a new sensorium, that is, new 'ways of being together', alongside other perceptual tools. This is mediated in the first instance by television, then by computers, and then by the convergence of television and computers in an accelerated alliance between audiovisual and informational speeds: 'A family resemblance links the variety of screens that bind together our work, home, and leisure experiences' (Ferrer, 1995: 155, 1996). Cutting across and reconfiguring our very bodily relations, the virtual city, in contrast to the mediated city, now no longer requires assembled bodies; it wants them interconnected.

There is nothing comparable to television's flow (Barzoletti, 1986) to demonstrate for us the hooking mechanisms (the coupling, in a linguistic sense) between the spatial discontinuity of the domestic scene and that continuum of images which indiscriminately mixes genres and programmes. The diversity of stories and narratives found in the scheduling matters less than the permanent glowing presence of the screen: what holds the viewer is not so much any discursive content as the uninterrupted flow of images. Beatriz Sarlo (1993) is right to affirm that without 'zapping' television was incomplete, since it is this which makes the orgasmic flow possible – not only that internal to televisual discourse, but also that of the viewer's construction of a discourse out of fragments or 'scraps' of news reports, soap operas, quiz shows and concerts. Over and above the apparent democratization introduced by technology, the social scene is doubly illuminated by the metaphor of the zapper. First, it is with bits and pieces, with scraps, junk and disposable objects that much of the population reinforces the hovels it inhabits, stitching together the *nous* needed to survive, and pulling together the know-how needed to handle urban opacity. Moreover, there is a clear link connecting those modes of seeing explored by TV viewers – which cuts across the palimpsest of genres and discourses – with certain nomadic modes of inhabiting the city. It is akin to that of the migrant who is compelled to unending migration within the city while the urban sprawl absorbs each successive invasion and forces up prices. It is above all epitomized by the gangs of displaced youngsters who constantly change their meeting-places.

The new generations are responding particularly to the insecurity implied by this de-centred, de-spatialized mode of life and are reconfiguring notions of sociality. These tribes have bonds arising neither from a fixed territory nor a rational and long-standing consensus, but rather from age and gender, aesthetic range and sexual tastes, lifestyles and social exclusions (Maffesoli, 1990; Pérez Tornero, 1996). Facing up to the spread of anonymity that massification brings, and deeply connected with the culture-world of information technology and the audiovisual, the heterogeneity of the urban tribes reveals the profound reconfiguration of sociality and the radical scope of the transformations that our 'we-ness' is undergoing.

These changes, at least as far as young people's world is concerned, point toward the emergence of sensibilities that are 'disconnected from the forms, styles, and practices of the hoary traditions that define "culture", and whose subjects are constituted by way of a connection/disconnection with officialdom' (Ramirez and Muñoz, 1995: 60). In the empathy of the young with technological culture – which encompasses the information absorbed by adolescents in their relationship with television, and the ease with which they can enter into, and negotiate their way through, the complexity of computer networks – what is in play is the emergence of a new sensibility composed by a dual cognitive and expressive complicity: it is in their stories and images, their sounds, and in the fragmentation and speed of the techno-culture that today's young find their language and rhythm. We are on the cusp of the formation of hermeneutic communities which respond to new ways of perceiving and narrating their own identity. We are witnessing the forging of identities ever less rooted in the past, more precarious and yet also more flexible, capable of amalgamating, of allowing to coexist within a single subject, elements from highly diverse cultural universes.

In various previous works, having contrasted the 'virtual city' to what I called the 'mediated city' – the Paris of Baudelaire deciphered by Benjamin – my recent readings of the latter have led me, to a considerable extent, to deconstruct that opposition. It had prevented me from recognizing that 'to blow up the *reified continuity* of history is also to explode the homogeneity of the epoch, whose very existence is saturated by the present' (Benjamin, 1997: 492). That explosion opens up the eye of the needle: we can now step through the apparent coherence of a present governed by a logic of homogeneity, and become sensitive to its blind-spots, gaps and incoherences. These now offer our chance of inventing/constructing futures. The political project that once animated the mediated city now cuts across and introduces tensions into the contradictory cultural text of the virtual city. But this is also expressed in other 'symbolic geographies' that dislocate the process of political representation: that is because of the intense, unstable forms of recognition appealed to today by those who are struggling to construct new forms of community and identity that are destabilizing our mediated experience of the city.

Note

* Translated from Spanish by Scott Oliver and Philip Schlesinger.

References

Achugar, H. (1997) 'Parnasos fundacionales, letra, nación y Estado en el siglo XIX', *Revista Iberoamércicana.*
Alfaro, R. Ma. (1998) *Redes solidarias, culturas y multietnicidad.* Quito: Ocic-AL/Uclap.
Bartra, R. (1999) *La sangre y la tinta: ensayos sobre la condición postmexicana.* México: Oceano.
Barzoletti, G. (ed.) (1986) *Il palinsesto: testo, apparati e generi della televisione.* Milano: Franco Angeli.
Baudrillard, J. (1981) *Simulacres et simulation.* Paris: Galilée.
Baudrillard, J. (1984) *Les Stratégies fatales.* Paris: Grasset.
Baudrillard, J. (1994) *Le Crime parfait.* Paris: Galilée.
Bauman, Z. (1993) *La sfida dell'etica.* Milano: Feltrinelli.

Bauman, Z. (1998) *O malestar na pós-modernidade*. Rio de Janeiro: Jorge Zaar.
Bayardo, R. and Lacarrieu, M. (eds) (1997) *Globalización e identidad cultural*. Buenos Aires: Ciccus.
Beck, U. (1998) *La sociedad del riesgo*. Barcelona: Paidos.
Bellah, R. (1985) *Habits of the Heart*. Berkeley: University of California Press.
Benjamin, W. (1970) 'These on the Philosophy of History', in *Illuminations*. London: Fontana.
Benjamin, W. (1989) *Paris, capitale du XIX siècle: le livre des passages*. Paris Du Cerf.
Benjamin, W. (1997) *Le Livre des passages*. Paris: Du Cerf.
Bhabha, H. (1990) *Nation and Narration*. London and New York: Routledge.
Brunner, J. J. (1996) *Cartografías de la modernidad*. Santiago de Chile: Dolmen.
Castells, M. (1998) *La era de la información*. Aianza: Madrid.
Ferrer, C. (1995) 'Taenia saginata o el veneno en la red', *Nueva Sociedad* 140.
Ferrer, C. (1996) *Mal de ojo: el drama de la mirada*. Buenos Aires: Colihue.
Flifisch, A. (1984) *Problemas de la democracia y la política democrática en América Latina*. Santiago: Flasco.
Follari, R. and R. Lanz (1998) *Enfoques sobre la mostmodernidad en América Latina*. Caracas: Sentido.
García Canclini, N. (1982) *Las culturas populares en el capitalismo*. Mexico: Neuva Imagen.
García Canclini, N. (1982) *Culturas híbridas*. México: Grijalbo.
Giddens, A. (1995) *La transformación de la intimidad*. Madrid: Cátedra.
Giddens, A. (1997) *Modernidad e identidad del yo*. Barcelona: Peninsula.
González Stephan, B., Lasarte, J., Montaldo, G. and J. Ma. Daroqui (eds) (1995) *Esplendores y miserias del siglo XIX: cultura y sociedad en América Latina*. Caracas: Monteávila.
Habermas, J. (1975) *Problemas de legitimación en el capitalismo tardío*. Buenos Aires: Amarrortu.
Habermas, J. (1989) *El discurso filosófico de la modernidad*. Madrid: Turnas.
Hall, S. (1999) *A identidade cultural na pós-modernidade*. Rio de Janeiro: D.P. & Editora.
Harvey, D. (1989) *The Condition of Postmodernity*. Cambridge: Blackwell.
Hobsbawm, E. (1996) 'La política de la identidad y la izquierda', *Nexos* 224: 34–47.
Jameson, F. (1992) *El postmodernismo o la lógica cutlural del capitalismo avanzado*. Barcelona: Paidos.
Kymlicka, W. (1996) *Ciudanía multicultural*. Barcelona: Paidos.
Laclau, E. (1996) *Emancipación y diferencia*. Buenos Aires: Ariel.
Lauer, M. (1982) *Crítica de la artesanía: plástica y sociedad en los andes peruanos*. Lima: Desco.
Lechner, N. (1990) *Los patios interiores de la democracia*. Santiago: Flacso.
Lipovetsky, G. (1992) *Le Crépuscule du devoir*. Paris: Gallimard.
Maffesoli, M. (1990) *El tiempo de las tribus*. Barcelona: Icaria.
Maldonado, T. (1997) *Critica della ragione informatica*. Milan: Feltrinelli.
Mead, M. (1971) *Cultura y compromiso*. Barcelona: Granica.
Monguin, O. (1995a) *Vers la troisième ville*. Paris: Hachette.
Monguin, O. (1995b) 'Le Spectre du multiculturalisme américain', *Esprit* 6: 16–25.
Monsiváis, C. (1982) 'Notas sobre el Estado, la cultura nacional y las culturas populares', *Cuadernos políticos* no. 38.

Monsiváis, C. (1992) 'De la cultura mexicana en vísperas del tratado de libre comercio', in G. Guevera (ed.) *La educación y la cultura ante el tratado de libre comercio*. Mexico: Nueva Imagen.
Mouffe, C. (1996) 'Por una política de la identidad nómada', *Debate feminista* 14: 3–14.
Novaes, A. (1983) *A nacional e o popular na cultura brasileira*. São Paulo: Brasiliense.
Pérez Tornero, J. M. (1996) *Tribus urbanas: el ansia de la identidad juvenil*. Barcelona: Paidos.
Pimentel, L. A. (1996) 'Otredad', *Debate feminista*, vol. 13.
Postman, N. (1994) *Tecnópolis*. Barcelona: Círculo de Lectores.
Ramírez, S. and S. Muñoz (1995) *Trayectos del consumo*. Calí: Univalle.
Rojo Arias, S. (1996) 'La historia, la memoria y la indentitdad en los comunicados del EZLN', *Debate Feminista*.
Sábato, H. (1989) 'Pluralismo y nación', *Punto de Vista* no. 34.
Sarlo, B. (1993) *Escenas de la vida postmoderna*. Buenos Aires: Ariel.
Schmúcler, H. (1988) 'Los familiares del totalitarismo: nación, nacionalismo y pluridad', *Punto de Vista* no. 33.
Schwartz, R. (1987) 'Nacional por sustracción', Punto de Vista no. 28.
Serres, M. (1990) *Diálogo sobre a ciência, a cultura e o tempo*. Lisboa: Instituto Piaget.
Taylor, C. (1998) *Multiculturalismo: lotte per il riconscimento*. Milan: Feltrinelli.
VV.AA. (1996) 'Multiculturalismo: justicia y tolerancia', *Isegoria* 14.
Wiewiorka, M. (1997) *Une societé fragmentée? Le multiculturalisme en débat*. Paris: La Découverte.

73
THE THREE AGES OF INTERNET STUDIES
Ten, five and zero years ago

Barry Wellman

Source: *New Media & Society* 6(1) (2004): 123–9.

Pre-history, 10 years ago

Permit me as a tribal elder to exceed my bounds and think back to the state of scholarship in our field 10 years ago. Although Murray Turoff and Roxanne Hiltz had published their prophetic *The Network Nation* in 1978, it was pre-internet history then.[1]

As one of the first social scientists to be involved in internet research, I went to biannual gatherings of the then-tribe: CSCW (computer-supported cooperative work), conferences that were dominated by computer scientists writing 'groupware' applications. Lotus Notes derivations were in vogue. Lab studies were the predominant research method of choice, summarized in Lee Sproull and Sara Kiesler's *Connections* (1991).

I remember standing lonely and forlorn at the microphone during a comments period at the CSCW 1992 conference. Feeling extremely frustrated, I exclaimed:

> You don't understand! The future is not in writing stand-alone applications for small groups. It is in understanding that computer networks support the kinds of social networks in which people usually live and often work. These social networks are not the densely-knit, isolated small groups that groupware tries to support. They are sparsely-knit, far-reaching networks, in which people relate to shifting relationships and communities. Moreover, people don't just relate to each other online, they incorporate their computer-mediated communication into their full range of interaction: in-person, phone, fax, and even writing.

I pleaded for paying more attention to how people actually communicate in real life. But this approach was disparagingly referred to as 'user studies', much less exciting than writing new computer applications.

Conference participants listened politely and went back to developing applications. I even helped to develop one, for it was exciting and fun to collaborate with computer scientists and to be one of the few sociologists who built stuff. Maybe we would get rich and famous. Our *Cavecat/Telepresence* desktop videoconferencing systems were stand-alone groupware at their then-finest (Buxton, 1992; Mantei *et al.*, 1991). But they never got out of the laboratory.

The first age of internet studies, punditry rides rampant

Yet, economic forces were already fueling the turn away from stand-alone groupware towards applications that supported social networks. This was the proliferation of the internet as it became more than an academic chatroom. Unlike groupware, the internet was open-ended, far-flung, and seemingly infinite in scope. The internet became dot.com-ed, and the boom was on by the mid-1990s.

The internet was seen as a bright light, shining above everyday concerns. It was a technological marvel, thought to be bringing a new Enlightenment to transform the world. Communication dominated the internet, by asynchronous email and discussion lists and by synchronous instant messaging and chat groups. All were supposedly connected to all, without boundaries of time and space. As John Perry Barlow, a leader of the Electric Frontier Foundation, wrote in 1995:

> With the development of the Internet, and with the increasing pervasiveness of communication between networked computers, we are in the middle of the most transforming technological event since the capture of fire. I used to think that it was just the biggest thing since Gutenberg, but now I think you have to go back farther.
>
> (1995: 36)

In their euphoria, many analysts lost their perspective and succumbed to presentism and parochialism. Like Barlow, they thought that the world had started anew with the internet. They had gone beyond groupware, and realized that computer-mediated communication – in the guise of the internet – fostered widespread connectivity. But like the groupware folks, they insisted on looking at online phenomena in isolation. They assumed that only things that happened on the internet were relevant to understanding the internet. Their initial analyses of the impact of the internet were often unsullied by data and informed only by conjecture and anecdotal evidence: travelers' tales from internet *incognita*. The analyses were often utopian.

They extolled the internet as egalitarian and globe-spanning, and ignored the way in which differences in power and status might affect interactions both online and offline. The dystopians had their say too, worrying that:

> while all this razzle-dazzle connects us electronically, it disconnects us from each other, having us 'interfacing' more with computers and TV screens than looking in the face of our fellow human beings.
> (Texas broadcaster Jim Hightower, quoted in Fox, 1995: 12)

Pundits and computer scientists alike were still trying to get a handle on what was happening without taking much account of social science knowledge. In my frustration, I began to issue manifestos in the guise of scholarly articles. Two papers presented my case based on my 30-plus years of experience as an analyst, studying communities as social networks. 'An Electronic Group is Virtually a Social Network' (1997) contrasted groups and groupware with social networks and social networkware. It asserted that the internet was best seen as a computer-supported social network, in fact, the world's largest component (to use graph theoretical language, which describes a network where all points are ultimately connected, directly or indirectly). 'Net Surfers Don't Ride Alone' (with Milena Gulia, 1999) took aim at the vogue for calling every interaction online a 'community'. It argued that the internet was not the coming of the new millennium, despite the gospel of *Wired* magazine (the *Vogue* of the internet), but was a new technology following the path of other promoters of transportation and communication connectivity, such as the telegraph, railroad, telephone, automobile, and airplane. It showed how community dynamics continued to operate on the internet – this was not a totally new world – and how intertwined offline relationships were with online relationships.

The second age of internet studies, systematic documentation of users and uses

The second age of internet studies began about five years ago. Around 1998, government policymakers, commercial interests and academics all realized the need for systematic accounts of the internet. If the internet boom were to continue, it would be good to describe it rather than just to praise it and coast on it. But the flames of the dot.com boom dimmed early in 2000, and with it the internet came down to earth. The pages of *Wired* magazine shrank 25 percent from 240 pages in September 1996 to 180 pages in September 2001, and yet another 17 percent to 148 pages in September 2003: a decline of 38 percent since 1996.

At the same time, the use of the internet kept growing. However, its proliferation has meant that it no longer stands alone, if it ever did. It has become embedded in everyday life. The ethereal light that dazzled from above has become part of everyday things. We have moved from a world of internet wizards to a world of ordinary people routinely using the internet. The internet has become an important thing but not a special thing. It has become the utility of the masses rather than the plaything of computer scientists.

Moreover, the uses of the internet kept expanding and democratizing. The initial 'killer applications' of communication were joined by information via the Netscape/Internet Explorer enabled world wide web. Search engines, such as AltaVista and then Google, moved web exploring beyond a cognoscenti's game of memorizing arcane URLs and IP addresses. Still later, web logs moved web creation beyond institutional designers' expertise to everyperson's soapbox.

The second age of internet studies has been devoted to documenting this proliferation of internet users and uses. It has been based heavily on large-scale surveys, originally done by marketing-oriented firms (and with some bias towards hyping use), but increasingly done by governments, academics, and long-term enterprises such as the Pew Internet & American Life Project (http://www.pewinternet.org) and the World Internet Project (http://www.worldinternetproject.net). These studies have counted the number of internet users, compared demographic differences, and learned what basic things people have been doing on the internet. For example, we now know that a majority of adults in many developed countries have used the internet, and that women are coming to use the internet as much as men in many developed countries. However, the socioeconomic gap persists in most countries even with increasing use, because poorer people are not increasing their rate of use as much as wealthier, better-educated ones (Chen and Wellman, 2004).

Neither the utopian hopes of Barlow nor the dystopian fears of Hightower have been borne out. Despite Barlow's hopes, the internet has not brought a utopia of widespread global communication and democracy. Despite Hightower's fears, high levels of internet use have not lured people away from in-person contact. To the contrary, it seems as if the more people use the internet, the more they see each other in person (distance permitting) and talk on the telephone (see the studies in Wellman and Haythornthwaite, 2002). This may be because the internet helps arrange in-person meetings and helps maintain relationships in between meetings (Haythornthwaite and Wellman, 1998). It may also mean that gregarious, extroverted people will seize on all media available in order to communicate (Kraut *et al.*, 2002).

To the surprise of some, the purportedly global village of the internet has not even destroyed in-person neighboring. In 'Netville', a suburb near Toronto, the two-thirds of the residents who had always-on, super-fast internet access knew the names of three times as many neighbors as their unwired counterparts, spoke with twice as many, and visited the homes of 1.5 times as many (Hampton and Wellman, 2003). Yet, the globe-spanning properties of the internet are obviously real, nowhere more so than in the electronic diasporas that connect émigrés to their homeland. In so doing, they enable diasporas to aggregate and transmit reliable, informal news back to often-censored countries (Miller and Slater, 2000; Mitra, 2003).

The dawning of the third age – from documentation to analysis

It has been easy until now. At first, no data were needed, just eloquent euphoria. The second age was low-hanging fruit with analysts using standard social scientific methods – and some concepts – to document the nature of the internet.

Now, the real analysis begins with more focused, theoretically-driven projects. For example, our NetLab is currently looking at the kinds of relationships that the internet does (and does not) foster, and how transnational entrepreneurs operate intercontinentally, both online and offline. As an overarching thought, we believe that the evolving personalization, portability, ubiquitous connectivity, and wireless mobility of the internet is facilitating a move away from interactions in groups and households, and towards individualized networks. The internet is helping each person to become a communication and information switchboard, between persons, networks, and institutions.

What of groupware, where I started a decade ago? As none of us predicted then, groupware transmuted into social network software as both individuals and organizations feel a need to contact dispersed others. The need for this has received great publicity: Between June and September 2003, Google reported about 9700 stories about Duncan Watts and associates' tracing of how the internet connects unknown persons in 'small worlds' (Dodds *et al.*, 2003). Social network software exists to connect the hitherto unconnected, helping people to make new ties. It comes in two flavors:

1 Friendship makers (such as friendster.com) which put friends of friends in contact or uses collaborative filtering (such as match.com and lavalife.com) to connect people with similar interests. My students report this as effective and enjoyable as going to bars or other 'meat [meet] markets', and more efficient;
2 Corporate network programs which are used to portray the social (dis)integration of workgroups or to help access knowledge in sprawling organizations (and not 'who knows who knows what' as IKNOW puts it: Contractor *et al.*, 1998; see also Nardi *et al.*, 2001).

I am not standing alone any more. Groups have clearly become individualized networks; on the internet and off of it (Wellman, 2001, 2002). The person has become the portal.

Acknowledgements

My thanks to *Cavecat/Telepresence* colleagues who first involved me in this area: Ronald Baecker, Bill Buxton, Janet Salaff, and Marilyn Mantei Tremaine. Bernie Hogan and Phuoc Tran gave useful comments on an earlier draft. Bell University Labs, Communication and Information Technologies Ontario, and the Social Science and Humanities Research Council of Canada have been the principal supporters of our NetLab research.

Note

1 Hiltz and Turoff named their book after my 'The Network City' paper (Craven and Wellman, 1973) – which had nothing explicitly to do with computer networks but everything to do with a network conception of communities.

References

Barlow, J. P. (1995) 'Is There a There in Cyberspace?', *Utne Reader* (March–April), 50–6.
Buxton, B. (1992) 'Telepresence: Integrating Shared Task and Person Spaces', paper presented at the Proceedings of Graphics Interface 1992, May, Vancouver.
Chen, W. and B. Wellman (forthcoming, 2004) 'Charting Digital Divides Within and Between Countries', in W. Dutton, B, Kahin, Ramon O'Callaghan and AndrewWyckoff (eds) *Transforming Enterprise*. Cambridge, MA: MITPress.
Contractor, N. S., D. Zink and M. Chan (1998) 'IKNOW: A Tool to Assist and Study the Creation, Maintenance, and Dissolution of Knowledge Networks', in T. Ishida (ed.) *Community Computing and Support Systems, Lecture Notes in Computer Science 1519*, pp. 151–64. Berlin: Springer-Verlag.
Craven, P. and B. Wellman (1973) 'The Network City', *Sociological Inquiry* 43(1): 57–88.
Dodds, P. S., R. Muhamad and D. Watts (2003) 'An Experimental Study of Search in Global Social Networks', *Science* 301(8): 827–9.
Fox, R. (1995) 'Newstrack', *Communications of the ACM* 38(8): 11–12.
Hampton, K. and B. Wellman (2003) 'Neighboring in Netville: How the Internet Supports Community and Social Capital in a Wired Suburb', *City and Community* 2(3): 277–311.
Haythornthwaite, C. and B. Wellman (1998) 'Work, Friendship and Media Usefor Information Exchange in a Networked Organization', *Journal of the American Society for Information Science*, 49(12): 1101–14.
Hiltz, S. R. and M. Turoff (1978) *The Network Nation*. Reading, MA: Addison-Wesley.
Kraut, R., S. Kiesler, B. Boneva, J. Cummings, V. Helgeson and A. Crawford (2002) 'Internet Paradox Revisited', *Journal of Social Issues* 58(1): 49–74.
Mantei, M., R. Baecker, A. Sellen, W. Buxton, T. Milligan and B. Wellman (1991) 'Experiences in the Use of a Media Space. Reaching Through Technology', *Proceedings of the CHI '91 Conference*, pp. 203–8. Reading, MA: Addison-Wesley.
Miller, D. and D. Slater (2000) *The Internet: An Ethnographic Approach*. Oxford: Berg.

Mitra, A. (2003) 'Online Communities, Diasporic', in K. Christensen and Daniel Levinson (eds) *Encyclopedia of Community*, vol. 3 (4 vols), pp. 1019–20. Thousand Oaks, CA: Sage.

Nardi, B., S. Whittaker and H. Schwartz (2001) 'It's Not what You Know, It's who You Know: Work in the Information Age', *First Monday*, URL (consulted 5 January 2002): http://www.firstmonday.org/issue5_5/nardi/index.html.

Sproull, L. and S. Kiesler (1991) *Connections*. Cambridge, MA: MIT Press.

Wellman, B. (1997) 'An Electronic Group is Virtually a Social Network', in S. Kiesler (ed.) *Culture of the Internet*, pp. 179–205. Mahwah, NJ: Lawrence Erlbaum.

Wellman, B. (2001) 'Physical Place and Cyberspace: the Rise of Personalized Networks', *International Urban and Regional Research* 25(2): 227–52.

Wellman, B. (2002) 'Little Boxes, Glocalization, and Networked Individualism', in M. Tanabe, P. van den Besselaar and T. Ishida (eds) *Digital Cities II: Computational and Sociological Approaches*, pp. 10–25. Berlin: Springer.

Wellman, B. and M. Gulia (1999) 'Net Surfers Don't Ride Alone: Virtual Communities as Communities', in B. Wellman (ed.) *Networks in the Global Village*, pp. 331–66. Boulder, CO: Westview.

Wellman, B. and C. Haythornthwaite (eds) (2002) *The Internet in Everyday Life*. Oxford: Blackwell.

74

WHERE INFORMATION SOCIETY AND COMMUNITY VOICE INTERSECT

Ramesh Srinivasan

Source: *The Information Society* 22(5) (2006): 355–65.

Information and communication technology (ICT) development initiatives have begun to acknowledge the power and importance of cultural and community-focused belief systems. Yet the vast majority of such initiatives tend to preidentify developmental goals that communities hold. Paulo Freire's writings have influenced development initiatives by introducing the possibility of working with communities to orient projects. While these "participatory" initiatives have involved soliciting community feedback relative to a research project whose goals were formulated in the university or development institution, they do not go far enough to harness actual visions held by communities. It is important to conceptualize a model and methodology of engaging communities to develop and articulate their own goals of information access and ultimately, an indigenous approach toward cultural, political, and economic aspects of development. This approach holds promise to sustain communities within a return on the investment and efforts of the researcher or institution. This article closes by describing a current initiative in Southern India that reflects the described methodology.

Pedagogy and the community voice

Paulo Freire's theory reveals the potential of engaging in informatioln and communication technology (ICT) development efforts that release the authorship and classificatory abilities of communities in praxis with researchers (Freire, 1968/2002). This enables the development of information systems and initiatives that remove the dichotomies of "oppressor–oppressed" to allow a constructive dialogue wherein shared visions and aspirations emerge.

Freire argues that education is always a political act, used to maintain the status quo or generate social, political, cultural, or economic change. A dialectical relationship characterizes the relationship between a teacher, the oppressor, and the student, the oppressed. It is dialectical in that the actions and thoughts of each are expressed relative to the acknowledgement of the other. He was critical of the "banking education," wherein learners are asked to file and silently absorb the deposits that they are imparted from the oppressor. The oppressor denies the legitimacy of the oppressed's voice by assuming that learning, development, and progress are only achievable via the intervention of the oppressor. This is a relationship that identifies the individual being acted on as an "object" and the lecturing teacher as the "subject." The lecture is a pedagogical process that requires the oppressed to suppress their voices and reactions. Learning rewards those who are best at emulating the paradigm introduced dogmatically. This is a great injustice because Freire believes that the great trait all human beings are born with is vocation, the ability to verbalize and articulate their own beliefs and reflections. This great potential held by all beings is described as *conscientizao*, the acknowledgment and action against oppressive elements of reality.

> The teacher issues communiques and makes deposits which the students patiently receive, memorize, and repeat. This is the "banking" concept of education, in which the scope of action allowed to the students extends only as far as receiving, filing, and storing the deposits. They do, it is true, have the opportunity to become collectors or cataloguers of the things they store. But in the last analysis, it is the people themselves who are filed away through the lack of creativity, transformation, and knowledge in this (at best) misguided system. For apart from inquiry apart from the praxis, individuals cannot be truly human. Knowledge emerges only through invention and re-invention, through the restless, impatient, continuing, hopeful inquiry human beings pursue in the world, with the world, and with each other.
>
> (Freire, 1968/2002, p. 72)

The pedagogy of the oppressed consists of two stages. These are "(1) the oppressed unveil the world of oppression and through the praxis commit themselves to its transformation, and (2) In the second stage, in which the reality of oppression has already been transformed, this pedagogy ceases to belong to the oppressed and becomes a pedagogy of all people in the process of permanent liberation" (Freire, 1968/2002, p. 36). Therefore, freedom from the oppression, defined as the restriction of the voice of the oppressed, is overcome via praxis, the act of reflection that dilutes the hierarchical and predefined student–teacher relationship into one of coproducer. As the extent of oppression is realized, the oppressed may begin to articulate their own voices and participate in the pedagogical process. Freedom entails rejecting the image of the oppressor and instead embracing the autonomy and collective responsibility common to all human beings. The dialectical relationship is enhanced as only the oppressed can free their oppressor and vice versa. The oppressor is freed from the power struggle of dehumanization, which limits meanings, and from a materialistic belief that *to be is to have*. Symmetrically, the oppressor can help free the oppressed from the trauma of hegemony, and the self-degradation that accompanies it.

The banking model is described as information transfer, and parallels international information development initiatives that presume that access to externally authored information is the only means by which the global progress of the "information society" may be achieved (Webster, 2003). In Freire's model, the problematic here is not one of information transfer, but the directionality of it, and the means by which this information is constructed and imparted. He argues: "Liberating education consists in acts of cognition, not transferals of information. It is a learning situation in which the cognizable object intermediates the cognitive actors-teacher on the one hand and students on the other" (Freire, 1968, p. 79).

According to Leeman (2004), banking education ensures the continuation of an oppressive society by:

- Mythologizing reality—"something to which people, as mere spectators, must adapt."
- Resisting dialogue.
- Treating students as objects of assistance.
- Inhibiting creativity.
- Failing to acknowledge humans as historical beings.

Freire therefore advocates a system of liberating education that treats oppressors and oppressed as equals within the learning process. "Through dialogue, the teacher of the students and student of the teacher cease to exist and a new term emerges: teacher-student and student-teacher. The teacher is . . . one who is himself taught in dialogue with the students, who in turn while being taught also teach" (Freire, 1968/2002, p. 80).

"Problem-posed education" is a partnership between teacher and student that democratizes content, how it is produced and valued, and focuses the education and learning around the here and now. In other words, instead of subscribing to an alien and historical formality, education is grounded in knowledge of the environments, peoples, epoch, and so on. In this sense, any of the participants may be more educated based on their own individual experiences, and the pedagogical process does not carry with it a historical model of power that suppresses the indigenous voice. Freire's model of thematic education extends this by conceiving of students as co-investigators with the teacher, and that together cross-cutting teams of students and teachers lead thematic investigations that they can present to the entire community. This process is reflexive, as throughout all must reexamine their roles, motivations, and principles, and therefore authentically commit themselves to the people. This commitment is the essence of the moral and emotional fabric that Freire concludes is consistent with his approach, and treats "people" as "us" rather than "other."

Reactions to Freire—approaching ICTs and development

Several effective critiques emerge that can work to augment this largely inspiring model. I wish to lay these out so as to further clarify the application of the model to the ICT development scenario.

First is the polarity between the oppressor and oppressed, to which Freire fails to add much texture. His concepts fall into the traditional Hegelian dialectic that lacks investigation into the multiple layers of meaning that generate the communities of oppressors and oppressed. Issues of gender, race, and cultural epistemology within each certainly would play a role in the actions taken and assumptions embedded within the pedagogical process. The universalization of the oppressed and oppressor does not interrogate the nature of the interconnections between the two categories and the mobility that may exist within these two categories. In different cultural scenarios, the oppressor and oppressed classes have been reversed at various times, through such processes as reverse discrimination. For example, previously repressed classes may revolt, take power, and then oppress the former oppressors. Access and power are different across gender roles in all societies, and the means by which the oppressor–oppressed relationship model plays out is likely radically different across different ethnicities and geographies.

Second, Freire speaks very little about agency and resistance that may exist prior to the process of dual transformation that involves collapse of hierarchy and embrace of praxis. He acknowledges that full-scale revolutions led by the oppressed transfer the title of oppressor from one group to another. Yet oppressed peoples even without a full revolt still maintain agency that enables tacit and constructive types of resistance. In the ICT domain alone, a number of examples exist that reveal the presence of marginalized peoples via the Web (Mitra, 1997) and use of the internet to catalyze grass-roots activism around an indigenous cause (Cleaver, 1998). There is ample evidence that local peoples theorize in their communities as part of their community life, and articulate and interpret these experiences through various modes that may not be familiar or commonplace among the oppressors (Dei, 1988). Even the labeling of oppressor on the non-indigenous is a victimizing process that fails to recognize the multiplicity of means by which pedagogy has proceeded and motivations that may not be overtly or tacitly malicious.

Third, Freire's concept of information is much too simplistic, and assumes information transfer as inextricably linked to oppression, rather than a recentering of traditional central–peripheral power dynamics (Castells, 1997). Freire's approach can be bolstered through initiatives that recognize communities and researchers collectively as information producers and cocreators. This understands that information and media can be created and adopted by communities themselves (Miller & Slater, 2000; Nelson, 1996; Appadurai, 1998), and that knowledge can be situated within the localized cultural scenarios in which the development project is based. It can further be bolstered through information projects that engage communities to serve as the classifiers and categorizers of the databases of their information systems, allowing knowledge to be presented and represented around local, culturally specific discourses and priorities.

These critiques aside, Freire's approach is extremely valuable in conceiving ICT development projects built around community visions. This approach, by focusing on different cultural belief systems, supplements the traditional discourse around networks and power that Castells (1997), for example, has popularized. Visvanathan has argued that accompanying the structural shifts in Castells's analysis of the diffusion of information must be a sociology and theory of knowledge (Visvanathan, 2002). This is the recognition that the network impacts not only the diffusion of information and power, but also the diffusion of multiple epistemologies that emerge from different local, cultural perspectives that are distinct from traditional Western assumptions behind science and technology (Boast *et al.*, 2006). It raises the importance of engaging alternative voices and epistemologies to impact and influence ICT initiatives.

Freire reveals that ICT development projects must directly engage the voices, categorical notions and discourses directly from communities themselves and bridge stratifications between the community and the organization, government, or researcher. Existing research has recognized community voices and established participatory dialogues, but has yet to use this process to define the ultimate goals and methodologies for ICT development projects.

Freire's conceptual approach reorients the perspective to focus ICT development projects around dialogue, praxis, and coproduction. This article extends the approach without overtly embracing many of the polarizing motivations, labels, and dichotomies that are justifiably criticized within *Pedagogy of the Oppressed*. It is important to conceptualize a model and methodology of engaging communities to develop and articulate their own visions and goals of information access and, ultimately, an indigenous approach toward cultural, political, and economic aspects of development. This approach holds promise to sustain within communities the returns on the investment and efforts of the researcher or institution.

This article elucidates such an approach by (1) introducing challenges and paradigms within current ICT development research, (2) reframing the discourse and introducing further examples that can be evaluated relative to Freire's ideas, and (3) describing an approach that can more deeply embody the ideas of Freire while providing an overview of a current initiative in Southern India that reflects the approach of this article.

ICT development: challenges and paradigms

A strong thrust in ICT development research is focused on bridging the "digital divide" of technology access. As this divide is considered to reify and augment existing global economic stratifications, the goal has been to stimulate development by providing equal information access. However, little has been said regarding the perspectives and authorship that lie behind this information. We need to keep in mind that development requires the generation of community capacities toward self-sustaining economy. It encompasses material and immaterial understandings (Menou, 1985, 1993; Sen, 1999), and recognizes the role of information as an ability to harness community knowledge and activity (Boulding, 1996).

Scholars celebrate the potential laden in ICT initiatives to engage and revitalize national infrastructures within the developing world:

> No single collection, user interface, or set of system capabilities will serve young and old, novice and expert, artist and physicist.... Yet people of varying backgrounds and skills, speaking different languages, have similar information needs.... The prospect of a global digital library presents several opportunities. One is to make information resources accessible to particular user communities while at the same time making those same resources accessible to a broader, ill-defined and perhaps unknown audience.
>
> (Borgman, 2000, p. 208)

However, when shifting from the unit of the nation or university to a particular village or community, information access initiatives encounter problems and fail for a variety of reasons (Heeks, 1999). Many researchers have not directly considered culture as a factor that mediates the acceptance of the technology or the ability to absorb it within locally identified visions and developmental goals (Eres, 1981, p. 1). It has been argued that these have been pushed forward with Western paradigms and, at worst, are imperialist and generate dependency on the technology providers (Escobar, 1995; Ferguson, 1990). These events have underscored the realities of technology transfer being not merely an exchange that is political or economic, but a profoundly cultural process.

In reaction to these dominantly top-down ICT initiatives, other researchers have adopted participatory positions that attempt to steer initiatives by receiving community input. They have recognized that ICT researchers have an important role in giving voice to the poor and enabling them to empower themselves as active information providers rather than passive information recipients (Heeks, 1999). Locally contextualized and authored information, therefore, can be comprehended, adopted, and acted on more than information accessed from an alien context. This approach can enable communities to trust the information they receive, act on it, and have the confidence and security to believe that the project serves their own indigenous and collective needs (Heeks, 1999).

For example, Puri and Sahay (2003) describe how the approach of communicative action (Habermas, 1984) can allow geographical information system (GIS) technology to be applied in locally relevant manners. Villagers in Anantapur (Andhra Pradesh, India) were encouraged to codevelop a strategy with researchers to resolve land degradation issues within the region. The process involved interviews, discussions and meetings, and the sharing of community-created maps that demonstrate local approaches toward land care. The goals were to engage in a participatory process to elicit the community's own systems of knowledge and apply these to the land degradation research.

> There exists the need to develop design strategies that can foster mutual sharing of different forms of knowledge and practices, and create conditions in which effective communication can take place. ... Information systems development approaches have generally been based on perspectives of purposive-rational action within an ontology of technical knowledge.... These researchers further argue that the nature and scope of such participation fails to consider the practical knowledge of users, and also does not afford the opportunity for "open and informed debate" between development groups and users.
> (Puri & Sahay, 2003, pp. 183–84)

Therefore, the theory of communicative action for information systems, articulated by Hirschheim and Klein (1999), values open communication between community members and researchers. It is based around four major paraphrased principles:

1 Equal opportunity to all participants to raise issues, points, and counterpoints to other views in discussion.
2 All participants are on an equal footing with respect to power positions.
3 All participants can question the clarity, veracity, sincerity, and social responsibility of the actions proposed.
4 All participants can have an equal opportunity to articulate feelings or doubts or concerns.

Kanungo's studies (2004) of villager-owned and operated knowledge centres (kiosks) within Pondicherry, Tamil Nadu (India), complement the Anantapur example. Kanungo points out that historically ICT initiatives have historically been framed within institutional, governmental, and laboratory environments. Therefore, these strategies lack the adaptability to succeed within the field. An emancipatory information system, in contrast, can sustain community because it considers the community as an integral part of a network (with other villages, researchers, nongovernmental orgazations [NGOs], etc.) that achieves the development goal.

> As of now, the principal catalyst is the [research foundation] with the villagers being aware that they own, and are responsible for, the KC.... Sustainability emerges as the critical factor that will influence how information and information technology resources are managed in the post-experimental phase. The information village is need-based and community owned.... Emergent behaviors and roles of participants in the information villages project point to the development of a collective mind that is focused on the willful improvement of life.
>
> (Kanungo, 2004, pp. 416–417)

NGOs have to balance similar complexities to effectively receive funding yet empower local communities (Lewis & Madon, 2002; Hulme & Edwards, 1995). This "upward and downward accountability" presents a dilemma that is critical for all development initiatives—justifying results to receive financial support and institutional approval while still doing justice to the needs of the community. NGOs have emerged as the popular agent of development initiatives and often are at the mercy of donor agendas (Hulme & Edwards, 1997). To survive, as with all development initiatives, it is clear that NGOs must adopt convergent solutions that respect the voices of both community members and donors.

Lewis and Madon (2004) point out that NGOs and information systems are embedded within larger social systems that include technologies, organizations, environments, politics, and so on. Therefore, simply presuming that a technology would drive social change is naive. Instead, it is the interplay between the technology and human sociocultural action and interpretation that is important (Avgerou, 2002; Williams & Edge, 1999; Giddens, 1984). Researchers therefore argue that NGOs also have much to gain via more effective uses of information systems (Edwards & Hulme, 1992) that are stronger at "analyzing the various layers of context to the societies in which they work" (Lewis & Madon, 2004, p. 121).

With the preceding ICT development examples, the paradigm of participatory development is invoked. Participatory rural appraisal (PRA) is a widely adopted method of engaging the poor to articulate and express their own needs that can in turn inform policy and practice. Advocates argue that this approach embodies the ideas of Freire, in its understanding that values, goals, and visions are different across culture and environment. By engaging the community to describe its own vision, the development professional can intervene in areas that hold direct and indigenous cultural resonance (Chambers, 1994; Kramsjo & Wood, 1992).

> The differences between top-down reductionist definitions and objectives, and poor people's realities (are striking).... The challenges are paradigmatic: to reverse the normal view, to upend perspectives, to see things the other way round, to soften and flatten hierarchy, to adopt downward accountability, to change behavior, attitudes and beliefs, and to identify and implement a new agenda.
> (Chambers, 1997, p. 196)

An issue PRA researchers face is the criticism of homogenizing the term community, without addressing the differences and dynamics within this construct (Gujit & Shah, 1998). The mythical notion of community cohesion ignores how power is adopted and manifested within the community (Cooke & Kothari, 2001), formulaically assumes the realities of "community life" (Cleaver, 2001), and equates participation with salvation (Francis, 2001). Clearly, the definition and approach toward community is a complex issue that warrants further research.

Where do the presented methods and theories stand relative to Freire's vision? I believe that while they are admirable in their advocacy of community cooperation, they do not go far enough. Missing within the Anantapur and Pondicherry cases is the discussion of whether the basic framework emerges from the community's point of view. Including the community to resolve a problem that is externally identified and framed may not fully satisfy Freire's vision of praxis. It presents the goal of developing ICT initiatives that approach the community without prejudging what its development needs are. Therefore, rather than positioning community input within a predefined technology or development goal, I advocate a process of praxis with community members that generates visions, technologies, and methodologies while recognizing and working across the structures of power and difference that exist within the community (Srinivasan, 2006). Simply assuming that the community will provide open, free feedback on an initiative that is already formulated by the NGO or researcher is unrealistic, and does not fully adhere to the depth of Freire's ideas. Instead, engaging communities themselves to create their own information and media, and to share these in a constructive dialogue, can be the step that allows the discovery of visions and methodologies for ICT development.

Therefore, several key issues emerge with respect to ICT initiatives. These include:

1. Access to what? : Providing a simple "black-box" Internet access solution is not inherently connected to a community's vision or needs.
2. Preadjudication of access topics, technologies, or development goals: In some cases, researchers have presumed that certain types of access are appropriate for a specific community. This is dangerous as it does not derive from a process where the community is itself making decisions regarding what it wishes to access.
3. Externalization and ritualism (Loegelin, 1992; Appadurai, 2004): Scholars have found that many ritualized, oral communities are missing the capacity to directly aspire to visions (Ong, 1988; Goody & Watt, 1968) that may be different than a ritualized history. However, some promise lies in approaches that engage communities to create and document information about their lives and collectively reflect on this (Srinivasan & Huang, 2005; Donald, 1993). This approach may engage communities to externalize notions that remained buried and laden within a collective habitus (Bourdieu, 1990).

ICT-initiative examples

In this section, I present three ICT development initatives that have influenced this paper and the initiative described at its conclusion. Each connects to the introduced theories and methodologies in their consideration of the community, its belief systems, and its broader context. But do they truly embody the position Freire has introduced of developing visions and goals from the community's own voice and objectives?

Indigenous video and television

Terrence Turner's work with the Kayapo people of central Brazil is a benchmark in this research (Turner, 1992). The purposes of his work were to stimulate a video-creating process to articulate and advance various political and cultural agendas held by the community. Introducing the technology of the video camera to the Kayapo translated into an involvement and documentation of the negative effects of governmental hydroelectric dam schemes. The video documentation was brought back to the community by the appointed video creators and informed the different tribes of the impending danger. Moreover, the Kayapo had found that using their video cameras allowed them to interview and question Brazilian bureaucrats and politicians with a level of legitimacy that the government official would have to answer. Ultimately, this work translated into an international exposure for these peoples, as they were able to demonstrate their land rights issues on an international stage that could supersede even the Brazilian national government.

The work of Eric Michaels and the Warlpiri Aborigines of Western Central Australia also merits mention. A technological solution involved the creation of a low-frequency, low-power community transmitter that would allow community members to select from a variety of locally produced programs. This process generated an expansion of topics covered through these video programs and, correspondingly, shifts within social organizations of the community to accommodate the television feed. Fascinatingly, the dominantly oral cultures of these aboriginal communities smoothly transition into the electronic systems of video infrastructure.

> There is no necessary translation from orality to electronics; we are instead seeing an experimental phase involving the insertion of the camera into the social organization of events.
> (Michaels *et al.*, 1994, p. 65)

The examples of the Kayapo and Warlpiri reveal the potential of indigenous created media and information. They reveal the potential by which local populations can create, circulate, and benefit from indigenous information and media. Applying these initiatives to Freire's approach, however, reveals that neither directly places the community's voice at the forefront. Turner's intervention is largely described as a response to a situation of land loss, and the instruction of video making was at least initially based around these needs. And with the Warlpiri, the creation of an indigenous television station is powerful as an infrastructure but does not necessarily entail the release of community voice and the dilution of oppressor/oppressed polarities. Both projects, however, reveal constructive paths that enable the release of community-created information, and, as such, stand somewhere in between the stark dichotomy of oppressor/oppressed laid out by Freire.

NGO mediation—the case of Jana Sahayog

In a Bangalore (India) urban slum region, Madon and Sahay write of Jana Sahayog, an NGO that has tactically taken a community information-focused approach to mediate the relationship between governmental initiatives and the realities faced by slum dwellers (Madon & Sahay, 2002). The interventions employ a variety of informational tactics, including (1) using audio in folk formats to alert slum dwellers of their rights, (2) creating a community newspaper that can allow community members to respond to conditions in which they feel themselves wrapped while being kept abreast of goings-on outside of the settlement, and (3) presenting documented measurements of slum conditions relative to governmental guidelines.

> Prior to the establishment of Jana Sahayog, basic information about the slums was produced by the government and was neither shared with other organizations nor made available to slum dwellers in a way that they could understand or respond to. . . . Since Jana Sahayog came into existence, information flow has gradually increased in the direction of the slum dwellers.
> (Madon & Sahay, 2002, p. 18)

Thus through such informational initiatives, Madon and Sahay invoke Castells's model of networks and power (Castells, 1997) to argue that NGOs can alter structures of power so that information flows toward and from the periphery, rather than solely residing at and circulating within the central node of the government.

Community-modeled ontology projects (Village Voice and Tribal Peace)

The previous two examples focus specifically on the development of a collection of community-generated information/media pieces that are disseminated within the community. The Village Voice and Tribal Peace projects complement these efforts by focusing not simply on indigenous authorship, but also on classification, categorization, description, and representation of these pieces and how they are shared. Different cultures manifest distinctly through the means by which they conceive of and categorize knowledge, whether it be in terms of the environment, health, geography, or other topics (Levi-Strauss, 1962; Turnbull, 2004; Watson & Chambers, 1989). Standards and classifications are emblematic of a social process, and exact great power over the cognition and understandings of inclusion and exclusion (Star, 1989; Bowker & Star, 1999). Moreover, the potential of working with different categorical discourses recognizes communities as multiple and differentiated, rather than as a universalized "oppressed" people. Each community naturally maintains its own epistemologies and priorities, and acknowledging these differences adds depth to Freire's argument.

Information systems via their use of databases potentially enable classifications and discourses to be represented by communities through an approach described in previous research as "fluid ontologies" (Srinivasan & Huang, 2005), or the representation of information system content according to fluid, elicited descriptions articulated by community. This process engages communities to not only create their own media and information, but also to iteratively design the architecture by which these voices are represented and disseminated. This design emerges through the shared reflection around community-created information and media, building on the work in "activity theory" of Cole and Engestrom (1993) and Engestrom (1999), who have explained the means by which collaborative activity can reconcile a diversity of interests and create representations that are inclusive, dynamic, and fluid.

Both these projects were focused on engaging disenfranchised communities (Somali refugees in the Boston area and 19 Native reservations in San Diego County) to create self-reflective media related to community issues in whatever manner the author chose. With both communities, an easily developed fluency with video literacy and creation enabled a collection of local narratives. As content was aggregated in both projects, a clear structure and range of topics and concepts began to emerge. This arose as community members began to view content created by one another (over the Web, in collective meetings, and on local cable access television channels) and discuss topics and possibilities that had never been vocalized according to the participants.

> During these discussions, the community would come to a consensus on whether an issue that had come up should be included in the ontology. For example, one story was set at a Somali youth party. It showed teenage men and women dancing together dancing to hip hop music. The idea of a youth dance party without Somali music was disagreeable to some of the participants because of its disrespect to the Islamic taboo of pre-marital relationships, while most of the youth at the meeting argued that one could have a pre-marital relationship without being disrespectful to Muslim culture. During this discussion, the participants decided that issues of religious tradition, sexuality, and generational differences were relevant to the ontology.
>
> (Srinivasan, 2004, p. 104)

Ontology was understood in this research as the community's identification of a structure of collective priorities that emerges from the reflective process of viewing community-created content. As members watched videos, listened to recordings, and viewed collective content, this ontology was elicited and formed the basis of both the Tribal Peace (www.tribalpeace.org) and Village Voice systems. It continues to be reformed as new information and media enter the system and the community's priorities and representations change accordingly. This research is discussed in great detail across several other published works (Srinivasan, 2004; Srinivasan & Huang, 2005), but points to the possibility of engaging communities to externalize issues through information authorship and representation.

The diagram in Figure 1 was therefore created across initial sets of community meetings (with open invitation for any to participate). These meetings were led by community leaders, with the researcher only present as an observer (Srinivasan, 2004). Participants were instructed to view, reflect, and derive a structural relationship of all relevant themes, topics, and their interrelations. This initial ontology was encoded into the development of

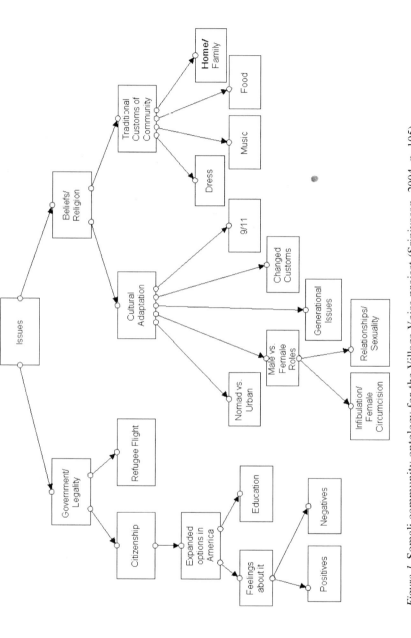

Figure 1 Somali community ontology for the Village Voice project (Srinivasan, 2004, p. 105).

the initial Village Voice ICT system, where community members could submit and annotate information (relative to this ontology) and browse the information of others by selecting topics of their choice from this community ontology. It was found in research that placing the community in control of its own ontology and system architecture resulted in greater participation and system usage relative to the standard indexing technique of keywords (Srinivasan, 2004).

Relating these examples to Freire

Each of these projects speaks to Freire's vision of praxis and the collaborative construction of knowledge. However, Jana Sahayog, Turner's work with the Kayapo, and the Village Voice/Tribal Peace engage community voice tactically, rather than instrumentally. Similar to the Anantapur and Pondicherry examples, objectives of land reclamation, government initiative responses, and so on had been predecided in these projects, and were not the emergent praxis that Freire describes.

Reconciling community voice with information access

Given these issues, I reintroduce my hypothesis that ICT development initiatives driven by community-created content may allow community members themselves to identify and pursue information access indicators that serve collective community needs. This identification may be accomplished by considering the idea of ontology introduced in the Tribal Peace and Village Voice projects, because the aspirations and priorities that emerge from the reflective stages of authoring and sharing information can transform into a structure of information access goals.

This theory is to be explored in the context of the Village Incubator (VI) research project based in Southern India. The research, in its initial stages, involves an engagement with two village communities that lack written literacy, basic education skills, and other indicators that are often emphasized in development interventions. As a number of communities operate within oral traditions that maintain a mythic and mimetic basis of ritualizing knowledge and its transmission, even Western liberal approaches toward development that ask communities to declare their own visions have tended to fail (Ong, 1988; Goody & Watt, 1968). Personal exchange norms and institutionalized practices instead dictate activity within such communities (Greif, 2002), rather than notions of transformation and planning. Indeed, many development projects presuppose that these shifts can only occur within communities that embrace the literacy of writing and reading. These projects have failed in their resonance with communities, and require the development of external symbolic systems that endanger traditions and are at best slowly adopted (Donald, 1993).

Southern India—information development and community voice[1]

The Village Incubator project seeks to determine whether the two communities in question can articulate and develop their own visions by creating, sharing, and reflecting on video, image, and audio information, and thereby actualize Freire's ideals. It is a collaborative effort between researchers and community members that will only proceed when community-derived goals and visions are expressed to researchers. Several villages in connection with the research partner NGO (Byrraju Foundation[2]) have expressed interest in working with the NGO and researchers on developing technologies that can serve their own indigenous needs. There is receptiveness to new approaches that enable the introduction of technologies that serve local developmental goals.

The work of several visual anthropologists (including the already discussed work of Turner with the Kayapo, Eric Michaels with the Warlpiri [Michaels *et al.*, 1994] and Sol Worth with the Navajo [Worth & Adair, 1972]) has shown how indigenous video and information can catalyze community activity and reflection. To realize Freire's theories, neither the researcher nor the NGO will make instrumental assumptions of community goals or visions, and instead both recognize that these will emerge over time and community reflection. It is therefore a project that is based around the praxis of dialogue between the researcher and NGO with a diverse set of community members. The project will proceed as follows:

- Two villages of several possibilities will be selected in Southern India (Andhra Pradesh and Tamil Nadu). Both villages will be selected based on the maintenance of preliterate oral traditions and a long, sustaining poverty and also the ease by which the NGO and researcher can access the field sites.
- Interns will be selected via the NGO to live within these communities and build relationships with community members that in turn can over time facilitate the deployment of the project. The relationship building will laterally work across the power structures and relationships within the community by taking an open and inclusive approach (Srinivasan, 2005).
- Video and other visual technologies (photograph-focused, perhaps sound-focused) will be provided to community members if the project and relationships develop appropriately to make this step feasible.
- Little doctrinaire instruction will be given on the use of these technologies or the imposition of values of what is or is not adequate use. Only operational training (of functionality and range of use) will be provided.
- The goal at this point will be to study the nature of the externalized information production process, how it diffuses within the community,

how it might transform collective visions and activities, and how a corpus may be assembled from different media pieces created by community members. In previous research, I had observed that the process of assemblage and media creation could generate discourse, dialogue, and other elements of public space—for instance, how taboo and ritualized topics were uncovered and reframed by a refugee community (Srinivasan, 2004).

- After these initial stages, the goal will be to study how the collection of media produced content will transform into mobilized community goals and an ICT project that can harmonize with these. This process will focus on community meetings to articulate shared priorities, notions, and conceptualizations that emerge from the creation of these multiple videos and their sharing.
- Evaluations of this research will be periodically be conducted, based on (1) whether information access indicators are identified, (2) the level of engagement the community maintains in creating information and accessing the chosen sources, and (3) the integration and stewardship of new initiatives that relate to collectively identified visions. This step may involve an analysis of how the process connects to existing community infrastructures and practices (such as schools, religious festivals, social and political meetings, and so on). These evaluations will identify whether the ICT initiative can sustain independently of the constant presence of the researcher or NGO partner.

Points of departure—Freire[3] and the trajectory of ICT development

Freire's *Pedagogy of the Oppressed* holds dramatic impact in the domain of global information development research efforts. He introduced a model of engagement with communities that recognizes development as a shared process of construction where communication and reflection uncover deeper wisdom. While Freire largely frames his model in binary and dialectical terms (such as oppressor–oppressed) and advocates an oppressed-led transition, it still informs a critical research agenda that integrates information and development. It opens up new ways of thinking in which development is not seen as merely information transfer, but as a process where communities can develop their own authorship and classifications.

Village Incubator is but a first attempt to weave Freire's ideas explicitly within ICT development research. Communities that author, circulate, and classify information represent a departure from the banking model of education that dismisses the community or student as a passive recipient. Described initiatives have ranged from rather blind impositions of information technologies onto developing communities to more sensitized informational projects that cultivate community-created information. Yet the fact is that most well-intentioned projects are visioned independent of the community–researcher praxis. In that regard, while they may not directly reify models of stratification and subservience, they do not forge new relationships and a codiscovery of ICT development goals and processes. In contrast, the Village Incubator project presents an opportunity for interested communities to engage the NGO, researcher, or other external institution with a sense of their own visions. This can help researchers develop ICT initiatives with communities that can sustain and resonate with local, cultural realities and beliefs.

Importantly, Freire's inspirations reconcile questions of cultural and pedagogical studies with information research by highlighting their interconnections within projects emerging from the vernacular of the community. Research that presents the community with the objective of leading its own endeavors begins to open up important answers to multidisciplinary questions, including (1) how do belief systems originate and circulate in communities, (2) how do communities conceive of memory and archival knowledge, (3) what types of visual and audio technologies work with different types of cultural systems, and (4) how can development indicators be elicited that are informationally oriented, economically oriented, and culturally oriented?

Is it possible to engage in ICT development research that is community-focused yet still engages the goals of access and connection that dominate information society agendas? Is it possible for a productive linkage to be formed between the hypotheses of this article and beneficial elements of resource-sharing that remain global priorities within the United Nations, World Bank, and other institutions? Such solutions may be realized in further research that conceives of an information society that accommodates multiple epistemologies, contexts, and cultural realities (Srinivasan, 2006; Visvanathan, 2002). Such answers present possibilities for convergent, praxis-oriented solutions in future ICT development research.

Notes

1 This project was inspired by collaborative efforts conducted with the Kozmetsky Global Collaboratory (KGC), based at Stanford University.
2 http://www.byrrajufoundation.org
3 The author wishes to acknowledge the collaborative discussions and work conducted by the Co-Divine project team, as part of the Kozmetsky Global Collaboratory at Stanford University.

References

Appadurai, A. 1998. *Modernity at large, Cultural dimensions of globalization.* Minneapolis: University of Minnesota Press, 1998.

Appadurai, A. 2004. The capacity to aspire: Culture and the terms of recognition. In *Culture and public action: A cross-disciplinary dialogue on development policy*, eds. V. Rao and M. Walton, pp. 59–85. Stanford, CA: Stanford University Press.

Avgerou, C. 2002. *Information systems and global diversity*. Oxford: Oxford University Press.

Boast, R., Bravo, M., and Srinivasan, R. 2006. Return to Babel: Emergent diversity, digital resources, and local knowledge. *The Information Society*, under review.

Borgman, C. 2000. *From Guttenberg to global information infrastructure: Access to information in the networked world*. Cambridge, MA: MIT Press.

Boulding, K. E. 1996. The economics of knowledge and the knowledge of economics. *American Economic Review* 56(2):1–13.

Bourdieu, P. 1990. *The logic of practice*. Stanford, CA: Stanford University Press.

Bowker, G. C., and Star, S. L. 1999. *Sorting things out: Classification and its consequences*. Cambridge, MA: MIT Press.

Castells, M. 1997. *The power of identity*. Oxford: Blackwell.

Chambers, R. 1994. Participatory rural appraisal (PRA): Challenges, potentials and paradigms. *World Development* 22(10):1437–1454.

Chambers, R. 1997. *Whose reality counts? Putting the first last*. London: Intermediate Technology.

Cleaver, H. 1998. The Zapatista effect: The Internet and the rise of an alternative political fabric. *Journal of International Affairs* 51(2):621–640.

Cleaver, F. 2001. Institutions, agency and the limitations of participatory approaches to development. In *Participation: The new tyranny?*, eds. B. Cooke and U. Kothari, pp. 36–55. London: Zed Books.

Cole, M., and Engestrom, Y. 1993. A cultural-historical approach to distributed cognition. In *Distributed cognitions: Psychological and educational considerations*, ed. G. Salomon, pp. 1–46. Cambridge: Cambridge University Press.

Cooke, B., and Kothari, U., eds. 2001. *Participation: The new tyranny?* London: Zed Books.

Dei, G. J. S. 1988. Crisis and adaptation in a Ghanaian forest community. *Anthropological Quarterly* 61(2):63–72.

Donald, M. 1993. *Origins of the modern mind: Three states in the evolution of culture and cognition*. Cambridge, MA: Harvard University Press.

Edwards, M., and Hulme, D. 1992. *Making a difference: NGOs and development in a changing world*. London: Earthscan.

Engestrom, Y. 1999. Activity theory and individual and social transformation. In *Perspectives on activity theory*, eds. Y. Engestrom, R. Miettinen, and R. L. Punamaki, pp. 19–38. Cambridge, MA: Cambridge University Press.

Eres, B. K. 1981. Transfer of information technology to less developed. countries: A system approach. *Journal of the American Society of Information Science and Technology* 32(2):97–102.

Escobar, A. 1995. *Encountering development: The making and unmaking of the third world*. Princeton, NJ: Princeton University Press.

Ferguson, J. 1990. *The anti-politics machine: Development, depoliticisation, and bureaucratic power in Lesotho*. Cambridge: Cambridge University Press.

Francis, P. 2001. Participatory development at the World Bank: The primacy of process. In *Participation: The new tyranny?*, eds. B. Cooke and U. Kothari, pp. 72–87. London: Zed Books.

Freire, P. 2002. *Pedagogy of the oppressed*, trans. Myra Bergman Ramos. New York: Continuum. (Originally published 1968)
Giddens, A. 1984. *The constitution of society*. Berkeley: University of California Press.
Goody, J., and Watt, I. 1968. *Literacy in traditional societies*. London: Cambridge University Press.
Greif, A. 2002. *Institutions and impersonal exchange: From communal to individual responsibility*. Working paper. Stanford, CA: Stanford University.
Gujit, I., and Shah, M. 1998. Waking up to power, conflict and process. In *The myth of community*, eds. I. Gujit and M. Shah, pp. 1–23. London: Intermediate Technology.
Habermas, J. 1984. *The theory of communicative action: Reason and rationalization of society*, vol. I. Boston: Beacon Press.
Heeks, R. 1999. *Information and communication technologies, poverty, and development*. Development Informatics Working Paper Series, Institute for Development Policy and Management, University of Manchester, Manchester, UK.
Hirscheim, R., and Klein, H. 1994. Realizing emancipatory principles in information systems development: The case for ETHICS. *MIS Quarterly* 18(1):83–109.
Hulme, D., and Edwards, M. 1995. *NGOs—Performance and accountability: Beyond the magic bullet*. London: Earthscan.
Hulme, D., and Edwards, M. 1997. *Too close for comfort? NGOs, states and donors*. London: Macmillan.
Kanungo, S. 2004. On the emancipatory role of rural information systems. *Information Technology and People* 17(4):407–422.
Kramsjo, B., and Wood, G. 1992. *Breaking the chains. Collective action for social justice among the rural poor of Bangladesh*. London: Intermediate Technology.
Leeman, P. 2004. Book review: Pedagogy of the oppressed. http://fcis.oise.utoronto.ca/~dschugurensky/freire/pl.html
Lewis, D., and Madon, S. 2004. Information systems and nongovernmental development organisations: Advocacy, organisational learning and accountability in a southern NGO. *The Information Society* 20(2):117–126.
Levi-Strauss, C. 1962. *The savage mind*. Chicago: University of Chicago Press.
Loegelin, M. 1992. *Interformation et development: étude synthetique des lignes de force du discourse universitaire*. Institut Universitaire de Technologie B, Départment Carrieres de l'information et de la communication, Université de Bourdeaux.
Madon, S., and Sahay, S. 2002. An information-based model of NGO-mediation for the empowerment of slum dwellers in Bangalore. *The Information Society* 18(1): 13–20.
Menou, M. J. 1985. An overview of social measures of information. *Journal of the American Society of Information Science and Technology* 36(3):169–177.
Menou, M. J. 1993. *Measuring the impact of information on development*. International Development Research Centre, Ottawa, ON, Canada.
Michaels, E., Langton, M., and Hebdige, D. 1994. *Bad aboriginal art: Tradition, media, and technological horizons*. Minneapolis: University of Minnesota Press.
Miller, D., and Slater, D. 2000. *The Internet: An ethnographic approach*. New York: Berg.
Mitra, A. 1997. Virtual commonality: Looking for India on the Internet. In *Virtual culture*, ed. Steve Jones, pp. 55–79, London: Sage.

Nelson, D. 1996. Maya hackers and the cyberspatialised nation state: Modernity, ethnostalgia, and a lizard queen in Guatemala. *Cultural Anthropology* 11(3):287–308.

Ong, W. J. 1988. *Orality and literacy: The technologizing of the word*. London: Routledge.

Puri, S. K., and Sahay, S. 2003. Participation through communicative action: A case study of GIS for addressing land/water management in India. *Information Technology for Development* 10:179–199.

Sen, A. K. 1999. *Development as freedom*. New York: Knopf.

Srinivasan, R. 2004. Reconstituting the urban through community-articulated digital environments. *Journal of Urban Technology* 11(2):93–111.

Srinivasan, R. 2005. *Weaving spatial, digital and ethnographic processes in community-driven media design*. Doctoral dissertation, Harvard University, Cambridge, MA.

Srinivasan, R. 2006. Ethnomethodological architectures—Information systems driven by cultural and community visions. *Journal of the American Society of Information Science and Technology*, in press.

Srinivasan, R., and Huang, J. 2005. Fluid ontologies for digital museums. *International Journal on Digital Libraries* 5(3):193–205.

Star, S. L. 1989. The structure of ill-structured solutions: Boundary objects and heterogeneous distributed problem solving. In *Distributed artificial intelligence*, eds. L. Gasser and M. Huhns, pp. 37–54. London: Pitman.

Turnbull, D. 2004. Performative and propositional knowledges: Niche construction, contingency, emergence, multiplicity, and the implications for reconceiving knowledge. In *Proceedings of 4S/EASST*, Paris, France.

Turner, T. 1992. Defiant images: The Kayapo appropriation of video. *Anthropology Today* 8(6):5–16.

Visvanathan, S. 2002. Knowledge and information in the network society. *Creative Commons*. http://www.india-seminar.com/2001/503/503%20shiv%20visvanathan.htm

Watson, H., and Chambers, D. 1989. *Singing the land, Signing the land*. Melbourne: Deakin University Press.

Webster, F. 2003. Information society. In *International encyclopedia of information and library science*, 2nd ed., eds. J. Feather and R. P. Sturges. pp. 1338–1357. New York: Routledge.

Williams, R., and Edge, D. 1999. The social shaping of technology. In *Information and communication technologies: Visions and realities*, ed. W. Dutton, pp. 53–68, Oxford: Oxford University Press.

Worth, S., and Adair, J. 1972. *Through Navajo eyes: An exploration in film communication and anthropology*. Bloomington: Indiana University Press.

75

NATION AND DIASPORA

Rethinking multiculturalism in a transnational context

Karim H. Karim

Source: *International Journal of Media and Cultural Politics* 2(3) (2007): 267–82.

Abstract

Multiculturalism has redefined the nation as comprising a culturally pluralist population. However, the increased linkages between countries, produced by accelerated globlisation, have also engendered intricate transnational networks between diasporas residing in several states. The telephone, internet, satellite television and other media help construct a web of connections among these 'transnations' enabling them to maintain and enhance their cultural identities. Diasporas have creatively engaged with transnational media and are participating in a 'globalisation-from-below'. An increasingly cosmopolitan outlook has been fostered by the intercontinental links. But multiculturalism policies tend erroneously to continue viewing members of immigrant communities as having engaged in a one-way trajectory that breaks ties with their past. The current conceptualisation of multiculturalism as fixed within the context of the nation-state does not allow for a well-considered response to the transnational contexts in which immigrants live out their lives. Some migrant-producing states have begun to address these circumstances, but those of immigrant-receiving governments have generally been reluctant to acknowledge them.

Multiculturalism appears today to have become like the elephant of the old Sufi tale, in which six blind men who touched its individual parts were convinced that it was, respectively, a wall, a snake, a spear, a tree trunk, a rope, and a fan. The policy is variously thought of as designed to improve race relations, promote affirmative action, mitigate communal conflict, recognize difference, encourage good citizenship, support national cohesion, foster social integration and enjoin cultural assimilation. And even though its emphasis has differed between countries, the implicit understanding seems to be that multiculturalism is the same around the world.

The multiculturalism policy first emerged in Canada in the early 1970s when official British-French biculturalism was replaced with multiculturalism in recognition of the 'contributions of the other ethnic groups' (Government of Canada 1970).[1] It grew out of the particular historical circumstances of the country, but also was a response to the universal tension between the nation-state and its cultural diversity. That the concept spread around the world comes as no surprise: it has been perceived as a way to reconcile the contradiction between the political fiction of a unitary national population and its pluralist reality.

But the nature of the policy as it developed in various countries has been shaped by respective historical, socio-political and demographic circumstances. Even in traditional immigrant-receiving states such as Canada and Australia, multiculturalism differs in the manners in which it is applied. The approach of Britain, with its history of resettling Commonwealth citizens within its shores, remains markedly distinct from that of other European countries. Asian countries such as India and Singapore, which do not allow large-scale immigration, have used the term 'multiculturalism' to describe the management of their long-existing cultural diversity.

The UK's model of multiculturalism came under severe attack following the suicide bombings of the London transport system by four British-born Muslims in July 2005. The apparent failure to secure the loyalty of these individuals was viewed as a general inability of the policy to engage successfully with the racial and religious diversity of the national population (Jones 2005; Roche 2005). The murder in Amsterdam of controversial film maker Theo van Gogh by a Moroccan-Dutch Muslim in 2004 elicited a similar critique of multiculturalism in the Netherlands (Hylarides 2005; Baker 2004), which has incorporated it into its particular 'pillarized' social policy. However, this was not the first time that multiculturalism had come under attack either in these countries or elsewhere. It has long been contested, even in the country of its birth (Karim 2003).

Although the conceptualisation and practice of multiculturalism varies between countries, the critiques of specific controversies tend to be generalized to the idea as a whole as they are reported in the transnational media. Within this discourse, it is not the policy of the specific state that comes under attack, but multiculturalism as a general notion. Difference, affirmative action, anti-racism, integration, assimilation, social cohesion or communal harmony may be favoured by particular governments, but critics often do not seem to make distinctions.

It is ironic that whereas commentators take a global view of multiculturalism, they do not contextualize the policy within processes of globalisation. The primary reference for its locus, even for most academics studying the issue, is the nation-state. This is so despite multiculturalism being largely a response to transnational migration and increasingly inflected by diasporic factors. The continued attachment of the second and later generations descended from immigrants to the ancestral country can often be attributed to the advancements in transportation and communication that enables them to travel physically and vicariously to the homeland. This paper seeks to explore the conceptual placement of multiculturalism within the nation-state and the strong emergence of global diasporic linkages, and then to suggest a rethinking of the policy within a transnational context.

Nations

All nations are imaginary (Anderson 1983). The concept of the nation-state, which emerged in 17th century Europe, was based on the general idea of a shared ethnicity of the population that lived within a particular territory (Renan 1990; Smith 1989). The ancient Greek word *ethnos*, from which ethnic is derived, denotes 'nation'. Ideas of the nation-state have involved the coalescence of ethnicity and territory to imply the existence of an ancestral homeland belonging to a particular people having kinship ties that are reflected in a common language and culture.

But this idea has been consistently problematic. Nations in reality have not been containers of 'pure ethnicities'. Because of the tendency of human beings to migrate and to intermarry, there have rarely existed territories that are ethnically homogenous – despite the attempts by some to 'cleanse' them. Cultural and linguistic particularities may be eliminated over time through the assimilation of variant groups, but new waves of migration tend to ensure diversity within national populations.

Colonialism replicated European forms of governance around the world. This included the separation of related peoples' identities and relationships by marking out fixed (although not completely immutable or impermeable) national borders, which were to be maintained even after independence. Educational systems help to ensure that the global system of nation-states are accepted by all peoples as 'natural' (Blaut 1993).

Contemporary states often sustain themselves with an adherence to a distinctive mythology, symbolism and culture associated with an ancient past. Populations are mobilized to believe in their authenticity through educational and mass communication systems (Smith 1989: 361). National mass media systems emphasize the concept of the nation-state as the primary and natural form of polity. They play this role with the continual highlighting of national symbols ranging from the prominent portrayal of national leaders in regular news bulletins to the frequent retelling of tales gleaned from the national mythology in dramatic programs (to say nothing of the ubiquity of the national flag and references to national institutions). Images of the map of the state in relation to others clearly demarcate the citizens of various countries as Canadians, Kenyans, Indians etc. A nation becomes a naturalized political, geographic and ethno-cultural entity, which is distinct from all other nations in the imagination of not only its own residents that those of others (the system of nation-states exists by mutual recognition.).

But this modernist imaginary appears to have become muddled with postmodernist ambiguities that crept in during the last decades of the twentieth century. The increased recognition of ethno-cultural diversity within national borders under policies of multiculturalism has seriously challenged the idea of a nation as ethnoculturally homogenous. Multiculturalism redefined the nation as comprising an ethnically pluralist populace. In practical terms, this new approach seeks to contain conflicts between competing ethnic groups within a state and effectively harness their skills as well as their intellectual and economic resources. Nevertheless, the primary cultural values of a country's dominant ethnic groups remain hegemonic even as some aspects of minorities' cultural heritage are incorporated into the national symbolic landscape, particular forms of racial discrimination are outlawed, and certain measures are instituted to enable greater minority participation in the public sphere.

In reality, the acknowledgement of ethno-cultural minorities within nation-states has occurred mainly because of the need for manual and skilled labour, not only in Northern countries but also in those like Malaysia that have embarked on ambitious programs of transforming their economies technologically. Long-standing ethnic diversity, which was often not valued in previous times, is now often seen as a vital national asset and showcased to the world. The public imagery and imaginaries of many nations have come to include a multi-ethnic population and a diversity of cultures.

Transnations/diasporas

Contemporary changes in the idea of the nation are occurring in a time when transnational communications are increasingly enabling individuals and communities to remain in touch across the seas. The telephone, internet, satellite television and other media help construct a web of connections among ethnic diasporas living in various parts of the world, making their cultural assimilation into national populations more difficult. These 'transnations', as Arjun Appadurai terms them, extend around the planet with the help of modern-day communications. Giving the example of the USA but citing what is almost universally true, he notes, 'No existing conception of Americaness can contain this large variety of transnations' (1996: 172). They reside in one country but also straddle across many others.

Like nations, diasporas are frequently described as 'imagined communities' (De Santis 2003; Tsaliki 2003). Borrowing from Benedict Anderson (1983), this characterisation emphasizes both, the improbability of first-hand acquaintance of all members of the group with each other and their adherence to a common set of cultural references. Diasporic links are enhanced by the simultaneous consumption of the same media content by members of a global community. However, as with an ethnic group, membership within a particular diaspora is based on a belief about a common descent whose veracity is often obscured by the mists of time.

Unlike a nation's traditional placement within a defined location, transnations are deterritorialized communities. Migration removes the diasporic members from the homeland; but they transport with them its imaginary, which they frequently invoke in their lands of settlement. (Some view themselves as exiles, dreaming of returning to ancestral home sometime in the future). This contributes to their desire for media content and other cultural products that celebrate their emotional links to the old country.

However, cultural goods and services do not only originate from the homeland but are exchanged in the world-wide networks of settlements that constitute the transnations (Cunningham and Nguyen 2003). For some groups, politics in the homeland or in other parts of the diaspora are of abiding interest, especially in times of crisis (Bunt 2003). Media are often used to mobilize support for the homeland causes (Hassanpour 2003, Santianni 2003). The utilisation of media by transnations challenge the incorporation of immigrant groups into the countries of settlement. But before examining this issue further, it is useful to explore the relationship of diasporic cultures with global structures and globalisation.

Diasporic cultures and global structures

The large migrations of the preceding centuries were a consequence of colonisation and trading connections as well as of the steady improvements in transportation. More recent human flows from Africa, Asia and Latin America to Europe, North America and Australasia seem to have been prompted in part by the economic involvement of the latter in the formed.[2] The 'off-shoring' of production, foreign investment into export-oriented agriculture and the power of multinationals in the consumer markets of developing countries have often led to mass movements of people (Sassen 1996).

During the 18th and 19th centuries, the extensive movements of slaves from Africa, indentured labourers from Asia and settlers from Europe resulted in new economic growth in the 'New World', while displacing aboriginal economic infrastructures. Even after slavery and indentured labour were outlawed, the flows from Southern countries were stopped by immigrant-receiving countries whose governments favoured European newcomers. In the 1950s and 1960s, people from Southern countries began to relocate in larger numbers in the North with the elimination of race-based restrictions to immigration.

These movements have created diasporas whose members are located around the world. However, the characteristics of all such transnations are not the same; indeed, major differences exist even within respective diasporas. Complex historical, social and cultural dynamics in specific groups have shaped identities within diasporas. Mandaville views these communities as being continually 'constructed, debated and reimagined' (2003: 135). To appreciate better, how individual diasporians situate their own selves, researchers need to understand how worldwide communities are internally layered according to periods of migration, the historical receptivity of host societies to various waves of migration and the continuation of the diaspora's links with the home country and with other parts of the transnation. These sociological factors have produced a range of differences in the strength of such groups' internal and external attachments. The characteristics of diasporas are also shaped by factors such as the extent of the retention of ancestral customs, language and religion, marriage patterns and the ability to communicate within the diaspora.

Multiculturalism policies tend erroneously to view members of immigrant communities as having engaged in a one-way move that break all ties with their past. Migrants often follow non-linear routes, frequently backtracking and returning to particular sites on the planet in sequences that vary between persons and groups. Apart from their multifarious connections with the land of origin, world-wide diasporas develop intricate networks linking their various settlements. The resulting identities are complex and dynamic – sharing different cultural characteristics with specific parts of their transnational community and simultaneously with the respective national populations of whom they have become a part.

They carry documentation attesting to their membership in a national group, but usually not to that which identifies them with a diaspora. Their relationships with various groups are subject to change in accordance with events in an individual's or community's life. A person's multi-layered identity may from time to time shift the hierarchy of attachments modulated by ethnicity, religion, nation as well as other forms of belonging. Some may relate to a religious diaspora that is more ethnically diverse than an ethnocultural group; others may feel comfortable engaging with several diasporas or with a conglomeration of groups from a geographical region (including an entire continent).

Some cultural studies and postcolonial perspectives have tended to view diasporas as standing in opposition to global and national hegemonies – of the empire striking back. Jon Stratton and Ien Ang suggest that for the postcolonial immigrant to Britain 'what the diasporic position opens up is the possibility of developing a post-imperial British identity, one based explicitly on an acknowledgement and vindication of the "coming home" of the colonized Other' (1996: 383, 384). Despite having left the old nation, the migrant finds it difficult to completely become a part of the new nation; diaspora existentially becomes the cultural border between the country of origin and that of residence – Homi Bhabha's 'third space' (1994), one of intense, cutting-edge creativity born out of the migratory angst of not feeling at home neither here nor there.

The romanticism about diasporic opposition to global capitalism notwithstanding, there are many examples of diasporic participation in transnational economic activity. From the 18th century banking network of the Rothschilds to the more recent global family businesses like Li Ka Shing, diasporic clans have been important players in high capitalism. At 450 billion dollars, the annual economic output in the early 1990s of the 55 million overseas Chinese was estimated to be roughly equal to that of the 1.2 billion people in China itself (Seagrave 1995). However, studies that focus primarily on the economic features of diasporas tend to overlook the significant internal disparities in wealth, education and social status. Ray (2003) addresses some of the socio-economic disjunctures between the multi-generational, lower-caste Fiji Indian immigrants to Australia and upper caste Hindu high technology workers who arrive directly from India.

Globalising from below

Richard Falk distinguishes between 'globalisation-from-above' and 'below'. The 'collaboration between leading states and the main agents of capital formation' characterizes the former (1993: 39). Transnational corporations are also major participants in the globalisation of communication. They include global news agencies, giant advertising companies, media and telecommunications corporations as well as non-communications global firms that are engaged in massive cross-border information flows.

'Globalisation-from-below' is carried out mainly by organisations that do not have strong links with governments or large corporations. They include transnational civil society bodies like Amnesty International and Greenpeace and relief agencies such as the International Committee for the Red Cross and Médecins Sans Frontières. Academic and professional associations, religious organisations, diasporic groups etc. also participate in 'globalisation-from-below' by developing lateral communication links between members in various parts of the world. They may not directly oppose international governmental activities or transnational corporations, but they are nevertheless distinct from them.[3]

Instead of dwelling on physically reversing geopolitical configurations of migrations, much of the cultural production of most diasporas involves the creation of imaginative space alongside existing mappings. In the face of the homogenizing forces of globalisation, diasporas, as deterritorialized nations, are seeking ways of 'reterritorialising' and 're-embedding' their identities in other imaginings of space (Lull 1995: 159). Displaced from their homelands, they find that 'Ethnicity is the necessary place or space' (Hall 1997: 184) from which they can speak to counteract dominant discourses. Hall views this process as operating 'on the terrain of "the global postmodern"' (184), which 'is an extremely contradictory space' (187), whereas he acknowledges the danger of extreme nationalism in ethnic assertion he also identifies the immense opportunities for the empowerment of the local, in contrast to the polarized scenario of Benjamin Barber's 'jihad vs. McWorld' (1995).

Notwithstanding the predictions of the declining influence of borders under pressures of globalisation, the spaces of nation-states largely continue to remain exclusive. But diasporas present a significant challenge to this territoriality by seeking to produce their own interstitial spaces that link national and transnational milieus. They make connections between the local and the global, between the colonial and the post-colonial.

The cultural power of British imperialism has been such that African and Asian children being educated in many former colonies tend to know more about the fauna and flora of England than that of their own countries. They are steeped in the details of British history. The old colonial capital of London remains central and the rest peripheral in many minds around the Commonwealth. But this imaginative geography is being increasingly challenged in the contemporary cultural production of diasporas. Claudia Egerer (2001) comments on the writing of Hanif Kureishi (who was born in England and has Pakistani ancestry), saying that he remaps the city with his narrative. He superimposes a postcolonial reading on the metropolitan centre, producing a new geography and new modulations of cultural power. Nevertheless, Eurocentric worldviews still remain globally hegemonic. Diasporic re-imaginings of space do not necessarily displace the dominant geography, but what emerges in vibrant bodies of literature and other arts is the co-existence of a multiplicity of cultural cartographies.

Migrant communities make homes in milieus that are removed from the homeland. John Wise (2000) writes about the ways in which the infusion of a space with one's own rhythms is integral to marking it out as one's home. (Re)territorialisation occurs through sounds and movement – cadencies and action. The languages, accents and rituals spoken and performed in a space establish its cultural connections to its occupants and give it an identity. Diasporas (re)create home by instilling such resonance into the spaces: they do it with their languages, customs, art forms, arrangement of objects and ideas. Their media, especially the electronic, reterritorialize the diaspora through the resonance of electromagnetic frequencies. However, the milieus that diasporas seek to create are not bounded by the borders of nation-states – their rhythms resonate transnationally to mark out the non-terrestrial spaces that stretch out inter-continentally.

Such 'supraterritoriality' (Scholte 1996) of diaspora is created and sustained by imaginatively transforming a milieu – this is not a physical place but an existential location dependent continually on the resonance of cultural practices. Diasporas account for space as an existential location as they seek to redefine and transform their existence from under the historical conditions of colonialism and/or the current exigencies of globalisation-from-above. These dynamics of spatialisation are imaginative; they usually do not involve the appropriation of territory but carry out an engagement with dominant cartographies. The diaspora exists virtually in the relationships maintained in a transnational milieu, held together by and in the intercontinental '"space of flows" – in mass media, telecommunications, computer connections and the like – [which] is a realm where religions, nations, classes, genders, races, sexualities, generations and so on continuously overlap and interrelate to produce complex and shifting identities and affiliations' (Scholte 1996: 597).

Diaspora's media

Diasporic media have sought out the most efficient and cost-effective means of communication due to the relatively small and widely scattered nature of the communities which they serve. Technologies that allow for narrowcasting to target specific audiences rather than those that provide the means for mass communication have generally been favoured. The particular challenges they face in reaching their audiences have spurred ethnic media frequently to be at the leading edge of technology adoption. Many families in the Indian community in Southall, England, obtained VCRs as early as 1978 'well before most households in Britain' (Gillespie 1995: 79).

While authorities in developing and developed countries had expressed fears that digital broadcasting satellites (DBS) would erode their sovereignty by transmitting foreign programming to their populations in unregulated manners, this technology is providing remarkable opportunities for diasporic communities. Ethnic broadcasters, previously having limited access to space on the electromagnetic spectrum in Northern countries, are finding much greater options opening up for them through DBS. For example, in the 1990s, a centre-right government in France actively encouraged the country's main broadcast regulator, the Conseil Supérieur de l'Audiovisuel, to exclude Arabic stations from licensed cable networks. The response of Maghrebi immigrant families was to subscribe in large numbers to DBS services which provide them programming from Arab countries across the Mediterranean Sea (Hargreaves and Mahdjoub 1997).

Diasporic programming using this technology has grown exponentially in the last few years, well ahead of many mainstream broadcasters in some cases. Even as mainstream networks in Europe were making plans to introduce digital broadcasting, the Arab-owned and operated Orbit TV in Rome had begun by 1994 to provide extensive programming via DBS to Arab communities both in Europe and the Middle East. One of the most fascinating uses of DBS technology in the Middle Eastern context is MED-TV, a Kurdish satellite television station (Hassanpour 2003). This is a case of a diaspora within and without the divided homeland attempting to sustain itself and to counter forceful suppression with the use of communications technology. MED-TV faces resistance not only from governments of various states straddling Kurdistan, but also from anti-terrorist police forces in the UK, Belgium and Germany.

Television programs produced in India are broadcast to its diaspora. Strong subscriber bases have developed for channels such as Zee, Sony, Star Plus and B4U (Thuss 2005). They include not only Indians but others with origins in Pakistan, Bangladesh, Sri Lanka, Nepal and Afghanistan. These communities include significant proportions of middle and upper middle class households that are able to pay for multiple services. The channels are carried on international networks like Sky in Europe and Asia as well as other providers such as DISH and ATN in North America. Cable and satellite services in the North have realized the viability of ethnic channels and are making them an integral part of their services.

The transnational diasporic commercial broadcasting infrastructure has become integral to the global economy. Niche marketers are actively using advertising on ethnic radio and television as a way to reach growing minority populations in a time of fragmenting audiences. The largest Spanish-language US network, Univisión has a growing number of stations and has affiliates, and is also carried on hundreds of cable systems in the country with massive viewership in centres with concentrations of Hispanics (Collins 1996: C6; also see Dávila 2001).

Either Univisión or Telemundo, the second-largest Spanish-language network in the US, is available on almost every cable system in Latin America. Local television stations regularly run stories from Univisión or Telemundo's nightly newscasts for their own use, giving these Hispanic American networks a degree of credibility and visibility that their mainstream (English-speaking) US counterparts do not enjoy (Rohter 1996). The picture that Latin Americans see of American society in these North–South news flows is very different from that presented by the mainstream global TV news agencies. Univisión and Telemundo adhere to Latin American news values that favour greater analysis than that offered by mainstream American television.

Diasporas are also making extensive use of the Internet. It seems especially suited to the needs of transnational communities, allowing for relatively easy connections for individuals residing in various continents. The broadcast model of communication, apart from offering limited access to minority groups, is linear, hierarchical and capital intensive. On-line media, on the other hand, allow relatively easier access and are nonlinear, largely non-hierarchical and relatively cheap. The ability to exchange messages with family members and friends on the other side of the planet and to have access to community information almost instantaneously changes the dynamics of diaspora, allowing for qualitatively and quantitatively enhanced linkages.

Diasporic website and blog content largely consists of cultural, heritage, genealogical and religious information. The availability of the technology in developing countries is lagging far behind industrialized ones. Consequently, members of diasporic groups in the North are the most active in producing cultural resources on the Web. A primary motivation on the part of immigrant communities seems to be survival in the face of the overwhelming output of the dominant culture and the limitations of their own access to the cultural industries in countries of settlement.

There appears to be an attempt by diasporic participants in cyberspace to create a virtual community that supposedly eliminates the distances that separate them in the real world. The global dispersion from the home country over a period of several generations is also seemingly reversed by bringing together disparate members of the ethnic group to interact in an electronic 'chat room'. Time and space are erased in this scenario to reconstitute parts of the community and to exchange cultural knowledge held in the diaspora. Chat sites allow far subscribers, many of whom tend to be of particular ethnic, cultural or religious backgrounds, to communicate from any place where they have access to the Internet. Discussions range on topics that include culture, literature, entertainment, politics and current events in the countries of origin and settlement.

With immigrants being able to obtain cultural materials with growing ease from other parts of the world through access to new media, governments are finding it increasingly difficult to compel them to assimilate into the dominant national culture. The current conceptualisation of multiculturalism within the context of the nation-state does not allow for a well-considered response to the transnational contexts in which immigrants live out their lives. Policy makers will have to account for the ways in which the diasporic aspects of individuals' worldviews influence the ways in which they act as citizens of their new countries.

Reconceptualising multiculturalism in the 21st century

Diasporas have grown significantly in recent times, with extended families, friends and business partners settling in separate continents. Their members have been able to maintain contact with each other through contemporary communication technologies and have developed the sense of being global communities. However, the scholarly and media debates on multiculturalism remain almost untouched by the overwhelming evidence of the transnational connections that immigrant individuals and groups maintain. Leading commentators such as Taylor (1992), Kymlicka (1995), Parekh (2000) and Sen (2006) do not go beyond the national context in their respective explorations of multiculturalism. Their critical contributions have significantly advanced the understanding of the sociopolitical factors that have led to the emergence of the policy and its implications on the societies which they have studied. They cite the role of increased transnational migration and they turn towards multiculturalism as a way to deal with inter-ethnic problems. But they all seem to seal the migrants conceptually within the borders of the countries in which they settle. The policy becomes primarily located within the nation-state; multiculturalism is largely expected to serve as a sociopolitical framework to guide inter-cultural relations in the new country not as a way to engage with global realities.

The European Union appears to be the site of the emergence of multiple layers of citizenship (Heater 1999) but is struggling with ways in which it can engage with non-European immigrants. Even as issues such as national values and social cohesion are raised in debates about settling immigrants, very little attention is given to the possible influence of their transnational and cosmopolitan outlooks on the resistance to dominant national discourses. Focused primarily on developing ways to integrate immigrants into the nation, policymakers do not appear to concern themselves with the extra-national worldviews of the latter. Newcomers are expected to adopt the dominant values and culture of their new country in due course, and cut their ties with the old one. This belief goes against the workings of human psychology – an individual's worldview can be modulated but it usually cannot be erased. The socialisation carried out in the formative years influences the rest of one's life.

This is not to say that no one is able to change and adapt to new circumstances. Immigrants have indeed been successful in integrating in their countries of settlement by internalising new social expectations and developing new modes of behaviour. This includes learning the local language, modulating one's accent, internalising the dominant social discourses and even consciously turning away from previous ways of thinking. However, these changes are difficult for people who move to a new country after their formative years. Nevertheless, it is impossible for a person to remain impervious to the norms of the society of settlement if she is to be able to function within it. Even the individuals most resistant to change do undergo some personal transformation.

Prior to the onset of the Internet and satellite television, it was difficult for immigrants to remain in daily contact with the home country. It was therefore possible for policymakers to conceive of a complete assimilation of newcomers into the receiving society. This was achieved to some extent with earlier European immigrants to countries like the US, especially beginning with the second generation. However, the new technologies have now made the 'melting pot' model largely untenable. Inter-continental transportation has also become also much faster and relatively cheaper, enabling migrants to peregrinate frequently between the new and old countries.

What has emerged is a cosmopolitan outlook fostered by a global mobility. Not only are middle and upper class migrants able physically to travel back and forth with some regularity, they can keep in touch with family and friends on a constant basis through the internet-based media. The concept of citizenship with respect to a single country is becoming increasingly strained under these circumstances. People who have diasporic connections around the world tend to view themselves as citizens of the world. They have family and friends in several countries, where they may also conduct business. A significant number of diasporic individuals hold dual and some even multiple citizenships, whereas governments view persons as subjects of specific jurisdictions, members of diasporas (as well as other persons such as members of the transnational corporate elite who are based in various countries for long periods) increasingly view themselves as cosmopolitan citizens (Breckenridge *et al.* 2002).

Several migrant-producing states have realized the value of establishing diaspora policies that mobilize emigrants to invest in the home country and lobby for its interests in the new one (Smith 2000). Various governments, such as those of India and Israel, have developed elaborate policies to engage with their respective global diasporas and have designated cabinet ministers to oversee their implementation. According to Aihwa Ong (1999), East Asian and South-East Asian governments appear to be accommodating diasporic Chinese entrepreneurs who conduct business in their diaspora in these regions. Colombia, the Dominican Republic and Italy permit diasporic members to vote in national elections in home states. A number of the migrant-producing states are actively using transnational media to enhance their respective diasporas' sense of belonging to the transnation.

The system of nation-states is currently undergoing profound changes in the way that it deals with its central goals of territorial domination administrative control, consolidation of collective cultural identity and the achievement of political legitimacy (Benhabib 2002). Various pressures of globalisation, including diasporic transnationalism, are prompting it to revisit these objectives. The transformative changes wrought by new modes of communication and transportation are also forcing a consideration of the deterritorialisation of governance (Held 1999). Multiculturalism, as conceived within traditional notions of the nation-state, is out of step with the thinking about multi-layered forms of cultural attachment that it has helped to put into motion. The multiculturalists who seek to foster policies that respond to contemporary circumstances

> plead for the *pluralization* of cultural identities; they demand the *decentering* of administrative uniformity and the creation of *multiple* legal and jurisdictional hierarchies; they ask for the *devolution*

of democratic power to regions or groups; and they welcome the *weakening* of the bond between continuing territorial residency and citizenship responsibilities.

Benhabib 2002: 181

It appears that it is the outdated multiculturalism policies that have failed in engendering an integrative sense of citizenship for contemporary times, not multiculturalism as a philosophical project.

The exclusive claim that the nation-state (as conceived presently) makes on the loyalty of the individual citizen is at odds with diasporic cosmopolitanism. Supporters of the inwardly-oriented nation-state are concerned about its possible demise if validity is accorded to the transnational linkages of its constituent groups. We appear to be at a historical moment which is demanding a substantial overhauling of the internal and external structuring of the nation-state. It is clear that a major rethinking is necessary in order to address the growing political impasse between the vertical structure of the nation-state and the horizontal pull of transnations.

It seems that the contrived nature of the nation-state is no longer able to maintain the fiction of internal monoliths. Populations' diversity and their global links have been a reality for a long time. Capitalism has brought us to a stage where transnational networks have become necessary to the economic survival of the nation. Even as elites vacillate in their support for globalisation, its infrastructure – particularly transnational media – is knitting the entire planet ever so closely. Migration has also become an integral feature of the contemporary international system. The economies of developed countries would not be able to function without the constant infusion of labour from poorer states, which themselves are increasingly dependent on emigrants' remittances.

In the face of these economic realities, the supporters of the traditional nation-state seek to maintain the purity of their nations. The likes of Samuel Huntington (2004) bewail the perceived loss of Anglo-American identity of the United States as a result of Hispanic immigration. Multiculturalism is viewed as a threat that destroys social cohesion. Rather than 'integration', American policymakers and opinion leaders still talk about 'assimilation' (supposedly into the mythical melting pot). There is a growing antipathy towards those who are viewed as 'unmeltable', such as Muslims.

It is interesting that among the only cases in which government policymakers discuss transnationalism and diaspora seriously are those related to security issues, whereas governments have the necessary task of preventing terrorism, they do not seem to appreciate the need to understand better the nature of diasporas. The contemporary dynamics of globalisation and technological development make it impossible to corral minority groups within borders of countries. Diasporic spaces overlap with other forms of transnational connections. The multiple layering of intercontinental communications networks appears to have become an intrinsic feature of globalisation; diasporic media using satellite and internet technologies are piggybacking on the structures established and maintained by governments and corporations: globalisation-from-above and globalisation-from-below do not always work in opposition.

A special issue of the *Journal of Communication Inquiry* titled 'Communicating the "New Patriotism": What Does It Mean to be a Citizen in a Global Context?', (published in October 2003) 'showed forms of patriotism to be relational and negotiative within contemporary processes of globalisation, rather than emphasising a rise of patriotism at the expense of or as oppositional to global processes' (Gavrilos 2003: 334). Multiculturalism has been viewed by governments as a mode of promoting citizenship. Some policymakers are coming to realize that multiculturalism has to address the increasing cosmopolitanism fostered by the diasporic consciousness if it is to be relevant in the contemporary socio-political and technological environment. Older conceptions of citizenship are becoming increasingly irrelevant with the growing acceptance that individuals have multi-layered identities. The nation-state is slowly coming to be re-conceptualized in accordance with the transnational media, transportation, commercial and social links of its residents in some quarters. However, governments of immigrant-producing and receiving states have yet to address the need to engage in international discussions about the implications of transnational diasporas and contemporary cosmopolitanism for the role of the nation-state in the 21st century. Such deliberations are necessitated not only by the important considerations of citizenship but also its implications for immigration, foreign policy, security and sovereignty.

Notes

1 Multiculturalism became policy in 1971, when it was announced by the Prime Minister in the Canadian parliament. *The Canadian Multiculturalism Act* was passed in 1988, remaining to this day the only full-fledged law on the policy in any country.
2 There are, of course, also notable migrations within continents to the more prosperous countries.
3 Falk tends to limit his conception of 'globalization-from-below' to groups actively involved in countering the influence of governments and large corporations, but I would like to extend this category also to those who do not necessarily do so.

References

Anderson, B. (1983), *Imagined Communities: Reflections on the Origin and Spread of Nationalism*, London: Verso.
Appadurai, A. (1996), *Modernity at Large: Cultural Dimensions of Globalization*, Minneapolis, MN: University of Minnesotta.

Baker, M. (2004), 'Netherlands: Dutch Immigration (Part 1) – The Death Of Multiculturalism', *Radio Free Europe*, http://www.rferl.org/featuresarticle/2004/11/922941ab-4df5-47ef-87da-1d726d9fldb0.html. Accessed 8 April 2006.
Barber, B. (1995), *Jihad vs. McWorld,* New York: Times Books/Random House.
Benhabib, S. (2002), *The Claims of Culture: Equality and Diversity in the Global Era*, Princeton: Princeton University Press.
Bhabha, H. K. (1994), *The Location of Culture*, London: Routledge.
Blaut, J. M. (1993), *The Colonizer's Model of the World: Geographical Diffusionism and Eurocentric History*, New York: Guilford.
Breckenridge, C., Pollock, S., Bhabha, H. and Chakrabarty, D. (eds.) (2002), *Cosmopolitanism*, Durham, NC: Duke University Press.
Bunt, G. R. (2003), *Islam in the Digital Age: E-Jihad, Online Fatwas and Cyber Islamic Environments*, London: Pluto Press.
Collins, G. (1996), 'Advertising: Information Resources Takes Aim at the Ethnic Market, and Nielsen', *New York Times*, Section 3, p. 3.
Cunningham, S. and Nguyen, T. (2003), 'Actually Existing Hybridity: Vietnamese Diasporic Music Video', in K. H. Karim (ed.), *The Media of Diaspora*, London: Routledge, pp. 119–132.
Dávila, A. (2001), *Latinos Inc.: The Marketing and Making of a People*, Berkeley: University of California Press.
De Santis, H. (2003), 'Mi programa es su programa: Tele/visions of a Spanish-language Diaspora in North America', in K. H. Karim (ed.), *The Media of Diaspora*, London: Routledge, pp. 63–75.
Egerer, C. (2001), 'Ambivalent Geographies: The Exotic as Domesticated Other', *Third Text*, 55, pp. 15–28.
Falk, R. (1993), 'The Making of Global citizenship', in J. Brecher, J. Childs and J. Cutler (eds.), *Global Visions: Beyond the New World Order*, Boston: South End Press, pp. 39–50.
Gavrilos, D. (2003), 'Communicating the "New Patriotism": What Does It Mean to Be a Citizen in a Global Context?', *Journal of Communication Inquiry*, 27: 4, pp. 333–336.
Gillespie, M. (1995), *Television, Ethnicity and Cultural Change*, London: Routledge.
Government of Canada, Royal Commission on Bilingualism and Biculturalism. (1970), *Book IV: The Cultural Contributions of the Other Ethnic Groups*, Ottawa: Information Canada.
Hargreaves, A. G. and Mahdjoub, D. (1997), 'Satellite Television Viewing among Ethnic Minorities in France', *European Journal of Communication*, 12: 4, pp. 459–477.
Hassanpour, A. (2003), 'Diaspora, Homeland and Communication Technologies', in K. H. Karim (ed.), *The Media of Diaspora*, London: Routledge, pp. 76–88.
Hall, S. (1997), 'The Local and the Global: Globalization and Ethnicity', in A. McClintock, A. Mufti and E. Shohat (eds.), *Dangerous Liaisons: Gender, Nation, and Postcolonial Perspectives*, Minneapolis: University of Minnesota, pp. 173–187.
Heater, D. (1999), *What is Citizenship?*, London: Polity.
Held, D. (1999), *Global Transformations: Politics, Economics and Culture*, Stanford, CA: Stanford University Press.
Huntington, S. P. (2004), *Who Are We?—The Challenges to America's National Identity*, New York: Simon & Schuster.

Hylarides, P. C. (2005 Feb), 'Multiculturalism in the Netherlands and the Murder of Theo van Gogh', *Contemporary Review*, http://www.findarticles.com/p/articles/mi_m2242/is_1669_286/ai_n13661901. Accessed 8 April 2006.

Jones, G. (2005, Aug. 3), 'Multicultural Britain is not working, says Tory chief', *News Telegraph*, http://www.telegraph.co.uk/news/main.jhtml?xml=/news/2005/08/03/ndavis03.xml. Accessed 8 April 2006.

Kymlicka, W. (1995), *Multicultural Citizenship: A Liberal Theory of Minority Rights*, Oxford: Oxford University Press.

Karim, K. H. (2003, Feb.), 'The Multiculturalism Debate in Canadian Newspapers: The Harbinger of a Political Storm?', *Journal of International Migration Issues*, 3: 3/4, pp. 439–455.

Lull, J. (1995), *Media, Communication, Culture: A Global Approach*, New York: Columbia.

Mandaville, P. (2003), 'Communication and Diasporic Islam: A Virtual Ummah?', in K. H. Karim (ed.), *The Media of Diaspora*, London: Routledge, pp. 135–147.

Ong, A. (1999), *Flexible Citizenship*, Durham, NC: Duke University Press.

Parekh, B. (2000), *Rethinking Multiculturalism: Cultural Diversity and Political Theory*, Cambridge, MA: Harvard University Press.

Ray, M. (2003), 'Nation, Nostalgia and Bollywood: In the Tracks of a Twice-Displaced Community', in K. H. Karim (ed.), *The Media of Diaspora*, London: Routledge, pp. 21–35.

Renan, E. (1990), 'What is Nation?', in H. Bhabha (ed.), *Nation and Narration*, London: Routledge, pp. 8–22.

Roche, M. (2005, Aug. 19), 'Le modèle multicultural britanique en crise', *Le Monde*, http://www.fsa.ulaval.ca/personnel/vernag/eh/F/cause/lectures/mod%E8le%20multiculturel%20britannique.htm. Accessed 8 April 2006.

Rohter, L. (1996, Dec. 15), 'Broadcast News: In Spanish, It's Another Story', *New York Times*, section 4, pp. 1, 6.

Santianni, M. (2003), 'The Movement for a Free Tibet: Cyberspace and the Ambivalence of Cultural Translation', in K. H. Karim (ed.), *The Media of Diaspora*, London: Routledge, pp. 189–202.

Sassen, S. (1996), *Losing Control? Sovereignty In an Age of Globalization*, New York: Columbia University Press.

Seagrave, S. (1995), *Lords of the Rim*, New York: G.P. Putnam.

Sen, A. (2006), *Identity and Violence: The Illusion of Destiny*, New York: WW. Norton.

Scholte, J. A. (1996), 'The Geography of Collective Identities in a Globalizing World', *Review of International Political Economy*, 3: 4, pp. 565–607.

Smith, A. D. (1989), 'The Origins of Nations', *Ethnic and Racial Studies*, 12: 3, pp. 340–367.

Smith, T. (2000), *Foreign Attachments: The Power of Ethnic Groups in Making of American Foreign Policy*, Cambridge: Harvard University Press.

Stratton, J. and Ang, I. (1996), 'On the Impossibility of a Global Cultural Studies: "British" Cultural Studies in an "International Frame"', in D. Morley and K.-H. Chen (eds.), *Stuart Hall: Critical Dialogues in Cultural Studies*, London: Routledge, pp. 361–391.

Taylor, C. (1985), *Multiculturalism and the Politics of Recognition*, Princeton: Princeton University Press.

Thuss, D. (2005), 'The Transnationalization of Television: The Indian Experience', in J. K. Chalaby (ed.), *Transnational Television Worldwide: Towards A New Media Order*, London: I.B. Tauris, pp. 156–172.

Tsaliki, L. (2003), 'Globalisation and Hybridity: The Maintenance of a National and Cultural Identity', in K. H. Karim (ed.), *The Media of Diaspora*, London: Routledge, pp. 163–176.

Wise, J. M. (2000), 'Home: Territory and Identity', *Cultural Studies*, 14: 2, pp. 295–310.

Part 10

GENDER AND THE CYBORG

76

GENDER AND THE INFORMATION SOCIETY

A socially structured silence

Sue Curry Jansen

Source: *Journal of Communication* 39(3) (1989): 196–215.

The price paid for the absence of a critical consciousness about gender in discussions of communications and technology is the reproduction of old patterns of power and privilege in the social distribution of knowledge.

Technological designs are also social designs. Cultural values, economic interests, and political decisions are as integral to their composition as mathematical calculations, motors, cams, circuits, and silicon chips.

During the past decade, debates provoked by commercial and military designs for a coming "information age" or "information society" have become prime sites for international political, economic, and cultural struggles. These struggles, in turn, have provided the auspices and impetus for ambitious agendas of politically engaged critical communications research. Theoretically rich, this research is beginning to deliver systematic assessments of the institutional architecture, economic constituents, technological possibilities, and occupational and class arrangements of emerging national and global structures of information-capitalism. The international character of this research has been especially salutary in exposing the eurocentric values, priorities, and biases that condition the development of designs for global information systems—values such as technical progress, economic growth, productivity, efficiency, and control. Nevertheless, this body of theory and the empirical assessments it has produced have remained largely silent about a crucial dimension of the power-knowledge of the information age: its gender politics.

The sources of this exclusion, this socially structured silence, are both transparent and puzzling. They are transparent because, in a sense, social and linguistic constructions of the term "technology" in Western languages and discourse practices mandate this silence. Even a cursory review of the scholarly literature on technology reveals that constitution of the terms "woman" and "technology" are not separate practices; they are related terms in a vocabulary of power-relations that defines the objects men make and manipulate and the work they do as "technical"; conversely, this vocabulary treats the objects women make and manipulate and the work they do as "nontechnical," "natural," sometimes even "nurturing," "humane," or "humanistic" (23, 60, 63, 84, 96). This practice is also, of course, congruent with theoretical conventions in economics, sociology, and history, which consider men's paid labor as productive and part of a nation's economy, and women's unpaid labor as reproductive and outside calculations of gross national products.

As a result of these constitutive practices, histories of Western technology have been histories of male activities. They examine the tools and techniques that have built industry and advanced warfare. They do not examine birthing, cooking, or child care skills or devices (58, 63, 68, 92, 111). Often these histories are secured by evolutionary assumptions that carry unexamined androcentric (and eurocentric) cargoes. When histories of technology mention women (and they do so rarely), women are usually conceived as "consumers" of technology, as users of telephones, typewriters, and facsimile machines.[1]

In short, it is easy to understand why mainstream debates on technology have ignored the question of gender. The established categories and conventions of Western languages and thought direct attention away from this question. The silence that results is so pervasive and deeply entrenched that feminist writer Jane Caputo (12, p. 487) describes the advanced technologies it produces as "phallotechnologies."

Nevertheless, the unreflective replication of these practices in critical theories and assessments of information technologies is puzzling and counterproductive, for a number of reasons. First, when communications scholars invade territories already occupied by other disciplines, they incur special obligations to survey the communicative features of those territories. When they study technology, they are therefore presumably required to display greater linguistic reflexivity than scientists, engineers, technologists, or historians.

Second, critical communications theorists, especially neo- or post-Marxists and postmodernists, directly and aggressively challenge the Enlightenment-based vocabulary of power-knowledge that supports these linguistic practices (e.g., 21, 25, 81, 94, 99, 100).

Third, many critical communications scholars publicly profess support for the egalitarian goals of feminism. Yet these practices obstruct realization of those goals.

Fourth, critical researchers are interested in what Harry Braverman (10) characterized as "de-skilling" processes in communications industries

(29, 106). The gendering of skills is particularly pronounced in technology-intensive industries, especially computer and other electronics industries (14, 62, 80). Computer industries appear to be undergoing de-skilling processes that are broadening and "feminizing" the bases of their pyramids of power and profit (30, 54, 80).

Fifth, studies of the history and social effects of the computer revolution suggest that the knowledge "lost" in the digitalization of information may be the humanistic knowledge that has preserved many cherished values of Western civilization (18, 64, 85, 107). These are the same values that were marginalized and feminized by gendered discourses on technology (phallotexts?) during the industrial revolution (60, 73, 93, 98, 110).

Sixth, putting the new wine of critical and cultural theory in the old bottles of patriarchal linguistic categories inhibits, perhaps even precludes, the kinds of radical reconceptualizations of structures of everyday life—of authority, difference, community, and relations with the nonhuman environment—valorized by current critical and postmodernist perspectives within communications studies (81). In sum, the absence of a critical consciousness regarding the gendering of technological discourse concedes contestable territory to technological designs that reproduce old patterns of power and privilege.

The socially structured silences supported by gendered vocabularies of power and knowledge are such consistent and persistent furnishings of discussions of technology within the communications literatures that Cheris Kramarae (59, p. ix) has issued "a challenge and invitation to malestream researchers to question, for example, the assumption that men in the West have a location which is separate and adequate for theorizing about communications and technology without consideration of the origin of the imposed hierarchical social divisions of such polar terms as female/male, East/West, and Black/white."

This article will take up Kramarae's challenge, with some caveats. In my view, adequate response to Kramarae's question requires the articulation of new languages, paradigms, and politics for creating and studying technologies. This is work that cuts across disciplines, work that requires an epochal change in consciousness and generations of effort. This article will offer some preliminary reflections on the nature of that work and suggest some resources that may provide productive points of departure. Like the mainstream texts it criticizes, this text is also skewed by its positioning within a Western vantage point. It too contains silences that require critique, correction, and amendment by other "others" (76, 101).[2] Although I am convinced that further development of critical and cultural perspectives in communications is contingent upon adequate theorizations of the gender question, I do not think that viable feminist rethinkings of technology can be achieved without effecting a *partial* truce with malestream research. Mainstream discourse on technology has ignored the world of the everyday, the private sphere, the traditional sites of female-gendered skills; however, within feminist perspectives, the public sphere remains undertheorized (24, 96). This dialectical tension needs to be redressed and used creatively.

At the present juncture in the struggle to articulate new vocabularies for constituting dialogues on technology, feminist choices are limited. To engage in creditable discussions of technology, we must use the language of the authoritative discourses—what Mikhail Bakhtin (2, p. 342) called "the word of the fathers." There are four major ways of coming to terms with this language: (a) surrendering; (b) escaping to the interior, where separate feminist colonies and critical codes can be established; (c) infiltrating the ranks in order to engage in what Umberto Eco (20, p. 135) calls "semiological guerrilla warfare"; or (d) "commuting" between points (b) and (c).[3] In my judgment, the last option is the most responsible posture. The first two, by leaving the boys alone with some very dangerous toys, may increase the risks of ecological and nuclear disaster (e.g., 15, 19, 90). The third approach can stand alone, but it stands in the middle of the dialectical process; it can deconstruct the old ways, but it lacks the creative resources necessary to empower a new vision. The trick, then, is to take from mainstream discourses without being (entirely) taken in by them. This is not an easy task, but it is one that is consistent with the professed dicta of critical and postmodernist cultural theories, which include theoretical, methodological, and ideological reflexivity.[4]

In the remainder of this article, I will try to put some additional teeth in Kramarae's challenge by briefly reviewing some recent feminist deconstructions of the epistemological "location" of white, Western, males. These deconstructions suggest that, like black females from the East, members of the malestream also see from particular vantage point or perspective that influences what and how they see. Then, I will consider some reasons which suggest that the language and models of communications may be especially resistant to displays of the perspectivity of knowledge. Finally, I will identify some ways in which such displays may be used to secure new models of systematic (even "objective" and scientific) knowledge that are responsive to postcolonialist and feminist perspectives.

A virtual revolution in feminist thought about thought has taken place since the publication of Carolyn Merchant's *Death of Nature* in 1980. Recent feminist analyses of the founding texts of modern science have established their historicity and intertextuality as well as their strategic positioning within debates involving church, state, commerce, witchcraft, and alchemy (9, 35, 56, 72).[5] Feminist recoveries of the submerged texts that informed the gender politics of early science demonstrate that scientific reasoning is grounded in metaphors and mythos, drawn from the Inquisition, that were designed to purge male fears of the diabolical powers of witches, place the promises and potions of scientists beyond inquisitors' suspicions, and remove the mystique of "mother" earth so that her resources could be exploited by commerce.

In short, these studies have demonstrated that "nature" is a social category. Its representation in the definitive texts of Western science was constructed from the specific reference point of a particular group of males who were interested in escaping the inquisitor's sword and developing mining resources. By exposing this reference point (and subsequent ones) from which the discourses of Western science have been articulated, feminist critics believe they have established that there is no "organic or natural standpoint" from which any of us can apprehend nature or the social world (33, p. 75; see also 65). This insight has, in turn, led such thinkers as Sandra Harding, Jane Flax, Donna Haraway, Evelyn Fox Keller, Hilary Rose, Susan Bordo, and others to radically problematize established/malestream concepts of observation, empiricism, and objectivity (9, 25, 26, 30, 32, 44, 45, 72, 73).

According to the new feminist epistemologies, the models, theories, and methodologies of modern science and technology bear the scars of their troubled history. Both Baconian empiricism and Cartesian rationalism carry their inscriptions (9, 56, 72). These inscriptions, in turn, skew the kinds of problems that interest scientists and the kinds of methods they use to study these problems (5, 33, 34, 35, 36, 56, 57). The new feminist perspectives trace these inscriptions to what Sandra Harding (35, p. 104) calls the primitive "totemic" of gender; they maintain that gender is the *difference* that has made the difference in the generative categories, rules, and structures of Indo-European languages.[6] They point out that within these languages, woman is constructed as the "other." Man's subjectivity is established by marking its difference from the "objects" of his gaze, desire, affection, or contempt. Woman is conceived as the negative pole in a series of hierarchical oppositions that result from this semiotic occlusion—activity/passivity, culture/nature, head/heart, logos/pathos. Within this code, only those who control the power to name remain unmarked, unmediated, and disembodied (34).

Conceived in this way, gender does not simply classify body types or prescribe norms for their representation; it "inflects an entire universe of objects and behaviors with masculine or feminine attributes, most of which remain unstated" (1, p. 2). Feminist deconstructions of this symbolic economy explode the myth of male "aperspectivity": the claim that the dominant view is the unbiased view. They reject the premise that the "neutral observer" is neutral and neuter (67). In short, they identify the all-seeing eye that informs the objective logics of mainstream science as the eye of the patriarch.

Feminist re-visions of the logic of science are not merely theoretical or meta-theoretical undertakings. Many of the authors of these revisions are practicing scientists. Citing the achievements of Rachel Carson, Barbara McClintock, and Jane Goodall, feminist scientists assume that some forms of inquiry can be better served by attempts to understand and preserve rather than master and control nature. They seek to expand the methods, metaphors, and models of science.

Thus, for example, Ruth Hubbard (47) tells a new story of embodiment. Hubbard reconceives the female egg as an active partner in the process of fertilization rather than as a passive princess waiting patiently for the sperm prince to awaken her from her slumbers. Hubbard looks at what happens to scientific questions when the gender totemic is treated as a null hypothesis: what happens when we look at similarities instead of differences in males and females of the same species.

Sarah Blaffer Hrdy (46) examines the mating behaviors of monkeys and discovers that females are not nearly as discreet, selective, or unappreciative of the pleasures of the flesh as male scientists since Darwin have claimed. Evelyn Fox Keller and Catherine E. Grontowski (57) speculate on what physics would sound or feel like if it had been constructed on aural or tactile instead of the spatial metaphors favored by men. Ann Oakley (83) displays the masculinist assumptions of standard interview protocols in social science and proposes a dialogic approach for research on women that is contiguous with female-gendered communicative patterns.

Except for primatology, however, the feminist epistemological challenge has had little impact on mainstream science (5). Social science has also largely resisted its incursions, except for gender studies, which continue to be marginalized (74).[7] The humanities, however, have proven more hospitable to the new feminist constructions of knowledge. In fields like philosophy, history, and literary theory—fields that have always preserved some space for the "subjective" (in the terms of androcentric discourse, the "feminine") —the feminist challenge has brought about a renewal of creative energies, which, in turn, have opened new areas of inquiry. Within feminist scholarship itself, the authority of the old androcentric and eurocentric models has been permanently displaced. The feminist epistemological critique has demonstrated that, in the words of John Hillman (43, p. 250), "the specific consciousness we call scientific, Western and modern is the long sharpened tool of the masculine mind that has discarded parts of its own substance, calling it 'Eve,' 'female' and 'inferior.' "

Mainstream communications research has been somewhat receptive to reformist efforts that stress the salience of gender-related variables in studies of language patterning, interpersonal, visual, and some facets of organizational communications; however, it has been virtually untouched by attempts to change conventional research designs to accommodate feminist epistemologies (88). Like other disciplines secured by social science orientations, communications is heavily invested in objectivist theories of knowledge: they provide the auspices for its disciplinary boundaries, textual authority, institutional positioning, and funding resources. However, there may be an additional reason for this insularity. The language and models of mainstream communications studies may be especially resistant to displays of the perspectivity of knowledge because of their special relationship to Cartesian concepts of "information."

David Bloor (6) has pointed out that every field has its "origin myth," which it makes major investments in protecting. These myths launder the past. They cleanse the record of the confusions, conflicts, and defeats that accompany the births of all disciplines. They tell more palatable and palpable stories of disciplinary origins, provide props for paradigmatic thinking, endow heirs to the tradition with a collective identity and sense of purpose, and foster temptations to hubris. "In the beginning," many mainstream communications textbooks tell us, there was Claude Shannon's (95) mathematical theory of communications. Everett Rogers (89) explains, "Shannon's information theory in the 1950's offered the potential of unifying not only the field of communications but also the social sciences and other sciences." Alas, a snake appeared in the garden. "When this theoretical approach to communication was institutionalized in U.S. universities," Rogers reports, "it was mainly absorbed into existing departments of speech and journalism, transforming them but also being bifurcated by this placement in an existing university organizational structure." According to Rogers, the result is a "Balkanization of communication research and theory," which produces "a low degree of coherence to communication research" (89, p. 210). But the dream of a unified science of information lives on in the hearts of the faithful (see, e.g., 3; cf. 85).

Subscription to this origin myth is not universal even within the mainstream, and the mainstream itself is becoming increasingly difficult to locate. Nevertheless, the origin myth has had significant currency within the field. Like origin myths in other disciplines, it has provided scholars seeking to distance themselves from the mainstream with a benchmark (and straw man) with which to chart their critical departures. In short, whether as ticket or target, communications scholars have strong attachments to information theory.

Information theory may represent the purest articulation—the exemplary model—of what Susan Bordo (9, p. 439) characterizes as "the Cartesian masculinization of thought." René Descartes (1596–1650) entered Western philosophy at a crucial juncture. The growing influence of mechanistic models and metaphors was undermining the authority of the organic world view that had secured Francis Bacon's (1561–1626) justification of scientific inquiry. The achievements of mechanistic science occurred at the same time that the great "witch craze" swept across Europe, claiming (according to conservative estimates) between 50,000 and 300,000 lives; and, as H. R. Trevor-Roper (102, p. 91) points out, the fury of the craze was not entirely "separable from the intellectual and spiritual life of those years." The Inquisitioners required assurance that scientists were doing God's work. Cartesian dualism provided this assurance by valorizing an approach to inquiry that emphasizes separation and difference, and establishes firm boundaries between man and nature (the "other" that in the gendered inflections of seventeenth-century France also included "woman"). The Cartesian method separates reason and emotion, and extols detached, dispassionate, calculating, and abstract modes of cognition; within the ethos of this quasi-secular form of Puritanism, embodiment became an obstacle to reason. The Cartesian recipe maps the coordinates upon which Shannon defined his mathematical theory of information and Alan Turing devised his theory of computational numbers and conceived of his "logic machine"; their work, in turn, provided partial blueprints for development of the modern digital computer (7, 77).

Realization of the Cartesian dream of a clean machine of reason had profound philosophical, mathematical, theological, political, economic, and social implications. These implications have been extensively explored in the literature on the computer revolution (see, e.g., 7, 18, 26, 75, 77, 103, 107, 108). However, the implications for the gendering of information have been neglected. By relocating the sites of numbers and arithmetic operations from mind to electronic circuits, Shannon and Turing's clean machines reduce the concept of information to the kinds of messages these circuits can accommodate. Magoroh Maruyama (71, p. 29) describes the truncated form of information valorized by information theory as "classificatory information"; he points out that this mode of reasoning is only one of the forms of information routinely used by humans (in the West) to organize and analyze data.[8] Maruyama reports that, unlike their electronic surrogates, human "information processors" also regularly rely upon "relational," "relevance," and "contextual informations" in making sense and reaching decisions.

J. David Bolter (7) and John Durham Peters (85) demonstrate that the information of information theory (Maruyama's "classificatory information") is a distinctly modern, Western, market-oriented construct that is *represented* in discourses of power as the issue of an immutable, universal, evolutionary logic. Nevertheless, the information technologies it produces bear the marks of their social genesis. Thus, for example, Bolter points out that computer operating systems such as MS-DOS, UNIX, and CPM are based upon the rules of the "command" and "control" functions of military hierarchies and business accounting systems.

My analysis of the epistemological and methodological assumptions of information theory indicates that information theory invites recruitment to representation within discourses of power (51; see also 22, 85). The quest for a unified science embraces methodological imperialism in its search for the "one true story"—the master narrative—of human reason. It also engages in a reductionism that would purge all informations except "classificatory information" from inclusion within the master narrative. Thus, for example, artificial intelligence modelers claim that all "interesting" forms of human intelligence can be captured within computer programs (75). The social counterpart of this methodological imperative is an appropriationist logic (the Western gaze) that seeks to master all it surveys—even the extraterrestrial (e.g., the Star Wars weapon system).

My studies of the constituents of "classificatory information" suggest that it is a gendered construct (49, 50, 51). My analyses of the assumptions and rule structures reified by computer logics indicate that "classificatory information" is the kind of information well-educated Western men draw upon most frequently in analyzing data. Using Carol Gilligan's (31) studies of gendered modes of reasoning, I compared the kinds of information that can be accommodated by information theory with the kinds of informations Gilligan's subjects relied upon in reaching moral decisions. Unlike Maruyama, Gilligan reduced reasoning patterns to two major types: what she calls a "morality of rules" and an "ethic of responsibility." She found that men generally relied upon the morality of rules, while women usually referred to an ethic of responsibility in reaching moral decisions.[9] The rules that guide Gilligan's masculine-gendered mode of reasoning are the same rules that construct "classificatory information." Conversely, the principles that guide the ethic of responsibility, Gilligan's feminine-gendered mode of reasoning, are based upon forms of information that cannot be readily accommodated by information theory: what Maruyama called "relevance," "contextual," and "relational informations."

Because Gilligan abstains from rendering a definitive judgment regarding the origins of these gendered differences in reasoning patterns, her findings remain open to essentialist interpretations. My studies and the feminist epistemological studies reviewed in this article generally favor cultural rather than biological interpretations of these differences.[10] They indicate that differential socialization, gendered language structures, and specific events in Western history have played powerful roles in generating these differences; however, they also suggest that these patterns are amenable to intervention and revision. Nevertheless, these studies do support the conclusion that the information of information theory is gendered. That is, they confirm Kramarae's characterization of the mainstream of communications research as a "malestream"; and they provide a warrant for extending feminist semiological warfare to the overfed but undernourished modern concept of "classificatory information."

Current, laudable concerns within social science and education for reforming gender-biased educational practices, gender inequities in access to information technologies, gender-based segmentation of technical skills, and gendered mentoring systems in science and engineering deal only with symptoms. These concerns seldom adequately grasp or treat the causes of these inequities.[11] However, this does not mean that these causes are beyond treatment, nor does it provide *any* warrants for feminist boycotts of information technologies. To the contrary, it recommends nothing less than a renaissance in the ways we conceive, create, code, use, and theorize technologies, gender, information, epistemology, and communications.

The challenges new feminist epistemologies pose to mainstream and critical communications research on the new technologies are, of course, only part of a much larger international and interdisciplinary response to the perceived depletion or corruption of the legacy of the Western Enlightenment. Poststructuralism, postmodernism, and some forms of social constructivism share feminism's skepticism of universal and universalizing claims about existence, language, reason, science, and progress; these perspectives also conceive of their critical projects as forms of resistance to the reified fictions of the naturalized, essentialized *human* of humanism that has historically denied the subjectivity of women, blacks, sexual minorities, and members of non-Western cultures.

In short, a broad and varied intellectual constituency is struggling to articulate epistemological stances that recognize the irreducible differences and radical multiplicity of local cultures. Biologist Donna Haraway (34, p. 579) describes the stakes of this struggle:

> "our" problem is, how to have *simultaneously* an account of radical historical contingency for all knowledge claims and knowing subjects, a critical practice for recognizing our own "semiotic technologies" for making meanings *and* a no-nonsense commitment to faithful accounts of a "real" world, one that can be partially shared and that is friendly to earthwide projects of finite freedom, adequate material abundance, modest meaning in suffering, and limited happiness.

The critique of gendered technologies and information theory developed in this article indicates that existing modernist/masculinist "semiotic technologies" exclude female-gendered beings, modes of reasoning, and skills from their discourses. Poststructuralists such as Jacques Lacan and Jacques Derrida would argue that such exclusions are inescapable; they claim that the feminine is characterized by the impossibility of representation (53, 66). The French feminist version of this argument conceives of language as a "binary trap"; the most radical form of the argument mandates creation of a new language (*l'écriture féminine*) secured in the prelinguistic imagery of female bodily pleasures and drives (53).

Anglo-American feminists nave been less mystical and, in my judgment, more pragmatic in confronting the problem of (mis)representation. They have conceived women's language as a submerged or residual practice residing largely outside of the discourses of power (and theory), but nevertheless integral to the creation and sustenance of the "everyday world" (82, 84, 90, 91, 96). Rather than an empty term in what Hélène Cixous and Catherine

Clément (13) call a "phallogocentric" language, malestream languages and philosophies, as Anglo-American feminists point out, contain well-established conventions for representing women. These conventions inscribe woman as "embodied" (albeit from the limited perspective of the male gaze).

Feminist materialism treats this sexist precedent as a semiotic opportunity —a dialectical opening or staging ground—for making a necessary epistemological correction. As the ones "who are not allowed *not* to have a body," a finite position, and situationally embedded knowledges, female thinkers are well placed within the struggle to articulate responsible post-Cartesian and perhaps postmodern theories of knowledge (34, p. 575).[12] Haraway (34, p. 580) describes the paradox: "We need the power of modern critical theories of how meanings and bodies get made, not in order to deny meanings and bodies, but in order to build meanings and bodies that have a chance for life."[13] In short, feminist critics need to use these critical theories to document the embodiment of male knowledge, including what Nancy Hartsock (38) describes as abstract masculinity.

The immediate feminist linguistic, artistic, and technological project requires women to claim the power to reinscribe and re-present women's experience of embodiment and skill.[14] The larger feminist, poststructuralist, and postmodernist epistemological projects require recognition of the embodiment of all knowledge: recognition that white men do not have the eyes of gods or cyclops. Like the vision of women, walleyed pike, and turkey vultures, the vision of human male is embodied, finite, and situationally embedded. No one sees from nowhere. Men, even accomplished scholars like Bacon, Descartes, Turing, and Shannon, view the world from specific, human, vantage points. Therefore, we require epistemologies that can account for positioning: what Haraway calls "situated" or "embodied" knowledges. We need to be able to locate the sources of all knowledge claims in order to rationally assess their truth value. Recognition of the situational embeddedness of knowledge does not require acceptance of relativism or rejection of the quest for "objective" knowledge. Haraway (34, p. 584) points out that

> the alternative to relativism is not totalization and single vision, which is always finally the unmarked category whose power depends on systematic narrowing and obscuring. The alternative to relativism is partial, locatable, critical knowledges sustaining the possibility of webs of connections called solidarity in politics and shared conversations in epistemology. Relativism is a way of being nowhere while claiming to be everywhere equally. The "equality" of positioning is a denial of responsibility and critical inquiry. Relativism is the perfect mirror twin of totalization in the ideologies of objectivity; both deny the stakes in location, embodiment, and partial perspective; both make it impossible to see well. Relativism

and totalization are both "god tricks" promising vision from everywhere and nowhere equally and fully, common myths in rhetorics surrounding Science. But it is precisely in the politics and epistemology of partial perspectives that the possibility of sustained, rational, objective inquiry rests.

Accepting epistemologies that recognize the embodiment and situational and linguistic embeddedness of knowledge does not require rejecting science. To the contrary, it demands finally that we display fidelity to a long-professed but seldom-honored covenant of malestream science: the idea that science is an ongoing, open-ended process that is never subject to final closure, a process that is fueled by criticism and delighted by surprise. Within the objectivity of situated knowledge, there are no unproblematic "objects" (34). All objects and observations are mediated by language, culture, and vantage points. The purpose of conducting semiological guerrilla warfare within the territories of mainstream science is not to bring down the house of science but to remodel and expand it: to create what Harding (35, pp. 243–251) calls a "successor science."

What would this successor science do for communications studies? It would open up an enormous array of new research questions, and it would radically alter the ways we approach and frame those questions. It would make epistemological and linguistic reflexivity routine features of all our inquiries. It would restore methodology to the privileged position it held in nineteenth-century articulations of warrants for the "human sciences" (17, 86). It would not require wholesale rejection of the achievements of mainstream theory and research. The vision that secures the achievements of Bacon, Descartes, Darwin, Turing, and Shannon is skewed, partial, and incomplete, but it is also extraordinarily acute, insightful, and productive. A successor science would not discard the man with his myopia; however, it would require regrounding and resituating the claims of mainstream science within a responsible theory of knowledge. That is, it would provide a warrant for fully embracing what Bloor (6, p. 1) calls "the strong program" in the sociology of knowledge.

This successor science would reopen the questions and perhaps reclaim the values marginalized by the twin triumphs of industrialism and instrumental rationality. Instead of settling for the fast foods of the easily processed and encoded message systems of "classificatory information," it would provide entry to the lavish banquet of research possibilities provided by more holistic reintegrations of "classificatory," "contextual," "relational," "relevance," and other information and communicative modes and practices. It would empower ongoing interrogations of the design codes and communicative models embodied in plans for global information systems. In sum, it would do what male critics of instrumentalism such as Max Weber,

Karl Jaspers, Karl Mannheim, Max Horkheimer, Theodor Adorno, Lewis Mumford, and Jürgen Habermas have long recommended: subordinate instrumental or "functional" forms of rationality to the claims of "substantive" rationality (44, 45, 52, 69, 78, 105). That is, it would require us to reflect upon and justify the ends as well as the means of technological decisions.

What kinds of information technologies would a successor science support? Beyond debates related to the future of reproductive technologies, feminist theory has not yet directly addressed this question. Nevertheless, informed speculation is possible. Technologies are extensions of structures of power and capital as well as derivatives of scientific discourses. Women and men in Western cultures have, of course, been differentially situated in relation to structures of wealth and power.

As a result of their subordinate position in these relations, women have developed alternative information networks and conceived of alternative social designs, e.g., witchcraft, keening rites, old wives' tales, midwifery, motherwit, communal laundering activities, sewing circles, moral uplift movements, and consciousness-raising groups. They have created and circulated handcrafted information systems: recipes, home remedies, samplers, quilts, letters, publications, performances, and works of art. Women have also "misused"/reconfigured malestream information technologies to serve alternative purposes. Thus, for example, Lana Rakow (87) points out that the telephone was initially conceived as a tool of business; American women transformed it into a household necessity. Judy Smith and Ellen Balka (97) report that a similar process is at work on a much smaller scale today as women reconfigure computer networking to accommodate feminist "chatting." Feminist-informed technologies would presumably incorporate elements drawn from these alternative networks, designs, artifacts, and uses.

Female-gendered articulations of principles of social order tend to rely on decentralized, egalitarian decision-making processes; they emphasize personal responsibility and interactional processes rather than formal rules; they treat skills and knowledge as resources to be pooled to enhance group efforts; they avoid hierarchical arrangements and formal divisions of labor; when divisions of labor are introduced, vertical rather than horizontal structures are often adopted so that creative and routine aspects of task forces can be distributed among all members (8, 24).

These principles reflect gendered differences in orientations to power and authority, where men in groups assume that a general, captain, coach, or dean will lead the charge, women usually conceive of power as a process rather than a privilege of office or person. Thus, for example, conceiving of power from a feminist perspective, Hartsock defines it in terms of empowerment: "To lead is to be at the center of a group rather than in front of others" (37, p. 118).

A feminist design aesthetic would presumably favor development of decentralized, egalitarian, accessible, process-oriented information technologies that advance expressive as well as instrumental values (48, 90, 91). Such an aesthetic would subvert, invert, or divert the design logic that has fostered development of the capital-intensive information systems which currently facilitate global control systems. It would challenge the single-minded, malestream commitment to what Mumford (78) calls "authoritarian technics," system-centered, immensely powerful, but inherently unstable technologies. Instead, a feminist design aesthetic would presumably seek to realize the telos of "democratic technics": it would articulate social designs that incorporate human-centered, diverse, resourceful, and durable technologies.[15]

A design aesthetic that is "friendly to earthwide projects of finite freedom, adequate material abundance, modest meaning in suffering, and limited happiness" cannot simply substitute one partial perspective for another. We face problems that require global action: the nuclear threat, environmental contamination, world hunger, global warming. Instrumental thinking created these problems, and instrumental thinking will be required to redress them; but, unless instrumentalism is resituated within grammars of human motives, relationships, values, concepts of community, and social responsibility, we are all imperiled by the emerging global structures of information-capitalism.

T. S. Eliot asked,

> Where is the life we have lost in living,
> Where is the wisdom we have lost in knowledge,
> Where is the knowledge we have lost in information?

A successor science urges us to find out.

Notes

1 For a provocative interpretation of the multiple connotations of the coding of women as "consumers" of technologies, see Campbell and Wheeler (11).
   Even some revisionary histories of technology unreflexively adopt mainstream framing conventions that render women invisible. Thus, for example, a 1987 volume entitled *The Social Construction of Technological Systems* (4) ignores the question of gender except for brief references to women as a "social group" that may require special consideration in explaining some parts of the development of the bicycle.
2 Constitution of the category of non-Western peoples as other "others" is problematic. Within the writings of white feminists, this discursive practice replicates the appropriationist frames of white, Western, masculinist logic (cf. 76).
3 The "commuter" image is developed by Bette Kauffman (55) in describing the psychic and practical strategies women artists use in pursuing careers within male-dominated art worlds.
4 An excellent demonstration of the advantages of this kind of "commuting" is provided by Carol Cohn (15) in her provocative deconstruction and critique of the role played by metaphors of sex and death in articulations of the "rational

world" of defense intellectuals. Cohn uses the trope of a spy to retain a critical perspective while traveling between the two worlds of feminism and militarism. In my own studies of the language of the artificial intelligence movement (49, 50, 51), I have found that "commuting" provides insulation against the traps of technical *cum* promotional languages, stimulates imagination by juxtaposing alien worlds, and precludes premature foreclosures of critical momentum.

5 My brief assay of the growing literature on gender, science, and epistemology cannot begin to do justice to the diversity or complexity of the arguments articulated by feminist scientists, historians of science, and philosophers. Some essential sources are Bleier (5), Bordo (9), Flax (27, 28), Haraway (33, 34), Harding (35), Harding and Hintikka (36), Keller (56), Keller and Grontowski (57), Merchant (72), and Rose (90, 91).

6 This claim is secured in the linguistic postulate which asserts that phonemes and signs achieve intelligibility only through difference; in Saussure's words, "whatever distinguishes one sign from the others constitutes it" (quoted in 40, p. 28).

7 In sociology, however, this may be changing; consider Hess's (42) 1989 Presidential Address to the Eastern Sociological Association.

8 Maruyama (71, p. 29) lists the following epistemological assumptions as constituent features of "classificatory information": "(1) the universe consists of substances or objects which obey the law of identity and mutual exclusiveness and can be classified into a hierarchy of categories, subcategories, and supercategories; (2) the information value of a 'message' increases with the categorical specification of the message; or a message's information value is greater if it describes an event which has a lower probability (for example, 'it snowed in Florida in summer' has a higher information value than 'it snowed in Quebec during the winter'); (3) a piece of information has an objective meaning which is universally understandable, without reference to other pieces of information; (4) discrepancies within messages or differences between messages must have been caused by error; therefore, the discrepant positions should be discarded as inaccurate."

9 Within Gilligan's (31) scheme, the "morality of rules" is based on the following assumptions: thinking is goal-oriented; a hierarchical order of (universal) rules guides decision making; decisions are made by identifying available means and applying the rules to identify the appropriate (moral/utilitarian) choice; available means can be articulated; articulation of means involves resolution of ambiguities; the hierarchy of rules is used to infer relations among alternatives; and the rules are used as templates for understanding new, unusual, or ambiguous situations. Principles of justice, equality, and fairness are formalized in the rules; decision making is conceived as an attempt to realize these values. In contrast, the "ethic of responsibility" is embedded in "web-like relations" rather than hierarchies or formal rules; it emphasizes contextual reasoning and equivocation; stresses care, attachment, affiliation, and interdependence; conceives of power as nurturance; embraces principles of equity and nonviolence; and defines self in relationships with others. Both of these modes of reasoning are systematic, internally consistent, and rational, but they frequently lead to different decisions.

10 Monique Wittig (109, p. 10) forcefully asserts the sociological argument: "The *ideology of sexual difference* functions as censorship in our culture by masking, on the ground of nature, the *social opposition between men and women*. Masculine/feminine, male/female are the categories which serve to conceal the fact that the difference is social" (emphases in original). Whether the origins are in biology, culture, or both, feminist interventions have demonstrated that androcentric texts and practices are subject to revision.

11 Thus, for example, Sherry Turkle's (104, pp. 41–61) studies of computational reticence suggest that for some women technophobia may be partly based in their discomfort with the martial language and macho metaphors of hackers. For example, women may be repelled by concepts like "sport death"; they may prefer to "communicate" rather than "command." Turkle sees this female computational reticence as a transitional phenomenon that will disappear as female socialization offers greater opportunities to interact with formal systems. Because Turkle believes that users impute their own meanings to what she calls "intimate machines," she is optimistic about this outcome. I am less sanguine. Users do indeed bring their own meanings to machines, but the designs of information machines also set limits. That is, they may exercise a kind of ersatz Sapir-Whorf effect whereby some meanings and uses can be much more readily accommodated than others. Some users may create their own codes, but most do not. The kind of accommodation to formal systems Turkle anticipates may be an accommodation to the appropriationist logic valorized by Minsky (75), Moravec (77), and others.

12 Feminists give postmodernism a mixed review. Some readily embrace what Teresa de Lauretis (16, p. x) describes as "a possible love affair between feminism and postmodernism." Others (cf. 28, 33, 35) embrace it with some qualifications. Still others (cf. 39, 41) rigorously reject it. Hawkesworth (41, p. 557) succinctly states the feminist case against postmodernism: "At a moment when the preponderance of rational and moral argument sustains prescriptions for women's equality, it is a bit too cruel a conclusion and too reactionary a political agenda to accept that reason is impotent, that equality is impossible. Should postmodernism's seductive text gain ascendancy, it will not be an accident that power remains in the hands of the white males who currently possess it.... In confrontations with power, knowledge and rational argumentation alone will not secure victory, but feminists can use them strategically to subvert male dominance and to transform oppressive institutions and practices."

13 George Lakoff's (61) studies of language and metaphor also make a strong case for developing a theory of language based upon embodiment; his argument is developed without reference to the feminist literature.

14 This project is, of course, well under way in literature and the arts. It is making significant inroads in discourses on reproduction and reproductive technologies (cf. 70). Feminist film theory and filmmaking has also been influenced by this project. Thus, for example, Teresa de Lauretis's (16) deconstruction of the male voyeuristic gaze of film technologies and conventions has inspired some experimental feminist filmmakers to articulate feminist alternatives.

15 Among historians of technology, Mumford (78, 79) is singular in recognizing the gendered constituents of technological designs; he associates androcentric cultures and technologies with authoritarian politics and conversely relates the ascendancy of "the feminine principle" to the development of democratic technics. Moreover, he does so within a conceptual framework that survives the test of feminist critique (cf. 92).

References

1 Armstrong, Nancy. "The Gender Bind: Women and the Disciplines." *Genders* 3, Fall 1988, pp. 1–23.

2 Bakhtin, Mikhail. *The Dialogic Imagination.* Austin: University of Texas Press, 1981.

3. Beniger, James R. *The Control Revolution.* Cambridge, Mass.: Harvard University Press, 1986.
4. Bijkei, Wiebe E., Thomas P. Hughes, and Trevor Pinch (Eds.). *The Social Construction of Technological Systems.* Cambridge, Mass.: MIT Press, 1987.
5. Bleier, Ruth (Ed.) *Feminist Approaches to Science.* New York: Pergamon Press, 1986.
6. Bloor, David. *Knowledge and Social Imagery.* London: Routledge & Kegan Paul, 1977.
7. Bolter, J. David. *Turing's Man: Western Culture in the Computer Age.* Chapel Hill: University of North Carolina Press, 1984.
8. Bookman, Ann and Sandra Morgen (Eds.). *Women and the Politics of Empowerment.* Philadelphia: Temple University Press, 1988.
9. Bordo, Susan. "The Cartesian Masculinization of Thought." *Signs* 11(3), 1986, pp. 439–456.
10. Braverman, Harry. *Labor and Monopoly Capital: The Degradation of Work in the Twentieth Century.* New York: Monthly Review Press, 1974.
11. Campbell, Beatrix and Wendy Wheeler. "Filofaxions." *Marxism Today*, December 1988, pp. 32–33.
12. Caputo, Jane. "Seeing Elephants: The Myths of Phallotechnology." *Feminist Studies* 14(3), Fall 1988, pp. 487–524.
13. Cixous, Hélène and Catherine Clément. *The Newly Born Woman.* Minneapolis: University of Minnesota Press, 1986.
14. Cockburn, Cynthia. *Machinery of Dominance: Women, Men and Technical Know-How.* London: Pluto Press, 1985.
15. Cohn, Carol. "Sex and Death in the Rational World of Defense Intellectuals." *Signs* 12(4), 1987, pp. 687–718.
16. de Lauretis, Teresa. *Technologies of Gender: Essays on Theory, Film, and Fiction.* Bloomington: Indiana University Press, 1987.
17. Dilthey, Wilhelm. *Pattern and Meaning in History.* Edited by H. P. Rickman. New York: Harper & Row, 1962.
18. Dreyfus, Hubert L. *What Computers Can't Do: The Limits of Artificial Intelligence.* New York: Harper & Row, 1979.
19. Easlea, Brian. *Fathering the Unthinkable: Masculinity, Scientists and the Nuclear Arms Race.* London: Pluto Press, 1983.
20. Eco, Umberto. *Travels in Hyper-Reality.* New York: Harcourt Brace Jovanovich, 1986.
21. Edelman, Murray. *Political Language: Words that Succeed and Politics that Fail.* New York: Academic Press, 1977.
22. Edwards, Paul N. "Border Wars: The Science and Politics of Artificial Intelligence." *Radical America* 19(6), 1985, pp. 39–50.
23. Eisenstein, Zillah (Ed.). *Capitalist Patriarchy and the Case for Socialist Feminism.* New York: Monthly Review Press, 1979.
24. Ferguson, Kathy. *The Feminist Case Against Bureaucracy.* Philadelphia: Temple University Press, 1984.
25. Finlay, Marike. *Powermatics: A Discursive Critique of New Communications Technology.* London: Routledge & Kegan Paul, 1987.
26. Fjermedal, Grant. *The Tomorrow Makers: A Brave New World of Living-Brain Machines.* New York: Macmillan, 1986.

27 Flax, Jane. "Political Philosophy and Patriarchal Unconscious." In Sandra Harding and Merrill B. Hintikka (Eds.), *Discovering Reality.* Dordrecht: D. Reidel, 1983.
28 Flax, Jane. "Postmodernism and Gender Relations in Feminist Theory." *Signs* 12, Summer 1987, pp. 621–643.
29 Freiberg, J. W. *The French Press: Class, State and Ideology.* New York: Praeger, 1981.
30 Garson, Barbara. *The Electronic Sweatshop.* New York: Simon and Schuster, 1988.
31 Gilligan, Carol. *In a Different Voice.* Cambridge, Mass.: Harvard University Press, 1982.
32 Habermas, Jürgen. *Knowledge and Human Interests.* Boston: Beacon Press, 1971.
33 Haraway, Donna. "A Manifesto for Cyborgs: Science, Technology, and Socialist Feminism in the 1980s." *Socialist Review* 80, 1985, pp. 65–107.
34 Haraway, Donna. "Situated Knowledge: The Science Question in Feminism and the Privilege of Partial Perspective." *Feminist Studies* 14(3), 1988, pp. 575–599.
35 Harding, Sandra. *The Science Question in Feminism.* Ithaca, N.Y.: Cornell University Press, 1986.
36 Harding, Sandra and Merrill B. Hintikka (Eds.). *Discovering Reality.* Dordrecht: D. Reidel, 1983.
37 Hartsock, Nancy. "Staying Alive." In *Building Feminist Theory: Essays From Quest.* New York: Longman, 1981, pp. 117–118.
38 Hartsock, Nancy. *Money, Sex, and Power: Toward a Feminist Historical Materialism.* New York: Longman, 1983.
39 Haug, Frigga et al. *Female Sexualization.* London: Verso, 1987.
40 Hawkes, Terrence. *Structuralism and Semiotics.* Berkeley: University of California Press, 1977.
41 Hawkesworth, Mary E. "Knowers, Knowing, Known: Feminist Theory and Claims of Truth." *Signs* 14(3), Spring 1989, pp. 533–557.
42 Hess, Beth B. "Beyond Dichotomy: Making Distinctions and Recognizing Differences." Presidential address to the Eastern Sociological Society, Boston, 1989.
43 Hillman, James. *The Myth of Analysis.* New York: Harper & Row, 1972.
44 Horkheimer, Max. *Eclipse of Reason.* New York: Seabury Press, 1974.
45 Horkheimer, Max and Theodor W. Adorno. *Dialectic of Enlightenment.* New York: Herder and Herder, 1972.
46 Hrdy, Sarah Blaffer. "Empathy, Polandry, and the Myth of the Coy Female." In Ruth Bleier (Ed.), *Feminist Approaches to Science.* New York: Pergamon Press, 1986, pp. 119–146.
47 Hubbard, Ruth, Mary Sue Henifin, and Barbara Fried. *Biological Woman—The Convenient Myth.* Cambridge, Mass.: Schenkman, 1982.
48 Jagger, Alison M. "Love and Knowledge: Emotion in Feminist Epistemology." *Inquiry* 32(2), June 1989, pp. 161–176.
49 Jansen, Sue Curry. "Science, Gender, and a Feminist Sociology of Science: The Case of Artificial Intelligence." Paper presented to the American Sociological Association, Chicago, 1987.
50 Jansen, Sue Curry. "The Ghost in the Machine: Artificial Intelligence and Gendered Thought Patterns." *Resources for Feminist Research/Documentation sur la Recherche Feminist* 17(4), December 1988, pp. 4–7.

51 Jansen, Sue Curry. "Mind Machines, Myth, Metaphor, and Scientific Imagination." Paper presented to the International Communication Association, San Francisco, May 1989.
52 Jaspers, Karl. *Man in the Modern Age.* Garden City, N.Y.: Anchor Books, 1957.
53 Juncker, Clara. "Writing (With) Cixous." *College English* 50(4), April 1988, pp. 424–436.
54 Karpf, Anne. "Recent Feminist Approaches to Women and Technology." In Maureen McNeil (Ed.), *Gender and Expertise.* London: Free Association Books, 1987.
55 Kauffman, Bette J. "'Woman Artist': Communicating Social Identity." Dissertation in progress, Annenberg School of Communications, University of Pennsylvania, 1989.
56 Keller, Evelyn Fox. *Reflections on Gender and Science.* New Haven, Conn.: Yale University Press, 1985.
57 Keller, Evelyn Fox and Catherine E. Grontowski. "The Mind's Eye." In Sandra Harding and Merrill B. Hintikka (Eds.), *Discovering Reality.* Dordrecht: D. Reidel, 1983.
58 Kramarae, Cheris. "Gotta Go Myrtle, Technology's at the Door." In Cheris Kramarae (Ed.), *Technology and Women's Voices: Keeping in Touch.* New York: Routledge & Kegan Paul, 1988.
59 Kramarae, Cheris. "Preface." In Cheris Kramarae (Ed.), *Technology and Women's Voices: Keeping in Touch.* New York: Routledge & Kegan Paul, 1988.
60 Kuhn, Annette and Ann Marie Wolpe (Eds.). *Feminism and Materialism: Women and Modes of Production.* London: Routledge & Kegan Paul, 1978.
61 Lakoff, George. *Women, Fire, and Dangerous Things: What Categories Reveal About the Mind.* Chicago: University of Chicago Press, 1987.
62 Liff, Sonia. "Gender Relations in the Construction of Jobs." In Maureen McNeil (Ed.), *Gender and Expertise.* London: Free Association Books, 1987.
63 Linn, Pam. "Gender Stereotypes, Technology Stereotypes." In Maureen McNeil (Ed.), *Gender and Expertise.* London: Free Association Books, 1987.
64 Lyotard, Jean-François. *The Postmodern Condition: A Report on Knowledge.* Minneapolis: University of Minnesota Press, 1984.
65 MacCormack, Carol P. "Nature, Culture and Gender: A Critique." In Carol P. MacCormack and Marilyn Strathern (Eds.), *Nature, Culture and Gender.* Cambridge: Cambridge University Press, 1980.
66 McDermott, Patricia. "Post-Lacanian French Feminist Theory: Lucy Irigaray." *Women and Politics* 7(3), Fall 1987, pp. 47–64.
67 MacKinnon, Catherine A. "Feminism, Marxism, Method and the State: An Agenda for Theory." *Signs* 7(3), Spring 1982, pp. 515–544.
68 McNeil, Maureen (Ed.). *Gender and Expertise.* London: Free Association Books, 1987.
69 Mannheim, Karl. *Ideology and Utopia.* New York: Harcourt, Brace, 1936.
70 Martin, Emily. *The Woman in the Body: A Cultural Analysis of Reproduction.* Boston: Beacon Press, 1987.
71 Maruyama, Magoroh. "Information and Communication in Poly-Epistemological Systems." In Kathleen Woodward (Ed.), *The Myths of Information.* Milwaukee: University of Wisconsin Press, 1980, pp. 28–40.

72 Merchant, Carolyn. *The Death of Nature: Women, Ecology and the Scientific Revolution.* New York: Harper & Row, 1980.
73 Miller, Jean Baker. *Toward a New Psychology of Women.* London: Penguin, 1978.
74 Millman, Marcia and Rosabeth Moss Kanter. *Another Voice: Feminist Perspectives on Social Life and Social Science.* Garden City, N.Y.: Anchor Doubleday, 1975.
75 Minsky, Marvin. *Society of Mind.* New York: Simon and Schuster, 1987.
76 Mohanty, Chandra. "Under Western Eyes." *Boundary* 2/3, 1984, pp. 333–358.
77 Moravec, Hans. *Mind Children: The Future of Robot and Human Intelligence.* Cambridge, Mass.: Harvard University Press, 1988.
78 Mumford, Lewis. "Authoritarian and Democratic Technics." *Technology and Culture* 5(1), Winter 1964, pp. 1–8.
79 Mumford, Lewis. *Technics and Civilization.* New York: Harcourt, Brace, 1964 [1934].
80 Nash, Jane and Maria Patricia Fernandez-Kelly. *Women, Men and the International Division of Labor.* Albany: State University of New York Press, 1983.
81 Nelson, Cary and Lawrence Grossberg. *Marxism and the Interpretation of Culture.* Urbana: University of Illinois Press, 1988.
82 Oakley, Ann. *The Sociology of Housework.* New York: Pantheon, 1975.
83 Oakley, Ann. "Interviewing Women: A Contradiction in Terms." In Helen Roberts (Ed.), *Doing Feminist Research.* London: Routledge & Kegan Paul, 1981.
84 O'Brien, Mary. *Reproducing the World: Essays in Feminist Theory.* Boulder, Colo.: Westview Press, 1989.
85 Peters, John Durham. "Information: Notes Toward a Critical History." *Journal of Communication Inquiry* 12(2), 1988, pp. 9–23.
86 Polanyi, Michael. *The Study of Man.* Chicago: University of Chicago Press, 1963.
87 Rakow, Lana. "Women and the Telephone: The Gendering of a Communications Technology." In Cheris Kramarae (Ed.), *Technology and Women's Voices: Keeping in Touch.* New York: Routledge & Kegan Paul, 1988, pp. 207–228.
88 Rakow, Lana. "From the Feminization of Public Relations to the Promise of Feminism." Paper presented to the International Communication Association, San Francisco, May 1989.
89 Rogers, Everett M. "Communication: A Field of Isolated Islands of Thought." In Brenda Dervin, Lawrence Grossberg, Barbara J. O'Keefe, and Ellen Wartella (Eds.), *Rethinking Communication, Volume 1: Paradigm Issues.* Newbury Park, Cal.: Sage, 1989.
90 Rose, Hilary. "Hand, Brain and Heart: A Feminist Epistemology for the Natural Sciences." *Signs* 9(1), 1983, pp. 73–90.
91 Rose, Hilary. "Beyond Masculinist Realities: A Feminist Epistemology for the Sciences." In Ruth Bleier (Ed.), *Feminist Approaches to Science.* New York: Pergamon Press, 1986.
92 Rothschild, Joan. "Introduction: Why Machina Ex Dea?" In Joan Rothschild (Ed.), *Machina Ex Dea: Feminist Perspectives on Technology.* New York: Pergamon Press, 1983.
93 Rowbotham, Sheila. *Hidden from History: Rediscovering Women in History from the Seventeenth Century to the Present.* New York: Random House, 1974.

94 Schiller, Herbert I. *Who Knows: Information in the Age of the Fortune 500.* Norwood, N.J.: Ablex, 1981.
95 Shannon, Claude. "The Mathematical Theory of Communication." In Claude Shannon and Warren Weaver, *The Mathematical Theory of Communication.* Urbana: University of Illinois Press, 1964 [1948].
96 Smith, Dorothy E. *The Everyday World as Problematic: A Feminist Sociology.* London: Open University/Milton Keynes, 1988.
97 Smith, Judy and Ellen Balka. "Chatting on a Feminist Computer Network." In Cheris Kramarae (Ed.), *Technology and Women's Voices: Keeping in Touch.* New York: Routledge & Kegan Paul, 1988, pp. 82–97.
98 Smith-Rosenberg, Carroll. "The Feminist Reconstruction of History." *Academe,* September–October 1983, pp. 26–37.
99 Smythe, Dallas. *Dependency Road: Communications, Capitalism, Consciousness, and Canada.* Norwood, N.J.: Ablex, 1981.
100 Smythe, Dallas. "Needs Before Tools? The Illusions of Electronic Democracy." Paper presented to the International Communication Association, Honolulu, May 1985.
101 Spivak, Gayatri Chakravorty. *In Other Worlds: Essays in Cultural Politics.* New York: Routledge, 1988.
102 Trevor-Roper, H. R. *The European Witch-Craze of the Sixteenth and Seventeenth Centuries.* New York: Harper & Row, 1969.
103 Turkle, Sherry. *The Second Self: Computers and the Human Spirit.* New York: Simon and Schuster, 1984.
104 Turkle, Sherry. "Computational Reticence: Why Women Fear the Intimate Machine." In Cheris Kramarae (Ed.), *Technology and Women's Voices: Keeping in Touch.* New York: Routledge & Kegan Paul, 1988.
105 Weber, Max. *The Theory of Social and Economic Organization.* Glencoe, Ill.: Free Press, 1964.
106 Webster, Frank and Kevin Robins. *Information Technology: A Luddite Analysis.* Norwood, N.J.: Ablex, 1986.
107 Weizenbaum, Joseph. *Computer Power and Human Reason.* San Francisco: W. H. Freeman, 1976.
108 Wiener, Norbert. *God and Golem, Inc. A Comment on Certain Points Where Cybernetics Impinges on Religion.* Cambridge, Mass.: MIT Press, 1964.
109 Wittig, Monique. "On the Social Contract." *Feminist Issues* 9(1), Spring 1989, pp. 2–12.
110 Zaretsky, Eli. *Capitalism, the Family and Personal Life.* London: Pluto Press, 1976.
111 Zimmerman, Jan. *The Technological Woman: Interfacing with Tomorrow.* New York: Praeger, 1983.

77

A CYBORG MANIFESTO

Science, technology, and socialist-feminism in the late twentieth century[1]

Donna J. Haraway

Source: Donna J. Haraway (1991) *Symians, Cyborgs, and Women: The Reinvention of Nature*, New York: Routledge, pp. 149–82.

An ironic dream of a common language for women in the integrated circuit

This chapter is an effort to build an ironic political myth faithful to feminism, socialism, and materialism. Perhaps more faithful as blasphemy is faithful, than as reverent worship and identification. Blasphemy has always seemed to require taking things very seriously. I know no better stance to adopt from within the secular-religious, evangelical traditions of United States politics, including the politics of socialist feminism. Blasphemy protects one from the moral majority within, while still insisting on the need for community. Blasphemy is not apostasy. Irony is about contradictions that do not resolve into larger wholes, even dialectically, about the tension of holding incompatible things together because both or all are necessary and true. Irony is about humour and serious play. It is also a rhetorical strategy and a political method, one I would like to see more honoured within socialist-feminism. At the centre of my ironic faith, my blasphemy, is the image of the cyborg.

A cyborg is a cybernetic organism, a hybrid of machine and organism, a creature of social reality as well as a creature of fiction. Social reality is lived social relations, our most important political construction, a world-changing fiction. The international women's movements have constructed 'women's experience', as well as uncovered or discovered this crucial collective object. This experience is a fiction and fact of the most crucial, political kind. Liberation rests on the construction of the consciousness, the imaginative apprehension, of oppression, and so of possibility. The cyborg is a matter of fiction and lived experience that changes what counts as women's experience in the late twentieth century. This is a struggle over life and death, but the boundary between science fiction and social reality is an optical illusion.

Contemporary science fiction is full of cyborgs – creatures simultaneously animal and machine, who populate worlds ambiguously natural and crafted. Modern medicine is also full of cyborgs, of couplings between organism and machine, each conceived as coded devices, in an intimacy and with a power that was not generated in the history of sexuality. Cyborg 'sex' restores some of the lovely replicative baroque of ferns and invertebrates (such nice organic prophylactics against heterosexism). Cyborg replication is uncoupled from organic reproduction. Modern production seems like a dream of cyborg colonization work, a dream that makes the nightmare of Taylorism seem idyllic. And modern war is a cyborg orgy, coded by C^3I, command-control-communication-intelligence, an $84 billion item in 1984's US defence budget. I am making an argument for the cyborg as a fiction mapping our social and bodily reality and as an imaginative resource suggesting some very fruitful couplings. Michael Foucault's biopolitics is a flaccid premonition of cyborg politics, a very open field.

By the late twentieth century, our time, a mythic time, we are all chimeras, theorized and fabricated hybrids of machine and organism; in short, we are cyborgs. The cyborg is our ontology; it gives us our politics. The cyborg is a condensed image of both imagination and material reality, the two joined centres structuring any possibility of historical transformation. In the traditions of 'Western' science and politics – the tradition of racist, male-dominant capitalism; the tradition of progress; the tradition of the appropriation of nature as resource for the productions of culture; the tradition of reproduction of the self from the reflections of the other – the relation between organism and machine has been a border war. The stakes in the border war have been the territories of production, reproduction, and imagination. This chapter is an argument for *pleasure* in the confusion of boundaries and for *responsibility* in their construction. It is also an effort to contribute to socialist-feminist culture and theory in a postmodernist, non-naturalist mode and in the utopian tradition of imagining a world without gender, which is perhaps a world without genesis, but maybe also a world without end. The cyborg incarnation is outside salvation history. Nor does it mark time on an oedipal calendar, attempting to heal the terrible cleavages of gender in an oral symbiotic utopia or post-oedipal apocalypse. As Zoe Sofoulis argues in her unpublished manuscript on Jacques Lacan, Melanie Klein, and nuclear culture, *Lacklein*, the most terrible and perhaps the most promising monsters in cyborg worlds are embodied in non-oedipal narratives with a different logic of repression, which we need to understand for our survival.

The cyborg is a creature in a post-gender world; it has no truck with bisexuality, pre-oedipal symbiosis, unalienated labour, or other seductions to organic wholeness through a final appropriation of all the powers of the parts into a higher unity. In a sense, the cyborg has no origin story in the Western sense – a 'final' irony since the cyborg is also the awful apocalyptic *telos* of the 'West's' escalating dominations of abstract individuation, an ultimate self untied at last from all dependency, a man in space. An origin story in the 'Western', humanist sense depends on the myth of original unity, fullness, bliss and terror, represented by the phallic mother from whom all humans must separate, the task of individual development and of history, the twin potent myths inscribed most powerfully for us in psychoanalysis and Marxism. Hilary Klein has argued that both Marxism and psychoanalysis, in their concepts of labour and of individuation and gender formation, depend on the plot of original unity out of which difference must be produced and enlisted in a drama of escalating domination of woman/nature. The cyborg skips the step of original unity, of identification with nature in the Western sense. This is its illegitimate promise that might lead to subversion of its teleology as star wars.

The cyborg is resolutely committed to partiality, irony, intimacy, and perversity. It is oppositional, utopian, and completely without innocence. No longer structured by the polarity of public and private, the cyborg defines a technological polis based partly on a revolution of social relations in the *oikos*, the household. Nature and culture are reworked; the one can no longer be the resource for appropriation or incorporation by the other. The relationships for forming wholes from parts, including those of polarity and hierarchical domination, are at issue in the cyborg world. Unlike the hopes of Frankenstein's monster, the cyborg does not expect its father to save it through a restoration of the garden; that is, through the fabrication of a heterosexual mate, through its completion in a finished whole, a city and cosmos. The cyborg does not dream of community on the model of the organic family, this time without the oedipal project. The cyborg would not recognize the Garden of Eden; it is not made of mud and cannot dream of returning to dust. Perhaps that is why I want to see if cyborgs can subvert the apocalypse of returning to nuclear dust in the manic compulsion to name the Enemy. Cyborgs are not reverent; they do not re-member the cosmos. They are wary of holism, but needy for connection– they seem to have a natural feel for united front politics, but without the vanguard party. The main trouble with cyborgs, of course, is that they are the illegitimate offspring of militarism and patriarchal capitalism, not to mention state socialism. But illegitimate offspring are often exceedingly unfaithful to their origins. Their fathers, after all, are inessential.

I will return to the science fiction of cyborgs at the end of this chapter, but now I want to signal three crucial boundary breakdowns that make the following political-fictional (political-scientific) analysis possible. By the late twentieth century in United States scientific culture, the boundary between human and animal is thoroughly breached. The last beachheads of uniqueness have been polluted if not turned into amusement parks – language, tool use, social behaviour, mental events, nothing really convincingly settles the separation of human and animal. And many people no longer feel the need for such a separation; indeed, many branches of feminist culture affirm the pleasure of connection of human and other living creatures. Movements for animal rights are not irrational denials of human uniqueness; they are a clear-sighted recognition of connection across the discredited breach of nature and culture. Biology and evolutionary theory over the last two centuries have simultaneously produced modern organisms as objects of knowledge and reduced the line between humans and animals to a faint trace re-etched in ideological struggle or professional disputes between life and social science. Within this framework, teaching modern Christian creationism should be fought as a form of child abuse.

Biological-determinist ideology is only one position opened up in scientific culture for arguing the meanings of human animality. There is much room for radical political people to contest the meanings of the breached boundary.[2] The cyborg appears in myth precisely where the boundary between human and animal is transgressed. Far from signalling a walling off of people from other living beings, cyborgs signal disturbingly and pleasurably tight coupling. Bestiality has a new status in this cycle of marriage exchange.

The second leaky distinction is between animal-human (organism) and machine. Pre-cybernetic machines could be haunted; there was always the spectre of the ghost in the machine. This dualism structured the dialogue between materialism and idealism that was settled by a dialectical progeny, called spirit or history, according to taste. But basically machines were not self-moving, self-designing, autonomous. They could not achieve man's dream, only mock it. They were not man, an author to himself, but only a caricature of that masculinist reproductive dream. To think they were otherwise was paranoid. Now we are not so sure. Late twentieth-century machines have made thoroughly ambiguous the difference between natural and artificial, mind and body, self-developing and externally designed, and many other distinctions that used to apply to organisms and machines. Our machines are disturbingly lively, and we ourselves frighteningly inert.

Technological determination is only one ideological space opened up by the reconceptions of machine and organism as coded texts through which we engage in the play of writing and reading the world.[3] 'Textualization' of everything in poststructuralist, postmodernist theory has been damned by Marxists and socialist feminists for its utopian disregard for the lived relations of domination that ground the 'play' of arbitrary reading.[4] It is certainly true that postmodernist strategies, like my cyborg myth, subvert myriad organic wholes (for example, the poem, the primitive culture, the biological organism). In short, the certainty of what counts as nature – a source of insight and promise of innocence – is undermined, probably fatally. The transcendent authorization of interpretation is lost, and with it the ontology grounding 'Western' epistemology. But the alternative is not cynicism or faithlessness, that is, some version of abstract existence, like the accounts of technological determinism destroying 'man' by the 'machine' or 'meaningful political action' by the 'text'. Who cyborgs will be is a radical question; the answers are a matter of survival. Both chimpanzees and artefacts have politics, so why shouldn't we (de Waal, 1982; Winner, 1980).

The third distinction is a subset of the second: the boundary between physical and non-physical is very imprecise for us. Pop physics books on the consequences of quantum theory and the indeterminacy principle are a kind of popular scientific equivalent to Harlequin romances[5] as a marker of radical change in American white heterosexuality: they get it wrong, but they are on the right subject. Modern machines are quintessential microelectronic devices: they are everywhere and they are invisible. Modern machinery is an irreverent upstart god, mocking the Father's ubiquity and spirituality. The silicon chip is a surface for writing; it is etched in molecular scales disturbed only by atomic noise, the ultimate interference for nuclear scores. Writing, power, and technology are old partners in Western stories of the origin of civilization, but miniaturization has changed our experience of mechanism. Miniaturization has turned out to be about power; small is not so much beautiful as pre-eminently dangerous, as in cruise missiles. Contrast the TV sets of the 1950s or the news cameras of the 1970s with the TV wrist bands or hand-sized video cameras now advertised. Our best machines are made of sunshine; they are all light and clean because they are nothing but signals, electromagnetic waves, a section of a spectrum, and these machines are eminently portable, mobile – a matter of immense human pain in Detroit and Singapore. People are nowhere near so fluid, being both material and opaque. Cyborgs are ether, quintessence.

The ubiquity and invisibility of cyborgs is precisely why these sunshine-belt machines are so deadly. They are as hard to see politically as materially. They are about consciousness – or its simulation.[6] They are floating signifiers moving in pickup trucks across Europe, blocked more effectively by the witch-weavings of the displaced and so unnatural Greenham women, who read the cyborg webs of power so very well, than by the militant labour of older masculinist politics, whose natural constituency needs defence jobs. Ultimately the 'hardest' science is about the realm of greatest boundary confusion, the realm of pure number, pure spirit, C^3I, cryptography, and the preservation of potent secrets. The new machines are so clean and light. Their engineers are sun-worshippers mediating a new scientific revolution associated with the night dream of post-industrial society. The diseases evoked by these clean machines are 'no more' than the minuscule coding changes of an antigen in the immune system, 'no more' than the experience of stress. The nimble fingers of 'Oriental' women, the old fascination of little Anglo-Saxon Victorian girls with doll's houses, women's enforced attention to the small take on quite new dimensions in this world. There might be a cyborg Alice taking account of these new dimensions. Ironically, it might be the unnatural cyborg women making chips in Asia and spiral dancing in Santa Rita jail[7] whose constructed unities will guide effective oppositional strategies.

So my cyborg myth is about transgressed boundaries, potent fusions, and dangerous possibilities which progressive people might explore as one part of needed political work. One of my premises is that most American socialists and feminists see deepened dualisms of mind and body, animal and machine, idealism and materialism in the social practices, symbolic formulations, and physical artefacts associated with 'high technology' and scientific culture. From *One-Dimensional Man* (Marcuse, 1964) to *The Death of Nature* (Merchant, 1980), the analytic resources developed by progressives have insisted on the necessary domination of technics and recalled us to an imagined organic body to integrate our resistance. Another of my premises is that the need for unity of people trying to resist world-wide intensification of domination has never been more acute. But a slightly perverse shift of perspective might better enable us to contest for meanings, as well as for other forms of power and pleasure in technologically mediated societies.

From one perspective, a cyborg world is about the final imposition of a grid of control on the planet, about the final abstraction embodied in a Star Wars apocalypse waged in the name of defence, about the final appropriation of women's bodies in a masculinist orgy of war (Sofia, 1984). From another perspective, a cyborg world might be about lived social and bodily realities in which people are not afraid of their joint kinship with animals and machines, not afraid of permanently partial identities and contradictory standpoints. The political struggle is to see from both perspectives at once because each reveals both dominations and possibilities unimaginable from the other vantage point. Single vision produces worse illusions than double vision or many-headed monsters. Cyborg unities are monstrous and illegitimate; in our present political circumstances, we could hardly hope for more potent myths for resistance and recoupling. I like to imagine LAG, the Livermore Action Group, as a kind of cyborg society, dedicated to realistically converting the laboratories that most fiercely embody and spew out the tools of technological apocalypse, and committed to building a political form that actually manages to hold together witches, engineers, elders, perverts, Christians, mothers, and Leninists long enough to disarm the state. Fission Impossible is the name of the affinity group in my town. (Affinity: related not by blood but by choice, the appeal of one chemical nuclear group for another, avidity.[8]

Fractured identities

It has become difficult to name one's feminism by a single adjective – or even to insist in every circumstance upon the noun. Consciousness of exclusion through naming is acute. Identities seem contradictory, partial, and strategic. With the hard-won recognition of their social and historical constitution, gender, race, and class cannot provide the basis for belief in 'essential' unity. There is nothing about being 'female' that naturally binds women. There is not even such a state as 'being' female, itself a highly complex category constructed in contested sexual scientific discourses and other social practices. Gender, race, or class consciousness is an achievement forced on us by the terrible historical experience of the contradictory social realities of patriarchy, colonialism, and capitalism. And who counts as 'us' in my own rhetoric? Which identities are available to ground such a potent political myth called 'us', and what could motivate enlistment in this collectivity? Painful fragmentation among feminists (not to mention among women) along every possible fault line has made the concept of *woman* elusive, an excuse for the matrix of women's dominations of each other. For me – and for many who share a similar historical location in white, professional middle-class, female, radical, North American, mid-adult bodies – the sources of a crisis in political identity are legion. The recent history for much of the US left and US feminism has been a response to this kind of crisis by endless splitting and searches for a new essential unity. But there has also been a growing recognition of another response through coalition – affinity, not identity.[9]

Chela Sandoval (n.d., 1984), from a consideration of specific historical moments in the formation of the new political voice called women of colour, has theorized a hopeful model of political identity called 'oppositional consciousness', born of the skills for reading webs of power by those refused stable membership in the social categories of race, sex, or class. 'Women of color', a name contested at its origins by those whom it would incorporate, as well as a historical consciousness marking systematic breakdown of all the signs of Man in 'Western' traditions, constructs a kind of postmodernist identity out of otherness, difference, and specificity. This postmodernist identity is fully political, whatever might be said about other possible postmodernisms. Sandoval's oppositional consciousness is about contradictory locations and heterochronic calendars, not about relativisms and pluralisms.

Sandoval emphasizes the lack of any essential criterion for identifying who is a woman of colour. She notes that the definition of the group has been by conscious appropriation of negation. For example, a Chicana or US black woman has not been able to speak as a woman or as a black person or as a Chicano. Thus, she was at the bottom of a cascade of negative identities, left out of even the privileged oppressed authorial categories called 'women and blacks', who claimed to make the important revolutions. The category 'woman' negated all non-white women; 'black' negated all non-black people, as well as all black women. But there was also no 'she', no singularity, but a sea of differences among US women who have affirmed their historical identity as US women of colour. This identity marks out a self-consciously constructed space that cannot affirm the capacity to act on the basis of natural identification, but only on the basis of conscious coalition, of affinity, of political kinship.[10] Unlike the 'woman' of some streams of the white women's movement in the United States, there is no naturalization of the matrix, or at least this is what Sandoval argues is uniquely available through the power of oppositional consciousness.

Sandoval's argument has to be seen as one potent formulation for feminists out of the world-wide development of anti-colonialist discourse; that is to say, discourse dissolving the 'West' and its highest product – the one who is not animal, barbarian, or woman; man, that is, the author of a cosmos called history. As orientalism is deconstructed politically and semiotically, the identities of the occident destabilize, including those of feminists.[11] Sandoval argues that 'women of colour' have a chance to build an effective unity that does not replicate the imperializing, totalizing revolutionary subjects of previous Marxisms and feminisms which had not faced the consequences of the disorderly polyphony emerging from decolonization.

Katie King has emphasized the limits of identification and the political/poetic mechanics of identification built into reading 'the poem', that generative core of cultural feminism. King criticizes the persistent tendency among contemporary feminists from different 'moments' or 'conversations' in feminist practice to taxonomize the women's movement to make one's own political tendencies appear to be the *telos* of the whole. These taxonomies tend to remake feminist history so that it appears to be an ideological struggle among coherent types persisting over time, especially those typical units called radical, liberal, and socialist-feminism. Literally, all other feminisms are either incorporated or marginalized, usually by building an explicit ontology and epistemology.[12] Taxonomies of feminism produce epistemologies to police deviation from official women's experience. And of course, 'women's culture', like women of colour, is consciously created by mechanisms inducing affinity. The rituals of poetry, music, and certain forms of academic practice have been pre-eminent. The politics of race and culture in the US women's movements are intimately interwoven. The common achievement of King and Sandoval is learning how to craft a poetic/political unity without relying on a logic of appropriation, incorporation, and taxonomic identification.

The theoretical and practical struggle against unity-through-domination or unity-through-incorporation ironically not only undermines the justifications for patriarchy, colonialism, humanism, positivism, essentialism, scientism, and other unlamented -isms, but *all* claims for an organic or natural standpoint. I think that radical and socialist/Marxist-feminisms have also undermined their/our own epistemological strategies and that this is a crucially valuable step in imagining possible unities. It remains to be seen whether all 'epistemologies' as Western political people have known them fail us in the task to build effective affinities.

It is important to note that the effort to construct revolutionary standpoints, epistemologies as achievements of people committed to changing the world, has been part of the process showing the limits of identification. The acid tools of postmodernist theory and the constructive tools of ontological discourse about revolutionary subjects might be seen as ironic allies in dissolving Western selves in the interests of survival. We are excruciatingly conscious of what it means to have a historically constituted body. But with the loss of innocence in our origin, there is no expulsion from the Garden either. Our politics lose the indulgence of guilt with the *naïveté* of innocence. But what would another political myth for socialist-feminism look like? What kind of politics could embrace partial, contradictory, permanently unclosed constructions of personal and collective selves and still be faithful, effective – and, ironically, socialist-feminist?

I do not know of any other time in history when there was greater need for political unity to confront effectively the dominations of 'race', 'gender', 'sexuality', and 'class'. I also do not know of any other time when the kind of unity we might help build could have been possible. None of 'us' have any longer the symbolic or material capability of dictating the shape of reality to any of 'them'. Or at least 'we' cannot claim innocence from practising such dominations. White women, including socialist feminists, discovered (that is, were forced kicking and screaming to notice) the non-innocence of the category 'woman'. That consciousness changes the geography of all previous categories; it denatures them as heat denatures a fragile protein. Cyborg feminists have to argue that 'we' do not want any more natural matrix of unity and that no construction is whole. Innocence, and the corollary insistence on victimhood as the only ground for insight, has done enough damage. But the constructed revolutionary subject must give late-twentieth-century people pause as well. In the fraying of identities and in the reflexive strategies for constructing them, the possibility opens up for weaving something other than a shroud for the day after the apocalypse that so prophetically ends salvation history.

Both Marxist/socialist-feminisms and radical feminisms have simultaneously naturalized and denatured the category 'woman' and consciousness of the social lives of 'women'. Perhaps a schematic caricature can highlight both kinds of moves. Marxian socialism is rooted in an analysis of wage labour which reveals class structure. The consequence of the wage relationship is systematic alienation, as the worker is dissociated from his (sic) product. Abstraction and illusion rule in knowledge, domination rules in practice. Labour is the pre-eminently privileged category enabling the Marxist to overcome illusion and find that point of view which is necessary for changing the world. Labour is the humanizing activity that makes man; labour is an ontological category permitting the knowledge of a subject, and so the knowledge of subjugation and alienation.

In faithful filiation, socialist-feminism advanced by allying itself with the basic analytic strategies of Marxism. The main achievement of both Marxist feminists and socialist feminists was to expand the category of labour to accommodate what (some) women did, even when the wage relation was subordinated to a more comprehensive view of labour under capitalist patriarchy. In particular, women's labour in the household and women's activity as mothers generally (that is, reproduction in the socialist-feminist sense), entered theory on the authority of analogy to the Marxian concept of labour. The unity of women here rests on an epistemology based on the ontological structure of 'labour'. Marxist/socialist-feminism does not 'naturalize' unity; it is a possible achievement based on a possible standpoint rooted in social relations. The essentializing move is in the ontological structure of labour or of its analogue, women's activity.[13] The inheritance of Marxian humanism, with its pre-eminently Western self, is the difficulty for me. The contribution from these formulations has been the emphasis on the daily responsibility of real women to build unities, rather than to naturalize them.

Catherine MacKinnon's (1982, 1987) version of radical feminism is itself a caricature of the appropriating, incorporating, totalizing tendencies of Western theories of identity grounding action.[14] It is factually and politically wrong to assimilate all of the diverse 'moments' or 'conversations' in recent women's politics named radical feminism to MacKinnon's version. But the teleological logic of her theory shows how an epistemology and ontology – including their negations – erase or police difference. Only one of the effects of MacKinnon's theory is the rewriting of the history of the polymorphous field called radical feminism. The major effect is the production of a theory of experience, of women's identity, that is a kind of apocalypse for all revolutionary standpoints. That is, the totalization built into this tale of radical feminism achieves its end – the unity of women – by enforcing the experience of and testimony to radical non-being. As for the Marxist/socialist feminist, consciousness is an achievement, not a natural fact. And MacKinnon's theory eliminates some of the difficulties built into humanist revolutionary subjects, but at the cost of radical reductionism.

MacKinnon argues that feminism necessarily adopted a different analytical strategy from Marxism, looking first not at the structure of class, but at the structure of sex/gender and its generative relationship, men's constitution and appropriation of women sexually. Ironically, MacKinnon's 'ontology' constructs a non-subject, a non-being. Another's desire, not the self's labour, is the origin of 'woman'. She therefore develops a theory of consciousness that enforces what can count as 'women's' experience – anything that names sexual violation, indeed, sex itself as far as 'women' can be concerned. Feminist practice is the construction of this form of consciousness; that is, the self-knowledge of a self-who-is-not.

Perversely, sexual appropriation in this feminism still has the epistemological status of labour; that is to say, the point from which an analysis able to contribute to changing the world must flow. But sexual objectification, not alienation, is the consequence of the structure of sex/gender. In the realm of knowledge, the result of sexual objectification is illusion and abstraction. However, a woman is not simply alienated from her product, but in a deep sense does not exist as a subject, or even potential subject, since she owes her existence as a woman to sexual appropriation. To be constituted by another's desire is not the same thing as to be alienated in the violent separation of the labourer from his product.

MacKinnon's radical theory of experience is totalizing in the extreme; it does not so much marginalize as obliterate the authority of any other women's political speech and action. It is a totalization producing what Western patriarchy itself never succeeded in doing – feminists' consciouness of the non-existence of women, except as products of men's desire. I think MacKinnon correctly argues that no Marxian version of identity can firmly ground women's unity. But in solving the problem of the contradictions of any Western revolutionary subject for feminist purposes, she develops an even more authoritarian doctrine of experience. If my complaint about socialist/Marxian standpoints is their unintended erasure of polyvocal, unassimilable, radical difference made visible in anti-colonial discourse and practice, MacKinnon's intentional erasure of all difference through the device of the 'essential' non-existence of women is not reassuring.

In my taxonomy, which like any other taxonomy is a re-inscription of history, radical feminism can accommodate all the activities of women named by socialist feminists as forms of labour only if the activity can somehow be sexualized. Reproduction had different tones of meanings for the two tendencies, one rooted in labour, one in sex, both calling the consequences of domination and ignorance of social and personal reality 'false consciousness'.

Beyond either the difficulties or the contributions in the argument of any one author, neither Marxist nor radical feminist points of view have tended to embrace the status of a partial explanation; both were regularly constituted as totalities. Western explanation has demanded as much; how else could the 'Western' author incorporate its others? Each tried to annex other forms of domination by expanding its basic categories through analogy, simple listing, or addition. Embarrassed silence about race among white radical and socialist feminists was one major, devastating political consequence. History and polyvocality disappear into political taxonomies that try to establish genealogies. There was no structural room for race (or for much else) in theory claiming to reveal the construction of the category woman and social group women as a unified or totalizable whole. The structure of my caricature looks like this:

socialist feminism – structure of class // wage labour // alienation
labour, by analogy reproduction, by extension sex, by addition race
radical feminism – structure of gender // sexual appropriation //
objectification
sex, by analogy labour, by extension reproduction, by addition race

In another context, the French theorist, Julia Kristeva, claimed women appeared as a historical group after the Second World War, along with groups like youth. Her dates are doubtful; but we are now accustomed to remembering that as objects of knowledge and as historical actors, 'race' did not always exist, 'class' has a historical genesis, and 'homosexuals' are quite junior. It is no accident that the symbolic system of the family of man – and so the essence of woman – breaks up at the same moment that networks of connection among people on the planet are unprecedentedly multiple, pregnant, and complex. 'Advanced capitalism' is inadequate to convey the structure of this historical moment. In the 'Western' sense, the end of man is at stake. It is no accident that woman disintegrates into women in our time. Perhaps socialist feminists were not substantially guilty of producing essentialist theory that suppressed women's particularity and contradictory interests. I think we have been, at least through unreflective participation in the logics, languages, and practices of white humanism and through searching for a single ground of domination to secure our revolutionary voice. Now we have less excuse. But in the consciousness of our failures, we risk lapsing into boundless difference and giving up on the confusing task of making partial, real connection. Some differences are playful; some are poles of world historical systems of domination. 'Epistemology' is about knowing the difference.

The informatics of domination

In this attempt at an epistemological and political position, I would like to sketch a picture of possible unity, a picture indebted to socialist and feminist principles of design. The frame for my sketch is set by the extent and importance of rearrangements in world-wide social relations tied to science and technology. I argue for a politics rooted in claims about fundamental changes in the nature of class, race, and gender in an emerging system of world order analogous in its novelty and scope to that created by industrial capitalism; we are living through a movement from an organic, industrial society to a polymorphous, information system – from all work to all play, a deadly game. Simultaneously material and ideological, the dichotomies may be expressed in the following chart of transitions from the comfortable old hierarchical dominations to the scary new networks I have called the informatics of domination:

Representation	Simulation
Bourgeois novel, realism	Science fiction, postmodernism
Organism	Biotic component
Depth, integrity	Surface, boundary
Heat	Noise
Biology as clinical practice	Biology as inscription
Physiology	Communications engineering
Small group	Subsystem
Perfection	Optimization
Eugenics	Population Control
Decadence, *Magic Mountain*	Obsolescence, *Future Shock*
Hygiene	Stress Management
Microbiology, tuberculosis	Immunology, AIDS
Organic division of labour	Ergonomics / cybernetics of labour
Functional specialization	Modular construction
Reproduction	Replication
Organic sex role specialization	Optimal genetic strategies
Biological determinism	Evolutionary inertia, constraints
Community ecology	Ecosystem
Racial chain of being	Neo-imperialism, United Nations humanism
Scientific management in home / factory	Global factory / Electronic cottage
Family / Market / Factory	Women in the Integrated Circuit
Family wage	Comparable worth
Public / Private	Cyborg citizenship
Nature / Culture	Fields of difference
Co-operation	Communications enhancement
Freud	Lacan
Sex	Genetic engineering
Labour	Robotics
Mind	Artificial Intelligence
Second World War	Star Wars
White Capitalist Patriarchy	Informatics of Domination

This list suggests several interesting things.[15] First, the objects on the right-hand side cannot be coded as 'natural', a realization that subverts naturalistic coding for the left-hand side as well. We cannot go back ideologically or materially. It's not just that 'god' is dead; so is the 'goddess'. Or both are revivified in the worlds charged with microelectronic and biotechnological politics. In relation to objects like biotic components, one must think not in terms of essential properties, but in terms of design, boundary constraints, rates of flows, systems logics, costs of lowering constraints. Sexual reproduction is one kind of reproductive strategy among many, with costs and benefits as a function of the system environment. Ideologies of sexual reproduction can no longer reasonably call on notions of sex and sex role as organic aspects in natural objects like organisms and families. Such reasoning will be unmasked as irrational, and ironically corporate executives reading *Playboy* and anti-porn radical feminists will make strange bedfellows in jointly unmasking the irrationalism.

Likewise for race, ideologies about human diversity have to be formulated in terms of frequencies of parameters, like blood groups or intelligence scores. It is 'irrational' to invoke concepts like primitive and civilized. For liberals and radicals, the search for integrated social systems gives way to a new practice called 'experimental ethnography' in which an organic object dissipates in attention to the play of writing. At the level of ideology, we see translations of racism and colonialism into languages of development and under-development, rates and constraints of modernization. Any objects or persons can be reasonably thought of in terms of disassembly and reassembly; no 'natural' architectures constrain system design. The financial districts in all the world's cities, as well as the export-processing and free-trade zones, proclaim this elementary fact of 'late capitalism'. The entire universe of objects that can be known scientifically must be formulated as problems in communications engineering (for the managers) or theories of the text (for those who would resist). Both are cyborg semiologies.

One should expect control strategies to concentrate on boundary conditions and interfaces, on rates of flow across boundaries – and not on the integrity of natural objects. 'Integrity' or 'sincerity' of the Western self gives way to decision procedures and expert systems. For example, control strategies applied to women's capacities to give birth to new human beings will be developed in the languages of population control and maximization of goal achievement for individual decision-makers. Control strategies will be formulated in terms of rates, costs of constraints, degrees of freedom. Human beings, like any other component or subsystem, must be localized in a system architecture whose basic modes of operation are probabilistic, statistical. No objects, spaces, or bodies are sacred in themselves; any component can be interfaced with any other if the proper standard, the proper code, can be constructed for processing signals in a common language. Exchange in this world transcends the universal translation effected by capitalist markets that Marx analysed so well. The privileged pathology affecting all kinds of components in this universe is stress – communications breakdown (Hogness, 1983). The cyborg is not subject to Foucault's biopolitics; the cyborg simulates politics, a much more potent field of operations.

This kind of analysis of scientific and cultural objects of knowledge which have appeared historically since the Second World War prepares us to notice some important inadequacies in feminist analysis which has proceeded as if the organic, hierarchical dualisms ordering discourse in 'the West' since Aristotle still ruled. They have been cannibalized, or as Zoe

Sofia (Sofoulis) might put it, they have been 'techno-digested'. The dichotomies between mind and body, animal and human, organism and machine, public and private, nature and culture, men and women, primitive and civilized are all in question ideologically. The actual situation of women is their integration/exploitation into a world system of production/reproduction and communication called the informatics of domination. The home, workplace, market, public arena, the body itself – all can be dispersed and interfaced in nearly infinite, polymorphous ways, with large consequences for women and others – consequences that themselves are very different for different people and which make potent oppositional international movements difficult to imagine and essential for survival. One important route for reconstructing socialist-feminist politics is through theory and practice addressed to the social relations of science and technology, including crucially the systems of myth and meanings structuring our imaginations. The cyborg is a kind of disassembled and reassembled, postmodern collective and personal self. This is the self feminists must code.

Communications technologies and biotechnologies are the crucial tools recrafting our bodies. These tools embody and enforce new social relations for women world-wide. Technologies and scientific discourses can be partially understood as formalizations, i.e., as frozen moments, of the fluid social interactions constituting them, but they should also be viewed as instruments for enforcing meanings. The boundary is permeable between tool and myth, instrument and concept, historical systems of social relations and historical anatomies of possible bodies, including objects of knowledge. Indeed, myth and tool mutually constitute each other.

Furthermore, communications sciences and modern biologies are constructed by a common move – *the translation of the world into a problem of coding*, a search for a common language in which all resistance to instrumental control disappears and all heterogeneity can be submitted to disassembly, reassembly, investment, and exchange.

In communications sciences, the translation of the world into a problem in coding can be illustrated by looking at cybernetic (feedback-controlled) systems theories applied to telephone technology, computer design, weapons deployment, or data base construction and maintenance. In each case, solution to the key questions rests on a theory of language and control; the key operation is determining the rates, directions, and probabilities of flow of a quantity called information. The world is subdivided by boundaries differentially permeable to information. Information is just that kind of quantifiable element (unit, basis of unity) which allows universal translation, and so unhindered instrumental power (called effective communication). The biggest threat to such power is interruption of communication. Any system breakdown is a function of stress. The fundamentals of this technology can be condensed into the metaphor C^3I, command-control-communication-intelligence, the military's symbol for its operations theory.

In modern biologies, the translation of the world into a problem in coding can be illustrated by molecular genetics, ecology, sociobiological evolutionary theory, and immunobiology. The organism has been translated into problems of genetic coding and read-out. Biotechnology, a writing technology, informs research broadly.[16] In a sense, organisms have ceased to exist as objects of knowledge, giving way to biotic components, i.e., special kinds of information-processing devices. The analogous moves in ecology could be examined by probing the history and utility of the concept of the ecosystem. Immunobiology and associated medical practices are rich exemplars of the privilege of coding and recognition systems as objects of knowledge, as constructions of bodily reality for us. Biology here is a kind of cryptography. Research is necessarily a kind of intelligence activity. Ironies abound. A stressed system goes awry; its communication processes break down; it fails to recognize the difference between self and other. Human babies with baboon hearts evoke national ethical perplexity – for animal rights activists at least as much as for the guardians of human purity. In the US gay men and intravenous drug users are the 'privileged' victims of an awful immune system disease that marks (inscribes on the body) confusion of boundaries and moral pollution (Treichler, 1987).

But these excursions into communications sciences and biology have been at a rarefied level; there is a mundane, largely economic reality to support my claim that these sciences and technologies indicate fundamental transformations in the structure of the world for us. Communications technologies depend on electronics. Modern states, multinational corporations, military power, welfare state apparatuses, satellite systems, political processes, fabrication of our imaginations, labour-control systems, medical constructions of our bodies, commercial pornography, the international division of labour, and religious evangelism depend intimately upon electronics. Microelectronics is the technical basis of simulacra; that is, of copies without originals.

Microelectronics mediates the translations of labour into robotics and word processing, sex into genetic engineering and reproductive technologies, and mind into artificial intelligence and decision procedures. The new biotechnologies concern more than human reproduction. Biology as a powerful engineering science for redesigning materials and processes has revolutionary implications for industry, perhaps most obvious today in areas of fermentation, agriculture, and energy. Communications sciences and biology are constructions of natural-technical objects of knowledge in which the difference between machine and organism is thoroughly blurred; mind, body, and tool are on very intimate terms. The 'multinational' material organization of the production and reproduction of daily life and the symbolic organization of the production and reproduction of culture and imagination seem equally implicated. The boundary-maintaining images of base and superstructure, public and private, or material and ideal never seemed more feeble.

I have used Rachel Grossman's (1980) image of women in the integrated circuit to name the situation of women in a world so intimately restructured through the social relations of science and technology.[17] I used the odd circumlocution, 'the social relations of science and technology', to indicate that we are not dealing with a technological determinism, but with a historical system depending upon structured relations among people. But the phrase should also indicate that science and technology provide fresh sources of power, that we need fresh sources of analysis and political action (Latour, 1984). Some of the rearrangements of race, sex, and class rooted in high-tech-facilitated social relations can make socialist-feminism more relevant to effective progressive politics.

The 'homework economy' outside 'the home'

The 'New Industrial Revolution' is producing a new world-wide working class, as well as new sexualities and ethnicities. The extreme mobility of capital and the emerging international division of labour are intertwined with the emergence of new collectivities, and the weakening of familiar groupings. These developments are neither gender- nor race-neutral. White men in advanced industrial societies have become newly vulnerable to permanent job loss, and women are not disappearing from the job rolls at the same rates as men. It is not simply that women in Third World countries are the preferred labour force for the science-based multinationals in the export-processing sectors, particularly in electronics. The picture is more systematic and involves reproduction, sexuality, culture, consumption, and production. In the prototypical Silicon Valley, many women's lives have been structured around employment in electronics-dependent jobs, and their intimate realities include serial heterosexual monogamy, negotiating childcare, distance from extended kin or most other forms of traditional community, a high likelihood of loneliness and extreme economic vulnerability as they age. The ethnic and racial diversity of women in Silicon Valley structures a microcosm of conflicting differences in culture, family, religion, education, and language.

Richard Gordon has called this new situation the 'homework economy'.[18] Although he includes the phenomenon of literal homework emerging in connection with electronics assembly, Gordon intends 'homework economy' to name a restructuring of work that broadly has the characteristics formerly ascribed to female jobs, jobs literally done only by women. Work is being redefined as both literally female and feminized, whether performed by men or women. To be feminized means to be made extremely vulnerable; able to be disassembled, reassembled, exploited as a reserve labour force; seen less as workers than as servers; subjected to time arrangements on and off the paid job that make a mockery of a limited work day; leading an existence that always borders on being obscene, out of place, and reducible to sex. Deskilling is an old strategy newly applicable to formerly privileged workers. However, the homework economy does not refer only to large-scale deskilling, nor does it deny that new areas of high skill are emerging, even for women and men previously excluded from skilled employment. Rather, the concept indicates that factory, home, and market are integrated on a new scale and that the places of women are crucial – and need to be analysed for differences among women and for meanings for relations between men and women in various situations.

The homework economy as a world capitalist organizational structure is made possible by (not caused by) the new technologies. The success of the attack on relatively privileged, mostly white, men's unionized jobs is tied to the power of the new communications technologies to integrate and control labour despite extensive dispersion and decentralization. The consequences of the new technologies are felt by women both in the loss of the family (male) wage (if they ever had access to this white privilege) and in the character of their own jobs, which are becoming capital-intensive; for example, office work and nursing.

The new economic and technological arrangements are also related to the collapsing welfare state and the ensuing intensification of demands on women to sustain daily life for themselves as well as for men, children, and old people. The feminization of poverty – generated by dismantling the welfare state, by the homework economy where stable jobs become the exception, and sustained by the expectation that women's wages will not be matched by a male income for the support of children – has become an urgent focus. The causes of various women-headed households are a function of race, class, or sexuality; but their increasing generality is a ground for coalitions of women on many issues. That women regularly sustain daily life partly as a function of their enforced status as mothers is hardly new; the kind of integration with the overall capitalist and progressively war-based economy is new. The particular pressure, for example, on US black women, who have achieved an escape from (barely) paid domestic service and who now hold clerical and similar jobs in large numbers, has large implications for continued enforced black poverty *with* employment. Teenage women in industrializing areas of the Third World increasingly find themselves the sole or major source of a cash wage for their families, while access to land is ever more problematic. These developments must have major consequences in the psychodynamics and politics of gender and race.

Within the framework of three major stages of capitalism (commercial/early industrial, monopoly, multinational) – tied to nationalism, imperialism, and multinationalism, and related to Jameson's three dominant aesthetic periods of realism, modernism, and postmodernism – I would argue that specific forms of families dialectically relate to forms of capital and to its political and cultural concomitants. Although lived problematically and unequally, ideal forms of these families might be schematized as (1) the patriarchal nuclear family, structured by the dichotomy between public and private and accompanied by the white bourgeois ideology of separate spheres and nineteenth-century Anglo-American bourgeois feminism; (2) the modern family mediated (or enforced) by the welfare state and institutions like the family wage, with a flowering of a-feminist heterosexual ideologies, including their radical versions represented in Greenwich Village around the First World War; and (3) the 'family' of the homework economy with its oxymoronic structure of women-headed households and its explosion of feminisms and the paradoxical intensification and erosion of gender itself. This is the context in which the projections for world-wide structural unemployment stemming from the new technologies are part of the picture of the homework economy. As robotics and related technologies put men out of work in 'developed' countries and exacerbate failure to generate male jobs in Third World 'development', and as the automated office becomes the rule even in labour-surplus countries, the feminization of work intensifies. Black women in the United States have long known what it looks like to face the structural underemployment ('feminization') of black men, as well as their own highly vulnerable position in the wage economy. It is no longer a secret that sexuality, reproduction, family, and community life are interwoven with this economic structure in myriad ways which have also differentiated the situations of white and black women. Many more women and men will contend with similar situations, which will make cross-gender and race alliances on issues of basic life support (with or without jobs) necessary, not just nice.

The new technologies also have a profound effect on hunger and on food production for subsistence world-wide. Rae Lessor Blumberg (1983) estimates that women produce about 50 per cent of the world's subsistence food.[19] Women are excluded generally from benefiting from the increased high-tech commodification of food and energy crops, their days are made more arduous because their responsibilities to provide food do not diminish, and their reproductive situations are made more complex. Green Revolution technologies interact with other high-tech industrial production to alter gender divisions of labour and differential gender migration patterns.

The new technologies seem deeply involved in the forms of 'privatization' that Ros Petchesky (1981) has analysed, in which militarization, right-wing family ideologies and policies, and intensified definitions of corporate (and state) property as private synergistically interact.[20] The new communications technologies are fundamental to the eradication of 'public life' for everyone. This facilitates the mushrooming of a permanent high-tech military establishment at the cultural and economic expense of most people, but especially of women. Technologies like video games and highly miniaturized televisions seem crucial to production of modern forms of 'private life'. The culture of video games is heavily orientated to individual competition and extraterrestrial warfare. High-tech, gendered imaginations are produced here, imaginations that can contemplate destruction of the planet and a sci-fi escape from its consequences. More than our imaginations is militarized; and the other realities of electronic and nuclear warfare are inescapable. These are the technologies that promise ultimate mobility and perfect exchange – and incidentally enable tourism, that perfect practice of mobility and exchange, to emerge as one of the world's largest single industries.

The new technologies affect the social relations of both sexuality and of reproduction, and not always in the same ways. The close ties of sexuality and instrumentality, of views of the body as a kind of private satisfaction- and utility-maximizing machine, are described nicely in sociobiological origin stories that stress a genetic calculus and explain the inevitable dialectic of domination of male and female gender roles.[21] These sociobiological stories depend on a high-tech view of the body as a biotic component or cybernetic communications system. Among the many transformations of reproductive situations is the medical one, where women's bodies have boundaries newly permeable to both 'visualization' and 'intervention'. Of course, who controls the interpretation of bodily boundaries in medical hermeneutics is a major feminist issue. The speculum served as an icon of women's claiming their bodies in the 1970s; that handcraft tool is inadequate to express our needed body politics in the negotiation of reality in the practices of cyborg reproduction. Self-help is not enough. The technologies of visualization recall the important cultural practice of hunting with the camera and the deeply predatory nature of a photographic consciousness.[22] Sex, sexuality, and reproduction are central actors in high-tech myth systems structuring our imaginations of personal and social possibility.

Another critical aspect of the social relations of the new technologies is the reformulation of expectations, culture, work, and reproduction for the large scientific and technical work-force. A major social and political danger is the formation of a strongly bimodal social structure, with the masses of women and men of all ethnic groups, but especially people of colour, confined to a homework economy, illiteracy of several varieties, and general redundancy and impotence, controlled by high-tech repressive apparatuses ranging from entertainment to surveillance and disappearance. An adequate socialist-feminist politics should address women in the privileged occupational categories, and particularly in the production of science and technology that constructs scientific-technical discourses, processes, and objects.[23]

This issue is only one aspect of enquiry into the possibility of a feminist science, but it is important. What kind of constitutive role in the production of knowledge, imagination, and practice can new groups doing science have? How can these groups be allied with progressive social and political movements? What kind of political accountability can be constructed to tie women together across the scientific-technical hierarchies separating us? Might there be ways of developing feminist science/technology politics in alliance with anti-military science facility conversion action groups? Many scientific and technical workers in Silicon Valley, the high-tech cowboys included, do not want to work on military science.[24] Can these personal preferences and cultural tendencies be welded into progressive politics among this professional middle class in which women, including women of colour, are coming to be fairly numerous?

Women in the integrated circuit

Let me summarize the picture of women's historical locations in advanced industrial societies, as these positions have been restructured partly through the social relations of science and technology. If it was ever possible ideologically to characterize women's lives by the distinction of public and private domains – suggested by images of the division of working-class life into factory and home, of bourgeois life into market and home, and of gender existence into personal and political realms – it is now a totally misleading ideology, even to show how both terms of these dichotomies construct each other in practice and in theory. I prefer a network ideological image, suggesting the profusion of spaces and identities and the permeability of boundaries in the personal body and in the body politic. 'Networking' is both a feminist practice and a multinational corporate strategy – weaving is for oppositional cyborgs.

So let me return to the earlier image of the informatics of domination and trace one vision of women's 'place' in the integrated circuit, touching only a few idealized social locations seen primarily from the point of view of advanced capitalist societies: Home, Market, Paid Work Place, State, School, Clinic-Hospital, and Church. Each of these idealized spaces is logically and practically implied in every other locus, perhaps analogous to a holographic photograph. I want to suggest the impact of the social relations mediated and enforced by the new technologies in order to help formulate needed analysis and practical work. However, there is no 'place' for women in these networks, only geometrics of difference and contradiction crucial to women's cyborg identities. If we learn how to read these webs of power and social life, we might learn new couplings, new coalitions. There is no way to read the following list from a standpoint of 'identification', of a unitary self. The issue is dispersion. The task is to survive in the diaspora.

> *Home*: Women-headed households, serial monogamy, flight of men, old women alone, technology of domestic work, paid homework, re-emergence of home sweat-shops, home-based businesses and telecommuting, electronic cottage, urban homelessness, migration, module architecture, reinforced (simulated) nuclear family, intense domestic violence.
>
> *Market*: Women's continuing consumption work, newly targeted to buy the profusion of new production from the new technologies (especially

as the competitive race among industrialized and industrializing nations to avoid dangerous mass unemployment necessitates finding ever bigger new markets for ever less clearly needed commodities); bimodal buying power, coupled with advertising targeting of the numerous affluent groups and neglect of the previous mass markets; growing importance of informal markets in labour and commodities parallel to high-tech, affluent market structures; surveillance systems through electronic funds transfer; intensified market abstraction (commodification) of experience, resulting in ineffective utopian or equivalent cynical theories of community; extreme mobility (abstraction) of marketing/financing systems; inter-penetration of sexual and labour markets; intensified sexualization of abstracted and alienated consumption.

Paid Work Place: Continued intense sexual and racial division of labour, but considerable growth of membership in privileged occupational categories for many white women and people of colour; impact of new technologies on women's work in clerical, service, manufacturing (especially textiles), agriculture, electronics; international restructuring of the working classes; development of new time arrangements to facilitate the homework economy (flex time, part time, over time, no time); homework and out work; increased pressures for two-tiered wage structures; significant numbers of people in cash-dependent populations world-wide with no experience or no further hope of stable employment; most labour 'marginal' or 'feminized'.

State: Continued erosion of the welfare state; decentralizations with increased surveillance and control; citizenship by telematics; imperialism and political power broadly in the form of information rich/information poor differentiation; increased high-tech militarization increasingly opposed by many social groups; reduction of civil service jobs as a result of the growing capital intensification of office work, with implications for occupational mobility for women of colour; growing privatization of material and ideological life and culture; close integration of privatization and militarization, the high-tech forms of bourgeois capitalist personal and public life; invisibility of different social groups to each other, linked to psychological mechanisms of belief in abstract enemies.

School: Deepening coupling of high-tech capital needs and public education at all levels, differentiated by race, class, and gender; managerial classes involved in educational reform and refunding at the cost of remaining progressive educational democratic structures for children and teachers; education for mass ignorance and repression in technocratic and militarized culture; growing anti-science mystery cults in dissenting and radical political movements; continued relative scientific illiteracy among white women and people of colour; growing industrial direction of education (especially higher education) by science-based multinationals (particularly in electronics- and biotechnology-dependent companies); highly educated, numerous élites in a progressively bimodal society.

Clinic-hospital: Intensified machine–body relations; renegotiations of public metaphors which channel personal experience of the body, particularly in relation to reproduction, immune system functions, and 'stress' phenomena; intensification of reproductive politics in response to world historical implications of women's unrealized, potential control of their relation to reproduction; emergence of new, historically specific diseases; struggles over meanings and means of health in environments pervaded by high technology products and processes; continuing feminization of health work; intensified struggle over state responsibility for health; continued ideological role of popular health movements as a major form of American politics.

Church: Electronic fundamentalist 'super-saver' preachers solemnizing the union of electronic capital and automated fetish gods; intensified importance of churches in resisting the militarized state; central struggle over women's meanings and authority in religion; continued relevance of spirituality, intertwined with sex and health, in political struggle.

The only way to characterize the informatics of domination is as a massive intensification of insecurity and cultural impoverishment, with common failure of subsistence networks for the most vulnerable. Since much of this picture interweaves with the social relations of science and technology, the urgency of a socialist-feminist politics addressed to science and technology is plain. There is much now being done, and the grounds for political work are rich. For example, the efforts to develop forms of collective struggle for women in paid work, like SEIU's District 925,[25] should be a high priority for all of us. These efforts are profoundly tied to technical restructuring of labour processes and reformations of working classes. These efforts also are providing understanding of a more comprehensive kind of labour organization, involving community, sexuality, and family issues never privileged in the largely white male industrial unions.

The structural rearrangements related to the social relations of science and technology evoke strong ambivalence. But it is not necessary to be ultimately depressed by the implications of late twentieth-century women's relation to all aspects of work, culture, production of knowledge, sexuality, and reproduction. For excellent reasons, most Marxisms see domination best and have trouble understanding what can only look like false consciousness and people's complicity in their own domination in late capitalism. It is crucial to remember that what is lost, perhaps especially from women's points of view, is often virulent forms of oppression, nostalgically naturalized in the face of current violation. Ambivalence towards the disrupted unities mediated by high-tech culture requires not sorting consciousness into categories of 'clear-sighted critique grounding a solid political epistemology' versus 'manipulated false consciousness', but subtle understanding of emerging pleasures, experiences, and powers with serious potential for changing the rules of the game.

There are grounds for hope in the emerging bases for new kinds of unity across race, gender, and class, as these elementary units of socialist-feminist analysis themselves suffer protean transformations. Intensifications of hardship experienced world-wide in connection with the social relations of science and technology are severe. But what people are experiencing is not transparently clear, and we lack sufficiently subtle connections for collectively building effective theories of experience. Present efforts – Marxist, psychoanalytic, feminist, anthropological – to clarify even 'our' experience are rudimentary.

I am conscious of the odd perspective provided by my historical position – a PhD in biology for an Irish Catholic girl was made possible by Sputnik's impact on US national science-education policy. I have a body and mind as much constructed by the post-Second World War arms race and cold war as by the women's movements. There are more grounds for hope in focusing on the contradictory effects of politics designed to produce loyal American technocrats, which also produced large numbers of dissidents, than in focusing on the present defeats.

The permanent partiality of feminist points of view has consequences for our expectations of forms of political organization and participation. We do not need a totality in order to work well. The feminist dream of a common language, like all dreams for a perfectly true language, of perfectly faithful naming of experience, is a totalizing and imperialist one. In that sense, dialectics too is a dream language, longing to resolve contradiction. Perhaps, ironically, we can learn from our fusions with animals and machines how not to be Man, the embodiment of Western logos. From the point of view of pleasure in these potent and taboo fusions, made inevitable by the social relations of science and technology, there might indeed be a feminist science.

Cyborgs: a myth of political identity

I want to conclude with a myth about identity and boundaries which might inform late twentieth-century political imaginations. I am indebted in this story to writers like Joanna Russ, Samuel R. Delany, John Varley, James Tiptree, Jr, Octavia Butler, Monique Wittig, and Vonda McIntyre.[26] These are our story-tellers exploring what it means to be embodied in high-tech worlds. They are theorists for cyborgs. Exploring conceptions of bodily boundaries and social order, the anthropologist Mary Douglas (1966, 1970) should be credited with helping us to consciousness about how fundamental body imagery is to world view, and so to political language. French feminists like Luce Irigaray and Monique Wittig, for all their differences, know how to write the body; how to weave eroticism, cosmology, and politics from imagery of embodiment, and especially for Wittig, from imagery of fragmentation and reconstitution of bodies.[27]

American radical feminists like Susan Griffin, Audre Lorde, and Adrienne Rich have profoundly affected our political imaginations – and perhaps restricted too much what we allow as a friendly body and political language.[28] They insist on the organic, opposing it to the technological. But their symbolic systems and the related positions of ecofeminism and feminist paganism, replete with organicisms, can only be understood in Sandoval's terms as oppositional ideologies fitting the late twentieth century. They would simply bewilder anyone not preoccupied with the machines and consciousness of late capitalism. In that sense they are part of the cyborg world. But there are also great riches for feminists in explicitly embracing the possibilities inherent in the breakdown of clean distinctions between organism and machine and similar distinctions structuring the Western self. It is the simultaneity of breakdowns that cracks the matrices of domination and opens geometric possibilities. What might be learned from personal and political 'technological' pollution? I look briefly at two overlapping groups of texts for their insight into the construction of a potentially helpful cyborg myth: constructions of women of colour and monstrous selves in feminist science fiction.

Earlier I suggested that 'women of colour' might be understood as a cyborg identity, a potent subjectivity synthesized from fusions of outsider identities and in the complex political-historical layerings of her 'biomythography', *Zami* (Lorde, 1982; King, 1987a, 1987b). There are material and cultural grids mapping this potential, Audre Lorde (1984) captures the tone in the title of her *Sister Outsider.* In my political myth, Sister Outsider is the offshore woman, whom US workers, female and feminized, are supposed to regard as the enemy preventing their solidarity, threatening their security. Onshore, inside the boundary of the United States, Sister Outsider is a potential amidst the races and ethnic identities of women manipulated for division, competition, and exploitation in the same industries. 'Women of colour' are the preferred labour force for the science-based industries, the real women for whom the world-wide sexual market, labour market, and politics of reproduction kaleidoscope into daily life. Young Korean women hired in the sex industry and in electronics assembly are recruited from high schools, educated for the integrated circuit. Literacy, especially in English, distinguishes the 'cheap' female labour so attractive to the multinationals.

Contrary to orientalist stereotypes of the 'oral primitive', literacy is a special mark of women of colour, acquired by US black women as well as men through a history of risking death to learn and to teach reading and writing. Writing has a special significance for all colonized groups. Writing has been crucial to the Western myth of the distinction between oral and written cultures, primitive and civilized mentalities, and more recently to the erosion of that distinction in 'postmodernist' theories attacking the phallogo-centrism of the West, with its worship of the monotheistic, phallic, authoritative, and singular work, the unique and perfect name.[29] Contests for the meanings of writing are a major form of contemporary political struggle. Releasing the play of writing is deadly serious. The poetry and stories of US women of colour are repeatedly about writing, about access to the power to signify; but this time that power must be neither phallic nor innocent. Cyborg writing must not be about the Fall, the imagination of a once-upon-a-time wholeness before language, before writing, before Man. Cyborg writing is about the power to survive, not on the basis of original innocence, but on the basis of seizing the tools to mark the world that marked them as other.

The tools are often stories, retold stories, versions that reverse and displace the hierarchical dualisms of naturalized identities. In retelling origin stories, cyborg authors subvert the central myths of origin of Western culture. We have all been colonized by those origin myths, with their longing for fulfilment in apocalypse. The phallogocentric origin stories most crucial for feminist cyborgs are built into the literal technologies – technologies that write the world, biotechnology and microelectronics – that have recently textualized our bodies as code problems on the grid of C^3I. Feminist cyborg stories have the task of recoding communication and intelligence to subvert command and control.

Figuratively and literally, language politics pervade the struggles of women of colour; and stories about language have a special power in the rich contemporary writing by US women of colour. For example, retellings of the story of the indigenous woman Malinche, mother of the mestizo 'bastard' race of the new world, master of languages, and mistress of Cortés, carry special meaning for Chicana constructions of identity. Cherríe Moraga (1983) in *Loving in the War Years* explores the themes of identity when one never possessed the original language, never told the original story, never resided in the harmony of legitimate heterosexuality in the garden of culture, and so cannot base identity on a myth or a fall from innocence and right to natural names, mother's or father's.[30] Moraga's writing, her superb literacy, is presented in her poetry as the same kind of violation as Malinche's mastery of the conqueror's language – a violation, an illegitimate production, that allows survival. Moraga's language is not 'whole'; it is self-consciously spliced, a chimera of English and Spanish, both conqueror's languages. But it is this chimeric monster, without claim to an original language before violation, that crafts the erotic, competent, potent identities of women of colour. Sister Outsider hints at the possibility of world survival not because of her innocence, but because of her ability to live on the boundaries, to write without the founding myth of original wholeness, with its inescapable apocalypse of final return to a deathly oneness that Man has imagined to be the innocent and all-powerful Mother, freed at the End from another spiral of appropriation by her son. Writing marks Moraga's body, affirms it as the body of a woman of colour, against the possibility of passing into the unmarked category of the Anglo father or into the orientalist myth of 'original illiteracy' of a mother that never was. Malinche was mother here, not Eve before eating the forbidden fruit. Writing affirms Sister Outsider, not the Woman-before-the-Fall-into-Writing needed by the phallogocentric Family of Man.

Writing is pre-eminently the technology of cyborgs, etched surfaces of the late twentieth century. Cyborg politics is the struggle for language and the struggle against perfect communication, against the one code that translates all meaning perfectly, the central dogma of phallogocentrism. That is why cyborg politics insist on noise and advocate pollution, rejoicing in the illegitimate fusions of animal and machine. These are the couplings which make Man and Woman so problematic, subverting the structure of desire, the force imagined to generate language and gender, and so subverting the structure and modes of reproduction of 'Western' identity, of nature and culture, of mirror and eye, slave and master, body and mind. 'We' did not originally choose to be cyborgs, but choice grounds a liberal politics and epistemology that imagines the reproduction of individuals before the wider replications of 'texts'.

From the perspective of cyborgs, freed of the need to ground politics in 'our' privileged position of the oppression that incorporates all other dominations, the innocence of the merely violated, the ground of those closer to nature, we can see powerful possibilities. Feminisms and Marxisms have run aground on Western epistemological imperatives to construct a revolutionary subject from the perspective of a hierarchy of oppressions and/or a latent position of moral superiority, innocence, and greater closeness to nature. With no available original dream of a common language or original symbiosis promising protection from hostile 'masculine' separation, but written into the play of a text that has no finally privileged reading or salvation history, to recognize 'oneself as fully implicated in the world, frees us of the need to root politics in identification, vanguard parties, purity, and mothering. Stripped of identity, the bastard race teaches about the power of the margins and the importance of a mother like Malinche. Women of colour have transformed her from the evil mother of masculinist fear into the originally literate mother who teaches survival.

This is not just literary deconstruction, but liminal transformation. Every story that begins with original innocence and privileges the return to wholeness imagines the drama of life to be individuation, separation, the birth of the self, the tragedy of autonomy, the fall into writing, alienation; that is, war, tempered by imaginary respite in the bosom of the Other. These plots are ruled by a reproductive politics – rebirth without flaw, perfection, abstraction. In this plot women are imagined either better or worse off, but all agree they have less selfhood, weaker individuation, more fusion to the oral, to Mother, less at stake in masculine autonomy. But there is another route to having less at stake in masculine autonomy, a route that does not pass through Woman, Primitive, Zero, the Mirror Stage and its imaginary. It passes through women and other present-tense, illegitimate cyborgs, not of Woman born, who refuse the ideological resources of victimization so as to have a real life. These cyborgs are the people who refuse to disappear on cue, no matter how many times a 'Western' commentator remarks on the sad passing of another primitive, another organic group done in by 'Western' technology, by writing.[31] These real-life cyborgs (for example, the Southeast Asian village women workers in Japanese and US electronics firms described by Aihwa Ong) are actively rewriting the texts of their bodies and societies. Survival is the stakes in this play of readings.

To recapitulate, certain dualisms have been persistent in Western traditions; they have all been systemic to the logics and practices of domination of women, people of colour, nature, workers, animals – in short, domination of all constituted as others, whose task is to mirror the self. Chief among these troubling dualisms are self/other, mind/body, culture/nature, male/female, civilized/primitive, reality/appearance, whole/part, agent/resource, maker/made, active/passive, right/wrong, truth/illusion, total/partial, God/man. The self is the One who is not dominated, who knows that by the service of the other, the other is the one who holds the future, who knows that by the experience of domination, which gives the lie to the autonomy of the self. To be One is to be autonomous, to be powerful, to be God; but to be One is to be an illusion, and so to be involved in a dialectic of apocalypse with the other. Yet to be other is to be multiple, without clear boundary, frayed, insubstantial. One is too few, but two are too many.

High-tech culture challenges these dualisms in intriguing ways. It is not clear who makes and who is made in the relation between human and machine. It is not clear what is mind and what body in machines that resolve into coding practices. In so far as we know ourselves in both formal discourse (for example, biology) and in daily practice (for example, the homework economy in the integrated circuit), we find ourselves to be cyborgs, hybrids, mosaics, chimeras. Biological organisms have become biotic systems, communications devices like others. There is no fundamental, ontological separation in our formal knowledge of machine and organism, of technical and organic. The replicant Rachel in the Ridley Scott film *Blade Runner* stands as the image of a cyborg culture's fear, love, and confusion.

One consequence is that our sense of connection to our tools is heightened. The trance state experienced by many computer users has become a staple of science-fiction film and cultural jokes. Perhaps paraplegics and other severely handicapped people can (and sometimes do) have the most intense experiences of complex hybridization with other communication devices.[32] Anne McCaffrey's pre-feminist *The Ship Who Sang* (1969) explored the consciousness of a cyborg, hybrid of girl's brain and complex machinery, formed after the birth of a severely handicapped child. Gender, sexuality, embodiment, skill: all were reconstituted in the story. Why should our bodies end at the skin, or include at best other beings encapsulated by skin? From the seventeenth century till now, machines could be animated – given ghostly souls to make them speak or move or to account for their orderly development and mental capacities. Or organisms could be mechanized – reduced to body understood as resource of mind. These machine/organism relationships are obsolete, unnecessary. For us, in imagination and in other practice, machines can be prosthetic devices, intimate components, friendly selves. We don't need organic holism to give impermeable wholeness, the total woman and her feminist variants (mutants?). Let me conclude this point by a very partial reading of the logic of the cyborg monsters of my second group of texts, feminist science fiction.

The cyborgs populating feminist science fiction make very problematic the statuses of man or woman, human, artefact, member of a race, individual entity, or body. Katie King clarifies how pleasure in reading these fictions is not largely based on identification. Students facing Joanna Russ for the first time, students who have learned to take modernist writers like James Joyce or Virginia Woolf without flinching, do not know what to make of *The Adventures of Alyx* or *The Female Man*, where characters refuse the reader's search for innocent wholeness while granting the wish for heroic quests, exuberant eroticism, and serious politics. *The Female Man* is the story of four versions of one genotype, all of whom meet, but even taken together do not make a whole, resolve the dilemmas of violent moral action, or remove the growing scandal of gender. The feminist science fiction of Samuel R. Delany, especially *Tales of Nevèrÿon*, mocks stories of origin by redoing the neolithic revolution, replaying the founding moves of Western civilization to subvert their plausibility. James Tiptree, Jr, an author whose fiction was regarded as particularly manly until her 'true' gender was revealed, tells tales of reproduction based on non-mammalian technologies like alternation of generations of male brood pouches and male nurturing. John Varley constructs a supreme cyborg in his arch-feminist exploration of Gaea, a mad goddess-planet-trickster-old woman-technological device on whose surface an extraordinary array of post-cyborg symbioses are spawned. Octavia Butler writes of an African sorceress pitting her powers of transformation against the genetic manipulations of her rival (*Wild Seed*), of time warps that bring a modern US black woman into slavery where her actions in relation to her white master-ancestor determine the possibility of her own birth (*Kindred*), and of the illegitimate insights into identity and community of an adopted cross-species child who came to know the enemy as self (*Survivor*). In *Dawn* (1987), the first instalment of a series called *Xenogenesis*, Butler tells the story of Lilith Iyapo, whose personal name recalls Adam's first and repudiated wife and whose family name marks her status as the widow of the son of Nigerian immigrants to the US. A black woman and a mother whose child is dead, Lilith mediates the transformation of humanity through genetic exchange with extra-terrestrial lovers/rescuers/destroyers/ genetic engineers, who reform earth's habitats after the nuclear holocaust and coerce surviving humans into intimate fusion with them. It is a novel that interrogates reproductive, linguistic, and nuclear politics in a mythic field structured by late twentieth-century race and gender.

Because it is particularly rich in boundary transgressions, Vonda McIntyre's *Superluminal* can close this truncated catalogue of promising and dangerous monsters who help redefine the pleasures and politics of embodiment and feminist writing. In a fiction where no character is 'simply' human, human status is highly problematic. Orca, a genetically altered diver, can speak with killer whales and survive deep ocean conditions, but she longs to explore space as a pilot, necessitating bionic implants jeopardizing her kinship with the divers and cetaceans. Transformations are effected by virus vectors carrying a new developmental code, by transplant surgery, by implants of microelectronic devices, by analogue doubles, and other means. Laenea becomes a pilot by accepting a heart implant and a host of other alterations allowing survival in transit at speeds exceeding that of light. Radu Dracul survives a virus-caused plague in his outerworld planet to find himself with a time sense that changes the boundaries of spatial perception for the whole species. All the characters explore the limits of language; the dream of communicating experience; and the necessity of limitation, partiality, and intimacy even in this world of protean transformation and connection. *Superluminal* stands also for the defining contradictions of a cyborg world in another sense; it embodies textually the intersection of feminist theory and colonial discourse in the science fiction I have alluded to in this chapter. This is a conjunction with a long history that many 'First World' feminists have tried to repress, including myself in my readings of *Superluminal* before being called to account by Zoe Sofoulis, whose different location in the world system's informatics of domination made her acutely alert to the imperialist moment of all science fiction cultures, including women's science fiction. From an Australian feminist sensitivity, Sofoulis remembered more readily McIntyre's role as writer of the adventures of Captain Kirk and Spock in TV's *Star Trek* series than her rewriting the romance in *Superluminal.*

Monsters have always defined the limits of community in Western inclinations. The Centaurs and Amazons of ancient Greece established the limits of the centred polis of the Greek male human by their disruption of marriage and boundary pollutions of the warrior with animality and woman. Unseparated twins and hermaphrodites were the confused human material in early modern France who grounded discourse on the natural and supernatural, medical and legal, portents and diseases – all crucial to establishing modern identity.[33] The evolutionary and behavioural sciences of monkeys and apes have marked the multiple boundaries of late twentieth-century industrial identities. Cyborg monsters in feminist science fiction define quite different political possibilities and limits from those proposed by the mundane fiction of Man and Woman.

There are several consequences to taking seriously the imagery of cyborgs as other than our enemies. Our bodies, ourselves; bodies arc maps of power and identity. Cyborgs are no exception. A cyborg body is not innocent; it was not born in a garden; it does not seek unitary identity and so generate antagonistic dualisms without end (or until the world ends); it takes irony for granted. One is too few, and two is only one possibility. Intense pleasure in skill, machine skill, ceases to be a sin, but an aspect of embodiment. The machine is not an *it* to be animated, worshipped, and dominated. The machine is us, our processes, an aspect of our embodiment. We can be responsible for machines; *they* do not dominate or threaten us. We are responsible for boundaries; we are they. Up till now (once upon a time), female embodiment seemed to be given, organic, necessary; and female embodiment seemed to mean skill in mothering and its metaphoric extensions. Only by being out of place could we take intense pleasure in machines, and then with excuses that this was organic activity after all, appropriate to females. Cyborgs might consider more seriously the partial, fluid, sometimes aspect of sex and sexual embodiment. Gender might not be global identity after all, even if it has profound historical breadth and depth.

The ideologically charged question of what counts as daily activity, as experience, can be approached by exploiting the cyborg image. Feminists have recently claimed that women are given to dailiness, that women more than men somehow sustain daily life, and so have a privileged epistemological position potentially. There is a compelling aspect to this claim, one that makes visible unvalued female activity and names it as the ground of life.

But *the* ground of life? What about all the ignorance of women, all the exclusions and failures of knowledge and skill? What about men's access to daily competence, to knowing how to build things, to take them apart, to play? What about other embodiments? Cyborg gender is a local possibility taking a global vengeance. Race, gender, and capital require a cyborg theory of wholes and parts. There is no drive in cyborgs to produce total theory, but there is an intimate experience of boundaries, their construction and deconstruction. There is a myth system waiting to become a political language to ground one way of looking at science and technology and challenging the informatics of domination – in order to act potently.

One last image: organisms and organismic, holistic politics depend on metaphors of rebirth and invariably call on the resources of reproductive sex. I would suggest that cyborgs have more to do with regeneration and are suspicious of the reproductive matrix and of most birthing. For salamanders, regeneration after injury, such as the loss of a limb, involves regrowth of structure and restoration of function with the constant possibility of twinning or other odd topographical productions at the site of former injury. The regrown limb can be monstrous, duplicated, potent. We have all been injured, profoundly. We require regeneration, not rebirth, and the possibilities for our reconstitution include the utopian dream of the hope for a monstrous world without gender.

Cyborg imagery can help express two crucial arguments in this essay: first, the production of universal, totalizing theory is a major mistake that misses most of reality, probably always, but certainly now; and second, taking responsibility for the social relations of science and technology means refusing an anti-science metaphysics, a demonology of technology, and so means embracing the skilful task of reconstructing the boundaries of daily life, in partial connection with others, in communication with all of our parts. It is not just that science and technology are possible means of great human satisfaction, as well as a matrix of complex dominations. Cyborg imagery can suggest a way out of the maze of dualisms in which we have explained our bodies and our tools to ourselves. This is a dream not of a common language, but of a powerful infidel heteroglossia. It is an imagination of a feminist speaking in tongues to strike fear into the circuits of the super-savers of the new right. It means both building and destroying machines, identities, categories, relationships, space stories. Though both are bound in the spiral dance, I would rather be a cyborg than a goddess.

Notes

1 Research was funded by an Academic Senate Faculty Research Grant from the University of California, Santa Cruz. An earlier version of the paper on genetic engineering appeared as 'Lieber Kyborg als Göttin: für eine sozialistisch-feministische Unterwanderung der Gentechnologie', in Bernd-Peter Lange and Anna Marie Stuby, eds, Berlin: Argument-Sonderband 105, 1984, pp 66–84. The cyborg manifesto grew from my 'New machines, new bodies, new communities: political dilemmas of a cyborg feminist', 'The Scholar and the Feminist X: The Question of Technology', Conference, Barnard College, April 1983.

The people associated with the History of Consciousness Board of UCSC have had an enormous influence on this paper, so that it feels collectively authored more than most, although those I cite may not recognize their ideas. In particular, members of graduate and undergraduate feminist theory, science, and politics, and theory and methods courses contributed to the cyborg manifesto. Particular debts here are due Hilary Klein (1989), Paul Edwards (1985), Lisa Lowe (1986), and James Clifford (1985).

Parts of the paper were my contribution to a collectively developed session, 'Poetic Tools and Political Bodies: Feminist Approaches to High Technology Culture', 1984 California American Studies Association, with History of Consciousness graduate students Zoe Sofoulis, 'Jupiter space'; Katie King, 'The pleasures of repetition and the limits of identification in feminist science fiction:

reimaginations of the body after the cyborg'; and Chela Sandoval, 'The construction of subjectivity and oppositional consciousness in feminist film and video'. Sandoval's (n.d.) theory of oppositional consciousness was published as 'Women respond to racism: A Report on the National Women's Studies Association Conference'. For Sofoulis's semiotic-psychoanalytic readings of nuclear culture, see Sofia (1984). King's unpublished papers ('Questioning tradition: canon formation and the veiling of power'; 'Gender and genre: reading the science fiction of Joanna Russ'; 'Varley's *Titan* and *Wizard*: feminist parodies of nature, culture, and hardware') deeply informed the cyborg manifesto.

Barbara Epstein, Jeff Escoffier, Rusten Hogness, and Jaye Miler gave extensive discussion and editorial help. Members of the Silicon Valley Research Project of UCSC and participants in SVRP conferences and workshops were very important, especially Rick Gordon, Linda Kimball, Nancy Snyder, Langdon Winner, Judith Stacey, Linda Lim, Patricia Fernandez-Kelly, and Judith Gregory. Finally, I want to thank Nancy Hartsock for years of friendship and discussion on feminist theory and feminist science fiction. I also thank Elizabeth Bird for my favourite political button: 'Cyborgs for Earthly Survival'.

2 Useful references to left and/or feminist radical science movements and theory and to biological/biotechnical issues include: Bleier (1984, 1986), Harding (1986), Fausto-Sterling (1985), Gould (1981), Hubbard *et al.* (1982), Keller (1985), Lewontin *et al.* (1984), *Radical Science Journal* (became *Science as Culture* in 1987), 26 Freegrove Road, London N7 9RQ; *Science for the People*, 897 Main St, Cambridge, MA 02139.

3 Starting points for left and/or feminist approaches to technology and politics include: Cowan (1983), Rothschild (1983), Traweek (1988), Young and Levidow (1981, 1985), Weizenbaum (1976), Winner (1977, 1986), Zimmerman (1983), Athanasiou (1987), Cohn (1987a, 1987b), Winograd and Flores (1986), Edwards (1985). *Global Electronics Newsletter*, 867 West Dana St, #204, Mountain View, CA 94041; *Processed World*, 55 Sutter St, San Francisco, CA 94104; ISIS, Women's International Information and Communication Service, PO Box 50 (Cornavin), 1211 Geneva 2, Switzerland, and Via Santa Maria Dell'Anima 30, 00186 Rome, Italy. Fundamental approaches to modern social studies of science that do not continue the liberal mystification that it all started with Thomas Kuhn, include: Knorr-Cetina (1981), Knorr-Cetina and Mulkay (1983), Latour and Woolgar (1979), Young (1979). The 1984 Directory of the Network for the Ethnographic Study of Science, Technology, and Organizations lists a wide range of people and projects crucial to better radical analysis; available from NESSTO, PO Box 11442, Stanford, CA 94305.

4 A provocative, comprehensive argument about the politics and theories of 'postmodernism' is made by Fredric Jameson (1984), who argues that postmodernism is not an option, a style among others, but a cultural dominant requiring radical reinvention of left politics from within; there is no longer any place from without that gives meaning to the comforting fiction of critical distance. Jameson also makes clear why one cannot be for or against postmodernism, an essentially moralist move. My position is that feminists (and others) need continuous cultural reinvention, postmodernist critique, and historical materialism; only a cyborg would have a chance. The old dominations of white capitalist patriarchy seem nostalgically innocent now: they normalized heterogeneity, into man and woman, white and black, for example. 'Advanced capitalism' and postmodernism release heterogeneity without a norm, and we are flattened, without subjectivity, which requires depth, even unfriendly and drowning depths. It is time to write *The Death of the Clinic*. The clinic's methods required bodies and

works; we have texts and surfaces. Our dominations don't work by medicalization and normalization any more; they work by networking, communications redesign, stress management. Normalization gives way to automation, utter redundancy. Michel Foucault's *Birth of the Clinic* (1963), *History of Sexuality* (1976), and *Discipline and Punish* (1975) name a form of power at its moment of implosion. The discourse of biopolitics gives way to technobabble, the language of the spliced substantive; no noun is left whole by the multinationals. These are their names, listed from one issue of *Science:* Tech-Knowledge, Genentech, Allergen, Hybritech, Compupro, Genen-cor, Syntex, Allelix, Agrigenetics Corp., Syntro, Codon, Repligen, MicroAngelo from Scion Corp., Percom Data, Inter Systems, Cyborg Corp., Statcom Corp., Intertec. If we are imprisoned by language, then escape from that prison-house requires language poets, a kind of cultural restriction enzyme to cut the code; cyborg heteroglossia is one form of radical cultural politics. For cyborg poetry, see Perloff (1984); Fraser (1984). For feminist modernist/postmodernist 'cyborg' writing, see HOW(ever), 871 Corbett Ave, San Francisco, CA 94131.

5 The US equivalent of Mills & Boon.
6 Baudrillard (1983). Jameson (1984, p. 66) points out that Plato's definition of the simulacrum is the copy for which there is no original, i.e., the world of advanced capitalism, of pure exchange. See *Discourse* 9 (Spring/Summer 1987) for a special issue on technology (cybernetics, ecology, and the postmodern imagination).
7 A practice at once both spiritual and political that linked guards and arrested anti-nuclear demonstrators in the Alameda County jail in California in the early 1980s.
8 For ethnographic accounts and political evaluations, see Epstein (forthcoming), Sturgeon (1986). Without explicit irony, adopting the spaceship earth/whole earth logo of the planet photographed from space, set off by the slogan 'Love Your Mother', the May 1987 Mothers and Others Day action at the nuclear weapons testing facility in Nevada none the less took account of the tragic contradictions of views of the earth. Demonstrators applied for official permits to be on the land from officers of the Western Shoshone tribe, whose territory was invaded by the US government when it built the nuclear weapons test ground in the 1950s. Arrested for trespassing, the demonstrators argued that the police and weapons facility personnel, without authorization from the proper officials, were the trespassers. One affinity group at the women's action called themselves the Surrogate Others; and in solidarity with the creatures forced to tunnel in the same ground with the bomb, they enacted a cyborgian emergence from the constructed body of a large, non-heterosexual desert worm.
9 Powerful developments of coalition politics emerge from 'Third World' speakers, speaking from nowhere, the displaced centre of the universe, earth: 'We live on the third planet from the sun' – *Sun Poem* by Jamaican writer, Edward Kamau Braithwaite, review by Mackey (1984). Contributors to Smith (1983) ironically subvert naturalized identities precisely while constructing a place from which to speak called home. See especially Reagon (in Smith, 1983, pp. 356–68). Trinh T. Minh-ha (1986–87).
10 hooks (1981, 1984); Hull *et al.* (1982). Bambara (1981) wrote an extraordinary novel in which the women of colour theatre group, The Seven Sisters, explores a form of unity. See analysis by Butler-Evans (1987).
11 On orientalism in feminist works and elsewhere, see Lowe (1986); Said (1978); Mohanty (1984); *Many Voices, One Chant: Black Feminist Perspectives* (1984).
12 Katie King (1986, 1987a) has developed, a theoretically sensitive treatment of the workings of feminist taxonomies as genealogies of power in feminist ideology

and polemic. King examines Jaggar's (1983) problematic example of taxonomizing feminisms to make a little machine producing the desired final position. My caricature here of socialist and radical feminism is also an example.

13 The central role of object relations versions of psychoanalysis and related strong universalizing moves in discussing reproduction, caring work, and mothering in many approaches to epistemology underline their authors' resistance to what I am calling postmodernism. For me, both the universalizing moves and these versions of psychoanalysis make analysis of 'women's place in the integrated circuit' difficult and lead to systematic difficulties in accounting for or even seeing major aspects of the construction of gender and gendered social life. The feminist standpoint argument has been developed by: Flax (1983), Harding (1986), Harding and Hintikka (1983), Hartsock (1983a, b), O'Brien (1981), Rose (1983), Smith (1974, 1979). For rethinking theories of feminist materialism and feminist standpoints in response to criticism, see Harding (1986, pp. 163–96), Hartsock (1987), and H. Rose (1986).

14 I make an argumentative category error in 'modifying' MacKinnon's positions with the qualifier 'radical', thereby generating my own reductive critique of extremely heterogeneous writing, which does explicitly use that label, by my taxonomically interested argument about writing which does not use the modifier and which brooks no limits and thereby adds to the various dreams of a common, in the sense of univocal, language for feminism. My category error was occasioned by an assignment to write from a particular taxonomic position which itself has a heterogeneous history, socialist-feminism, for *Socialist Review*. A critique indebted to MacKinnon, but without the reductionism and with an elegant feminist account of Foucault's paradoxical conservatism on sexual violence (rape), is de Lauretis (1985; see also 1986, pp. 1–19). A theoretically elegant feminist social-historical examination of family violence, that insists on women's, men's, and children's complex agency without losing sight of the material structures of male domination, race, and class, is Gordon (1988).

15 This chart was published in 1985. My previous efforts to understand biology as a cybernetic command-control discourse and organisms as 'natural-technical objects of knowledge' were Haraway (1979, 1983, 1984). The 1979 version of this dichotomous chart appears in this vol., ch. 3; for a 1989 version, see ch. 10. The differences indicate shifts in argument.

16 For progressive analyses and action on the biotechnology debates: *GeneWatch, a Bulletin of the Committee for Responsible Genetics*, 5 Doane St, 4th Floor, Boston, MA 02109; Genetic Screening Study Group (formerly the Sociobiology Study Group of Science for the People), Cambridge, MA; Wright (1982, 1986); Yoxen (1983).

17 Starting references for 'women in the integrated circuit': D'Onofrio-Flores and Pfafflin (1982), Fernandez-Kelly (1983), Fuentes and Ehrenreich (1983), Grossman (1980), Nash and Fernandez-Kelly (1983), Ong (1987), Science Policy Research Unit (1982).

18 For the 'homework economy outside the home' and related arguments: Gordon (1983); Gordon and Kimball (1985); Stacey (1987); Reskin and Hartmann (1986); *Women and Poverty* (1984); S. Rose (1986); Collins (1982); Burr (1982); Gregory and Nussbaum (1982); Piven and Coward (1982); Microelectronics Group (1980); Stallard *et al.* (1983) which includes a useful organization and resource list.

19 The conjunction of the Green Revolution's social relations with biotechnologies like plant genetic engineering makes the pressures on land in the Third World increasingly intense. AID's estimates (*New York Times*, 14 October 1984) used at the 1984 World Food Day are that in Africa, women produce about 90 per cent

of rural food supplies, about 60–80 per cent in Asia, and provide 40 per cent of agricultural labour in the Near East and Latin America. Blumberg charges that world organizations' agricultural politics, as well as those of multinationals and national governments in the Third World, generally ignore fundamental issues in the sexual division of labour. The present tragedy of famine in Africa might owe as much to male supremacy as to capitalism, colonialism, and rain patterns. More accurately, capitalism and racism are usually structurally male dominant. See also Blumberg (1981); Hacker (1984); Hacker and Bovit (1981); Busch and Lacy (1983); Wilfred (1982); Sachs (1983); International Fund for Agricultural Development (1985); Bird (1984).

20 See also Enloe (1983a, b).
21 For a feminist version of this logic, see Hrdy (1981). For an analysis of scientific women's story-telling practices, especially in relation to sociobiology in evolutionary debates around child abuse and infanticide, see this vol., ch. 5.
22 For the moment of transition of hunting with guns to hunting with cameras in the construction of popular meanings of nature for an American urban immigrant public, see Haraway (1984–5, 1989b), Nash (1979), Sontag (1977), Preston (1984).
23 For guidance for thinking about the political/cultural/racial implications of the history of women doing science in the United States see: Haas and Perucci (1984); Hacker (1981); Keller (1983); National Science Foundation (1988); Rossiter (1982); Schiebinger (1987); Haraway (1989b).
24 Markoff and Siegel (1983). High Technology Professionals for Peace and Computer Professionals for Social Responsibility are promising organizations.
25 Service Employees International Union's office workers' organization in the US.
26 King (1984). An abbreviated list of feminist science fiction underlying themes of this essay: Octavia Butler, *Wild Seed, Mind of My Mind, Kindred, Survivor*; Suzy McKee Charnas, *Motherliness*; Samuel R. Delany, the Neverÿon series; Anne McCaffery, *The Ship Who Sang, Dinosaur Planet*; Vonda McIntyre, *Superluminal, Dreamsnake*, Joanna Russ, *Adventures of Alix, The Female Man*; James Tiptree, Jr, *Star Songs of an Old Primate, Up the Walls of the World*; John Varley, *Titan, Wizard, Demon*.
27 French feminisms contribute to cyborg heteroglossia. Burke (1981); Irigaray (1977, 1979); Marks and de Courtivron (1980); *Signs* (Autumn 1981); Wittig (1973); Duchen (1986). For English translation of some currents of francophone feminism see *Feminist Issues: A Journal of Feminist Social and Political Theory*, 1980.
28 But all these poets are very complex, not least in their treatment of themes of lying and erotic, decentred collective and personal identities. Griffin (1978), Lorde (1984), Rich (1978).
29 Derrida (1976, especially part II); Lévi-Strauss (1961, especially 'The Writing Lesson'); Gates (1985); Kahn and Neumaier (1985); Ong (1982); Kramarae and Treichler (1985).
30 The sharp relation of women of colour to writing as theme and politics can be approached through: Program for 'The Black Woman and the Diaspora: Hidden Connections and Extended Acknowledgments', An International Literary Conference, Michigan State University, October 1985; Evans (1984); Christian (1985); Carby (1987); Fisher (1980); *Frontiers* (1980, 1983); Kingston (1977); Lerner (1973); Giddings (1985); Moraga and Anzaldúa (1981); Morgan (1984). Anglophone European and Euro-American women have also crafted special relations to their writing as a potent sign: Gilbert and Gubar (1979), Russ (1983).
31 The convention of ideologically taming militarized high technology by publicizing its applications to speech and motion problems of the disabled/differently abled

takes on a special irony in monotheistic, patriarchal, and frequently anti-semitic culture when computer-generated speech allows a boy with no voice to chant the Haftorah at his bar mitzvah. See Sussman (1986). Making the always context-relative social definitions of 'ableness' particularly clear, military high-tech has a way of making human beings disabled by definition, a perverse aspect of much automated battlefield and Star Wars R&D. See Welford (1 July 1986).
32 James Clifford (1985, 1988) argues persuasively for recognition of continuous cultural reinvention, the stubborn non-disappearance of those 'marked' by Western imperializing practices.
33 DuBois (1982), Daston and Park (n.d.), Park and Daston (1981). The noun *monster* shares its root with the verb *to demonstrate*.

Bibliography

Athanasiou, Tom (1987) 'High-tech politics: the case of artificial intelligence', *Socialist Review* 92: 7–35.
Bambara, Toni Cade (1981) *The Salt Eaters.* New York: Vintage/Random House.
Bird, Elizabeth (1984) 'Green Revolution imperialism, I & II', papers delivered at the University of California, Santa Cruz.
Bleier, Ruth (1984) *Science and Gender: A Critique of Biology and Its Themes on Women.* New York: Pergamon.
——, ed. (1986) *Feminist Approaches to Science.* New York: Pergamon.
Blumberg, Rae Lessor (1981) *Stratification: Socioeconomic and Sexual Inequality.* Boston: Brown.
—— (1983) 'A general theory of sex stratification and its application to the positions of women in today's world economy', paper delivered to Sociology Board, University of California at Santa Cruz.
Burke, Carolyn (1981) 'Irigaray through the looking glass', *Feminist Studies* 7(2): 288–306.
Burr, Sara G. (1982) 'Women and work', in Barbara K. Haber, ed. *The Women's Annual, 1981.* Boston: G.K. Hall.
Busch, Lawrence and Lacy, William (1983) *Science, Agriculture, and the Politic of Research.* Boulder, CO: Westview.
Butler, Octavia (1987) *Dawn.* New York: Warner.
Butler-Evans, Elliott (1987) 'Race, gender and desire: narrative strategies and the production of ideology in the fiction of Toni Cade Bambara, Toni Morrison and Alice Walker', University of California at Santa Cruz, PhD thesis.
Carby, Hazel (1987) *Reconstructing Womanhood: The Emergence of the Afro-American Woman Novelist.* New York: Oxford University Press.
Christian, Barbara (1985) *Black Feminist Criticism: Perspectives on Black Women Writers.* New York: Pergamon.
Clifford, James (1985) 'On ethnographic allegory', in James Clifford and George Marcus, eds *Writing Culture: The Poetics and Politics of Ethnography.* Berkeley: University of California Press.
—— (1988) *The Predicament of Culture: Twentieth-Century Ethnography, Literature, and Art.* Cambridge, MA: Harvard University Press.
Cohn, Carol (1987a) 'Nuclear language and how we learned to pat the bomb', *Bulletin of Atomic Scientists*, pp. 17–24.

—— (1987b) 'Sex and death in the rational world of defense intellectuals', *Signs* 12(4): 687–718.
Collins, Patricia Hill (1982) 'Third World women in America', in Barbara K. Haber, ed. *The Women's Annual, 1981.* Boston: G.K. Hall.
Cowan, Ruth Schwartz (1983) *More Work for Mother: The Ironies of Household Technology from the Open Hearth to the Microwave.* New York: Basic.
Daston, Lorraine and Park, Katherine (n.d.) 'Hermaphrodites in Renaissance France', unpublished paper.
de Lauretis, Teresa (1985) 'The violence of rhetoric: considerations on representation and gender', *Semiotica* 54: 11–31.
—— (1986a) 'Feminist studies/critical studies: issues, terms, and contexts', in de Lauretis (1986b), pp. 1–19.
——, ed. (1986b) *Feminist Studies/Critical Studies.* Bloomington: Indiana University Press.
Derrida, Jacques (1976) *Of Grammatology*, G. C. Spivak, trans. and introd. Baltimore: Johns Hopkins University Press.
D'Onofrio-Flores, Pamela and Pfafflin, Sheila M., eds (1982) *Scientific-Technological Change and the Role of Women in Development.* Boulder: Westview.
Douglas, Mary (1966) *Purity and Danger.* London: Routledge & Kegan Paul.
—— (1970) *Natural Symbols.* London: Cresset Press.
DuBois, Page (1982) *Centaurs and Amazons.* Ann Arbor: University of Michigan Press.
Duchen, Claire (1986) *Feminism in France from May '68 to Mitterrand.* London: Routledge & Kegan Paul.
Edwards, Paul (1985) 'Border wars: the science and politics of artificial intelligence', *Radical America* 19(6): 39–52.
Enloe, Cynthia (1983a) 'Women textile workers in the militarization of Southeast Asia', in Nash and Fernandez-Kelly (1983), pp. 407–25.
—— (1983b) *Does Khaki Become You? The Militarization of Women's Lives.* Boston: South End.
Epstein, Barbara (forthcoming) *Political Protest and Cultural Revolution: Nonviolent Direct Action in the Seventies and Eighties.* Berkeley: University of California Press.
Evans, Mari, ed. (1984) *Black Women Writers: A Critical Evaluation.* Garden City, NY: Doubleday/Anchor.
Fausto-Sterling, Anne (1985) *Myths of Gender: Biological Theories about Women and Men.* New York: Basic.
Fernandez-Kelly, Maria Patricia (1983) *For We Are Sold, I and My People.* Albany: State University of New York Press.
Fisher, Dexter, ed. (1980) *The Third Woman: Minority Women Writers of the United States.* Boston: Houghton Mifflin.
Flax, Jane (1983) 'Political philosophy and the patriarchal unconscious: a psychoanalytic perspective on epistemology and metaphysics', in Harding and Hintikka (1983), pp. 245–82.
Foucault, Michel (1963) *The Birth of the Clinic: An Archaeology of Medical Perception*, A. M. Smith, trans. New York: Vintage, 1975.
—— (1975) *Discipline and Punish: The Birth of the Prison*, Alan Sheridan, trans. New York: Vintage, 1979.

—— (1976) *The History of Sexuality*, Vol. 1: *An Introduction*, Robert Hurley, trans. New York: Pantheon, 1978.
Fraser, Kathleen (1984) *Something. Even Human Voices. In the Foreground, a Lake.* Berkeley, CA: Kelsey St Press.
Fuentes, Annette and Ehrenreich, Barbara (1983) *Women in the Global Factory.* Boston: South End.
Gates, Henry Louis (1985) 'Writing "race" and the difference it makes', in '*Race', Writing, and Difference*, special issue, *Critical Inquiry* 12(1): 1–20.
Giddings, Paula (1985) *When and Where I Enter: The Impact of Black Women on Race and Sex in America.* Toronto: Bantam.
Gilbert, Sandra M. and Gubar, Susan (1979) *The Madwoman in the Attic: The Woman Writer and the Nineteenth-Century Literary Imagination.* New Haven, CT: Yale University Press.
Gordon, Linda (1988) *Heroes of Their Own Lives. The Politics and History of Family Violence, Boston 1880–1960.* New York: Viking Penguin.
Gordon, Richard (1983) 'The computerization of daily life, the sexual division of labor, and the homework economy', Silicon Valley Workshop conference, University of California at Santa Cruz.
—— and Kimball, Linda (1985) 'High-technology, employment and the challenges of education', Silicon Valley Research Project, Working Paper, no. 1.
Gould, Stephen J. (1981) *Mismeasure of Man.* New York: Norton.
Gregory, Judith and Nussbaum, Karen (1982) 'Race against time: automation of the office', *Office: Technology and People* 1: 197–236.
Griffin, Susan (1978) *Woman and Nature: The Roaring Inside Her.* New York: Harper & Row.
Grossman, Rachel (1980) 'Women's place in the integrated circuit', *Radical America* 14(1): 29–50.
Haas, Violet and Perucci, Carolyn, eds (1984) *Women in Scientific and Engineering Professions.* Ann Arbor: University of Michigan Press.
Hacker, Sally (1981) 'The culture of engineering: women, workplace, and machine', *Women's Studies International Quarterly* 4(3): 341–53.
—— (1984) 'Doing it the hard way: ethnographic studies in the agribusiness and engineering classroom', paper delivered at the California American Studies Association, Pomona.
—— and Bovit, Liza (1981) 'Agriculture to agribusiness: technical imperatives and changing roles', paper delivered at the Society for the History of Technology, Milwaukee.
Haraway, Donna J. (1979) 'The biological enterprise: sex, mind, and profit from human engineering to sociobiology', *Radical History Review* 20: 206–37. (This vol. pp. 43–68.)
—— (1983) 'Signs of dominance: from a physiology to a cybernetics of primate society', *Studies in History of Biology* 6: 129–219.
—— (1984) 'Class, race, sex, scientific objects of knowledge: a socialist-feminist perspective on the social construction of productive knowledge and some political consequences', in Violet Haas and Carolyn Perucci (1984), pp. 212–29.
—— (1984–5) 'Teddy bear patriarchy: taxidermy in the Garden of Eden, New York City, 1908–36', *Social Text* 11: 20–64.

—— (1989b) *Primate Visions: Gender, Race, and Nature in the World of Modern Science.* New York: Routledge.

Harding, Sandra (1986) *The Science Question in Feminism.* Ithaca: Cornell University Press.

—— and Hintikka, Merill, eds (1983) *Discovering Reality: Feminist Perspectives on Epistemology, Metaphysics, Methodology, and Philosophy of Science.* Dordrecht: Reidel.

Hartsock, Nancy (1983a) 'The feminist standpoint: developing the ground for a specifically feminist historical materialism', in Harding and Hintikka (1983), pp. 283–310.

—— (1983b) *Money, Sex, and Power.* New York: Longman; Boston: Northeastern University Press, 1984.

—— (1987) 'Rethinking modernism: minority and majority theories', *Cultural Critique* 7: 187–206.

Hogness, E. Rusten (1983) 'Why stress? A look at the making of stress, 1936–56', unpublished paper available from the author, 4437 Mill Creek Rd, Healdsburg, CA 95448.

hooks, bell (1981) *Ain't I a Woman.* Boston: South End.

—— (1984) *Feminist Theory: From Margin to Center.* Boston: South End.

Hrdy, Sarah Blaffer (1981) *The Woman That Never Evolved.* Cambridge, MA: Harvard University Press.

Hubbard, Ruth, Henifin, Mary Sue, and Fried, Barbara, eds (1982) *Biological Woman, the Convenient Myth.* Cambridge, MA: Schenkman.

Hull, Gloria, Scott, Patricia Bell, and Smith, Barbara, eds (1982) *All the Women Are White, All the Men Are Black, But Some of Us Are Brave.* Old Westbury: The Feminist Press.

International Fund for Agricultural Development (1985) *IFAD Experience Relating to Rural Women, 1977–84.* Rome: IFAD, 37.

Irigaray, Luce (1977) *Ce sexe qui n'en est pas un.* Paris: Minuit.

—— (1979) *Et l'une ne bouge pas sans l'autre.* Paris: Minuit.

Jaggar, Alison (1983) *Feminist Politics and Human Nature.* Totowa, NJ: Roman & Allenheld.

Jameson, Fredric (1984) 'Post-modernism, or the cultural logic of late capitalism', *New Left Review* 146: 53–92.

Kahn, Douglas and Neumaier, Diane, eds (1985) *Cultures in Contention.* Seattle: Real Comet.

Keller, Evelyn Fox (1983) *A Feeling for the Organism.* San Francisco: Freeman.

—— (1985) *Reflections on Gender and Science.* New Haven: Yale University Press.

King, Katie (1984) 'The pleasure of repetition and the limits of identification in feminist science fiction: reimaginations of the body after the cyborg', paper delivered at the California American Studies Association, Pomona.

—— (1986) 'The situation of lesbianism as feminism's magical sign: contests for meaning and the U.S. women's movement, 1968–72', *Communication* 9(1): 65–92.

—— (1987a) 'Canons without innocence', University of California at Santa Cruz, PhD thesis.

—— (1987b) *The Passing Dreams of Choice . . . Once Before and After: Audre Lorde and the Apparatus of Literary Production*, book prospectus, University of Maryland at College Park.
Kingston, Maxine Hong (1977) *China Men*. New York: Knopf.
Klein, Hilary (1989) 'Marxism, psychoanalysis, and mother nature', *Feminist Studies* 15(2): 255–78.
Knorr-Cetina, Karin (1981) *The Manufacture of Knowledge*. Oxford: Pergamon.
—— and Mulkay, Michael, eds (1983) *Science Observed: Perspectives on the Social Study of Science*. Beverly Hills: Sage.
Kramarae, Cheris and Treichler, Paula (1985) *A Feminist Dictionary*. Boston: Pandora.
Lange, Bernd-Peter and Stuby, Anna Marie, eds (1984) *1984*. Berlin: Argument Sonderband 105.
Latour, Bruno (1984) *Les microbes, guerre et paix, suivi des irréductions*. Paris: Métailié.
—— and Woolgar, Steve (1979) *Laboratory Life: The Social Construction of Scientific Facts*. Beverly Hills: Sage.
Lerner, Gerda, ed. (1973) *Black Women in White America: A Documentary History*. New York: Vintage.
Lévi-Strauss, Claude (1971) *Tristes Tropiques*, John Russell, trans. New York: Atheneum.
Lewontin, R. C., Rose, Steven, and Kamin, Leon J. (1984) *Not in Our Genes: Biology, Ideology, and Human Nature*. New York: Pantheon.
Lorde, Audre (1982) *Zami, a New Spelling of My Name*. Trumansberg, NY: Crossing, 1983.
—— (1984) *Sister Outsider*. Trumansberg, NY: Crossing.
Lowe, Lisa (1986) 'French literary Orientalism: The representation of "others" in the texts of Montesquieu, Flaubert, and Kristeva', University of California at Santa Cruz, PhD thesis.
McCaffrey, Anne (1969) *The Ship Who Sang*. New York: Ballantine.
Mackey, Nathaniel (1984) 'Review', *Sulfur* 2: 200–5.
MacKinnon, Catherine (1982) 'Feminism, marxism, method, and the state: an agenda for theory', *Signs* 7(3): 515–44.
—— (1987) *Feminism Unmodified: Discourses on Life and Law*. Cambridge, MA: Harvard University Press.
Many Voices, One Chant: Black Feminist Perspectives (1984) *Feminist Review* 17, special issue.
Marcuse, Herbert (1964) *One-Dimensional Man: Studies in the Ideology of Advanced Industrial Society*. Boston: Beacon.
Markoff, John and Siegel, Lenny (1983) 'Military micros', paper presented at Silicon Valley Research Project conference, University of California at Santa Cruz.
Marks, Elaine and de Courtivron, Isabelle, eds (1980) *New French Feminisms*. Amherst: University of Massachusetts Press.
Merchant, Carolyn (1980) *The Death of Nature: Women, Ecology, and the Scientific Revolution*. New York: Harper & Row.
Microelectronics Group (1980) *Microelectronics: Capitalist Technology and the Working Class*. London: CSE.
Mohanty, Chandra Talpade (1984) 'Under western eyes: feminist scholarship and colonial discourse', *Boundary* 2, 3 (12/13): 333–58.

Moraga. Cherríe (1983) *Loving in the War Years: lo que nunca pasó por sus labios.* Boston: South End.
—— and Anzaldüa, Gloria, eds (1981) *This Bridge Called My Back: Writings by Radical Women of Color.* Watertown: Persephone.
Morgan, Robin, ed. (1984) *Sisterhood Is Global.* Garden City, NY: Anchor/ Doubleday.
Nash, June and Fernandez-Kelly, Maria Patricia, eds (1983) *Women and Men and the International Division of Labor.* Albany: State University of New York Press.
Nash, Roderick (1979) 'The exporting and importing of nature: nature-appreciation as a commodity, 1850–1980', *Perspectives in American History* 3: 517–60.
National Science Foundation (1988) *Women and Minorities in Science and Engineering.* Washington: NSF.
O'Brien, Mary (1981) *The Politics of Reproduction.* New York. Routledge & Kegan Paul.
Ong, Aihwa (1987) *Spirits of Resistance and Capitalist Discipline: Factory Workers in Malaysia.* Albany: State University of New York Press.
Ong, Walter (1982) *Orality and Literacy: The Technologizing of the Word.* New York: Methuen.
Park, Katherine and Daston, Lorraine J. (1981) 'Unnatural conceptions: the study of monsters in sixteenth- and seventeenth-century France and England', *Past and Present* 92: 20–54.
Perloff, Marjorie (1984) 'Dirty language and scramble systems', *Sulfur* 11: 178–83.
Petchesky, Rosalind Pollack (1981) 'Abortion, anti-feminism and the rise of die New Right', *Feminist Studies* 7(2): 206–46.
Piven, Frances Fox and Coward, Richard (1982) *The New Class War: Reagan's Attack on the Welfare State and Its Consequences.* New York: Pantheon.
Preston, Douglas (1984) 'Shooting in paradise', *Natural History* 93(12): 14–19.
Reskin, Barbara F. and Hartmann, Heidi, eds (1986) *Women's Work, Men's Work.* Washington: National Academy of Sciences.
Rose, Hilary (1983) 'Hand, brain, and heart: a feminist epistemology for the natural sciences', *Signs* 9(1): 73–90.
—— (1986) 'Women's work: women's knowledge', in Juliet Mitchell and Ann Oakley, eds, *What Is Feminism? A Re-Examination.* New York: Pantheon, pp. 161–83.
Rose, Stephen (1986) *The American Profile Poster: Who Owns What, Who Makes How Much, Who Works Where, and Who Lives with Whom?* New York: Pantheon.
Rossiter, Margaret (1982) *Women Scientists in America.* Baltimore: Johns Hopkins University Press.
Rothschild, Joan, ed. (1983) *Machina ex Dea: Feminist Perspectives on Technology.* New York: Pergamon.
Russ, Joanna (1983) *How to Suppress Women's Writing.* Austin: University of Texas Press.
Sachs, Carolyn (1983) *The Invisible Farmers: Women in Agricultural Production.* Totowa: Rowman & Allenheld.
Said, Edward (1978) *Orientalism.* New York: Pantheon.
Sandoval, Chela (1984) 'Dis-illusionment and the poetry of the future: the making of oppositional consciousness', University of California at Santa Cruz, PhD qualifying essay.

—— (n.d.) *Yours in Struggle: Women Respond to Racism, a Report on the National Women's Studies Association.* Oakland, CA: Center for Third World Organizing.

Schiebinger, Londa (1987) 'The history and philosophy of women in science: a review essay', *Signs* 12(2): 305–32.

Science Policy Research Unit (1982) *Microelectronics and Women's Employment in Britain.* University of Sussex.

Smith, Barbara, ed. (1983) *Home Girls: A Black Feminist Anthology.* New York: Kitchen Table, Women of Color Press.

Smith, Dorothy (1974) 'Women's perspective as a radical critique of sociology', *Sociological Inquiry* 44.

—— (1979) 'A sociology of women', in J. Sherman and E. T. Beck, eds *The Prism of Sex.* Madison: University of Wisconsin Press.

Sofia, Zoe (also Zoe Sofoulis) (1984) 'Exterminating fetuses: abortion, disarmament, and the sexo-semiotics of extra-terrestrialism', *Diacritics* 14(2): 47–59.

Sofoulis, Zoe (1984) 'Jupiter Space', paper delivered at the American Studies Association, Pomona, CA.

—— (1987) 'Lacklein', University of California at Santa Cruz, unpublished essay.

Sontag, Susan (1977) *On Photography.* New York: Dell.

Stacey, Judith (1987) 'Sexism by a subtler name? Postindustrial conditions and postfeminist consciousness', *Socialist Review* 96: 7–28.

Stallard, Karin, Ehrenreich, Barbara, and Sklar, Holly (1983) *Poverty in the American Dream.* Boston: South End.

Sturgeon, Noel (1986) 'Feminism, anarchism, and non-violent direct action polities', University of California at Santa Cruz, PhD qualifying essay.

Sussman, Vic (1986) 'Personal tech. Technology lends a hand', *The Washington Post Magazine*, 9 November, pp. 45–56.

Traweek, Sharon (1988) *Beamtimes and Lifetimes: The World of High Energy Physics.* Cambridge, MA: Harvard University Press.

Treichler, Paula (1987) 'AIDS, homophobia, and biomedical discourse: an epidemic of signification', *October* 43: 31–70.

Trinh T. Minh-ha (1986–7) 'Introduction', and 'Difference: "a special third world women issue"', *Discourse: Journal for Theoretical Studies in Media and Culture* 8: 3–38.

——, ed. (1986–7) *She, the Inappropriate/d Other, Discourse* 8.

Weizenbaum, Joseph (1976) *Computer Power and Human Reason.* San Francisco: Freeman.

Welford, John Noble (1 July, 1986) 'Pilot's helmet helps interpret high speed world', *New York Times*, pp. 21, 24.

Wilfred, Denis (1982) 'Capital and agriculture, a review of Marxian problematics', *Studies in Political Economy* 7: 127–54.

Winner, Langdon (1977) *Autonomous Technology: Technics out of Control as a Theme in Political Thought.* Cambridge, MA: MIT Press.

—— (1986) *The Whale and the Reactor.* Chicago: University of Chicago Press.

Winograd, Terry and Flores, Fernando (1986) *Understanding Computers and Cognition: A New Foundation for Design.* Norwood, NJ; Ablex.

Wittig, Monique (1973) *The Lesbian Body*, David LeVay, trans. New York: Avon, 1975 (*Le corps lesbien*, 1973).

Women and Poverty, special issue (1984) *Signs* 10(2).

Wright, Susan (1982, July/August) 'Recombinant DNA: the status of hazards and controls', *Environment* 24(6): 12–20, 51–53.
—— (1986) 'Recombinant DNA technology and its social transformation, 1972–82', *Osiris*, 2nd series, 2: 303–60.
Young, Robert M. (1979, March) 'Interpreting the production of science', *New Scientist* 29: 1026–8.
—— and Levidow, Les, eds (1981, 1985) *Science, Technology and the Labour Process*, 2 vols. London: CSE and Free Association Books.
Yoxen, Edward (1983) *The Gene Business*. New York: Harper & Row.
Zimmerman, Jan, ed. (1983) *The Technological Woman: Interfacing with Tomorrow*. New York: Praeger.

78

WHAT DO WE KNOW ABOUT GENDER AND INFORMATION TECHNOLOGY AT WORK?

A discussion of selected feminist research

Juliet Webster

Source: *European Journal of Women's Studies* 2(3) (1995): 315–34.

Introduction

The emergence in the late 1970s of information and communication technologies (ICTs) prompted enormous interest in computer technologies and their effects upon work. Many early studies of automated work, its characteristics and its implications for the experiences of workers were, however, concerned almost exclusively with the nature of work done by men; the debate on the 'labour process' which took place particularly in Britain and America was male dominated in its theorization, its conceptual categories and its empirical focus. Empirically, the focus was on occupations dominated by men, in particular on skilled craft work, and assumptions were often made that the impacts of automation would be the same for *all* workers as they were for male workers. Conceptual constructs such as 'skill', which were important measures of change in work processes, were treated unproblematically, with little awareness of the ways in which these were social constructions arising from unequal levels of bargaining power between men and women. And at a theoretical level, there was a generalized ignorance of the ways in which gender relations are at the very centre of the process of technological change.

Since these early studies, feminists and others concerned specifically with the computerization of women's work have taken issue with some of the key assumptions and findings of this body of work. They sought, firstly, to make a corrective to the almost exclusive empirical focus on men's jobs by conducting studies of the automation of women's work; secondly, to develop conceptual tools which would enable us to understand how the process of technological change might be different in relation to women's work than it is in relation to men's work; and, thirdly, to urticulate the relationship between gender and technology, and particularly to analyse the ways in which technologies, similarly to jobs, come to be gendered – that is, to have gender relations and divisions of labour embedded within them.

This article provides a selective overview of feminist research conducted since information technologies were introduced into the first workplaces at the end of the 1970s. It offers a synthesis of this literature and highlights some of the key theoretical and empirical contributions which have advanced our understanding of the gender–technology relationship.

Specifically, the article examines the two-fold nature of the gender–technology relationship and the way in which this has been theorized and examined empirically. It considers some 'impact' studies of information technology upon gendered divisions of labour and gender relations, and outlines some of the intellectual advances that have been made in our understanding of the sexual division of labour through these studies. It also considers the growing volume of work dealing with the shaping of information technology (IT) at work by gender, and in particular the growing range of empirical studies which have charted this shaping, both of technological artefacts and of processes of technological change more broadly.

Changing technology, changing gender

The concept of 'gender' has been theorized in many different ways by feminist thinkers. These can be summarized as 'gender structure' (or the sexual division of labour), 'gender symbolism' (the meanings according to which human beings think about and organize social activity) and individual gender' (the personal gender identity of an individual) (see Harding, 1986: 18). Though all are important for our understanding of gender and its relationship to other social phenomena, such as technology, this article is concerned only with the first of these aspects, namely, with 'gender structure', i.e. the gendering of the division of labour and of labour processes.

Furthermore, it is worth noting that neither 'technology' nor 'gender relations' are static phenomena. Both have been subject to profound changes as they are negotiated and renegotiated with each other, and within the rest of the social world (Cockburn and Ormrod, 1993; Tijdens, 1994). This also implies that, as Henwood (1993) has pointed out, we have to conceptualize technology and gender as continually shifting. Certainly, the shift in perspectives on gender relations is evident in the selection of literature reviewed here. Some of the early 'impact' studies of IT treat gender relations as passive recipients of changes wrought by technology and/or by capital (e.g. Braverman, 1974; Cooley, 1980; Bird, 1980; Huws, 1980; Softley, 1985; Wernecke, 1983; Women's Voice, 1979). More recently, gender relations have been conceptualized in a more dynamic way, as continually constituting and reconstituting themselves, and their role in actively defining and shaping the nature and direction of technological change is more clearly recognized (Cockburn, 1983; Cockburn and Ormrod, 1993; Wajcman, 1991; Murray, 1993).

In addition, we have witnessed a period of such dramatic technological change over the past 15 years that our approach to 'technology' must be equally dynamic. An unprecedented pace of change has occurred in the types of hardware, software and expertise that constitute computers since the 'microelectronics revolution' first took place at the end of the 1970s. The early mainframe systems of the 1970s and 1980s (and their particular principles of centralization and remoteness from users) have given way to distributed processing, personal computing systems and IT networks (Tijdens, 1994). These are important changes, with potentially important consequences for women. Yet technologies, and their effects, are all too readily accepted as given in feminist research (Henwood, 1993), with the result that there is little, if any, awareness of the implications of such developments for the experience of women at work or for the continued embedding of gender relations of expertise, knowledge and power within these systems.

The dynamism of gender relations is made clearer in feminist studies; patterns of male domination and female subordination are recognized as constantly shifting over time and across cultures. Feminists point to a plurality of masculinities and femininities (Wajcman, 1991; Cockburn and Ormrod, 1993). If technologies are imbued with male values, then these are not fixed but are dynamic and find different expression in technologies in different eras and cultures.

These points are of both theoretical and empirical significance, and are important to bear in mind when considering the insights offered by studies of the gender–technology relationship as it is worked out, in practice, in the workplace. The following part of the article discusses this research and assesses its contribution to our thinking.

Changes in labour processes?

The early 1980s saw a blossoming of workplace ethnographies of women's work which attempted to provide a corrective to the predominance of studies focusing exclusively on the work processes of men (Herzog, 1980; Cavendish, 1981; Pollert, 1981; Westwood, 1984). The early studies concentrated on women's manual work, and were not specifically concerned with the implementation of computer technologies; nevertheless, these studies offered important insights into the specific ways in which women's work is organized and controlled, and their relationship to production technologies. Pollert's (1981) study of a tobacco factory and Cavendish's (1981) research into the production of components for car assembly reveal a strongly gendered division of labour based on assumptions about women's 'natural' manual dexterity and their lack of aptitude for handling technology. Pollert describes a highly segregated, long-established division of labour between the highly mechanized, capital-intensive tasks performed by men and the non-mechanized, labour-intensive work performed by women. In Cavendish's study, the work performed by women, though requiring a considerable degree of manual dexterity, was defined as less skilled than men's work. The contribution of these studies, aside from their ethnographic value, was to call early attention to women's exclusion from technologies, technical know-how and skill. They also served to warn of the vulnerability of women workers in low grade, low paid occupations. According to Armstrong (1982), labour-intensive work is inherently more insecure than capital-intensive work, due to short-term changes in demand and to long-term pressures for automation. These warnings were underlined by Wernecke (1983), who cautioned that, in the office, it would be secretaries and typists who would be most vulnerable to the deleterious effects of computerization.

Indeed, it was in the office that researchers first examined the impact of IT upon women's jobs (Bird, 1980; Barker and Downing, 1980; West, 1982; Greve, 1986; Webster, 1986). Early research attempted to enumerate the likely effects on levels of employment, but failed to reach firm conclusions (Leeds TUCRIC, 1982). Later research (Tijdens, 1994) has also identified no significant loss of employment. The effects of computerization on the work process of women office workers proved easier to assess, largely through case studies. Here, the implementation of IT, specifically in the form of word processing, was generally found to have little impact; the organization of office work and particularly the sexual division of labour remained intact (Silverstone and Towler, 1984; Webster, 1990; Liff, 1993). Research into the automation of clerical work confirmed the low status of women, and highlighted a particular set of managerial practices designed to control and subordinate these workers – a system of patriarchal control creating and drawing upon the peculiarly gendered character of office roles and relationships (Barker and Downing, 1980).

Barker and Downing, among others (e.g. Women's Voice, 1979; Morgall, 1981; Softley, 1985) predicted, however, that the introduction of new technology into the office would bring about the demise of these patriarchal relations of control and their replacement with more 'mechanical' control structures, together with a deskilling of secretarial work similar to that identified by Braverman (1974) in relation to male craft work. Other research has suggested that this 'homogenization' of office work and manual work has not occurred (Lie and Rasmussen, 1985; Webster, 1990). Thus, while patriarchal control of women office workers has persisted, this, paradoxically, has permitted women to continue to exercise some of their former technical skills and control over the labour process. (This does not mean that women's office work has ever been defined as 'skilled', despite the fact that many office tasks do indeed require technical training, manual dexterity, discretion and judgement. Women's office work has always provided a strong example of how women's work comes to be devalued simply because it is women who perform it [Phillips and Taylor, 1980].) Overall, in fact, there is little evidence to suggest that computerization has caused straightforward deskilling of women office workers. Rather, its impact has been shown to be highly contingent upon the context within which it is introduced, for example, upon the types of jobs performed (Wagner, 1985; Webster, 1990), and upon longer term rationalization processes at work (Crompton and Jones, 1984).

In accounts of technological change it is, in fact, often forgotten that work restructuring is set in motion by managements in order to achieve their desired organization of work and technical division of labour, not an imperative of new technology alone. In the context of the low wage, low skill status of much women's work, it may not make sense for managements to embark on expensive and disruptive programmes of work rationalization in order to achieve productivity gains unless these offset the costs of such programmes. Feminist accounts of technological change have restored an awareness of the different imperatives relating to the costs and control of male and female workers, rather than assuming that managements will use identical strategies of work rationalization for female as for male workers. They have been careful to distinguish between the labour costs of women and men, and particularly to address the ways in which employers make use of differentially priced labour power in particular circumstances, often using women as a cheaper or more reliable option than machinery.

Shifting spatial divisions of labour

On a global scale, there is more convincing evidence for a dramatic restructuring of work. Capitals conventionally roam the globe in search of ever cheaper arenas in which to carry out production. Information and communications technologies have facilitated this process, permitting the relocation of corporate activities away from the more expensive regions in the so-called 'First World', either to less favoured regions within the same countries (Henwood and Wyatt, 1986; Goldstein, 1989), or to entirely different countries in the Third World (Grossman, 1979; Fuentes and Ehrenreich, 1983; Mitter, 1986; Posthuma, 1987; Common Interests, 1991). As well as the infamous use of young, 'docile', non-unionized South-East Asian women for microelectronics manufacture, telecommunications technologies have facilitated the relocation of data entry jobs, clerical jobs and garment production into low wage, low overhead regions, most notably the Caribbean, Latin America, South-East Asia, India and, most recently, China. Although jobs initially most significantly affected have been those in the clerical, textiles and electronics industries, few occupations seem to be immune to this dispersal of work and to its coordination by means of computer and satellite technology. Even software production is now being fragmented and subcontracted to India, China and South-East Asia (Heeks, 1993).

Such relocation clearly provides dramatic cost savings to employers (Mitter, 1986). However, while adding a racial dimension to the restructuring of work (and therefore compelling us to address race as well as gender issues in our analysis of technological change), it does nothing to alter the sexual division of labour or the low status of women's work, either in the First or in the Third World.

Similarly, research into new technology homeworking reveals a locational restructuring of work, but little change in the low grade status of women's work. For example, Huws's (1984) study of clerical home-working in Britain found that the majority of homeworkers were married women in their mid-30s. In addition to the routine and intense nature of the work itself, the women in her study were low paid, isolated, non-unionized and uncertain as to the status of their employment. Routinized and increasingly intense labour processes, together with low pay and lack of unionization are conditions of work which are typical of women's clerical work in general, but for homeworkers these conditions were exacerbated by their isolation from other workers and their inability to organize collectively in any way. In their Australian research, Wajcman and Probert (1988) found that the sexual division of labour operating in society at large was reproduced in the types of homeworking jobs that men and women did, and they found marked differences in working conditions between them. Men were to be found mainly in professional occupations (such as management, computer programming and systems analysis) working from home, while women were located largely in clerical occupations, and were married with young children. Like female homeworkers in the traditional sweated industries, they were typically paid at piece rates and earned substantially less than comparably skilled workers working in offices, and, in addition, they had to meet their own overhead costs – heating, lighting and power for machines. The male professionals, on the other hand, were typically self-employed, and were able to exploit the skill shortage in their type of work, earning more working at home than working from an office and with lower overhead costs. According to recent research into teleworking in Britain, this pattern of occupational segregation among teleworkers does not appear to have substantially altered (Huws, 1993; Fothergill, 1994). Moreover, Fothergill's research shows that, in Britain, men and women are currently being propelled into teleworking for very different, and not entirely surprising, reasons: men often becoming self-employed teleworkers after having been made redundant from their jobs, and women taking up teleworking in order to combine childcare with work. This does not prove to be as convenient as it would appear. Teleworking women with children were found to work extremely diverse and unpredictable hours, as they seized opportunities when their children were at school or in bed to work without interruptions. Furthermore, according to Huws, women are increasingly debarred from using teleworking to combine work with childcare; she points to cases where having young children is a disqualification for employment as a teleworker (Huws, 1993: 52). One of the few 'perks' of this kind of work for women is, it would seem, being eroded.

Research into teleworking is, in Britain at least, still in its infancy. However, to date, it indicates that much teleworking, while facilitated by ICTs, has revolved around work which has been conducted from home for some time – especially self-employed clerical and professional work. What has been decisive in influencing employers' strategies regarding telework has not been technology so much as socioeconomic factors such as the need to reduce building overheads or to restructure companies (Haddon and Silverstone, 1993). Moreover, teleworking has not had the impact on daily life that its potential flexibility promised, and seems merely to capture and relocate workplace divisions of labour into the home. This touches broader issues about the origins of such divisions of labour and of women's occupational segregation more generally. The usual focus of feminist attention has been with the role of domestic labour in shaping women's occupational positions; the transference of workplace divisions of labour into the domestic sphere reverses this focus.

Conclusions on the restructuring of women's jobs

What have we learned about the effect of new technologies on women's jobs? First, research has challenged assumptions that the diffusion of IT would result in fundamental changes in the sexual division of labour, either leading to an increasing degradation of work and the substitution of male labour with cheap, unskilled female labour, or creating a multiskilled, multitasking, undifferentiated workforce. Instead, it has demonstrated decisively that gendered divisions of labour and patterns of work organization are not readily dislodged by the implementation of information, or any other, technologies. The pattern of evidence suggests that the introduction of new technologies does not substantially undermine sexual divisions in the labour market, the gendering of occupations allocated to men and women, or the social construction of skill. Instead, the sexual division of labour appears to have been left very much intact by the introduction of technology, with women remaining concentrated in low grade, low paid jobs, most notably in the service sector, within service occupations in the manufacturing sector and in semi-skilled, labour-intensive production, assembly and packing jobs in the mass production industries. (See especially Game and Pringle [1983] for several case studies which confirm this conclusion.)

The second insight contributed by feminist research into the process of technological change is that women's relationship to technology in the workplace, as elsewhere, is overwhelmingly one of separation and exclusion. Women's exclusion from technology was identified in the ethnographic research of Pollert and Cavendish, but it was only with Cockburn's (1983, 1985) work that a thoroughgoing attempt was made to theorize the gender–technology relationship in terms of the dynamics operating between capital and labour, and women and men. She provided, first, descriptive case study evidence of the impact of new technology upon the sexual division of labour and skills, particularly in the printing industry (Cockburn, 1983). Secondly, she highlighted the way in which the process of technological change was itself conditioned by the struggles of skilled men to retain the basis for their exclusive craft privileges. Thirdly, she articulated at a theoretical level the construction of male and female gender identities in relation to technological competence and asserted the masculinity of technology as a social product (Cockburn, 1985).

Cockburn's (1983) research into technological change in typesetting described attempts by newspaper employers to replace hot metal typesetting – work traditionally carried out by skilled craftsmen and from which women had always been excluded – with cold electronic composition. The employers saw this technical change as enabling them to replace the men with cheaper women workers. The very design of the new machinery – with QWERTY keyboards and altogether lighter handling – had built into it the wherewithal to undermine the traditional allocation of skilled jobs to a powerful group of highly unionized male craft workers, and thus their exclusive rights to this craft. The male compositors fought to defend their position by having sole rights to use the computer typesetting equipment, and their strategy of resistance continued to centre around the exclusivity of their skills and the barring of women from the trade. In many workplaces, they succeeded, though the old material basis of their craft had now been eliminated. In fact, for the craftsmen these changes were highly emasculating.

Cockburn's later (1985) work developed her ideas about the construction of male identity in terms of technical competence and skills. In general, physical strength, initiative and technological competence materially distinguish the work of men and women. Women are not typically found in jobs using technological skills, not because there is anything 'natural' in this state of affairs, but because men have appropriated these skills. Social and cultural relations within and outside the workplace have defined men as technologically capable, have allowed them to organize to secure rewards in the labour market, and have served to exclude women from technological know-how and from the rewards commensurate with this know-how. The exclusive access of men to technological competence has been a key source of men's power over women and of their capacity to command higher incomes and scarce jobs. Men and women, therefore, have very different relationships to technical knowledge and to machinery, and it is these relationships which in part constitute their gender identities:

> Technology enters into our sexual identity: femininity is incompatible with technological competence; to feel technically competent is to feel manly.
>
> (Cockburn, 1985: 12)

Cockburn's analysis has recently invited some critique. In particular, her tendency to underplay the differences between men's jobs and thus to overstate the distinctions between men's and women's work has been found problematic. Not all men's jobs are skilled and involve the type of craft control Cockburn describes (West, 1990), and indeed technology can also be used by some men to dominate others (Wajcman, 1991). Class differences (and also ethnic and generational differences) give rise to different versions of masculinity, such that it may be more useful to think in terms of 'masculinities' (Wajcman, 1991: 40). Nevertheless, her analysis is one of the most sustained attempts to formulate the gender–technology relationship. Here, gender relations are not simply the passive recipients of change brought about through the introduction of technology, but themselves critically shape the process of technological change, the institutions and the practices involved.

The social shaping of technology and the role of gender

The 'social shaping of technology' perspective would appear to address such challenges to conventional thinking on the one-way relationship between technology and gender relations. This perspective was explicitly developed as an antithesis to technological determinism and was intended to challenge notions of the social 'impact' of technologies which did not recognize their social context and the social and economic factors involved in their development.

The social shaping of technology approach draws upon a range of conceptual traditions, including the sociology of scientific knowledge and 'social constructionism' articulated by Callon (1987), Latour (1987) and others, the sociology of industry (Noble, 1979), and evolutionary economics (Nelson and Winter, 1977). It contends that technological change is a complex social activity involving struggle, interest articulation and learning, that different actors possess differential, socially defined levels of expertise and that technological change is not a linear process, but takes place across networks of actors in an iterative way, and that all this significantly affects the form and content of emerging technologies.

However, most 'social shaping' and 'social constructionist' accounts remain stubbornly silent on matters of gender (and race) (Liff, 1990; Horn, 1994). This omission is all the more surprising since the creation and consumption of technologies, including IT, is subject to an extreme sexual division of labour. It has therefore been the concern of feminist scholars to emphasize the centrality of gender relations in constituting technologies – through the institutions, values and divisions of labour involved (Cockburn, 1983, 1985; McNeil, 1987; Harding, 1991; Wajcman, 1991). Feminist interest in the gender relations of technology in fact developed first out of an analysis of the exclusion of women from science and of the gendered nature of scientific knowledge and activity. Following from this, feminists began in the 1980s to examine the position of women in technological jobs, and the wider question of the impact of gender relations on the design and production of technology and hence the gendered nature of technology.

Examination of technological artefacts has shown that occupational sex-typing provides the basis for the design of technologies applied to particular jobs. In some cases this has generated technologies which embody the features of work done primarily or exclusively by women, in other words, technologies which are designed and marketed for use by women workers. For example, histories of the typewriter and, more recently, the word processor have shown how established working patterns and skills in 'women's' office jobs have come to be embedded in the tools which are developed for them. Features like the size and weight of typewriters (Knie, 1992), the QWERTY keyboard (David, 1985) and function keys on dedicated work processors, all reflect the sex-typing of office jobs, assumptions that they will be used primarily by women with touch-typing skills (Webster, 1993) but without technical competence (Hofmann, 1994) and assumptions about the 'tight' character of the work that women are fitted for.

Technologies may also be designed in order to undermine the sex-typing of certain occupations. Cockburn's (1983) work on the development and application of computerized typesetting systems in the printing industry (discussed earlier in this article) provides strong evidence of this purpose. These systems were designed expressly to depart from the old linotype devices which relied on skilled, male craft labour, marked by long apprenticeships, strong trade union organization and which required a combination of physical strength and manual dexterity for their operation. This was a design, then, which had gender and class struggles at its very heart. Moreover, there was nothing inevitable about it. Electronic circuitry could have been used in conjunction with the old linotype keyboards, and, indeed, the firm Linotype did manufacture such a device. The purpose (even if not the initial outcome) of designing electronic systems with smaller, light-to-operate, QWERTY-style keyboards was to deskill male craft labour and ultimately to replace it with relatively unskilled female labour.

If gendered divisions of labour are involved in the conception and design of technologies, then they are certainly involved in the actual production of them. In IT, there is a sharp sexual division between men, who are principally involved in the design, development, marketing, selling, installation, management and servicing of systems, and women, who are concentrated in the low skilled assembly of them (Goldstein, 1989; Cockburn and Ormrod,

1993). Again, essentialist assumptions of men's and women's 'natural' abilities underlie this division. On the one hand, as we have seen, men are seen as having an inherent affinity with technology, while on the other, it is supposed that women have the nimble fingers and patience necessary for the microscopic assembly of minute components. Moreover, in the employment of women in the Third World in sweated, routinized, integrated circuit assembly work, racial stereotypes are heaped upon gender stereotypes and economic imperatives. While the electronics multinationals clearly perceive the cost benefits of this cheap source of labour, together with the absence of trade unionism or worker militancy, they are also attracted by the particular 'docility' of South-East Asian women (Grossman, 1979; Fuentes and Ehrenreich, 1983).

Gender relations have also profoundly affected the pace and direction of technological change in the workplace. As we have seen, the conditions of women's paid employment – the casualized, unskilled and relatively cheap nature of female labour in certain industries, together with use of labour control practices which are primarily patriarchal in nature – have often cut across moves towards the rationalization of these production processes through automation. This has meant that the diffusion of new technologies has often been slower in many jobs in which female labour is concentrated than it has been in jobs dominated by men.

Most fundamentally, however, research has pointed to the gendered nature of technology in general. Rather than examining how women could be more equitably treated by an essentially neutral technology, many feminists now argue that Western technology itself embodies patriarchal values. In particular, the strong military-industrial orientation of modern technology is seen as being symptomatic of the male dominance of technology, and of the masculinity of technological processes and products. Technology is seen as deeply implicated in the masculine project of the domination and control of women and nature. According to Arnold and Faulkner (1985: 22), for example,

> Technology is central to the immense productive dynamism of capitalism ..., but it is also more than this: it is a vital aspect of modern patriarchy. It enables men to exercise unprecedented domination over the natural world and over society. In the capitalist period, more than any other previous epoch, technology has excluded and alienated women; it has become *masculine*.

Technology is seen as masculine, first, in the institutions and processes which generate and perpetuate it, and second, in the values which underlie it. Socialist feminists have reminded us that the relations of production are constructed as much out of gender divisions as class divisions. In this vein, Cockburn (1983, 1985) and Arnold and Faulkner (1985) see women's exclusion from technology as a consequence of the gender division of labour and the male domination of skilled trades that have developed under capitalism. The gender division of labour which developed in the factory, in which women were excluded from craft skills and from access to technology, meant that the machinery introduced was designed by men with men in mind, either by the capitalist inventor/ entrepreneur, or by skilled craftsmen. Industrial technology from its origins thus reflected male power as well as capitalist domination.

The masculine culture of technology is fundamental to the way in which the gender division of labour is still being reproduced today. 'The social institutions of technology are, like most institutions in society, dominated by men' (Arnold and Faulkner, 1985: 18). Feminists have pointed to a variety of barriers to women's access to technology, from social attitudes, to girls' education, to the teaching of engineering and technology in post-school education, to the employment policies of firms (for an overview of this work, see Kirkup and Keller, 1992). Technology has come to be defined as an activity appropriate for men, and at the same time, to be part of the definition of masculinity (Murray, 1993). On the other hand, women are notably absent from the design of technologies, and from decision-making concerning their implementation. Indeed, they are largely the recipients of technology, often defined as marginal to it, and as simply 'unskilled' users (Tijdens, 1994). Cockburn (1985) has suggested that women, as well as finding themselves barred from technological opportunities, actively resist entering technological fields because of the cultural incompatibility with femininity. In the 'producers'/'users' dichotomy of technology, women are overrepresented in the latter group just as men are in the former.

In addition to the institutional domination of technology by men, it has been asserted that technology is redolent with 'male values'. Cooley (1980), one of the most prominent writers on technology and the labour process, argues that technology has the male values of objectivity, rationality, strength, competition and domination built into it and is starved of the so-called female values of intuition, subjectivity, tenacity and compassion. Similarly, eco-feminists, though coming at the question from a very different perspective, equate women with a closeness to nature. They contend that the technologies that men have created are based on the domination of nature paralleling their domination of women. Their analysis focuses particularly on military technologies, which they see as 'products of a patriarchal culture that speaks violence at every level' (King, 1983: 126).

Does the problem lie in men's domination of technology, or is technology inherently masculine? This remains one of the critical questions for feminists and others concerned with an understanding of the interaction of gender relations and technology. The difficulty with the 'technology as masculine' approach is that it views masculinity and femininity as natural biological and psychological attributes, and fails to examine the ways in which, through socialization and social processes which restrict women to the private domain, men and women have become associated with 'masculine' and 'feminine' values in the first place (Wajcman, 1991). Nevertheless, the strength of this approach is that it goes beyond what Henwood (1993) has dubbed the 'women in technology' policy approach, in which the problem is seen as simply being women's exclusion from technological work and in which change is understood as coming about through increased access and further equal opportunities policies. Despite the essentialism in the 'technology as masculine' approach, an analysis of technology as embodying patriarchy points at the very least to a serious lack of regard for women's needs and priorities in technological innovation and design.

'Feminist' systems design: addressing the needs of women

It is in recognition of this failure of conventional technological design to meet the needs of women, and of the intriguing prospect that different design priorities might produce different technological artefacts, that researchers have recently embarked on 'human-centred' computer systems design projects (Vehviläinen, 1991; Greenbaum and Kyng, 1991; Green *et al.*, 1993; Probert and Wilson, 1993). Human-centred systems design projects originated in Scandinavia, and must be seen partly in the context of the particular industrial relations and political environment there. Early initiatives in the 1970s and 1980s aimed to address the problems of work fragmentation and deskilling often brought about by new technologies, and to formulate design strategies for avoiding them (Ehn and Kyng, 1985). They were participative, involving collaboration between employers and trade unions or labour organizations, and strongly multidisciplinary, stressing the importance of combining organizational and technical knowledge to develop systems and jobs which would improve or maintain, and not degrade, the quality of working life.

Many of the initiatives developed in Scandinavia and later in Britain and Germany concentrated on workplaces dominated by men in strong craft unions. Drawing upon the methods developed in these projects, several further projects sought to inject a gender perspective into systems design. It has been argued that important organizational, communications and interpersonal aspects of women's work are invisible to managers and systems designers; these projects have attempted to empower women workers in the process of systems design using techniques which draw upon these invisible but long-established competences which women bring to bear upon their work. These initiatives, while drawing upon early human-centred systems projects, have also been concerned to differentiate women's concerns and their experience in relation to computer technology (Green *et al.*, 1993).

Perhaps the most significant contribution of this body of work has been in the development of new *processes* of systems design rather than in their *outcomes*. 'Woman-centred' design methods include 'study circles' (Vehviläinen, 1986), concentration upon the people using the systems rather than upon the artefacts ultimately created in the design process (Bødker and Greenbaum, 1993) and upon the 'shared knowledge' of office workers rather than the 'authoritative knowledge' of systems developers (Suchman and Jordan, 1989), and the prototyping of technical solutions (Hales and O'Hara, 1993). However, the outcomes in terms of technological artefacts have been less distinct from their conventional counterparts, perhaps unsurprisingly given the continuing context of class and patriarchal relations within which they were developed (Green *et al.*, 1993). In this context, it is also worth noting the potential importance of moves in conventional systems design towards end-user computing, which has removed much of the mystique and inaccessibility of early computing systems. Given the significant over-representation of women within the user rather than the producer role with regard to IT, how will such developments affect women's relationship to, and experience of, them?

Conclusion: the gender–technology relationship

The project of feminist analysis of technology and gender over the last decade and a half has been to develop an understanding of women's, and, to a lesser extent, men's, relationship to technology. This article has set out to chart the major insights with which this analysis has supplied us. Feminists have begun to elucidate the particular implications of new technologies for women's jobs and for the sexual division of labour. Their research points to the enduring nature of this division, to the continuing ways in which women's work is ascribed a low skill status, to women's continuing exclusion from the processes of design and decision-taking about technology in the workplace, and to a host of long-established patterns of work organization in women's jobs which seem to have been barely affected by the process of technological change but which seem much more strongly related to the overall strategic objectives of employers. Instead, feminist research has pointed to the ways in which jobs and technologies have historically come to be gendered in ways which have crucially conditioned the effects of technological change on women's (and men's) jobs. In doing so, it has challenged simplistic suggestions that the process of technological change is associated with a straightforward breakdown of the sexual division of labour; these fail to take account of the very real differences in women's and men's relationships to technology and to the organization of paid work.

Indeed, the lesson of feminist analysis of these developments is surely that women's relationship to paid work, and to the technologies which are the tools of that work, cannot be understood in isolation from the other components of their social life. Particularly critical in this picture is the role of women's *unpaid* labour. This shapes their employment status and thus secures their subordination in paid labour. In doing so, it operates in conjunction with factors *within* workplaces, such as the process of occupational sex-typing and the exclusion of women from technology. And women's subordination in the workplace is in turn rooted in a host of broader social institutions, such as the family, the education system and the state. The strength of feminist analysis is that, in stark contrast to conventional labour sociology or economics research focusing on men's jobs, it places great emphasis upon the interaction of the public and the private domains of women's lives and the ways in which they combine to shape women's relationships to work and technology.

On the other side of the coin, feminist analysis has begun to point to the ways in which the gendered nature of society influences technological development and, by implication, the impact of technologies. Here, it offers a corrective to the woeful gender-blindness of the social shaping and social constructionist approaches to the development of technologies. However, neither of these perspectives has yet incorporated the issue of gender or race into their analyses, despite the fact that it is now well recognized that technological artefacts have gender relations actually embedded within them, and also that the institutions of technology, the acquisition of technological know-how and indeed the very culture of technology itself have come to be dominated by men at the expense of women. This has been the particular contribution of feminist writers to our understanding of the creation and development of new technologies. This identification of the processes whereby technology has become 'masculine' also provides some explanation as to why the introduction of technologies has had differential impacts on women's and men's jobs, and why it has been experienced differently by men and women. And it alerts us to the fact that technologies are no more gender neutral than they are neutral in any other sense. Analysis of the development and impact of technologies upon work must therefore take into account not only the class relations within which they are introduced, but also the gender relations of the workplace, of technology itself and of society at large.

References

Armstrong, P. (1982) 'If It's Only a Woman it Doesn't Matter So Much', pp. 27–43 in J. West (ed.), *Work, Women and the Labour Market*. London: Routledge.

Arnold, E. and W. Faulkner (1985) 'Smothered by Invention: The Masculinity of Technology', pp. 18–50 in W. Faulkner and E. Arnold (eds), *Smothered by Invention: Technology in Women's Lives*. London: Pluto Press.

Barker, J. and H. Downing (1980) 'Word Processing and the Transformation of Patriarchal Relations of Control in the Office', *Capital and Class* 10: 64–99.

Bird, E. (1980) *Information Technology in the Office: The Impact on Women's Jobs*. Manchester: Equal Opportunities Commission.

Bødker, S. and J. Greenbaum (1993) 'Design of Information Systems: Things versus People', pp. 53–63 in E. Green *et al.* (eds), *Gendered by Design: Information Technology and Office Systems.* London: Taylor and Francis.
Braverman, H. (1974) *Labor and Monopoly Capital.* New York: Monthly Review Press.
Callon, M. (1987) 'Society in the Making: The Study of Technology as a Tool for Sociological Analysis', pp. 83–103 in W. E. Bijker, T. P. Hughes and T. J. Pinch (eds), *The Social Construction of Technological Systems.* London: MIT Press.
Cavendish, R. (1981) *Women on the Line.* London: Routledge.
Cockburn, C. (1983) *Brothers: Male Dominance and Technological Change.* London: Pluto.
Cockburn, C. (1985) *Machinery of Dominance: Women, Men and Technical Knowhow.* London: Pluto Press.
Cockburn, C. and S. Ormrod (1993) *Gender and Technology in the Making.* London: Sage.
Common Interests (1991) *Women Organising in Global Electronics.* London: Women Working Worldwide.
Cooley, M. (1980) *Architect or Bee? The Human/Technology Relationship.* Slough: Langley Technical Services.
Crompton, R. and G. Jones (1984) *White Collar Proletariat.* London: Macmillan.
David, P. A. (1985) 'Clio and the Economics of QWERTY', *Economic History* 25(2): 332–7.
Ehn, P. and M. Kyng (1985) 'Trade Unions and Computers: The Scandinavian Collective Resources Approach', paper presented at the FAST conference 'The Press and the New Technologies – the Challenge of the New Knowledge' 7–9 November, Brussels.
Fothergill, A. (1994) 'Telework: Women's Experiences and Utilisation of Information Technology in the Home', pp. 175–89 in A. Adam and J. Owen (eds), *Breaking Old Boundaries: Building New Forms*, Proceedings of the 5th IFIP International Conference on Women, Work and Computerization (2–5 July), Manchester.
Fuentes, A. and B. Ehrenreich (1983) *Women in the Global Factory.* Boston, MA: South End Press.
Game, A. and R. Pringle (1983) *Gender at Work.* London: Pluto.
Goldstein, N. (1989) 'Silicon Glen: Women and Semiconductor Multinationals', pp. 111–28 in D. Elson and R. Pearson (eds), *Women's Employment and Multinationals in Europe.* London: Macmillan.
Green, E., J. Owen and D. Pain (eds) (1993) *Gendered by Design: Information Technology and Office Systems.* London: Taylor and Francis.
Greenbaum, J. and M. Kyng (eds) (1991) *Design at Work: Co-operative Design of Computer Systems.* Hillsdale, NJ: Lawrence Erlbaum.
Greve, R. (1986) *Women and Information Technology: A European Overview.* Luxembourg: Commission of the EC.
Grossman, R. (1979) 'Women's Place in the Integrated Circuit', *South East Asia Chronical* 66: 2–17.
Haddon, L. and R. Silverstone (1993) 'Telework and the Changing Relationship of Home and Work', paper presented to the PICT National Conference 'European Dimensions in Information and Communication: Panacea or Pandora's Box?' (19–21 May), Kenilworth.

Hales, M. and P. O'Hara (1993) 'Strengths and Weaknesses of Participation: Learning by Doing in Local Government', pp. 153–72 in E. Green *et al.* (eds), *Gendered by Design: Information Technology and Office Systems.* London: Taylor and Francis.
Harding, S. (1986) *The Science Question in Feminism.* Milton Keynes: Open University Press.
Harding, S. (1991) *Whose Science? Whose Knowledge? Thinking from Women's Lives.* Milton Keynes: Open University Press.
Heeks, R. (1993) 'Software Subcontracting to the Third World', pp. 236–50 in P. Quintas (ed.), *Social Dimensions of Systems Engineering: People, Processes, Politics and Software Development.* London: Ellis Horwood.
Henwood, F. (1993) 'Establishing Gender Perspectives on Information Technology: Problems, Issues and Opportunities', pp. 31–52 in E. Green *et al.* (eds), *Gendered by Design: Information Technology and Office Systems.* London: Taylor and Francis.
Henwood, F. and S. Wyatt (1986) 'Women's Work, Technological Change and Shifts in the Employment Structure', pp. 106–37 in R. Martin and B. Rowthorn (eds), *The Geography of De-industrialisation.* London: Macmillan.
Herzog, M. (1980) *From Hand to Mouth.* Harmondsworth: Penguin.
Hofmann, J. (1994) 'Two Versions of the Same: The Text Editor and the Automatic Letter Writer as Contrasting Conceptions of Digital Writing', pp. 219–34 in A. Adam and J. Owen (eds), *Breaking Old Boundaries: Building New Forms*, Proceedings of the 5th IFIP International Conference on Women, Work and Computerization (2–5 July), Manchester.
Horn, D. G. (1994) 'Review of Weibe Bijker and John Law (eds), *Shaping Technology/Building Society: Studies in Sociotechnical Change*', *Science, Technology and Human Values* 19(3): 386–8.
Huws, U. (1980) *Your Job in the Eighties.* London: Pluto Press.
Huws, U. (1984) *The New Homeworkers: New Technology and the Changing Location of the White Collar Workers.* London: Low Pay Unit.
Huws, U. (1993) 'Teleworking in Britain: A Report to the Employment Department', Employment Department Research Series No. 18.
King, Y. (1983) 'Toward an Ecological Feminism and a Feminist Ecology', pp. 118–29 in J. Rothschild (ed.), *Machina ex Dea: Feminist Perspectives on Technology.* New York: Pergamon Press.
Kirkup, G. and L. S. Keller (eds) (1992) *Inventing Women: Science, Technology and Gender.* Cambridge: Polity Press.
Knie, A. (1992) 'Yesterday's Decisions Determine Tomorrow's Options: The Case of the Mechanical Typewriter', pp. 161–72 in M. Dierkes and U. Hoffman (eds), *New Technology at the Outset: Social Forces in the Shaping of Technological Innovations.* Frankfurt: Campus Verlag.
Latour, B. (1987) *Science in Action: How to Follow Scientists and Engineers through Society.* Milton Keynes: Open University Press.
Leeds TUCRIC (1982) *New Technology and Women's Employment: Case Studies from West Yorkshire.* Leeds: Leeds Trade Union Community Resource and Information Centre.
Lie, M. and B. Rasmussen (1985) 'Office Work and Skills', in A. Olerup *et al.* (eds), *Women, Work and Computerisation: Opportunities and Disadvantages.* Amsterdam: North-Holland.

Liff, S. (1990) 'Gender and Information Technology: Current Research Priorities, Strengths, Gaps and Opportunities', paper presented to second PICT Workshop on Gender and IT, November/December 1989.

Liff, S. (1993) 'Information Technology and Occupational Restructuring in the Office', pp. 95–110 in E. Green *et al.* (eds), *Gendered by Design: Information Technology and Office Systems.* London: Taylor and Francis.

McNeil, M. (ed.) (1987) *Gender and Expertise.* London: Free Association Books.

Mitter, S. (1986) *Common Fate, Common Bond: Women in the Global Economy.* London: Pluto Press.

Morgall, J. (1981) 'Typing our Way to Freedom', *Feminist Review* 9: 87–103.

Murray, F. (1993) 'A Separate Reality: Science, Technology and Masculinity', pp. 64–80 in E. Green *et al.* (eds), *Gendered by Design: Information Technology and Office Systems.* London: Taylor and Francis.

Nelson, R. and S. Winter (1977) 'In Search of a Useful Theory of Innovation', *Research Policy* 6: 36–76.

Noble, D. F. (1979) 'Social Choice in Machine Design: The Case of Automatically Controlled Machine Tools', pp. 18–50 in A. Zimbalist (ed.), *Case Studies on the Labor Process.* New York: Monthly Review Press.

Phillips, A. and B. Taylor (1980) 'Sex and Skill: Notes towards a Feminist Economies', *Feminist Review* 6: 79–88.

Pollert, A. (1981) *Girls, Wives, Factory Lives.* London: Macmillan.

Posthuma, A. (1987) 'The Internationalisation of Clerical Work', University of Sussex Science Policy Research Unit Occasional Paper No. 24.

Probert, B. and B. Wilson (1993) 'Gendered Work', pp. 1–19 in B. Probert and B. Wilson (eds), *Pink Collar Blues: Work, Gender and Technology.* Melbourne: Melbourne University Press.

Silverstone, R. and R. Towler (1984) 'Secretaries at Work', *Ergonomics* 27(5): 557–64.

Softley, E. (1985) 'Word Processing: New Opportunities for Women Office Workers?', pp. 222–37 in W. Faulkner and E. Arnold (eds), *Smothered by Invention: Technology in Women's Lives.* London: Pluto.

Suchman, L. and B. Jordan (1989) 'Computerisation and Women's Knowledge', pp. 153–60 in K. Tijdens *et al.* (eds), *Women, Work and Computerisation: Forming New Alliances.* Amsterdam: North-Holland.

Tijdens, K. (1994) 'Behind the Screens: The Foreseen and Unforeseen Impact of Computerisation on Female Office Workers' jobs', pp. 132–9 in T. Eberhart and C. Wächter (eds), *Proceedings of the 2nd European Feminist Research Conference: Feminist Perspectives on Technology, Work and Ecology*, 5–9 July, Graz, Austria.

Vehviläinen, M. (1986) 'A Study Circle Approach as a Method for Women to Develop their Work and Computer Systems', paper presented at IFIP Women, Work and Computerization conference (August), Dublin.

Vehviläinen, M. (1991) 'Gender in Information Systems Development', in I. V. Eriksson *et al.* (eds), *Women, Work and Computerization: Understanding and Overcoming Bias in Work and Education.* Amsterdam: North-Holland.

Wagner, J. (1985) 'Women in the Automated Office.', pp. 53–64 in A. Olerup *et al.* (eds), *Women, Work and Computerisation: Opportunities and Disadvantages.* Amsterdam: North-Holland.

Wajcman, J. (1991) *Feminism Confronts Technology*. Pennsylvania: Penn State University Press.
Wajcman, J. and B. Probert (1988) 'New Technology Outwork', pp. 51–67 in E. Willis (ed.), *Technology and the Labour Process: Australian Case Studies*. Sydney: Allen and Unwin.
Webster, J. (1986) 'Word Processing and the Secretarial Labour Process', pp. 114–31 in K. Purcell, S. Wood, A. Waton and S. Allen (eds), *The Changing Experience of Employment: Restructuring and Recession*. London: Macmillan.
Webster, J. (1990) *Office Automation: The Labour Process and Women's Work in Britain*. Hemel Hempstead: Harvester Wheatsheaf.
Webster, J. (1993) 'From the Word Processor to the Micro: Gender Issues in the Development of Information Technology in the Office', pp. 111–26 in E. Green et al. (eds), *Gendered by Design: Information Technology and Office Systems*. London: Taylor and Francis.
Wernecke, D. (1983) *Microelectronics and Office Jobs: The Impact of the Chip on Women's Employment*. Geneva: International Labour Office.
West, J. (1982) 'New Technology and Women's Office Work', pp. 61–79 in J. West (ed.), *Work, Women and the Labour Market*. London: Routledge and Kegan Paul.
West, J. (1990) 'Gender and the Labour Process: A Reassessment', pp. 244–73 in D. Knights and H. Willmott (eds), *Labour Process Theory*. London: Macmillan.
Westwood, S. (1984) *All Day Every Day*. London: Pluto Press.
Women's Voice (1979) 'Job Massacre at the Office', pamphlet. London: Women's Voice.

79

REFLECTIONS ON GENDER AND TECHNOLOGY STUDIES

In what state is the art?

Judy Wajcman

Source: *Social Studies of Science* 30(3) (2000): 447–64.

Abstract

This Comment reflects upon the relationship between gender and technology, and how it has been theorized in recent decades. I argue that while feminist approaches have had considerable influence on mainstream social studies of science and technology, tensions remain. I go on to explore the proliferation of feminist research which conceptualizes technology as culture. I suggest that the contemporary focus on cultural representation and consumption, exciting and productive as it is in many respects, has contributed to the neglect of design studies. These are necessary to fully elucidate how gender relations figure in the construction of technology.

John Glenn's return visit to outer space on 7 November 1998 served as a reminder that the conquest of space through technology has remained a predominantly male enterprise. Yet, in 1960, 13 women pilots were judged to be NASA's top astronauts – better than the Mercury Seven male astronauts who were later immortalized in print and on film. The women pilots, who stayed on the ground, were judged as more suitable than the men for space travel: for example, they required less oxygen per minute and had a much higher tolerance to sensory deprivation. However, within a few months of passing all the medical and scientific tests, the women were told they would not be part of the space race. They were the right stuff, but the wrong sex.[1]

This story of the forgotten women astronauts may be seen as part of the feminist project to uncover and recover women 'hidden from history'. It also graphically illustrates that there is nothing natural or inevitable about the ways in which technology is identified as masculine, and masculinity is defined in terms of technical competence. History might have been otherwise. If a woman, rather than a man, had been the first American in space, the masculine culture of technology might have been disrupted, or at least destabilized.

This event prompted me to reflect on how the relationship between gender and technology has been theorized over the last 20 years or so. In 1987, Sara Delamont commented on the gender-blindness of science studies at that time.[2] Since then, a whole new field of social studies of technology has been developed. As we enter the 21st century it is important to subject this field to similar questioning, and see if it has replicated the *lacunae* identified in science studies.

Looking back over contributions to this journal during the last decade, it is clear that there is a growing awareness of feminist issues. However, a rather small proportion of the main substantive papers (excluding shorter communications, reviews, and the like) systematically incorporate a gender analysis. Taking a broad definition that also includes papers sensitive to gender issues or about women, there were 9 (6.6%) such papers out of 136. This excludes editions of the journal devoted to symposia, none of which problematized gender as a central concern. What is it about social studies of technology that might account for this imbalance?

In this paper I want to look at how gender and technology studies emerged, the extent to which this theme has been taken up within mainstream technology studies and, in the final section, I will indicate the breadth of recent feminist literature on technology. I hope to show that there is more scope for cross-fertilization between feminist studies of technology and the mainstream S&TS tradition. During the 1990s there has been a lively debate between various strands of feminism and other social studies of technology.[3] Many of the issues that I raise here have now been taken on board.[4] However, I will argue that there are limitations in influential approaches in the field which remain obstacles to a fruitful dialogue.

Technology and the sexual division of labour

Like many of my feminist contemporaries, I came to gender and technology studies from having been immersed (in the 1970s) in Marxist labour process debates about production. The argument here was that class conflict shapes technology in the workplace.[5] Capitalism continuously applies new technology designed to fragment and de-skill labour, so that labour becomes cheaper and subject to greater control. Technological revolution was understood to be a trait of capital accumulation processes. Although this theoretical approach had been reasonably sophisticated in its analysis of the capital–labour relation, feminists questioned the notion that control over the labour process operates independently of the gender of the workers who are being controlled.

This, for me, was where the feminist sociological project began, as a critique of the gender-blindness of Marxism. Feminist sociological work pointed out that the division of labour characterizing paid occupations was a sexual hierarchy, and that its gendered nature was not incidental.[6] Both employers as employers, and men as men, were shown to have an interest in creating and sustaining occupational sex-segregation. Time and time again, gender was shown to be an important factor in shaping the organization of work that resulted from technological change. In sum, we argued that the relations of production are constructed as much out of gender divisions as out of class divisions.

And if the workplace is patriarchal, then what about the domestic sphere? Feminists pointed out that the labour process, as defined in mainstream work, ignored a significant part of all labour – the unpaid labour done by women in the home. Feminist interest in domestic technology can be traced back to the debate about housework as a key element of women's oppression. By the 1970s, housework was recognized as 'work' and had become the object of serious academic study by historians and sociologists.[7] We argued that paid work could not be understood without reference to women's unpaid work in the home, and that the sexual division of labour separated women from control over the technologies they used, both at the workplace and at home. Much of the early work came from feminist historians of technology working in North America, and it was the journal *Technology and Culture* that contained the first pieces on the history of domestic technology.[8] Dominating the debates was the apparent paradox that mechanization of the home had not substantially decreased the amount of time women spend on household tasks.

Looking back over the literature of this period, I see that it clearly reflects the major preoccupations of feminist scholars of the time. New cross-disciplinary research areas were charted so as to counter the masculine bias in various academic subjects and the invisibility of women's lives.[9] Feminism was concerned to show what being a woman might imply, and how women's lives were shaped by various social forces. Feminist sociologists' work was mainly focused on explanations at the level of social structure – so arguments in terms of the sexual division of labour, both in the labour market and in domestic work, figured strongly in these writings. In line with this, feminist technology studies were mainly concerned with the impacts of technology on women's lives.[10] So how technological change would impact on gender relations at work and at home were obvious questions.

The concern with the 'effects' of technology on society reflected the naive technological determinism that prevailed in the social sciences at the time.[11]

Beyond this, some contributors were prone to adopt a naïve version of the social shaping perspective. As Anne-Jorunn Berg notes:

> The somehow taken for granted character of technology rendered technology in theoretical terms a more or less vague extension of various patriarchal and/or capitalist structures.[12]

As a result, feminist approaches mainly dismissed technoscience as inherently patriarchal and malignant. Traces of this inheritance are evident in my own work.[13] While clearly critical of a radical or ecofeminist position which rejects technology in favour of a return to a mythical natural state, the general tone of this feminist approach is rather pessimistic about the possibilities of redesigning technologies for gender equality: its emphasis is perhaps too heavily on how technological developments will reproduce gender hierarchies, rather than on the possibility that gender relations may be transformed by new technologies. Also, while the intrinsic indeterminacy of technology is acknowledged, not enough attention is paid to women's agency. There has been much criticism of the all-too-common tendency to treat women as the passive victims of technology.[14] For all this, it is clear that we were asking the right questions and were influential in setting a very productive feminist research agenda. This intellectual project was an emanation of second-wave feminism, as was the associated political project of building women's technical knowledge and expertise.

By the late 1980s, attention in feminist technology studies was tending to shift away from the focus on women *and* technology. It was moving instead to examine the very processes by which technology is developed and used, and those by which gender is constituted. Both these themes were already established in studies of how technology is shaped by gender relations.[15] However, they received fresh impetus from two theoretical developments – the new sociology of technology, and the postmodern turn in feminist theory.

Social studies of technology

Over the last two decades, Science and Technology Studies (S&TS) has become an established discipline. Several schools of theory have emerged, but two approaches have been particularly influential in relation to feminist studies.

The first is the 'social construction of technology' (SCOT) perspective, developed by Trevor Pinch and Wiebe Bijker.[16] In common with the social shaping approach, the SCOT approach emphasizes that technological artefacts are open to sociological analysis, not just in their usage, but especially with respect to their design and technical content: it draws heavily upon earlier work applying a sociological perspective to scientific knowledge. Pinch and Bijker take up the notion of 'symmetry' of explanation, and argue that symmetry means avoiding explaining the success or failure of technologies by whether or not they work: and, for them, 'machines "work" because they have been accepted by relevant social groups'.[17] While this particular formulation may underplay the materiality of machines,[18] the concept of the 'interpretative flexibility' of technology is widely seen as SCOT'S most useful addition to feminist debates.[19]

Interpretative flexibility refers to the way in which different groups of people involved with a technology can have very different understandings of that technology, including different understandings of its technical characteristics. Thus users can radically alter the meanings and deployment of technologies. How then can SCOT account for the stabilization or 'closure' mechanisms in the creation of a new technology? Pinch and Bijker's answer is in terms of 'relevant social groups' sharing the same set of meanings, and attaching them to a specific artefact. Relevant social groups are typically identified empirically as the actors that participate in the negotiations or controversies around a specific technology. As women are usually absent from these groups, there was a tendency to overlook the need for a gender analysis of the technology – a point I will return to below.

The other main approach that has been taken up by feminists is 'actor-network theory' (ANT), developed variously by scholars such as Michel Callon, Bruno Latour and John Law.[20] ANT exposed the fallacy of construing technology and society as separate spheres, influencing each other. Rather, the metaphor of a 'heterogeneous network' conveys the view that technology and society are mutually constitutive: both are made of the same stuff – networks linking human beings and non-human entities. The technological, instead of being a sphere separate from society, is part of what makes large-scale society possible. Through describing the network, ANT considers how some actors become decision-makers while others do not. Their most controversial idea, that we cannot deny *a priori* that non-human actors or 'actants' can have agency, has helped us to understand the role of technology in producing social life.

The conception of the non-human as actant reinforces an action-orientation. ANT considers how users of technologies are configured by various agents in the process of development and design, production, marketing, distribution, sales, maintenance, and so on. Designers define the potential actors or users of their technologies in various ways, and inscribe this vision of the world in the technical content of the new object. As Michel Callon expresses it: 'Machines carry the word of those who invented, developed, perfected and produced them . . . the machine is a spokesperson'.[21] This 'script' or 'scenario', in Madeleine Akrich's terms, is written, or 'inscribed', into technology.[22] But, as with the notion of 'interpretative flexibility', the 'script' or 'inscription' is open to various translations. The user interacts with the pre-inscribed artefact, and can challenge and renegotiate the meanings and uses of the artefact. This idea, that consumers are an integral part of the process of technological development, has been important for feminist research, as we shall see.

From gender-blind to gender-aware

Within these mainstream bodies of work, the ways in which technological objects may be shaped by the operation of gender interests or identities have not been a central focus. Despite the emphasis on the way innovations are socially shaped, it has been largely incumbent on feminists to demonstrate that this 'social' is also a matter of gender relations. So what is it about social studies of technology that has made it hard for us to think about gender issues? Several problems are involved, and I will outline them below.

To begin with, the marginalization of gender in both SCOT and ANT constructivist studies of technology is indicative of a general problem with their methodology. This is related to the conception of power deployed by theorists in this genre. Using a conventional notion of technology, these writers were concerned to identify and study the social groups or networks that actively seek to influence the form and direction of technological design. Their focus on observable conflict led to a common assumption that gender interests were not being mobilized. What many have overlooked is the fact that the exclusion of some groups, while not empirically discernible, may nevertheless have an impact upon the processes of technological development.[23] To adopt the terminology of Steven Lukes, action-oriented approaches are insufficiently 'radical', restricting their analyses to the two observable dimensions of power and neglecting a third, structural dimension.[24]

While the effects of structural exclusion on technological development are not easy to analyse, they should not be overlooked. Feminists have stressed that women's absence from spheres of influence is a key feature of gender power relations. Few women feature among the principal actors in technological design, as the sexual division of labour has excluded them from entering science, engineering and management.[25] As several commentators have pointed out, the problem with a primary focus on 'relevant social groups' in the process of technological development is how to take account of those actors who are routinely marginalized or excluded from a network.[26]

Within the broad social shaping approach, feminists have found it relatively easy to discuss systematic male domination over women as a sex in terms parallel to class exploitation. Just as capitalists are deemed to have a relatively stable set of interests in maximizing profits, so we could talk of men's interests as a sex being institutionalized. The concept of patriarchy was often deployed as a shorthand for institutionalized power relations between men and women where gender is a property of institutions and historical processes, as well as of individuals. However, this was not meant to imply that men are a homogeneous group. For example, in *Feminism*

Confronts Technology, I stressed that men's interests are not all identical, and that when it comes to influencing the design and development of a specific technology, some groups will have more power and resources than others. So, long before the so-called 'postmodern challenge', 'difference' within the category of men, and between women, was already widely recognized.

By contrast, ANT was more strongly influenced by a Foucauldian concept of power, where power is represented as capacity and effectiveness. Latour, for instance, suggests that power is not a possession – indeed it must be treated as 'a consequence rather than a cause of action'.[27] Elsewhere, Latour has argued that such constellations as classes, countries, kings or laboratories should not be treated as the cause of subsequent events, but rather as a set of effects.[28] In other words, they should be seen as the consequence of a set of heterogeneous operations, strategies and concatenations. The job of the investigator, then, is not to discover final causes, but to unearth these schemes and expose their contingency. John Law agrees that power is indeed the product of a set of (strategy-dependent) relations but, he argues, this does not mean that it cannot be stored and used for certain purposes.[29]

In my view, an overemphasis on the enabling aspects of power can make it awkward to address the obduracy of the link between men and technology. Feminists' traditional concerns with women's access to technology, the differential impact of technology on women, and the patriarchal design of technologies, have all sat uneasily with this analysis of technology. While ANT perceives that artefacts embody the relations that went into their making, and that these relations prefigure relations implied in the use and non-use of artefacts, it is less alert to the inevitable gendering of this process. ANT does not always recognize that the stabilization and standardization of technological systems necessarily involve negating the experience of those who are not standard, 'a destruction of the world of the non-enrolled'.[30]

A central argument of much feminist theory has been that men are set up as the norm against which women are measured and found wanting. Indeed, this thesis is at the core of my recent book, *Managing Like a Man*, which is about the male definition of management.[31] An investigation into senior managers in multinational corporations, it shows how the hegemonic organizational culture incorporates a male standard which positions senior women managers as out of place. A parallel argument can be made that the standardization of networks implicitly places men's experiences and men's investments at the centre, without acknowledging their specificity. The corollary is the simultaneous denial of other realities, such as women's. So, while it is true that the imputation of social interests to social structures and institutions is always contestable and difficult to specify, there are nevertheless important contexts where feminist analysis has no choice but to invoke 'interests explanations'.[32]

The absence of women from view is also a function of the concentration on issues of design. Innovation studies have underplayed the importance of enrolling other groups in the alliance of forces that enables a technological innovation to succeed. Agents in ANT are most commonly male heroes, big projects and important organizations, in what Susan Leigh Star has described as a 'managerial or entrepreneurial' model of actor networks.[33] There is a striking parallel here with Sara Delamont's point about the bias in science studies 'towards exciting, high status men working in elite centres of "big science" excellence', rather than the routine science in which most women are involved.[34] Once the lens is widened to include manufacturing operatives, marketing and sales personnel, and the consumers and end-users of technologies, women's work immediately comes into view. More women are literally present, the further downstream you go from the design process. Women are the hidden cheap labour force that produces technologies, the secretaries, cleaners and cooks, they are part of the sales force, and the main users of domestic and reproductive technologies. The undervaluing of women's 'unskilled' and delegated work serves to make them invisible in mainstream technology studies.

Finally, constructivist studies have generally assumed that gender has little bearing on the development of technology because the masculinity of the actors involved was not made explicit.[35] It might be seen as ironic that the focus on agency has rarely sensitized these authors to issues of gendered subjectivity. However, most scholars are habituated to consider gender issues only when their subjects are women. So one strategy for incorporating a gender perspective into technology studies, as in other areas of social science, has been to study places where women are. This work has done much to compensate for past neglect, but it has also unfortunately reinforced the perception that gender is only an issue where the research subjects are female. Gender thus becomes a variable to explain women's difference – in this case, to explain why contemporary Western femininity involves being ill-suited to technological pursuits.

A full theoretical integration of the analysis of gender into technology studies requires an understanding that both men and women have gender identities which structure their experiences and their beliefs. Then we can begin to explore the significance of technology in the formation of subject identity for both sexes. Feminists have long argued that the symbolic representation of technology is sharply gendered. Men's affinity with technology is now seen as integral to the constitution of male gender identity and the culture of technology. Engineering is a particularly intriguing example of an archetypically masculine culture where mastery over technology is a source of both pleasure and power for the predominantly male profession.[36] This is not to say that there is one masculinity or one form of technology: rather, it is to note that in contemporary Western society, hegemonic masculinity, the culturally dominant form of masculinity, is still strongly associated with technical prowess and power.[37] To be in command of the very latest technology signifies being involved in directing the future, so it is a highly valued and mythologized activity. More research is needed that explores how technologies operate as a site for the production of gendered knowledge and knowledge of gender.

Feminist research in the S&TS tradition

Much empirical research on gender and technology is now engaging with these issues, and can partly be seen as a response to the problems outlined above. More attention has been given to the development and diffusion processes of specific technologies in an attempt to deconstruct the designer/user divide.[38] In the limited space available here, I will only briefly outline the approach taken in three of these projects.

One exemplary study that deliberately set out to combine an innovation study with a user study is that by Cynthia Cockburn and Susan Ormrod, who trace the trajectory of the microwave oven from its conception right through to its consumption. Well aware that the standard S&TS focus on invention underplays the role of women, the authors unravel the way that the sexual division of labour is mapped on to each stage in the journey of a domestic technology. Like other domestic technologies, the microwave is designed by men in their capacity as engineers and managers, people remote from the domestic tasks involved, for use by women in their capacity as houseworkers. Where women do enter the picture (apart from on the production line), it is primarily as home economists. Cockburn and Ormrod observe that the cooking expertise of the home economists is crucial to the successful design of the artefact. The women see themselves as doing 'a kind of engineering or science',[39] but it is not acknowledged as such by the predominantly male culture of engineers. Their technical skills are undervalued because of the strong association of cooking with femininity. As a result, even at the one point when women enter the innovation process, they wield little influence over the development of new technologies. What is so original about Cockburn and Ormrod's microwave study is that it follows the gendering processes through the various stages of the artefact's life. It recognizes that gendering does not begin and end with design and manufacturing: domestic technologies are also encoded with gendered meanings during their marketing, retailing and appropriation by users. While the technology is made into a physical object during production, the symbolic meanings attaching to it are continually being negotiated and reinvented. In particular, Cockburn and Ormrod explore the extent to which interpretative flexibility exists once a given commodity reaches the hands of the consumer. Marketing and retailing play a key rôle in framing demand: 'there is an unclear dividing line between accurately *representing* the customer, *constructing* the customer and *controlling* the customer'.[40] Thus, for Cockburn and

Ormrod, marketing and consumption are all part of the social shaping of technology.

While the microwave study set out to demonstrate how gendering processes affect every stage in the life of a technology, its analysis is stronger in relation to the gendered construction of the potential users than in relation to the machine's design. It does not fully succeed in showing, in any detailed sense, how the development of the microwave reflected designers' assumptions about the gendered characteristics of the prospective users. Much of what goes on inside the black box of innovation remains a mystery.

Studies on cervical cancer screening by Monica Casper and Adele Clarke, and by Vicky Singleton and Mike Michael, are similarly concerned with the processes whereby technologies are deployed and appropriated by users.[41] These studies, the latter explicitly informed by an ANT approach, share with the microwave study the choice of a routine, mundane technology as opposed to heroic technoscience. They eschew the 'executive approach' that would necessarily focus on male technoscientists, instead widening the lens to incorporate women 'downstream'. Casper and Clarke's study is about how a rather recalcitrant tool, the 'Pap smear', became the major cancer screening technology in the world. They argue that several sets of concrete practices or 'tinkering' have been used to make the Pap smear appear to be the right tool for the job. One such practice has been the gendering of the division of labour in cytological screening. It appears that the success of the Pap smear depended on the feminization of the job of technician, with its accompanying low pay for difficult work. This makes clear the centrality of women's undervalued work in the standardization of a technology. The authors also explore the rôle of the women's health movement and public health activists, those outside the usual boundaries of the network, in successfully reshaping elements of the tool.

Their findings echo those of Singleton and Michael's earlier study, which analyzes the UK Cervical Screening Programme as a durable actor-network. This study focuses on the pivotal part played by general practitioners, who are themselves enrolled in the programme and enrol women to participate: it highlights the way ANT tends to overlook not only those whoare at the margins of a given network, but also the fact that people can possess different attributes, and be operating in several different domains at once. Indeed, the durability of the network depends on the possibility that general practitioners can be both the harshest critics and the most ardent supporters of the network – that is, they can occupy the margins and the core at the same time. Rather than viewing a network as victorious once and for all, this approach suggests that ambivalence, marginality and the multiple identities of actors/actants actually reinforce and sustain the network.

In neither of these accounts of cervical screening programmes is the scientist or the executive given primacy. What is curious is the absence of any discussion of how this technology is part of a long history of medical procedures designed for use exclusively on women's bodies. The gendering of the technical innovation itself is somehow taken for granted. However, the way gender is theorized in these studies does represent an encouraging advance over previous work. Early feminist studies of gender and technology tended to theorize gender as a fixed and unitary phenomenon, which exists prior to and independently of technology, and then becomes embedded within it. We then explained the success of a technology in terms of the economic or political interests of powerful groups, typically regarding these interests as established, and in need of no further explanation. Against this, recent feminist scholars such as Judith Butler argue that men's and women's interests are not objectively given but are collectively created.[42] Influenced by poststructuralism, they conceive of 'gender as a performance', so as to stress that gender is not fixed in advance of social interaction, but is constructed *in* interaction. One acts or performs gender, and demonstrates one's gender identity. Gender is a social achievement.

This notion of 'gender as doing' fits well with ANT's view of society as a *doing* rather than a *being*. The construction of gender identities, like that of technologies, is a moving relational process achieved in daily social interactions. The question is now posed in terms of 'how interests are shaped together with the technology-in-the-making'.[43] It follows from this that gendered conceptions of users are fluid, and subject to a variety of interpretations. Therefore the relationship between particular gender power interests and their inscription in technological innovation is treated with much more subtlety and complexity. This model of technological development enables us to understand technologies and interests as products of mutual alliances and dependencies among groups involved in the specific technology. Thus technologies and new forms of gender relations and gendered cultures are co-produced.

Technology as culture

Over the last decade there has been an explosion of feminist writing on technology, much of it being carried out at some conceptual distance from the sociology of science and technology which developed during this same period. This writing is explicitly informed by a combination of cultural studies, anthropology and postmodern philosophy.[44] Reflecting the postmodern emphasis on discourse, technology is conceptualized as an object of consumption, as a text and as a communication medium. Indeed, this work refuses to allow any distinction between the material and the cultural, and instead treats technology as a seamless fusion of material and cultural. Its contribution to previous feminist analysis is the concern with how technology as culture is implicated in the construction of subjective gender identities.

The most influential feminist commentator writing in this vein is Donna Haraway.[45] She argues that we should embrace the positive potential of technoscience, and is sharply critical of those who reject technology. Famously, she prefers to be a 'cyborg' – a hybrid of organism and machine parts – rather than an ecofeminist 'goddess'. She notes the great power of science and technology to create new meanings and new entities, to make new worlds. Genetic engineering, reproductive technology and the advent of virtual reality are all seen as fundamentally affecting the basic categories of 'self and 'gender'. She positively revels in the very difficulty of predicting what technology's effects will be, and warns against any purist rejection of the 'unnatural', hybrid, entities produced by biotechnology.

Most of this recent feminist literature is about biomedical technologies and information technologies. The increasing preoccupation in sociological theory with the body and sexuality has been paralleled by research on biomedical technologies – technologies for the body. There are many studies of childbirth and contraception, *in vitro* fertilization, cosmetic surgery and genetic engineering.[46] While reproductive technologies have long been of central concern to feminist studies, there has been a major shift in the analysis employed. Earlier work on the impact of reproductive technologies on women assumed that the body is biologically given and fixed. Over the last decade or so, feminists have begun to argue that there is now no such thing as the natural, physiological body. One consequence of this work is that the conventional distinction between sex (natural) and gender (social) has been thoroughly contested and deconstructed. Technologies, like science, are now seen as contributing to the stabilization of the body. With the rise of modern science, bodies have become objects that can be transformed with an increasing number of tools and techniques. Modern bodies are made and remade through science and technology; they too are technological artefacts.

The common focus of these studies is scientific theories and medical texts, and how these are implicated in the cultural production of images and meanings of sex and the body. On the whole, however, what is revealed is the effects of bio-technology, its impact on our bodies, our sense of self and our social relations.

Information and communication technologies comprise the other substantial research field in the sociology of technology. There is a profusion of studies on the Internet, cyberspace and virtual reality. Popular writers such as Nicholas Negroponte and Howard Rheingold proclaim that innovations in this area will result in either a utopian or dystopian transformation of society and the individual.[47] Much of the research has been concerned with the cultural consequences of the diffusion and consumption of information and communication technologies for the family, rather than gender *per se*. For example, Roger Silverstone and Eric Hirsch focus on the 'changing character of our own domesticity, both inside and outside the home, and on the changing character of the social groups – principally the family – that still define much of its character'.[48] Similarly, the latest British Economic and

REFLECTIONS ON GENDER AND TECHNOLOGY STUDIES

Social Research Council programme on technology, called 'Virtual Society?', is about whether 'there are fundamental shifts in how people behave, organise themselves and interact as a result of the new electronic technologies'. The programme appears to contain little in the way of a gender analysis.[49]

Once again we are more likely to see a feminist inflection in this work on information and communication technologies when the research is conducted by feminists. In the same way as biomedical technologies are seen as potentially emancipating women by transforming the relations between the self, the body and machines, so too is the Internet. In *Life on the Screen: Identity in the Age of the Internet*, Sherry Turkle enthuses about the potential for people 'to express multiple and often unexplored aspects of the self, to play with their identity and to try out new ones'.[50] It is the increasingly interactive and creative nature of computing technology that now enables millions of people to live a significant segment of their lives in virtual reality. Moreover, it is in this computer-mediated world that people experience a new sense of self that is decentred, multiple and fluid. In this respect, Turkle argues, the Internet is the material expression of the philosophy of postmodernism.

Interestingly, the gender of Internet users mainly features in Turkle's chapter about virtual sex. Cyberspace provides a risk-free environment where people can engage in the intimacy they both desire and fear. Turkle argues that people find it easier to establish relationships online and then pursue them off-line. Yet, for all the celebration of the interactive world of cyberspace, what emerges from her discussion is that people engaging in Internet relationships really want the full embodied relationship. Like many other authors, Turkle argues that gender-swapping, or virtual cross-dressing, encourages people to reflect on the social construction of gender, to acquire 'a new sense of gender as a continuum'.[51] However, she does not consider the possibility that gender differences in the constitution of sexual desire and pleasure influence the manner in which cybersex is used.

Allucquere Rosanne Stone also celebrates the myriad ways modern technology is challenging traditional notions of gender identity: 'In cyberspace the transgendered body is the natural body'.[52] For example, her discussion of phone and virtual sex describes how female sex workers disguise crucial aspects of identity and can play at reinventing themselves. She takes seriously the notion that virtual people or selves can exist in cyberspace, with no necessary link to a physical body. As an illustration of this, Stone's narrative about the cross-dressing psychiatrist has become an apocryphal feminist tale. It is the story of Julie Graham, who described herself as a New York neuropsychologist who never saw anyone in person because of her disfigurement. She successfully projected her personality and had a flourishing social life on the Internet, giving advice to many women who confided in her.[53] When Julie was exposed years later as a middle-aged male psychiatrist, many women who had sought her advice felt deeply betrayed and violated.

Julie's case is generally taken to show that the subject and the body are no longer inseparable; that cyberspace provides us with novel free choices in selecting a gender identity irrespective of our material body. However, this story can be read in a radically different manner, one that questions the extent to which the cyborg can escape the biological body. Although Julie's electronic manifestation appears at first sight to subvert gender distinctions, Ruth Oldenziel points out that it ultimately reinforced and reproduced these differences.[54] For the women seeking Julie's advice, her gender was crucial. They wanted to know that there was a woman behind the name; this is what prompted their intimacies. Julie's gender guided their behaviour and their mode of expression: 'It rendered her existence, no matter how intangible and "unreal" Julie appeared at first, extremely physical and genuine'.[55]

Relationships on the Internet are not as free of corporeality as Stone suggests. There is evidence that many more men adopt a female persona than *vice versa*, and this may be another way for men to assert their domination over female bodies. After all, if technologies are inscribed with gender relations in their design, then the culture of computing is predominantly the culture of the white American male.[56] As Oldenziel explains:

> The electronic environment largely simulates the outside, physical world, for in the end technical processes and objects are all products of human labor that create a world that goes as far, or better still, no further than our own imagination.[57]

It is not surprising that the typical Internet user world-wide remains a young, white, educated male in Western societies,[58] and that a major use of the Internet is to access pornography, designed for a predominately male audience. It is, though, disappointing that these facts go largely unremarked in the literature.[59]

New communication technologies have certainly brought about new techniques for sociality and new ways of gender-bending. The latter does, of course, have a rich cultural history. For example, one thinks of the way some 19th-century women novelists were able to exploit new printing technologies to establish themselves as successful male writers. Similarly, the Internet can be a site for the creation of new feminist communities, and a new tool for political organizing. Authors such as Sadie Plant and Dale Spender are excited by the possibilities that the World Wide Web offers to women.[60] The message is that young women in particular are colonizing cyberspace where, like gravity, gender inequality is suspended. While there is a thrilling quality to these pioneering endeavours, we must not be hypnotized by the hype that is now ubiquitous. While it is deeply unfashionable to be critical, there is a risk that concentration on the Internet as the site of transformative feminist politics may exaggerate its significance.

Conclusion

As a result of the sociological and feminist research carried out in the last decades of the 20th century, we now have a much more complex understanding of gender, of technology and of the mutually constitutive relationship between them. Increasingly, we now work from the basis that neither masculinity, femininity nor technology are fixed, unitary categories, but that they contain multiple possibilities and are constructed in relation to each other. At the same time, there has been a rejection of the technophobia evident in earlier feminist writing in favour of a popular cyberfeminism that embraces new technology as a source of empowerment for women. While much contemporary academic feminist writing on technology is not connected to feminist political activism in the same way that it was in the 1970s and 1980s, it may foster a critical optimism about the prospects for changing women's relationship to machinery. Long denied the opportunity to conquer outer space, in cyberspace women can at least nourish the dream of a world free from gender hierarchies.

This is a good moment to reflect on where feminist sociological research might head in the future. We may be coming full circle. We began by criticizing the early concern with the impact of technology on society, much of it being implicitly about consumption. We then turned to look at the social relations of technical design and innovation. Now much feminist work is explicitly concerned with consumption or cultural representation. Certainly it is the case that the simple divide between consumption and production has been deconstructed, and we now accept that design, production and consumption are profoundly interactive. However, while, at a theoretical level, we all take for granted that gender and technology are mutually constitutive, I would still argue that the weight of empirical research is on how technology shapes gender relations, rather than on how gender relations are shaping the design of technologies. My hope is that a fully rounded understanding of the relationship between gender and technology will strengthen feminist voices within sociology of technology debates, and so help fashion our future.

Notes

I would like to thank Wendy Faulkner, John Law, Donald MacKenzie, Sally Wyatt and the anonymous referees for commenting on an earlier version of this paper.

1 'Right Stuff Wrong Sex', BBC Radio 4 Broadcast, 24 April 1997.
2 Sara Delamont, 'Three Blind Spots? A Comment on the Sociology of Science by a Puzzled Outsider', *Social Studies of Science*, Vol. 17, No. 1 (February 1987), 163–70.
3 See, for example, Keith Grint and Rosalind Gill (eds), *The Gender–Technology Relation* (London: Taylor & Francis, 1995), and Steve Woolgar (ed.), 'Feminist and Constructivist Perspectives on New Technology', Special Issue, *Science, Technology, & Human Values*, Vol. 20, No. 3 (Summer 1995), 283–385.

4 See, for example, Ronald Kline and Trevor Pinch, 'Users as Agents of Technological Change: The Social Construction of the Automobile in the Rural United States', *Technology and Culture*, Vol. 37, No. 4 (October 1996), 763–95; John Law and John Hassard (eds), *Actor Network Theory and After* (Oxford: Blackwell, 1999).
5 Harry Braverman, *Labor and Monopoly Capital: The Degradation of Work in the Twentieth Century* (New York: Monthly Review Press, 1974); David Noble, *Forces of Production: A Social History of Industrial Automation* (New York: Knopf, 1984).
6 Veronica Beechey, *Unequal Work* (London: Verso, 1987); Cynthia Cockburn, *Brothers: Male Dominance and Technological Change* (London: Pluto Press, 1983); Heidi Hartmann, 'Capitalism, Patriarchy, and Job Segregation by Sex', *Signs: Journal of Women in Culture and Society*, Vol. 1, No. 3 (1976), 137–67.
7 See, for example, Christine Bose, Philip Bereano and Mary Malloy, 'Household Technology and the Social Construction of Housework', *Technology and Culture*, Vol. 25, No. 1 (January 1984), 53–82; Ruth Schwartz Cowan, *More Work for Mother: The Ironies of Household Technology from the Open Hearth to the Microwave* (New York: Basic Books, 1983); Ann Oakley, *The Sociology of Housework* (London: Martin Robertson, 1974).
8 See, for example, Alison Ravetz, 'Modern Technology and an Ancient Occupation: Housework in Present-Day Society', *Technology and Culture*, Vol. 6, No. 2 (Spring 1965), 256–60.
9 For example, Cambridge Women's Studies Group (eds), *Women in Society* (London: Virago, 1981).
10 See, for example, Wendy Faulkner and Eric Arnold (eds), *Smothered by Invention: Technology in Women's Lives* (London: Pluto Press, 1985); Joan Rothschild (ed.), *Machina Ex Dea: Feminist Perspectives on Technology* (New York: Pergamon Press, 1983).
11 According to this standpoint, technology was a separate sphere, developing independently of society, following its own autonomous logic, and then having 'effects' on society: see Donald MacKenzie and Judy Wajcman, 'Introductory Essay', in MacKenzie and Wajcman (eds), *The Social Shaping of Technology* (Milton Keynes, Bucks.: Open University Press, 1985), 2–25, at 4–5.
12 Anne-Jorunn Berg, *Digital Feminism* (Trondheim: Centre for Technology and Society, Norwegian University of Science and Technology, Report no. 28, 1996), 20.
13 Judy Wajcman, *Feminism Confronts Technology* (Cambridge: Polity Press, 1991).
14 This was particularly evident in feminist writing in the 1980s on reproductive technology: see, for example, Gena Corea et al., *Man-Made Women: How New Reproductive Technologies Affect Women* (London: Hutchinson, 1985).
15 See the 1985 edition of MacKenzie & Wajcman (eds), op. cit. note 11, especially Cynthia Cockburn's contributions ('Caught in the Wheels: The High Cost of being a Female Cog in the Male Machinery of Engineering', 55–65; 'The Material of Male Power', 125–46), and her books *Brothers*, op. cit. note 6, and *Machinery of Dominance* (London: Pluto Press, 1985).
16 Trevor J. Pinch and Wiebe E. Bijker, 'The Social Construction of Facts and Artefacts: Or How the Sociology of Science and the Sociology of Technology Might Benefit Each Other', *Social Studies of Science*, Vol. 14, No. 3 (August 1984), 399–441, reprinted in Bijker, Thomas P. Hughes and Pinch (eds), *The Social Construction of Technological Systems: New Directions in the Sociology and History of Technology* (Cambridge, MA: MIT Press, 1987), 17–50.
17 Wiebe Bijker, *Of Bicycles, Bakelites, and Bulbs: Toward a Theory of Sociotechnical Change* (Cambridge, MA: MIT Press, 1995), 270.

18 See the new 'Introduction' to the revised edition of Donald MacKenzie and Judy Wajcman (eds), *The Social Shaping of Technology* (Milton Keynes, Bucks.: Open University Press, 1999), 3–27, esp. 22.
19 See, for example, the Introduction to Cynthia Cockburn and Susan Ormrod, *Gender and Technology in the Making* (London: Sage, 1993), 1–15, at 8–9.
20 Michel Callon, 'Some Elements of a Sociology of Translation: Domestication of the Scallops and the Fisherman of St Brieuc Bay', in John Law (ed.), *Power, Action and Belief: A New Sociology of Knowledge?* (London: Routledge & Kegan Paul, 1986), 196–229; Callon, 'The Sociology of an Actor-Network: The Case of the Electric Vehicle', in Callon, Law and Arie Rip (eds), *Mapping the Dynamics of Science and Technology* (Basingstoke, Hants.: Macmillan, 1986), 19–34; Bruno Latour, *Science in Action* (Milton Keynes, Bucks.: Open University Press, 1987); Latour, *The Pasteurization of France* (Cambridge, MA: Harvard University Press, 1988); Law, 'Technology and Heterogeneous Engineering: The Case of Portuguese Expansion', in Bijker, Hughes & Pinch (eds), op. cit. note 16, 111–34; Law & Hassard (eds), op. cit. note 4.
21 As quoted in Berg, op. cit. note 12, 39.
22 Madeleine Akrich, 'The De-Scription of Technical Objects', in Wiebe Bijker and John Law (eds), *Shaping Technology/Building Society: Studies in Sociotechnical Change* (Cambridge, MA: MIT Press, 1992), 205–24.
23 See Langdon Winner, 'Upon Opening the Black Box and Finding it Empty: Social Constructivism and the Philosophy of Technology', *Science, Technology, & Human Values*, Vol. 18, No. 3 (Summer 1993), 362–78; Stewart Russell, 'The Social Construction of Artefacts: A Response to Pinch and Bijker', *Social Studies of Science*, Vol. 16, No. 2 (May 1986), 331–46.
24 Steven Lukes, *Power: A Radical View* (London: Macmillan, 1974). Lukes is providing a formal analysis of the dimensions of power, and does not himself discuss gender issues. However, much feminist research has been concerned with gender structures, and approaches that fail to find a place for this level of analysis will fail to do justice to feminist critiques.
25 See Mary Frank Fox, 'Gender, Hierarchy, and Science', in Janet Chafetz (ed.), *Handbook of the Sociology of Gender* (New York: Kluwer Academic/Plenum Publishers, 1999), 441–57, and Fox, 'Women in Science and Engineering: Theory, Practice, and Policy in Programs', *Signs*, Vol. 24, No. 1 (1998), 201–23.
26 Sandra Harding, *Whose Science? Whose Knowledge?* (Milton Keynes, Bucks.: Open University Press, 1991), and Susan Leigh Star, 'Power, Technology and the Phenomenology of Conventions: On Being Allergic to Onions', in John Law (ed.), *A Sociology of Monsters: Essays on Power, Technology and Domination* (London: Routledge, 1991), 26–56.
27 Bruno Latour, 'The Powers of Association', in Law (ed.), op. cit. note 20, 264–80, at 264.
28 Latour (1988), op. cit. note 20.
29 John Law, 'Theory and Narrative in the History of Technology: Response', *Technology and Culture*, Vol. 32, No. 2, Pt 1 (April 1991), 377–84.
30 Star, op. cit. note 26, 49.
31 Judy Wajcman, *Managing Like a Man: Women and Men in Corporate Management* (Cambridge: Polity Press, 1998).
32 See Steven Shapin's discussion of such explanations in his 'Following Scientists Around', *Social Studies of Science*, Vol. 18, No. 3 (August 1988), 533–50. See also Wiebe Bijker and John Law's discussion of the problematic structure/agency distinction in their 'Postscript' to Bijker & Law (eds), op. cit. note 22.
33 Star, op. cit. note 25, 26.

34 Delamont, op. cit. note 2, 166. See also Margaret Rossiter, *Women Scientists in America: Struggles and Strategies to 1940* (Baltimore, MD: Johns Hopkins University Press, 1982).
35 See, for example, Callon, 'Sociology of an Actor-Network', and Latour (1987, 1988), all opera cit. note 20.
36 Sally Hacker, *Pleasure, Power and Technology* (Boston, MA: Unwin Hyman, 1989); Wendy Faulkner, 'The Power *and* the Pleasure? A Research Agenda for "Making Gender Stick" to Engineers', *Science, Technology, & Human Values*, Vol. 25, No. 1 (Winter 2000), 87–119; Ruth Oldenziel, *Making Technology Masculine: Men, Women, and Modern Machines in America* (Amsterdam: Amsterdam University Press, 1999).
37 See Wajcman, op. cit. note 13, Chapter 6.
38 See authors such as Berg, op. cit. note 12; Danielle Chabaud-Rychter, 'Women Users in the Design Process of a Food Robot: Innovation in a French Domestic Appliance Company', in Cynthia Cockburn and Ruza Furst-Dilic (eds), *Bringing Technology Home: Gender and Technology in a Changing Europe* (Milton Keynes, Bucks.: Open University Press, 1994), 77–93; the contributors to Merete Lie and Knut Sørensen (eds), *Making Technology Our Own? Domesticating Technology into Everyday Life* (Oslo: Scandinavian University Press, 1996); Lucy Suchman, 'Working Relations of Technology Production and Use', in MacKenzie & Wajcman (eds), op. cit. note 18, 258–65; and Juliet Webster, *Shaping Women's Work* (Harlow, Essex: Longman, 1995).
39 Cockburn & Ormrod, op. cit. note 19, 94.
40 Ibid., 109 (emphasis in original).
41 Monica Casper and Adele Clarke, 'Making the Pap Smear into the "Right Tool" for the Job: Cervical Cancer Screening in the USA, circa 1940–95', *Social Studies of Science*, Vol. 28, No. 2 (April 1998), 255–90; Vicky Singleton and Mike Michael, 'Actor-Networks and Ambivalence: General Practitioners in the UK Cervical Screening Programme', *ibid.*, Vol. 23, No. 2 (May 1993), 227–64.
42 See, for example, Judith Butler, *Gender Trouble* (New York: Routledge, 1990). Her emphasis on performance can be traced back at least to Erving Goffman's dramaturgical model: E. Goffman, *Interaction Ritual* (New York: Anchor Books, 1967).
43 Nelly Oudshoorn, *Beyond the Natural Body: An Archaeology of Sex Hormones* (London: Routledge, 1994), 82.
44 See, for example, Linda L. Layne (ed.), 'Anthropological Approaches in Science and Technology Studies', Special Issue, *Science, Technology, & Human Values*, Vol. 23, No. 1 (Winter 1998), 4–128; also Sarah Franklin's review essay on anthropological writing, 'Science As Culture, Cultures Of Science', *Annual Review of Anthropology*, Vol. 24 (1995), 163–84. Interestingly, a recent successful anthropology journal entitled *Journal of Material Culture* (Sage) is 'concerned with the relationship between artefacts and social relations... and explores the linkage between the construction of social identities and the production and use of material culture'. I am thinking here of authors such as Sadie Plant, 'On the Matrix: Cyberfeminist Simulations', in Rob Shields (ed.), *Cultures of the Internet* (London: Sage, 1996), 170–83; Allucquere Rosanne Stone, *The War of Desire and Technology at the Close of the Mechanical Age* (Cambridge, MA: MIT Press, 1995); and Sharon Traweek, *Beamtimes and Lifetimes: The World of High Energy Physics* (Cambridge, MA: Harvard University Press, 1988).
45 Donna Haraway, 'A Manifesto for Cyborgs: Science, Technology, and Socialist Feminism in the 1980s', *Socialist Review*, Vol. 15, No. 2 (1985), 65–108, and Haraway, *Modest_Witness@Second_Millennium.FemaleMan@Meets_OncoMouse™: Feminism and Technoscience* (New York: Routledge, 1997).

46 See, for example, Marc Berg and Annemarie Mol (eds), *Differences in Medicine: Unraveling Practices, Techniques and Bodies* (Durham, NC: Duke University Press, 1998); Adele Clarke and Joan Fujimura (eds), *The Right Tools for the Job: At Work in Twentieth-Century Life Sciences* (Princeton, NJ: Princeton University Press, 1992); Sarah Franklin, *Embodied Progress: A Cultural Account of Assisted Conception* (London: Routledge, 1997); Singleton & Michael, op. cit. note 41; Casper & Clarke, op. cit. note 41; Oudshoorn, op. cit. note 43; and Barbara Katz Rothman, *Genetic Maps and Human Imagination: The Limits of Science in Understanding Who We Are* (New York: W.W. Norton, 1998).
47 Nicholas Negroponte, *Being Digital* (Sydney: Hodder & Stoughton, 1995); Howard Rheingold, *The Virtual Community* (New York: Harper, 1994).
48 Roger Silverstone and Eric Hirsch, 'Introduction', in Silverstone and Hirsch (eds), *Consuming Technologies: Media and Information in Domestic Spaces* (London: Routledge, 1992), 1-11, at 3.
49 This is particularly disappointing given that a feminist group did critique the last large ESRC technology project, the 'Programme on Information and Communication Technologies' (PICT), on precisely these grounds. See Sonia Liff's report: 'Stunted Growth or Slow Development? The Coverage of Gender Issues within ESRC-Funded Research on Information Technology' (Swindon, Wilts.: ESRC/PICT Archives, 1990).
50 Sherry Turkle, *Life on the Screen: Identity in the Age of the Internet* (New York: Simon & Schuster, 1995), 12.
51 Ibid., 314.
52 Stone, op. cit. note 44, 180.
53 Ibid., Chapter 3.
54 Ruth Oldenziel, 'Of Old and New Cyborgs: Feminist Narratives of Technology', *Letterature D'America*, Vol. 14, No. 55 (1994), 95-111.
55 Ibid., 103.
56 See the collection edited by Susan Leigh Star, *The Cultures of Computing* (Oxford: Blackwell, 1995).
57 Oldenziel, op. cit. note 54, 104.
58 UNDP, *Human Development Report* (New York: United Nations, 1999).
59 A notable exception is Graham Thomas and Sally Wyatt, 'Access is Not the Only Problem: Using and Controlling the Internet', in Wyatt *et al.* (eds), *Technology and In/equality: Questioning the Information Society* (London: Routledge, forthcoming 2000).
60 Sadie Plant, *Zeros and Ones: Digital Women and the New Technoculture* (London: Fourth Estate, 1997); Dale Spender, *Nattering on the Net: Women, Power and Cyberspace* (Melbourne: Spinifex, 1995).

80

AN INTERRUPTED POSTCOLONIAL/FEMINIST CYBERETHNOGRAPHY

Complicity and resistance in the "cyberfield"

Radhika Gajjala

Source: *Feminist Media Studies* 2(2) (2002): 177–93.

Introduction

In this paper, I will discuss a situation that I refer to as the "SAWnet refusal." The situation arises out of my attempt at a cyberethnography of the electronic discussion group SAWnet (South Asian Women's Network), and it raises complex issues in relation to feminist ethnography and feminist Internet research. Briefly stated, what happened was that in the spring of 1994 I began to research a South Asian women's e-mail discussion list. In the summer of 1995, this study was interrupted (this is what I refer to as the "refusal") and my attempt at studying the group failed. However, the discussions leading to the failure highlighted several important issues in relation to ethnographic practices online and to feminist practices of re-presentation that I explore here.

This experience raises a number of important questions. How do ethnographic practices and the ethnographer evolve in an online context? How are they revolutionized? What constitutes the field and how do we define its boundaries? Further, can we transpose concerns that arise out of RL ("real life") anthropology or face-to-face ethnography onto the study of virtual communities without seriously considering the very important differences between the nature of face-to-face interaction and virtual interaction and thus confuse the issues? When can RL anthropological and critical issues be considered relevant to online ethnography? (See David Jacobson (1999) for a discussion of some of these issues.) Considering the interactive nature of online participation, questions arise as to who is an ethnographer, who qualifies to be a "native" informant, and what the options are for refusing to be a subject. For instance, in my experience with the SAWnet list, I was an active participant posting fiction and poetry, sharing a common ethos with other list-members and thus in many ways I was considered to be "an insider." It was only when I announced my researcher role and SAWnettors began to consider the implications of being written about that I became some what of an "outsider." The medium (the Internet with its lack of face-to-face contact), the transnational nature of access to the community I was studying, the fact that I had been a participant on SAWnet since 1993 and was a South Asian woman—these factors further complicated the ethnographic experience. Yet another complication with online ethnography is related to the matter of feminist e-spaces: What does it mean to define a "safe" women-only social space? What are the inclusions and exclusions implicit in the notion of being "safe" online? Who speaks for whom? Because of these and other contradictions that emerged in this situation, my efforts at studying the group failed. I will explore some of the possible reasons for my failure to undertake a cyberethnography in this paper. Specifically, I will focus on the ways in which conducting ethnography in cyberspace is distinctly different from "real life" ethnography while also underscoring some issues/problematics that are specific to the technology/medium.

My work on SAWnet is unique and different from several feminist analyses of women-centered e-spaces that exist (Susan Herring 1996; Dale Spender 1995; Barbara Warnick 1999) because it engages with the specific context of my intervention as a researcher and the response of list-members to being researched. This situation demanded that I interrogate the process and assumptions behind academic feminist ethnographies. The paper also highlights issues related to the politics of enunciation within diasporic spaces while questioning the possibility for a true "cyborg-diaspora" online. Issues of voice and voicelessness, as well as of marginalization, ventriloquizing, and Othering based on gender, race, class, and geographical location emerge as central concerns.

Feminist diasporas in cyberspace

In examining various populations online, it is important to keep in mind the economic, political, and cultural forces that drive globalization and the resulting immigration from third-world regions to various parts of the world. The lure of cyberspace, not unlike the lure of immigrating to the US, promises a dream of individual freedom and upward mobility that becomes a possibility for the culturally or ideologically assimilated and materially privileged Other. The "global village" is performed once the Other has melted down and become deracinated and degendered and is allowed the freedom to "express" his or her cultural difference within the appropriate, politically correct, postmodern, apparently multicultural (yet ahistorical and celebratory) paradigm. In the context of the Internet and Indians from the South Asian subcontinent, for instance, Vinay Lal writes:

> It is the agenda of the "Internet elites," if they may be so termed, that dictates the modernization and liberalization of the Indian economy, and it is their interests and ambitions that have led to the emergence of the cell phone culture while the greater part of the country remains without reliable ordinary telephone service. The development of an internationally renowned software industry even while nearly 50% of the Indian population remains mired in poverty is yet another of the anomalies engendered by the culture of the Internet elites. Their mobility in cyberspace furnishes them with opportunities to work within the world of international finance and business; like the elites of the First World, they are beginning to live in time, and space poses no barriers for them . . . The timespace compression that cyberspace typifies only works to the advantage of these elites.
>
> (1999: 140)

Cyberspace provides a very apt site for the production of shifting yet fetishized frozen homes (shifting as more and more people get online and participate, frozen as their narratives remain on websites and list archives through time in a timeless floating fashion) by and for such South Asian diasporics. It is here that their narratives potentially function as those of native informants for researchers and policy makers from "first-world" regions. E-mail lists like SAWnet become conveniently available to researchers wishing to point to the "diversity" of women's voices in cyberspace. For instance, Leslie Shade (1993) and Lisa Gerard (1999–2000) have referred to SAWnet as one of several examples of how women network online while avoiding commodification. While referring to SAWnet as a successful woman's space, it is not implied that SAWnet is used as a representative example of "third-world" women's empowerment through the Internet. The fact that spaces such as SAWnet are often seen as the only easily available sign-posts of diversity and multiculturalism online is highly problematic (see Deepika Bahri 2001; Radhika Gajjala 1998; Lal 1999; and Amit S. Rai 1995 for more on this).

Yet cyberspace is also a "space" which contains the *possibility* for disruptive cyborg-diasporic encounters (Indira Karamcheti 1992). It is a space where the diasporic stories of the past (often told as if they were stories from the present) and of places left behind can reach the actual physical (socio-cultural in flux) places that are fetishized in the memory/nostalgia of the model native (diasporic) informants. The real places, however, are not the same (obviously) as in the memory of the diasporic storyteller. In cyborg-diaspora, those who have left home have taken on the role of native informant. They speak and thus silence narratives from "back home" within a powerfield that celebrates the "Westernized" as "progressive" and degrades the "third world" as "underdeveloped." Unused to having their narratives challenged in shared public spaces, the cyborg-diaspora potentially faces the "real" in the form of counternarratives from those "back home."

South Asian diaspora online, therefore, exists between notions of "home" and "being away." Even though many from actual South Asian geographical (home) locations are connected and online, their discourse is still framed by notions of home and being away; not-having-left-home-yet (or-at-all) and having arrived (i.e., "made it") in the Western world. This discourse prevails because South Asian presence online is dominated by subject positions located in diaspora. Further, in many instances, the term "South Asia" is used as a catchall phrase that in reality covers mostly Indian concerns. South Asian subjectivities that emerge online are continually negotiating "model minority" performances and essentialized cultural performances based on fetishized, mummified notions of "home" traditions and cultural practices. These performances, rather than being "outside of" and "on the periphery of" the colonial imaginary, are central to the re-installment, maintenance, and continuation of colonial discourses that situate the third-world subject as an essentialized exotic Other within hierarchies privileging a certain view of Modernity as progressive and desirable. These self-narratives by model native informants who have moved "away" from home yet fetishize "home," while celebrating their moving away and the arriving as progressive (upward social mobility), perform the dual and simultaneous function of "modernization" and "exoticization" of the "third-world" (underdeveloped) subject. These negotiated performances do not occur "through the heroic act of an individual (the migrant), but through the forming of [virtual, cyborg] communities that create multiple identifications through collective acts of remembering in the absence of a shared knowledge or a familiar terrain" (Sara Ahmed 1999: 329) and through collective acts of storytelling and sharing of knowledge and experience of the "unfamiliar" and "new" terrains. One such community online is SAWnet. What makes it different from other South Asian online spaces is that it is a women-only e-mail discussion list.

But the mere act of sharing these narratives online does not create a disruptive cyberdiaspora. South Asians in diaspora have produced and continue to produce such narratives even when not online or "connected" via modern telecommunication systems. The narratives and the sharing within these diasporic communities are not "new"—it is the possibility of disruption implied in the notion of cyborg-diaspora through the speed, potential interactivity, and access of the Internet communication as well as the publicness of online interaction that is "new."

In pre-Internet interaction, face-to-face presentation norms and ceremonial group performances of cultural identity within physically/geographically contained places ensured that to a certain extent, the boundaries could be maintained in the production of somewhat essentialized categories of "home" and "not home," or the "at home" and the "outside of home." Coherent, unified, homogenized categories could be invoked to explain away contradictions. In cyberspace, however, the model of interaction blurs boundaries in certain ways. Such a blurring of boundaries in cyberspace necessitates a rethinking of feminist methodologies for the study of various (cyber)cultural spaces.

Feminist media studies and cyberethnography

Concerns raised by my experience with SAWnet are not new to feminist media researchers who have undertaken ethnographies of popular culture audiences. Some concerns that arise in my work also are ones faced by scholars such as Andrea Press and Liz Cole (1999) during their encounters with audiences. Researching women's ideas regarding abortion debates and their sense of identity as formed through interpersonal dialogue and exposure to cultural images on television and other mass media, Press and Cole faced certain challenges. For instance, they needed to examine their own "unvoiced experiences" and worldview in relation to that of their subjects (Press and Cole 1999: x). The challenges that they faced have their basis in the contradictions between the feminist ideals of empowerment, protection, empathy, and understanding of women on the one hand and the "objectivity" demands on researchers on the other. These challenges led to an interrogation of their positionality as researchers and as feminists. They were faced with having to make choices for which their academic, scholarly "methods" literature and training had not prepared them. "On their [i.e., the subjects'] territory, in their homes," write Press and Cole, "we were stripped of authority and the illusion of objectivity." In addition, their "subjects had in effect restored our subjectivity, thereby complicating the whole practice and meaning of research" (1999: ix). Their experiences highlighted the fact that researchers' subjectivities are produced within historical and structural constraints, making it impossible for them to adopt a "view from nowhere" stance. The importance of contextual, self-reflexive ethnographies examining the political economy and cultural dynamics of the Internet (cyberspace) cannot be over-stated.

My specific case study began in the spring of 1994, when Istarted to research SAWnet, a South Asian women's e-mail discussion list. This study was to be a part of a larger project that would focus on the centrality of notions of gender and sexuality and the importance of representations of the "subaltern" in the formulation of online group identities. Specifically, I was hoping to see if SAWnet could be truly dialogic and empowering to women irrespective of race, class, sexuality, and geographic location. In 1995, the study was interrupted in what I can only describe as an extremely productive but also provocative manner by some of the participants of the e-mail discussion list.

My attempts at studying this group took several forms. During the summer of 1994, I posted a survey on SAWnet to find out if the nature of the online community had changed since the time of its formation. At the time, I indicated that I intended to write at least a magazine article about SAWnet using data from the survey. Interest in the changing nature of the group led me to try to find out if any members felt dissatisfied with how the group was interacting. I wanted to see if there were discourses that were being marginalized. This prompted me to investigate the possibilities for dialogic interaction within an online community like SAWnet. Although I was aware of the rule on SAWnet that posts could only be shared with non-members of SAWnet if the poster gave permission, I did not imagine that writing a description of SAWnet would be a problem for any of its members, since this does not involve the use of anyone's messages on SAWnet.[1]

During the spring of 1995, when an anthropologist from New Zealand (a non-South Asian) announced her intention to write a paper about the community, some of the members of SAWnet began to question her methods and motives in relation to her location and representational practices. At the time, I reminded members of my own ongoing study and offered copies of my work in-progress. My entry into the discussions regarding SAWnet contributed to and further complicated the discussion, partly because it was not possible to position me as an outsider. It was known to members that I was of South Asian origin and that I had not initially joined the discussion list with the intention of studying it. I had a history of interaction as an "insider." The discussions led to a vote, after which members decided not to allow anyone to make "global statements" about SAWnet, that is, "no one is allowed to generalize based on any of the posts on the discussion list." A policy was developed that individual members would have to grant permission for use of their messages. The current SAWnet policy statement linked to the SAWnet website records this policy decision (SAWnet 2002).

The three options suggested and voted for were:

1 Studies of SAWnet are specifically forbidden.
2 Studies of SAWnet are permitted, as long as no post is quoted without explicit permission from its author.
3 SAWnet should be studied, but SAWnet members together will choose someone to study us. Only that person has the authority to do the study.

There were about 350 members at the time of the vote, out of which 69 voted. Out of this 69, 39 voted for option 1, 29 voted for option 2, and 1 voted for option 3.[2]

This policy decision is what I have referred to as "the SAWnet refusal." A project that began as an attempt to study South Asian women's use of and inhabitation of the Internet resulted in a situation in which a variety of issues were raised that problematized and rearticulated concerns central to feminist ethnography and the politics of the Internet. Both Internet researchers and feminist researchers face issues related to subjects "talking back," questioning and displacing the researcher's authority. In the case of feminist scholars, this occurs because of the contradictory demands between feminist ideals of dialogic engagement and the implicit demand of mainstream social science for the researcher to hide her subjectivity in an effort to appear to be "unbiased." With research conducted in Internet spaces, the interactive nature of the medium potentially leads to a questioning of the researcher's conceptual and methodological assumptions by "subjects."

Concerns and dialogues regarding women-only safe spaces originating in second-wave feminisms are played out in various ways in relation to women and cyberspace. There is a body of work examining women's use of the Internet that invokes past feminist debates regarding the need for safe spaces for women, while engaging and questioning the (im)possibilities of safe women-only spaces online. For instance, Kristine Blair and Pamela Takayoshi (1999) argue that "websites written by and for women that offer women spaces for active participation in the construction of more productive, supportive, and encouraging subject positions for women and girls" (1999: 6).

Women on SAWnet were/are aware of these discussions circulating around women's use of the Internet. The origin of SAWnet as a women-only e-mail discussion list occurred in response to the perceived marginalization of women's voices and women's issues on Usenet bulletin boards such as soc.culture.indian, amongst others. In addition, my engagement with SAWnet also demonstrates that all safe spaces have, implicit within their formations, certain ideologies and visions that exclude and disenfranchise some members. For instance, the implicit heterosocial framing of most discussions in this space excludes the possibility that South Asian lesbians might find this women-only list to be a safe place. Feminist researchers of the Internet have also examined such processes of inclusion and exclusion where the creation of a supposedly safe space for specific groups of women leads to exclusionary, homogenizing identification practices that are oppressive to certain members of the groups (see Joanne Addison and Susan Hilligoss 1999; Radhika Gajjala 2001). In addition, my experience with SAWnet highlights the fact that a women-only e-mail list is not necessarily a safe space or a private space. This is true despite the rule on SAWnet that "posts are private and should not be forwarded without the author's permission," because of the nature of the medium/technology through which communication was taking place. The implicit protection promised by the rules framing the formation of the virtual community seemed to have lulled the participants into thinking that e-mail discussions were like conversations in a friend's living room, where their privacy could not be invaded by unwanted researchers or nasty encounters that might have "real life" (RL) consequences beyond the artificial boundaries of cyberspace. The project, therefore, underscores the fragility/impossibility of constructing a female safe space online.

How then might this technology alter participation and interpersonal communication in the public arena—does all space become public? Ideas of private/public, closed and open spaces are blurred and reconfigured. The consequences of the blurring of these binaries are yet to be examined and understood. In addition, the site of cyberspace now brings us face-to-face with and forces us to articulate the *fact* of multiple subject positions (and the unequal power relations which permit their voicing and silencing)—based in contexts mediated by class, gender, geographical location, race, caste, and other unequal power relations.[3] Such identities have always existed, but have not often been performed in legitimized public spaces. In cyberspace there is a less clear line between "legitimate" and "illegitimate," authorized and unauthorized public spaces. Yet the fact that cyberspace is still characterized by Anglo-American (masculine) academic and corporate hegemony sees to it that the few inconsistencies are either erased or ignored in various re-writings and re-wirings of cyberspace.

It is true that there is now an increasing, even overwhelming, amount of research being done on the Internet (feminist, critical, and mainstream). However, in the early 1990s Internet researchers had very few prior studies on which to draw in order to inform the methodologies used to study sociocultural formations online. My work on SAWnet began in 1994 amidst much hype (even among critical researchers) regarding virtual community and hypertext (see George Landow 1992; Howard Rheingold 1993). At the time, there were few precedents available for what it might mean to "study" a dynamic Internet community from a postcolonial feminist perspective.[4] My initial attempts therefore drew on a combination of survey method and textual analyses.

Although "method" for Internet studies and for doing research in cyberspace (Jacobson 1999) is still much debated and discussed (see, for example, discussions on lists such as A(o)IR), there are several prior studies for feminist researchers of the Internet to draw upon now. For example, media scholars have studied Usenet groups, Web-based "communities," MUDs, and MOOs (see Chris Boese 1998–2000; Laura J. Gurak 1997). Researchers have used textual and discourse analysis to examine websites (Blair and Takayoshi 1999). Others have investigated adolescent girls' use of the Internet (such as the "Cybergrrls" phenomena) and their access to the Internet and technology (Chris Sauer 2001). Additionally, there have been rhetorical analyses of women-centered sites (Warnick 1999). Feminist researchers have examined women's Internet presence from a variety of disciplinary and cross-disciplinary perspectives. For example, there are feminist researchers whose work is categorized as being about computer-mediated communication and women (Herring 1996); cyberfeminisms (Radhika Gajjala and Annapurna Mamidipudi 1999; Kira Hall 1996; Jenny Sunden 2001;

Faith Wilding and Maria Fernandez 1999); development, globalization, and women (Wendy Harcourt 1999); feminist Internet studies (Liesbet van Zoonen 2001); race, gender, sexuality, and cyberculture (Bettina Heinz, Gu Li, Ako Inuzuka, and Roger Zender 2002; Beth Kolko, Lisa Nakamura, and Gil Rodman 2000); digital labor and women (Ursula Biemann 1999); and so on. Of course, all these labels and categories are probably individual negotiations of disciplinarity, as many feminist scholars are required to situate their work and justify it within authorized "disciplines."[5] It is not my intention to provide an extensive detailing and critique of the literature available, but to point to some of the diversity of feminist perspectives on studying the Internet currently available.

My examination of the SAWnet refusal is situated at the intersection of feminist media studies and postcolonial communication research. I draw some of my theoretical insights from postcolonial theory and subaltern studies (Anannya Bhattacharjee 1992, 1997; Partha Chatterjee 1989; Chandra Mohanty 1993; Uma Narayan 1989; Kum Kum Sangari and Sudesh Vaid 1989; Gayatri Spivak and Elizabeth Grosz 1990). However, I also draw from feminist cultural anthropology (Ruth Behar and Deborah Gordon 1996; Mary John 1996; Judith Stacey 1988; Kamala Visweswaran 1994) and feminist philosophy (Linda Alcoff 1991–2; Lorraine Code 1998; Sandra Harding 1998; Narayan 1989). In each of these conceptual approaches, I draw upon ideas about "speaking for," "speaking to," "speaking with," and "speaking about" human subjects of research. Such issues are already well known to many feminist Internet researchers (see Laura Augustin 1999).

In an attempt to examine my relations with the women I was writing about, I asked questions about my own location within the South Asian diasporic community. How did my own "discrepant dislocations" (John 1996) and personal history within Indian society and Indian diasporic communities affect my approach to an ethnography of South Asians? What were my hidden presumptions/assumptions and biases?

"Contrary to the assumptions that brought some of us to the US," writes Mary John in relation to her own experience as an anthropologist of South Asian origin researching members of a South Asian community in the US,

> we may thus find ourselves forced to contend with our places of departure, asked to function as native informants from "elsewhere." From what position of authority would we speak? The very attempt to become such cultural representatives, the faltering of our memory, must, then, lead to a different realization: the need for an examination of the historical, institutional, and social relations that have, in fact, produced subjects also quite unlike "the native informant" of old.
>
> (John 1996: 23)

Questions regarding ethnography and representation are complicated by the nature of the medium for communication, which blurs various categories such as public/private, audience/author, producer/consumer, and text/human subject. For example, there was some confusion on the part of SAWnet members with regard to SAWnet interactions being texts. If I had been studying documents written by these women and published in printed form, there would have been no doubt about the documents being texts. However, while studying texts produced in interaction on e-mail lists, the researcher necessarily takes on an "approach in which the object of study is a process (the changing text) rather than a project (the static text)" (Espen J. Aarseth 1994: 82).

My discussion here regarding SAWnet tries to respect members' wishes by not using messages about personal lives without their permission. My intention, contrary to what some SAWnet members may have suspected, was not (and still is not) to write an exposé of the South Asian female mind and life. It was also never my intention to expose any confidences members may have shared about their private lives. Judith Stacey (1988), in her article "Can There Be a Feminist Ethnography?," suggests that the feminist ethnographer's dilemma is that "feminist researchers are apt to suffer the delusion of alliance more than the delusion of separateness" (1988: 22). The ethnographer, in such cases, "betrays" (and perhaps even feels betrayed by) a feminist principle and by the subjects of her ethnographic study. In such instances, John (1996) argues, there is no getting away from the fact that "feminist goals of 'authenticity, reciprocity, and intersubjectivity' might be even more dangerous than the masculinist, objectifying methods they criticize, precisely because professed beliefs of mutual respect are apt to hide relations of authority, exploitation, and manipulation unavoidable in fieldwork (1996: 118). However, feminist ethnographers such as Behar and Gordon (1996) and Stacey (1988) have also argued for the necessity of a dialogue between feminist ideals and ethnographic methodologies. Moreover, engagement with postmodern approaches emphasizes the partialness and situatedness of any type of representation, while underscoring the power relations at play in the very process of representation (see Behar and Gordon 1996).

Feminist betrayals?

Around the time that SAWnet group members were discussing researchers who wished to study the group (in 1995), I e-mailed a scholarly paper I had written to some members that contained an analysis of South Asian women. In the paper, I positioned Indian women as faced by the "dark side of epistemic privilege" (Narayan 1989). I wrote that Indian women are faced with the tension between Indian nationalism's discursive positioning of the "Bharatiya Nari" (Woman of Bharat/India) and Western feminism's complicity with colonial discourses. The Indian woman's expression of agency is complicated by the fact that both these discourses speak *for* and *about* her, but do not allow her to speak for herself. My study was thus an attempt to examine the emergence of the kinds of South Asian female subject positions that were enabled within the context of SAWnet and how individual posters discursively negotiated agency.

My description of South Asian women and of SAWnet caused some controversy. My own complicity as a creative writer and as an academic in producing certain images of South Asian women became an issue that members wished to interrogate. As a result, I was prompted to revisit and analyze various texts that I had written about SAWnet in my previous work (Gajjala 1998). What happened in response to my description of SAWnet and of South Asian women could be interpreted as an attempt by certain participants of SAWnet to define and control community. But it was also a panic. Some of the members were clearly upset when they realized that despite the illusion, SAWnet is not a safe haven for women.

The objections to my study of SAWnet revolved around questions regarding methodology, concern over privacy, and anxieties about how I would represent members. Questions regarding the methodology were primarily framed within the science vs. non-science debate. Members who questioned my methodology wanted to know how I would "validate" my findings and make sure that I was presenting the "correct" picture of SAWnet since my audience might not be able to verify the truth of what I was saying by accessing the archives of SAWnet.[6] JV, a member of SAWnet who responded to several drafts of my work before and after the SAWnet refusal to allow me to continue to study the group, writes:

> Looking back, I feel that the debate that ended in the decision for "the vote" arose largely because some of the dominant personalities at the time were resistant to others' attempts to characterize the S Asian women's community (or at least the community comprised of sawnettors) . . . perhaps out of a somewhat naive fear of misrepresentation, or out of a distrust of (and disdain for?) the field (and jargon) you represented. That is, in addition to other variables, the debate was very much also one of the "proper" way to do "scientific" research (I remember at least the most vocal opponent was in the hard sciences).

Some women did not think I should be representing them and making generalizations about their lives. They felt that what I had written was not their experience. Most importantly, they were concerned that my narrative regarding South Asian women would be received as representative, whether I intended it to be so or not. There was also anxiety expressed about the possibility that my disclaimers would make no difference to an audience that would readily generalize based on one or two academic studies.

Some of the women who were objecting to the study appeared to have felt betrayed by a co-member (not just as a co-member of SAWnet, but a co-member of the South Asian community). During discussions that occurred after some members had read the papers that another researcher (who was a non-South Asian academic woman also attempting to study SAWnet at that time) and I had e-mailed to them, several issues concerning power and representation were raised. Such reactions highlight several important questions concerning broader, contemporary issues raised in critical, post-colonial ethnography and feminist anthropology, especially since, as JV suggests, "the vehemence of the reaction [could have been] in part exacerbated by the fact that just around that time the white (?) researcher had wanted to do so as well." This once again invokes controversies and discussions ongoing within feminist theory and anthropology about the politics of location and representation of "third-world" women and black women by white feminist ethnographers.

Kamala Visweswaran (1994) has suggested that ethnographers need to consider ways to "disrupt" their own authority as ethnographers, thus allowing for a questioning of the work. In her essay "Betrayal: An Analysis in Three Acts," she argues for a deconstructive ethnography where the ethnographer pays careful attention to silences, refusals, and betrayals. How is a "disruption of authority" possible? As a participant ethnographer and as a "third-world" academic producing my work within the Western academy, my encounter with SAWnet raises several concerns about audiences. Visweswaran discusses (in the context of her work as a feminist anthropologist) the struggles and difficulties she faces as an intellectual who locates herself "in a field of power (the West) and in the production of a particular knowledge (about the East)" (1994: 25). She advances the case for "a critical feminist epistemology that finds its stakes, as with other interested and subversive epistemologies . . . and, as Haraway puts it, 'situated knowledge'" (1994: xx). Kirin Narayan (1997), another anthropologist concerned with issues related to participant observation, argues for the "*enactment of hybridity* in our texts" (emphasis in the original). This hybridity is intended as a negotiation between "the world of engaged scholarship and the world of the everyday." She writes:

> What we must focus on is the quality of relations with the people we seek to represent in our texts: are they viewed as mere fodder for professionally self-serving statements about a generalized Other, or are they accepted as subjects with voices, views, and dilemmas—people to whom we are bonded through ties of reciprocity and who may even be critical of our professional enterprise?
>
> (Narayan 1997: 23)

These and other related strategies are useful for the ethnographer who is a participant-observer. But how would I build this "quality of relations" with women I know mainly (if not solely) through my e-mail communication with them? Consequently, one of the steps I took was to continually share my drafts of this work with women who were willing to respond publicly to my call for participation. I also tried to supplement e-mail interaction with face-to-face encounters with South Asian women. I have shown drafts of this project to several South Asian women both in the US and when I visited India. I have incorporated critiques I received as part of an interrogation of my academic and creative work about South Asian women into the study (Gajjala 1998).

In the context of the larger South Asian diaspora community of which SAWnet is very much a part, I feel that the story of the refusal needs to be told. On the one hand, it is a story of a group of postcolonial women refusing to be subjects of academic studies and showing that they are very articulate and able to express themselves. On the other hand, there is the issue of the attempt and perceived need of immigrant communities to control the image of community. Behind this need lies a history of complex postcolonial identity negotiations within a mainstream Western power field. I agree to a certain extent with Ananda Mitra when he writes in his study of Indian newsgroups online that "[t]he fact that the diasporic Indians now occupy a new space in America and Western Europe demands the production of a specific 'face,'" [and] this need should not simply be read as a stereotypical "Eastern" need to "save face" (1997: 70). Instead, it should be explored in depth in relation to the larger South Asian diasporic communities and their history in relation to political and cultural domination by Western and European nations. Nor should this be simplistically celebrated as "resistance." As a South Asian woman and a participant of SAWnet, I am very sympathetic to some of the protests. However, I feel that the protests should not be merely confined to SAWnet archives, but should be instead spoken about outside of the virtual group. My reasoning for this is that the experience of my refusal exposes many of the complexities and contradictions about South Asian diasporic socio-cultural spaces.

It was my face-to-face meetings with several SAWnet members at The South Asia Conference 1996 that made me rethink my position with regard to SAWnet. I met members there who were very interested in the project. I don't think they were all necessarily in favor of it. However, in my face-to-face meetings with these women, I could see them as multidimensional human beings, something I was unable to do through reading their posts on SAWnet. I better understood women who might not want to be fitted into a simple "yes" or absolute "no" answer on a questionnaire. On the other hand, there were others who put the whole project in perspective for me. They made me realize that efforts by some SAWnet members to silence me might have had to do with power issues related to my location within the South Asian immigrant community in the US. One woman clearly pointed out to me that there was a connection between what I had experienced on SAWnet and the "habit of ex-nomination" that Annanya Bhattacharjee (1992) describes. What I had to say, both in my creative work and in my academic description, did not fit in with the notion of a model immigrant community. Also, it could be that as a graduate student (low income) and non-immigrant (which is the equivalent of "low status" in the eyes of many South Asian immigrants), I was probably not very highly placed within in the diasporic South Asian social hierarchy in North America.

As I write this, I remain a part of SAWnet (albeit a very infrequent poster, mostly because I have many other lists to manage and to which I contribute, and I am no longer a graduate student). I continue to be one of the volunteer moderators (I first volunteered for SAWnet sometime in 1994 and last moderated in April 1997 and November 2001). The moderator of the month (MoM) is entrusted with the password for the list, which gives her access to all the SAWnet subscriber information. She is also responsible for ensuring that SAWnet policies are enforced with regard to who is allowed to subscribe to the list and who is not. I can only wonder why, when I have made it quite clear to the participants of SAWnet that I continue to write about the group, no one has protested about the fact that I am still one of the moderators for the list. I do not, however, assume that this is a sign of approval for my work on SAWnet. Perhaps by not excluding me from moderating or participating on the list, there is an attempt to avoid or ignore the fact that I continue to write about SAWnet. An alternative explanation is that a list that strives to be democratic and that now has more than 700 members with varied viewpoints on the issue of studying SAWnet makes it difficult for just a handful of women to arbitrarily decide to expel me. In 2002, website maintainers of SAWnet have listed my online publication to the SAWnet website at http://www.umiacs.umd.edu/users/sawweb/sawnet/awards.html. In addition, there have been others who have written about and described SAWnet in print publications. The above URL includes some of these citations.

If in 1995 some members of SAWnet regarded my research as a form of "betrayal," what then does "betrayal" mean in the context of SAWnet? For Stacey, "fieldwork represents an intrusion and intervention into a system of relationships, that the researcher is far freer than the researched to leave. The inequality and the potential treacherousness of this relationship is inescapable" (1988: 23). In the case of a virtual community, however, both the researcher and researched are free to leave. As Ananda Mitra points out, "there is no Internet audience[/participant]who is also not empowered to become an agent to mold the space as he or she wishes" (1997: 60). In the case of the real life community in which this virtual community (SAWnet) is imbedded, neither my resistant subjects nor I, as researcher, can "leave." Undoubtedly, my work is an intrusion and an intervention into a system of relationships as they existed prior to discussions about my study in the autumn of 1995. Some might have even considered my study to be an invasion of privacy. However, it is not an intrusion and intervention in the sense that it would be if I were doing an ethnography of a RL community. In fact, from what I can see, the posters on SAWnet continue with no obvious "institutional" memory of having been "intruded upon" as new members generate discussions on topics similar and dissimilar to what has been discussed on SAWnet nearly a decade ago, and old members continue to participate.

Confusion between "real" and virtual spaces continues even in current debates concerning privacy on the Internet. Internet exchanges are very often assumed to be like telephone exchanges or personal, hard-copy letters. We tend to forget that unlike our telephone interactions, our online interactions are recorded in print and are stored in a system that can be accessed by system managers and hackers. They can be retrieved and viewed at any time in the future.

What is also important to note here is that few of the women on SAWnet are likely to be materially or culturally "underprivileged." Unlike the case of anthropology of the materially and culturally "Other," virtual presence—the very fact that someone is online and actively participating—situates the ethnographic subject in a social space of material and cultural privilege with access to the same (or similar) power structures as the researcher. They, as much as I, are anthropologists, reporting not just about our own diasporic communities, within and outside them as participant-observers, but also "anthropologists in reverse" (John 1996) who carry back "field notes" about our host society/culture back to our birth-countries. As I have argued elsewhere (Gajjala 1998), e-mail lists, Usenet bulletin boards, websites, web-conferences, and so on can be regarded as ethnographies of the self and of the other. With reference to SAWnet, I have reported:

> SAWnet itself [i]s a space of representation. This is by virtue of its being a discursive space that depends on some shared conceptions of identity—imagined, as you note . . . In effect, SAWnet itself exists because of our self-representations within real life communities AS S. Asian women . . .
>
> ("C" as quoted in Gajjala 1998)

Our narratives on SAWnet are often appropriated and re-appropriated in various ways within the hegemonic frameworks that favor "Western" structures of thought and cultures. Our words are quite often given more weight than those of a less culturally/materially privileged woman speaking from the geographical "third world." The attribution of "authenticity" to our narratives and the investment of various audiences ("first-world" global policy-makers, for instance) in naming our narratives as those of the "unheard" must be questioned.

Sara Suleri, Trinh Minh-ha and others have discussed the process by which non-Western (non-white, non-bourgeoisie) women are "Othered" and "interpellated by difference" (cited in John 1996). At the same moment as we are "Othered" we also learn to be the ideal Other, complicitous with the existing status quo and the process of "Othering" men and women of lesser material and cultural privilege. As representative native informants or ideal reporters from the "third world," we have been indoctrinated into the cultural and linguistic system through our postcolonial education and our "sanctioned ignorances" (John 1996). We learn to produce narratives about our so-called Othered selves that will fit appropriately within hegemonic narratives concerning "third-world" cultures. It is this habitual, even unwitting, complicity that needs to be interrogated.

Conclusion

This paper was not about "the subaltern."[7] The "subaltern" does not have a voice online in the same sense as female South Asian intellectuals and professionals, who form the majority of members on SAWnet, do. What I have focused on here is the privilege of being able to speak and to write in hegemonic spaces which are nonetheless situated "in a field of power (the West) and in the production of a particular knowledge (about the East)" (Visweswaran 1994).[8] Yet my paper also talks about silences—the unsaid and the cannot-be-said. I have examined the positions of authority that we as members of SAWnet have been given, have taken, or have enabled, and asked, at whose expense are we able to speak? Implicitly, I have also questioned how we might be able to negotiate from within our speech and our silences in order to transform or disrupt Western hegemony. To that end, I argue for the need to negotiate from within existing hegemonic structures so as to disrupt narratives that circulate about South Asian women. My research examines South Asian women's resistance to such narratives as well as their complicity (at times) with them. As a member of SAWnet pointed out in response to one of my papers concerning the discussion group, "[i]f we remain silent, that is not going to make the subaltern heard" ("C" quoted in Gajjala 1998).

It is therefore important for South Asian women to examine the speaking roles we are assigned as well as the locations from which we speak. As a non-subaltern "third-world" woman as "Other" to the Western woman, I find a point of entry into the hegemonic sphere enabled by a history of relative cultural and material privilege. However, I, and other women like me, must remember that our speech could be viewed and used as representative of subaltern women who are not located within the same sphere of material and cultural privilege that we inhabit. As a participant ethnographer within a South Asian community, it is from a questioning and sometimes hesitant position of authority that I speak. Although this speaking could no doubt be considered by some as a potential betrayal of community on one level, my silence most certainly would be a betrayal of another kind.

Acknowledgements

This paper is based on my dissertation "The SAWnet Refusal: An Interrupted Cyberethnography" chaired by Roberta Astroff.

Versions of this essay have been presented at various academic conferences. I wish to thank discussants and participants for their feedback and helpful suggestions. Special thanks to SAWnet members who encouraged me to continue with the project and those who resisted the idea of being studied, the founders as well as continuing members and moderators of SAWnet—without whom "SAWnet" would not exist.

I am most grateful to writing group members of the Institute of Culture and Society at Bowling Green State University, Lisa McLaughlin, Cynthia Carter, the anonymous reviewers, and Robert Ochieng for their assistance in the process of putting this paper together.

Notes

1 I had asked and received permission to use the posts I used in my paper.
2 See Gajjala (1998) at http://www.cyberdiva.org/erniestuff/sanov.html.
3 It is not my intention here to celebrate mobility of multiple subjectivities in an elite manner. While the fact of multiple subject positions is a fact for all, the ability/authority to perform them in an expression of individualistic freedom is available to a few women and men of privilege. The very conditions enabling the freedom, agency, and mobility for the privileged few of the world are indeed dependent upon the immobility, victimization, and poverty of certain sections of the world's population.
4 I use the term both in relation to temporal consciousness and epistemological concerns arising from the notion. See Deepika Bahri and Mary Vasudeva (1996) for further discussions of the notion of "post-colonial/postcolonial."
5 Here I invoke Lisa McLaughlin's definition of "disciplinarity," and "refer to the theories, practices, and institutional arrangements that discriminate among forms of knowledge, specify knowledge and knowledge relationships that coalesce around "objects of study," and demarcate boundaries within which knowledges may take on the appearance of coherence" (1995: 145).
6 Incidentally, to my knowledge, at present, any woman can become a member of SAWnet and ask to receive a copy of all past SAWnet digests. Therefore, any woman can "verify" that the discussion I am writing about really did occur.
7 See Spivak (1988) and Sandhya Shetty and Elizabeth Bellamy (2000) for relevant discussions of "the subaltern" and Spivak's answer to the question "Can the subaltern speak?"
8 Here terms such as "West" and "East" are used by Visweswaran to connote a power imbalance between the "North" and the "South," etc. While I sometimes revert to using all these categories to describe the hierarchy, I wish to express my dissatisfaction and discomfort with existing labels that end up as sweeping generalizations in the minds of the not-always-so-careful readers. The problem, of course, is that academic labels currently available to describe various material and

cultural hierarchies tend to generate a problematic "which could only be resolved by the search for or construction of a self-enclosed, isolated identity" (Lawrence Grossberg 1993: 1).

References

Aarseth, Espen J. 1994. "Nonlinearity and Literary Theory," in George Landow (ed.) *Hyper/Text/Theory*, pp. 51–86. Baltimore, MD: Johns Hopkins University Press.

Addison, Joanne and Susan Hilligoss. 1999. "Technological Fronts: Lesbian Lives 'On the Line,'" in Kristine Blair and Pam Takayoshi (eds.) *Feminist Cyberscapes: Mapping Gendered Academic Spaces*, pp. 21–40. Stamford, CT: Ablex.

Ahmed, Sara. 1999. "Home and Away: Narratives of Migration and Estrangement." *International Journal of Cultural Studies* 2 (3): 329–47.

Alcoff, Linda. 1991–2. "The Problem of Speaking for Others." *Cultural Critique* 20 (Winter): 5–32.

Augustin, Laura. 1999. "They Speak, but Who Listens?," in Wendy Harcourt (ed.) *Women@Internet*, pp. 149–55. London: Zed Press.

Bahri, Deepika. 2001. "The Digital Diaspora: South Asians in the New Pax Electronica," in Makarand Paranjpe (ed.) *In Diaspora: Theories, Histories, Texts*, pp. 222–32. New Delhi: Indialog Publications.

Bahri, Deepika and Mary Vasudeva (eds.). 1996. *Between the Lines: South Asians and Postcoloniality*. Philadelphia, PA: Temple University Press.

Behar, Ruth and Deborah Gordon (eds.). 1996. *Women Writing Culture*. Berkeley, CA: University of California Press.

Bhattacharjee, Anannya. 1992. "The Habit of Ex-nomination: Nation, Woman and the Indian Immigrant Bourgeois." *Public Culture* 5 (1): 19–44.

Bhattacharjee, Anannya. 1997. "The Public/Private Mirage: Mapping Homes and Undomesticating Violence Work in the South Asian Immigrant Community," in Jacqui Alexander and Chandra Mohanty (eds.) *Feminist Genealogies, Colonial Legacies, Democratic Futures*, pp. 308–29. New York: Routledge.

Biemann, Ursula. 1999. "Performing the Border," in Cornelia Sollfrank and Old Boys Network (eds.) *Next Cyberfeminist International*, pp. 36–40. Hamburg: Hein & Co.

Blair, Kristine and Pamela Takayoshi (eds.). 1999. *Feminist Cyberscapes: Mapping Gendered Academic Spaces*. Stamford, CT: Ablex.

Boese, Chris. 1998–2000. *The Ballad of the Internet Nutball: Chaining Rhetorical Visions from the Margins of the Margins to the Mainstream in the Xenaverse*. PhD Dissertation, Rensselaer Polytechnic Institute, Troy, NY. On-line. Available: http://www.nutball.com/dissertation/index.htm (March 30, 2002).

Chatterjee, Partha. 1989. "The nationalist resolution of the women's question," in Kum Kum Sangari and Sudesh Vaid (eds.) *Recasting Women*, pp. 232–53. New Delhi: Kali for Women.

Code, Lorraine. 1998. "Voice and Voicelessness: A Modest Proposal?," in Janet Kourany (ed.) *Philosophy in a Feminist Voice: Critiques and Reconstructions*, pp. 204–30. Princeton, NJ: Princeton University Press.

Gajjala, Radhika. 1998. *The SAWnet Refusal: An Interrupted Cyberethnography*. PhD Dissertation, University of Pittsburgh, Pittsburgh, PA.

Gajjala, Radhika. 2001. "Studying Feminist E-Spaces: Introducing Transnational/ Postcolonial Concerns," in Sally Munt (ed.) *Technospaces*, pp. 113–26. London: Continuum International.

Gajjala, Radhika and Annapurna Mamidipudi. 1999. "Cyberfeminism, Technology and International 'Development.'" *Gender and Development* 7 (2): 8–16.

Gerard, Lisa. 1999–2000. "'Diets Suck!' and Other Tales of Women's Bodies on the Web." *Works and Days* 17/18: 33–36.

Grossberg, Lawrence. 1993. "Cultural Studies and/in New Worlds." *Critical Studies in Mass Communication* 10: 1–22.

Gurak, Laura J. 1997. *Persuasion and Privacy in Cyberspace: The Online Protests over Lotus MarketPlace and the Clipper Chip*. New Haven, CT: Yale University Press.

Hall, Kira. 1996. "Cyberfeminism," in Susan Herring (ed.) *Computer-mediated Communication: Linguistic, Social and Cross-cultural Perspectives*, pp. 148–55. Amsterdam: John Benjamins Publishing Co.

Harcourt, Wendy (ed.). 1999. *Women@Internet*. London: Zed Press.

Harding, Sandra. 1998. *Is Science Multicultural? Postcolonialisms, Feminisms and Epistemologies*. Bloomington: Indiana University Press.

Heinz, Bettina, Gu Li, Ako Inuzuka, and Roger Zender. 2002. "Under the Rainbow Flag: Webbing Global Gay Identities." *International Journal of Sexuality and Gender Studies* 7 (2–3): 107–24.

Herring, Susan. 1996. "Posting in a Different Voice: Gender and Ethics in CMC," in Charles Ess (ed.) *Philosophical Perspectives in Computer Mediated Communication*, pp. 115–45. New York: SUNY Press.

Jacobson, David. 1999. "Doing Research in Cyberspace." *Field Methods* 11 (2): 127–45.

John, Mary. 1996. *Discrepant Dislocations: Feminism, Theory and Postcolonial Histories*. Berkeley: University of California Press.

Karamcheti, Indira. 1992. "The Shrinking Himalayas." *Diaspora* 2 (2): 261–76.

Kolko, Beth, Lisa Nakamura, and Gil Rodman (eds.). 2000. *Race in Cyberspace*. New York: Routledge.

Lal, Vinay. 1999. "The Politics of History on the Internet: Cyber-Diasporic Hinduism and the North American Hindu Diaspora." *Diaspora* 8 (2): 137–72.

Landow, George. 1992. *Hypertext: The Convergence of Contemporary Critical Theory and Technology*. Baltimore, MD: Johns Hopkins University Press.

McLaughlin, Lisa. 1995. "Feminist Communication Scholarship and 'The Woman Question' in the Academy." *Communication Theory* 5: 144–61.

Mitra, Ananda. 1997. "Virtual Commonality: Looking for India on the Internet," in Steven Jones (ed.) *Virtual Culture: Identity and Communication in Cybersociety*, pp. 55–79. London: Sage.

Mohanty, Chandra Talpade. 1993. "Defining Genealogies: Feminist Reflections on Being South Asian in North America," in The Women of South Asian Descent Collective (eds.) *Our Feet Walk the Sky: Women of the South Asian Diaspora*, pp. 351–58. San Francisco: Aunt Lute.

Narayan, Kirin. 1997. "How Native is a 'Native' Anthropologist?," in Louise Lamphere, Helena Ragone, and Patricia Zavella (eds.) *Situated Lives: Gender and Culture in Everyday Life*, pp. 23–41. New York: Routledge.

Narayan, Uma. 1989. "The Project of Feminist Epistemology: Perspectives from a Non-western Feminist," in Alison Jaggar and Susan Bordo (eds.) *Gender/Body/Knowledge: Feminist Reconstructions of Being and Knowing*, pp. 256–69. New Brunswick, NJ: Rutgers University Press.

Press, Andrea and Elizabeth Cole. 1999. *Speaking of Abortion: Television and Authority in the Lives of Women*. Chicago: University of Chicago Press.

Rai, Amit S. 1995. "In On-line: Electronic Bulletin Boards and the Construction of a Diasporic Hindu Identity." *Diaspora* 4 (1): 31–57.

Rheingold, Howard. 1993. *The Virtual Community: Homesteading on the Electronic Frontier*. New York: Harper Perennial.

Sangari, Kum Kum and Sudesh Vaid. 1989. *Recasting Women*. New Delhi: Kali for Women.

Sauer, Chris. 2001. *Removing the Mask of Silence: Counteracting Gender Bias through a Cybergrrl Classroom*. PhD Dissertation, Bowling Green State University.

SAWnet. 2002. On-line. Available: http://www.umiacs.umd.edu/users/sawweb/sawnet/ (March 31, 2002).

Shade, Leslie. 1993. "Gender Issues in Computer Networking," presented at "Community Networking: The International Free-Net Conference", Carleton University, Ottawa, Canada, August 17–19.

Shetty, Sandhya and Bellamy, Elizabeth J. 2000. "Postcolonialism's Archive Fever." *Diacritics* 30 (1): 25–48.

Spender, Dale. 1995. *Nattering on the Net: Women, Power and Cyberspace*. Australia: Spinifex.

Spivak, Gayatri Chakravorty. 1988. "Can the Subaltern Speak?" in Cary Nelson and Lawrence Grossberg (eds.) *Marxism and the Interpretation of Culture*, pp. 271–313. Urbana, IL: University of Illinois Press.

Spivak, Gayatri Chakravorty and Elizabeth Grosz. 1990. "Criticism, Feminism, and the Institution," in Sarah Harasym (ed.) *The Postcolonial Critic: Interviews, Strategies, Dialogues*, pp. 1–16. New York: Routledge.

Stacey, Judith. 1988. "Can There Be a Feminist Ethnography." *Women's Studies International Forum* 11 (1): 21–27.

Sunden, Jenny. 2001. "What Happened to Difference in Cyberspace? The (Re)turn of the She-Cyborg." *Feminist Media Studies* 1 (2): 215–32.

van Zoonen, Liesbet. 2001. "Feminist Internet Studies." *Feminist Media Studies* 1 (1): 67–72.

Visweswaran, Kamala. 1994. *Fictions of Feminist Ethnography*. Minneapolis: University of Minnesota Press.

Warnick, Barbara. 1999. "Masculinizing the Feminine: Inviting Women On Line 1997." *Critical Studies in Mass Communication* 16 (1): 1–19.

Wilding, Faith and Maria Fernandez. 1999. "Feminism, Difference, and Global Capital," in Cornelia Sollfrank and Old Boys Network (eds.) *Next Cyberfeminist International*, pp. 22–24. Hamburg: Hein & Co.

81

GENDERING THE INTERNET
Claims, controversies and cultures

Liesbet van Zoonen

Source: *European Journal of Communication* 17(1) (2002): 5–23.

Abstract

In this article the mutual shaping of the Internet and gender is analysed. Common claims that the Internet constitutes a masculine or contrarily a feminine environment are critically discussed, as well as the cyberfeminist contention that the Internet enables new identities not limited by gender. It is argued instead that gender and the Internet are multidimensional concepts that are articulated in complex and contradictory ways. Drawing from cultural and technology studies, we assume that the gendered meanings of the Internet arise particularly at the moment of 'domestication'. In-depth interviews with young couples are used to illustrate how the social, symbolic and individual dimensions of gender interact with everyday uses and interpretations of the Internet, showing four types of articulations constituting traditional, deliberative, reversed and individualized use cultures. Whereas male usage primarily explains these types, the interviews show that this does not automatically result in the construction of a masculine domain in the household. It opens up space for shared and feminine appropriations as well.

Internet is a contested medium as far as its social cultural meanings and significance are concerned. A core issue in the debate is the meaning of the Internet for gender: how does gender influence Internet communication, contents and use, and – the other way around – how do Internet communication, contents and use impact upon gender? In the terms common to cultural studies of technology, what is at stake is the *mutual shaping* of gender and the Internet (see van Oost, 1995). The Internet arose in the early 1960s out of the collaboration of American universities and the Pentagon (see Naughton, 1999). It thus has its roots in the so-called military–industrial complex, which according to many feminist critics inevitably constitutes it as a medium deeply embedded in masculine codes and values (see van Zoonen, 1992).

In recent years, however, other feminist authors have reclaimed the Internet as a technology close to the core qualities of femininity (e.g. Spender, 1995). Yet other, cyberfeminist authors contend that it enables a transgression of the dichotomous categories of male and female, constructing transgender or even genderless human identities and relations (e.g. Braidotti, 1996). This article discusses these three claims on the gender codes of the Internet, and shows that interpretations of the Internet as masculine, feminine or even transgender are based on limited conceptualizations of both gender and technology. An alternative analysis based on particular use cultures of the Internet in everyday life shows how both technology and gender are multi-dimensional processes that are articulated in complex and contradictory ways which escape straightforward gender definitions. To begin with, I briefly review the gender codes of the Internet's enabling technologies: the telephone and the computer.

Gender codes of enabling technologies

At the end of the 19th century the telephone appeared in American society. The technology was still in its infancy: one needed operators to connect calls, there were still few subscribers, there were more party lines than private lines and competition between telephone companies was fierce (Fischer, 1992). It was in that situation that one of the independent telephone companies in Indiana called a hearing of the Indiana Public Service Commission about acceptable uses of the telephone. The company objected to women's uses of the telephone in particular: women talked for long periods on the telephone about supposedly trivial matters and this was not what the medium was meant for, so the company claimed (Rakow, 1988). The telephone had indeed been propagated by the burgeoning industry as a medium for practical management and household purposes; businessmen were the first target groups. Exhibits, telephone vendors and advertisements in trade journals all claimed that the telephone would 'increase efficiency, save time, and impress customers' (Fischer, 1992: 66). As far as women were addressed in this early period, the business of the household was emphasized: 'the telephone could help the affluent household manager to accomplish her task' (Fischer, 1992: 67). Many women, however, had a completely different appreciation of the new medium and used it for 'social purposes': keeping in touch with family and friends, exchanging personal experiences and the latest community news, and – in the more rural areas – using it as a companion in lonely times.

Industry leaders and professionals objected to such uses of the telephone. They considered chatting on the telephone as 'one more female foolishness' (Fischer, 1992: 231). In trade journals and advertisements 'talkative women and their frivolous electrical conversations about inconsequential personal subjects were contrasted with the efficient task-oriented, worldly talk of business and professional men' (Marvin, 1988: 23). Complaints were issued in newspapers about 'women's habits of talking on the phone for "futile motives"' (Martin, 1988: 96). In the popular literature of that time the image of women's telephonic longwindedness had become a common joke (Brooks, 1977), the quintessential and early expression of it in Mark Twain's short sketch *A Telephone Conversation*. In such a context one can understand why the Indiana phone company thought it necessary to discipline women's telephone behaviour through calling a public hearing. There was a more blunt financial motive as well: users were charged for the numbers of calls they made, not for the length of them. It appeared at the hearing, however, that ordinary telephone subscribers had no objection to the way women used the telephone, 'so the commission ruled it could do nothing' (Rakow, 1988: 220). It did not take long for the telephone industry to adjust their marketing efforts to the way women used the telephone, recognizing the possible profits in such use. Around the 1920s, marketing changed its emphasis from the telephone as a practical device to a medium for comfort, convenience and conversation (Fischer, 1992). Nowadays it is hard to imagine the telephone as anything else then a medium to maintain social contact. It is therefore not a far-fetched conclusion to say that 'women subscribers were largely responsible for the development of a culture of the telephone' (Martin, 1991: 171, quoted in Fischer, 1992: 236), as we know it today.

The gender codes of the computer emerged quite differently and turn the light to another historical scene, set in mid-19th-century, upper-class England. At a dinner party hosted by Mary Somerville, a woman whose mathematical work was used at Cambridge, one of the people attending was Charles Babbage who played a leading role in the scientific and technical development of the period. Nowadays he is credited with having developed the first calculator and the first blueprint for a computer. At the dinner party, he told his audience about a machine he had built – the Difference Engine – which was capable of making various calculations and tables. Among the attentive listeners were Lady Byron and her 18-year-old daughter, Ada. Lady Byron was a gifted mathematician herself and known in high society as the Princess of Parallelograms. Her daughter definitively inherited her intellectual gifts and had at the age of 13 produced a design for a flying machine. Ada and her mother were fascinated by Babbage's ideas and went to see the Difference Engine in his studio. One of the observers of that scene remembers 'Miss Byron, young as she was, understood its workings, and saw the great beauty of its invention' (Moore, 1977: 44, quoted in Plant, 1998: 47). Ada and Babbage developed a close friendship and exchanged in the years to come a voluminous correspondence about mathematics and logic. Although it was highly unusual in these Victorian times for women to take an interest in science, Ada was encouraged by her mother and her later husband William King, Earl of Lovelace to pursue her studies in mathematics. Her mother's encouragement was hardly disinterested; she was afraid that Ada would become a poet like her father, the infamous Lord Byron. He had brought discredit on the family by his love affair with his half sister, after whom Ada was named. To counter any poetic tendencies, Lady Byron encouraged Ada to go to public lectures on mathematics and correspond with mathematicians. Women then were not allowed to attend university or join scientific societies. Ada, nevertheless, obtained a highly acclaimed position among the mathematicians of these times: 'Beautiful, charming, temperamental, an aristocratic hostess, mathematicians of the time thought her a magnificent addition to their number' (Babbage Pages, n.d.). Much more than with her beauty and charm, however, Ada impressed the mathematics community with her work on the second of Babbage's famous machines, the Analytical Engine. Babbage himself had great difficulty explaining to lay audiences what exactly the machine could do and how it differed from his first endeavour, the Difference Engine. Ada became an outspoken advocate of Babbage's invention. She translated an Italian paper about the Engine and added her own extensive notes to it, which were three times longer than the original text. The notes contained a set of instructions for how to use the Engine. Nowadays we would consider such instructions to be a computer program and for that reason Ada has been credited with being the first computer programmer in history. 'Ada understood the potential power of a computing machine such as envisioned by Babbage – one that had internal memory, could make choices and repeat instructions – and she foresaw its application in mathematical computation, artificial intelligence and even computer music' (Freeman, 1996). Babbage's Analytical Engine and Ada's work on it disappeared from the public eye until 1937, when his unpublished notebooks were discovered. Ada's contribution to computer history has been acknowledged by various sources, most notably the American Defence Department which named its primary programming language, ADA, after her.

We can consider the telephone and the computer as respectively the mother and the father of the Internet, the global network of computers that came into being in the early to mid-1960s. The child is some 40 years old then but its gender is still undecided. Starting out as the masculine technology associated with the military–industrial complex, it has in recent years been reclaimed as a typical expression of femininity, by feminists and market researchers alike (van Zoonen, 2001a). It might even escape these categories and produce completely new transgender or even genderless codes of human identity and communication. In the following sections I discuss these claims in more detail.[1]

Gender codes and the Internet: femininity

Several highly reputed feminist scholars have claimed that the Internet is a woman's medium. This belief has become so widespread and largely undisputed that long-time feminist critic of technology Ellen Balka (1997) recently exclaimed: 'Where have all the feminist technology critics gone?' She argues that earlier critical views on information technologies have given way to an optimism that is seduced by the radical potential of the World Wide Web. Dale Spender (1995), for instance, made an early feminist claim on the Internet as a medium especially relevant for individual and collective networking of women, and also for other subordinated groups, for that matter. Sherry Turkle, professor in the sociology of science at the MIT and author of an influential book on the construction of identities through Internet communication (Turkle, 1995), claims that one needs an ethic of community, consensus and communication on the Internet and this is what she thinks women in particular are good at (quoted in Jenkins, 1999: 332). Similarly, Sadie Plant (1998), acclaimed in the British press as the most radical 'techno theorist' of the day, sees femininity to be the core element of network technology, which she considers to build on women's relation to weaving. Other authors have compared the experience of the Net, the immersion of its user in its textual, visual and virtual realities, to that of the foetus in the womb. Internet experience is considered analogous to the secure and unconstrained experience of the maternal matrix that offers an escape from the constraints of the body (Smelik, 2000).

Side-stepping for a moment the gender essentialism contained in such views and looking at the pragmatic effects of such arguments, we can see how authors like Spender, Turkle and Plant are working towards a redefinition of the Internet from the exclusively masculine domain born out of the American military–industrial–academic complex towards its feminine antithesis of peaceful communication and experimentation. Thinking back on the history of the telephone, for instance, and the way women had to fight their way into its acceptable use (Martin, 1991), thinking of the masculine culture that still encapsulates the computer, thinking more generally of the way technology has been made masculine throughout its history (Oldenziel, 1999), one can recognize the relevance of such a project of redefinition.

Feminist authors who claim the Internet to be a woman's medium find themselves in an unexpected and unsolicited alliance with Internet marketing researchers. They too claim the Internet to be a 'woman's world' (VODW, 1999) and female users of the World Wide Web are thought to be distinct in their goals and online behaviour. Several marketing studies claim to show women are more interested than men in personal interaction and support (e.g. email, chat groups and forums). They seek to build a personal relation with a site and feel strongly connected to online communities. In a trend report conducted for the German women's magazine *Freundin* (translation:

Girl Friend), it is argued that womanhood offers many opportunities nowadays and very few disadvantages, new technologies like the Internet make life easier, enhance the possibilities for communication and offer new possibilities for consumption: 'The new media enlarge women's horizons and scope of action. Women will shape the nature of the Net economy' (Wipperman, 2000). At present, marketing research constructs women as communicative consumers for whom the Internet provides opportunities never had before. This picture is so convincing that many e-commerce strategies are built on it: the American portal women.com, for instance, offers not only an enormous amount of online content (over 90,000 pages) on traditional women's concerns but also forums and chatline possibilities on a variety of traditionally gendered topics.

Gender codes and the Internet: masculinity

Only 10 years ago, the dominant feminist vision on new information and communication technologies (ICTs) was that they were male dominated. Structural, social-psychological and cultural factors rooted in a patriarchal society were all seen to prevent women from gaining access to ICTs, both as producers and as users (see van Zoonen, 1992). The claims of the Internet being a technology true and close to women and femininity might thus come as a surprise since the structural, social-psychological and cultural factors that explained women's reticence towards ICTs in the early 1990s have not changed dramatically yet. Looking at the actor networks, texts, representations and communicative practices on the Internet there is little reason to think it provides a whole new gender context in comparison with earlier ICTs.

The so-called 'actor network' of human and technical actors involved in the development of the Internet as a technology is almost 100 percent male. In John Naughton's (1999) brief history of the Internet only one woman is found, Nicola Pellow, who was involved in the development of HTML in the 1980s.[2] Male dominance in ICT research and development is not likely to change. On the contrary, the number of women studying and working in the sector in the US has fallen from 30 percent in 1989 to 15 percent in 1999 (Nua, 1998) and similar downward trends have been noted in Europe. The image of the IT sector turns out to be a strong prohibitive factor for women who associate IT work with long working hours, unsociable male colleagues and a male chauvinist culture. Evidence of the latter can be seen, for instance, in a recent discussion in the hacker community about the role of women. In hacker news network, editor Eric Parker describes women in the hacker community as 'scene whores':

> They are a real threat. They waste our time, ruin friendships, cause chaos between hackers, and generally ruin periods of our life. A

sure sign after being compromised by a scene whore, after they are done with you, is when you go to talk to friends you have neglected during the period compromise, and they say 'Welcome back, we missed you.'

(Parker, 2000)

As this quote shows, in terms of texts, representations and communicative practices the Internet is also not simply a women's haven. Although there are few systematic analyses of the representations and constructions of gender on the Internet, there is enough evidence about (child) pornography, right-wing extremism, sexual harassment, flaming and other unpleasantness to disclaim any utopian vision of the Internet as an unproblematic feminine environment. It is telling that an important women's movement on the net, that of the webgrrls, had to name itself 'grrls', instead of 'girls' because searching on the net for 'girls' mainly produces sex sites and very little relevant material for women (Sherman, 1998). An important source on gender patterns in online communication comes from computer-mediated communication (CMC) studies. Email, chat boxes, news groups, discussion lists are all examples of CMC. Several researchers have analysed the communicative practices in CMC, finding feminine discourse in groups dominated by women: apologetic, consensual and communicative language patterns are typical for them. Masculine discourse occurs in male groups; it is found to be factual, action oriented, impersonal, argumentative, sometimes rude and aggressive. Masculine discourse is seen in most mixed-gender groups as well, making it difficult if not impossible for women to participate fully in such groups (for an overview, see Postmes *et al.*, 2000).

There seems thus as much evidence for the claim that the Internet is masculine and a male world, as there is for the claim that it is feminine and a female world. There is yet another claim to the gender of the Internet, and that is that it has no gender, or better that it is a gender laboratory, a playground for experimenting with gender symbols and identity, a space to escape from the dichotomy of gender and the boundaries produced by physical bodies.

Gender codes and the Internet: cyberfeminism

Cyberfeminism is a term for a variety of academic and artistic practices that centre around and in the Internet, and other new technologies. Some authors even have it that 'after years of post-structuralist theoretical arrogance, philosophy lags behind art and fiction in the difficult struggle to keep up with today's world' (Braidotti, 1996). Whether art or philosophy is the motor, cyberfeminism is the current version of one of the key feminist essentials to connect theory with practice. The year 1997 even witnessed the beginning of Cyberfeminist International during the renowned art fair

Documenta in Kassel, Germany. Cyberfeminism is very much in debate but has some defining common features. Transgender politics or gender bending is one of them, referring to the possibilities that the new technologies offer to escape from bodily gender definitions and construct new gender identities, or even genderless identities. Technophilia is another defining factor of cyberfeminism, accepting and celebrating the fact that technology is no longer an external factor to the human body but has become an integral part of it. Donna Haraway's writing on cyborgs offers the almost canonical frame of reference here, the cyborg being 'a cybernetic organism, a fusion of the organic and the technical forged in particular, historical, cultural practices' (Haraway, 1997: 51). Thinking of pacemakers, hearing aids and even glasses, cyborgs are completely ordinary as well as the subject of science fiction such as *Robocop* and *Total Recall*.

Cyberfeminism on the Internet is found among others in the so-called Multi User Dungeons (MUDs). MUDs have attracted the attention of many feminist authors and seem to have become paradigmatic for the Internet as a laboratory for gender. MUDs are text-based, virtual games which may have the different purposes of seeking adventure and killing monsters, of socializing with others and building new communities. They also offer a tool for teaching by constructing virtual classrooms. One usually does not access a MUD through the World Wide Web, but links up through Telnet. When logging on for the first time, one chooses a name for the character one wants to be and keeps that name for the duration of the game, which can – in fact – go on for years. It is precisely this choice of identity at the beginning of the game that the MUD reputation of being a laboratory for gender experiments comes from. Women play as men, men operate as women, others choose multiple identities like Laurel and Hardy, or try what it means to operate as an 'it'. Sherry Turkle's (1995) book *Life on the Screen: Identity in the Age of the Internet* offers the most extensive account of gender experience in the MUDs, concluding that MUDs provide a postmodern utopian space in which existing social boundaries and dichotomies cease to have relevance. In the words of Turkle: 'MUDs are proving grounds for an action based philosophical practice that can serve as a form of consciousness raising about gender issues' (Turkle, 1995: 214).

Whereas life in the MUDs challenges gender identities, other forms of cyberfeminism undermine existing gender symbols and representations in different ways. Parody and irony are the postmodern stylistic devices used to construct typical cyber varieties of gender, that are neither traditional nor feminist. It is expressed in its terminology of geekgrrls, bitches, riotgrrls, guerila grrls and other cybergrrls, terms which indicate an escape both from traditional gender relations and from common feminist practice. Ladendorf (2000) shows how their sites use images of the female body from the 1950s, the ultimate decade of traditional gender patterns, and other icons and stylistic devices of pop culture to construct a new particular cyberculture of womanhood. Their sites contain a rich variety of gender challenges and contestations popular among young women. As a result of the latter, some of them have been taken over by commercial entrepreneurs, which has modified their vanguard character (van den Boomen, 1997).

Gender and technology: multidimensional concepts

The Internet is thus claimed as feminine, masculine and as beyond gender. The easy solution to these contradictions would be to say that the Internet is so vast and complex that all three positions are true and exist easily alongside each other. And for one part, it is indeed as simple as that. However, we do need to complicate that other part in order to make sense of the varied and contradictory articulations of gender and the Internet. One thing that is striking if we recapitulate the feminine, masculine and transgender features of the Internet, is that in all three claims different dimensions of gender are used as decisive evidence. In gender theory gender is understood as referring to three dimensions: social structures which relegate women and men to different social positions, individual identities and experience of what it means to be a woman or a man, and symbolic organization of society in which several dualities like nature/culture, private/public, leisure/work, coincide with female/male. The claims that the Internet is a masculine domain are strongly supported by the fact that the overwhelming majority of actors in design and production are male – an argument which evokes gender as social dimension – and that texts, representations and communicative practices are masculine – a claim that is built on the symbolic dimensions of gender. Gender as identity does not appear in the picture here, which leads to a well-known dilemma in the research on women working in the communication industries, namely that their participation and positive experience can only be explained by assuming masculine identities in them (van Zoonen, 1988, 1994). Similarly, the claim that the Internet is feminine is built on a limited conceptualization of gender, in particular on gender as identity. The Internet's supposed femininity is said to be located in the communicative, consensual and community-building aspects, features which are thought by feminist and marketing researchers alike to be constitutive parts of feminine identities. Such an understanding, however, ignores the social fact of male-dominated actor networks, and the symbolic reconstructions of traditional gender on the levels of texts and representations. Cyberfeminism, finally, in its aims to undermine the concept of gender in all its dimensions all together, operates particularly at the level of representations, and is much less concerned with social actors or individual identities.

When it comes to understanding technology, masculine, feminine and transgender conceptualizations of the Internet differ in their understanding of where gender is located in the circuit of culture that constitutes the Internet.

I borrow the idea of technology as constituted in a circuit of culture from Du Gay *et al.* (1997), who use the Sony Walkman as a case study of the way meanings of technological artefacts emerge. Five cultural processes are identified – representation, identity, production, consumption and regulation – which when applied to the Internet raise questions as to how the Internet is represented and which representations it carries, what social identities are associated with it, how it is produced and consumed, and what mechanisms regulate its distribution and use. In a study of the mutual shaping of gender and the magnetron, Cynthia Cockburn and Susan Ormrod (1993) have used a similar approach defining mutual shaping as taking place in a sequence of moments in the life trajectory, or the biography of a technological artefact, which runs from design, development, production and marketing, to distribution, sales, use and domestication. Thinking back once again to the claims of the Internet being respectively feminine, masculine and beyond gender, we can see that these claims are in fact all built on a partial understanding of the Internet as a socially constructed technology. The claims for masculinity are located in the moments of design, development and production, and in the moments of representation. The claims for femininity are mainly located in the moments of marketing, distribution and use, whereas cyberfeminism manifests itself foremost in moments of representation.

Mutual shaping

What then would be an alternative approach to the mutual shaping of gender and the Internet which takes into account the different dimensions of gender as well as the circuit of culture that constitutes the Internet? The theoretical issue behind that question concerns how social meanings of technology come into being, and whether there is a decisive moment in the circuit of culture that is particularly relevant in relation to the gendering of technology. Histories of technologies all seem to point in the direction of the moments of usage that may be the most important in the development of social meanings. Thinking back on the history of the telephone, it was the usage of women that turned the technology into a sociable instrument. Thinking back on the history of the computer, the early and key presence of Ada Lovelace in research and development did not result in the construction of the computer as feminine. The history of the radio suggests that its initial two-way interactive nature, providing communicative possibilities much like today's Internet, disappeared under pressure of usage patterns in the family which turned the radio into a passive receiving practice (Moores, 1988). Television's history shows similarly its adaptation to circumstances of use in the family (van Zoonen and Wieten, 1994). Silverstone and Hirsch (1992), in their studies of domestic technologies, have coined such adaptations as a process of domestication in which technologies are incorporated into the routines of daily life. Domestication is not a smooth linear process, but has – especially at the early stages of the introduction of a technology – the nature of a struggle for meaning, a process of framing which even after meanings have become more solid and consensual, is never finished and always under contestation. Other authors use other concepts for the same process: Ruth Schwartz Cowan (1987), for instance, speaks of the consumption junction in which technologies acquire meanings, and Everett Rogers (1983) has referred to the everyday use of technology in terms of the reinvention of technology.

These studies all suggest that the decisive moment in the circuit of culture is in the moment of consumption, when technologies are domesticated in everyday lives. In these everyday lives gender appears in its three dimensions simultaneously; whereas social structures, individual identities and symbolic representations of gender may be analytically distinguished, in the concrete social practices of the everyday they work inextricably together in their interpellation and positioning of women and men. How these three dimensions come into play in concrete everyday situations was the object of an exploratory qualitative study we conducted among 24 young Dutch couples, between 20 and 30 years old, living together without children. In-depth interviews were held and transcribed about the uses and interpretations of various ICTs in their households, with particular attention to their uses of the Internet. The analysis followed an accumulation of analytic procedures, analogous to techniques proposed by Strauss and Corbin (1990) to develop 'grounded' theory. Each conversation fragment in the interview was first represented as a unique proposition. As a second step in the analysis, these propositions were then clustered according to similarities in content. Finally the interviews were considered in terms of discursive styles characterizing the specific interactions between the couples.[3] The outcomes show how specific family relations result in different articulations of gender and the Internet, which – in their turn – inspire new rituals and relations within the household. The dimensions of gender that come to the fore in this process appear to vary across households, resulting in the reconstruction of four kinds of articulations which we labelled as traditional, deliberative, individualized and reversed IT cultures in the household.

Articulating gender and the Internet in everyday life

The various ways in which gender and the Internet appeared to be articulated in the 24 households we studied, could be summarized as four 'media cultures': First, there is a fairly straightforward *traditional* culture in which computer and the Internet are considered to be the domain of the male partner in the household. He uses them most often, knows most about it and is highly interested in these new technologies. In the most extreme cases, he monopolizes the computer and the Internet:

GENDERING THE INTERNET

Man: Actually I work alone on it. Occasionally Ingrid would like to send a mail or so, but we do that together. She will tell me what has to be in it, and then I will do the actual sending. She has become more interested in the Internet. Before she didn't pay any attention to the computer, but now once in a while she likes to send a mail, or look up some information, for the holidays or so.

Woman: Well, as he says, I don't use it very often. I don't understand much of it yet. I think if I knew more about it, I would use it more as well. Now I always need Norman's help, to mail and stuff. That is because my work does not involve computers, his does.

In this interview fragment we see how the social position of one of the partners (he works with computers, she doesn't) translates into a traditional culture at home around the computer and the Internet. Thus the social dimension of gender comes into play here, normalizing and legitimizing the specific media culture of these two partners and coding the Internet and PC at a symbolic level as male territory in the household. Most couples whose computer and Internet use could be typified in these traditional terms, recognized the traditional nature of their use, but did not consider it very problematic. That might testify to a relatively neat fit between the social, symbolic and individual (identity) dimension of gender, although the acknowledgement of the traditional nature of these arrangements also shows that this arrangement is no longer self-evident. What is further striking in this fragment is that the Internet has drawn the woman to the computer, negotiating the former exclusively male codes of the PC.

In other cases, the media culture could be typified as *deliberative*: the partners negotiate about the use of the PC and the Internet, and also consider them to be a subject of common concern:

Woman: I like the PC best for the Internet applications. You do too, don't you Marc?
Man: Yes, some e-mail as well.
Woman: And to look up things for the holidays, or about living or gardening and stuff.
Man: It is about the same for me, sometimes some random clicking and surfing, but the novelty has worn off a bit and now we don't use it that frequently anymore.

This interview fragment shows clearly how PC and Internet use are instrumental in constructing a sense of togetherness among the partners ('*we* don't use it that frequently anymore'), instead of them being the domain of the male partner as in more traditional use cultures. The collective identity as a couple overwrites in this case the individual (gender) identities of the partners. A deliberative use culture is simplified because most couples in this study identified the PC and the Internet with work or school-related tasks. That makes their use relatively easy to prioritize: work or studies take precedence over surfing or gaming. Notwithstanding the gender neutrality of such a priority, it turns out to be male biased in the context of Dutch households where – even among young couples – men are the main or primary providers:

Woman: He usually has more important things to do on it than I have, I only want to [go on the] Internet a bit. So he goes first and I will do something else.

When the partners have equal careers, there is greater potential conflict about PC and Internet use. However, most couples then look for practical solutions. An extra PC or laptop is bought or brought in from work. The media culture than changes from a deliberative into an *individualized* culture:

Man: She is writing her thesis at the moment and if she is really busy with it, I'll take a laptop home from work.

In such individualized cultures gender as a factor that regulates the access to and use of the PC and Internet at home disappears into the background. Gender as a factor in the individual use and interpretations of the PC and Internet, as a dimension of the user's gender identity does remain relevant, but is no longer constructed in interaction with the partner.

In two extraordinary cases, women took the lead in PC and Internet use: they were the most important users and also the ones to make the decisions. In both cases, however, the male partners appeared to have jobs in which they worked with computers all day. Not wanting to spend their leisure time in such a way, the home PC and the Internet became available to the female partners, both at the time of the interview immersed in writing their final theses:

Man: I work with computers all day and really don't want to go home to stare at that screen once again.
Woman: And I am writing my thesis at present, so really need to be able to work on it full time.

In these two cases, we see how the social position of the partners can also result in a reversal of the traditional use culture around the PC and the Internet, which indicates that even one, single dimension of gender, i.e. the social one, does not result in a univocal articulation of the technology.

The four use cultures vary as to how gender and the Internet are mutually shaped. It is tempting to conclude that in three out of the four cultures, male usage offers the main explanation for the specific articulations we found: in a traditional culture the male partner claims the PC and the Internet as his domain, while in the reversed culture it is the lack of a claim by the male partner which enables women to dominate the PC and Internet. In addition, in the deliberative culture negotiation disappears as soon as one of the partners can occupy the PC and the Internet because of work or school requirements. This systematically favours the partner with the highest income, most of the time – especially in Dutch gender relations – the man. Only in the individualized use culture, in which both partners use their own appliances, does the male grip on the PC and the Internet use seem to dissolve. Although such a conclusion is partly warranted, it is insufficient in its denial of the active role that women play in the construction of the PC and the Internet as male. Women's distance from the computer is not only the result of processes of exclusion, but can also be interpreted as part of a conscious gender strategy. Turkle (1988) has shown how women use their reticence towards computers as evidence of their true identity as a woman. After all, an interest or even a passion for computers does not align well with traditional understandings of femininity. Gray (1992) has concluded similarly that women sometimes use their technical inabilities to make their husbands take up their share of domestic duties. If they showed technical capacities themselves, they feared they would be confronted with even more work, now related to the domestic technologies. Turkle's and Gray's observations are further indicators of the complex, situational and relational character of the articulations of gender and the Internet.

Conclusion

The interviews have shown the complexity of articulations of gender and the Internet at the micro-level of everyday lives. Nevertheless, at the macro-level of social discourse there are rather univocal claims about the Internet being masculine, feminine or transgender. These claims do have their value as part of the social struggle about the meaning of the Internet: the claim of it being feminine redefines technology as a domain appropriate for women; the observations of it being masculine puts oppressive and sexist practices on and behind the Net on political and social agendas; and cyberfeminism challenges us to move beyond the dual categories of gender. In analytical terms, however, these three claims fall short because of their limited conceptualization of gender and their insufficient approach of technology. Instead, we proposed a multidimensional understanding of the mutual shaping of gender and technology, in which it is claimed that in the end the social meanings of the Internet will emerge from particular contexts and practices of usage. We have seen from the brief discussion of the interviews that the mutual shaping that takes place in the domestication of the Internet in households of young heterosexual couples tends to frame it in traditional gender terms. Especially in its connection to the PC, our results show the Internet being taken up as an extension of male territory in the household. This does not necessarily lead to the exclusion of women since men are also seen to consciously leave the PC to their partners. Neither are women passive partners in this process. They actively take part in interactions which constitute their respective gender identities with regard to use of the PC and Internet.

Like every academic study, this one has its particular location in time but for two reasons the longevity of the analysis presented here may be briefer than usual with academic work. The use of the Internet at present takes place mainly through the PC and it is particularly the masculine codes of the PC that resound in the everyday use cultures we found around Internet use. In the future, however, the Internet is expected to be an ordinary extension of each and every communication technology – television, (mobile) telephone, radio, etc. – and even of most other domestic technologies from refrigerator to microwave and washing machine. Each of these appliances have their own gendered uses and gender codes which will result in new and different articulations of gender with the Internet. Second, the individualization of media use in the household can be expected to increase. Many households at present have two television sets and a mobile phone for each family member. It is only a matter of time before this trend extends to a multiple presence of PCs and Internet access, making Internet use in everyday life much more individual than we found in the current interviews. Such individualization may yet again change the articulations of gender and Internet and disconnect them from the interaction between partners.

Notes

1 I have also discussed these claims in van Zoonen (2001a).
2 The author himself went to some trouble to find more women in Internet history but could not find them. Email exchange, 1999; and see www.briefhistory.com
3 This procedure has been applied successfully in other work on the use of ICTs, e.g. van Zoonen (2001b), van Zoonen and Aalberts (forthcoming).

References

Babbage Pages (n.d.) available at: www.ex.ac.uk/BABBAGE/ada.html (consulted 23 May 2001).
Balka, E. (1997) *Computer Networking: Spinsters on the Web. Resources for Research and Action.* Ottawa: CRIAW/ICREF.
Braidotti, R. (1996) 'Cyberfeminism with a Difference'; available at: www.let.uu.nl/women's_studies/rosi/cyberfem.htm (consulted 23 May 2001).
Brooks, J. (1977) 'The First and Only Century of Telephone Literature', pp. 208–24 in I. de Sola Pool (ed.) *The Social Impact of the Telephone.* Cambridge, MA: MIT Press.

Cockburn, C. and S. Ormrod (1993) *Gender and Technology in the Making*. London: Sage.
Du Gay, P., S. Hall, L. Janes, H. Mackay and K. Negus (1997) *Doing Cultural Studies: The Story of the Sony Walkman*. London: Sage.
Fischer, C. (1992) *America Calling: A Social History of the Telephone to 1940*. Berkeley: University of California Press.
Freeman, E. (1996) 'Ada and the Analytical Engine', *Educom Review* March/April.
Gray, A. (1992) *Video Playtime. The Gendering of a Leisure Technology*. London: Routledge.
Haraway, D. (1997) *Modest_Witness@Second_Millennium. Female Man Meets Onco Mouse*. London: Routledge.
Jenkins, H. (1999) 'Voices From the Combat Zone: Game Grrlz Talk Back', pp. 328–41 in J. Cassels and H. Jenkins (eds) *From Barbie to Mortal Kombat: Gender and Computer Games*. Cambridge, MA: MIT Press.
Ladendorf, M. (2000) 'Pin-Ups and Grrls. The Pictures of Grrlzines', paper presented at the Crossroads in Cultural Studies Conference, Birmingham.
Martin, M. (1988) '"Rulers of the Wires"? Women's Contribution to the Structure of Communication', *Journal of Communication Inquiry* 12(2): 89–103.
Martin. M. (1991) *Hello Central: Gender, Technology and Culture in the Formation of the Telephone System*. Montreal: McGill/Queen's University Press.
Marvin, C. (1988) *When Old Technologies Were New*. New York: Oxford University Press.
Moores, S. (1988) 'The Box on the Dresser: Memoirs of Early Radio and Everyday Life', *Media, Culture & Society* 10(1): 23–40.
Naughton, J. (1999) *A Brief History of the Future: The Origins of the Internet*. London: Weidenfeld and Nicolson.
Nua (1998) 'It's an Image Thing', Nua Internet Surveys; available at: www.nua.ie/surveys/?f=VS&art_id=886595295&rel=true (consulted 28 April 2000).
Oldenziel, R. (1999) *Making Technology Masculine*. Amsterdam: Amsterdam University Press.
Parker, E. (2000) http://www.projectgamma.com/news/archive/2000/january/ 0110100-1539.shtml
Plant, S. (1998) *Zeros and Ones: Digital Women and the New Technoculture*. London: Fourth Estate.
Postmes, T. (2000) 'Social Psychological Approaches to ICT'; available at: www.infodrome.nl
Rakow, L. (1988) 'Women and the Telephone: The Gendering of a Communications Technology', pp. 207–29 in C. Kramarae (ed.) *Technology and Women's Voices: Keeping in Touch*. New York: Routledge and Kegan Paul.
Rogers, E. (1983) *The Diffusion of Innovations*. New York: Free Press.
Schwartz Cowan, R. (1987) 'The Consumption Junction: A Proposal for Research Strategies in the Sociology of Technology', in W. Bijker, T. Hughes and T. Pinch (eds) *The Social Construction of Technological Systems*. Cambridge, MA: MIT Press.
Sherman, A. (1998) *Cybergrrl: A Woman's Guide to the World Wide Web*. New York: Ballantine Books.
Silverstone, R. and E. Hirsch (eds) (1992) *Consuming Technologies: Media and Information in Domestic Spaces*. London: Routledge.

Smelik, A. (2000) 'Die virtuele matrix. Het lichaam in cyberpunkfilms', *Tijdschrift voor Genderstudies* 3(4): 4–13.
Spender, D. (1995) *Nattering on the Net: Women, Power and Cyberspace*. North Melbourne: Spinifex Press.
Strauss, A. and J. Corbin (1990) *Qualitative Data Analysis*. Beverly Hills, CA: Sage.
Turkle, S. (1988) 'Computational Reticence: Why Women Fear the Intimate Machine', pp. 41–61 in C. Kramarae (ed.) *Technology and Women's Voices*. London: Routledge.
Turkle, S. (1995) *Life on the Screen: Identity in the Age of the Internet*. New York: Simon and Schuster.
Van den Boomen, M. (1997) 'Grrls en bitches: postfeministische e-zines', *Lover* 24(3): 8–10.
Van Oost, E. (1995) 'Over vrouwelijke en mannelijke dingen', in M. Brouns, M. Verloo and M. Grunell (eds) *Vrouwenstudies in de jaren negentig. Een kennismaking vanuit verschillende disciplines*. Bussum: Coutinho.
Van Zoonen, L. (1988) 'Rethinking Women and the News', *European Journal of Communication* 3(1): 35–53.
Van Zoonen, L. (1992) 'Feminist Theory and Information Technology', *Media, Culture & Society* 14(1): 9–31.
Van Zoonen, L. (1994) *Feminist Media Studies*. London: Sage.
Van Zoonen, L. (2001a) 'Feminist Internet Studies', *Feminist Media Studies* 1(1): 67–72.
Van Zoonen, L. (2001b) 'Een computer kan niet knuffelen. De betekenis van internet voor communicatie en identiteit' [A Computer Cannot Give You a Hug: Rethinking Communication and Identity Through the Internet], pp. 71–90 in H. Bouwman (ed.) *Communicatie in de informatiesamenleving* [Communication in the Information Society]. Utrecht: Lemma.
Van Zoonen, L. and C. Aalberts (forthcoming) 'The Uses of Interactive Television in the Everyday Lives of Young Couples', in M. Consalvo (ed.) *Women and Everyday Uses of the Internet: Agency and Identity*. New York: Peter Lang.
Van Zoonen, L. and J. Wieten (1994) 'It Wasn't Exactly a Miracle: The Introduction of Television in the Netherlands', *Media, Culture & Society* 17(3): 641–60.
VODW (1999) 'Internet: It's a Woman's World', VODW Making Waves New York; available at: www.vodw.com/makingwaves/ (consulted 28 April 2000).
Wipperman, P. (2000) *Millenium Frauen.com. Weibliche Strategien für das digitale Zeitalter*. Trendbüro Hamburg/freundin Verlag Gmbh.

Part 11

PRIVACY AND SURVEILLANCE

82

THE SURVEILLANCE SOCIETY
Information technology and bureaucratic social control

Oscar H. Gandy, Jr.

Source: *Journal of Communication* 39(3) (1989): 61–76.

Advanced electronic technologies "dramatically increase the bureaucratic advantage" in the workplace, marketplace, and government by enabling—and encouraging—increasingly automatic methods of surveillance of the individual that the U.S. legal system cannot control.

Information has become an essential resource for the bureaucratic management of the global political economy. Perceptive analysts (2, 22, 38) recognize that the real source of growth in both the information work force and the development of information technologies is not to be found in any transformed consumer demand, but in the continually expanding surveillance requirements of multinational corporate enterprise. Indeed, for some observers, "information society" is a misnomer that hides the extent to which industrial societies have in fact become surveillance societies (11).

Surveillance, like propaganda, is a term that has taken on an unfortunate negative connotation. The idea of surveillance brings to mind images of the undercover police agent or counterspy rather than more acceptable images of the journalist, researcher, or communication specialist performing, in Harold Lasswell's term, "the surveillance of the environment." Charles Wright (55) has asked,

> what are the consequences of conducting surveillance through the process of mass communications instead of through some alternative system, such as a private intelligence network? That is, what are the results of treating information about events in the environment as items of news to be distributed indiscriminately,

simultaneously and publicly to a large, heterogeneous, anonymous population?.

(p. 17)

In this article we ask, similarly: What are the consequences of conducting surveillance through the system and logic of corporate and state bureaucracies? These bureaucracies treat information about a large heterogeneous population as data to be jealously guarded—shared with other bureaucracies when there is the promise of mutual gain and shared with individuals only under the threat of penalties established by law.

One consequence is an increasing inequality between those who provide and those who gather personal information. By confining their analyses to the structure and performance of markets and regulatory environments, the usual assignments of information inequality—to the "haves" and the "have-nots," the technological elites and the technopeasants, the pedestrians and the wizards—largely miss the point. The inequality that best describes the information age is not the rift between castes or classes but the widening chasm of power between individuals and bureaucratic organizations (33).

Here we attempt to describe how communications and information technologies are being used to increase the reach and influence of bureaucratic surveillance. Computerization and the speed of telecommunications networks have been combined in ways that dramatically increase the bureaucratic advantage. The current legal system is hopelessly inadequate to the challenge of controlling the "technologies of control" (54).

Modern surveillance technology is an integrated system of hardware and software that includes devices for sensing, measuring, storing, processing, and exchanging information and intelligence about the environment. For the most part the "new" technologies make the pursuit of information through surveillance more extensive, more efficient, and less obtrusive than former methods, because advanced electronics allows innovations not originally designed for surveillance to be integrated into the pool of surveillance resources.

These devices serve a variety of purposes, from noting the presence or absence of persons or objects to determining their identity or status, including their state of mind. Cameras now require little or no light, and microminiaturized versions can be easily hidden from sight; listening devices can hear conversations in rooms many hundreds of yards away; and scientific instruments can examine bodily fluids and genetic material at the molecular level. We include here the scanners that read the Universal Products Code (UPC) on commercial products in the supermarket as well as the infrared detectors that count the number of patrons for museum exhibits. The common quality is that these devices are more sensitive than ever before and overcome previous limits of time, space, and distance in gathering information about individuals (25). Associated technologies also allow for the storage, retrieval, and processing of these data gained through surveillance of the environment.

Increasingly, telecommunications networks allow data to be shared among systems and across distances (32) and among government agencies, contractors, and clients (48, pp. 58–60). The reach and efficiency of such systems allow a virtually unified data base to be created, even though the actual files may reside in the memories of quite distant machines.

Sophisticated analytical software also makes possible the dynamic processing and display of intelligence based on correlating thousands of discrete bits of information about the targets of surveillance. "Expert systems"—computer software applications that incorporate the expertise of an analyst—are able to process available data, issue diagnoses, and direct the actions of other devices or persons. By reducing the time and cost associated with moving from data gathering to decision making and by centralizing control (36), they make surveillance more efficient. Thus, analysis can estimate the probability that an individual will pursue a particular course of action that either serves the interests of the controller or represents an unacceptable level of risk; the analysis can even suggest where additional data would be necessary (47). The marriage of computers and telecommunications (37) is the major material force in the new technology of surveillance.

The new technologies have transformed the nature of surveillance in important ways. Contemporary surveillance derives from Bentham's early nineteenth-century Panopticon, an architectural design for a prison where inmates were (or would believe that they were) being watched by unseen eyes The Panopticon was also to be a laboratory for testing approaches to modifying behavior. Through "its preventative character, its continuous functioning, and its automatic mechanisms," the device would ensure desirable conduct (12, p. 206).

Similarly, the new surveillance can be thought of as a form of "remote sensing" where the observer is never seen. Information is processed by unknown, faceless technicians and specialists who have no direct, personal knowledge of or concern for their data subjects. The superior technology available to the surveillance agency enables it to generate intelligence about an individual that even the individual does not possess. For example, remote laboratories that perform blood tests on job applicants may discover the presence of life-threatening diseases about which the individual has had not the slightest warning sign. If the tests have been performed without the subject's consent—such as tests for AIDS in those jurisdictions that bar requirements for HIV testing as a condition of employment—the results may never even be revealed to the individual.

The new surveillance is increasingly automatic and is triggered by the data subject. Thus, a person who enters a parking garage, office, or secure floor using a magnetically striped card initiates the creation of a record noting the date and time of entry and exit. The act of logging on to a computer system begins the documentation of files entered, keystrokes and errors made, and messages sent and received. "Station message detail recorders" on office telephone systems can record the number, time, and duration of all calls placed from any instrument. Advanced audience assessment devices record which television programs are being viewed—or at least, on the basis of their scanned images, who is present in the room. If the system is uncertain, its on-screen display can inquire about who entered or left the room. Individuals participate voluntarily in much of contemporary surveillance, even if not with fully informed consent.

The analysis of surveillance data, too, has become more automatic (26). Cross-matching computer files has become routine in the government provision of services. Eligibility, or "front-end" verification, is used to compare an applicant's file with the files of banks, employers, insurance companies, or others who might provide evidence of unreported resources. Cross-matching might also reveal the absence of matches where they are expected, as in the case of claims for dependent children who do not appear on any school registration lists. Such matches need not be initiated by any particular application but may be the result of a bureaucrat's "hunch" about where evidence of illegality might be found. Illegality is assumed, and all individuals in a particular file are subjected to this "search" without their knowledge or consent. And, as soon as the existence of a new data base becomes known, its potential for providing additional information about a data subject is assessed, and the demand for more matches grows.

Contemporary surveillance is directed toward preventing or avoiding loss or injury, rather than detecting crime that has already occurred. Individuals are no longer brought under surveillance merely to determine whether they have committed a crime; bureaucratic surveillance is initiated more frequently to determine if an individual has even the *potential* to commit a criminal act. And, as we have seen, the definition of criminal behavior may expand as telematics improves the capacity of the system to survey and discipline (47).

For example, Credit Bureau Incorporated, with files on 142 million consumers, offers a service called Delinquency Alert System (DAS). DAS provides a rating that the creditor can use in deciding whether to extend or limit credit to persons who, though not currently delinquent, might be at risk given the nature of their expenditures and accounts (5). The same kind of predictive models are used to assess the riskiness of assigning bail to persons charged with crimes and the punitive orientation of prospective jurors.

These analytical models generate "types" or classes of persons, rather than specific individuals, and anyone falling within those groups comes under suspicion and hence surveillance. Thus, males of a certain age, skin color, and point of origin have an increased likelihood of being searched, or at least questioned, by customs and security agents at international airports. In the southeastern part of the United States, certain models of automobile have a greater probability of being stopped by police if their drivers are black or Latino. These narcotics interdiction and antiterrorist profiles have their equals in the Internal Revenue Service scans of tax returns and in the routine processing of applications for credit cards. The ostensible purpose is the same—to predict and prevent.

The capacity to predict also provides the opportunity to control. In James Beniger's perspective (4), information technologies are control technologies, which reduce the costs of uncertainty by establishing routines that efficiently "preprocess" and classify, and thereby help to rationalize various activities in the environments of complex, interconnected systems. But his naturalistic model largely ignores the political and economic impact of these modes of control. As state and private bureaucracies seek to control the social environment in which they function, they must also, as John Kenneth Galbraith suggests, plan the behavior of the people within them (15, pp. 39–40). As the power of the corporate bureaucracy grows in relation to individuals and to smaller competitors, it also grows relative to the power of the state (1).

Thus, surveillance that ostensibly predicts and prevents also makes the individual citizen, worker, or consumer the target of bureaucratic control. If, as Frank Webster and Kevin Robins suggest (51, pp. 49–73), information technology is a complex social relation, then its development and spread reflect the design and interests of bureaucracies and, increasingly, the consent and assistance of a "disciplinary state" that contains dissent and opposition from those least well served by the information revolution.

The spread of computerization throughout the bureaucratic infrastructure changes the bureaucracy while it increases the bureaucracy's power relative to other organizations and to the individuals who are its employees, clients, or suppliers. Telecommunications networks extend the advantages of economies of scale and scope that computerization confers on an organization. Under the guise of decentralization and independence, this coordination function reinforces the power and influence of centralized authority (6). The massive scale of transnational operations requires private global networks; meanwhile, the organization can use its oligopsony power to extract discounts and special favors from service providers (37, 39).

Once a network and computerized data base have been established, the marginal cost of adding additional bits of information declines, so large organizations gather more information and discard less (23). The organization need not have an immediate need or application for any particular item of information its network collects, because storage and access are cheap relative to collection. The nature of multivariate analytical and predictive models is such that information already in storage becomes more valuable as new information is added to the data base.

Because of the monopoly power of corporate bureaucracies and the authority and autonomy of state bureaucracies, the theoretical restraints of the market have little effect on their surveillance activities. Similarly, the peculiar qualities of information (3), including the substantial externalities associated with its collection and use, lead organizations in general (and monopoly firms in particular) to collect more information than is socially optimal. By the same token, because each isolated bit of information on the citizen/consumer has such a seemingly small "privacy cost" and because monitoring the bureaucracy's use of that information has a high cost, individuals are incapable of acting in their own interests. Indeed, because individuals are "contract term takers" (23), and because they are usually required to provide personal information as a condition of service, resistance is perhaps even irrational. Examining information technology as a social relation in three environments—the workplace, the marketplace, and government—shows how the concerns of the individual are increasingly subjected to the unobtrusive powers of bureaucratic surveillance.

Although pre-employment background searches have become routine, it is on the job that surveillance becomes total and continuous. A study by the Office of Technology Assessment (45) notes that "electronic monitoring is only one of a range of technologies used in today's workplace to gather information about the work process or to predict work quality based on personal characteristics of the workers" (p. 12; see also 27). The surveillance of workers in the information age begins well before they enter the office or factory. The growth in pre-employment drug tests (43), psychological screening batteries (18), and searches of credit bureau files and arrest records reflects not only the advances of computer-aided analyses but also the declining costs of collecting, storing, and processing data thought to be relevant to employment decisions.

On the job, in pursuit of greater efficiency in production and management, both large and small employers use computer-based systems to record and compare workers' output against standards or goals and to link their individual responses to changes in the work environment. It is ironic, perhaps, that the sector of the work force under the most complete and continuous surveillance is that which contains the largest contingent of information workers—workers whose very purpose is the collection and processing of data.

The growing importance of telemarketing and the inbound processing of orders and claims for banking, insurance, and investment organizations has increased management's claims that surveillance of the telephone worker is necessary to maintain standards and efficiency. The Communications Workers of America estimates that nearly 15 million telephone workers are being secretly "bugged," either automatically by an electronic supervisor or by anonymous quality-assessment personnel. These remote supervisors, often located in phone centers hundreds of miles from the workers being observed, listen in on conversations to evaluate how well employees are following the predetermined scripts and how well they are maintaining the appropriate tone and quality of voice (7).

Setting aside concerns about gains in productivity, Andrew Clement's (6) examination of the progress of office automation focuses instead on the exercise of control over the labor process. More than 80 percent of white-collar workers are expected to have computerized work stations by the end of the century, and such systems facilitate the collection and analysis of a variety of work and nonwork activities in the modern office. As higher and higher levels of the organization become connected to the electronic umbilical, it becomes possible "for technical forms of workplace control to be extended to occupational ranks that previously had not been exposed to such techniques" (6, p. 233). The spread of personal computers throughout the office represented something of a temporary loss of this surveillance potential. However, local area networks capable of integrating PCs that use different communications protocols will restore their preferred managerial status as "intelligent terminals."

Surveillance technology in the realm of consumer behavior has the potential to exceed the effects identified for the workplace, because while not everyone is gainfully employed, nearly everyone is an actual or potential consumer. The control of mass consumption involves using information about consumers, including data about the extent to which they have been exposed to persuasive messages, as well as indices of their responsiveness to such appeals. "People meters" represent a shift from measuring households to measuring individuals; some versions, reflecting the primary purpose of assessment, provide ratings of commercials as well as news and entertainment programs. The importance of comprehensive, continuous audience surveillance is reflected in the steady pressure to develop overnight ratings in all television markets and to include estimates of cable and VCR usage in those packages.

Advances in digital communications technologies, especially in terms of their addressability and verifiability (17), allows market research to apply the sophisticated techniques of social science to the surveillance of consumers in order to predict and control their behavior. The preprocessing or classification component of control identified by Beniger (4) finds its contemporary reflection in the sophisticated segmentation of consumer markets on the basis of data gathered from surveys, experiments, and continuous monitoring of the marketplace (10, 14, 29).

Television audiences are classified on the basis of individual interests, needs, and orientations (13) through a technique called geodemographic clustering. The PRIZM target marketing system, developed by the Claritas Corporation, utilizes data collected by the U.S. Census Bureau and numerous other sources of public and private consumer surveillance to classify each of the nation's 250,000 neighborhoods (52). This preprocessing of a vast, heterogeneous population into one of 40 consumption-related categories or types helps those who plan targeted commercial and political appeals.

The computer facilitates the use of older communications channels to support market research. Just as UPC codes pinpoint the identity of products as they are passed over the laser scanners in the supermarket, similar bar codes identify the consumer who has submitted a coupon received in the mail or pulled out of a magazine. When matched with store price and where it was redeemed, the coupon also helps estimate the price and income elasticity of demand for such goods. The storage capacity of these computers allows lists of such coupon responders to be inexpensively reproduced and sold to others in the business community. Each week, the *Friday Report*, a newsletter of the direct marketing industry, reports on dozens of available lists at prices ranging from $45 to $100 per thousand names.

Kevin Wilson (54) focuses our attention on the home as a site for many computer-based information systems, or "technologies of control." Interactive home networking systems are subject to, if not a direct product of, efforts to "transform human activities into marketable commodities" (p. 9). Their "impact on techniques of public surveillance will be felt most strongly as these systems increase points of contact between client and agency, because there is no practical limit to the types of information which will circulate through interactive systems" (p. 95).

Spiros Simitis, a law professor and Data Protection Commissioner for the West German state of Hesse, takes a similar view of interactive systems (41). Many modern cable systems are already capable of providing a variety of services, from catalogue shopping and data retrieval to the monitoring of fire and burglar alarms. Because use of these services is quickly and efficiently recorded in the system's computer, Simitis concludes that where "anonymity was once the rule, complete transparency now dominates.... Videotex is, therefore, further proof of the steady, but often imperceptible, transition in social control from physical coercion to observation and surveillance" (41, p. 729).

The U.S. government is both the single largest user and the greatest supporter of the development of computer and telecommunications systems' surveillance capacities. The federal government operated an estimated 27,000 large mainframe computers in 1985, serving some 173,000 terminals (46). A survey of 12 cabinet-level departments and 13 independent agencies by the U.S. Office of Technology Assessment found 539 records systems, with 3.5 billion records subject to the guidelines of the Federal Privacy Act of 1974.[1] More than half of these systems had been fully or partially computerized by 1985 (44, p. 40).

This massive collection of data does not begin to describe the surveillance activity of the federal bureaucracy, which is also the primary gatherer of social and behavioral statistics. The $3.2 billion estimate of federal government expenditures for information dissemination in fiscal year 1987 provides a sense of the size of the data pool that the government collects or causes to be collected on its behalf (48). Many of these data do not qualify as records under the Privacy Act, as they do not identify individual data persons, but they are no less part of the government's surveillance function.

The Department of Defense is the largest collector and distributor of information within the government. Its surveillance requirements are global, and from time to time it has been actively involved in domestic political surveillance of civilians (9). It is joined by the Central Intelligence Agency, the National Security Agency, and the Federal Bureau of Investigation as major collectors of information used for surveillance. In 1988, for example, the FBI successfully avoided facing restrictions on its "Library Awareness Program," which sought the assistance of librarian-informers in keeping track of foreigners and others who might gain access to information that threatens national security (21).

The Internal Revenue Service is the major civilian collector of personal data within the government. To extend its reach and to improve the ability of its analytical models to identify nonreporters or underreporters, the IRS has sought—occasionally with the consequence of adverse publicity (49)—to use private data bases that contain considerable detail about citizens' expenditures and income.

In response to recommendations of the President's Private Sector Survey on Cost Control (the Grace Commission), politicians suggested establishing federal mandates for performing extensive matching of public and private files to detect fraud, waste, and abuse at the state level. This requirement, which became part of the Deficit Reduction Act of 1984 (PL 98–369), serves as yet another economic spur to adopt practices that have their own economic incentives.

Surveillance systems and techniques are also used to manufacture political consent by manipulating public opinion (28). The skillful provision of information subsidies through a variety of information channels has been shown to influence public policy (16).

The same segmentation and targeting approaches that help to market commercial goods and services are regularly used to market political candidates and positions on policy referenda. A special licensing agreement with Claritas Corporation allows Targeting Systems Incorporated to apply the geodemographic clustering method to political issues (52). PRIZM cluster analysis helps political consultants decide where more data are needed or where it makes sense to simply ignore the resident population. Concern that the cluster method would be used to win elections appears to have been unfounded, as politicians find the data gathering too expensive for most local campaigns. Instead, "cluster targeting has found a more receptive target among corporate clients attempting to influence public policy and arouse the citizenry" (52, p. 221). With each election and referendum vote, fresh data about the similarity of political behavior within clusters improve the precision of the PRIZM data base.

The bureaucracies of the state and the private corporations have amassed an almost unimaginable technological advantage when compared with the resources of the average individual. Within the sphere of bureaucratic organizations, too, inequality is the rule rather than the exception. The largest firms have the most powerful, sophisticated, and fully integrated systems of surveillance that money can afford. The presence of personal computers in the homes of a few million consumers is no more of a threat to TRW than the presence of even greater number of VCRs and cameras is to CBS. Indeed, as Wilson and others have argued, the spread of such systems increases the potential of surveillance.

It is difficult to gauge the extent to which the U.S. population accepts such disparity in technological systems as the natural, evolutionary, and inevitable consequence of economic growth. Some individual concerns about privacy have surfaced in a variety of national opinion surveys over the years.

A rather narrow search of the Roper Center data base for the years 1975–1986 produced some useful indicators of concern (34). According to Walker Research's Marketing Research Industry Image studies, for example, an increasing share of respondents—between 25 and 28 percent in 1978–1984—agreed that "polls or research surveys are an invasion of privacy."[2] However, an overwhelming majority of respondents (81 percent) in a 1986 study (40) still agreed that "the research industry serves a useful purpose," although this figure represented a slight decline. Indeed, a slightly increased proportion (82 percent) of Americans apparently believed that "polls and research surveys are used to help manufacturers produce better products," while only 44 percent believed that polls and surveys help "manufacturers sell consumers products they don't want or need."

In 1983, under the sponsorship of the Southern New England Telephone Company, the Harris organization surveyed nearly 1,300 telephone households to explore knowledge and opinions about technology and privacy (20). As in previous surveys, the extent of concern about privacy was quite high. Forty-eight percent of respondents were very concerned and 29 percent were somewhat concerned about "threats to your personal privacy in America today." While 68 percent agreed that they begin surrendering their privacy when they enter the credit system, nearly the same proportion (67 percent) believed that personal information was being kept in files for purposes unknown to them.

Respondents seemed to have a fairly well developed understanding of how information about their past behavior could be gathered and included in a master file, and 78 percent of those polled indicated that such files would represent an invasion of their privacy. Eighty percent of the respondents also agreed that computers have made it "much easier for someone to obtain confidential personal information about persons improperly." Seventy-seven percent agreed that selling information about a person's credit standing would be a serious invasion of privacy—yet the sale of access to such information is precisely what credit bureaus do. The inconsistency in these responses is also evident in the fact that 80 percent of the respondents claim never to have been the victim of an improper invasion of privacy.

A more theoretically sophisticated study by Eugene Stone *et al.* (42) found quite distinct differences in attitudes associated with different kinds of organizations likely to threaten individual privacy. Respondents were asked about the extent to which they believed that they themselves, rather than bureaucratic organizations, had control over how information about them would be gathered and used. The data suggest that the more people seem to "value informational privacy the less control they believe they actually have over personal information" (42, p. 464). This is consistent with data reported by Alan Westin (53) that linked concerns about privacy with feelings of alienation and distrust of government and other powerful forces in society. Respondents were more confident about their ability to personally control information relative to employers than to the IRS, insurance companies, credit grantors, law enforcement agencies, or lending institutions.

Privacy legislation has done little to preserve or to extend the rights and freedoms that were envisioned when the laws were initially passed. Bureaucratic practice and the incentives of managers to extend the reach and influence of their agencies have led to the eventual normalization of "exceptions," which soon become the bureaucratic paths around the legislative barriers (11). When a data protection or privacy commission is established, complacent citizens and politicians presume that the problem has gone away. Yet the limited resources and hostile environment such efforts will encounter guarantee that they will lose their edge over time.

In addition, the bulk of legislative action at the federal level has been directed toward government actions, all but ignoring the activities of corporate bureaucracies, which have a far more extensive reach.[3] As the movement toward commoditization and privatization spreads and deepens, the need for legislative attention to corporate practices will grow, although "attempts to restore privacy and individual autonomy by dismantling bureaucracies as such are doomed to failure" (30, p. 288).

Even if it weren't for the continued pressure of bureaucratic expansion, much recent legislation that on its face promises to protect the rights of privacy is seriously flawed and serves primarily to legitimate the very assaults the laws were designed to prevent. For example, the Electronic Communications Privacy Act (ECPA) of 1986 (HR 4952) has been heralded as a tremendous success, the result of historic cooperation between government and often-competing industry groups. But while Congress was extending the reach of outdated prohibitions against unwarranted wiretapping to include the emerging digital communications systems, the legislation also considered the disclosure of record content and transactions. The legislative analysis interprets the Act's nondisclosure section (section 2702) as formally establishing the right of those data managers to treat the fact of transaction as information that can then be divulged to third parties. Thus, it further legitimates the use of such transaction information in creating mailing lists, complete with electronic addresses of "persons fitting broad demographic criteria."

James Katz's evaluation of the ECPA (24) finds that the tightening of some restrictions, such as those on unauthorized access, has been accompanied by some weakening of the safety net with regard to government access. This weakening is accomplished by increasing the range of activities that qualify for state surveillance, easing the requirements for gaining court orders, and improving the state's ability to gain access to usage data. Katz also sees the ECPA legislation as explicitly recognizing the economic rationale behind the legitimization of surveillance: "If it could be shown that a technology gives birth to new industries, improves the trade balance, increases industrial efficiency, and creates meaningful jobs, the privacy costs would be more willingly accepted by the polity" (24, p. 362).

Along similar lines, the so-called "Bork Bill," rushed through Congress following an uproar over a newspaper's publication of Supreme Court nominee Robert Bork's video rental records, legitimizes industry practice. The Video Privacy Protection Act (S 2361) is read by some as limiting video stores' ability to rent lists of their customers (21); but the list industry saw the bill as a historic reversal of threatening trends in the struggle for rights in consumer transaction records. In its initial form, the proposed legislation would have required video stores to obtain a customer's expressed consent before renting his or her name to a direct marketer. In its final form, the legislation places the responsibility on customers to indicate that they do not want their names used; otherwise, the rental firms (and, by implication, any other transaction records keepers) may sell or transfer lists of customers who regularly view particular kinds of videotapes. The prohibition from releasing information about which particular titles are viewed is of no significant consequence. In the view of one industry analyst, with the passage of this legislation, "we have built a Congressional endorsement and trade-off which should carry us into the next century" (50).

The legislative burden is placed squarely on the shoulders of citizen-consumers, who generally have only limited awareness of the nature of the list industry and of the opportunities that might be available for them to have their names withdrawn from the lists. National surveys and industry reports suggest that, even though there is growing resentment of "junk mail" and unsolicited telephone calls (31), individuals tend not to request or even to indicate that they would like to have their names removed from lists.

Kevin Wilson (54), extending the analysis of James Rule (35), sees public demand for protection against surveillance weakening at a time when the need for coordination and compliance spurs on its growth. From this perspective, surveillance works through its ability to maintain the internalization of the rules. Legislation that protects against the occasional "abuses" of the surveillance merely provides a social justification for its extension in this "improved" form.

Other legislation that specifically addresses the problems of data sharing fails to take into account the changing nature of U.S. industry. While there may continue to be some restrictions on sharing customer lists between organizations, it would be unimaginable to think that such restrictions would apply *within* firms. Vertical integration and horizontal conglomeration are creating a structure in which quite diverse organizations under the same corporate umbrella can be expected to collect, process, and share internally quite comprehensive information about individuals gleaned from their transaction records. Thus, a model conglomerate of the future will have banking and financial services, credit cards, travel and insurance, and the traditional automotive and consumer retail service records. In addition, it will support an expanding line of entertainment and information businesses, from cable television and videocassette rental (from automatic kiosks) to videotex, electronic mail, and data base gateway services. The possibilities for cross-marketing on the basis of information available to such a firm stagger the imagination—and would be absolutely invisible to the majority of consumers.

Finally, existing legislation uniformly limits the reach of data protection to "individually identifiable information." Such restrictions provide no limits on the collection, distribution, and use of information about "groups" of any size or definition beyond those that have won some degree of protection through political action (e.g., blacks, women, the elderly). Thus, the characteristics of communities or neighborhoods, defined in terms of five-digit zip codes, have no limits in privacy claims. On the basis of indices developed through "anonymous" data aggregation, geodemographic targeting (52) can proceed unabated to "redline" particular communities as being ineligible for investment, unwise for travel, and unlikely as prospects for political mobilization. Economic, social, and political discrimination simply take on new forms as they grow and spread.

What hope is there for resistance to the spread of surveillance? Priscilla Regan (33) suggests that, ironically, 'liberal democracies, whose *raison d'être* is the protection of the individual, are rendered virtually impotent in the face of bureaucratic power" because their institutions were designed at a time when bureaucratic power did not exist (p. 360). But to the extent that reports of public sentiment reflect a genuine understanding of and resentment toward the growing disparity in power that is facilitated and extended by surveillance, there is always the potential for resistance. Resistance may be mobilized in response to well-publicized cases of abuse, or it may come in response to the reemergence of a "literature of alarm" (33, p. 24) like that which accompanied the dramatic spread of computerization throughout the government bureaucracy in the 1960s and 1970s. The potential for resistance is always present, and the rather high level of awareness and concern suggests that it rests just beneath the surface, waiting to be released.

Notes

1 The Privacy Act, passed in 1974, sought to restrict the collection and sharing of personal information by the federal government to the purposes for which it had been gathered; it was supposed to require the informed consent of the citizen for such use. The Act was passed before computerization of records had become widespread within the government bureaucracy, and it also included a number of exceptions, including a blanket exclusion for what an agency might declare to be a "routine use." These exceptions have become the rule, necessitating the passage of more specific legislation controlling the use of government data bases for matching.
2 This finding is consistent with evidence of the growing number of people who refuse to participate in opinion surveys. The differential rates of survey nonresponse between the United States, Canada, and Britain have been attributed in part to differences in national response to the census from 1930 to 1980 (19).
3 Legislative attempts to preserve privacy in the consumer realm in the United States include efforts to restrict government access to data held in private files. These include the Right to Financial Privacy Act and the Electronic Funds Transfer Act of 1978. Specific acts, concerned primarily with ensuring the accuracy of banking, credit, and employment data held in private records, have emerged since the passage of the Privacy Act. Compilations of state and federal privacy laws are published regularly by the *Privacy Journal*. The protection offered by these laws pales in comparison with those recommended by the Council of Europe for its members. For discussion of the Data Protection Convention and the need for its revision, see (8).

References

1 Adams, Walter and James W. Brock. *The Bigness Complex: Industry, Labor, and Government in the American Economy.* New York: Pantheon Books, 1986.
2 Arriaga, Patricia. "Towards a Critique of the Information Economy." *Media, Culture & Society* 7, 1985, pp. 271–296.
3 Babe, Robert E. "Information Industries and Economic Analysis: Policymakers Beware." In Oscar Gandy, Jr., Paul Espinosa, and Janus Ordover (Eds.), *Proceedings from the Tenth Annual Telecommunications Policy Research Conference.* Norwood, N.J.: Ablex, 1983, pp. 123–136.
4 Beniger, James R. *The Control Revolution: Technological and Economic Origins of the Information Society.* Cambridge, Mass.: Harvard University Press, 1986.

5 "Changes Affecting Credit Bureaus." *Privacy Journal* 14(7), May 1988, p. 11.
6 Clement, Andrew. "Office Automation and the Technical Control of Information Workers." In Vincent Mosco and Janet Wasko (Eds.), *The Political Economy of Information.* Madison: University of Wisconsin Press, 1988, pp. 217–246.
7 Communications Workers of America. *Fact Sheet: Secret Monitoring in the Workplace.* Washington, D.C.: CWA, 1987.
8 Council of Europe. *New Technologies: A Challenge to Privacy Protection?* Strasbourg: Council of Europe, 1989.
9 Donner, Frank J. *The Age of Surveillance: The Aims and Methods of America's Political Intelligence System.* New York: Knopf, 1980.
10 Engel, James F., Henry Fiorillo, and Murray A. Cayley (Eds.). *Market Segmentation: Concepts and Applications.* New York: Holt, Rinehart & Winston, 1972.
11 Flaherty, David H. "The Emergence of Surveillance Societies in the Western World: Toward the Year 2000." *Government Information Quarterly* 5(4), 1988, pp. 377–387.
12 Foucault, Michel. *Discipline and Punish: The Birth of the Prison.* New York: Random House, 1977.
13 Frank, Ronald E. and Marshall G. Greenberg. *The Public's Use of Television: Who Watches and Why.* Beverly Hills, Cal.: Sage, 1980.
14 Frank, Ronald, William Massey, and Yoram Wind. *Market Segmentation.* Englewood Cliffs, N.J.: Prentice-Hall, 1972.
15 Galbraith, John Kenneth. *Economics and the Public Purpose.* Boston: Houghton Mifflin, 1973.
16 Gandy, Oscar H., Jr. *Beyond Agenda Setting: Information Subsidies and Public Policy.* Norwood, N.J.: Ablex, 1982.
17 Gandy, Oscar H., Jr., and Charles E. Simmons. "Technology, Privacy and the Democratic Process." *Critical Studies in Mass Communication* 3(2), June 1986, pp. 155–168.
18 Gardner, Susan. "Wiretapping the Mind: A Call to Regulate Truth Verification in Employment." *San Diego Law Review* 21(2), March 1984, pp. 295–323.
19 Goyder, John and Jean Leiper. "The Decline in Survey Response: A Social Values Interpretation." *Sociology* 19(1), February 1985, pp. 55–71.
20 Louis Harris and Associates. "The Road After 1984: The Impact of Technology on Society." Study conducted for Southern New England Telephone for presentation at the Eighth Annual Smithsonian Symposium, December 1983.
21 "In Congress." *Privacy Journal* 14(11), October 1988, p. 7.
22 Jonscher, Charles. "Information Resources and Economic Productivity." *Information Economics and Policy* 1, 1983, pp. 13–35.
23 Jussawalla, Meheroo and Chee-Wah Cheah. *The Calculus of International Communications.* Littleton, Colo.: Libraries Unlimited, 1987.
24 Katz, James E. "US Telecommunications Privacy Policy: Socio-Political Responses to Technological Advances." *Telecommunications Policy*, December 1988, pp. 353–368.
25 Marx, Gary T. *Under Cover: Police Surveillance in America.* Berkeley: University of California Press, 1988.
26 Marx, Gary T. and Nancy Reichman. "Routinizing the Discovery of Secrets: Computers as Informants." *Software Law Journal* 1(1), Fall 1985, pp. 95–121.

27 Marx, Gary T. and Sanford Sherizen. "Monitoring on the Job: How to Protect Privacy as Well as Property." *Technology Review*, November/December 1986, pp. 63–72.
28 Meadow, Robert G. (Ed.). *New Communication Technologies in Politics.* Washington, D.C.: Washington Program of the Annenberg School of Communications, 1985.
29 Meyers, James H. and Edward M. Tauber. *Market Structure Analysis.* Chicago: American Marketing Association, 1977.
30 Moore, Barrington, Jr. *Privacy: Studies in Social and Cultural History.* Armonk, N.Y.: M. E. Sharpe, 1984.
31 Nadel, Mark S. "Rings of Privacy: Unsolicited Telephone Calls and the Right of Privacy." *Yale Journal on Regulation* 4, 1986, pp. 99–128.
32 Pacific Bell. *Pacific Bell's Response to the Intelligent Network Taskforce Report.* Sacramento, Cal.: Pacific Bell, 1988.
33 Regan, Priscilla. "Public Use of Private Information: A Comparison of Personal Information Policies in the United States and Britain." Unpublished doctoral dissertation, Cornell University, Ithaca, New York, 1981.
34 Roper Center for Public Opinion Research. University of Connecticut, Storrs. Search completed for the author on November 2, 1987.
35 Rule, James B. *Private Lives and Public Surveillance: Social Control in the Computer Age.* London: Allen Lane, 1973.
36 Rule, James, Douglas McAdam, Linda Stearns, and David Uglow. "Documentary Identification and Mass Surveillance in the United States." *Social Problems* 31(2), December 1983, pp. 222–234.
37 Schiller, Dan. *Telematics and Government.* Norwood, N.J.: Ablex, 1982.
38 Schiller, Dan. "How to Think About Information." In Vincent Mosco and Janet Wasko (Eds.), *The Political Economy of Information.* Madison: University of Wisconsin Press, 1988, pp. 27–43.
39 Schiller, Herbert I. *Information and the Crisis Economy.* Norwood, N.J.: Ablex, 1984.
40 Schleifer, Stephen. "Trends in Attitudes Toward and Participation in Survey Research." *Public Opinion Quarterly* 50, 1986, pp. 17–26.
41 Simitis, Spiros. "Reviewing Privacy in an Information Society." *University of Pennsylvania Law Review* 135, 1987, pp. 707–746.
42 Stone, Eugene, H. Gueutal, D. Gardner, and S. McClure. "A Field Experiment Comparing Information-Privacy Values, Beliefs and Attitudes Across Several Types of Organizations." *Journal of Applied Psychology* 68(3), 1983, pp. 459–468.
43 "Testing for Drug Use in the American Workplace: A Symposium." *Nova Law Review* 11(2), Winter 1987.
44 U.S. Congress. Office of Technology Assessment. *Electronic Records Systems and Individual Privacy.* OTA-CIT-296. Washington, D.C.: U.S. Government Printing Office, June 1986.
45 U.S. Congress. Office of Technology Assessment. *The Electronic Supervisor: New Technologies, New Tensions.* OTA-CIT-333. Washington, D.C.: U.S. Government Printing Office, September 1987.
46 U.S. Congress. Office of Technology Assessment. *Defending Secrets, Sharing Data: New Locks and Keys for Electronic Information.* OTA-CIT-310. Washington, D.C.: U.S. Government Printing Office, October 1987.

47 U.S. Congress. Office of Technology Assessment. *Criminal Justice. New Technologies and the Constitution. OTA-CIT-366.* Washington, D.C.: U.S. Government Printing Office, 1988.
48 U.S. Congress. Office of Technology Assessment. *Informing the Nation: Federal Information Dissemination in an Electronic Age. OTA-CIT-396.* Washington, D.C.: U.S. Government Printing Office, October 1988.
49 U.S. Congress. Senate. Committee on Governmental Affairs. Hearing, June 6, 1984. *Computer Matching: Taxpayer Records.* Washington, D.C.: U.S. Government Printing Office, 1984.
50 "Video Privacy Protection Act of 1988." *Friday Report,* November 11, 1988, p. 1.
51 Webster, Frank and Kevin Robins. *Information Technology: A Luddite Analysis.* Norwood, N.J.: Ablex, 1986.
52 Weiss, Michael J. *The Clustering of America.* New York: Harper & Row, 1988.
53 Westin, Alan, Louis Harris and Associates, and Sentry Insurance. *A National Opinion Research Survey of Attitudes Toward Privacy.* Stevens Point, Wisc: Sentry Insurance, 1979.
54 Wilson, Kevin G. *Technologies of Control: The New Interactive Media for the Home.* Madison: University of Wisconsin Press, 1988.
55 Wright, Charles R. *Mass Communication: A Sociological Perspective.* New York: Random House, 1959.

83

AN ELECTRONIC PANOPTICON?

A sociological critique of surveillance theory

David Lyon

Source: *Sociological Review* 41(4) (1993): 653–78.

Abstract

The concept of an electronic Panopticon is making increasingly frequent appearances within analyses of electronic surveillance. This paper traces briefly the history of the Panopticon from Jeremy Bentham to Michel Foucault and through a series of case studies shows how the idea seems relevant in the context of computer databases. It is argued that while the Panopticon has some salience to electronic surveillance, particularly through its enhanced capacity for invisible monitoring of personal details, the notion of a 'societal Panopticon' is sociologically mistaken. Nonetheless, where vestiges of the Panopticon are present within electronic surveillance, they present a challenge to social analysis and to political practice.

Every now and then a concept catches the sociological imagination because it seems to capture neatly some feature of contemporary society. 'Anomie', 'network', 'labelling', 'mass society' and many others qualify as examples. The Panopticon holds promise as just such a concept. Originating as Jeremy Bentham's eighteenth century architectural plan for a prison, the Panopticon became the centrepiece of Michel Foucault's theory of surveillance. Although Foucault made no allusion to computers, the Panopticon now makes frequent appearances in discussions of electronic surveillance.

While in some respects the prison plan failed – Bentham found it hard to sell the idea of prisoner 'solitude' and the organization-style of a capitalist factory for instance – Foucault holds that its principles have actually diffused through numerous social spheres. Today this is taken further, such that the ultimate realization of the panoptic is facilitated by information technology. By electronic mediation society itself becomes a panoptic prison. So it is said.

The image of the electronic Panopticon has been used to good effect in a number of studies documenting the social aspects of computerization. A few examples give their flavour. Shoshana Zuboff's celebrated ethnography of computer-based technologies in the workplace draws on the panoptic metaphor to show how managers maintain control. New technology renders workers' activities transparent to management, inducing conformity to a degree undreamed of two centuries ago, or even two decades ago (Zuboff, 1988). Gary Marx's analysis of American undercover police practices documents the emergence of a 'new surveillance' based primarily on computer technology that is subtle, decentralized and increasingly permeates society at large. Its lineage may be traced from the Panopticon, through the maximum security prison to the 'maximum security society' (Marx, 1988).

In a Canadian context Vincent Mosco sees the Panopticon operating through the computerization of marketing techniques, a process that he and others refer to as 'social management' (Mosco, 1989). What Foucault calls the 'capilliary level' of the social organism, that is, the minutiae of everyday life routines, is penetrated by the new surveillance. In parallel with commercial developments, of course, is the massive electronic enhancement of government data-collection practices. Rob Kling, for example, asks, 'Have computerized information systems effectively transformed Bentham's panoptic principle from a strategy which is only feasible in village-scale settings to a routine means of mass surveillance by modern states?' (Kling, 1986: 3).

As these examples show, the 'panoptic', which is how I shall refer to the principles of the Panopticon, has been applied to diverse social spheres, not all of which would normally be associated with each other. It is also being used in ways that draw together the analysis of new technology, social change and relations of power. Moreover, with a few exceptions, the panoptic comes to us not direct from the eighteenth century, but mediated by Foucault.

While many wide-eyed predictions about the coming of an information society are overblown and sociologically deficient (see Lyon, 1988), there can be little doubt that new technology is implicated in contemporary social transformations, and that this has consequences for social control. If sociology is to remain abreast of current developments, analytical leverage must be gained on the question of how these are connected. The panoptic has been seized upon as a likely conceptual candidate, linking the changing technologies of surveillance with the debate over the information society and, more broadly, post-modernity.

Its attractiveness to social theory lies in the ways it epitomizes the disciplinary approaches of modernity, as we shall see. It expresses neatly the Enlightenment concern with empirical observation and classification, related to the rational reproducing of social order. And the idea of exploiting uncertainty in the observed as a way of ensuring their subordination has obvious resonance with current electronic technologies that permit highly unobtrusive monitoring of data subjects in a variety of social contexts. Finally, we shall see that postmodern preoccupations with the decentred subject are also echoed here. If our supposedly personal details of intimate everyday life circulate beyond our control within remote computer databases, where now is the human self?

The panoptic, I shall argue, has considerable illuminative power as a descriptive metaphor, maybe more than those derived from Orwell or Kafka. Thus we shall explore the different dimensions of the panoptic, as applied to new forms of electronic surveillance. The big question, however, is, how adequate is the panoptic as an explanatory concept? Is it at all useful in understanding contemporary forms of social control or is its relevance merely residual? Can it fulfil the various roles asigned to it by recent social analysts? Or is its rhetorical reach rather more limited?

In what follows I shall first look at the panoptic in the work of Bentham and Foucault, then examine electronic surveillance as panoptic power, and thirdly, assess the sociological usefulness of the concept by asking three questions: Can the panoptic be generalized across different social spheres? Does it match the empirical realities of social order in today's advanced societies? Does the panoptic yield a complete picture of the origins and nature of surveillance?

The Panopticon from Bentham to Foucault

Bentham published his plan for the Panopticon penitentiary in 1791. Essentially, it was for a building on a semi-circular pattern with an 'inspection lodge' at the centre and cells around the perimeter. Prisoners, who in the original plan would be in individual cells, were clearly open to the gaze of the guards, or 'inspectors' but the same was not true of the view the other way. By a carefully contrived system of lighting and the use of wooden blinds, officials would be invisible to the inmates. Control was to be maintained by the constant sense that prisoners were watched by unseen eyes. There was nowhere to hide, to be private. Not knowing whether or not they were watched, but obliged to assume that they were, obedience was the prisoners' only rational option. Hence Bentham's Greek-based neologism; the Panopticon, or all-seeing place (Bentham, 1843).

The Panopticon was to be a model prison, a new departure, a watershed in the control of deviance and a novel means of social discipline. Bentham invested more time and energy in this than any other project – and, as

Gertrude Himmelfarb observes, 'mourned its failure more passionately' (Himmelfarb, 1968: 32). He saw in it 'a great and new invented instrument of government' and believed the panoptic principle held promise of 'the only effective instrument of reformative management.' In a closing eulogy, that he later repeated in the preface, he made the famous claim,

> 'Morals reformed – health preserved – industry invigorated – instruction diffused – public burthens lightened – Economy seated, as it were, upon a rock – the gordian knot of the Poor Laws not cut, but untied – all by a simple idea in Architecture!'
> (Bentham, 1843: 39)

Bentham's apparently utopian enthusiasm for the Panopticon had personal, political and cultural origins. Personally, he hoped to reap financial benefit from an entrepreneurial stake in the project, and to raise his status profile from being its first director. Politically, the Panopticon promised a local, non-religious reform over against the Evangelical and transportation-to-Australia alternatives currently on offer. And culturally, the Panopticon epitomised the kind of 'social physics' so popular with the *philosophes* of his day. It neatly translated La Mettrie's *L'Homme Machine* into an architectural reality.[1]

Ironically, while it appears that no prison was ever built exactly along the lines Bentham had in mind, and he certainly failed to persuade the British government to invest in it, the principles embodied in the Panopticon were to have a widespread influence. The key principle was inspection, though inspection of a specific kind. Bentham's Panopticon represented a secular parody of divine omniscience and the observer was also, like God, invisible. Thus,

> '... the more constantly the persons to be inspected are under the eyes of the persons who should inspect them, the more perfectly will the purpose of the establishment be attained.
> (Bentham, 1843: 40)

And if such constant supervision proves impossible, prisoners should be given the *impression* that the gaze is unwavering.

Bentham's innovation, then, was not just to inspect, or even to ensure that the gaze is asymmetrical, but to use uncertainty as a means of subordination. The asymmetrical gaze created uncertainty which in turn produced surrender. Asymmetrical surveillance joined the whole modern project of destroying the certainties of alternative powers, wherever they still lurked (see Bauman 1988b, 1991). Which is why the Panopticon *principles* were so significant. The question is, are they still so?

The inspection principle suited other purposes than prisons, according to Bentham. Of course they did! Indeed, he got the original idea of the Panopticon from his brother's workshop in Russia. And he advertised the virtues of the panoptic as being appropriate for any context in which supervision was required: for

> '... punishing the incorrigible, guarding the insane, reforming the vicious, confining the suspected, employing the idle, maintaining the helpless, curing the sick, instructing the willing in any branch of industry, or training the rising race in the path of education'.
> (Bentham, 1843: 40)

As we shall see, Foucault argues that panoptic control has indeed become significant in many of these spheres.

Two other principles attached to the panoptic in the specific context of the penitentiary. One was the 'solitude' or isolation of inmates, the other, allowing the prison to be run as a private enterprise by outside contractors. Solitude would extend even to having private toilets for prisoners, and to holding chapel services from a central position above the inspection lodge, without prisoners moving from their cells. Inmates were to be atomised, secluded. As for running the prison by contract, this would possibly enable profit to be made and prison governors to be held in unaccustomed esteem.

Bentham cheerfully defended his Panopticon from any misplaced liberal attack. Might it be thought 'despotic,' or might the result of 'this high-wrought contrivance ... be constructing a set of *machines* under the similitude of *men*?' (Bentham, 1843: 64). Let people think so if they wish. Such criticisms miss the point, namely, 'would happiness be most likely to be increased or decreased by this discipline?' Here is control, and clean control at that. Much better, he commented, than something like Addison's – bizarre-sounding – proposal to 'try virginity with lions'. 'There you saw blood and uncertainty: here you see certainty without blood' (Bentham, 1843: 64). Of course, uncertainty still exists for those subjected to the Panopticon regime. Indeed, the 'machine' depends on it. Certainty resides in the system, and, one might add, with the inspector, the one 'in the know'.

This kind of certainty, sought by Bentham in the Panopticon, epitomises for Foucault the social disciplines of modernity. Whereas in earlier times punishment is public and brutal, modernity introduced clean and rational forms of social control. The unruly crowd is rendered manageable; no plots of escape from prison, no danger of contagion if they are patients, no mutual violence if they are mad, no chatter if schoolchildren and no disorders or coalitions if workers. The crowd is replaced by a 'collection of separated individualities' (Foucault, 1979: 201). As Foucault says, Bentham made 'visibility a trap'.

In the following important quotation Foucault summarises his understanding of the major effect of the Panopticon:

to induce in the inmate a state of conscious and permanent visibility that assures the automatic functioning of power. So to arrange things that the surveillance is permanent in its effects, even if it is discontinuous in its action; that the perfection of power should tend to render its actual exercise unnecessary; that this architectural apparatus should be a machine for creating and sustaining a power relation independent of the person who exercises it; in short, that the inmates should be caught up in a power situation of which they themselves are the bearers.

(Foucault, 1979: 201)

In the Panopticon discipline crossed what Foucault calls a 'disciplinary threshold' in which the 'formation of knowledge and the increase of power regularly reinforce each other in a circular process' (Foucault, 1979: 204). Older, more costly and violent forms of power fell into disuse and were superseded by 'a subtle, calculated technology of subjection' (Foucault, 1979: 221).

Sociology is indebted to Foucault for his theory of surveillance, touching as it does on both aspects of its power; the accumulation of information and the direct supervision of subordinates. The former is found in the detailed files held on each Panopticon inmate, the latter in the architectural potential of the building itself. Acknowledging Foucault's contribution, Anthony Giddens observes that in modern times 'disciplinary power' is characterised by 'new modes of regularizing activities in time-space' (Giddens, 1985: 183). Observation – metaphorically if not literally[2] – is central to these modes, and thus the Panopticon epitomises such disciplinary power.

However, Foucault also insists that this kind of disciplinary power is typically present throughout the institutions of modernity, in all kinds of administrative contexts. 'Is it surprising', asks Foucault rhetorically,

'that the cellular prison, with its regular chronologies, forced labour, its authorities of surveillance and registration, its experts in normality ... should have become the modern instrument of penality?'

But not only that, he goes on;

'Is it surprising that prisons resemble factories, schools, barracks, hospitals, which all resemble prisons?'.

(Foucault, 1979: 228)

What for Bentham was an aspiration is for Foucault a social reality – the panoptic principle diffusing different institutions. This assumption, often questioned within the sociology of administrative power, must be re-addressed in the context of electronic surveillance.[3]

Curiously enough, Foucault himself seems to have made no comments about the relevance of panoptic discipline to the ways that administrative power has been enlarged and enhanced by computers especially since the 1960s. Yet surely we see here nothing less than the near-perfection of the principle of discipline by invisible inspection via information-gathering. Or do we? As we noted above, today no shortage exists of social analysts prepared to complete Foucault by making the connections explicit. Thus we turn next to explore the extent of that link; may we think of electronic surveillance as panoptic power?

Electronic surveillance: panoptic power?

In what ways, and in what contexts, might electronic surveillance display panoptic features? No consensus exists about either question. Different analysts focus on different aspects of panopticism that reappear or are reinforced by computers: the invisibility of the 'inspection', its automatic character, the involvement of subjects in their own surveillance and so on. Equally, different analysts emphasize different spheres of operation of the putative panopticon: in workplace organization and especially, electronic monitoring, in criminal records and policing, in consumer behaviour and transactions and in the myriad administrative activities of the state.

In order to obtain some analytical purchase on the question of electronic panopticism, this section of the paper makes use of Giddens's distinction between two major axes of surveillance. He proposes that sociology consider two levels: First, surveillance is the accumulation of coded information, seen in what he calls the 'internal pacification' of nation-states. This is bound up with the growth of bureaucratic administration, defence, and policing. Secondly, surveillance refers to the direct monitoring of subordinates within the capitalistic workplace that has become the key to management in the twentieth century (Giddens, 1985: 14–15, 172f.).

Giddens admits that the two senses of surveillance belong quite closely together. Indeed, only thought of together can the twin processes of surveillance illuminate the historical association of the capitalistic labour contract with the state monopoly of violence. Still, he maintains that they should be analytically distinct. We shall begin by following this distinction, and respecting it, looking first at the treatment of criminality and deviance as a central aspect of 'state' surveillance. Secondly, we shall examine the putative panopticism of capitalistic situations, starting with the workplace. However, this may oblige us to rethink the Giddens distinction, for two reasons: One, capitalism in the late twentieth century focuses at least as much 'management' attention on the marketplace as the workplace. Two, the application of information technologies may be encouraging a convergence between different surveillance activities.

1. Internal pacification

The persistence of panoptic principles in contemporary society has been noted both by those studying general trends in social control – such as Stanley Cohen – and by others examining specific practices involving new technology and policing. Cohen, for instance, investigating the shift towards crime control 'in the community' (inclusivist, as opposed to exclusionary) notes the ways that panoptic ideas are present in methods of 'technological incapacitation' (Cohen, 1985: 222). Radio telemetry, or electronic tagging allows relatively minor offenders to live 'freely' at home, or even to go to work while wearing a computerized device on the ankle. This tag involuntarily obliges him or her to remain in touch with some central control. Cohen relates this to the panoptic in that the wearer is (potentially) constantly supervised, participates in the process, but cannot verify it.

Gary Marx's analysis of American undercover policy work takes this much further, noting numerous ways in which electronic technologies portend what he calls a 'new surveillance'. They transcend darkness, distance and time, are invisible (or low visibility), involuntary, capital rather than labour intensive, involve decentralized self-policing, introduce suspicion of whole categories of persons rather than targeting specific individuals, and are both more intensive and extensive (Marx, 1988: 207f.). He sees the state's traditional monopoly over the means of violence giving way to new controls; manipulation not coercion, computer chips not prison bars, remote and invisible tethers, not handcuffs or straitjackets. He cautions that these panoptic shifts may be 'diffusing into the society at large' (Marx, 1988: 220).

In another American study, Diana Gordon subjects the National Crime Information Center (NCIC) to analysis as a panoptic 'machinery of power' (Gordon, 1986).[4] Her central concern is simply expressed:

> 'With the national computerized system, the entire function of crime-control, not just the prison, becomes a "panoptic schema", with the record a surrogate for the inmate and all of law enforcement as warden'.
>
> (Gordon, 1986: 487)

Gordon is at pains to argue that the presence of panoptic tendencies spells dangers often unperceived by those working closest to the NCIC. Certain social structural changes may be occurring, she suggests, and therefore it is mistaken to see the issue as merely one of infringing civil liberties. For instance, in many states at least a third of criminal record requests are for non-criminal purposes, above all employment and licensing. As with Marx, Gordon believes that the effects are societal: 'And then we are all enclosed in an electronic Panopticon' (Gordon, 1986: 487).

The distinctions between criminal records databases and more general computerized systems for government administration have become increasingly blurred over the past few decades, especially as computer-matching has become a more widespread practice. This refers to the linking of records from different databases to track offenders or to limit abuse, such as tax evasion or welfare fraud. Employment records may be checked, for example, to prevent welfare claims being made by people receiving salaries (see Reichman, 1987, Information and Privacy Commissioner, 1991).

In an article which claims that modern surveillance systems derive from the Panopticon, Oscar Gandy suggests several other ways that new technologies extend its reach within a government context (Gandy, 1989). Apart from the massive databases of the Department of Defense, the Central Intelligence Agency, the National Security Agency and the Federal Bureau of Investigation, Internal Revenue is a major collector of personal data, used to identify nonreporters and underreporters. Political parties also seek to strengthen their position by using computerized surveillance methods to affect public opinion (see also Meadow, 1985, Weiss, 1988).

2. Control within capitalism

The debate over whether or not the adoption of new technologies represents intensified workplace control within capitalism is complex and inconclusive. Shoshana Zuboff's ethnography, *In the age of the smart machine* takes the view that computers in the workplace have a transformative capacity. Paralleling authority as the 'spiritual basis of power' she examines technique as the 'material basis of power'. The key to contemporary management technique, she argues, is panopticism, enabled by the use of new technologies.

The extremely precise computer systems of today's organizations permit minute monitoring of events and performances within the workplace. At one of the workplaces investigated by Zuboff, a highly automated pulp mill, a small explosion occurred in the early hours of the morning. By scrutinizing the 'Overview System', a bird's eye view of the whole operation, constantly recorded at five-second intervals, management could determine the exact cause of the accident; equipment failure, poor decisionmaking, or a sleepy operator? (Zuboff, 1988: 315–317). Workers at such sites are thus highly transparent to management even in the apparently small details of day-to-day routine. This heightened visibility, also noted by researchers looking at computerization in much smaller contexts such as restaurants and taxicab companies (Rule and Attewell, 1989) Zuboff connects with the panoptic.

Other aspects of panoptic power are clearly visible in Zuboff's account of the computerized workplace. In particular, she discusses the allure of panopticism for management, which – neatly echoing Bentham – is the 'promise of certain knowledge'. Increased reliance upon the 'facts' produced by the computer systems generates new management styles, in her account. Employee performance appears as 'objective' data, which often correlates with another panoptic feature, the certainty of punishment. Apparently, the firing process tends to be shortened from around a year from the start of the dispute to something much more immediate (Zuboff, 1988: 326).

Operators within the ubiquitous digital 'gaze' of such computer systems, and without the more familiar face-to-face relationships with superiors may seek modes of resistance, but compliance appears more common. Information systems 'can transmit the presence of the omniscient observer and so induce compliance without the messy conflict-prone exertions of reciprocal relations' (Zuboff, 1988: 323). Zuboff comments that in workplaces where workers as well as management had access to the personal data collected on the systems, 'anticipatory conformity' was exhibited, showing that the standards of management had been internalized by workers. This gain seems to be a case of Foucault's 'normalizing discipline' of the panoptic.

Interestingly enough, Zuboff does not try to generalize her findings to a societal level, she sees no need to. For her, the transformations within the workplace are striking enough. Her modesty may be wise. Others, however, have argued that some of the kinds of management strategies made possible by the use of information technology are now being applied in the marketplace as well as in the workplace. In this way, it is suggested, the panoptic power of surveillance spills over into society at large, only now the vehicle is commercial organization, not government administration.

The link is made directly by Frank Webster and Kevin Robins, who argue that information technologies facilitate the massive extension of Taylorist principles of scientific management from the realm of production into the realm of consumption. As they say,

> '"Teleshopping", global and targetted advertizing, and electronic market research surveillance, all combine to establish a more "efficient" network marketplace'.
>
> (Webster and Robins, 1989)

In this case surveillance is accomplished by means of gathering transactional information (see Burnham, 1983) such as itemized telephone bills, credit card exchanges and bank withdrawals. This is Mosco's 'social management' or what Gandy calls the 'panoptic sort'. This

> ... 'sort refers to the all-seeing technology of market segmentation, where all available information is potentially useful in constructing a profile and assigning [sorting] an individual to a particular classification'.
>
> (1991: 20)

As with the electronic extension of criminal records systems mentioned above, social management is the springboard for considering society itself as panoptic. 'On the basis of the "information revolution"', assert Robins and Webster, 'not just the prison or the factory, but the social totality comes to function as a hierarchical and disciplinary Panoptic machine' (1988: 72). The so-called wired city renders consumers visible to unverifiable observers by means of their purchases, preferences and credit ratings. Private, sequestered, decentralized activities, the mundane routines of everyday life are as it were in view, continuously and automatically.

Following Foucault, Webster and Robins point to no single power source, although the capitalist system of discipline is what they see being panoptically augmented. There is, they say, 'no single omniscient inspective force'. Nonetheless, 'society as a whole comes to function as a giant panoptic mechanism' in which, to pursue the analogy, hapless consumers find themselves in atomized – designer? – cells at the periphery. More optimistically, Gandy sees signs of consumer revolt surfacing to counteract perceived threats of computerized classifications (1991: 16).

This picture is very similar to one painted, in richer Foucaldian colours, by Mark Poster. For him the world of consumer surveillance amounts to a 'Superpanopticon' (1989: 122) because the panoptic now has no technical limitations. The Panopticon was invented for a new industrial capitalist society. Today the 'population participates in its own self-constitution as subjects in the normalizing gaze of the Superpanopticon' (Poster, 1990: 97). Poster's analysis occurs in the context of a study of the 'mode of information' which, he explains, 'designates social relations mediated by electronic communications systems which constitute new patterns of language' (1989: 123).

The technology of power in Poster's Superpanopticon does two things. It imposes a norm, disciplining its subjects to participate by filling forms, giving social insurance numbers, using credit cards. But it also helps to constitute complementary selves for those subjects, the sum, as it were, of their transactions. New individuals are created who bear the same names but who are digitally shorn of their human ambiguities and whose personalities are built artificially from matched data. Artificial they may be, but these computer 'selves' have a part to play in determining the life-chances of their human namesakes. Thus are subjects constituted and deviants defined within the Superpanopticon.

Evaluating electronic Panopticism

It is clear that, for the authors mentioned here at least, the panoptic offers a powerful and compelling metaphor for understanding electronic surveillance. The prison-like society, where invisible observers track our digital footprints does indeed seem panoptic. Bentham would surely smile wryly if he saw us complying with institutional norms as we use barcoded library books or note telephone caller IDs before accepting a call. The familiar distinctions between public and private life dissolve as both government and corporation ignore old thresholds, garnering personal data of the most mundane and intimate kinds.

Beyond the metaphor, a model of power also lies in the concept of the panoptic. The normalizing discipline, the exaggerated visibility of the subject, the unverifiability of observation, the subject as bearer of surveillance, the quest for factual certainty, all are important aspects of the panoptic as model of power. The question is, to what extent are all these necessarily present in each electronic surveillance context? Would the claim be sociologically warranted that electronic surveillance is panoptic power?

To answer this question satisfactorily, three others must be addressed. First, *can the panoptic be generalized over different social spheres?* From the above discussion it is evident that analysts using the panoptic image think of electronic surveillance as a process that spills over conventional social – and thus sociological – boundaries. Diana Gordon remarks that because diverse databases, found in government and commercial organizations, are enabled to 'talk' with each other, crime control affects all of us: 'And then we are all enclosed in an electronic Panopticon'. Robins and Webster, likewise, focus attention on ways that management styles developed in the workplace now encroach electronically on the daily domestic lives of consumers. For them, this is one crucial factor that makes the Panopticon an appropriate 'central figure for understanding the modalities of power in the "information society"' (1988: 62).

Electronic technologies do seem to facilitate convergence of practices over different and once-distinct institutional areas. Zuboff notes that within the workplace alone older divisions are fading as information technology is applied. 'Continuous process' and 'discrete parts' manufacturing, which developed separately to address different problems of production now find work-tasks and work-organization becoming more alike with the coming of computer integrated manufacturing (1988: 415–422). Again, similar techniques are used for matching disparate data to target tax-evaders within government administration as to target potential consumers with income-and-lifestyle-specific direct mailing (eg Stix, 1991: 152–153). Incidentally, members of both groups are frequently unaware that they are under surveillance.

For Foucault, the Panopticon epitomises the disciplinary network of social relations seen not only in prisons but in the capitalist enterprise, military organization and in a multitude of state-run institutions. It does not wait for offenders to act, but classifies and situates before any 'event', producing not 'good citizens' but a 'docile deviant population' (see Dandeker, 1990: 27). Despite Foucault's opposition to what he calls 'totalizing', he frequently gives the impression that the panoptic prison has been made redundant through the development of a disciplinary network on a societal scale: the Panopticon-at-large. Analysts of electronic surveillance may be forgiven for picking up a relatively undifferentiated view of power from Foucault.

This view has not been without critics, among them Anthony Giddens. The nub of Giddens' criticism is that, one, we must differentiate between the means of economic production and the political means of administration and two, that prisons are qualitatively different from other social organizations. With respect to the first, the fact that, during the nineteenth century, locales were established in which regular observation of activities could take place with the purpose of control makes the workplace and the state similar, but not the same. According to Giddens, workplace subordination rests on a hidden exploitative relation, unlike the nation state, which ultimately depends for its power on a monopoly of the 'means of violence'.

Regarding the nature of prisons, Giddens points out that inmates have to spend all their time there; they are what Goffman calls 'total institutions'. Contrast schools, business firms or other civil organizations, where only a part of the day is spent, and where disciplinary power is far more diffuse. Thus for Giddens,

> 'Foucault is mistaken in so far as he regards "maximized" disciplinary power of this sort [i.e. panoptic] as expressing the general nature of administrative power within the modern state.
> (1985: 185)

Giddens's critique is well taken, at least insofar as it touches on preelectronic features of modern social institutions. Foucault, and his followers, do exaggerate the centrality of the panoptic within the disciplinary apparatus of modernity. But perhaps just as Foucault was making a rhetorical point over against those who would stress the humanitarian motives in founding early prisons, so today those who would characterize electronic surveillance as panoptic perhaps do so in a *salutary* fashion, over against others who regard it as benign, or who believe that privacy laws offer adequate social safeguards for it or personal protection from it. Electronic technologies *do* seem to diffuse surveillance throughout society in new ways.

As we have seen, Giddens's neat theoretical distinctions do begin to blur when confronted with the realities of contemporary electronic surveillance. Increasingly, disciplinary networks *do* connect employment with civil status or consumption with policing. Moreover, the very processes of time-space distanciation so ably analysed by Giddens may well be undergoing further alteration. Once, this characteristically modern geographical and temporal 'stretching' of social relations was facilitated by changes in transport and communications (see Innis, 1951). Now, the advent of information technologies enables novel configurations. The worker could once leave the capitalistic enterprise behind at the factory gates. Now it follows her home as a consumer. The same home was once regarded as a private haven. The computerized 'king' may now enter the 'Englishman's home' at will. Indeed, the householder carries him in, disguised as a social insurance number. The distinctions discussed by Giddens still retain their salience for much of society today, one suspects. It is an empirical question how long they will continue to do so in the same ways as surveillance is progressively augmented by information technology.

Even if new technology does facilitate a novel penetration of the mundane routines of everyday life, however, it is not clear that this in itself augments a general societal panopticism. For Bentham and the other bearers of modernity have in a sense done their work. Citizens of the advanced societies are already expert-dependent in a radical sense. We cannot but rely upon those 'in the know', the experts (Bauman, 1991; Giddens, 1990).

Equally, electronic panopticism may turn out to be a vestigial residue of modernity's – Benthamite – utopian hunger for certitude. The ghost of the unseen inspector may continue to haunt specific milieux, such as Zuboff's pulp mill, courtesy of computer-power. (Even here, we might be forgiven for wondering whether the panoptic metaphor is allowed too free an explanatory rein: do managers really seek 'total control'? Perhaps they just want efficiency, of which increased worker-transparency is a spin-off.) It may even contribute to new forms of categorizing subjects across different spheres and thus serve to sustain social control, but this still does not add up to the more apocalyptic vision of a societal Panopticon. Nonetheless, even such 'panoptic residues' raise significant sociological queries.

This discussion of historical changes and of consumerism in particular brings me to my second question; *does the panoptic do justice to the realities of social order in capitalist societies today?* Numerous plausible answers have been given to the classic sociological query of how social order is maintained. To be worth anything, the answer must connect directly with contemporary realities.

In this section I draw upon the idea that consumerism contributes heavily to the maintenance of social order today. Zygmunt Bauman, for instance, argues that contemporary social life is characterized increasingly by a duality between what he refers to as the 'seduced' and the 'repressed'. Social integration is achieved above all by means of market dependency. Social skills and economic capacity entitle the majority to consume; they are the seduced. The minority, the new poor (or what others have dubbed the underclass)[5] are subjected to tight normative regulation, not least of a panoptic variety. In Bauman's view this immediately poses a further problem for the panoptic; if society is becoming more prison-like, then why is modern life for the majority not more unpleasant? (Bauman, 1987; 1988a; 1988b).

If we grant that social order and integration are achieved through consumerism, and that only deviants – flawed consumers – experience old-fashioned panoptic discipline[6] what are we to make of the apparent panopticism of consumer surveillance? One difficulty is that the nature of such surveillance has still to be clarified. Power relations may be present in commercial surveillance, but power to do what, exactly? Poster's 'Superpanopticon' is said to 'impose norms', but does it? Surely all it can do is supply a structure, but even then, it is one within which real choices still are made (see Featherstone, 1987).

It may turn out that the clues to this puzzle lie with Jean Baudrillard's advice to 'forget Foucault' (1987). For Baudrillard, Foucault's mistake is to ignore the *simulations* of power seen in the proliferating media of electronic communications and information technologies. Perhaps an alternative to the panoptic lies here (Kellner, 1989: 133)? The data-images constructed by corporations are indeed mere *simulacra*, and they only become apparent to their 'real' subjects when junk mail or unsolicited telephone marketers appear. If so, Poster's Superpanopticon refers to a 'virtual world' of data images, where discipline is equally 'virtual' unless the real subject deviates or a computer error occurs.

Another way forward is to stay with Foucault, but to seek nuance within his theory. The disciplines that shape most of our lives may well exhibit some panoptic features, but are they all as focused and carceral as some disciples of Foucault would have us believe? In an article (that has the intrinsic attraction of including a sociology of Disneyworld) Clifford Shearing and Philip Stenning highlight an important distinction in Foucault's theory of discipline. They point out that Foucault worked with both a generic concept of discipline as well as (the more fully worked out) 'historically specific examination of it in the context of carceral punishment' (Shearing and Stenning, 1985: 336).

Foucault's 'physics or anatomy of power, technology' represents the generic mode of discipline, of which the panoptic is merely a type. Discipline is dispersed throughout the micro-relations that constitute society. It is not, for Foucault, 'from above', like monarchical power. This embeddedness of power, say Shearing and Stenning, is what makes the panopticon the exemplar of discipline. They go on to contrast the *moral* discipline of carceral punishment – for example in the Panopticon – with the merely *instrumental* discipline manifest in other locations such as factories, hospitals or workshops. Their own investigations of private security and control companies in Canada reveal a discipline that is strictly instrumental, not moral in basis. As they say, 'Within private control the instrumental language of profit and loss replaces the moral language of criminal justice' (1985: 339–40).

The distinction between moral 'soul-training' of carceral discipline and the instrumental discipline of private security systems is a useful one (even though it seems to me that again it takes us well beyond the familiar Foucault of the panoptic). Shearing and Stenning generalize further from the instrumental model, via a brief case-study of Disneyworld, to what they see as 'the dominant force in social control'. Less like Orwell's nightmare, much more like Huxley's *Brave New World*, here is consensually-based control in which 'people are seduced into conformity by the pleasures offered by the drug "soma" rather than coerced into compliance by threat of Big Brother, just as people are today seduced to conform by the pleasures of consuming the goods that corporate power has to offer' (347, see also Mugford and O'Malley, 1991).

Here then is a plausible answer to the question about the reproduction of social order in the capitalist societies of the late twentieth century. Paradoxically, the panoptic may not be an appropriate image on account of its capacity to make 'society like a prison' so much as because of the embedded nature of its discipline.[7] However, this does not mean that we can safely forget the panoptic. Carceral discipline, perhaps relating to residual moral categories, may well still be experienced by Bauman's 'repressed'. But, as I stressed above, this is a residual not a general, let alone an expanding category. It is here that we find most signs of the panoptic as it appears in most of Foucault's *Discipline and Punish*. But as the repressed are frequently, as Bauman puts it, 'flawed consumers', a question arises as to how far even the normative discipline meted out to them is actually moral and not merely instrumental. The norms from which they deviate are essentially rooted in consumer skills. It is participation in society as consumers from which they are primarily excluded, through lack of credit-worthiness, welfare dependence, and so on.

As it could be argued that the application of information technology encourages the extension of *instrumental* discipline (see, eg Zuboff, 1988: chapter nine), the question of whether this constitutes a dominant trend becomes even more pressing. The Lyotardian lament for the loss of the (moral) 'metanarratives' of modernity and their replacement with the (instrumental) categories of computerized control (Lyotard, 1984) may become an increasingly important site for sociological investigation.

If Bauman is right about the dual system of control, then as he says, this raises further questions about political power, democratic institutions and citizenship. This brings us to the last question I wish to address regarding the panoptic qualities of electronic surveillance. *Does the panoptic yield a complete picture of the origins and nature of surveillance?* Of course, this question has already received a partial – and negative – answer, but now I want to focus on the ambiguities or paradoxes of surveillance, and on what Giddens calls the 'dialectic of control' (1985: 10–11). This also involves our looking not only at where Foucault obtained his conception of the panoptic, but where Bentham got it from in the first place.

We may grant that Foucault theorized a more general view of disciplinary power than that embodied in the Panopticon. But he certainly gave the impression that citizens of modern nation-states find themselves increasingly to be the subjects of centralized carceral discipline. And, for someone who spent precious little time considering how the warm 'bodies' of which he wrote might *respond* to such discipline, he made a curious closing comment in *Discipline and Punish:*

> 'In this central and centralized humanity, the effect and instrument of complex power relations, bodies and forces subjected by multiple forces of "incarceration", objects for discourses that are themselves elements for this strategy, we must hear the distant roar of battle'.
> [my emphasis] (Foucault, 1979: 308)

It is not clear that the roar of battle was as loud as Foucault predicted, or so distant. If the 'battle' is one of revolt against discipline, then this assumes, further, that discipline is viewed by subjects in an entirely negative light, and that there would be a considerable time-lag between the imposition of discipline and the battle. However, one could equally argue, on sound historical grounds, that changing processes of social control always occur in the context of struggle and that the contest is confused, ambiguous and recursive.

Abercrombie, Hill and Turner, in their study of *Sovereign Individuals of Capitalism,* spotlight what they call the 'Foucault paradox'. The much-prized achievement of (welfare) citizenship in modern societies could 'only become effective if accompanied by the growth of a state bureaucracy capable of enforcing these rights in practice' (1986: 179, see also Shils, 1975). In other words, the burgeoning panopticism of nineteenth century institutions emerged hand-in-hand with collective discourses of social rights. They bore a reciprocal relation to one another. Recognizing people as unique identities to ensure that each is treated equally simultaneously makes their control that much easier.

Giddens generalizes this phenomenon in his 'dialectic of control', in which all strategies of control 'call forth counter-strategies on the part of subordinates' (1985: 11). Of course, Giddens hangs onto human agency here, a premiss abandoned in Foucault's work. Giddens sees the build-up of administrative power as accompanied by expanding reciprocal relations between rules and ruled. Equally, he regards modern management practices as involving reciprocity. Strategies and counter-strategies are in constant tension with each other. In this account, Foucault's battle is neither distant nor, necessarily, roaring.

However, a further question raised by this paper remains; does surveillance alter its character as information technology facilitates its further reach and efficiency? If, as I have suggested, the answer is, yes, then how might this affect the dialectic of control, the Foucault paradox? Palpable social and personal benefits undoubtedly accompany the use of information technology in surveillance systems. Gary Marx, for instance, acknowledges that it is effective in apprehending criminals, detecting corruption, preventing crime, verifying arms control and monitoring health (1988: 220). Users of credit cards find them convenient and reliable; many are grateful for the ease with which shopping, banking or travel can be accomplished using computer-based equipment. We could go on. Whatever the deeper consequences for the quality of life, none of the above is generally regarded as negative. Similarly, with respect to government databanks, the principle of equal treatment, noted by Abercrombie, still obtains, information technology notwithstanding. Indeed, some evidence indicates that many *prefer* the enhanced anonymity of electronic processing of their personal details.

Fears and anxieties about electronic surveillance, and critiques of or resistance to it arise from specific aspects of its panoptic character. Opponents of the new surveillance deplore the fact that it depends upon categories, that no knowledge of the individual is required, that it is increasingly instrumental, that areas of personal life once thought to be inviolably private are invaded and that it effectively erodes personal and democratic freedoms. Foucault offers little help at this point, not only because he did not comment on computer technologies, but more profoundly, because he never examined the basis of his own 'moral outrage' against the Panopticon (see Jay, 1989).

Critics of electronic surveillance could do worse than to turn again to Bentham to define the object of their ire. After all, as Foucault rightly observed, Bentham's work does indeed mark a watershed in the understanding of social control. In the Panopticon the issues are sharply etched. What contemporary commentators object to is both prefigured in the Panopticon and emphasized by the electronic. Bentham, following the Cartesian logic that regarded human beings as machines whose activities could be measured and controlled, wrote impersonality, abstract classification and automatic power into the Panopticon. Precisely these features reappear, now digitally inscribed and intensified, in the new, computer-run surveillance.

Bentham's project was nothing less than a secular utopia, a model society-in-miniature, cut loose from any theological moorings that might complicate his claim that the Panopticon stood as the solution par excellence to the human condition (see Strub, 1989, Crimmons, 1986). In the crucial principle of inspection he explicitly parodied the doctrine of divine omniscience, taking it to be an unsurpassed means of moral control. What he conveniently ignored, though, was the *personal* character of knowledge present even in the biblical quotations with which he ironically epigraphed his text. Consideration of such themes would yield fresh perspectives on the mutuality of knowing, 'watching over' for care as well as control, and 'overlooking' as forgiveness as well as monitoring. Hardly surprising, then, that the Panopticon excludes the personal and slips almost imperceptibly from moral to instrumental categories. It is equally unremarkable, given this backdrop, that today's actors in the surveillance drama have started to focus their criticisms on these aspects of electronic panopticism – perceived control by inspection and impersonal categorization.

While further implications of this analysis lie beyond the scope of this paper, what seems clear is that Foucault's understanding of the panoptic, though penetrating, is also found wanting. On the other hand, a fuller understanding of the Panopticon itself does yield both insight into the peculiarly modern varieties of surveillance and important clues as to what contemporary analysts and critics regret in the rise of *electronic* surveillance. How far electronic panopticism will develop – in the spheres where it is still found – before the dialectic of control starts to swing more decisively in favour of its subjects, and what difference *can* be made by those subjects, is one of the most interesting and important questions for current critical social analysis.[8] We shall have to look beyond Foucault, however, for the framing of a coherent critique.

Conclusion

The concept of an electronic Panopticon is appearing with increasing frequency in sociological analyses of computer-based surveillance. That it has metaphorical power is not in doubt. The question is, how far can the Panopticon serve as an explanatory concept? Our analysis of various studies using the Panopticon concept suggests three things:

One, electronic surveillance does exhibit panoptic qualities in certain settings. Above all, it still contributes to social control via invisible inspection and categorization. This is especially striking in the case of consumer surveillance, which has been expanding exponentially over the past decade and which is increasingly articulated with other kinds of surveillance. This in turn raises questions about the neat distinctions between 'data-gathering' and 'direct supervision', categories derived from pre-electronic times. However, we must still ask what sort of power lies here? And what are the connections between the virtual world of computer databases and civil society?

Two, seeing the Panopticon in a 'totalizing' way – as Foucault did, despite himself – deflects attention from other modes of social ordering. Those utilizing the concept have often failed to see how the Panopticon had already 'done its work', contributing to modernity's elimination of alternative powers and the creation of dependency, before being electronically enhanced. If it is correct to see consumerism as creating social order, providing integration, identity and the grounds of social inclusion, then burgeoning electronic surveillance must be analysed in relation to that.

Three, Foucault's failure to admit any basis for 'outrage' against the Panopticon inhibits the development of a properly critical theory of contemporary surveillance. The panoptic paradigm can only generate bad news. Seeing the Panopticon as a secular parody of divine omniscience, however, provides some crucial components of critique. The Panopticon was not a mere product of Bentham's disturbed imagination. It was a deliberately distorted inversion of an alternative social reality. Too few social theorists take us beyond the fears, threats, suspicion and constraints of the Panopticon to consider the place of love, care, trust and enabling within surveillance systems. Now, how far the use of electronic technologies tends to eliminate the latter is a question worth pursuing. Elsewhere.

Acknowledgements

I am grateful for comments on earlier drafts of this paper from Zygmunt Bauman, Gary Marx, Gayle MacDonald, Frank Pearce, Bob Pike and Laureen Snider.

Notes

1. Bentham's immodest ambitions for the Panopticon were connected with its role within contemporary agitation for prison reform in England. On Bentham's hopes of personal gain from involvement in the administration of the Panopticon see Lyon (1991).
2. Even when monitoring occurs via computer files we still use the literary idea of 'seeing' even though this is not literally occurring. Super*vision*, sur*veillance* itself, each have this connotation.
3. The Panopticon may also be seen in relation to other kinds of technique, particularly perhaps that using biotechnology. But the surveillance power of biotechnology depends, nonetheless, upon microelectronics. See Lyon (1992).
4. See also on Canada, Flaherty (1986) and on Britain, Campbell and Connor (1986).
5. The concept of an underclass is bedevilled by controversy, not least because it has been adopted by certain sympathists of both 'left' and 'right' politics. Interestingly, it represents another attempt conceptually to come to grips with an emergent social figuration in which not productivity ('class') but consumption becomes the criterion of participation.
6. Bauman's analysis helps to make good, for example, the work of Bourdieu (1984) which, while illuminating the consumer order, neglects to analyse those excluded from consumption.
7. As well as embeddedness, other features noted by Stenning and Shearing remain significant for the analysis of consumer surveillance: it is preventative, cooperative, non-coercive, consensual, non-carceral, instrumental, and effective.
8. I hint at how this might be provided in (1990). See also Fortner (1986: 1989). Some of the issues are discussed on a philosophical level in Brown (1990).

References

Abercrombie, N., S. Hill and B. Turner, (1986), *Sovereign Individuals of Capitalism*, London: Allen and Unwin. Baudrillard, J., (1987), *Forget Foucault*, New York: Semiotext(e), ET of *Oublier Foucault*, Paris: Éditions Galilée, 1977.
Bauman, Z., (1987), *Legislators and Interpreters*, Cambridge: Polity Press.

Bauman, Z., (1988a), 'Is there a post-modern sociology?' *Theory, Culture and Society* 5 (1): 217–37.
Bauman, Z., (1988b), *Freedom*, Milton Keynes: Open University Press.
Bauman, Z., (1991), *Modernity and Ambivalence*, Cambridge: Polity Press.
Bentham, J., (1843), *Jeremy Bentham: Collected Works* (ed. John Bowring), London.
Bourdieu, P., (1984), *Distinction: A Social Critique of the Judgement of Taste*, Cambridge MA: Harvard University Press.
Brown, G., (1990), *The Information Game: Ethical Issues in a Microchip World*, London and New York: Humanities Press.
Burnham, D., (1983), *The Rise of the Computer State*. New York: Vintage Books.
Campbell, D., and S. Connor, (1986), *On the Record: Computers, Surveillance and Privacy*. London: Michael Joseph.
Cohen, S., (1985), *Visions of Social Control*. New York: Basil Blackwell.
Crimmons, J., (1986), 'Bentham on religion: atheism and the secular society, *Journal of the History of Ideas*, 47: 95–110.
Dandeker, C, (1990), *Surveillance, Power and Modernity*, Cambridge: Polity Press.
Featherstone, M., (1987), 'Lifestyle and consumer culture', *Theory, Culture and Society*, 4: 55–70.
Flaherty, D., (1986), 'Protecting privacy in policy information systems', *University of Toronto Law Journal*, 36: 116–148.
Fortner, R., (1986), 'Physics and metaphysics in an information age', *Communication*, (9): 151–172.
Fortner, R., (1989), 'Privacy is not enough: personhood and high technology', *The Conrad Grehel Review*, Spring: 159–177.
Foucault, M., (1979), *Discipline and Punish*, New York: Vintage Books.
Gandy, O., (1989), 'The surveillance society: information technology and bureaucratic social control', *Journal of Communication*, 39 (3), repr. in M. Siefert et al. (eds). *The Information Gap*, New York: Oxford University Press, 1990: 61–76.
Gandy, O., (1991), 'The anticipatory response: Avoiding the destructive gales of popular resistance', paper from 19th Annual Telecommunications Policy Research Conference, Solomons Island MD, September.
Giddens, A., (1985), *The Nation-State and Violence*, Oxford: Polity Press.
Giddens, A., (1990), *The Consequences of Modernity*, Oxford: Polity Press.
Gordon, D., (1986), 'The electronic panopticon: a case-study of the development of the National Criminal Records System', *Politics and Society*, 15: 483–511.
Himmelfarb, Gertrude, (1968), *Victorian Minds*, New York: Knopf.
Information and Privacy Commissioner, (1991), *Privacy and Computer Matching*, Toronto: Information and Privacy Commissioner/Ontario.
Innis, H. A., (1951), *The Bias of Communication*, Toronto: University of Toronto Press.
Jay, M., (1989), 'In the empire of the gaze: Foucault and the denigration of vision in twentieth century thought', *in* L. Appignanesi, (ed.), *Postmodernism: ICA Documents*, London: Free Association Books.
Kellner, D., (1989), *Jean Baudrillard: From Marxism to Postmodernism and Beyond*, Cambridge: Polity Press.
Kling, R., (1986), 'Struggles for democracy in an information society' *The Information Society* 4 (1/2):
Lyon, D., (1988), *The Information Society: Issues and Illusions*, Oxford: Polity Press.

Lyon, D., (1990), 'Whither shall I flee?: Surveillance, omniscience and normativity in the panopticon', paper from British Sociological Association Theory and Religion Conference, Bristol University, January.

Lyon, D., (1991), 'Bentham's Panopticon: from moral architecture to electronic surveillance', *Queen's Quarterly*, 98 (3).

Lyon, D., (1992), "The New Surveillance: Electronic technologies and the Maximum Security Society', *Crime, Law and Social Change*, 17(2): 159–175.

Lyotard, J.-F., (1984), *The Postmodern Condition*, Manchester: University of Manchester Press.

Marx, G. T., (1985), 'The iron fist in the velvet glove: Totalitarian potentials within democratic structures' in J. F. Short jnr., (ed.), *The Social Fabric*, Beverly Hills: Wage.

Marx, G. T., (1988), *Undercover: Police Surveillance in America*, Berkeley: University of California Press.

Meadow, R. G., (ed.), (1985), *New Communications Technologies in Politics*, Washington DC: Washington Program of the Annenberg School of Communications.

Mosco, Vincent, (1989), *Pay-per Society*, Toronto: Garamond.

Mugford, S. and P. O'Malley, (1991), 'Heroin policy and deficit models' *Crime, Law and Social Change* 15 (1): 19–36.

Poster, M., (1989), *Critical Theory and Poststructuralism: In Search of a Context*, Ithaca: Cornell University Press.

Poster, M., (1990), *The Mode of Information*, Oxford: Polity Press.

Reichman, N., (1987), 'Computer matching: Towards computerized systems of regulation', *Law and Policy*, October: 387–415.

Robins, K. and F. Webster, (1988), 'Cybernetic capitalism: Information, technology and everyday life', *in* V. Mosco and J. Wasko (eds), *The Political Economy of Information*. Madison: University of Wisconsin Press.

Rule, J. and P. Attewell, (1989), 'What do computers do?' *Social Problems*, 36 (3): 225–240.

Shearing, C. and P. Stenning, (1985), 'From the Panopticon to Disneyworld: the development of discipline', *in* A. Doob and E. L. Greenspan (eds), *Perspectives in Criminal Law*, Toronto: Canada Law Books.

Shils, E., (1975), *Center and Periphery: Essays in Macrosociology*. Chicago: University of Chicago press.

Stix, G., (1991), 'Call and tell' *Scientific American*, April: 152–3.

Strub, H., (1989), 'The theory of panoptical control', *The Journal of the History of the Behavioral Sciences*, 25: 40–59.

Webster, F. and K. Robins, (1989), 'Plan and Control: towards a cultural history of the information society', *Theory and Society*, 18.

Weiss, M. J., (1988), *The Clustering of America*, New York: Harper and Row.

Zubboff, S., (1988), *In the Age of the Smart Machine*, New York: Basic Books.

84

THE DISTRIBUTION OF PRIVACY RISKS

Who needs protection?

Charles D. Raab and Colin J. Bennett

Source: *The Information Society* 14(4) (1998): 263–74.

It is commonly accepted that the use of personal information in business and government puts individual privacy at risk. However, little is known about these risks—for instance, whether and how they can be measured, and how they vary across social groups and the sectors in which personal data are used. Unless we can gain a purchase on such issues, our knowledge of the societal effects of information technology and systems will remain deficient, and the ability to make and implement better policies for privacy protection, and perhaps for a more equitable distribution of risk and protection, will remain impaired. The article explores this topic, examining conventional paradigms in data protection, including the one-dimensional view of the "data subject," that inhibit better conceptualizations and practices. It looks at some comparative survey evidence that casts light on the question of the distribution of privacy risks and concerns. It examines theoretical issues in the literature on risk, raising questions about the objectivity and perception of the risk of privacy invasion.

Introduction

This article discusses a relatively neglected topic in the study of information privacy and data protection: the risks posed to privacy by the use of personal information about individuals, the social distribution of these risks, and the ability of laws and practices of data protection systems to ameliorate differentials and thus to promote equality in the distribution of privacy. While threats to information privacy have gained in importance as an issue in the development of an "information society," there is little detailed knowledge about variations in the patterning of privacy and its protection across society. Public policy is therefore less precisely focused than it could be.

An examination of the distribution of privacy risks and protections would not only improve understanding about he effects of information technologies and processes upon society, but might have practical application as well. Privacy advocates and organizations such as Privacy International find it difficult to build coalitions on the very disparate issues to which new surveillance practices give rise. By identifying particularly vulnerable social groups, better knowledge might enhance the protection of their privacy through the activities of general civil liberties organizations or privacy advocates on behalf of such groups, and also affect the political processes through which privacy protection is arbitrated. However, there are many conceptual and empirical difficulties in gaining a purchase on this matter.

Not least of these is the problem of understanding and evaluating risk. Some attempt must be made—if not fully in this article—to come to grips with the way in which hazards are generated by information systems that deal in personal data. This is not only because the concept of risk pervades data protection regulations and rhetoric, and serves as a rationale for the design of protective devices, be they rules, codes of practice, standards, or privacy-enhancing technologies. It is also because the risks associated with the coming of "information society" lend themselves to analysis in terms of social-scientific themes, as Lyon (1994), Gandy (1993), Marx (1988), and others have shown.

The present article explores further some issues that were broached in earlier writing (Raab, 1995).[1] The invisibility of equity issues in data protection is explained and criticized, and the image of the "data subject" is examined with a view to its reconceptualization. In order to gain a closer purchase on the question of distribution, illustrations are cited from the growing body of survey research on privacy, which casts light on public attitudes toward, and knowledge of, privacy risks and privacy protection. The article then looks at the question of risk analysis in order to seek further points of orientation.

Differential risks and data protection

Regulatory bodies, users of personal data, and individual "data subjects" all play both conflictual and mutually reinforcing parts in data protection systems. However, they cannot easily answer the question, "Who gets what data protection?" Even though a principal aim of data protection policy is to safeguard the privacy of individuals, policymakers and official regulators are less able to achieve their objective to the extent that they only imperfectly monitor the effects that their own and others' activity has upon the privacy of those they aim to protect.[2] The strategies and operations of regulatory bodies may therefore be less effective than they could be. Data users are less able to gauge the impact of processing activities upon their clienteles, and to tailor their own compliance with the principles of data protection. For their part, individuals are less able to develop a critical awareness of their relative place in the distribution of privacy protection, and of their relationship to the systems in which their personal information is used. They, along with political actors and privacy advocates, are also less able to judge how well regulators and data users are protecting privacy.

In more academic terms, our knowledge of the privacy effect of information technology on society will remain one-dimensional without a more finely grained understanding of distributions and patterns. It is often believed that both privacy risks and data protection are unevenly spread across social categories. This assumption is open to fruitful hypothesizing and research, but there are few systematic studies to test it, with a view—in part—to informing regulatory policy and strategy. There is little reliable knowledge of whether the privacy of women, for example, is more often invaded than that of men; non-whites than whites; poor than rich; old than young; ill people than healthy; and so on. Similarly, the distribution of protection and safeguards is obscure.

Although such dichotomies are far too simple, impressionistic conventional wisdom can be cited on each side of those lines. For example, because the poor more often come into contact with welfare institutions that collect and use their personal details, it is thought that it is they, rather than the rich, who are more vulnerable to the state's misuse of personal information. State surveillance perhaps reinforces existing social stereotypes and categories (Gandy, 1993). On the other hand, it cannot simply be assumed that the poor have less information privacy, in an absolute sense. Those who are further up on the socioeconomic ladder are more likely to be part of the credit-card economy and to be targeted with considerable precision by direct marketers and the private sector in general, exposing them to risks. The Internet is used disproportionately by young, educated, middle-class males. Is it then this social category that is more vulnerable to the abuses of electronic mail or to the surveillance potential of the World Wide Web? With the likely burgeoning of electronic commerce, in what direction will the social—and global—patterning of risk be changed?

It may be easy to speculate that the market economy tends to produce higher levels of surveillance for the educated middle classes, whereas state institutions are more threatening for the poor, women, gays and lesbians, and so on. However plausible, this is guesswork, and there is no adequate investigation of whether variations reflect differences in the way social categories and groups participate in principal sectors of life, such as work, leisure, consumption, education, health care, public order, etc. Yet it is likely that the recording of sensitive information about HIV/AIDS, enforced subject-access requests for criminal or medical records, and the requirement to provide personal details in exchange for social benefits, consumer credit, or employment expose different sections of the population to different privacy risks, and some more than others. But we cannot yet fully map the dimensions of these disparities, devise policies and practices to deal with them, or evaluate the results of the latter. Such differentials may deny equity and have implications for privacy laws and regulations, data protection agencies, and self-regulating industries. While regulators are pressed to "do something about" mail-order firms, credit-card companies, health services, and others, remedying any structured inegalitarian effects of data collection, processing, or communication is very low on the policy agenda.

In sum, despite a few indications of a substantively differentiated approach, data protection discourse and practice have not generally developed in this direction. Laws are based on a general, procedural application of "fair information principles" to all personal data. The distinctions that are introduced do not clearly or primarily aim at achieving equity; nor have they supplanted the main framework of principles, described later. On the other hand, it is neither conceptually nor empirically easy to understand the social distribution of privacy and privacy protection. As will be shown, some studies and reports move in this direction. However, the difficulty of deriving clear interpretations from their findings reflects the complexities of grappling with different meanings of privacy, varying intersubjective evaluations of risks, and the vagaries of survey research.

The conventional data protection paradigm

Questions concerning the distribution of privacy risks and privacy protection have been obscured by theories and practices that have followed the conventional paradigm for discussions of privacy and data protection systems. The paradigm constructs issues in an adversarial mode—the individual ("data subject") versus the organization ("data user")—within a liberal conception of individual rights (Bennett, 1995). Privacy is seen as the right to be let alone (Warren & Brandeis, 1890) or to control the use of one's information (Westin, 1967). Individuals make claims (or have rights) to the privacy of their personal data against the needs (or rights) of others— typically, organizations—to collect, process, use, and communicate these data. Although some organizations are heavily involved in what is conventionally thought of as surveillance in the narrow sense, such as law-enforcement and order-maintaining agencies, all organizations that use personal data thereby carry out surveillance as construed more widely (Flaherty, 1989).

Writers such as Lyon (1994) and Rule *et al.* (1980) consider that the conventional paradigm merely manages surveillance, but does not stop its gradual spread. This is partly because the paradigm embodies "fair information principles" that are enshrined in the influential Organization for Economic Cooperation and Development (OECD) Guidelines (OECD, 1981) and in the Council of Europe Convention (Council of Europe, 1981), which are reflected in data protection laws everywhere. An approximate paraphrasing is that they require that data be fairly and lawfully obtained and processed; held, used, and disclosed only for lawful purposes; adequate, relevant, and not excessive; accurate and up to date; not held for longer than their purpose requires; held securely; and accessible to the data subject. But even if followed to the letter, these principles may still legitimate massive personal record-keeping systems. This is because they are largely *procedural*, "due process" principles and do not themselves address *substantive* issues and definitions of privacy (Bennett, 1992, 112). They treat all individuals or citizens alike as abstract "data subjects" without regard to categorical or other empirical variations in their exposure to risks, or their fears.

Some systems leave it largely to individuals themselves to pursue complaints and to seek remedies; this is especially so in the United States. On the other hand, many data-protection systems also involve public-policy initiatives to prevent privacy invasions and to strengthen individuals' control through the provision of regulatory machinery with preventative as well as corrective functions. Thus an official regulatory body can be a potentially powerful third player, arbitrating disputes, monitoring and influencing practice, and contributing to public-policy formation regarding applications of privacy-invasive technologies.

But it may be difficult, and indeed illegitimate, for such a body to pursue social-policy goals within the regulatory routines that follow the conventional paradigm, even where the personal values of data-protection officials incline in this direction, supported by research and pressure-group networks. In particular, there is little that would encourage or legitimize the applicability of criteria related to the social distribution of privacy risks, prevention, and remedies. Officials may have to adhere to administrative and legal norms or political expectations that mainly reinforce an unreconstructed, procedural and abstract, version of the paradigm. It could be argued that equity and other substantive goals are best left to the workings of the political process, rather than to the initiatives of regulators. There may be political demands that data protection's main purpose should be to facilitate the commercial or governmental exploitation of personal data. Regulators may thus be enjoined not to become "activists," but to function only in terms of the paradigm's procedural due process, and to seek "balances."

The question of equity is especially important in view of the prevailing doctrine of "balancing" between the privacy interests of data subjects and the information-processing interests and purposes of data users, however ambiguous this doctrine or however opaque the risk "balancing act" might be (Raab, 1993; Bennett, 1995; Adams, 1995). Given the state of what we may call "regulatory intelligence," discussed later, the practical effect of balancing is to pit the supposed against the known, the Identikit data subject against the drawn-from-life portrait of the data user. This gap might even be widening as more people assume "virtual identities" through their use of the Internet and engage in quasi-social interactions through electronic mail, newsgroups, and the World Wide Web.

In a given instance, a balancing regulator needs to judge whether a data subject's rights (or at least, claims) outweigh the interests of the data user, without bringing to bear a range of particular knowledge about the contending parties. This is a difficult judgement, even in the abstract. But in another sense—and this may be especially so when regulators seek to frame preventative policies, or to influence the development of technologies—balancing requires not only a conception of rights and legitimate interests, but some grasp of the distribution of hazards and fears as well. Because privacy rights do not necessarily prevail over other interests, without such knowledge it may be difficult to argue against data users' persuasive demonstration of the known and possibly measurable (or costable) harm to their activities if their use of personal data were restricted. This difficulty is especially likely to arise where government policy favors the maximal development of uses and flows of information by itself and others. Regulatory agencies may have little force in a world of public policy that normally gives much less credence to claims on behalf of information privacy, and in which public concern about privacy is only sporadic, weak, or obscurely expressed.

It is true, however, that existing data-protection systems have, indeed, developed a sense of variable risk, but they construe this in terms of different kinds of *data*, and not of different kinds of *persons*. Thus—despite the valid criticism that *any* data might be sensitive, depending upon the context in which it is used—the explicit recognition that some data are inherently sensitive plays a prominent part in data-protection theory and practice. These data include information revealing racial or ethnic origin, political opinions, religious or philosophical beliefs, trade-unionmembership, or concerning health or sex life. These are the "special categories" of data, the processing of which requires special rules under Article 8 of the European Union Directive (European Union, 1995).

In addition, privacy laws normally provide exemptions from, or relaxation of, the rules governing registration, processing or disclosure for classes of data that are regarded as relatively innocuous (e.g., payroll data, household management data). The United Kingdom Data Protection Registrar's thinking about the revision of the registration methods in the British system proposed a simplification predicated on the notion of differential risk across types of data (Office of the Data Protection Registrar, 1996).[3] In some systems, data that are considered especially sensitive, such as physical and mental health data, or genetic information, may even be withheld from the person concerned.

Provided that it can be shown to be sound, the recognition of differentially risky data could be an important conceptual underpinning for a sophisticated regime of privacy protection, and may simplify implementation.

However, it only implicitly and inferentially mobilizes an egalitarian principle in counteracting the effects of an uneven spread of social, economic, or other circumstances as they affect exposures to privacy dangers. Equity-oriented protections may therefore only arise *ad hoc* without contributing toward the formation of more explicit, coherent, and frequently used regulatory criteria. These criteria can only be developed by focusing on *persons at risk*, not risky data as such. But there is only an underdeveloped research base that could inform such a perspective, or that would be of interest to social scientists attempting to understand privacy in its social context.

Reconstructing the "data subject"

There is a disparity in regulatory intelligence: regulators appear to be more cognizant of the world of data users than of data subjects, and have built this knowledge into regulatory practice. It is rather like medieval maps of the world, where the contours of European lands were more accurately drawn than were the unexplored places beyond the seas. The "detectors" (Hood, 1983) used by policymakers and regulators are more highly developed to acquire information about data users than about those whose data are used; data protection systems are better oriented toward understanding the functional variety of data users than the sociological variety of data subjects and their concerns about invasions of privacy.[4] Sectoral approaches to data protection mean that data users—at least in the more significant industries and sectors such as direct marketing, credit referencing, banking and insurance, the police, and the major public services—are certainly more visible, and their interests more identifiable, than are those of the data subjects.[5]

If they are to act more effectively to protect privacy, policymakers and regulators need a more sophisticated understanding of the variety and attributes of those whose personal data are used. They are currently described in highly abstract terms as "data subjects," "persons," "individuals," "citizens," and "the public." A somewhat clearer picture is gained by reconceptualizing them in terms that map more closely onto then *sectors* of data usage. Sectoral approaches to data protection, which form part of the fine tuning of general rules to specific information practices, facilitate this. For example, banks, shops, and mail-order firms each have "customers," "credit (or loyalty) card holders"; the various social services deal with "clients," "claimants," "patients," etc. Education systems teach "students"; criminal justice systems have "suspects" and "offenders"; political systems involve "voters" and "taxpayers."

Understanding sectoral identities and attributes enables data users, regulators, and data subjects to organize their interactions, and helps to make more precise and predictable one's conduct and one's expectations of others. Claims and rights to privacy protection vary across these categories. Gandy (1993) shows how the "panoptic sort" identifies, classifies, and assesses people as part of surveillance and social control; from a critical perspective, this is the unacceptable practical face of such analyses. Nevertheless, privacy agencies may be able to target their advice and assistance to particular constituencies of subjects based on these more precise identifications. The further development of good information practice would involve data users in knowing more about the privacy concerns of, and risks to, their students, customers, patients, etc. Sectoral identities of the persons whose data are processed may thus be one route to useful knowledge for better information practices and better regulation.

But if each person is not simply a representative "data subject," neither is he or she simply a customer or taxpayer or voter. It is at least a plausible and researchable hypothesis that the data subject's *social* identities as young/old, rich/poor, healthy/ill, female/male, etc. generate, and help to explain, exposure to varying levels of danger through the processing of personal data in sectors that pose differential risks to privacy and in which the levels of privacy protection vary. Thus it is the *variety of types* of client, patient, etc. that needs investigation, beyond the mere sectoral assignment of the data subject. In terms of the hypothetical data subject that we have just mentioned, the fact that the person is (say) a woman between the ages of 18 and 25, has no higher education, works at a clerical job, and lives in a large city may help to explain the person's privacy circumstances, fears, and perceptions.

From the data subject's viewpoint, the sectoral approach points up the fact that, in daily life, the individual moves through sectoral contexts with different privacy configurations and may have varying attitudes toward these. She tells her doctor what she does not tell her bank. Her tutor does not have to know her financial details, but she cannot withhold these from the tax office. She does not want the benefits office to give her information to her landlord, but would not mind if her solicitor knows her shareholdings. She is more afraid of what her insurance company does with her personal data than what the driving-license bureau does. She thinks that her privacy is more at risk from direct marketers than from her pension fund. She enjoys the convenience of booking theater tickets by telephone with her credit card. Where possible, she may adopt selective strategies for controlling who knows what about herself, and her propensity to raise complaints may vary. She is unaware of many things that are being done "out there" with her data, and worries about some of the possibilities. But she is comfortable with the trade-offs that she makes and the risks that she believes she runs.[6]

This sectoral approach implies that a more sensitive and effective application of data protection principles may be achieved when the data user or regulator knows more about the circumstances and interests of data subjects in different social and economic contexts. It argues for a more precisely tuned appreciation of risks and harms. But the data subject is a *whole person*, with a set of social attributes and variable preferences, and cannot simply be represented as an aggregation of sectoral roles. This way of looking at it runs sociological variables across the sectors to produce a two-dimensional view, which is at least better than a one-dimensional view.[7] But the routinely recorded administrative statistics of data protection agencies have not normally been disaggregated sufficiently to allow for a more nuanced understanding, and for recombination in order to address the "whole person" question across sectors and social categories. Yet there is useful public-opinion survey evidence that provides a starting point for further investigation, insofar as it provides a more rounded sociodemographic view of the public. What does it indicate?

Some survey evidence

Only a few relevant research findings can be adduced here. In general, surveys bear out the generalization that levels of privacy concern are relatively high and are broadly similar across countries (Bennett, 1992, 37–43). While the definition of "privacy" may be ambiguous, surveys reveal perceptions of risk and attitudes toward particular aspects of data protection. They also tap the dimensions of fear and trust as well as showing the extent to which privacy is valued and its protection is seen as desirable. Let us look selectively at some of them.

Since 1986, the UK Data Protection Registrar has reported general findings among "members of the public," although these statistics are not broken down in order to show important demographic variations. Survey results fluctuate from year to year, sometimes reflecting the effects of advertising campaigns. In 1994 (Data Protection Registrar, 1994)[8] it was reported that protecting people's rights to personal privacy was a "very important" issue for 66% of the sample of 1,000 persons. Seventy-two percent were "very" or "quite" concerned about the amount of information that is kept about them by various organizations. Concern about the keeping of information without their knowledge was particularly high, ranging from 94 to 59%, with respect to details about savings, earnings, court judgments, credit ratings, one's visitors, and medical history. The proportions were lower with regard to education and job history, what one buys, club membership, TV viewing, newspaper reading, and age, ranging from 38 to 13%.[9] Doctors and the National Health Service were the organizations that respondents trusted most with their data (88%), and mail order companies the least (22%). Interestingly, this same rank ordering was found when questions about trust in different organizations were asked in Australia (Australia, Privacy Commissioner, 1995, 12) and in Canada (Ekos Research Associates, 1993, 20).

Although the British public were apparently very concerned about privacy, few respondents knew much about their rights. Only 47%—with prompting—were even aware of the Data Protection Act, although this was a significant increase from the 38% of the previous 2 years. Even smaller proportions of the "aware" minority knew what functions the act performed.[10] But the Registrar's published data are not disaggregated by sociodemographic variables, so we do not know who fears what, who trusts whom, and who knows what about their legal entitlements. A similar lack of awareness about privacy rights was discovered in Australia (Australia, Privacy Commissioner, 1995).

Some informative findings about social distributions of attitudes toward the provision of personal information are available in research conducted by outside organizations. In Britain, a survey carried out by the Henley Centre with the sponsorship of the Direct Marketing Association disaggregated findings by age, social class, and industrial sector. It identified consumers' fears about exclusion, inaccuracy, the passing on of information, and technology. Among the findings were that the fear of being labeled by companies was strongest among older and poorer people, but was a majority response in all categories. Inaccuracy was feared by the vast majority—89% overall; 87% opposed the passing on of information to other companies, and there was also a widespread fear of information technology's capability of linking data and compiling dossiers (Henley Centre, 1995, ch. 4).

The Harris–Equifax surveys in the United States, conducted by a leading credit referencing company in connection with Alan Westin, have provided data in general as well as in specific fields and sectors. The first in the series (Equifax, 1990) was a survey of over 2,000 consumers as well as a smaller number of data-using business executives. In 1991, Westin's analysis drew a distinction between "privacy fundamentalists" (25%), "the unconcerned" (18%), and "the pragmatic majority" (57%). "Fundamentalists" were the most distrustful of organizations and concerned about the use of data; at the other end of the scale, the "unconcerned" did not worry and valued consumption benefits and public order over their privacy. The "pragmatic" had more subtle and discriminating views concerning particular organizations, practices, and values (Harris–Equifax, 1991, 6–7).[11]

The 1994 survey (Equifax–Harris, 1994) of about 1,000 persons employed categories of age, education, race, sex, region, type of community, political philosophy, and household income.[12] It found that 84% of Americans were "very" or "somewhat" concerned about privacy threats. This was the highest percentage found in a number of surveys going back to 1978, with 71% of blacks "very" concerned, as compared with only 48% of whites. Those aged between 18 and 24 were less concerned than those aged 50–64, and those earning less than $15,000 per year were far more concerned than those earning over $75,000. College graduates were much less concerned than those who had never completed high school. In general, the arguably related variables of race, income, and level of education seem to explain variations in attitudes toward the use of personal data across a wide range of contexts and issues that include the use of social security numbers, a proposed national identification system, medical research, and utility services.

It is evident that trust plays an important part in individuals' perception of risk. Doctors and nurses were trusted with personal data far more than were mail-order companies, and in about the same proportions as in Britain. But the survey found that individuals' level of distrust in government and in technology—particularly high in the United States, and increasing over the years—correlated with their attitudes on privacy issues.[13] Comparisons with equivalent Canadian data have revealed similar correlations, perhaps in contrast to the conventional wisdom that Canadians are more trustful of government institutions than are Americans (Harris–Equifax, 1992, ix).

However, even some of the very distrustful were found among those who were prepared to accept particular uses of personal information on condition that safeguards were provided in the form of laws, remedies, and voluntary fair information practices applied by data users. The survey showed that willingness to change from opposition to acceptance was stronger among the demographic groups that were most worried about privacy threats: "These include African-Americans; respondents with less than high school education; Southerners; suburbanites; and persons 40–49 years of age" (Equifax–Harris, 1994, xix). Findings of this kind are particularly interesting because they suggest that the perceived level of risk cannot be taken as an unexplained prior condition, but interacts with safeguards and is influenced by the latter's availability.

A survey concerning health information in the United States showed that levels of concern for privacy differed according to income, gender, age, geographical region, level of education, and other variables (Harris–Equifax, 1993). Detailed comparisons of figures across survey years cannot be discussed here, but Westin's interpretative essay gives the following overview:

> Blacks are generally among the higher concerned groups on medical- and other privacy issues. Harris–Equifax surveys have shown low-income, low-education, and minority-racial groups to be among the most highly concerned about general privacy threats, violations of employee and consumer privacy rights, and government invasions of citizen privacy in law enforcement and social-program administration. It is not surprising, therefore, to find these sectors of the public scoring "high concern" on medical-privacy issues in the 1993 survey.
>
> (Harris–Equifax, 1993, 15)

Westin also points out that respondents with the least and the highest levels of education and of income were highly concerned to comparable degrees on many questions. This was surprising because other surveys have shown that high-income, well-educated people are not generally highly concerned about privacy. Westin's suggested explanation is that these groups:

> are among the heaviest users of mental health services and also report having their medical information improperly disclosed at rates much higher than the public. It may be that such respondents feel capable of defending their informational interests quite well in the employment and consumer contexts, and feel a part of the governing elite as far as general privacy concerns are involved. But, their use of mental health services and their adverse medical confidentiality experiences make them feel sensitive—and vulnerable —when medical and health information is involved.
>
> (Harris–Equifax, 1993, 15)

The survey is noteworthy for its focus on data practices, and on the attitudes of both the public and "leaders," in a specific and particularly important sector. Westin's interpretation is also especially germane in view of what has been said earlier about sectoral approaches and about the variations in the empirical patterning of individuals' participation in, and exposure to the privacy dangers in, informatized areas of social, economic, and governmental life.

Another survey, the 1993 Canadian Privacy Survey, also revealed group variations in fear of serious privacy invasions (Ekos Research Associates, 1993), but puts a somewhat different interpretation on them: one that is related more to powerlessness rather than to the degree of inclusion in information-using (and -misusing) systems. In general, the elderly, the less educated, women, and Francophones expressed higher levels of concern. But the authors see a "class cleavage in the nature and impact of privacy issues" (Ekos Research Associates, 1993, iii). They argue:

> For those in the less powerful and less privileged classes, ... powerlessness may be combining with a growing disillusionment with Government and other institutions, to produce a generalized fear.... At the same time, their economically marginal positions render them less capable of identifying and responding to these problems. For example, they are least capable of affording some of the new technologies designed to minimise privacy threats. They are also least likely to be subject to the irritants of marketing intrusions, since they are not attractive marketing opportunities. ... More privileged members of society, on the other hand, understand and experience privacy issues in a fundamentally different way. As consumers, they are the more likely users of the new

information technologies ... they endure the majority of telemarketing and charitable agency intrusions. Finally, they are also more interested in and capable of affording new privacy protection services.
(Ekos Research Associates, 1993, iii)

The Canadian report distinguishes among persons with different levels of concern over privacy, in terms of an exotically labeled fivefold typology based on factor analysis: "fearful regulators," "extroverted technophobes," "guarded individualists," "open pragmatists," and "the indifferent" (Ekos Research Associates, 1993, 34–38). The relationship between these divisions and sociodemographic characteristics of members of each category points up the complexity of privacy as a socially distributed value, and shows that generalizations about (say) women, the poorly educated, or the young cannot be made with confidence. The report plots the typological groups against seven sociodemographic variables, but there are no indications of statistical significance among the differences that are shown (Ekos Research Associates, 1993, 64).

Most Canadians do not appear to know how to handle privacy problems, according to this survey. Sixty-one percent would not know whom to turn to, although this varied by age (the older, the more knowledgeable) and region (Francophones felt better able). Knowledge of how technologies affect privacy was somewhat more widespread, but social-group differences were small. Awareness of the possibility for formal recourse was low, but again it was higher among Francophones. There was a strong desire for government legislation, although other protective strategies received support as well.

Three further illustrative surveys can be cited. A Dutch enquiry reported the results of a privacy questionnaire in terms of a range of variables including religious and political affiliation and several employment categories (Holvast *et al.*, 1989). An international European survey found that more women than men appear to be worried about leaving electronic tracks on information networks. Levels of concern correlate closely with age level of education across all countries. Awareness of data protection laws is variable and often low, although there are very high proportions in all countries—above 90%—who attach a high level of importance to privacy protection and think the European Union should ensure this (International Research Associates, 1997). In a Hungarian study, geographical, educational, age, and occupational factors were taken into account in analyzing responses to a questionnaire investigating issues concerned with the administrative use of personal data, including trust and safeguards (Székely, 1991). One finding was that persons' sensitivity about medical history, income, finances, family life, and personal past and future plans was related to age. Those over 66 were less demanding of information privacy; an explanation is:

> Elderly people, especially single ones, have to rely on other people's help and on medical and social services more intensively.... For all of this they have to give more information about themselves and to disclose an increasing number of dimensions of their private lives. To this is added their generally reduced incomes, and beyond a certain degree they are compelled to draw attention to this fact.
>
> (Székely, 1991, 19)

Sensitivity was found to be highest among the young, who are thought to have a greater need for "informational self-determination" on many categories of information. The less educated were also less sensitive; this is attributed to the lower levels of privacy in their families and communities, and to the lower frequency of their contacts with officialdom in which data might be disclosed. They also are considered to be less knowledge able about information processing and use (Székely, 1991, 19).

One aim of the enquiry was to identify and explain the circumstances of a social group who were particularly aware of the need for data protection and who demanded information privacy and autonomy. A subsample was identified. Its members were

> somewhat better informed, ... are more interested in the fate of their data, pay more attention to the differences between named and anonymous data processing, are bothered more by compulsory provision of data, and more strongly oppose the establishment of interconnection among registrations.... they place safety before comfort, prefer decentralized to centralised registration, and are suspicious about the computerised processing of personal data. Accordingly, they more strongly oppose an expansion of [State Office for Population Registering] activities, call for more information about their data, and almost 100 per cent of them oppose the selling of their personal data for various information services.
>
> (Székely, 1991, 37)

Contrary to the conventional wisdom that would suppose them to be politically active and technologically sophisticated young Budapest intellectuals, it was found that they were not significantly different from the whole sample in terms of the full range of sociodemographic variables. This is believed to reflect the nature of Hungarian society at the time of the survey, in which the opportunity for information privacy had not been available, and in which consciousness of data protection could be traced to "familial, religious, cultural and other traditions" (Székely, 1991, 37) rather than directly to the other variables. This configuration of high privacy awareness and desire is seen as constituting a new dimension in society.

Privacy risks revisited

The preceding discussion has concerned perceptions of privacy threats and of safeguards or protective measures that might mitigate the risks posed by personal information processes. In terms of its contribution to knowledge and policy, the state of research is somewhat encouraging, especially where surveys have used sectorization as well as sociodemographic breakdowns as analytical dimensions. Levels of knowledge and awareness of privacy threats, technological processes, and the administrative use of data have been ascertained, and the dimension of trust/distrust has been singled out as important, particularly in relation to perceived needs or demands for better privacy protection.

Evidence of this kind is highly relevant. It shows who feels threatened by privacy invasions, who knows about data protection, and who would be reassured by safeguards on the processing of personal data. These findings should ideally be run against actual patterns of involvement of different categories of data subject with various sectors of data usage, as does the Equifax–Harris (1996, 15–22) comparison among credit-card holders, direct-mail purchasers, and Internet users. More precise information might be difficult to obtain, but not impossible. Estimates might be available from data users whose knowledge of their clientele or customers includes relevant socioeconomic or other characteristics. Therefore—and especially if the question of equality is to be addressed—closer attention should be paid to differences that might give a purchase on systematic demographic variations that might help us to understand why some people feel more exposed than others. To a degree, some surveys already do this, providing explanations of attitudes. Important variables in the Equifax–Harris surveys, for example, are whether the respondent has or has not been a victim of a privacy invasion, and the relative importance of the consumer's own personal experiences with business firms in shaping attitudes.

However, an important limitation is that the results do not provide much information on the distribution of *data protection* as a specific service or regulatory function, or on the efficacy of data protection systems in coping with, or ameliorating, risks and fears. They cannot coherently answer the question, "Who gets what data protection?" Looking at it through this end of the telescope, the available knowledge about how privacy protection laws and systems work does not easily relate to the circumstances of particular individuals or groups, although it gives some insights into this. It was argued earlier that regulators have a clearer understanding of data users' practices than of data subjects. Moreover, these patterns of risk, protection, and perception may vary by sector, by country, and by type of person.

Thomas's (1928) aphorism, that situations defined as real are real in their consequences, should not leave us too upset if we cannot get very far beyond the plane of popular perceptions and attitudes toward privacy risks, and plausible explanations of them. Policymakers and privacy-regulating bodies, as well as data users themselves, need to respond to these fears, distrusts, and demands, however "unrealistic" these may be thought to be by those who would try to calculate risks. In our attempt to understand policy processes, we may then note that the organizational and regulatory response to opinions and attitudes, and not necessarily to what some would construe as "objective" fact, is a key component in shaping policy and in the political construction of privacy as a problem.

Still on the plane of perceptions and attitudes, the evidence shows that sensitivity to privacy issues does vary to some extent across the social spectrum. What it does not show is whether these differences correspond to differences in actual exposure to risk, although, as we have seen, there are plausible exposure-related reasons why the old, the ill, etc. feel vulnerable. It might be argued that we need some way of assessing "real" hazards, both generally and for different groups or categories of people; otherwise, we cannot say whether they—or government, politicians, privacy advocates, etc.—are under- or overreacting, pandering to popular fears, negligent in the face of threats, or tailoring policy appropriately.

There are parallels here to crime and the fear of crime—the "law and order" agenda—and connections with the problem of evaluating the "adequacy" of data protection (Raab & Bennett, 1996b). There are also issues concerning false consciousness and the propriety of "educating, agitating, and organizing" the public, engaging them in the political arena to gain better privacy protection, all on the basis of unfalsifiable assumptions. But conversely, there are also ethical issues about keeping people uninformed and therefore quiescent about dangers to which they may be exposed. Exaggeration of the risks or individuals' lack of concern for their privacy are both worrisome, as well as being data for sociological study.

Where do these issues lead us? Do we need, and can we obtain, "objective" knowledge of the variable hazards to which people are exposed through the collection and use of their personal details? Are we—whether inevitably or only currently—less able to show the distribution of privacy risk across society than we might be, say, to demonstrate the distribution of environmental hazards or physical safety? Is the attempt to understand the pattern of inequality and to determine more precisely how far we are from the *equal* protection of personal information doomed to failure? Are we left only with what people think or fear, rather than some "harder" reality? And if so, what then?

These are large questions that confront not only the state of the art of empirical research but the whole status of "objectivity" and "rationality" in social science. In particular, they are at the heart of contemporary controversy and debate in the literature on risk analysis and risk assessment.[14] Some take the view that the expert, objective determination of risk is the only reliable knowledge, and that lay people's subjective views—where they differ—should be discounted as error. This view has been challenged, and may even be superseded, by the view that "expert" knowledge is also to a degree subjective, value-laden, and dependent upon judgment. Because the distinction between the two forms of know ledge cannot be firmly established, there is no valid reason to exclude perceptions in assessing and managing risk (Royal Society, 1992, ch. 5; Slovic, 1987, 1997). As Beck observes, "The scientific concern . . . relies on social expectations and value judgements, just as the social discussion and perception of risks depend on scientific arguments . . . scientific rationality without social rationality remains *empty*, but social rationality without scientific rationality remains *blind*" (Beck, 1992, 30; emphasis in original).

On the other hand, risk management and policy are more complex given the diversity of risk perceptions across a population. Resolving these differences is a matter of political as well as scientific choice; the acceptability of a risk has to be answered in terms of "to whom, . . . when, and under what circumstances?" (Royal Society, 1992, 92). The policy and administrative dilemma is "how, in the face of such plurality, societal decisions about risks may be made that are both equitable, and in some way in the interests of all" (Royal Society, 1992, 124). There are group differences in risk perception that appear to be associated with individuals' membership in, or identification with, different groups or sociocultural categories and therefore with adherence to different beliefs and norms (Royal Society, 1992, 108). Although no specific research on privacy risk perception has been done to test this or other findings, risk research generally is persuasive in concluding that "purely psychological, individual-based analysis can account for only a part of risk perception and risk behavior" (Royal Society, 1992, 112). The individualist perspective of data protection and of many existing surveys tends to obscure these matters.

Recent writings on risk offer further helpful insights. Beck (1992) has noted the relationship between the paradigm of industrial or "class" society and the new paradigm of "risk society," which also involves issues of inequality. He recognizes disparities in the distribution of risks, and talks about "social risk positions" (Beck, 1992, 23) that follow class inequalities, but that might take a different path that rebounds on those who produce or gain from risks. He has particularly in mind pollution, ecological risks, etc., but as his argument thereby comprises situations that ignore national borders and are global, the case of perssonal information flows might be germane as well.

Especially interesting is his point that, with risk, "[k]nowledge gains a new political significance" (Beck, 1992, 23), and we are thus pointed toward the development of "a sociological theory of the origin and diffusion of *knowledge about risks*" (Beck, 1992, 24; emphasis in original). This is relevant to privacy risks because, as has often been pointed out, the lack of transparency of data processing means that individuals are not often able to understand what happens to their personal details once they are collected, or even to know when in fact they are being collected. This situation may breed rumor and thence fear, which is often registered in survey responses. Newspaper "horror stories" about privacy invasions and misuse of data, as well as personal or bar stories about these, and daily evidence of surveillance by means of closed-circuit cameras, may validate and shape the individual's perception of privacy threats, but they may not be accurate measures of the risks to which people are subjected.[15]

Yet these perceptions cannot be brushed aside by a "scientistic" determination of risk; they are real, and real in their consequences. Beck argues:

> [R]isk determinations are an unrecognized, still undeveloped symbiosis of the natural and human sciences, of everyday and expert rationality, of interest and fact. They are simultaneously neither simply the one nor only the other. They can no longer be isolated from one another through specialization, and developed and set down according to their own standards of rationality. They require a cooperation across the trenches of disciplines, citizens' groups, factories, administration and politics, or—which is the more likely —they disintegrate between these into antagonistic definitions and *definitional struggles.*
>
> (Beck, 1992, 28–29; emphasis in original)

We may infer from this that it is not futile to investigate actual risk patterns, seeking estimates of the probabilities, magnitudes, and distributions of risk according to a range of sociodemographic variables. It is also very worthwhile to investigate, as far as possible, the privacy implications of policies, information systems, and business processes in government and the private sector.[16] But we should not expect incontestable results that would resolve issues, settle all conflicts between data users and data subjects, or provide data protectors with reliable strategies. Adams holds that science cannot resolve disagreements about risk, "[b]ecause people are constantly responding to their circumstances, and thereby constantly altering each others' risk-taking environments . . . the future is constantly being reshaped by people's perceptions of it. Science has no firm ground on which to stand" (Adams, 1995, 194).

Drawing upon a typology derived from cultural theory,[17] Adams's (1995) distinction among types of perspectives on risk bears resemblance to some of the categories of privacy stances that we have seen in some of the survey research. Briefly, "individualists" play down risks, oppose regulation, and leave risk decisions to the market and individual discretion. "Hierarchists," on the other hand, seek the authoritative, scientific management of risk from the top down, with regulation grounded in "research to establish 'the facts' about both human and physical nature" (Adams, 1995, 41). "Egalitarians" perceive risks but are prudent and cautious, sometimes favoring regulation but sometimes opposing it on grounds that it inhibits other desirable behavior; they seek cooperation in reducing risk. "Fatalists" see an unpredictable world that they cannot affect, and therefore play no part in arguments about risk. Because they argue from different premises about the nature of the world, they disagree about matters that are fundamental to the question of risk, such as its acceptable level (Adams, 1995, 59). The decisions they take—the "balancing act in which perceptions of risk are weighed against propensity to take risk" (Adams, 1995, 15)—are filtered through their different cultural outlooks to produce different conclusions.

One consequence of this cultural model for our discussion of knowledge about "real" risks is that the outlook of the "hierarchists" is not privileged in the sociocultural construction of risk. Their resource—scientific research—may be no more a trump card than are privacy "rights." If the knowledge they possess about risks is deficient for the purpose of regulation, the call for "good science" is misplaced, in Adams's view:

> On occasion science may succeed in solving a problem by the discovery of new agreed "facts" which can serve as a basis for consensual action.... But in such cases science has simply removed the issue from the realm of risk; it has not solved the problem of how to proceed in the absence of agreed facts.
> (Adams, 1995, 195)

Douglas and Wildavsky (1982) make a similar point when they argue that risk assessment needs to take account of both subjective and objective aspects of problems, but that it would require settled societal values underpinning adequate methods of discovering facts and of making political decisions:

> That would be a trusting world, but it is not the one in which we live. There is neither agreement over appropriate methods to assess risks nor acceptance of the outcomes of public processes. Advanced techniques of risk assessment arrive in the very scene in which they are the least appropriate.
> (Douglas & Wildavsky, 1982, 68)

Conclusion

A firm stance on these issues cannot be taken in the absence of further investigation of privacy risks and perceptions. In the final analysis, however, although "good science" may not be able to sort out risk problems, *some* science may be better than no science, and increments of knowledge about exposures to privacy hazards and their distribution may help to put the claims of both the alarmist and the complacent into perspective. But little of such knowledge is available. Scientific research on issues such as road safety and environmental pollution—the usual cases in point in the risk literature—is far further down the path, even if that path is a false trail and an "objective" determination of risk, complete with cost-benefit analysis, is dangerously misleading. Privacy risks and their distribution have not yet enjoyed a widespread, evidenced discourse that might reveal where the areas of agreement and disagreement lie among protagonists with different outlooks, what "facts" can be accepted, what the range of risk probabilities and magnitudes might be, and what is plausible or far-fetched in regard to who gets what privacy.[18]

Therefore, survey and other evidence, and debates about the findings, might well suggest strategies for coping more effectively with risks and fears thrown up by information technology and its applications, and with disparities among social groups and categories in the protection of their personal information. These strategies could be employed not only by regulatory "hierarchists" but also by "pragmatists" or "egalitarians" in pursuit of their various objectives. "Individualists" or the "unconcerned" might even find that some research casts light on the feasibility of their position by showing the effect of certain solutions, such as privacy-enhancing technologies and market-based initiatives. "Fatalists," as Adams (1995) shows, sideline themselves in arguments of this kind, but better knowledge might show how their privacy, too, can be protected, as of right.

Debates about privacy are, in large part, debates about politics. Beyond research and strategies, in considering the distribution of privacy risks and of privacy protection, Douglas and Wildavsky's view should be borne in mind:

> Knowledge of danger is necessarily partial and limited: judgments of risk and safety must be selected as much on the basis of what is valued as on the basis of what is known. . . . Science and risk assessment cannot tell us what we need to know about threats of danger since they explicitly try to exclude moral ideas about the good life. . . . If we agreed on what polity we desired, we could consider what risks would be worth facing for establishing it.
> (Douglas & Wildavsky, 1982, 80–82)

Notes

1 Previous versions were given at the ETHICOMP96 Conference in Madrid, November 1996 (see Raab & Bennett, 1996a) and at the Conference on Risk, City University, London, June 1997. The authors are particularly grateful for comments from Paul Anand, Dag Elgesem, Jeroen van den Hoven, Simon Rogerson, and Paul Slovic.

2 The general problem of the measurement of the quality of data protection has been dealt with elsewhere (Raab & Bennett, 1996b).
3 "We propose to distinguish between sensitive and non-sensitive data, to focus on a list of 'sensitive' purposes, and discriminate between sensitive and non-sensitive data, sources and disclosures. . . . There will inevitably be different views as to which uses of data are particularly sensitive. . . . It is easy to make a case for any data to be classed as 'sensitive' . . . in many cases the sensitivity of data relates to the purpose for which it is held and its possible disclosures (Office of the Data Protection Registrar, 1996, paras. 4.6, 8.1, 9.1).
4 Interesting exceptions can be noted, illustratively. For example, there have been Australian surveys "identifying the privacy concerns of Aboriginal and Torres Strait Islander people in the Northern Territory," and examining the difficulties faced by people with disabilities in regard to access to medical records (Human Rights Australia, 1995, 9).
5 This does not necessarily mean that data users are particularly influential in the policy process, or that all data users are equally well-placed as policy actors. However, it is arguably the case that, in general, they are more able to mobilize for these purposes than is the public at large, as in other fields where citizens or consumers as such are among the less well-organized and less sophisticated political actors. It is, however, an open question whether any disparities in influence are reinforced by the disparity in regulatory intelligence.
6 On the question of individual choice, see Elgesem (in press).
7 A third dimension might be chronological, registering the improvement or worsening of risk-and-protection positions over time for categories of persons and within sectors.
8 The 1994 figures are shown here because they were more detailed than those published in subsequent years. No survey results were published in the Registrar's 1995 Annual Report.
9 No question was apparently asked about information concerning driving habits, video-surveillance data, or records of telephone calls—areas of data capture and processing that are becoming increasingly important.
10 Although the figures reported for 1997 (Data Protection Registrar, 1997, Appendix 8) are not directly comparable, public awareness (especially following advertising) has increased considerably to roughly two-thirds. But perhaps more disturbing is the 1994 finding that 40% of computer-record-holding small businesses, and 20% of large businesses, were unaware that they had to register their holdings with the Registrar. Ten years after the passage of the Act, only 43% and 72%, respectively, were aware that the act conferred rights on individuals. These proportions have varied over the years, and improved in 1997 following a media campaign.
11 The Equifax–Harris figures for 1996 were 24% "fundamentalists," 16% "unconcerned," and 60% "pragmatists" (Equifax–Harris, 1996, 13). The survey by the Henley Centre found 9% "fundamentalists," 8% "unconcerned," and 80% "pragmatists," although these proportions were only considered indicative (Henley Centre, 1995, 87–88).
12 Whether the categories used in such surveys are the relevant ones for an understanding of inequalities, whether the categories define actual social groups, and whether groups identified in other ways, including self-identification, would provide a better basis for analysis of inequalities are important methodological issues that cannot be discussed here.
13 "The higher a respondent's distrust, the more he or she is concerned about threats to privacy, opposed to new uses of personal information (especially through

information-technology applications), and in favor of legal and regulatory bans or controls on uses of personal information by business or government" (Equifax–Harris, 1994, xii).
14 See, for example, the Royal Society (1992).
15 Cf. the discussion of "risk communication" in the Royal Society (1992), ch. 5.
16 See the discussion of privacy impact analysis in Bennett (1995, ch. 6) and the literature cited therein; also see Stewart (1996).
17 See also the Royal Society (1992, 112–114) and the literature cited therein.
18 See, however, the philosophical discussion by Elgesem (1996) of privacy risks, their justification, and their acceptability with particular reference to registers of medical information for epidemiological research.

References

Adams, J. 1995. *Risk*. London: UCL Press.

Australia, Privacy Commissioner. 1995. *Community attitudes towards privacy*. Canberra: Human Rights Australia.

Beck, U. 1992. *Risk society*. London: Sage.

Bennett, C. 1992. *Regulating privacy*. Ithaca, NY: Cornell University Press.

Bennett, C. 1995. The Political Economy of Privacy. Hackensack, NJ: Center for Social and Legal Research, unpublished paper.

Council of Europe. 1981. *Explanatory Report on the Convention for the Protection of Individuals with Regard to Automatic Processing of Personal Data [includes Treaty No. 108]*. Strasbourg: Council of Europe.

Data Protection Registrar. 1994. *Tenth Report of the Data Protection Registrar June 1994*. HC 453, Session 1993–94. London: HMSO.

Data Protection Registrar. 1997. *The Thirteenth Annual Report of the Data Protection Registrar June 1997*. HC 122, Session 1996–97. London: The Stationery Office.

Douglas, M., and Wildavsky, A. 1982. *Risk and culture*, Berkeley, CA: University of California Press.

Ekos Research Associates. 1993. *Privacy revealed.* Ottawa: Ekos Research Associates, Inc.

Elgesem, D. 1996. Privacy, respect of persons, and risk. In *Philosophical perspectives on computer-mediated communication*, ed. C. Ess, pp. 45–56. Albany: State University of New York Press.

Elgesem, D. In press. Data protection and the limits of centralized risk assessment. In *A reader in information ethics*, eds. S. Rogerson and T. Bynum. Oxford: Blackwell.

Equifax. 1990. *The Equifax Report on Consumers in the Information Age*. Atlanta, GA: Equifax, Inc.

Equifax–Harris. 1994. *Equifax–Harris Consumer Privacy Survey 1994*. Atlanta, GA: Equifax, Inc.

Equifax–Harris. 1996. *The Equifax–Harris Consumer Privacy Survey 1996*. Atlanta, GA: Equifax, Inc.

European Union. 1995. Directive 95/46/EC of the European Parliament and the Council of 24 October 1995 on the protection of individuals with regard to the processing of personal data and on the free movement of such data. *Official Journal of the European Communities*. L281/31, 23/11/95.

Flaherty, D. 1989. *Protecting privacy in surveillance societies*. Chapel Hill, NC: University of North Carolina Press.
Gandy, O. 1993. *The panoptic sort*. Boulder, CO: Westview Press.
Harris–Equifax. 1991. *Harris–Equifax Consumer Privacy Survey*. Atlanta, GA: Equifax, Inc.
Harris–Equifax. 1992. *The Equifax Canada Report on Consumers and Privacy in the Information Age*. Ville d'Anjou: Equifax Canada.
Harris–Equifax. 1993. *Health Information Privacy Survey 1993*. Atlanta, GA: Equifax, Inc.
Henley Centre. 1995. *Dataculture*. London: Henley Centre for Forecasting, Ltd.
Holvast, J., van Dijk, H., and Schep, G. 1989. *Privacy Doorgelicht*. Onderzoeksrapport No. 71.'s-Gravenhage: SWOKA.
Hood, C. 1983. *The tools of government*. London: MacMillan. Human Rights Australia. 1995. *Privacy Commissioner—Seventh Annual Report on the Operation of the Privacy Act*. Canberra: Australian Government Publishing Service.
International Research Associates. 1997. *Information Technology and Data Privacy: Report Produced for the European Commission*. Brussels: INRA.
Lyon, D. 1994. *The electronic eye*. Cambridge: Polity Press.
Marx, G. 1988. *Undercover: Police surveillance in America*, Berkeley, CA: University of California Press.
Office of the Data Protection Registrar. 1996. *Heading for the Future: A Consultation Paper—A Proposal for Revision of Registration Methods under the Data Protection Act 1994*. Wilmslow: Office of the Data Protection Registrar.
Organization for Economic Cooperation and Development. 1981. *Guidelines on the Protection of Privacy and Transborder Flows of Personal Data*. Paris: OECD.
Raab, C. 1993. The governance of data protection. In *Modern governance*, ed. J. Kooiman, pp. 89–103. London: Sage.
Raab, C. 1995. Equality and privacy: Who gets what data protection? In *Privacy disputed*, eds. P. Ippel, G. de Heij, and B. Crouwers, pp. 111–122. Den Haag: SDU.
Raab, C., and Bennett, C. 1996a. Distributing privacy: Risks, protection and policy. In *Proceedings of ETHICOMP96—Values and Social Responsibilities of Computer Science*, ed. P. Barroso, pp. 336–350. Madrid: Universidad Complutense de Madrid.
Raab, C., and Bennett, C. 1996b. Taking the measure of privacy: Can data protection be evaluated? *International Review of Administrative Sciences*, 62(4): 535–556.
Royal Society. 1992. *Risk: Analysis, perception and management*, London: The Royal Society.
Rule, J., McAdam, D., Steams, L., and Uglow, D. 1980. *The politics of privacy*. New York: Mentor.
Slovic, P. 1987. Perception of risk. *Science* 236:280–285.
Slovic, P. 1997. Trust, emotion, sex, politics, and science: Surveying the risk-assessment battlefield. In *Environment, ethics and behavior*, eds. M. Bazerman, D. Messick, A. Tenbrunsel, and K. Wade-Benzoni, pp. 277–313. San Francisco: New Lexington Press.
Stewart, B. 1996. Privacy Impact Assessments. Paper presented to the Privacy Issues Forum, Christchurch, New Zealand, 13 June.

Székely, I., ed. 1991. *Information privacy in Hungary*. Budapest: Hungarian Institute for Public Opinion Research.
Thomas, W. 1928. *The child in America*. New York: Knopf.
Warren, S., and Brandeis, L. 1890. The Right to privacy. *Harvard Law Review* 4(5):193–220.
Westin, A. 1967. *Privacy and freedom*. London: Bodley Head.

85

TACTICAL MEMORY

The politics of openness in the construction of memory

Sandra Braman

Source: *First Monday* 11(7) (2006): n.p.

Abstract

Those in the openness movement believe that access to information is inherently democratic, and assume the effects of openness will all be good from the movement's perspective. But means are not ends, nothing is inevitable, and just what will be done with openly available information once achieved is rarely specified. One implicit goal of the openness movement is to create and sustain politically useful memory in situations in which official memory may not suffice, but to achieve this, openness is not enough. With the transition from a panopticon to a panspectron environment, the production of open information not only provides support for communities but also contributes to surveillance. Proprietary ownership of information is being challenged, but there is erosion of ownership in the sense of being confident in what is known. Some tactics currently in use need to be re-evaluated to determine their actual effects under current circumstances. Successfully achieving tactical memory in the 21st century also requires experimentation with new types of tactics, including those of technological discretion and of scale as a medium. At the most abstract level, the key political battle of the 21st century may not be between particular political parties or ideologies but, rather, the war between mathematics and narrative creativity.

"Memory is not just of the past, it's of the future, too."

— Douglas Woolf.

The openness movement is driven by the belief that access to information is inherently democratic, and riven by the assumption that all of the effects of openness will be good from the movement's perspective. But means are not ends, nothing is inevitable, and just what will be done with openly available information once achieved is rarely specified.

Information has many definitions — and all may be simultaneously in play — but its most fundamental is as a constitutive force in society (Braman, 1989). One implicit goal, therefore, is to use open information to create and sustain politically useful memory in situations in which official memory may not suffice. Memory is key because it is infrastructure, the informational structure critical to the individual and collective identities from which all agency springs. To achieve this type of memory, though, openness is not enough. Information and knowledge, tools and processes, require additional attention. It is here, between openness and infrastructure, that we find the space for doctrine (establishment of constitutional and constitutive principles), strategy (identification of long-term goals), tactics (choices regarding how to achieve strategic goals in a specific context with particular resources), and logistics (the material support systems upon which tactics rely).

In this article the focus is on tactics, "an arrangement of procedure with a view to achievement of specific ends" (*Oxford English Dictionary*). The history of tactics is one of ever-expanding foci and frames. In the military, for example — the domain in which tactical thinking has been the most highly developed — this began with attention to the volume of materials (soldiers, bullets, and armor), and subsequently turning to the problem of accuracy in use of those materials, the processes by which accurate weapons are produced, industrial strength in support of weapons production, and "Big Science" to improve industrial strength and generate weapons innovations (Beaumont, 1994; van Creveld, 1991). This history can be broken down into three stages of tactical evolution: clockwork, motor, and network (De Landa, 1991), with the last stage of particular interest from the perspective of the opportunities for tactical memory uses of openness in the first decades of the 21st century.

Information and communication have long been used for tactical purposes. Roman leaders carried detailed notes with them into the field (Lee, 1993), Napoleon established a special staff to collect tactical information, and the formal communications structures of diplomacy were established as the formal tactical component of an international system in which foreign relations was the strategic domain (Tran, 1987). Indeed, a tactical unit in the military can be defined as an information processing machine because it must include a means by which information is transmitted through a formation from leaders to soldiers and back in order to function (De Landa, 1991). While the question of whether or not machines will ever achieve an autonomous sense of consciousness remains unanswered, Dewdney (1998) describes smart tactical weapons — weapons that incorporate their own intelligent targeting and launch systems — as our first created forms of consciousness because they just live through the "I am" moment and then self-destruct.

In recent years we have begun to find the concept of tactics useful for thinking about cultural matters, and about the role of communication in society. The adaptation of biotechnology so that it is "appropriate" for indigenous, or "people's," environments, has been described as tactical (Kloppenburg and Burrows, 1996). Tactical voting is one of the three classic examples of lying and cheating in economic theory (Molho, 1997). Melucci's (1997) argument that the loci of social conflicts have shifted in many cases from overt political action to the linguistic and architectural codes that organize information leads to appreciation of the roles of language, knowledge production, and memory as tactical matters. Tactical media practitioners deliberately operationalize this insight (Garcia and Lovink, 1997).

Here we explore three problems that confront those attempting to use openness to create politically useful memory in the current environment and three limits to the effectiveness of current tactics in play. These difficulties provide the parameters of what may turn out to be the most significant political battle of the 21st century, the struggle between mathematics and narrative form. Three tactical recommendations are offered in response. Taken together, it is hoped that this analysis will provide some stimulus for thinking about the possibilities of tactical memory.

Three problems

Much of the activity within the openness movement is directed at removing long-standing barriers to information access, or at those being newly put in place in response to contemporary security concerns. However, even when there is openness, there are problems at each stage of the processes by which memory is developed — collecting, owning, and using the facts.

Collecting the facts

Jeremy Bentham's (1787) concept of the panopticon, popularized by Foucault (1979), is widely used to describe the nature of surveillance as a form of information collection in the contemporary environment. The concept as initially put forward included three elements. An architecture was suggested that allowed one person to monitor many persons simultaneously. The person watching was given an economic interest in the effectiveness of the monitoring. And those being watched could not see the watcher; because as a result it could not be known with certainty whether or not one was being watched at any given time, those being watched would be motivated to regulate their behavior at all times — in effect, watching themselves. Foucault-inspired analyses of have broadened the concept to include the dehumanizing fragmentation of the individuals into disparate informational elements. Common across all of these is identification of a subject to be the target of surveillance and then the establishment of a single monitor or an array of monitoring equipment that keeps the subject within its gaze.

Though the concept of the panopticon is regularly invoked in discussions of contemporary surveillance techniques, such as the use of video cameras to record activity in public places, Hookway (2000) argues persuasively that, instead, the panopticon has been replaced with the panspectron. In a panspectron, no surveillance subject is identified in order to trigger an information collection process. Rather, information is collected about everything and everyone all the time. A subject appears only when a particular question is asked, triggering data mining in information already gathered to learn what can be learned in answer to that question. While in the panopticon environment the subject knows that the watcher is there, in the panspectron environment one may be completely unaware that information is being collected.

When the concept of the panspectron was first introduced, a mere half dozen years ago, it may have seemed to many to have been "merely" theoretical, speculative, or at best predictive. Since that time, however, the use of familiar technologies such as video surveillance cameras has rapidly spread, new technologies such as RFID chips and ubiquitous embedded computing systems have come into use, and we are learning more and more about the practices and intentions of those involved with homeland and national security. Though in the past social and political values as translated into laws prevented maximization of the capabilities of digital technologies for the collection of information about individuals, for the nonce, fear of terrorism has trumped. Until and unless effective legal barriers are re-erected, which in turn will require a re-adjustment of power relations among branches of government and political parties, the panspectron is already a reality in areas such as electronic communications (including telephone calls) and financial records, and will increasingly become so in other aspects of our lives.

In a full panspectron, it is impossible to hide physically. Aerial surveillance using heat and other sensors can track movement through rooms in the home and identify the plants being grown, Internet service providers and other organizations are being pressured or required to maintain digital records of transactions and communications for at least two years, and RFID chips move with us through space. The privacy mechanisms that seem natural to us as biological creatures — turning off the lights and shuttering the windows, moving by night, whispering, hiding — are irrelevant although as organisms we still engage in these practices. In the digital environment, privacy, like invasions of privacy, is instead a mathematical matter. Those who are watching use algorithms to discern patterns and relationships that in turn identify specific observational targets, and algorithms are used again to track all of the activities, transactions, and communications of individuals once identified as of interest. Efforts to elude the panspectron, then, must also be mathematical, whether that is accomplished digitally (through, for example, encryption or anonymizing techniques) or behaviorally (by acting in a manner in which what one does is not discernible by the algorithms used for tracking and pattern recognition purposes).

The impacts of this development on our ability to use openness for tactical memory purposes are three. First, one-way surveillance when those surveilled are not even aware that information is being gathered generates a type of interpersonal relationship that was historically rare but has become increasingly dominant in the contemporary world (Calhoun, 1991). Second, citizens have lost the ability to choose which information will be available to others and which will not. And third, information deliberately provided to selected others and to the public becomes additional fodder for the panspectron, a problem revisited in more depth below.

Owning the facts

The central thrust of the openness movement, of course, is to confront means by which public access to information is restricted, and those involved with open source software have made abundantly clear the importance of openness in the processes by which information and knowledge are produced as well. Both of these have to do with ownership in the sense in which it is most commonly used, the legal right of possession, a meaning the *Oxford English Dictionary* traces back to the 16th century. A second meaning of ownership came into use in the 1980s, however, that should also be taken into account by the openness movement — being or feeling responsible for the resolution of a particular problem or issue. There are three ways in which this type of ownership of the facts has become problematic for those working with tactical memory: the possibility that one's memory will become criminalized; the practice of deliberately falsifying, or 'perturbing,' statistical records; and, the legal release of the national security establishment from the requirement of accuracy in the data used to justify surveillance of specific individuals and consequent treatment of those individuals by the national security and criminal justice systems.

Misappropriation by memory

Trade secrets is a way of protecting knowledge based in unfair competition law rather than intellectual property rights, but the recent trend, beginning with the seminal U.S. Supreme Court decision for the current trade secrets regime *Kewanee Oil Company v. Bicron Corporation* (1974), has been to treat trade secrets as property. Almost a century ago, however, even the U.S. Supreme Court recognized that trade secrets have as much to do with relationships as with property (*E.I. duPont de Nemours Powder Co. v. Masland*, 1917). For a long time trade secrets law distinguished between transferring knowledge in tangible forms (for example, in documents and other records) and in the intangible form of personal memory. Because it is often impossible to identify the sources of the knowledge one holds in memory, and to separate protectable knowledge from unprotectable knowledge in one's memory, courts were willing to consider cases involving the tangible transport of trade secrets but would not accept cases based on accusations of infringement of trade secrets via individual memory (Glahn and Shilling, 2002).

As constant and ever-quickening cycles of innovation have become central to economic success in information industries characterized by frequent employee mobility, however, concern over inappropriate knowledge transfer between corporations has become more extreme. The legal consequence has been a set of twin doctrines that address alleged transfers of trade secrets in the intangible form of personal memory — "misappropriation by memory" occurs when such knowledge has actually been used in a new setting, and fears of "inevitable disclosure" allow companies to act simply on the suspicion that such a transfer might take place (Hamler, 2000; Lowry, 1988; Saulino, 2002). In some cases the intention to use memory-based trade secrets of one firm on behalf of another is clear, as when the individuals in *Morlife v. Lloyd Perry* (1997) reconstructed a former employer's client list in order to use it for themselves. The issue is less clear when, as in the case of *SCO v. IBM* (currently set to go to trial in 2007), employees who moved from one corporation to another relied upon knowledge of open source code in both places (Rogers, 2003). Other cases have involved claims that disputed knowledge was gained over the course of a shared education and durable personal relationship, not trade secrets.

Though there are lots of different ways in which information accessed may be cognitively processed — or not — the documentation of access to potential sources of knowledge made possible by a panspectron environment will make it easier to levy charges of misappropriation by memory in future. This raises the threat of criminalization of memory, whether or not there was intentionality or conscious awareness of knowledge sources.

Perturbing the facts

While it is the point of databases to collect and make available accurate information, both privacy law and public opinion demand that those who do data mining do not invade the privacy of individuals in the process of developing analyses of the whole. One class of techniques developed in response to these concerns involves restricting queries in a variety of ways so that the combination of results from successive queries of data in the aggregate cannot yield information about individuals through the ways in which the results overlap. A second class of techniques involves literally falsifying the data itself, known as "perturbation." Approaches to perturbation include such techniques as swapping values between records and adding noise to the results of a query.

While acknowledging that perturbation degrades the quality of the statistics and admitting that the goals of providing high quality statistics and preventing the full or partial disclosure of individual details are mutually exclusive, a profusely cited work by Agrawal and Srikant (2000) further elaborates on a technique for perturbing data that adds and subtracts a random value from each individual record. Multiple iterations of producing a distribution based upon the resulting statistics are necessary in order to approximate with confidence the original distribution. Agrawal and Srikant emphasize that the distribution, but not the values in individual records, can be reconstructed in this way. Though it has been demonstrated that it is possible to retrieve original data from datasets distorted by adding random values (Kargupta et al., 2003) (thus vacating the purported utility of the technique for security purposes), and argued that not enough is known about the tradeoffs between data value and risk of privacy invasion (Iyengar, 2002), work on this approach continues.

Certainly these efforts have stimulated new thinking about how privacy should be defined for databases and their content. Dwork (2006), for example, proves that the goal of ensuring that nothing about an individual should be learnable from a database that can't be learned without access to the database is actually unachievable, making this an unworkable definition of database protection. Chawla et al., (2005) start by defining privacy as protection from being brought to the attention of others. From both perspectives, the availability of auxiliary information — information that is available from other sources to those who query databases — significantly diminishes the ability to statistically protect that data in the collection itself. This work is undertaken by mathematicians, with little attention to either legal or sociological analyses of the consequences of the effects of the approaches with which they are experimenting beyond the barrier question of the extent to which any given approach can effectively protect privacy. The work of philosopher Nissenbaum (2004) stands out in this literature for its inclusion of social theory and empirical evidence from the social sciences in her concept of contextual integrity — achieved when normative and distributive expectations are met in any given circumstances — for analysis of privacy threats from public surveillance.

Still, however, this step forward leaves a serious analytical lacuna in thinking through the ramifications for perturbing the data from a legal perspective, for loss of privacy is only one of the dangers that can arise for individuals from databases. Because access to resources and life opportunities often depends upon information in databases, several of the 18 data privacy laws currently in effect in the U.S. include a provision that offers opportunities to individuals to correct database errors when they are discovered. And in the current homeland security environment, the provision of inaccurate information to a database is defined as a terrorist activity. What provisions are in place to ensure that perturbed data at the individual level do not remain linked to the individual? How can individuals learn whether or not data about themselves in a database was perturbed after the point at which the accuracy of the information was checked? Tactical memory efforts can be undermined if data used for decisions-making purposes is deliberately altered in this way precisely because it is being made available.

Abandonment of the FBI accuracy requirement

In the homeland security environment, the Federal Bureau of Investigation (FBI) has an expanded mission that now includes national security matters as well as those of criminal justice, and a significantly eased situation regarding its ability to surveil. The National Crime Information Center (NCIC), created in 1967 to track criminal activity, is a key source of information that guides surveillance practices. In 1974 (with passage of the first U.S. Privacy Act), the FBI was required to assure the accuracy of the data it held, and in 1976 that database became computerized. However, in March of 2003, the Justice Department exempted the FBI's National Crime Information Center, along with its Central Records System and the National Center for the Analysis of Violent Crime, from the Privacy Act. This exemption was justified by the claim that it was necessary in order to avoid interference with the law enforcement functions and responsibilities of the FBI[1]. The Justice Department further claimed that the accuracy requirement should be dropped because it was impossible to determine in advance which information is accurate, relevant, timely, and complete.

This again creates a situation in which more information is available — at least to those in the security and criminal justice establishments — but the accuracy of that information drops in what can lead to a cascading chain of faulty processes of information collection. In worst-case scenarios, the ultimate result can be court cases in which this type of information is being used as evidence against the accused but — if collected under the provisions of the USA PATRIOT Act — the accused will not even be presented with an opportunity to know what evidence is being used or to challenge its facticity. Here the tactics of memory are clearly being used for strategic purposes.

Analogy and the law

Contemporary uses of analogy in legal thought are a good example of ways in which historically respected techniques can be inventively turned to new uses if there is political will. Analogy has long been considered a hallmark of legal reasoning even though analogical arguments are more persuasive than they are analytical (Weinreb, 2005). Deductive arguments can be subjected to the rules of formal logic and their conclusions empirically tested, as can the conclusions reached by inductive arguments, but analogical arguments are neither formally testable nor empirically verifiable. We have not developed techniques for evaluating the validity of analogical arguments, nor for determining the relative strength or weakness of any given analogy. Thus despite their importance in legal thought, formal models of legal decision-making and analysis instead focus on the tension between rules and standards. Still, analogical reasoning has been critical to legal thought because it provides a way for the law to grow and change in conformity with community views (Levi, 1949), it is a way of achieving a conclusion even when fundamental aspects of a case or problem may be only partially theorized (Sunstein, 1996), and it valuably serves when the pragmatic limit of social scientific knowledge is reached but a legal decision is still required (Geertz, 1983).[2]

In periods of open political revolution, those who come into power feel free to abandon parts or all of the pre-existing legal system. When significant or radical political transformations take place under the guise of business as usual, however, analogy becomes particularly valuable as a means of adjusting the legal system to new political realities. The concept of functionally equivalent borders is a recent U.S. example of how this can be done.

It has long been held that the Fourth Amendment's restrictions on searches don't apply to those entering the country; anyone can be subjected to routine and nonroutine searches at the border without a warrant and without any requirement to show "probable cause" (evidence of reasons to suspect illegal behavior). Though geopolitical borders can be marked precisely, in the 1970s courts began to use an "elastic border" notion because, it was argued, it was not always possible to conduct searches at the border itself (Sims, 1977). In 1973 the U.S. Supreme Court replaced the elastic border notion with the concept of a functionally equivalent border (*Almeida-Sanchez v. U.S.*). The concept was not clearly defined, requiring only that a search have some relationship to an international boundary (Ittig, 1973). Roving border patrols, the notion of an "extended border search," the assumption that an illegal alien is always at a border, and the development of free trade zones in each state provide additional flexibility in use of the concept.

Since 9/11, concerns about U.S. citizens who have relationships with foreign nationals suspect because of their own social networks introduces a border nexus into any related investigation. In order to ensure that dangerous people or materials do not enter the United States, the federal government now requires searches to take place in foreign ports and airports before transport to the country begins, effectively exporting the U.S. border around the world. And in 2005, Congress explicitly interpreted the Homeland Security Act of 2002 as giving permission to the Department of Homeland Security

(DHS) to exempt itself from U.S. law if deemed necessary in order to protect the border — in essence placing the DHS above the law[3].

Locations of geopolitical examples have long been examples of open information, but with this series of analogical and legal steps what we believe we know may no longer be so. With loss of the meaningful ownership of this type of open information, our ability to construct memories about cross-border relations declines and we are less able to use memory in politically effective ways.

Inference attacks

There is a long history of classifying information, but in recent years there has also been growing interest in the category of "sensitive but unclassified" (SBU) information — information to which the public has access but that can, in combination with other information or within a certain context of understanding, yield insights considered undesirable. To those in the national security establishment, the ability to generate such inferences is understood to be a form of attack. As described by computer scientists working to protect the security of single databases, an "inference attack" occurs when a user can derive an answer to an unauthorized question on the basis of the results of an authorized query. Those results may be positive (information produced) or negative (information that is not produced in response to a query) (Ishihara *et al.*, 2005). Interoperability between databases and other forms of data sharing across organizational boundaries increase the potential for such inferences (Mitra *et al.*, 2006). And because knowledge held by those who access data is key to the ability to draw inferences, the expanding universe of open access information — the goal and the result of the openness movement — again increases the danger of what are being defined as inference attacks.

Three classes of policies for protecting against inference and aggregation attacks are being publicly discussed (Strickland, 2005). There are policies that structure the information itself, policies that structure access to information, and policies that rely upon intermediaries for secure information sharing. The first class includes compartmentalizing data of different types whether via metadata tagging or the erection of internal database barriers; filtering or disguising data (including through the use of perturbation as discussed above); and, finding ways to identify data that might be sensitive given certain lines of inference. The second class includes traditional vetting and need to know approaches to determining who should be allowed to access certain data, relying upon roles to define who should have the right to know what information as circumstances shift, and event-triggered access as the most dynamic approach. The third class includes release controls such as vocabulary limits; secure multiparty computing that requires successful completion of joint functions in order to obtain a correct output;

the use of multidimensional classification systems; and, a variety of ways of combining these approaches.

Techniques for detecting the potential for inference include identifying diverse tags that can be mapped onto the same concept in an ontology ("ontological equivalence") (Kaushik et al., 2005) as well as analyzing logical, semantic, and mathematical relationships (Strickland, 2005). Memory-based reasoning can also be turned to this end. Those engaged in this activity, however, face a number of difficulties: more than one chain of inference may be involved in achieving any given conclusion. Relationships among data may derive from database design rather than explicit compartmentalization or tagging of the data. It may be possible to achieve a partial inference that has a reasonable degree of probability even when absolute certainty is not achieved. Most importantly, it is impossible to fully control for the user's domain knowledge; as a result, speculation regarding which information needs to be protected in order to prevent a certain type of inference from being developed may be completely inaccurate.

The last of these is of particular interest to those in the openness movement, for considerable effort is going into expanding the domain of user information that can be modeled in order to determine possible lines of inference. There has been considerable public debate about the increase in the collection about personal information, including such details as the Web sites one visits, since 9/11, and about the abandonment of barriers to the data matching across databases. These legal developments, in addition to the proactive efforts of those in the openness movement, continually expand the universe of information that can be mined for possible inference attacks.

Three limits

A number of current political tactics take advantage of — or insist upon — increased opportunities for openness in access to information and the processes of knowledge production. Voluntary exposure, efforts to democratize decision-making about scientific research and the uses of that research, and engaging in ephemeral rather than permanent actions and relationships are three such tactics. What are the strengths and weaknesses of each of these uses of openness in the face of the problems identified above?

Voluntary exposure

A decade ago we began to see the first experimentation with voluntary exposure as a means of creatively responding to encroachments on personal privacy with the Jennie-cam and other adventures involving constant recording of oneself or one's environs and the distribution of that information over the net. Today these have moved from the realm of the artist into everyday life; individuals share their personal cell phone calls loudly in public places, display intimate details about themselves regularly on MySpace, and publish their diaries or political thoughts as blogs. The term "sousveillance" has come into use to distinguish such practices from the involuntary exposure generated when surveillance is undertaken by others.

Most of this activity no longer carries an explicit political valence, but some of it does. Blogs offer a premiere example of voluntary exposure that is deliberately intended to counter perceived biases in media reportage about important political events and barriers to information flows about political realities, activities, and preferences on the ground. Global Voices (http://www.globalvoicesonline.org/), for example, is a highly sophisticated Web portal hosted by the Berkman Center for Internet and Society at Harvard Law School that offers access to blogs with news and political analysis from around the world. Managed by a former news agency bureau chief, this site is a boon to readers, who can trust the multiple layers of gatekeeping involved in choosing which bloggers to present from the myriad in any given region or on a particular topic. Growth in relationships among blog-active non-profits, effective social and political action driven by bloggers, eager participation in blogging conferences, and repeated take-up by the mainstream media of news stories and information first introduced in blogs (see, *e.g.*, Lawson-Borders and Kirk, 2005) all provide evidence that this site and related blogging activity are successfully taking advantage of the Web to enhance the diversity of information about political affairs and support the building of community among those with shared political views.

While blogs have enriched the public sphere, though, they are also themselves subjects of analysis. The intelligence community is deeply interested in bloggers representing a diversity of positions along the political spectrum in various parts of the world. For this community, blogs and blog portals like Global Voices provide an extremely efficient way of identifying individuals and groups of political interest as well as content that can be mined for data and possible lines of inference as part of the knowledge domain that constitutes the panspectron. It is possible that these uses of the voluntary exposure offered by the blogosphere could undermine the intentions of some of those who understand what they are doing to have a particular set of tactical uses in the political environment.

Openness in knowledge production

Wikipedia is one successful example of use of the Web for open knowledge production, and there are others. While there are critiques of this approach to participatory knowledge production, these share many features with critiques of other ways of producing information, and both techniques and norms for responding to criticisms and weaknesses are still developing. Compared to "Big Science," however, this process might be described as "small" in the sense that knowledge is contributed by individuals who voluntarily enter the conversation with what they bring to it and who refine that knowledge as a result of discussion with others who have also brought what they know to the table. In contrast, Big Science involves large amounts of money, highly developed organizational and experimental structures, many people engaged in coordinated collaborative activity, and hierarchical decision-making regarding which questions will be asked. The phrase "post-normal science" refers to the openness movement as it has engaged with Big Science.

The concept of post-normal science was born in environmentalism. The history of political protests against specific paths of scientific research goes back several decades in various forms of resistance to university acceptance of government funds for research in areas such as the development of nuclear weapons. It was fear over the release of genetically modified (GM) organisms into the environment, however, that stimulated the development of calls for participatory, or post-normal, science (Murdock, 2004). The ideal put forward by proponents of post-normal science is democratic decision-making about which large-scale scientific research governments would fund, as well as about how the results of research would be used. Most of those calling for post-normal science, however, focus on the effects of the uses of research results but direct their demands as well at research processes, conflating policy-making and knowledge production. If the ideal defined as "openness" were acted upon, the actual result would be closure of many important types of basic research. The notion of incorporating values and social preferences into research funding decisions is a good one, but doing so requires more than the one-step call for openness, and questions about the ethics and politics of uses of research results must involve quite other processes in order to be effective.

The ephemeral

Another tactic being used by those who are struggling to find effective modes of acting politically in the contemporary environment has been to engage in ephemeral rather than programmatic actions, and to build temporary rather than stable and enduring relationships and organizations. In a panopticon environment, these would be effective techniques. In a panspectron environment, however, this detail can become additional information for data mining.

The ephemeral is one form of the statistically improbable, a notion that has already been turned into a marketing tool by Amazon, which provides information on its Web site about the "statistically improbable phrases" that appear in books it sells. While poets since ancient times have striven to produce statistically improbable language in the form of unique expressions, in the panspectron tracking the use of such phrases allows another form of inference tracking. National security implications of the statistically improbable were introduced in the early 1990s, when "new security theory" was developed to cope with what were believed then to be post-Cold War conditions. One of the big problems for new security theory was identifying the enemy when the Soviet Union and communism no longer served, and in response four categories were identified: terrorists, those involved with drugs, those who economically threatened the U.S., and those whose behaviors were statistically unpredictable (Steele, 1990). Against this context, then, the very effort to act or relate in ephemeral ways as a tactic that takes advantage of an open environment can serve to draw attention to one's activities as a potential danger to the state. Meanwhile, when attorney general, John Ashcroft put forth the goal of building a national database that would include six degrees of separation in the information recorded. If this goal were reached, individuals on six different flights who sat in the same airplane seat, or six different renters of a particular apartment, would be linked even though in almost all such cases the relationships would be spurious.

Three recommendations

This brief investigation into threats to openness and weaknesses in tactics believed to take advantage of openness point to a dilemma for the openness movement: all structures of open content, all uses of open content, and all processes by which open content is acquired, developed, or created, are voluntary contributions to the panspectron that can then in turn be mined for analysis of possible inference attacks and identification of individuals who might be considered politically dangerous. This fact does not lead to the conclusion that openness is not desired, but it does suggest the need to develop additional tactics appropriate to the current environment. We can call these the techniques of tactical memory because they create and sustain politically effective memory. They include treatment of scale as a medium, technological discretion, and collaboration.

Scale as medium

Mandelbrot's (1977) visualization of fractals, forms that appear to be highly irregular at any single scale but which are self-replicating across scales, has helped us literally see how scale is a medium in itself. Learning to write offers an introduction to this notion as we first put letters into words, then words into sentences, sentences into paragraphs, and paragraphs into an overarching narrative structure. Thinking about genre, channels, and mediums in the digital environment has made grammatical relationships among these visible. We use the word grammar to refer to the construction of the sentences that are textual elements. Genre is in essence the grammar of narrative structure. Channels entail programming grammars within a given medium. Media are distinguished from each other by the grammar of their channels. In the pan-medium environment (Theall, 1999), distinct media, each with its own reach, types of access and borders, scale and scope, provide one grammar for our communicative and informational activities, and the emergent information architectures provided by semantic Web-type ontological efforts provide another. And scalability, of course — the ability to scale up a process or activity in terms of amount of information being processed or transmitted, the geographic or chronological reach of access and distribution, and/or the numbers of people simultaneously involved in content production and use — is a key evaluative criterion for digital content and processes.

Information search and collection systems each have their own scale, and the term granularity is used to refer to the scale of the datum-collecting mesh in use by any given system. Ulrich Beck (1992) examined the political ramifications of this when he powerfully uncovered inadequacies of the information collection mechanisms of the modern state in a world in which the critical causal mechanisms often cross boundaries of geopolitics, time, and organizational form; involve numerous causal mechanisms that interact in complex ways; and, may yield results that are themselves currently imperceptible. Schwenkel (2006) offers an example of the role of scale in the construction of memory with political value in her analysis of the way in which interpenetrated and transnational memories affect understandings of the history — and therefore the present — of Vietnam.

These features, however, also offer tactical possibilities if scale is understood as a grammar in itself. Because the mathematical techniques used to guide surveillance mechanisms and to mine data will each have their own granularity, continuous redesign of scale could provide relief from the algorithmic eye. Crossing scale can be treated as a medium in itself. In this domain artists may be the leaders in developing tactical memory techniques.

Technological discretion

Discretion is the space between what is intended, or possible, and what is actually done. Utopian visions of the changes to be wrought by new information technologies often founder on their failure to distinguish among the technological potential at the cutting edge of innovation in resource-rich situations (what we might call the technological horizon), what is logistically available to any given individual or community (the technological environment), and what is actually used by that individual or community[4]. In the moments in which choices are made in the formation of one's own information ecology vis-à-vis the potentials of the information environment, tactical decisions are possible. That discretion can be exercised both with new technologies, and with old.

The most obvious forms of technological discretion are the opportunities to choose which technologies one will engage in one's personal ecology, and how. One can choose to be networked all the time — or only a few minutes a day when actively communicating, perhaps from equipment devoted to this purpose alone. One can choose to be exposed to push media (such as that offered by television broadcasters), or pull media alone (choosing reading material or the Web sites one surfs). One can carry a GPS-enabled cellphone at all times, being constantly available for voice contact and visible to geographic location mechanisms, or not. Appreciation of the power in refusing to take up a technology suggests that some data analysis — and some policy goals — should be reconsidered.

Designers of new technologies have specific uses and effects in mind, but each also has unintended affordances. Experience in the digital environment, in fact, has invested the concept of affordances with new meaning. A relatively young word — the *Oxford English Dictionary* notes its first appearance only in 1879 — the concept has had its most active use among psychologists who, following Gibson (1966), have used it to refer to what organisms can perceive of an object's characteristics from the perspective of what they can do with those features. Optical information that shows an object to be rigid, flat, level, and extended, for example, will be interpreted as something upon which one can stand or sit. In today's environment, the notion of affordances has been taken up (see, *e.g.*, De Landa, 1991) to refer to new forms of utility individuals and groups discover as they play with the digital potential. E-mail itself developed out of the experience of scientists who used the affordances offered by a network established to exchange scientific data when they found that communicating interpersonally about that data — and then, in turn, about themselves and social affairs — improved their ability to conduct scientific analyses (Abbate, 1999). Over the past two decades, an entire culture has been built up devoted to exploring the affordances of the network environment, whether for the positive and creative purposes of hacking or for the more destructive ends of cracking. Discoveries made by those engaged in this activity have been so important that the scholarly literature on R&D now acknowledges that valuable innovation can be undertaken by users, and that what in the past had been described as misuses of technologies or failures to diffuse are in fact often moments of adaptation or a continuation of the innovation cycle.

Discretion can also be exercised to develop new uses of old technologies. The ancient practice of moving earth for purposes of ritual communication and scientific knowledge production is appearing again in contemporary art. The concept of spandrels, most commonly heard in discourse about architecture, refers to design features that have lost their original functions but that are still in use for aesthetic or other communicative purposes; an example of discretion in the use of a spandrel for purposes important to the sustenance of memory was the practice of hiding forbidden manuscripts inside of the bindings of books, where they often remained for many hundreds of years before being rediscovered, enabling lost history to be regained.

Storing information in the "underwriting" of palimpsests, media that have been written upon, erased, and written upon again, is as ancient as the use of the wax tablets from which the term derives but as newly available as storing critical information on hard drives in files that have been erased and overwritten, or in edits ostensibly removed from documents. Christopher Dewdney (1998) tells the wonderful story of the use of what he calls "Maginot Line" technologies when Persian rug-makers were able to use their skills in building coherent patterned wholes out of small fragments of material to reconstruct U.S. government documents destroyed by the CIA when the Shah of Iran fell.

Collaboration

Some of the oldest techniques of all remain valuable in the 21st century. Though asking two people with no pre-existing relationship to collaborate on building a consistent memory of an event may not yield results any better than what would be generated by each individual working alone, when friends are asked to engage in this exercise stronger, more detailed, and more coherent memories emerge (Andersson and Rönnberg, 1996). The effect is strengthened yet again when couples who have been married a long time are asked to report on shared memories; together, these couples do better on memory performance tests than many individuals who are much younger (Bower, 1997). Collaborations are also required in order to achieve success with many of the other techniques discussed above; in this sense, the distinction between individual and collective memory begins to fall away.

The implications for tactical memory are obvious: Sustain social networks over time. Collaborate on memory activities (downloading and circulating key documents, for example). And multiply content sites so critical memory can't be destroyed. Such collaborations may also extend to developing a sense of that which should be public memory and that which remains private. In many cultures there are distinctions between memories that you admit to, and those which are kept secret for tactical reasons. Just where to locate particular memories should be a critical part of our reconsideration of the boundaries between the public and the private in the 21st century.

The new twist on collaboration today, however, is that often the tools through which it is exercised are themselves digital in nature. This fact presents another challenge to those in the openness movement, for the software that supports specific modes of doing business and that enables interpersonal and group communications can itself now be patented.

One dilemma: mathematics vs. narrative creativity

"Poets are marching again upon the hills of history."

— Ed Sanders.

Openness, yes, but openness is only the beginning of the processes by which information acquires meaning and fulfills its role as a constitutive social force. The use of open information to build and sustain tactical memory, based on community experience rather than official fiat and self-consciously devoted to providing the infrastructure for effective political action, is implicitly one of the goals towards which the openness movement strives. While there is a rising tide of support for openness in many venues, there is also an array of practices and principles in play. With the transition from a panopticon to a panspectron environment, the production of open information becomes a contribution to surveillance efforts in addition to offering means by which communities can achieve their own goals and engage in public discourse about shared matters of public concern. Proprietary ownership of information is being challenged, sometimes successfully, but there is erosion of ownership in the sense of being confident in what is known: the effective location of something as basic as that of a geopolitical border has become elusive and unknowable, actions based on memory may be treated as illegal or a threat to national security simply because one's memory is involved, even official bodies are deliberately "perturbing" facts specifically because of openess, and the national security establishment need not require accuracy from the information it uses to identify individuals to be treated with suspicion.

All of the reasons why open information is desirable remain valid and openness continues to be a goal worth pursuing with energy. For purposes of tactical memory, though — community-based memory that can provide a foundation for politically effective action — some political tactics currently in use should be re-evaluated to determine their effects under current circumstances rather than as they may have worked under conditions of the past. The very traditional tactics of collaboration remain valuable, but it is also important to experiment with new types of tactics specific to the digital and network environment, including those of technological discretion and of scale as a medium.

At the most abstract level, the key political battle of the 21st century may not be between particular political parties or ideologies but, rather, the war between mathematics and narrative creativity. Data mining, searching for inference attacks, and surveillance are driven by mathematical algorithms. Against that context, it is narrative creativity, the ability to continually tell stories in new ways, that provides the means by which to elude the granularity and the logic of the mathematical nets used by those who would restrict public conversation and action to preferred forms.

Notes

1 *Federal Register*, 2003, pp. 14140–14141.
2 More cynically, Richard Posner (2002) admits that lawyers find analogical arguments irresistible because they allow attorneys to limit their reading to law books.

3 H. R. Conf. Rep. No. 109–72, 109th Cong., 1st Sess. 170–172 (2005).
4 What Nardi and O'Day (1999) usefully named the information ecology.

References

Janet Abbate, 1999. *Inventing the Internet.* Cambridge, Mass.: MIT Press.
Rakesh Agrawal and Ramakrishnan Srikant, 2000. "Privacy-preserving data mining," *Proceedings of the 2000 ACM SIGMOD International Conference on Management of Data,* volume 29, number 2, pp. 439–450.
Almeida-Sanchez v. United States, 413 U.S. 266, 272–73 (1973).
J. Andersson and J. Rönnberg. 1996. "Collaboration and memory: Effects of dyadic retrieval on different memory tasks," *Applied Cognitive Psychology,* volume 10, number 2, pp. 171–181.
Roger A. Beaumont, 1994. *War, chaos, and history.* New York: Praeger.
Ulrich Beck, 1992. *Risk society: Towards a new modernity.* Translated by Mark Ritter. London: Sage.
Jeremy Bentham, 1787. "Panopticon," In: Miran Bozovic (editor). *The panopticon writings.* London: Verso, 1995, pp. 29–95.
Bruce Bower, 1997. "Partners in recall: Elderly spouses build better memories," *Science News,* volume 11 (13 September), pp. 174–175.
Sandra Braman, 1989. "Defining information: An approach for policy-makers," *Telecommunications Policy,* volume 13, number 3, pp. 233–242.
Craig Calhoun, 1991. "Indirect relationships and imagined communities: Large-scale social integration and the transformation of everyday life," In: Pierre Bourdieu and James S. Coleman (editors). *Social theory for a changing society.* Boulder, Colo.: Westview Press, pp. 95–120.
Shuchi Chawla, Cynthia Dwork, Frank McSherry, Adam Smith, and Hoeteck Wee, 2005. "Toward privacy in public databases," presented to the Second Theory of Cryptography Conference, Cambridge (February), at http://theory.lcs.mit.edu/~asmith/PS/sdb-tcc-2005-almost-final-proceedings.pdf, accessed 9 August 2006.
Manuel De Landa, 1991. *War in the age of intelligent machines.* New York: Zone Books.
Christopher Dewdney, 1998. *Last flesh: Life in the transhuman era.* Toronto: McClelland and Stewart.
Cynthia Dwork, 2006. "Differential privacy," presented to the 33rd International Colloquium on Automata, Languages and Programming, S. Servolo, Venice (July), and at http://research.microsoft.com/research/sv/DatabasePrivacy/dwork.pdf, accessed 9 August 2006.
E.I. duPont de Nemours Powder Co. v. Masland, 244 U.S. 100 (1917).
Federal Register, 2003, pp. 14140–14141 (24 March).
Michel Foucault, 1979. "Panopticism," In: *Discipline and punish: The birth of the prison.* Translated by Alan Sheridan. New York: Vintage Books, pp. 195–230.
David Garcia and Geert Lovink, 1997. "The ABC of tactical media," first distributed via the nettime listserv; now available online at http://subsol.c3.hu/subsol_2/contributors2/garcia-lovinktext.html, accessed 9 August 2006.
Clifford Geertz, 1983. "Fact and law in comparative perspective," In: *Local knowledge: Further essays in interpretive anthropology.* New York: Basic Books, pp. 167–234.

James Jerome Gibson, 1966. *The senses considered as perceptual systems*. Boston: Houghton Mifflin.

Wilbur A. Glahn and Cameron G. Shilling, 2002. "The cutting edge of trade secret law," *Findlaw.com*, at http://library.findlaw.com/2002/Dec/20/132443.html, accessed 9 August 2006.

Nathan Hamler, 2000. "The impending merger of the inevitable disclosure doctrine and negative trade secrets: Is trade secret law heading in the right direction?" *Journal of Corporate Law*, volume 25 (Winter), pp. 383–405.

Branden Hookway, 2000. *Pandemonium: The rise of predatory locales in the postwar world*. Princeton, N.J.: Princeton Architectural Press.

Yasunori Ishihara, Shuichiro Ako, and Toru Fujiwara, 2005. "Security against inference attacks on negative information in object-oriented databases," *IEICE Transactions on Information and Systems*, volume E88-D, number 12, pp. 2767–2776.

Judith B. Ittig, 1973. "The rites of passage: Border searches and the Fourth Amendment," *40 Tennessee Law Review 329 (Spring)*.

Vijay S. Iyengar, 2002. "Transforming data to satisfy privacy constraints," *Proceedings of the Eighth ACM SIGKDD International Conference on Knowledge Discovery* (New York: ACM Press), pp. 279–288.

Hillol Kargupta, Souptik Datta, Qi Wang and Krashanmoorthy Sivakumar, 2003. "On the privacy preserving properties of random data pertubation techniques," *ICDM 2003: Third IEEE International Conference on Data Mining* (New York: IEEE), pp. 99–106.

Saket Kaushik, Wijesekera Duminda, and Paul Ammann, 2005. "Policy based dissemination of partial Web ontologies," *SWS '05: Proceedings of the 2005 ACM Workshop on Secure Web Services* (New York: ACM Press), pp. 43–62.

Kewanee Oil Company v. Bicron Corporation, 416 U.S. 470 (1974).

Jack Kloppenburg and Beth Burrows, 1996. "Biotechnology to the rescue? Twelve reasons why biotechnology is incompatible with sustainable agriculture," *Ecologist*, volume 26, number 2, pp. 61–68.

G. Lawson-Borders and R. Kirk, 2005. "Blogs in campaign communication," *American Behavioral Scientist*, volume 49, number 4, pp. 548–559.

A. D. Lee, 1993. *Information and frontiers: Roman foreign relations in late antiquity*. Cambridge: Cambridge University Press.

Edward Levi, 1949. *An introduction to legal reasoning*. Chicago: University of Chicago Press.

Suellen Lowry, 1988. "Inevitable disclosure trade secret disputes: Dissolution of concurrent property interests," *Stanford Law Review*, volume 40 (January), pp. 519–544.

Benoit B. Mandelbrot, 1977. *Fractals: Form, chance, and dimension*. New York: W.H. Freeman.

Prasenjit Mitra, ChiChun Pan, and Peng Liu, 2006. "Privacy preserving semantic dinteroperation and access control of heterogeneous databases," *Proceedings of the 2006 ACM Symposium on Information, Communication, and Computer Security* (New York: ACM Press), pp. 66–77.

Alberto Melucci, 1997. *Challenging codes: Collective action in the information age*. Cambridge: Cambridge University Press.

Ian Molho, 1997. *The economics of information: Lying and cheating in markets and organizations*. Oxford: Blackwell.

Morlife, Inc. v. Lloyd Perry, 56 Cal. App. 4th 1514 (1st Dist. Aug. 14, 1997).

Graham Murdock, 2004. "Popular representation and postnormal science: The struggle over genetically modified foods," In: Sandra Braman (editor). *Biotechnology and communication: The meta-technologies of information*. Mahwah, N.J.: Lawrence Erlbaum Associates, pp. 227–260.

Bonnie A. Nardi and Vicki L. O'Day, 1999. "Information ecologies: Using technology with heart," *First Monday*, volume 4, number 5 (May), at http://www.firstmonday.org/issues/issue4_5/nardi_contents.html, accessed 9 August 2006.

Helen Nissenbaum, 2004. "Privacy as contextual integrity," *Washington Law Review*, volume 79, pp. 119–157.

Richard A. Posner, 2002. *The problematics of moral and legal theory*. Cambridge, Mass.: Harvard University Press.

Douglas L. Rogers, 2003. "The SCO litigation: Maintaining walls around trade secrets or attacking the knowledge of those outside the walls?" *Intellectual Property & Technology Law Journal*, volume 15, pp. 1–15.

Jennifer L. Saulino, 2002. "Locating inevitable disclosure's place in trade secret analysis," *Michigan Law Review*, 2002 (March): pp. 1184–1214.

Christina Schwenkel, 2006. "Recombinant history: Transnational practices of memory and knowledge production in contemporary Vietnam," *Cultural Anthropology*, volume 21, number 1, pp. 3–30.

SCO v. IBM, case #2:03cv00294 DAK in the U.S. District Court Central Division, District of Utah (trial scheduled for 2007).

Harriet J. Sims, 1977. "Recent Developments," *George Washington Law Journal*, volume 65, p. 1641.

Robert David Steele, 1990. "Intelligence in the 1990's: Recasting national security in a changing world," *American Intelligence Journal*, volume 11, number 3, pp. 29–36.

Lee S. Strickland, 2005. *Secure information sharing: Balancing classification policies in an electronic era with new adversaries*. College Park: Center for Information Policy, University of Maryland; prepared for the Information Security Oversight Office, National Archives and Record Administration, at http://www.cip.umd.edu/reports/ISOO_report_final.pdf, accessed 9 August 2006.

Cass R. Sunstein, 1996. *Legal reasoning and political conflict*. New York: Oxford University Press.

Donald F. Theall, 1999. "The carnivalesque, the Internet and control of content: Satirizing knowledge, power and control," *Continuum: Journal of Media & Cultural Studies*, volume 13, number 2, pp. 153–164.

Martin L. Van Creveld, 1991. *Technology and war: From 2000 BC to the present*. Revised and expanded edition. New York: Free Press.

Lloyd L. Weinreb, 2005. *Legal reason: The use of analogy in legal argument*. Cambridge: Cambridge University Press.

86

THE SECRET SELF

The case of identity theft

Mark Poster

Source: *Cultural Studies* 21(1) (2007): 118–40.

> In the late 1990s, 'Identity Theft' became a crime in the United States. At that time 'Identity Theft' was determined to be the fastest rising crime in the country. It is a crime that depends on digital culture and networked computing. I ask how this crime works to redefine the nature of identity, how it exteriorizes identity, separating it from the interiority of consciousness and moving it into the realm of information machines. The implications of identity theft for privacy and security are also examined. I ask as well about the implications of such theft for an emerging Western and Global culture that relies increasingly on digital media, the interaction of humans and information machines.

Is secrecy possible under the gaze of transparency increasingly set in place by digital networks? One may argue that secrecy requires a private realm, whether this be the secure walls of the family home, a safety deposit box, or the inner recesses of consciousness. One may also argue that such conditions are melting away in an age when media, especially digital media, dissolve the border between the public and the private. In this essay I will examine the extraordinary case of 'identity theft' to illustrate the contemporary conditions of privacy and its lack, secrecy and its possible impossibility.

The recent construction of the crime of identity theft raises the paradoxical question of the security of identity. How can actions in the world impinge upon and even destabilize an individual's identity? Is not identity threatened primarily from interior upheavals such as crises of identity, traumatic loss of memory, disintegration of the personality as a consequence of mental breakdowns, psychoses, and the like? If one's identity is subject to the felony of theft (grand theft identity, one would surmise), is not the nature of identity itself called into question? When identity can be stolen like an automobile, a purse, or a credit card, then it must be a thing of this world, a piece of private property, an asset of some sort, a material possession. If that is the case, we must account for the construction of identity as an object, not as a subject.

The general culture regards identity as the basis of subjectivity, as the center of the self, its spiritual core. If that were true or the entirety of the issue, then 'identity theft' would clearly not be possible. When individuals construct their own identities, as current liberal ideology proclaims, the theft of identity is not even conceivable. We need then to account for a change in the nature of identity, its exteriorization and materialization, its becoming vulnerable to theft, its emergence as insecure – within the ideology of individualism itself. To achieve such an analysis I propose two steps. The first is to place the alteration of the construction of identity squarely within a Foucaultian framework of a technology of power. This affords the advantage of comprehending identity in its exteriorization to begin with, as a phenomenon instituted by discourses and practices, as a form of 'subjectivation'. Next we need to account for the role of information machines or media – what I call 'the mode of information' – in the process. Such a double strategy of interpretation allows 'identity' to emerge as a historical process, one neither naturalized nor universalized within the ideology of liberalism and its insistence on the always already given figure of identity within the individual. The innovation of identity theft as the materialization of identity appears then not as a fall from the grace of interior identity, as some malign feature of new media, but as the potential of every construction of identity, as the dangerous supplement to the positing of identity as the core of the self.

Prologue

Everyone knows about identity theft and probably has some degree of fear and insecurity because of it. People know about it and are anxious about it not because they have directly experienced identity theft but because the media have relentlessly informed them about it. The situation regarding identity theft is typical of insecurity in a heavily mediated age. Information machines – newspapers, magazines, television, radio, the Internet – constitute the discourses that (in)form subjects as participants in culture. Far more than oral, face-to-face networks, media disseminate cultural meanings and give shape to our insecurities. In the case of identity theft, Americans have seen television shows, heard radio newscasts, read magazines all of which present themselves as educating the public about events and situations, while at the same time these media produce a hyperreal effect that makes all-to-present a certain danger.

THE SECRET SELF: THE CASE OF IDENTITY THEFT

Advertisement

Figure 1 People Magazine 12 August 2003.

Here is an example of media induced anxiety from a Citibank advertisement published in *People Magazine* on 8 December 2003. Video versions of the similar material were broadcast on many networks television in late November and early December 2003, continuing well into 2004. In the following three photos, images of individuals are presented with text that somehow does not fit their appearance.

In figure 1, a middle-aged, conservatively dressed woman of color says 'I spent $2,342 on violent and suggestive video games'. In figure 2, a middle-aged portly white man says 'I had $23,000 worth of liposuction'. In figure 3, a young white woman, a girl-next-door type, says 'There are 3 warrants for

Advertisement

Figure 2 People Magazine 12 August 2003.

my arrest. One of them involves smuggling'. In each case the image does not fit the quote. This discordance is explained in the figure 4.

Figure 4 for the first time designates the source of the advertisement as Citibank. It reads, from the top, 'Identity theft. It can take your good credit rating. Never mind your good name'. At this point the reader may be able to decode the apparent contradiction in figures 1 to 3 between the image and the text. The identities of the three people have been stolen and the money was spent not by them but by the thieves. The advertisement, it might be noted, appropriates an artistic device made famous by René Magritte's 'Ceci n'est pas une pipe (1926)', one that was widely used in

THE SECRET SELF: THE CASE OF IDENTITY THEFT

Advertisement

Figure 3 People Magazine 12 August 2003.

conceptual art (see figure 5). The technique exploits the media specificity and difference between images and words, in Magritte's case to play with the opposing meanings or contradiction within the image, thereby destabilizing the viewer's reading and rendering impossible, some would say undecidable, a unified interpretation. The word, in this case 'pipe', can never be identical to the image of a pipe or to the referent pipe. Yet the image is that of a pipe. The text and image refute each other (Foucault 1983). The indexicality of the image and the referentiality of the text work against each another. This oppositional tension, however, points to the non-identity of word, image,

Figure 4 People Magazine 12 August 2003.

THE SECRET SELF: THE CASE OF IDENTITY THEFT

Figure 5 René Magritte, 'This is not a Pipe'.

and thing. It suggests both their relationality – words and images do refer to things – and their media specificity – as different media they are able to operate against each other.

Citibank's advertisement deploys, more modestly and with less artistic creativity, the media specificity of word and image to indicate the consequence of identity theft: a person's life may be taken away from them if someone else is able to use one's personal information for their own benefit. Thus in figure 1 $2,342 dollars were spent by a teen-age boy to buy video games, not the woman pictured in the ad; in figure 2 $23,000 were used by a woman for plastic surgery to improve her appearance, not by the man in the image; in figure 3, a convicted smuggler stole the identity of a prim looking young woman. The advertisement works its scary operations by stereotyping the texts and images. It could be that woman in figure 1 is a fan of video games, that the fat man in figure 2 was much fatter before liposuction, and that the innocent looking young woman in figure 3 was indeed a felon. Only the reader's cultural biases prevent an incorrect interpretation.

With figure 4 not only is the source of the advertisement made explicit, but the insecurity generated in the narrative of figures 1 to 3 is dissipated: Citibank will protect the reader from identity theft, guaranteeing one's safety as a consumer. The fear that was aroused in figures 1 to 3 through the contradiction of image and text is happily resolved. All one need do to achieve piece of mind and security of identity is to obtain a Citibank credit card. The financial corporation has made the world that much better and safer. And all of this happens just in time for Christmas shopping. Happy holidays!

In the televised versions, the promotion is more easily effective in producing the 'correct' interpretation by the viewer. In one of some dozen of these, a seated young, black woman speaks about spending a lot of money but the voice one hears is that of an older man, synchronized with the lip movements of the person in the video image.[1] Of course, the 'woman' might be a transsexual with a baritone voice. This possibility is not registered by the advertisement, working as it does with commonplace stereotypes. Granting this potential difficulty, the televised version deploys voice instead of text, with the specificity of the media resulting in a more obvious representation of contradiction and mismatched identity.

Although the ad, as moving image with sound, arouses the audience to immediate recognition of the double identity, thief and victim combined, it also generates in the viewer a strong feeling of the uncanny. In order to unify the image with the sound, the picture must express emotions that are consonant with the voice. In this case, the voice (of the thief) is gleeful. He has pulled off a successful robbery and is enjoying his stolen merchandise. But the woman in the image, synchronously mouthing the same words the male thief speaks, is also smiling even though she has no reason to be happy. There is a double contradiction in the advertisement: the man's voice speaks in the woman's body and the woman is smiling while the words she mouths indicate unfortunate circumstances. The second contradiction is rendered necessary in order to achieve the verisimilitude of the first contradiction. If the woman's expression was one of unhappiness, the identity of the thief would not fold into the identity of the victim. The result for the viewer is intense discomfort at the discordance being performed.

The televised advertisement deploys a conceit familiar in science-fiction films such as *The Invasion of the Body Snatchers* (1956). The victim's body has been taken over by the identity thief, although in the case of the Citibank ad, the voice of the thief substitutes for the voice of the victim. The uncanny feeling in the audience results from the hybrid victim's body-thief's voice. In the science fiction film, the victim's voice remains in the victim's body, with only a slight but important change in the tone of the voice, eerie and emotionless. In the televised ad, the voice (of the thief) and the facial expression (of the victim) retain their demonstrative qualities. The media specific merger of the voice and body produce a discomforting illusion of the theft not only of the identity but of the body as well. The thief's trace, however, is present in his or her voice. Identity theft is here represented visually and aurally not as a substitution of consciousnesses or information from one person to another but as a voice in the wrong body.

If the print advertisement suffers from the limitations of its media constraints, so the televised advertisement, in some ways more effective than the former, also cannot quite pull off the representation of identity theft. These media 'failures' suggest the difficulty of the cultural issue of identity theft: it contains so many irreconcilable fragments that its rupture through theft is not easily expressed in analogue media. One might well conclude that identity is impossible with digital media or networked computing. Only in that domain can the social markers of the physical world be nullified, only in that domain can theft of identity be represented and practiced. In this paper I want to explore the case of identity theft in relation to the media, networked computing in particular, and to inquire about the changed circumstances of security in the domain of the digitally constituted self.

Identity theft

One of the noteworthy aspects of identity theft is its sudden appearance in print media. On August 22, 2003, I searched for the term in several online databases and received surprising results. The Modern Language Association bibliography returned a result sum of zero. As of that date, we can conclude that no humanistic inquiry had been published on the topic. Two other bibliographic databases yield listing yielded the following figures:

	1987–1999	*2000–August 2003*
The Expanded Academic ASAP/Gale	39	144
Computer related magazines	18	56
Proquest ABI/INFORM	10	328

Almost none of the references dated before 1995 and through 1999 there were very few. Beginning in 2000 there is a flurry of articles that have 'identity theft' in the title, mostly in newspapers and popular weeklies. It is clear that 'identity theft' is a twenty-first century phenomenon. This fact is significant especially because it indicates a cultural lag in the use of the term because, as we shall soon see, it includes both digital crimes on the Internet and the theft of credit card information that occurs in more conventional public spaces. It took some time before the term 'identity theft' was adopted in the print media to apply to situations of stolen personal, credit information.

The popular media definition of identity theft specifies the appropriation of an individual's personal information to provide access for the criminal to credit lines, purchases and cash. The thief does not take material objects that belong to someone else, only 'information'. Here is one definition: 'With identity theft, a thief takes over a consumer's entire identity by stealing critical private information, such as the Social Security number, driver's license number, address, credit card number or bank account number. The thief can then use the stolen information to obtain illegal loans or credit lines to buy goods and services under the stolen name' (McNamara 2003). Identity theft then does not refer to the theft of credit cards and their use by the perpetrator. The crime might include taking a credit card but it is taken only for the information it provides the criminal, in particular account numbers. The false use of credit cards constitutes fraud (presenting oneself in a store as someone else and forging their signature on the credit slip) and is not generally included in the category 'identity theft'.

Other writers define the term somewhat differently. Jennifer Lee, writing in the *New York Times*, makes an interesting distinction between illegally using existing accounts or funds and creating new ones: 'Unlike identity theft, in which the criminal uses personal information to open and use accounts that are in the victim's name, account theft entails using stolen credit or A.T.M. cards, or financial records, to steal from the victim's existing accounts'. Identity theft is more serious, she continues because 'The scope of the problem is moving international and moving to larger rings of criminals' (Lee 2003). What Lee terms 'account theft' is thus a more traditional form of robbery while 'identity theft' designates acting in someone else's place to create financial instruments for illegal gain. Lee's distinction tends to hold in most of the media discussions of the crime, but it fails to discriminate between various uses of digital media.

Some reporters limit identity theft to those cases where the Internet is used to obtain personal information and restrict the illegal use of found or stolen credit cards to more traditional categories of transgression. The difficulty in sustaining this distinction is that even in those cases where a physical credit card is misappropriated, criminals very often use the card as information on the Internet to purchase goods, obtain loans, or secure new credit cards (Mihm 2003, p. 44). In either case, identity theft refers to stolen information that is deployed in a digital network illegally to obtain money and goods. In one of the few books devoted to the topic, Katalina Bianco defines identity theft as follows: 'Identity theft is a term used to refer to all types of crime in which someone wrongfully obtains and uses another person's personal data in a way that involves fraud or deception, typically for economic gain' (Bianco 2001, p. 1).

We may now return to the question of why the term 'identity theft' was not used until the 2000s. 'Identity Theft', like so many other practices on digital networks, was until recently not recognized as a crime. No one, before the widespread use of the Internet, did it nor was there a law against it. Thieves certainly used others' personal documents but they did not, until recently, extract personal information from these papers and cards to act economically in another's place. As Stephen Mihm explains, 'Existing federal legislation addressed only the fraudulent creation, use and transfer of identification documents, not the theft and criminal use of the underlying personal information, particularly Social Security numbers and dates of birth' (2003, p. 44). It was not until 30 October 1998 that the US legislature enacted the Identity Theft and Assumption Deterrence Act that covered the practices in question. Only after that date could one prosecute someone for identity theft. Newspapers began to discuss identity theft by and large only after it was designated a crime. There was thus something very new about identity theft. Only with digital networks could the crime of using someone's personal information for economic gain become a widespread practice. Digital information machines were then coupled with criminal intent to produce the innovation of identity theft.

And steal they did. In the short space of two or three years, identity theft went from an unrecognized practice to the fastest growing crime in the United States. In 2002, for example, there were 418,000 robberies in the country but 700,000 identity thefts, almost twice the number. One periodical reported that no less than seven million Americans thought they had been victims of identity theft (Livingston 2003). The statistics are astounding and frightening. Judging from newspaper and periodical reports, the likelihood is great the many if not most individuals will have their identity stolen in their lifetime. Which leads to some amusing and interesting speculations...

Perpetrators and their victims

Who commits the crime of identity theft? One might guess that such a high-tech crime would be enacted by computer specialists such as hackers. But this is not at all the case, judging from newspaper reports. Here is a list of categories of perpetrators gleaned from periodicals: a former college official, a former state worker, an ex-H&R Block manager, high-tech insiders, an Orange County Couple, prison workers, a student, the wife of an imprisoned gang leader, automobile dealership employees (with 1700 complaints in 2001) and, of course, Al-Qaeda terrorists. One article argued that identity theft is not normally the act of a lone individual, but requires the complicity of major financial institutions like banks and credit agencies. Sheila Cherry writes, 'Identity theft is only possible with the full cooperation of three major participants: the impostor, the creditor and the credit bureau. All are coconspirators and equally guilty of identity theft' (Cherry 2002). So much information is needed to carry out the felony that lax security procedures by large financial institutions is a condition for the crime. Insiders are naturally blamed for information leakage, not only from banks but also from government agencies. As one critic notes, 'There is widespread use of Social Security numbers in government and business databases, which hackers access illegally' (Anonymous 2003a). Sheila Cherry continues, '... others say the technology that gave government easier access to private information is in fact responsible for the epidemic of identity theft. Even the Department of Justice (DOJ) has warned of the insider problem caused by too many employees having too much access to personal information on citizens' (2002). The institutions that are responsible for our security – banks, insurance companies, government offices – turn out to be a major source of criminal activity in the area of identity theft.

If the list of perpetrators is long, the list of victims is even longer. Just about anyone is vulnerable to identity theft: surprising perhaps on the list are doctors and patients, army troops, even a UC Irvine faculty housing resident. The Police Department Crime Log of the University of California, Irvine reports under the category 'grand theft' the following: 'UCI affiliate reports credit card fraud by theft of identity in University Hills. Disposition: Report Taken'. One is apparently not safe anywhere. Many of the victims are accosted not in the street or in physical space but in virtual realm of the Internet. Cyberspace is a realm that cancels the borders between public and private, rendering all communications and all data on one's hard drive part of a shared electronic space. Although obstacles can be placed between one's computer and the global network, the basic architecture of the Internet is designed for open and rapid connections between all online computers. Firewalls and other techniques to limit outside access to one's local machine are means of partial isolation and protection. Many instances of identity theft are a consequence of open structure of the Internet. Scott Bradner observes '. . . a major reason for the dramatic increase in the threat [of identity theft] stems from the all-too-easy availability of personal information on computer systems connected to the Internet' (Bradner 2003). We can conclude from this that identity theft is a result of the new relation between humans and digital information machines, an interface that couples in a new synergy carbon based and silicon based beings. In the context of the human-computer interface, identity takes on a different configuration from that announced by Locke, expanded upon by Erikson, and politicized by the new social move-ments. The security of identity in the digital world is, as a consequence, a different matter from that in the physical world of extended objects. What is stolen is not one's consciousness but one's self as it is embedded in (increasingly digital) databases. The self constituted in these databases, beyond the ken of individuals, may be considered the digital unconscious.

Identity theft and its discontents

Victims Assistance of America, Inc. maintains a website that allows victims of identity theft to upload their stories. As one browses through the tales of loss, it becomes clear that identity theft turns people's lives upside down. After someone has amassed huge unpaid bills, all in your name, you often cannot get a mortgage or refinance your house for months while you try to clear your name. Meanwhile, you are harassed by collection agencies insisting you pay for charges you swear to them you did not make. A couple of incidents printed in *Consumer Reports* will suffice to get a feeling for the trials one undergoes as a victim of identity theft. 'Margaret Murray, a disabled homemaker from Spartanburg, SC, was arrested in front of her son after a thief passed bad checks in her name. Frances Green, a beautician from Jamaica, NY, discovered that the house she was about to buy had already been sold – to an ID thief posing as Green who, with a phony seller and fake lawyers, defrauded the mortgage company and ruined Green's credit' (Anonymous 2003b, p. 12). Here is the story of Bob Hartle of Phoenix, Arizona: 'Hartle spent nearly four years and $15,000 to restore his good name after an identity thief borrowed more than $100,000 in his name and then filed for bankruptcy. The impostor had also obtained five driver's licenses (and a speeding ticket) in Hartle's name, opened bank accounts, was hired and fired as Bob Hartle, and failed to pay state and federal taxes. The real Hartle says he contacted more than 100 people in his quest to repair the damage, including local law-enforcement agencies, the FBI and the US Secret Service's financial-crimes division' (Davis 1998). Stories like these are abundant in print and broadcast media.

The inconvenience and economic loss suffered by victims is enormous. It can take a victim several years to straighten out their situation. Often one does not discover the problem until months after the perpetrator has carried out the crime, an indication that the theft of identity is unconscious to the individual. And the loss is paid for by all consumers, amounting to an estimated $4.2 billion in 2003 (Davis 1998). Identity theft is thus far from a trivial problem, but one that increasingly characterizes digitally mediated society.

Genealogy of identity

An understanding of 'identity theft' can be helped by a clarification of the term 'identity'. To this end I will attempt a genealogy of the cultural figure of 'identity'. Genealogies are best carried out, if Foucault and Nietzsche are our guides, by going back to a point in history when the phenomenon in question appears to contemporary eyes as monstrous, as in the punishment of Damiens, the regicide. I will instead begin with the familiar and comfortable, with first the concepts of identity in Locke and Erickson, then a cultural history of the combination of identity with media in the nineteenth century, finally with the uses of identity in the late twentieth century in the so-called new social movements and in postmodern practices of popular culture and consumerism.

Locke and identity as consciousness

In the modern philosophical tradition there is a remarkably consistent use of the term 'identity' as an attribute of consciousness, a discursive line that begins quite abruptly with John Locke.[2] In Chapter 27 'Of Identity and Diversity' of volume 1 of *An Essay Concerning Human Understanding*, Locke first considers the question of identity or sameness in relation to all beings, not only humans. He argues that the sameness of anything is 'something that existed such a time in such a place, which it was certain, at that instant, was the same with itself, and no other' (Locke 1959, pp. 438–9). Here, as Koyré has so nicely demonstrated, is the coordinated, Cartesian world of time and space where any being can be fixed in its location (Koyré 1958). The world is here a three dimensional grid with each element or body occupying a unique and definite bit of space/time. For Locke, this condition applies equally to humans: 'for man it is the same as with everything else: [identity is] a participation of the same continued life, by constantly fleeting particles of matter, in succession vitally united to the same organized body' (Locke 1959, p. 444). Humans have an identity precisely because they can endure through time and in space.

As an aside I note that such a modern configuration of identity as sameness in time and space systematically excludes the dimension of time as change. Objects after all and contra Locke do not subsist in time. They alter in appearance, decay and disappear. Identity in Locke's sense persists only for the moment and, from a longer term point of view, is illusory. Indeed, digital technology introduces the morph as a visual refutation of the Descartes/Locke model of identity. As extended objects, digital morphs (Fisher 2000) alter seemingly at will, confounding the eye of the beholder with infinitely changing shapes, anticipated in imagination by Ovid's *Metamorphoses*. The modern Western concept of identity is in this sense a remarkable cultural construction that, when the time dimension is considered, appears ridiculous.

But the English philosopher, like his French forebear, René Descartes, recognizes the special quality of the human as a rational, self-conscious being whose identity must reflect this all-important attribute. So Locke contends that identity must include the *recognition* of sameness. He writes that a person is 'a thinking intelligent being, that has reason and reflection, and can consider itself as itself, the same thinking thing, in different times and places; which it does only by that consciousness which is inseparable from thinking, and, as it seems to me, essential to it . . .' (1959, p. 448–9). Unlike for Descartes for whom it is enough that a human think in order to be and have its essence in reason, for Locke, identity is secured through its enduring recognition by the self. Locke improves considerably upon Descartes for making identity central to the human self.

In addition, Locke insists that identity requires not only recognition, but, perhaps by dint of that, consciousness. Identity is an attribute of consciousness for him. In a remarkable passage, Locke formulates the cornerstone of the modern concept of identity:

> For, it being the same consciousness that makes a man be himself to himself, personal identity depends on that only, whether it be annexed solely to one individual substance, or can be continued in a succession of several substances . . . For it is by the consciousness it has of its present thoughts and actions, that it is *self to itself* now, and so will be the same self, as far as the same consciousness can extend to actions past or to come; and would be by distance of

time, or change of substance, no more two persons, than a man be two men by wearing other clothes to-day than he did yesterday, with a long or a short sleep between; the same consciousness uniting those distant actions into the same person, whatever substances contributed to their production.

(1958, pp. 450–2)

Regardless of changes in what he calls secondary attributes such as clothing, Locke defines identity as an interior quality of awareness. In this respect, the notion of sameness is not the same for all beings, he argues, against his earlier claim, but is unique for humans as distinct from other substances with respect to its property of consciousness. He writes: 'This may show us wherein personal identity consists: not in the identity of substance, but, as I have said, in the identity of consciousness...' (1958, p. 460).

A further complication of Locke's theory of identity, especially as it relates to the question of identity theft, is the connection he draws between the self and property (MacPherson 1962). In *The Second Treatise of Civil Government*, Locke grounds the basis of property in social wealth in the relation one has to oneself. In the first instance, property is ownership of the self by the self. He writes, '... every man has a property in his own person; this nobody has any right to but himself' (Locke 1937, p. 19). Acts of labor expand the domain of property to the objects worked on, such as land. Identity theft is therefore a violation of the primary relation one has to oneself, removing the ground for all subsequent forms of accumulation brought about through labor. If one's self has been stolen one cannot, given Locke's logic, amplify one's property through labor because there is no agent or ground for the addition. Identity theft undermines the capitalist basis for property and presents the paradoxical state of a body with no ability to accumulate wealth.

As philosophers are wont to do, Locke considers several objections to his concept of identity, dismissing each one in turn with arguments based in logic. The classic conditions of unreason that Descartes had noted are also debated by Locke, those of drunkenness and dreaming, for instance. Locke also, it might be noted as something of a remarkable curiosity, takes up the question of multiple personality, of 'two distinct incommunicable consciousnesses acting in the same body' (1958, p. 464). In the context of this study of identity theft in digital information technology, I cannot pursue in any detail Locke's analysis of two consciousness in one body, each quite unconscious of the other's existence. Suffice it to say that the question of multiple selves has been a major point of contention in many areas of discourse for the past three decades. Psychologists still ponder the possibility of multiple personalities without resolving the question firmly (Hacking 1995). Philosophers too have continued to debate the point, with postmodernists, like Gilles Deleuze and Félix Guattari outrageously announcing in the first lines of their celebrated work, *A Thousand Plateaus*, their own multiplicity: 'The two of us wrote *Anti-Oedipus* together. Since each of us was several, there was already quite a crowd' (Deleuze and Guattari 1987, p. 3). Multiple identities certainly complicate the question of identity theft. How many identities does a thief have to steal in order fully to render the robbery complete? And what would Citibank have to say about the issue?

Erikson and identity as ego

If John Locke linked identity with consciousness, the psychological implications of the move were not systematically developed until the work of Erik Erikson, for whom identity became, extending and replacing the Freudian concept of the ego, the central feature of individual psychology. Starting with *Childhood and Society* (1950), continuing in *Young Man Luther* (1958), and culminating in *Identity: Youth and Crisis* (1968), Erikson developed a concept of identity that was widely influential in the social sciences and in the general culture. If anyone can be said to have authored the term in twentieth century American society Erikson must be given credit for the accomplishment.

Erikson's position was associated with the ego psychology revision of psychoanalysis whose leading theorist was Heinz Hartmann (Hartmann 1964). Briefly, ego psychology altered psychoanalytic theory by diminishing the importance of the instincts, marginalizing the role of the unconscious, stressing position of the ego, and introducing a new preoccupation with social aspects of individual psychology. Each of these revisions of psychoanalysis contributed to the emergence of the question of identity. In post-World War II America, the leading psychological preoccupation was no longer, as it was in Victorian Europe, sexuality and its etiology but the coherence of the self. Americans, it would appear, felt lost, dazed and confused perhaps by the incredible success of the United States in world affairs, by the boundless power of the country, by the rapid changes that were being introduced in society and culture.

Erikson theorized identity explicitly as an addition to and revision of psychoanalysis, complaining that the lack of a concept of identity was a serious failure. With the goal of opening space in psychoanalytic theory for a concept of identity, he lambasted classic Freudian thought for its inadequate recognition of the social. He contended that the absence of a concept of identity in psychoanalysis is a direct consequence of its preoccupation with interior mental life at the expense of understanding the individual as immersed in a wider world: 'The traditional psychoanalytic method ... cannot quite grasp identity because it has not developed terms to conceptualize the environment. Certain habits of psychoanalytic theorizing, habits of designating the environment as "outer world" or "object world", cannot take account of the environment as a pervasive reality' (Erikson 1968, p. 24).

From his first formulations of the concept, Erikson characterized identity as an attribute of the ego. He wrote in 1950 'The sense of ego identity ... is the accrued confidence that the inner sameness and continuity prepared in the past are matched by the sameness and continuity of one's meaning for others ...' (Erikson 1963, p. 261). In 1968, almost 20 years later, he confirmed his earlier notion of identity, defining it in remarkably similar terms: 'Ego identity ... is the awareness of the fact that there is a self-sameness and continuity to the ego's synthesizing methods, the *style of one's individuality*, and that this style coincides with the sameness and continuity of one's *meaning for significant others* in the immediate community' (Erikson 1968, p. 50). One might quip that there is an identity to Erikson's concept of identity. One might also note the strong resonances in Erikson of Locke's notion of identity. 'Sameness', 'continuity' – these are the terms through which Locke theorized identity.

Ego identity was, for Erikson, not an easy accomplishment but a stage of life fraught with dangers. There was no assurance that identity would be achieved; fragmentation and confusion were equally possible as fates for the individual. Identity, for him, was a persistent issue throughout life but was especially acute during an individual's youth or adolescence. It was this time of life that marked a 'crisis' of identity. The individual was challenged to synthesize earlier psychic developments and achieve a stability of self that a century before might have been called 'character'. Erikson writes regarding the period of youth, 'It is the ego's function to integrate the psychosexual and psychosocial aspects on a given level of development and at the same time to integrate the relation of newly added identity elements with those already in existence ...' (1968, p. 162). If this task is successfully negotiated, the individual emerges with an identity enjoying three psychic strengths: 'a conscious sense of individual uniqueness', 'an unconscious striving for continuity', and 'a solidarity with a group's ideals' (Erikson 1968, p. 208). The American discourse on identity, by dint of Erikson's writing and its popularity, reinforced the Lockean version of identity as consciousness.

Identity in the United States, despite the psychic issues of crisis Erikson raised, by definition is secure since it refers to a quality of self-consciousness, an interior sense of unity, integrity, autonomy, determination. As we shall see this notion of identity carried over into the political realm in the 1970s and 1980s, just before the origin of the crime of identity theft.

Identity and theft

Although the main current of the modern definition of identity was associated with interior consciousness, there was a second cultural inscription of the term, one far less dominant than the first but nonetheless increasingly important as certain changes occurred in the configuration of political power beginning in the late eighteenth century. Starting at that time, the technology of power of sovereignty began to be supplemented with a new technology of power of governmentality, as Foucault names it (Foucault 1991). Governmentality refers to the policing of the population, the institution of surveillance mechanisms, the construction of extensive bureaucracies and social science disciplines to monitor many aspects of the health and welfare of all citizens. A new kind of power was thereby established that constructed each individual as a case. Potentially every individual would have a dossier filled with information that tracked them through their life course, recording significant events and changes in their circumstances. In other words, databases were set in place that identified individuals and traced their goings and comings. Each individual took on an additional identity, one inscribed in the ledgers of governments, insurance companies, workplaces, schools, prisons, the military, libraries – every institutionalized space in modern urban environments. In the words of Nikolas Rose, '. . . the ideas of identity and its cognates have acquired an increased salience in so many of the practices in which human beings engage. In political life, in work, in conjugal and domestic arrangements, in consumption, marketing, and advertising, in television and cinema, in the legal complex and the practices of the police, and in the apparatuses of medicine and health, human beings are addressed, represented, and acted upon *as if they were selves* of a particular type: suffused with an individualized subjectivity, motivated by anxieties and aspirations concerning their self-fulfillment, committed to finding their true identities and maximizing their authentic expression in their life-styles' (Rose 1998, pp. 169–170). In order for governmentality to be effective, media were necessary, media in the form of records that first were handwritten, later took the shape of print, and finally were digitized and computerized. In the nineteenth century, means were sought in new technologies to link the record of the individual with his or her body. Mechanisms of identification were needed to suture the individual with the record. At first, simple records were generated in the form of identity cards and passports, but later photography was adapted to police procedures and the uncertain science of finger-printing was added to the arsenal of practices of criminal investigation. For the most important individuals to be fixed into the media of record-keeping were criminals. Crimes against persons and especially against property militated strongly for apparatuses of identification.

With the emergence in the nineteenth century of anonymity in urban crowds, Tom Gunning observes, came '. . . bureaucratic means to trace and identify, such as medical documentation and the growing use of photographs in identity cards and passports, all of which demarcate a person as a unique entity' (1995, p. 23). Gunning argues that the photograph was central to constituting the individual as a unique identity and therefore to the origin of the modern *individual*. He continues, 'Such techniques of identification became necessary in the new world of rapid circulation and facilitated the circulation of the newly constituted individual through its circuits with a traceable accountability' (p. 23). He concludes as follows: 'The vulnerability of one's body to recording and classification developed into fantasies of universal observation not only through being photographed while under arrest but also through being caught in the act by photography' (p. 35). From the outset of modernity, media were coupled with identity and criminals were the leading figures in the new play of forces. As soon as an effort was made to identify individuals the focus on interior consciousness was inadvertently dislocated into the exterior mechanisms of analogue traces, as photographs, as finger-prints, eventually as DNA. What needs special emphasis in the context of my effort to make sense of the new crime of identity theft, is that individual identity is being transformed, by dint of information media, into something that both captures individuality and yet exists in forms of external traces.

Identity as resistance

The pre-history of identity theft cannot, however, be written as a linear evolution from the region of consciousness to the realm of the media. The narrative is much more complex. Just as highly sophisticated and fine-grained media were able to identify individuals with the least traces left behind by their bodies or in extensive databases, an opposing current developed that combined both earlier tendencies in Locke and Erikson of identity as consciousness, and the newer practice of identity as material, bodily trace. In the new social movements of the 1970s and 1980s and in the popular culture of the postmodern era, identity was reconfigured both as exterior sign or mediated trace and as intentional consciousness. In the protest movements that contested gender and race hierarchies, visible features of the individual such as body shape and skin color were linked with rebellious consciousness against forms of discrimination and oppression targeted to those traces. Identity politics was born. Ethnicity and race, gender and sexual orientation became pivots of resistance against discrimination, marginalization, and social injustice in countless forms. In fact, privileged positions of radicality were claimed across the board of these movements, assertions that one was especially able to recognize injustice and to struggle against it *because* of one's identity as Asian American (Lowe 1996), a woman (Hartsock 1997), a black woman (Collins 2000), queer (Warner 1993) and so on. In each case, critical consciousness is coupled with some aspect of bodily identity. A unity is fashioned from both the 'interior' of consciousness as identity and the 'exterior' of bodily characteristic. What is of special interest in the context of this study of identity theft is that such unity is in many cases regarded as unproblematic in the sense that resistive identity consciousness couples exactly with bodily characteristics *and* modes of oppression.[3] Identity is thus a double operation of material trace and consciousness bound together in a configuration that solidifies the figure of identity even as one enunciates opposition to its subjugation.

It is perhaps ironic that popular culture took a similar path in the 1980s also combining interior consciousness and external trace in a happy confluence of identity formation. Consumers and fans of celebrities began to link their identities with their purchases and their favorite pop stars. Consumers ostentatiously displayed the labels of the apparel, often purchased especially for the cultural capital afforded by the names of designers. In a parallel move, fans, mostly young ones, draped themselves in the trappings of favorite rock bands, sports teams, movie stars, television shows, and the like. In both cases, individuals sought public recognition of their identity in the objects they wore on their body. More modestly perhaps than the form of radicality ascribed to identity politics, popular culture modes of identity generally aspired only to attach the individual to the brand or band, claiming with pride primarily the cultural value or taste of the selection. Consumers then did not organize their resistance into political forms in order to celebrate their branded identities as foci of opposition. True enough there certainly were anti-capitalist and anti-corporate consumer protests perhaps most commonly associated with Ralph Nader and the cooperative movement. Moreover some critical theorists located resistance in all acts of consumption (de Certeau 1984). Yet the pattern of consumer identity construction was not deeply political in orientation.

The inscription of identity into the general culture of postmodernity entailed a mixture of materiality and consciousness. But this composite identity remained a construction for which the individual alone was regarded as responsible. The bodily aspect of identity folded into the conscious component. Identity remained the property of the individual, bordered and guarded by the skin and wrappings intentionally chosen by him or her. We shall now look at the question of identity theft and examine the ways identity takes on a decidedly different cast.

The phenomenon of identity theft in digital networks

After this review of the concept of identity and an examination of the practice of identity theft over the past decade, we may return to the media representation of identity theft and inquire about the consequences of identity theft for the formation of the subject. We have seen that identity theft posits identity as external to the consciousness of the self, altering a long, accepted usage of the term in modern society. Identity theft implies that identity consists of a series of numerical indicators (social security numbers, credit card numbers, driver's license numbers, bank account numbers, birth dates) and a series of personal information (name, address, mother's maiden name). These may be known to the consciousness of an individual, but they exist in computer databases, Internet sites, plastic cards, and other documents. The constituents of identity in the sense of identity theft exist therefore in information media and this media is dispersed across the globe.

With the emergence of the phenomenon of identity theft, the meaning of identity and its cultural instantiation is now doubled. Identity fragments into an aspect of consciousness (an awareness of continuity in time and space) and a complex of media content contained in information machines that combine to define an individual. This duality of identity, I contend, has not been recognized in cultural discourse, and its implications have not been explored. Instead the media representation of identity theft – and this is the chief argument of this essay – works to foreclose the duality, to conceal the difficulty of reconciling the definition of identity as consciousness with the definition of identity as digitized information, to expose the danger of the latter for the former and to defuse that danger, to familiarize the population with the phenomenon of identity theft and to normalize that phenomenon so that it appears as always already in the social fabric. In other words, the media representation of identity theft constitutes the crime as a new basis for insecurity and provides a solution to neutralize the threat through a subscription to the bank's credit card. The media discourse of the Citibank advertisement both in its print and its television examples performs the difficult, seemingly impossible cultural work of raising the specter of identity outside consciousness while confirming the security of identity within consciousness.

Yet the cat has escaped the bag. The recognition is dawning of a new mediascape with profound implications for culture, society and politics. The practice of identity theft is conditional upon the heterogeneity of identity, the imbrication of consciousness with information machines, the dispersal of the self across the spaces of culture, its fragmentation into bits and bytes, the nonidentical identity or better identities that link machines with human bodies in new configurations or assemblages, the suturing or cathecting of pieces of information in disjunctive time and scattered spaces. Some argue that such a figure of the self, often termed 'postmodern', is congruent with the exigencies of globalized capitalism. This may be so. But the terms of emerging cultural struggles must be fought not on the ground of returning to the conveniences of identity as interior consciousness. Instead critical discourse must find the bases for a happier inscription of identity in its conditions of coupling with machines, in its media unconscious, precisely against the effort of trajectories of globalization that would prefer the Citibank solution of an admission of multiplicity of the self but one shrouded in the comfort of unity and security within consciousness. We might then discover that the term 'identity' is not of much use as a critical category but rather designates the construction of the self in our current conjuncture, including our modes of subjectivation, the ways we practice the self upon ourselves.

In that case, the issue of secrecy would take on a new cast, perhaps one that is better understood in relation to digital technologies as the question of encryption. Here what is at stake is the hiding of zeros and ones, transforming the most transparent of codes into a form that cannot be deciphered. In that case the pertinent problem to pose is this: can identity be encrypted? No longer is the question one of reading the mind, of penetrating into consciousness to unveil its secrets, but of painstakingly decoding a message that is intentionally made opaque. Digital secrecy, when applied to identity, is indeed a possible impossibility.

Acknowledgements

I am grateful to Victoria Johnson, Annette Schlichter and Jon Wiener for their comments on earlier drafts of this paper.

Notes

This work is licensed under the Creative Commons Attribution-NonCommercial License. To view a copy of this license, visit http://creativecommons.org/licenses/by-nc/1.0 or send a letter to Creative Commons, 559 Nathan Abbott Way, Stanford, California 94305, USA.

1 Copies of the advertisements may be found at a website entitled, 'Upbeat and Downstairs' (http://daryld.com/citiads.php).
2 I am indebted to Etienne Balibar for pointing me to the extraordinary chapter in Locke that discusses the question of identity. Balibar himself treats the issue in relation to the question of property and its link to identity as in the following de?nition of identity he attributes to Locke: (1) that all the actions of the laboring body are accompanied with a conscious representation, or a representation of their meaning and their ends in consciousness – the ultimate site of personal identity; and (2) that this body forms an indestructible whole, that it is not split or broken but expresses a proper life in the continuity and diversity of the actions of what Locke metonymously called 'its hands' (Balibar 2002, p. 304).
3 There are numerous exceptions to this type of identity politics, perhaps best exempli?ed in and most often associated with the work of Judith Butler beginning with *Gender Trouble* (Butler 1990).

References

Anonymous (2003a) 'Identity Theft Fastest Growing White Collar Crime in Nation', *State Legislatures*, vol. 29, no. 4, p. 9.
Anonymous (2003b) 'Stop Thieves from Stealing You', *Consumer Reports*, pp. 12–17.
Balibar, E. (2002) '"Possessive Individualism" Reversed: From Locke to Derrida', *Constellations*, vol. 9, no. 3, pp. 299–317.
Bianco, K. (2001) *Identity Theft: What You Need to Know*, Chicago, CCH Incorporated.
Bradner, S. (2003) 'I Don't Want You to Be Me', *Network World*, Framingham.

Butler, J. (1990) *Gender Trouble: Feminism and the Subversion of Identity*, New York, Routledge.
Cherry, S. (2002) 'Al-Qaeda may be stealing your ID', *Insight on the News*, vol. 18, p. 18.
Collins, P. H. (2000) *Black Feminist Thought: Knowledge, Consciousness, and the Politics of Empowerment*, New York, Routledge.
Davis, K. (1998) 'Making Identity Theft a Crime', *Kiplinger's Personal Finance Magazine*, vol. 52, p. 16.
de Certeau, M. (1984) *The Practice of Everyday Life*, Berkeley, University of California Press.
Deleuze, G. & Guattari, F. (1987) *A Thousand Plateaus: Capitalism and Schizophrenia*, Minneapolis, University of Minnesota Press.
Erikson, E. (1963) *Childhood and Society*, New York, Norton.
Erikson, E. (1968) *Identity: Youth and Crisis*, New York, Norton.
Fisher, K. (2000) 'Tracing the Tesseract: A Conceptual Prehistory of the Morph', in *Meta-morphing: Visual Transformations in the Culture of Quick Change*, ed. V. Sobchack, Minneapolis, University of Minnesota Press, pp. 103–130.
Foucault, M. (1983) *This Is Not a Pipe*, Berkeley, University of California Press.
Foucault, M. (1991) 'Governmentality', in *The Foucault Effect*, ed. G. Burchell, Chicago, University of Chicago Press, pp. 87–104.
Gunning, T. (1995) 'Tracing the Individual Body: Photography, Detectives, and Early Cinema', in *Cinema and the Invention of Modern Life*, eds L. Charney & V. Schwartz, Los Angeles, University of California Press, pp. 15–45.
Hacking, I. (1995) *Rewriting the Soul: Multiple Personality and the Sciences of Memory*, Princeton, NJ, Princeton University Press.
Hartmann, H. (1964) *Essays on Ego Psychology: Selected Problems in Psychoanalytic Theory*, New York, International Universities Press.
Hartsock, N. (1997) 'The Feminist Standpoint: Developing the Ground for a Speci?cally Feminist Historical Materialism', in *The Second Wave: A Reader in Feminist Theory*, ed. L. Nicholson, New York, Routledge, pp. 216–240.
Koyré, A. (1958) *From the Closed World to the In?nite Universe*, New York, Harper and Row.
Lee, J. (2003) 'Identity Theft Victimizes Millions, Costs Billions', *New York Times*, New York, p. A20.
Livingston, B. (2003) 'Identity Theft Crisis', *eWeek*.
Locke, J. (1937) *Treatise of Civil Government and A Letter Concerning Toleration*, New York, Appleton-Century Crofts.
Locke, J. (1959) *An Essay Concerning Human Understanding*, New York, Dover.
Lowe, L. (1996) *Immigrant Acts*, Durham, Duke University Press.
MacPherson, C. B. (1962) *The Political Theory of Possessive Individualism*, New York, Oxford University Press.
McNamara, P. (2003) 'Net Buzz: Identity Theft', *Network World*, p. 56.
Mihm, S. (2003) 'Dumpster-Diving for Your Identity', *New York Times*, pp. 42–47.
Rose, N. (1998) *Inventing Our Selves: Psychology, Power, and Personhood*, Cambridge, Cambridge University Press.
Warner, M. (ed.) (1993) *Fear of a Queer Planet: Queer Politics and Social Theory*, Minneapolis, University of Minnesota Press.

INDEX

Adler, Mortimer I 108
Advertising: Control Revolution, during I 171; global marketing I 270; instrument of social control, as I 268–9; mind management I 270; psychological research, use of I 269
Africa as knowledge society II 388–415; affordability II 399–401; availability II 401–2; brain drain II 409–10; challenge to Africa II 395–6; defining knowledge society II 392; deliverability II 393–4, II 404–6; economic landscape II 390–2; four pillars of knowledge society II 393–5, 396–9; human capacity II 406–10; human intellectual capability II 394–5; ICTs and connectivity II 393; infrastructure II 393–4, 404–6; intellectual capacity II 406–10; lack of educated people II 407–8; language II 403–4; reality check II 388–415; relevance II 402–3; research and development II 408; technological landscape II 390–2; timelines II 402; usable content II 393, 399–404
Allocative resources I 261
Aloo, Fatma I 218
Animals: communication, and I 16
Anomie I 165; meaning I 165
Archaeology of the global era I 341–62; age of 'ideology' I 346–7; anti-intellectual populism I 344; asymmetrical planet I 356–8; Dialogue between Civilizations I 360; duty to remember I 345; 'end-of' thesis I 346–8; eschatology with a religious connotation I 343; forgetting history I 342–6; freedom of commercial speech I 353–4; global democratic marketplace I 353–4; global security I 351–2; global standard, search for I 354–5; global system with new global actors I 358–60; globalization I 341–2; independence, concept of I 343; "intellectual technology" I 347; management metaphors, rise of I 352–3; nation-state, territory of I 359; "network diplomacy" I 349; new messianism I 355–6; professional forecasters I 348–9; protests I 358; revolution in military affairs I 351–2; soft power networks I 349–51; UNDP assessment of globalization I 357; UNESCO World Report on Culture I 357; world economy as 'archipelago' I 357
Arrow, Kenneth: information, on I 90
Arts: financial support for I 51; reproduction via telecommunications I 252
Attention: aggregates I 23–24; attention frames I 17; world society, in I 17–18
Audience analysis I 15
Authoritative resources I 261
Automation: controlled society, and I 134

Baker, William C. I 112
Becker, Joseph I 113
Bell, Alexander Graham I 81, 171
Bell, Daniel I 2, 147, 159, 184, 241, 263
Bender, Roger I 143
Beniger, James I 4, 6

INDEX

Berleur, Jacques **I** 5
Books: mass production **I** 103; role of **I** 72–3
Braverman, Harry **I** 192
Burck, Gilbert **I** 96
Bureaucracy: control technology, and **I** 167; information economy, and **I** 99–100; rapid growth of **I** 166; rationalization, and **I** 166–8

Cable TV: minority groups, and **I** 50, *see also* Television
Canada: Telidon programme **I** 187
Capitalism: beyond industrial **I** 191–3; digital technologies, effect on **I** 5; disorganized, shift to **I** 260; expansion of logic of **I** 247; family capitalism **I** 119
Carlyle, Thomas **I** 102
Castells, Manuel **I** 6
Centralization: privacy, and **I** 118–19
Chandler, Alfred **I** 263
Chemical Abstract Service: computerization of **I** 106–7
Circuits of communication **I** 18–19
Cities: location of **I** 114–16
Clark, Colin **I** 94
Class analysis of communication **I** 363–75; deconstruction of information society discourse **I** 365; digitalisation and the death of distance **I** 372; digitalisation and the frictionless economy **I** 367–8; exploitation **I** 374; growth of consumer media **I** 370; information/copyright/creative industries as new growth sector **I** 368; information workers **I** 372–5; knowledge as core of value added **I** 366; mediacentric view of Information Society **I** 369–72; plurality boosters **I** 371; political economy of media **I** 365; Schumpeterian growth theory **I** 366–7; use of **I** 364
Clifton, Henry **I** 81
Cloutier, Jean **I** 243
Commons-based peer production and virtue **III** 391–417; Cluster I **III** 402; Cluster II **III** 402; Cluster III **III** 403; Cluster IV **III** 404; examples **III** 392–6; from structure to virtue **III** 405–10; principles **III** 397–400; public policy **III** 410–14

Communication: act of **I** 15–16; ages of media, table **I** 46; biological equivalences **I** 16–17; circuits of **I** 18; control, and **I** 161; democracy, and **I** 52–3; deregulation and privatization in **I** 250; detailed equivalences **I** 18–19; development, and **I** 49; effects of improvement in **I** 27–36; efficient **I** 21–3; fusion of technologies **I** 94; intellectual foundations of revolution in **I** 85–94; needs and values **I** 19–20; operationalizing new technology **I** 149–52; political economy of **I** 5; political theory, role in **I** 272–3; power distortion, and **I** 23; reactions to developments in **I** 236; realms of **I** 92; research on **I** 23; sentiment groups and publics **I** 24; skill, and **I** 22; social conflict, and **I** 20–21; social inequality, and **I** 4; social scientific study of **I** 3; specialists, categories of **I** 17; structure and function of **I** 15–26; substitute for transportation, as **I** 53–4; technological development, effects **I** 92–3; written and oral traditions, and **I** 3
Communication policy **III** 199–221; academic and public interest **III** 214–19; global information economy **III** 199–221; information, communication and participatory democracy **III** 201–2; information/communication as public utility **III** 212–13; information society **III** 208–10; post-telecommunication networks **III** 206–8; press **III** 202–3; public interest **III** 199–221; public interest in information society **III** 210–12; public interest research **III** 213–14; radio and television **III** 203–5
Communication, power and counter-power in the network society **I** 413–43; absence of given content in media **I** 416; blogs **I** 420–1; business media strategies **I** 425–7; communication as public space of network society **I** 430–2; credibility, trust and character **I** 417; crisis of political legitimacy **I** 418–19; electoral politics in age of

multimodal internet **I** 427–9; grassroots politics and the new media **I** 429–30; historical dynamics of counter-power **I** 431; interplay between political actors in new communication realm **I** 430; mass communication **I** 415–18; mass self-communication and counter-power **I** 421–4; media politics **I** 415–18; networks of opposition **I** 423–4; new technological framework **I** 414–15; power relations in new communication space **I** 425–30; rise of mass self-comunication **I** 419–21; scandal politics **I** 418–19; social movements **I** 422–3; social networking services **I** 426–7

Communications **II** 122–37; advertising expenditures **II** 128; audiences, nature of **II** 129; blindspot of economics **II** 122–37; bourgeois notion of free time and leisure **II** 133; demand management **II** 131; economic function of audience commodity **II** 134; exploring blindspot **II** 128–34; free lunch **II** 130; institutional analysis **II** 126–7; Marxist economics **II** 127–8; neoclassical economics **II** 123–6; service performed by advertiser **II** 131; time sold to advertiser **II** 132–3

Communications, rate of innovations in **I** 47

Communications media: development, role in **I** 49

Communications policy research **I** 45–57; benefits of **I** 54; dangers of **I** 55; developing countries **I** 49; established category, as **I** 45; Finland, in **I** 49; Japan, in **I** 49; MITRE Corporation **I** 47; multidisciplinary nature of **I** 55; NASA **I** 48; social philosophy, role of **I** 55; technological change, and **I** 46; United Nations **I** 48; US programs **I** 47–8; vertical integration issues **I** 51; World Bank **I** 49

Comparative advantage: concept of **I** 146; inequality, and **I** 147; rationale of **I** 146–9

Compunications **I** 93

Computer-aided-design-computer-aided-manufacture (CADCAM) **I** 200

Computer-mediated work **II** 464–84; automation of managerial assumptions **II** 467–8; birth of information environment **II** 476–9; deskilling of labour **II** 466–7; focus of managerial control **II** 481–3; listening to resistance **II** 479–80; management policies toward automation **II** 466–8; nature of organization and management **II** 483; new possibilities for supervision and control **II** 473–6; new worlds **II** 464–84; quality of employment relationship **II** 480–1; research sites **II** 471; social interaction affected **II** 472–3; substitution of labour **II** 466–7; work becomes abstract **II** 468–70

Computerization and social transformation **II** 439–63; academic discourse **II** 441–4; characterizing technological systems **II** 452–3; computerization as social and technical process **II** 453–4; conceptual issues **II** 451–6; discourse **II** 449–51; ideologies **II** 449–51; information and computer sciences **II** 456–58; managerial actions **II** 445–8; mobilizing ideologies **II** 450–1; popular discourse **II** 441–4; social organization of access to information **II** 453; social reinforcement **II** 448; social transformation **II** 439–41; technological utopianism **II** 450–1; transformed images **II** 444–5; web models **II** 454–6

Computers: coexistence with nature, and **I** 134; domestic importance **I** 143; interactive data retrieval **I** 92; mass society, and **I** 88–9; meshing with telephone **I** 92; modernization, and **I** 63–4; ultimate science, as **I** 134

Computopia **I** 128–38; Automated State, and **I** 134–5; citizen action, and **I** 135; concepts of **I** 130; controlled society, and **I** 134; equality of opportunity **I** 130–1; freedom of decision **I** 130–1; functional societies **I** 132–3; interdependent synergistic

societies **I** 132; time-value **I** 130; voluntary communities **I** 131–2
Consumer demand; changing nature of **I** 198
Consumption; systemizing management of **I** 268
Content analysis **I** 15
Control; planning, and **I** 261–4
Control analysis **I** 15
Control Revolution **I** 159–63; advertising **I** 171; beginnings of **I** 160; bureaucracy, and **I** 167; communication, and **I** 161; consumer feedback **I** 171; control, meaning **I** 161; crisis of control **I** 163–6; economic and political control **I** 160–1; Information Society, and **I** 173–7; new control technology **I** 168–73; production, control of **I** 168–9
Conversations: politics of **I** 222–4; West and non-West dialogue **I** 222
Copyright: communications policy issue, as **I** 51–2
Corporations: exploitation of information-related products **I** 191
Crawford, J. H. **I** 112
Critique of Information **I** 395–412; Adorno in the living room **I** 409–10; Baudelaire **I** 397–8; cyberpunk **I** 403–4; *flaneur* **I** 405; Lash, Scott **I** 395–412; McLuhan **I** 402; memory and mourning **I** 406–9; new sociality **I** 398–401; pattern recognition in *The Man Without Qualities* **I** 401–6; play and spatial materialism **I** 398–401
Critique of information economy **II** 263–83; employment by sectors **II** 271; four sector aggregation of US labour force **II** 270; information economy: basic premises **II** 264–6; information labour: productive or unproductive, whether **II** 268–73; information revolution or profitability revolution **II** 275–80; Marxian definition of productive and unproductive labour **II** 266–8; nature of information labour **II** 266–75; productive and unproductive labour, Mexico **II** 273; productive and unproductive labour, United States **II** 272;

unproductive labour and capital accumulation **II** 273–5
Cultural exports **I** 64; flow of culture **I** 222; ideological items, as **I** 144
Cultural propaganda **I** 65
Cultural studies: analytical traditions of **I** 5
Cybernetics **I** 83
Cybertechnologies: creation of wealth, and **I** 218; interaction, and **I** 218–19; quick and slow time, and **I** 216–17; surveillance, and **I** 219; war, and **I** 219–20
Cyborg manifesto **IV** 228–71; appearance of women as historical group **IV** 239; biological-determinist ideology **IV** 231; biotechnologies **IV** 242–3; boundary between physical and non-physical **IV** 232; category 'woman' **IV** 236; church **IV** 250; clinic-hospital **IV** 250; communications technologies **IV** 242; control strategies **IV** 241; cyborg imagery **IV** 258–9; cyborg, nature of **IV** 228–30; dualisms in Western traditions **IV** 255; emerging bases for new kinds of unity **IV** 251; feminist science **IV** 247; feminist taxonomies **IV** 235; feminization of poverty **IV** 245; fractured identities **IV** 233–9; home **IV** 248; homework economy outside the home **IV** 244–8; ideologies about human diversity **IV** 241; information of domination **IV** 239–44; ironic political myth **IV** 228; language politics **IV** 253; literary deconstruction **IV** 254–5; market **IV** 248–9; microelectronics **IV** 243; monsters **IV** 257–8; myth of political identity **IV** 251–9; oppositional consciousness **IV** 234–5; paid work place **IV** 249; political struggle, and **IV** 233; privatisation **IV** 246; radical feminism, and **IV** 236, 237; reformulation of expectations **IV** 247; school **IV** 249–50; science fiction **IV** 256–7; state **IV** 249; symbolic systems **IV** 252; technological determination **IV** 231–2; three major stages of capitalism **IV** 245; women in integrated circuit **IV** 248–51; women of colour **IV** 234–5, 252–3

Dalgarno, George **I** 107
Darby, Abraham **I** 81
Data processing: essential resource, as **I** 83–5
Data-havens **I** 65
de Chardin, Teilhard **I** 225
De Landa, Manuel **I** 6
Deciphering information technologies **I** 329–40; conditions for possibility of innovation **I** 334; knowledge, importance of **I** 335; measurement error **I** 333; modern societies as networks **I** 329–40; 'new economy' **I** 336; productivity paradox **I** 332–6; technological determinism **I** 330–2
Democracy: effects of communication, and **I** 52
Democracy, networks and power **III** 1–4; dialogue and political action **III** 3–4; public spheres of participation **III** 2–3; voice and decision making **III** 1–2
Democratic rationalization **III** 50–72; constructivism **III** 53–4; double aspect theory **III** 60–1; dystopian modernity **III** 52; Heidegger's "essence" of technology **III** 65–6; history or metaphysics **III** 66–8; indeterminism **III** 55–6; interpreting technology **III** 57–9; limits of democratic theory **III** 50–1; social relativity of efficiency **III** 61–2; technical code **III** 62–5; technological determinism **III** 52–3; technological hegemony **III** 59–60; technology, power and freedom **III** 50–72
Descartes **I** 107
Deskilling **I** 192, 199; microelectronics, and **I** 199
Developing nations: industry, relocation of **I** 148; information inequality, and **I** 192; information societies, as **I** 63
Development: role of communications in **I** 54; Westernization, as **I** 63
Dewey, John **I** 29, 108
Dibble, Julian **I** 225
Digital divide research **II** 416–35; achievements **II** 416–35; answers to basic questions **II** 428–30; basic questions **II** 418–19; empirical research **II** 430; material access **II** 420–3; motivational access **II** 423–5; shortcomings **II** 416–35; skills access **II** 425–6; types of access **II** 419–20; usage access **II** 426–8
Digital divides **II** 351–70; constructing **II** 356–61; dominant new media configurations **II** 361–3; knowledge societies **II** 351–70; new media rights and entitlements **II** 363–6; new media technologies and society **II** 353–6
Digitalization: impact **I** 176
Dorson, Richard **I** 34
Doxiades, C. A. **I** 116
Drucker, Peter: 'knowledge society' **I** 2
Durkheim, Emile **I** 163–4
Dynamo and computer **II** 38–47; "diffusion lags" **II** 42–3; electrification, history of **II** 40–1; "group drive" power transmission **II** 41; historical analogy **II** 45; information as economic commodity **II** 45; measurement biases **II** 43–4; modern productivity paradox **II** 38–47; relevance of historical studies **II** 39

Economic restructuring: spatial and managerial dimensions of **I** 209
Economics of knowledge codification and tacitness **II** 138–78; aim of skillful performance **II** 145; benefits **II** 165; boundaries in re-mapped knowledge space **II** 157–60; classification of knowledge and knowledge generation activity on two axes **II** 159; codification and tacitness reconsidered **II** 149–53; codified knowledge **II** 149–50; cognitive science **II** 141–3; costs **II** 165; costs and benefits in context of change **II** 169–71; costs and benefits in stable context **II** 165–9; displaced codebook **II** 156; economic determinants of codification **II** 163–71; endogeneity of tacitness-codification boundary **II** 163–5; foreseeable state of technology **II** 144; from evolutionary economics to management strategy and technology policy **II** 143–9; further work, direction of **II** 171–2; importance of tacit knowledge **II** 156; interactions with external

INDEX

phenomena **II** 161–3; new growth theory literature **II** 151; proposed topography **II** 153–7; public subsidy to science **II** 147; re-mapping, value of **II** 160–3; research activities, need for **II** 148; sociology of scientific knowledge **II** 141–3; tacit dimension **II** 141–9; tacit knowledge **II** 138–41; topography **II** 160–1; tree structure **II** 155; unarticulable knowledge **II** 152

Economics of technology sharing **II** 216–38; actors' strategies in open source **II** 219–22; appropriate public policies toward open source **II** 227–9; broader research agenda **II** 231–4; code release strategy **II** 222; commercial firms working and competing with open source **II** 222–4; customizing **II** 226; history of open source software **II** 217–19; legal system and open source **II** 224–5; "living symbiotically" **II** 222; motivation of open source contributions **II** 219–22; open source and academia **II** 233–4; open source working beyond software **II** 231–2; programmers' incentives **II** 220–1; realization of benefits **II** 232–3; relative quality of open source software **II** 225–7; security **II** 227; software patents and open source **II** 229–31; surveys **II** 221

Edison, Thomas Alva **I** 81

Education: computer-aided **I** 93, 205; home delivery of, impact **I** 51; self-servicing **I** 211

Effect analysis **I** 15

Eger, John **I** 145

Electricity: mass society, and **I** 88

Electronic panopticon **IV** 366–87; Bentham **IV** 368–70; computerization of marketing techniques **IV** 367; concept in sociological analyses **IV** 384; concept of **IV** 377; consumerism, and **IV** 379–80; control within capitalism **IV** 374–6; critics of electronic surveillance **IV** 383; 'dialectic of control' **IV** 382; disciplinary network of social relations **IV** 377; electronic surveillance **IV** 372–84; evaluating **IV** 376–84; Foucault **IV** 371–2; Foucault paradox **IV** 382; generalization over different social spheres **IV** 377; generic mode of discipline **IV** 380; internal pacification **IV** 373–4; modern surveillance methods **IV** 373–4; Poster's Superpanopticon **IV** 376; prisons, nature of **IV** 378; reproduction of social order **IV** 381; social aspects of computerization **IV** 367; sociological critique of surveillance theory **IV** 366–87; Taylorist principles, and **IV** 375; utopian hunger for certitude **IV** 379; workplace monitoring **IV** 374

Elites: knowledge elite **I** 120; masses, and **I** 119–20; technocracy **I** 193

Ellul, Jacques **I** 3

Employment: classification of labour **I** 59: growth in tertiary **I** 201; industrial organization, and **I** 207–9; informatics, and **I** 206; information economy, in **I** 100; information sector **I** 59; information as source of **I** 62; information work **I** 189–90; knowledge workers **I** 38–9; quality of **I** 209; second careers **I** 44; technological development, and **I** 199; women and IT **I** 192–3; work sharing **I** 249

Enclosure **III** 305–2; anti-monopoly **III** 320–4; beyond **III** 317–20; disaggregating freedom **III** 332–4; discovering e-commons **III** 329–32; first movement **III** 306–8; intangible commons **III** 311–13; intellectual property and distributed creativity **III** 313–17; legal realism for public domain **III** 332–34; recognizing public domain **III** 325–29; reifying the negative **III** 334–8; second movement **III** 305–52; tax on reading **III** 320–4

Energy: technological development **I** 110

English language: information rate of **I** 87

Equivalent enlightenment, principle of **I** 25

Everyday life online and offline **IV** 1–6; gender and the cyborg **IV** 6–7; literacy **IV** 5–6; mediation in information societies **IV** 4–5;

online activism **IV** 3–4; online engagement patterns **IV** 3; privacy and surveillance **IV** 7–8; virtuality and identity **IV** 2–3

Fast structural change and slow productivity change **II** 48–68; from 'electricals' to 'micro-electronics' **II** 50–3; from 'microelectronics' to 'IT' **II** 53–5; growth of FMS **II** 62; historical setting **II** 50–3; information technology, employment and productivity **II** 55–62; new information technologies **II** 49–55; organizational and social factors in moving from potential to actual productivity gains **II** 63–6; paradoxes in economics of information technology **II** 48–68; pervasive new technology system **II** 49–55; post-war growth in labour and capital productivity in UK **II** 60; productivity growth **II** 57; speed and difficulties of adjustment **II** 56; total factor productivity 1973–81 **II** 58; use of high-tech equipment **II** 61

Films: export of **I** 66

Finland: communications policy research **I** 49

Floridi, Luciano **I** 6

Ford, Henry **I** 247

Fordism: crisis of **I** 248; Gatesism, and **I** 253; meaning **I** 248

Freeman, Christopher **I** 4

Futurism: information society, roots of, and **I** 186

Gaia of civilisations **I** 229

Gantt, Henry L. **I** 267

Garnham, Nicholas **I** 5

Gates, Bill **I** 253

Gatesism **I** 253–4

Gender and information technology at work **IV** 272–90; changes in labour processes **IV** 274–6; changing technology, changing gender **IV** 273–4; construction of male identity **IV** 279; dynamism of gender relations **IV** 274; feminist research **IV** 272–90; 'feminist' systems design **IV** 284–5; gender-blindness **IV** 286; gender-technology relationship **IV** 285–6; gendered nature of technology **IV** 282; impact of IT upon women's jobs **IV** 275–6; 'male values' **IV** 283; masculine culture of technology **IV** 283; new technology homeworking **IV** 277–8; occupational sex-typing **IV** 281; production of technologies **IV** 281–2; restructuring of women's jobs **IV** 278–80; shifting spatial divisions of labour **IV** 276–8; social shaping of technology **IV** 280–4; teleworking **IV** 277–8; women-centred design methods **IV** 284–5; women's exclusion from technology **IV** 279; women's unpaid labour **IV** 285–6

Gender and technology **IV** 291–309; ANT **IV** 295–8; biomedical technologies **IV** 302; cervical cancer screening **IV** 300–1; cross-disciplinary research areas **IV** 293; domestic sphere **IV** 293; enabling aspects of power **IV** 297; feminist research in S&TS tradition **IV** 299–301; feminist writing **IV** 301–304; future of feminist sociological research **IV** 305; gender-blind to gender-aware **IV** 296–9; gender-blindness of Marxism **IV** 293; gender of Internet users **IV** 303; information and communication technologies **IV** 302–3; male definition of management **IV** 297; masculinity of actors involved **IV** 298; microwave oven **IV** 299–300; new communication technologies **IV** 304; SCOT **IV** 294–5; sexual division of labour **IV** 292–4; social studies of technology **IV** 294–6; structural exclusion **IV** 296; technological determinism **IV** 293–4; technology as culture **IV** 301–304; traditional notions of gender identity **IV** 303–4; women pilots **IV** 291–2

Gender and the information society **IV** 207–27; Cartesian masculinization of thought **IV** 213; "classificatory information" **IV** 215; feminist choices **IV** 210; feminist epistemological challenge **IV** 212; feminist materialism **IV** 217; feminist re-visions of logic of science **IV** 211–12; gendered vocabularies

of power and knowledge **IV** 209;
male activities **IV** 208; "nature" as
social category **IV** 211; "origin myth"
IV 213; semiotic technologies **IV** 216;
socially structured scheme **IV** 207–27;
successor science **IV** 218–19
Gendering the Internet **IV** 330–46;
articulating in everyday life
IV 340–3; Babbage, Charles
IV 332–3; claims **IV** 330–46;
complexity of **IV** 343; controversies
IV 330–46; cultures **IV** 330–46;
gender and technology:
multidimensional concepts
IV 338–9; gender codes:
cyberfeminism **IV** 336–8; gender
codes: femininity **IV** 334–5; gender
codes: masculinity **IV** 335–6; gender
codes of computer **IV** 332–3; gender
codes of enabling technologies
IV 332–5; longevity of analysis
IV 344; mutual shaping **IV** 339–40
General theory of information **I** 6
Gershuny, Jonathon **I** 4, 190
Giddens, Anthony **I** 261
Gifts, power of **II** 197–215; alt.Linux
II 203–6; digital gifts **II** 207; gift
economy **II** 201–6; gift giving as peer
review **II** 212–13; learning art of gift
giving **II** 203–6; message of openness
II 209; method **II** 199; newbie case
II 203–6; open source-actors and
stakeholders **II** 199–201; open source
software **II** 197–215; organizing
social relationships in open source
communities **II** 197–215; power in
gift economy **II** 206–12; virtual
collaboration **II** 210
Global position system (GPS): war,
and **I** 220
Global village **I** 3, 221, 236
Globalization **IV** 76–104; capitalist,
global movement against **IV** 88–93;
contested terrain, as **IV** 96;
contradictions **IV** 83–8;
depoliticization, and **IV** 87;
education, and **IV** 96–7;
environmental destruction **IV** 91;
from above **IV** 93; from below **IV** 86;
global justice **IV** 91; history of
United States, and **IV** 94; Internet
and terrorist groups **IV** 92; Marx
and Engels **IV** 94; objective

ambiguity **IV** 83–4; postmodernism,
and **IV** 95; poststructuralist theories
IV 81–2; restructuring of capitalism
IV 78–83; Seattle protests **IV** 90;
technological and economic
determinism **IV** 79–80; technological
revolution **IV** 78–83; terrorism,
and **IV** 84; theorizing **IV** 76–104;
turbulent processes **IV** 85; use of
Internet, and **IV** 89–91
Goethe: communication, on **I** 85–6
Golding, Peter **I** 4
Governing information societies
III 4–7; Internet governance
III 4–6; regulatory challenges
III 6–7
Greenberger, Dr Martin **I** 113
Growth of information work
I 284–308; allocation of occupations
to industrial and service sectors
I 299; analysis of four sectors of
workforce **I** 297–9; assigning
occupations from service sector to
industrial sector **I** 294–5; Bell, and
I 284–308; categories of workers
I 290; comparison of findings from
studies **I** 299–301; comparison of
information workers to government
information workers **I** 303;
conceptualisation **I** 286–91; earlier
findings **I** 291–2; early twentieth
century **I** 284–308; growth 1900–
1970 **I** 288; "information economy"
I 289; information work, meaning
I 291; measurement **I** 286–91;
measurement of numbers of workers
in composite occupations **I** 297–9;
modern management, and **I** 301–5;
"new knowledge" **I** 287; occupations
allocated 50% to industry and 50%
to information **I** 294; occupations
allocated 50% to service and 50% to
information **I** 293; OECD typology
I 289; percentages of US workforce
by sector 1900–1980 **I** 296;
percentages of US workforce by
sector 1900–1980 **I** 300; Porat, and
I 284–308; Porat's findings **I** 295–7;
Porat's typology **I** 292; sector
aggregation of US workforce
1900–1908 **I** 288; sector aggregation
of US workforce 1900–1980 **I** 296;
sector-re-aggregation of US

workforce 1900–1986 **I** 300; service occupations allocated to industry **I** 295; sources of bias in Porat's information occupations **I** 292–5; splitting occupational categories **I** 292–4; updates **I** 291–2

Healthcare: self-servicing **I** 211
Hirsch, Joachim **I** 260
Households: privitization of individual **I** 210
Human rights: information systems, and **I** 64
Human services **I** 81
Hyperindustrialization **I** 260

Identities **IV** 137–57; avatars of national communities **IV** 149–55; celebration of weak identities **IV** 141–2; collective demoralization **IV** 140–1; contemporary thought **IV** 144; devaluation of the national **IV** 152; dichotomy between rural and urban **IV** 146–7; disenchantment with world **IV** 140–1; ethnocentrism, and **IV** 148; expressivity, and **IV** 143; fashion, and **IV** 145; feminist perspectives **IV** 142–3; fundamentalisms as modes of resistance and belonging **IV** 138–9; globalization, and **IV** 139; Latin America **IV** 150–1; liberal rationalism, and **IV** 145–6; mediated city **IV** 155; new identities **IV** 141–3; new communities **IV** 137–57; new urban communities in the virtual city **IV** 152–5; old and new cultural communities **IV** 146–9; pathologies of modernity, and **IV** 140–1; precarious social order, where **IV** 150; reconfiguration of cultures **IV** 148; reconfiguration of notions of sociology **IV** 154; relationship between particularism and universalism **IV** 143–5; ruling conventions and reconfigurations in traditional communities **IV** 147–9; secret universality of which particularisms are made **IV** 143–6; sites of subject-formation **IV** 141–3; thick texture of debate **IV** 137–46; traditions **IV** 137–57; virtual city in formation **IV** 153

Identity theft **IV** 433–55; Citibank advertisements **IV** 435–8; digital networks, and **IV** 452–4; discontents, and **IV** 444–5; Erikson and identity as ego **IV** 448–9; genealogy of identity **IV** 445–52; governmentality, and **IV** 450; identity and theft **IV** 449–51; identity as resistance **IV** 451–2; knowledge of **IV** 434; Locke and identity as consciousness **IV** 45–448; meaning **IV** 441–2; media induced anxiety **IV** 435–41; new mediascape, and **IV** 453; perpetrators **IV** 443–4; statistics **IV** 443; sudden appearance in media **IV** 441; televised advertisements **IV** 439–40; victims **IV** 443–4

Ignorance: consqeuences of **I** 22
Ilm **I** 224
Inayatulla, Sohail **I** 7
Industrial Revolution **I** 155–6; bureaucracy, and **I** 166; social effects **I** 163
Industrial societies; characteristics of **I** 129; transformation in Western **I** 142–6
Industry: dominant industries **I** 81
Inequality: information inequality **I** 192; social *see* Social inequality
Inequality and the digital divide **II** 6–7
Informatics **I** 205–7; consumer uses of **I** 206; design of **I** 212; development of **I** 205; distribution of resources **I** 212; informatics languages **I** 245; job creation, and **I** 206; new type of writing, as **I** 244–5; social welfare, and **I** 210–11
Information **II** 69–92; characteristics in information economy **II** 84–8; collective good, as **I** 91; commodity, whether **I** 91; Commons' analysis **II** 80; consumption of capital and labour **I** 62; contribution to domestic production **I** 62; dimensions of **II** 72–3; economic resource, as **II** 85–6; economics of **I** 90–2; emerging dimension of institutional analysis **II** 69–92; ephemeral **II** 72; evolution of economic thinking **II** 73–7; exchange, and **II** 79–80; final consumer product, as **II** 86–7; free flow of **I** 151–2; general theory of *see* General theory of information

growth of **I** 104; Hayek on **II** 80–3; implications for industrial structure and market development **II** 87–8; inequality **I** 150–1; Innis, Harold A. **II** 77–9; institutions, and **II** 70–2; Keynesian analysis **II** 75–6; markets, and **II** 79–84; Marx on **II** 74–5; mass consumption, and **I** 268; neoclassical theory **II** 75; new socio-economic factor, whether **I** 190–1; physics and human behaviour, and **I** 87; political theory, role in **I** 272–3; post-industrial society, in **I** 80–3; public policy issues **II** 88–90; regulation, and **I** 263; replacement of labour by **I** 185; resource, as **I** 67; retrieval of, future problems **I** 102–6; sale of **I** 66; scientific exploitation of **I** 269; source of profit and employment, as **I** 62; storage **II** 73; uncertainty, and **I** 90–91; valuable commodity, whether **I** 61–3; Western monopolies, and **I** 142

Information and communication technology (ICT); humanization of **I** 4; Information Society policy, and **I** 3; transformative character of **I** 3

Information economy **I** 97–102, 241–2; economic magnitudes of **I** 96; future prospects **I** 100–1; growth in **I** 96; primary information sector **I** 98; secondary information sector **I** 98–9; sectors of **I** 97–8; workforce composition, and **I** 100

Information era **I** 215–34; limitations on futures **I** 216

Information poverty and political inequality **III** 15–31; average 1986 weekly expenditure on services **III** 26–7; citizenship in age or privatised communications **III** 15–31; percent of households in selected income groups 1986 owning communication and information facilities **III** 20; privatisation **III** 15–17

Information Revolution **I** 258; dark side of **I** 264–5; extension of old processes, as **I** 269; meaning **I** 258–9

Information services; types of **I** 64

Information Society; analytical purchase of concept **I** 5; beyond industrial capitalism **I** 191–3; 'computopia', as **I** 2; concept of **I** 183; Control Revolution, and **I** 173–177; critique of **I** 188–90; cultural history of **I** 258–83; discourse of **I** 239–46; economic activities, expansion of **I** 199; from post-industrialism to **I** 183–96; global implications of **I** 58–69; industrial societies becoming **I** 63; industrial society distinguished **I** 60; information inequality **I** 192; information values, and **I** 129; information work, importance of **I** 189; infrastructure for **I** 109–14; infrastructure of control **I** 4–5; injunction and prescription, as **I** 3; interconnected society, as **I** 239–41; labour force composition, and **I** 173–4; 'march through the sectors' **I** 190–1; measuring and mapping **I** 4; microprocessing technology, and **I** 176; moving target, as **I** 4; natural resources, and **I** 67; policy questions of **I** 109–14; political and economic dependency, and **I** 5; problematic, as a **I** 193–94; quantitative dimensions of **I** 94–101; research, influence of **I** 7; roots of idea **I** 184–6; social choice, and **I** 207–11; social framework of **I** 80–127; technocratic society, as **I** 67; vagueness of notion **I** 245–6

Information society and community voice **IV** 165–85; approaching ICTs and development **IV** 168–70; banking education **IV** 167; Byrragu Foundation **IV** 180–1; community-modeled ontology projects **IV** 176–9; dominantly top-down ICT initiatives **IV** 170–1; education as political act **IV** 166; ICT development: challenges and paradigms **IV** 170–4; ICT development projects **IV** 168–70; ICT initiative examples **IV** 174–9; indigenous video and television **IV** 174–5; Jana Sahayog **IV** 175–6; Kayago people **IV** 174–5; key issues with respect to ICT initiatives **IV** 174; NGO mediation **IV** 175–6; NGOs, and **IV** 172; pedagogy and the community voice **IV** 165–8; "problem-posed education"

INDEX

IV 167–8; reactions to Freire **IV** 168–70; reconciling community voice with information access **IV** 179; Somali community ontology for Village Voice project **IV** 178; Southern India-information development and community voice **IV** 180–1; theory of communicative action for information systems **IV** 171–2; trajectory of ICT development **IV** 181–2; Tribal Peace project **IV** 178–9; Village Voice project **IV** 176–9; Walpiri people **IV** 175

Information systems: human rights, and **I** 64

Information technology (IT): engineering of public opinion **I** 276; government policy, impact on **I** 187; regulation of political life, and **I** 276; social economics of **I** 197–214; social significance of **I** 183; women's employment opportunities, and **I** 192–3

Information theory **I** 86, 87, 215

Information work **I** 189–90; knowledge work distinguished **I** 190; occupations under **I** 202

Innis, Harold **I** 3; communication, on **I** 86

Institutional approach to communication and information policy **II** 93–110; beyond interests, ideas and technology **II** 93–110; determinants of US spectrum policies **II** 102–6; ideological approach **II** 97–8; institutions, incentives and policy choices **II** 99–102; interest-group approach **II** 95–7; taxonomy of theoretical approaches **II** 94–9; technological approach **II** 98–9; US broadcasters **II** 102–6

Intellectual property: production of knowledge, and **I** 85

Intellectual technology **I** 83, 172

Intelligent machines **I** 6

Interactivity **I** 242–4; egalitarian relationships, and **I** 244; positive value of **I** 243; social and cultural change, and **I** 242; technological determinism, and **I** 243; types of **I** 243–4

International Telecommunications Union (ITU) **I** 150

Internationalization **I** 250

Internet: anglicisation of language by **I** 220; anonymity, and **I** 217; communicative dialogues, and **I** 7; empowerment of women, and **I** 218; hegemony of West, and **I** 228; justice, and **I** 227; mass self communication, and **I** 6; transcendence, and **I** 226; undermining of despots by **I** 226; virtual realities **I** 217–18

Internet and US communication policy-making **III** 276–304; critical perspective **III** 276–304; democracy, scholarship and communication technology **III** 297–9; historical perspective **III** 276–304; new super powerful democratic technology **III** 287–91; policy and profit motive **III** 286; salvaging political culture **III** 292–6

Internet co-governance **III** 371–90; C_3 **III** 386–7; constructive co-existence **III** 376–7; different interpretations **III** 381–2; diffusion of governance **III** 378; from industrial society to information society **III** 377; future developments **III** 387; global governance **III** 377–9; growing complexity **III** 377; growing interdependence between two different worlds **III** 372–3; ICANN, making of **III** 380–1; "Internet Governance" **III** 379–80; M_3 **III** 383–6; M_3C_3 **III** 371–90; myth of unregulated internet **III** 371–2; public internet policy: United Nations **III** 373–4; real places **III** 375–6; technical internet policy **III** 374–5; united constituencies **III** 374–5; virtual spaces **III** 375–6; WGIG **III** 382; WSIS **III** 382

Internet connectivity among OECD countries **II** 328–50; correlation coefficients for all variables **II** 345; data **II** 334–7; description of variables, data sources **II** 344; economic factors **II** 332; existing technologies **II** 333; explaining differences **II** 328–50; explanatory factors **II** 335–7; findings **II** 337–9; findings from previous research

INDEX

II 331; Finland **II** 340–1; France **II** 341; human capital **II** 332; institutional legal environment **II** 333; methods **II** 334–7; OLS regression results for Internet hosts **II** 338; outcome variable **II** 335; textable propositions **II** 333–4; theoretical considerations **II** 331–4; United Kingdom **II** 340

Internet, public spheres and political communication **III** 170–89; civic cultures and political discussion **III** 183–6; deliberation **III** 170–89; democracy's communication spaces **III** 172–4; destabilized political communication **III** 174–6; dispersion **III** 170–89; limits of deliberative democracy **III** 181–3; multisector online public spheres **III** 176–8; two perspectives **III** 179–81

Internet, social implications **IV** 42–75; bountiful diversity **IV** 62–4; community **IV** 52–4; culture, impact on **IV** 62–4; deliberative democracy **IV** 58–9; "digital divide" in United States **IV** 46–8; electronic battleground **IV** 55–9; engaged public **IV** 57; evolving Internet **IV** 64–6; firm structure effects **IV** 61; flexible networks **IV** 59–62; global digital divide **IV** 48–9; hypersegmentation **IV** 62–4; impact on time use and community **IV** 50–5; industry specific effects **IV** 61–2; inequality in content providers' access to attention **IV** 49–50; informed public **IV** 56; Internet and inequality **IV** 45; limits on impact **IV** 59–60; major research questions **IV** 45–64; massification **IV** 62–4; organizations, impact on **IV** 59–62; panopticons **IV** 59–62; political polarization **IV** 57–8; politics, impact on **IV** 55–9; politics of the Internet **IV** 59; renewed public sphere **IV** 55–9; social capital formation **IV** 50–5; social isolation **IV** 50–5; theoretical context **IV** 44–5; time displacement **IV** 50–2; work group effects **IV** 60

Internet studies **IV** 158–64; dawning of third age **IV** 162; first age of **IV** 159–60; pre-history, 10 years ago **IV** 158–9; second age of **IV** 160–2; three ages **IV** 158–64

Inventing the global information future **II** 284–307; Cell A **II** 293–4; Cell B **II** 295–7; Cell C **II** 297–9; Cell D **II** 299–301; competition, cooperation and developing countries **II** 289–90; constructing scenarios **II** 291–3; critical uncertainties **II** 291; difficulty of predicting future **II** 285–8; driving forces **II** 291; future is path dependent **II** 301–2; leading issues for global information infrastructure **II** 288–9; scenario building **II** 290–1; scenario design **II** 291–3; scenarios **II** 293–301; scenarios beyond telecommunications **II** 303; technologies for better understanding future **II** 290

Islam: religious interpretation, and **I** 227–8

Japan; communications policy planning **I** 49; plan for information society **I** 186–7; Tam New Town **I** 187

Kitwood, Tom **I** 191

Knowledge; accumulation of **I** 77; "added value", as **I** 85; books, role of **I** 72–3; classes of production **I** 95–6; collective good, as **I** 91; consumption of **I** 77; current input **I** 77; estimating stock of human **I** 73–5; factor in production, as **I** 242; flow of, estimating **I** 76–7; growth of scientific **I** 104–5; knowledge elites **I** 120; meaning **I** 85; measurement of **I** 95–7; measuring society's stock of **I** 70–1; payment for search of **I** 91; phenomenological theory of **I** 74; post-industrial society, in **I** 83; production of **I** 85, **I** 91; replacement of **I** 77; sale of **I** 66; scientific journals **I** 71–2; stocks and flows of **I** 70–9; waste **I** 77

Knowledge and economies **II** 1–5; information, problem of **II** 2–3; institutional dynamics **II** 4–5; knowledge codification **II** 5; productivity paradox **II** 3–4

Knowledge-based economy **II** 111–21; batches **II** 118–19; codified knowledge **II** 112–15; flows

II 118–19; knowledge-based economy II 115–16; model of knowledge process II 116–17; pieces II 118–19; Sisyphus model II 111–21; tacit knowledge II 112–15; taxonomy of information II 117–18

Knowledge class I 186

Knowledge exports I 64

Knowledge society I 37–44; complexity of jobs I 39; knowledge industries I 37; knowledge opportunities I 38–9; knowledge workers, need for I 38; nature of jobs, and I 39; schooling, and I 41; skill, and I 38; years of working life I 40

Kondratiev wave I 191

Labour: productivity increases I 201; replacement by knowledge I 85, 185

Language: conversation, of I 223; informatics languages I 245; information rate of I 87; internet, effect on I 220; statistics of I 86–8

Lash, Scott I 6

Lasswell, Harold I 3

Law and borders III 222–65; absence of territorial borders in Cyberspace III 225–30; breaking down territorial borders III 223–30; copyright law III 234–6; cyberspace as a place III 230–2; cyberspace regimes III 232–6; internal diversity III 241–4; local authorities, foreign rules III 238–41; new boundary for Cyberspace III 230–6; responsible self-regulatory structures III 236–8; rise of law in Cyberspace III 222–65; territorial borders in "real world" III 223–5

Lazarsfeld, Fritz I 3

Leiss, William I 242

Leisure society I 249

Leontieff, Wassily I 89

Libraries: university holdings, growth of I 104

Library of Alexandria I 73

Life expectancies: reasons for increase I 40

Lifestyles: evolution of employment, and I 210

Link, Henry C. I 268

Linotype I 103

Lippmann, Walter I 274

Luhmann, Niklas I 6

Lyon, David I 5

Machlup, Fritz I 2, 95, 173; 'measuring the unmeasurable' I 2

McLuhan, Marshall I 221; 'global village' I 3

Maier, Charles I 267

Mail: electronic delivery of, effects I 50

Making sense of information age I 376–94; Castells I 383–5; causation I 379; class analysis I 386–7; cultural studies I 385–7, 389–90; culture I 385–7; ESRG research I 381–2; expansion of symbolic I 385–6; Information Society I 377–80; microelectronics revolution I 380–2; Network Society I 382–5; Post-Industrial Society, elements of I 379; production I 386; virtuality I 387–9; work/occupation I 386

Malik, Suhail I 6

Manufacturing: informatics equipment, of I 206; interdependencies with services, and I 4

Marconi, Guglielmo I 171

Martin, James I 239–40

Marvin, Caroline I 5

Masuda, Yoneji I 2, 187

Mattelart, Armand I 6

Media: political economy of I 5; social inequality, and I 4

Media analysis I 15

Media and public sphere III 73–85; conditions for democracy III 81; democratic accountability III 82; democratic politics III 78; economic systematicity III 82; Habermas III 73–85; Hegelian state versus civil society dichotomy III 76; Marxist theory of ideology III 77; mediated communication III 79; mediated symbolic forms III 79; pluralist political project III 83; "power container" III 82; rationality III 83–4; representation III 74; television III 75; universality III 80; validation of Enlightenment project III 84–5

Media literacy IV 105–17; access IV 108; analysis IV 108–9; beyond skills-based approach IV 110–11; challenge of new information and communication technologies **IV** 105–17; changing literacies **IV** 112–13; content creation **IV** 109–10; evaluation **IV** 109; from point to screen **IV** 111; individual uses **IV** 113–14; institutional uses **IV** 113–14; literacy useful term, whether **IV** 106–7; meaning **IV** 107–8; renewed debates over **IV** 105–6; transformative nature of Internet **IV** 111–12

Mediation of everyday life **IV** 118–36; active audience, notion of **IV** 130; anthropological critique **IV** 130–1; body **IV** 121; boundary between complicity and collusion **IV** 132; collusion in **IV** 118–36; communication **IV** 125; complicity as irony of position **IV** 131; complicity in **IV** 118–36; conditional trust **IV** 128; cultural vocabularies **IV** 133; distance and trust **IV** 125–9; ethics of everyday life **IV** 124–5; modernity, and **IV** 122–3; new forms of sociability **IV** 123–4; play theory **IV** 129; proper distance **IV** 127; proximity **IV** 126; refusal of paradox **IV** 120–1; relationship between individual and social **IV** 122; social **IV** 119; technological **IV** 119; trust in abstract system **IV** 127; weakness of media **IV** 130

Menou, Michel **I** 4
Merton, Robert **I** 3
Micro Revolution **I** 184
Microprocessing: impact **I** 176
Microvita **I** 229
Miege, Bernard **I** 5
Miles, Ian **I** 4, 190
Mind management **I** 270
MITRE Corporation: communications policy research program **I** 47–8
Models: society, of **I** 89–90
Morse, Samuel F. B. **I** 169
Muller-Thym, Prof. B. J. **I** 28
Multiple subjectivity and virtual community **IV** 28–41; avatars **IV** 35–7; cycling through **IV** 37–40; flexibility **IV** 34–5; MUDs **IV** 29–41; multiplicity **IV** 34–5; objects-to-think-with **IV** 32–4; online personae **IV** 29–32; self states **IV** 35–7; Trojan horses **IV** 34–5; windows **IV** 30

Mumford, Lewis **I** 263
Murdock, Graham **I** 4, 5–6; modern era, on **I** 5–6

NASA: telecommunications policy research **I** 48
Nation and diaspora **IV** 186–203; contrived nature of nation-state, and **IV** 199; cosmopolitan outlook **IV** 198; cultural power of British imperialism **IV** 193; DBS **IV** 194–5; diaspora **IV** 189–90; diaspora's media **IV** 194–6; diasporic cultures **IV** 190–2; European Union **IV** 197; global mobility **IV** 198; globalising from below **IV** 192–4; immigrant communities **IV** 190–1; Internet, use of **IV** 195–6; nations **IV** 188–9; patriotism, and **IV** 200; population movements **IV** 190–1; reconceptualising multiculturalism in 21st century **IV** 196–200; rethinking multiculturalism in transnational context **IV** 186–203; television programs **IV** 194–5; transnations **IV** 189–90; UK model of multiculturalism **IV** 187

National planning **I** 116–18; coordinated information **I** 117; indicative planning **I** 117; mobilized targets **I** 118; modelling and simulation **I** 117; national goals **I** 117

National sovereignty; free flow of information, and **I** 55
Nationalism; international communication, and **I** 52; print, and **I** 32
Neill, R. F. **I** 30
New ICTs and the codification of knowledge **II** 179–94; aid to individual memory **II** 180–3; aiding group memory **II** 183–5; codification of knowledge, and **II** 179–94; costs of electronic storage **II** 182; electronic files **II** 181; empirical investigation of knowledge codification **II** 190–1; 'groupware' **II** 189; purposes of ICTs **II** 181; simulation **II** 187–90; social memory **II** 185–7; specialization **II** 186; specialized languages **II** 187–90; symbolic communication **II** 187–90

New information and communication technologies (NICT) **I** 238
New Machine **I** 267
New mediation and direct representation **III** 86–108; accountability **III** 100–1; complexity **III** 94–5; discourses of mediation and representation **III** 89–91; plurality **III** 101–3; reality **III** 104; reconceptualizing representation **III** 99–105; reconceptualizing representation in digital age **III** 86–108; representation, information and communication **III** 87–9; re-presenting representation **III** 96–8; scale **III** 93–4; technocracy **III** 95–6; transcending representation **III** 91–6
New Technologies and economic development **II** 17–37; assimilation **II** 17–37; chain of relationships **II** 27; downswing characteristics **II** 26–7; Fourth Kondratiev **II** 28–31; income distribution **II** 29; institutional requirements for next upswing **II** 33–6; investment patterns **II** 23–4; Kondratiev **II** 17–19; mass production technological style **II** 31–2; model elements **II** 21–7; model of capitalist system **II** 20–1; occupational structure **II** 28–9; patterns of transformation **II** 27–8; processes of transformation **II** 27–8; product demand **II** 29–30; Schumpeter **II** 19–20; socio-institutional structures **II** 32–3; structural change **II** 17–37; Taylorism **II** 28–9; technological styles **II** 21–3; transformation process **II** 30–1; upswing characteristics **II** 24–6
Newspapers: mass production **I** 103

Oettinger, Anthony: communications policy program **I** 48; compunications **I** 93; information industries, on **I** 96–7
Open networking **II** 5–6
Organized complexity **I** 83

Parkinson's law **I** 28
Perception: inferring **I** 19
Planning: control, and **I** 261–4
Political authority in mediated age **III** 149–69; instructive examples of media-derived authority **III** 160–4; media, public opinion and authority **III** 154–60; nature of authority **III** 151–4; political communication in our time **III** 164–6
Pool, Ithiel de Sola **I** 3
Porat, Marc **I** 2, 97, 173, 189, 241
Postcolonial/feminist cyberethnography **IV** 310–29; authority of ethnographers **IV** 321; complicity and resistance in cyberfield **IV** 310–29; confusion between real and virtual spaces **IV** 324; ethnographer as participant-observer **IV** 321–2; feminist betrayals **IV** 319–25; feminist diasporas in cyberspace **IV** 311–14; feminist media studies **IV** 314–19; interrupted **IV** 310–29; method for Internet studies **IV** 317; objections to study of SAWnet **IV** 320; SAWnet **IV** 314–29; SAWnet refusal **IV** 310–29; South Asian diaspora community **IV** 322; south Asian diaspora online **IV** 313; "subaltern" **IV** 325; women-only safe spaces **IV** 316; women's use of Internet **IV** 316
Post-industrial society: axial principle of **I** 81; classification of economic sectors **I** 95; comparative schema of **I** 84; development of information society, and **I** 185; information and knowledge, and **I** 83–5; information as main asset of **I** 259; information and telecommunications in **I** 80–3; intellectual technology **I** 83; second coming of **I** 197–203
Post-war boom: end of **I** 203–5; female employment **I** 204; inflation, and **I** 204; technological change, and **I** 203
Postal system: development of **I** 169–70; mass mailing **I** 170
Poster, Mark **I** 7, 263
Potter, David **I** 268
Power, identity and new technology homework **II** 553–77; Gidden's theorization of power and identity **II** 555–60; identity **II** 565–8; 'new forms' of organizing **II** 553–77; power, question of **II** 562–5;

INDEX

research context **II** 560–1; research outcomes **II** 562–8; review of evidence **II** 572–4; time and space, effects **II** 565–8

Preprocessing **I** 167

Price, Derek de Solla **I** 104

Primary information sector **I** 58–9; goods **I** 58–9; services **I** 58

Printing press; effect on communications **I** 30; Gutenburg galaxy **I** 34; homogeneity and centralism, and **I** 31; mass mailing, and **I** 170; nationalism, and **I** 32; technological development **I** 103

Privacy: centralization, and **I** 118–19; surveillance **I** 219; transborder data flows, and **I** 65

Privacy risks **IV** 388–411; balancing regulator **IV** 392–3; Canadian Privacy Survey 1993 **IV** 399–400; conventional data protection paradigm **IV** 391–4; data protection **IV** 402; "data subject" **IV** 394–5; differential risks and data protection **IV** 389–91; diffusion of knowledge, and **IV** 404, 405; distribution **IV** 388–411; equity, and **IV** 392; evaluating **IV** 389; Harris-Equifax surveys **IV** 397–8; "hierarchies", and **IV** 405–6; Hungarian enquiry **IV** 400–1; investigation of risk patterns **IV** 405; "law and order" agenda, and **IV** 403; objective determination **IV** 403–4; patterns **IV** 390; politics, and **IV** 407; protection, need for **IV** 388–411; recognition of differentially risky data **IV** 393–4; reconstructing "data subject" **IV** 394–6; risk management and policy **IV** 404; sectoral identities and attributes **IV** 394–6; sensitivity to **IV** 403; strategies for coping with **IV** 407; survey evidence **IV** 396–401, 402; UK statistics **IV** 396–7; understanding **IV** 389

Production: control of **I** 168–9

Production function **I** 85; knowledge, and **I** 85

Production sites: relocation of **I** 141, 246

Professional-managerial class **I** 186

Professionalization: relabelling, as **I** 188

Propaedia **I** 108

Propaganda: cultural *see* Cultural propaganda; definition **I** 275; public opinion theory, and **I** 275

Public opinion theory **I** 275; study of propaganda, and **I** 275

Rail network: distribution of goods, and **I** 169; mass mailing, and **I** 170

Rationalization: bureaucracy, and **I** 166–8; computerization, and **I** 248; definition **I** 168; scientific and administrative **I** 273

Real-time politics **III** 109–48; assessment **III** 133–4; centralization **III** 114; comparing models **III** 121–6; digital embedding **III** 126–34; individual initiative **III** 113; institutions **III** 116–21; Internet and political process **III** 109–48; lateral relationships **III** 126–8; managerial democracy **III** 112; online discussion for a **III** 110; open information **III** 115; political community **III** 110–11; public policy **III** 114; referenda **III** 111–12; social equality **III** 115; spacing **III** 129–33; voting process **III** 112–13

Reason: Enlightenment ideal of **I** 274

Reconceptualizing digital divide **II** 371–87; acquisition of literacy **II** 381; information age town **II** 372–4; literacy **II** 379; literacy and ICT access **II** 382–4; literacy divide **II** 380–1; model computer lab **II** 374–5; models of access **II** 377–8; rethinking digital divide **II** 375–7; slum "Hole in the Wall" **II** 371–2; technology for social inclusion **II** 377

Refeudalisation **I** 273

Regulation: information as component of **I** 263

Reid, Alex: remote services research **I** 48

Research and development (R&D): political financing of **I** 188

Rethinking ICTs **III** 190–6; choices **III** 194–6; dependence **III** 192; dependence/autonomy **III** 193; ICTs on human scale **III** 190–6; uncertainty **III** 192; uncertainty/security **III** 194; vulnerability **III** 192; vulnerability/integrity **III** 193–4

Retirement: knowledge workers, and **I** 41
Riesman, David **I** 31
Roberts, Dr L. G. **I** 113
Robins, Kevin **I** 5
Rostow, W. W. **I** 31
Roszak, Theodore **I** 272
Rubin, Michael **I** 2
Rudenberg, H. Gunther **I** 143

Sardar, Zia **I** 217
Schement, Jorge **I** 6
Schiller, Herbert **I** 5, 191
Schramm, Wilbur **I** 3
Science: advance of technology, and **I** 82; definition **I** 82
Scientific journals: growth in number of **I** 71, 104
Scientific Management **I** 265–71; marketing, of **I** 271; productivity under **I** 267; system of consumption, and **I** 267
Segmentation, principle of **I** 31
Serbia: Belgrade revolt **I** 225–6
Service economy **I** 197; growth in employment in **I** 201; income elasticity of **I** 200; post-industrialist view of **I** 201; trends underpinning growth of **I** 200
Services: human **I** 81; interdependencies with manufacturing, and **I** 4; knowledge industries as **I** 37; post-industrial **I** 81; professional **I** 81
Shannon, Claude **I** 1, 86–7
Sloan, Alfred P. **I** 268; "Sloanism" **I** 268
Smith, Adam **I** 94, 128
Smith, Cyril Stanley **I** 81, 83
Smythe, Dallas **I** 5
Social change: long-run processes of **I** 203–7
Social conflict: communication, and **I** 20–1
Social inequality: comparative advantage doctrine, and **I** 147; innovations, and **I** 6; media and communication industry, and **I** 4
Social regulation: modes of **I** 250–1
Social welfare **I** 210–11; community care **I** 211; informatics, and **I** 211; self-service provision **I** 211

Societal transformations: appreciation of **I** 156; causes of **I** 156; pace of **I** 239; table of modern **I** 157–8
Society: elite and mass **I** 119–20; infrastructures **I** 109–10
Sociology of the future **I** 309–28; change **I** 320–2; continuities **I** 323–6; convergence of ICTs **I** 323–4; "death of work" **I** 322; demographic correlates of Internet access 1998 **I** 319; deregulation **I** 325; differentiation **I** 325; digital Athenian democracy **I** 320; disciplinary crisis **I** 310; EU expert group **I** 324–315; fallacies **I** 317–23; globalisation **I** 312; household ownership of communications facilities 1997–98: **I** 319; identity: fallacy of postmodern subject **I** 317; inequality **I** 318–19; information and communications technologies, and **I** 309–28; information society **I** 313–14; interpreting information society **I** 311–15; means and ends **I** 316–17; post-materialism **I** 311; power **I** 319–20; sociology of impatience **I** 323–6; technological determinism **I** 315; telegraphy **I** 316; trends **I** 323–6; two types of technology **I** 316–17
Soete, Luc **I** 4
Software: production of **I** 206
Sorby, Henry Clifton **I** 81
Spaeth, Anthony **I** 226
Speer, Albert: communications technology, on **I** 29
Stehr, Nico **I** 6
Stonier, Tom **I** 6, 259
Strategic information systems planning **II** 485–504; appropriate, choosing **II** 499–500; assessment **II** 492–3; barriers to **II** 490; broader conception **II** 495–500; business linkage **II** 493; components **II** 496; contingency framework **II** 500; current status **II** 492; development path **II** 488; management involvement **II** 491; revised 'stages of growth' model **II** 497–8; success factors **II** 490; successful implementation **II** 485–504; theory versus practice **II** 489–94

INDEX

Sub-Saharan Africa, impact of ICT **II** 308–27; action centred around users **II** 320–1; action centred around users and users' reactions **II** 313; actual impact **II** 313, 314, 315; application in local communities **II** 324; application in wider context **II** 324; constraints **II** 313, 319–20; data collection and analysis **II** 311–12; further areas of research **II** 325; informants' interpretations of actions and strategies against constraints **II** 322–3; infrastructure **II** 324; policy and management awareness **II** 321–4; potential impact **II** 313, 316–19; research methodology **II** 310–11; social feedback model of four core categories and external factors **II** 314

Surveillance: functions of communication **I** 25; mobilizing of administrative power, as **I** 262; new technologies, and **I** 219; state, role of **I** 271; totalitarian rule, and **I** 262

Surveillance society **IV** 349–65; analysis of data **IV** 352; Bork Bill **IV** 360; bureaucracy **IV** 353; capacity to predict **IV** 353; consumer behaviour **IV** 355; DAS **IV** 352; ECPA 1986 **IV** 359–60; Grace Commission **IV** 357; "individually identifiable information" **IV** 361; market research **IV** 355–6; modern surveillance technology **IV** 350–1; negative connotation **IV** 349; privacy legislation, and **IV** 359–62; PRIZM cluster analysis **IV** 357–8; public opinion, and **IV** 358–9; "remote sensing" **IV** 351; resistance to spread of surveillance **IV** 361; television audiences **IV** 355; teleworking **IV** 354–5; theoretical restraints of market **IV** 354; US Department of Defense **IV** 357; US government **IV** 356–8

Sweden: Terese project **I** 187

Systems theory **I** 6

Tactical memory **IV** 412–32; abandonment of FBI accuracy requirement **IV** 419; affordances **IV** 427; analogy and the law **IV** 419–20; blogs **IV** 423; classification of information **IV** 421–2; collaboration **IV** 428; collecting facts **IV** 414–16; ephemeral **IV** 424; Fourth Amendment **IV** 420; inference attacks **IV** 421–2; information and communication, use of **IV** 413–14; mathematics vs narrative creativity **IV** 428–9; misappropriation by memory **IV** 416–17; openness in knowledge production **IV** 423–4; owning the facts **IV** 416; panopticon **IV** 414–15; panspectrom **IV** 415–16; perturbing the facts **IV** 417–19; position of openness **IV** 412–32; post-normal science **IV** 424; scale as medium **IV** 425–6; spandrels **IV** 427; technological discretion **IV** 426–8; voluntary exposure **IV** 422–3

Taylor, Frederick Winslow **I** 265; "brain work", on **I** 265

Taylor, Richard **I** 4

Taylorism **I** 249; microelectronic reorganization of **I** 260; *see also* Scientific Management; social philosophy, as **I** 266–7; technological support, and **I** 266

Technocracy **I** 193

Technological colonialism **I** 66

Technological determinism **I** 6, 86; interactivity, and **I** 243; social shaping of new technology, and **I** 193

Technology and structures **II** 505–52; appropriation of structures **II** 510–12; artifact and use **II** 512–15; change in technologies-in-practice **II** 519–21; collaborative technology-in-practice within Iris **II** 522–5; collective problem-solving **II** 526, **II** 527; embodied structures **II** 507–10; emergent structures **II** 507–10; empirical examples **II** 521–37; enactment of structures **II** 510–12; enactment of structures in practice **II** 516; enactment of technologies in practice **II** 517; implications of practice lens **II** 537–45; improvisation technology-in-practice **II** 534–6; individual productivity **II** 530–2; limited-use technology-in-practice- **II** 527–30; Notes technology **II** 522, 523;

473

practice lens **II** 512–19; structuring of technologies-in-practice **II** 515–19; three technologies-in-practice within Alpha **II** 525–6; two technologies-in-practice within Zeta **II** 532–4; types of enactment **II** 540, 541
Tehranian, Majid **I** 222
Telecom crisis **III** 353–70; failure of neoliberal transformation **III** 362–5; liberalization **III** 358–60; methodology **III** 355; new strategies for next generation **III** 365–6; privatisation **III** 360–1; restructuring of global telecommunications system **III** 353–70; theoretical framework **III** 355; transformation of telecom industry **III** 356–61
Telecommunications: economic control, and **I** 170; international infrastructure **I** 121; literary and artistic works, and **I** 252; national information policy, and **I** 112; new infrastructure for **I** 205; post-industrial society, in **I** 80–3; teleprocessing, and **I** 93
Teledemocracy **III** 32–49; access to public records **III** 41–2; broadcasting **III** 39–41; early work on **III** 35; emerging applications of information technology **III** 38–45; governmental applications in 1990s **III** 40; interpersonal communications **III** 43–4; later work on **III** 36; monitoring **III** 44–5; political science research on **III** 32–49 specialized databases **III** 42–3; streams of literature **III** 34–8; surveying **III** 44–5; transactions **III** 41
Telegraph system **I** 169
Telephone: access to, globally **I** 216; meshing with computers **I** 92; technological innovation in **I** 93–4
Television: broadcasting ownership **I** 50; centralisation, and **I** 53; expansion through cable **I** 92; export of programs **I** 66; language policy **I** 53; minority groups, and **I** 50; pay-per-view **I** 252
Theological synergism **I** 128–38; rebirth of **I** 136–7
Theoretical knowledge; role of **I** 2
Totalitarianism: surveillance, and **I** 262

Touraine, Alain **I** 185–6
Training: communications media, for **I** 51
Transformation of open source software **II** 239–59; acceptable community values **II** 254–5; characterizing FOSS **II** 241–4; characterizing FOSS and OSS 2.0 **II** 242; characterizing OSS 2.0 **II** 251; deriving appropriate TCO measures **II** 253; elaboration of business models **II** 253; FOSS development process **II** 241–3; FOSS licensing **II** 244; FOSS product domain **II** 243; FOSS product support **II** 243–4; from bazaar process to bazaar product **II** 249; implementing whole product approach **II** 255; implications and challenges for practice **II** 254–6; implications and challenges for research and practice **II** 251–6; key issues for research and practice **II** 252; leveraging community software development **II** 248; leveraging open source brand **II** 248; market creation strategies in OSS 2.0 **II** 247–8; OSS 2.0 analysis and design **II** 244–5; OSS 2.0 business strategies **II** 246; OSS 2.0 development process **I** 245; OSS 2.0 licensing **II** 249–51; OSS 2.0 product domain **II** 246; OSS 2.0 Product support **II** 248–9; primacy FOSS business strategies **II** 243; safeguarding against IPR infringement **II** 256; stimulating open source invertical domains **II** 255–6; transferring lessons from open source to conventional development **II** 252–3; typology of OSS 2.0 licences **II** 250; value-added service-enabling in OSS 2.0 **II** 246–7; value for money **II** 254; value for money versus adhering to acceptable community values **II** 254; whole-product approach **II** 249
Transnational virtual community **IV** 17–27; fetishes, illusion and power in cyberspace **IV** 21–2; implications for culture, power and language **IV** 17–27; Internet **IV** 19–20; language and the transnational community **IV** 22–4;

transnationalism as an issue
IV 17–19; virtuality and symbolic-
cultural basis of transnational
community IV 19–20
Transportation: communication as
substitute for I 53–4
Tremblay, Gaetan I 6
Trotsky, Leon I 116
Tsoukas, Haridimos I 6
Turkle, Sherry I 226

United Nations (UN): communication
needs research I 48
United States: computer exports
I 63, 144; data-haven, as I 65;
information based economy, as
I 58; information society, as I 60–1;
post-war economy I 143; sector
aggregation of labour force I 59;
service society, as I 81

Values: communications, and I 20
van Dijk, Jan I 6
Virtual reality: sexual pleasure, and
I 218; world of men I 218
von Bekesy, Georg I 32

Walras, Leon I 108
War: cybertechnologies, and I 219–20
Watt, James I 128
Weaver, Warren I 1

Weber, Max I 160
Webster, Frank I 5
Weinberg, Alvin I 112
Weiner, Norbert I 1, 81: Brownian
motion, on I 82; cybernetics, theory
of I 83; society, work on I 1
Wells, H. G.; "world brain", on
I 113–14
Westernization: modernization and
development as I 63
Widespread organizational change
II 7–8
Winston, Brian I 6
Wirth, Louis I 116
Wolton, Dominique I 144–5
Women: deskilling, and I 193;
internet, and I 218; IT and
employment opportunities I 192–3;
post-war employment I 204; reduced
working lifetimes, and I 208–9
Workers, knowledge: I 38, 198, *see also*
Knowledge society; retirement, and
I 41
World Bank: communications policy
research I 49
Wright Brothers I 81

Zapatistas: internet, and I 227
Zones of cyberspace III 266–75;
closeness III 267–9; future
developments III 269–73